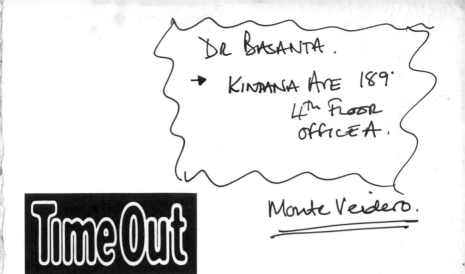

DR BASANTA.

→ KINTANA AVE 189.
4th FLOOR
OFFICE A.

Monte Veidero.

Time Out

Buenos Aires

timeout.com/buenosaires

Published by Time Out Guides Ltd, a wholly owned subsidiary of Time Out Group Ltd.
Time Out and the Time Out logo are trademarks of Time Out Group Ltd.

© **Time Out Group Ltd 2008**
Previous editions 2001, 2004, 2006.

10 9 8 7 6 5 4 3 2 1

This edition first published in Great Britain in 2008 by Ebury Publishing
A Random House Group Company
20 Vauxhall Bridge Road, London SW1V 2SA

Random House Australia Pty Limited 20 Alfred Street, Milsons Point, Sydney, New South Wales 2061, Australia
Random House New Zealand Limited 18 Poland Road, Glenfield, Auckland 10, New Zealand
Random House South Africa (Pty) Limited Isle of Houghton, Corner Boundary
Road & Carse O'Gowrie, Houghton 2198, South Africa

Random House UK Limited Reg. No. 954009

Distributed in USA by Publishers Group West
1700 Fourth Street, Berkeley, California 94710

Distributed in Canada by Publishers Group Canada
250A Carlton Street, Toronto, Ontario M5A 2L1

For further distribution details, see www.timeout.com

ISBN : 978-1-84670-058-3

A CIP catalogue record for this book is available from the British Library

Printed and bound by Firmengruppe APPL, aprinta druck, Wemding, Germany

The Random House Group Limited supports The Forest Stewardship Council (FSC), the leading international forest
certification organisation. All our titles that are printed on Greenpeace approved FSC certified paper carry the FSC
logo. Our paper procurement policy can be found at http://www.rbooks.co.uk/environment

Time Out carbon-offsets all its flights with Trees for Cities (www.treesforcities.org).

This publication complies with the IGM and was approved with the file number GG08 0813/5, May 2008.

Edited and designed by
Time Out Guides Limited
Universal House
251 Tottenham Court Road
London W1T 7AB
Tel +44 (0)20 7813 3000
Fax +44 (0)20 7813 6001
Email guides@timeout.com
www.timeout.com

Editorial
Editor Daniel Neilson
Managing Editor Mark Rebindaine
Copy Editor Patrick Welch
Proofreader Marion Moisy
Indexer Anna Norman

Managing Director Peter Fiennes
Financial Director Gareth Garner
Editorial Director Ruth Jarvis
Deputy Series Editor Dominic Earle
Editorial Manager Holly Pick
Assistant Management Accountant Ija Krasnikova

Design
Art Director Buenos Aires Gonzalo Gil
Designer Buenos Aires Javier Beresiarte
Art Director Scott Moore
Art Editor Pinelope Kourmouzoglou
Senior Designer Josephine Spencer
Graphic Designer Henry Elphick
Digital Imaging Simon Foster
Ad Make-up Federico Gilardi, Jodi Sher

Picture Desk
Picture Editor Jael Marschner
Deputy Picture Editor Katie Morris
Picture Researcher Gemma Walters
Picture Desk Assistant Marzena Zoladz

Advertising
Commercial Director Mark Phillips
International Advertising Manager Kasimir Berger
International Sales Executive Charlie Sokol
Advertising Sales (Buenos Aires) Mark Rebindaine
Advertising Assistant Kate Staddon

Marketing
Marketing Manager Yvonne Poon
Head of Marketing Catherine Demajo
Sales & Marketing Director, North America Lisa Levinson
Marketing Designers Anthony Huggins, Nicola Wilson

Production
Group Production Director Mark Lamond
Production Manager Brendan McKeown
Production Controller Caroline Bradford
Production Coordinator Julie Pallot

Time Out Group
Chairman Tony Elliott
Financial Director Richard Waterlow
Group General Manager/Director Nichola Coulthard
Time Out Magazine Ltd MD Richard Waterlow
Time Out Communications Ltd MD David Pepper
Time Out International MD Cathy Runciman
Group IT Director Simon Chappell

Contributors
Introduction Daniel Neilson. **History** Peter Hudson (*Hunting Falcons* Daniel Neilson; *Heroes and Villains* Ben Lerwill). **BA Today** Matt Chesterton. **Tango** Chris Moss. **Football** Matt Chesterton (*Derby days* Daniel Neilson). **A-Z BA Life** Matt Chesterton, Ismay Atkins. **Where to Stay** Matt Chesterton, Daniel Neilson, Cat Scully (*Sex in the city, Shooting stars* Daniel Neilson). **Sightseeing: Introduction** Matt Chesterton. **The Centre** Matt Chesterton, Brian Hagenbuch (*Mothers of reinvention?* Fiona McCann; *Walk on* Matt Chesterton) Dominic Thomas. **South of the Centre** Fiona McCann (*The other side of the tracks* Matt Chesterton); **North of the Centre** Chris Moss (*Walk on: Mind your manors* Fiona McCann; *Walk on: Step on the grass* Matt Chesterton). **West of the Centre** Declan McGarvey (*Bloom town* Brian Hagenbuch). **Along the River** Declan McGarvey, Matt Chesterton (*Shock of the new* Matt Chesterton). **Further Afield** Brian Hagenbuch. **Cafés, Bars & Pubs** Matt Chesterton, Bridget Gleeson, Daniel Neilson, Cat Scully, Mark Rebindaine (*Show me the dough, Sweeter things in life* Layne Mosler; *Wine: A bluffer's guide* Dan Perlman; *The new sushi?* Daniel Neilson). **Cafés, Bars & Pubs** Matt Chesterton, Bridget Gleeson, Daniel Neilson, Cat Scully (*Literary ramblings* Matt Chesterton). **Shops & Services** Florencia Bibas (*Made in Argentina* Cat Scully; *Street style* Bridget Gleeson, *Urban gauchos* Daniel Neilson). **Festivals & Events** Melanie Kramers. **Children** Cat Scully. **Clubs** Jack Coleman, Grant Dull (*Sound of the suburbs* Daniel Neilson). **Film** Brian Hagenbuch, Melanie Kramers (*Maradona, the documentary* Brian Hagenbuch). **Galleries** Matt Chesterton, Melanie Kramers (*Don't say it, spray it* Daniel Neilson). **Gay & Lesbian** Pablo de Luca, Gustavo Noguera (*Five star gay* Ella Lawrence). **Music** Brian Hagenbuch (*The chronicle of Colón* Bridget Gleeson, *Nowt queer as folk* Daniel Neilson). **Sport & Fitness** Mark Rebindaine, Cat Scully (*Mounted and monied* Melanie Kramers). **Tango** Chris Moss, Maggie Cowan-Hughes (*Changing of the guard* Jeffrey Tanenhaus). **Theatre & Dance** Brian Hagenbuch, Melanie Kramers (*Carnival kicks* Emmet Boland, Romina Robles, *Dancing on air* Melanie Kramers). **Trips Out of Town: Getting Started** Joshua Goodman. **Upriver** Emma Clifton, (*Fantasy islands* Chris Moss). **Country** Matt Chesterton (*Rolling over the ranch* Chris Moss). **Beach** Mark Rebindaine. **Uruguay** Gabriel Bialystocki, Mark Rebindaine, Cintra Scott (*The grape escape* Cat Scully). **Directory** Fiona McCann, Declan McGarvey.

Maps Nexo Servicios Gráficos, Luis Sáenz Peña 20, Piso 7 'B', Buenos Aires, Argentina (www.nexolaser.com.ar).

Photography by Marc van der Aa (artwork on page 133 by Mercedes Jáuregui), except: pages 15, 28, 34, 127, 137, 153, 177, 181, 185, 206, 213, 218, 230, 231, 245, 249, 251, 255, 257, 260, 270, 271, 273, 275, 277, 280, 285, 286; pages 10, 13, 16, 19, 20, 21, 31, 224 Clarín Contenidos; pages 214, 252 Bridget Gleeson; page 269 Emma Clifton; pages 183, 189 Tali Karszenbaum; page 288 Helen Lerwill. The following images were provided by the featured establishment/artist: pages 47, 55, 67, 69, 71, 237, 241, 246, 259.

The Editors would like to thank: Tribalwerks, Cathy Runciman, and all contributors to the previous edition of *Time Out Buenos Aires*, whose work forms the basis for parts of this book.

Contents

Introduction

Argentina's prodigal son, the writer Jorge Luis Borges, wrote in his poem, *The Mythical Founding of Buenos Aires*: 'Hard to believe Buenos Aires had any beginning/I feel it to be as eternal as air and water'. And as Argentina, and its epicentre Buenos Aires, approaches its bicentennial anniversary in 2010, as Borges imagined, it is hard to wander the streets of the capital and imagine that, with the exception of La Boca, San Telmo and some of downtown, 200 years ago, all this was, well, fields.

In two centuries of independence, *porteños*, as the city's residents are called, have developed some strong characteristics. They are gregarious, occasionally melancholy yet endlessly welcoming, and, as you meet and interact with them, it is likely an impromptu chat or drink with a talkative resident will be remembered long after your photo of the Casa Rosada has been relegated to the bottom drawer and you've forgotten your tango steps.

Buenos Aires, you see, is not a city to visit, but a city to live in. That is not to suggest everyone should quit their jobs, sell up and move to Argentina's capital, although people are in their droves, but that those who come should, whether visiting for three days or three months, take time to live like *porteños*. Be sure to visit the sites, take amusing perspective shots of the Obelisco, and watch a cheesy tango show, but also spend hours in coffee shops mulling over a novel, cheer along with fanatics at a football game, chat for hours after your steak dinner and stay up until dawn partying with BA's carefree and beautiful young crowd. This is how to get under the skin of an utterly, and wonderfully, beguiling city.

Through its chaotic and frenetic exterior, you will see that much of the city is beautiful, with grandiose buildings, world-class art galleries, fine restaurants and a thriving fashion industry. Yet those who come with the wince-inducing 'Paris of the South' tag in mind will be disappointed (if that's your bag, we suggest Paris). Buenos Aires, despite the occasional European pretence, is undoubtedly a Latin city, as anyone who takes time to explore neighbourhoods such as Once and Retiro will discover. And, like every other city in Latin America, it still has major problems with inequalities of wealth.

Buenos Aires is unpredictable. Sometimes frustratingly so, but more often thrillingly so. You never know what's around the next corner: a spontaneous tango display, a flash mob from BA's exciting theatre scene, a free concert by one of the world's leading artists, or maybe another protest.

This is why we adore Buenos Aires, and why we know you will too.

ABOUT TIME OUT GUIDES

This is the fourth edition of *Time Out Buenos Aires* , one of an expanding series of Time Out guides produced by the people behind the successful listings magazines in London, New York and Chicago. Our guides are all written and updated by resident experts, who have striven to provide you with all the most up-to-date information you'll need to explore the city or read up on its background, whether you're a local or a first-time visitor.

THE LIE OF THE LAND

Buenos Aires' grid system makes getting around the city relatively easy. We have divided the city into overall areas (the Centre, North of the Centre, South of the Centre, and so on), and then barrios or neighbourhoods within those (Recoleta, San Telmo, La Boca, Congreso, and so on). For more details, *see p74*. Every place is listed with its exact address – written in Spanish, to help you tell a taxi driver or ask a local. For listings of locations which are not precisely pinpointed on our street maps we have given the nearest two cross streets or intersection.

THE LOWDOWN ON THE LISTINGS

Above all, we've tried to make this book as useful as possible. Addresses, telephone numbers, websites, transport information, opening times, admission prices and credit card details are all included in our listings. And, as far as possible, we've given details of facilities, services and events, all checked and correct as we went to press. However, venues can change their arrangements, and during holiday periods some businesses and attractions have variable hours.

While every effort has been made to ensure the accuracy of information contained in this guide, the publishers cannot accept responsibility for any errors it may contain.

PRICES AND PAYMENT

The prices we have supplied should be treated as guidelines; volatile economic conditions can cause them to change. For most services we have published prices as they were quoted to us – in either Argentinian pesos (AR$) or US dollars (US$). This allows you to identify the places that are charging tourists dollar rates for their services (and often charging lower peso prices to locals). For ease of use, and because most visitors book their accommodation in advance, we have quoted rates for hotels and other lodging in US dollars. At the time of going to press, a US dollar was worth just over AR$3.

We have noted whether venues such as shops, hotels and restaurants accept the following credit cards: American Express (**AmEx**), Diners Club (**DC**), MasterCard (**MC**) and Visa (**V**). A few businesses may take travellers' cheques. If prices vary wildly from those we've quoted, ask whether there's good reason. If not, go elsewhere. We aim to give the best and most up-to-date advice, so we always want to know if you've been badly treated or overcharged.

TELEPHONE NUMBERS

To phone Buenos Aires from outside Argentina, dial your country's international exit code, then 54 (for Argentina), then 11 (for Buenos Aires) and finally the local eight-digit number, which we have given in all listings. If you are calling from within Argentina, but outside BA, you will need to add 011 before the eight-digit number. Within the city just dial the eight digits.

ESSENTIAL INFORMATION

For all the practical information you might need for visiting the city – including visa and customs information, emergency phone numbers, information on local weather, details of local transport, language tips and a selection of useful websites – turn to the **Directory** chapter at the back of the guide. It starts on page 293.

MAPS

The map section at the back of this book includes orientation and neighbourhood maps of the Buenos Aires area, and street maps of central BA, with a comprehensive street index. The street maps start on page 318, and now pinpoint the specific locations of hotels (❶), restaurants (❶) and cafés and bars (❶).

LET US KNOW WHAT YOU THINK

We hope you enjoy *Time Out Buenos Aires* , and we'd like to know what you think of it. We welcome tips for places that you consider we should include in future editions and take note of your criticism of our choices. You can email us at guides@timeout.com.

Advertisers

There is an online version of this guide, along with guides to 50 international cities, at **www.timeout.com**.

In Context

Features

Eva Perón addresses Buenos Aires from the balcony of the Casa Rosada.

History

It's amazing what you can fit in 500 years.

Stop and look up. The neighbourhoods of Buenos Aires are full of grand old buildings. Friezes, corner statues, iron and brasswork are overshadowed by fast-paced urbanity. Buses career around corners of cobblestone streets and old women furiously hose down mosaic tiles. Remnants of the city's heyday exist among the traffic jams and shantytowns. Buenos Aires used to be one of the world's richest cities. In 1910 Argentina was the ninth wealthiest nation, a country whose beef, grain and wool exports funded its growth, and its success rivalled that of other new nations in the Americas. It was seemingly self-sufficient, free from the heavy hand of Spain and European oppression. A haven for immigrants, its growing population churned out prosperity and culture. Sadly, the golden era was short-lived and like sand through their fingers, the citizens of Buenos Aires lost it all. Money, stability, safety all disappeared through decades of political corruption, mismanagement and God knows what else. Yet turn the corner and modern marvels of engineering stagger high into the Argentinian blue sky. There's the rumble of construction everywhere and a sense of a 'new era' is in the air. Porteños are a proud bunch and although they've had a heavy dose of bad luck, hopes of reviving rusty distinction are gathering momentum. Will the streets of Buenos Aires ever glitter again?

VIRGIN LANDS

For most *porteños* the city's history began when the European *conquistadors* arrived in the 16th century. But the land they conquered wasn't empty. The area stretching inland from the southern shore of the estuary of the Río de la Plata (River Plate) was populated by bands of hunter-gatherer Querandí who eked out a nomadic existence on the vast, grassy pampas.

The first Europeans botched their entrance spectacularly. Juan Díaz de Solís, a Portuguese navigator employed by the Spanish crown, landed in 1516, 24 years after Columbus reached the Americas. He and the rest of the landing party were killed and eaten by the indigenous tribes on the eastern bank of the River Plate. Nevertheless, successive waves of Spanish and Portuguese explorers sparked a race to colonise the area.

Spaniard Pedro de Mendoza arrived with between 1,200 and 2,000 soldiers and settlers in February 1536. The city and port of Santa María de los Buenos Ayres that he founded was probably located near what is now Parque Lezama. But after initial friendly contact, conflicts with the indigenous inhabitants further upriver grew. Some settlers resisted, but the main force of Spanish colonisation switched northwards and, in 1541, Domingo Martínez de Irala, commander of the garrison in Asunción, ordered the abandonment of Buenos Aires.

Settlement of what is now Argentina continued with the foundation of three regional capitals in the interior: Santiago del Estero, Tucumán and Córdoba. But it became clear that a port would be necessary to service the vast area to the south of the silver deposits of Potosi, and on 11 June 1580 Lieutenant Juan de Garay replanted the Spanish flag in the soil of Buenos Aires. The city was reborn.

But with no great fanfare. Until 1610 Buenos Aires had scarcely 500 inhabitants, few of whom dared or cared to venture into the as yet unsettled and uncultivated pampas, making them dependent on supply ships for survival. Unfortunately, these were infrequent; Spain sent virtually all its goods on a circuitous route, allowing voyages to Buenos Aires only every one or two years in an attempt to cut piracy.

SOWING THE SEEDS OF A NATION

From these humble beginnings Buenos Aires gradually grew in importance. By the 18th century, the process of taming the pampas was under way. Hardy settlers ventured out into the fertile plains and established what would become the vast *estancias* (cattle ranches) of the province, and the resultant trade in leather and dried beef continued to flow through Buenos Aires. In 1776, in recognition of the port's strategic position and in a bid to regain commercial control, Spain created the Virreinato del Río de la Plata (Viceroyalty of the River Plate), comprised of what are today Bolivia, Paraguay, Argentina and Uruguay, and finally separated it from Peruvian command.

The new authorities immediately set up free trade agreements with Chile, Peru and Spain, and during the last two decades of the 18th century the port boomed. The first of many waves of immigrants arrived from Europe. Buenos Aires became a bustling commercial centre, free from the strict social hierarchy that characterised its rivals in the interior. Its growing wealth funded an orphanage, a women's hospital, a shelter for the homeless and street lighting.

But the rapid growth also brought tensions. The new pro-free trade merchant class, mainly *criollos* (American-born Spanish) began to face off against the Spanish-born oligarchy that favoured Spain's monopoly. The creation of the city's first newspapers and the prospect of revolution and war in Europe also inspired heated debate about the country's future.

The empire-building British had ideas of their own and began to cast a covetous eye on Spain's colonies. In 1806, under the command of General William Carr Beresford, some 1,500 British troops entered Buenos Aires. The 'English Invasion' was a débacle.

With the blundering Brits sent home with their sabres between their legs, *porteño* resentment was focused once more on their Spanish rulers. Simmering tensions in the city were heightened by news that Napoleonic forces had triumphed in Spain. The *criollos* demanded that Viceroy Santiago de Liniers' successor, Baltasar Hidalgo de Cisneros, convene an open meeting of the city's governing body to consider the situation. Despite attempts by Spanish loyalists to restrict the size of the meeting, the vote was conclusive. The *criollos* declared the viceroy's reign to have expired and a junta (council) was elected to replace him. This marked a revolutionary transfer of power from the Spanish elite to the *criollos*.

'The *Revolución de Mayo* sparked a rise in anti-Spanish feeling.'

The loyalists made a last-ditch attempt at resistance, but a massive public protest backed by the *criollo* militia units on 25 May 1810 – in the square later to be named Plaza de Mayo in honour of the events that took place there – convinced them of the inevitable.

This conflict, henceforth to be known as the *Revolución de Mayo*, sparked a rise in anti-Spanish feeling. The country formally declared its independence in the northern province of Tucumán on 9 July 1816. On this day, celebrated annually as Argentina's independence day, the new nation announced its opposition to 'any other form of foreign domination'.

WET BEHIND THE EARS

Emboldened by having crushed the English invaders in the previous decade, *criollos* in Buenos Aires subsequently led the movement for independence from Spain, promising to consult the provinces later. But the city had scarcely 40,000 inhabitants, and the provinces, jealous of its power, were not easily convinced. The province of Córdoba staged a counter-revolution, led by Liniers, who was executed by the junta for his trouble.

The resulting civil war lasted ten years, during which the government, constituted in various guises in Buenos Aires, sought to assume all the rights and privileges of the former Spanish colonial authorities.

This period saw the establishment of professional armed forces led by General José de San Martín and the rise of the *caudillos*, provincial strongmen who brutally defended regional autonomy. In the name of Federalism, these opposed centralised Unitarian rule. San Martín, the son of Spanish officials, ensured his place in Argentina's pantheon of national heroes by joining the revolutionary cause and leading an advance across the Andes to liberate Chile.

In 1820 provincial forces defeated the nationalist army at Cepeda, outside Buenos Aires, and the centralist intentions of the city were scuppered. Thereafter the city suffered a period of turmoil. But by the end of 1820 order had been restored under Bernardino Rivadavia who dedicated the income from the customs house to improving the city, reorganising its government and justice system.

The intellectual, architectural and economic growth of the city, which now had over 55,000 inhabitants, contrasted with underdevelopment in the provinces. Nevertheless, relations with the rest of the country improved temporarily and Buenos Aires took on the responsibility for international relations as the new nation was recognised by the major foreign powers.

COMING UP ROSAS

Rivadavia became the first president of a united and independent Argentina in 1826, but a year later the provinces were again up in arms. Rivadavia's constitution was rejected by most of the provincial *caudillos*, led by Juan Manuel de Rosas and Juan Facundo Quiroga.

'Public documents, newspapers and letters had to start with "Long live the Federation and death to the savage Unitarians!"'

Two times governor of Buenos Aires, Rosas consolidated his strong following in the countryside by organising an expedition to exterminate the indigenous Araucano, who competed with the wealthy ranch owners for the region's cattle. During his 17-year reign, Rosas consolidated the power of the port and province of Buenos Aires. But he also imposed rigid censorship and ruled by murder and repression. All citizens were compelled to make public their support for Rosas by wearing a red Federalist ribbon (the Unitarian colours were sky-blue and/or white) and public documents, newspapers and personal letters were required to start with the forceful slogan 'Long live the Federation and death to the savage Unitarians!'

At the end of his second governorship Rosas left a country that was isolated and economically backward. But he had also, albeit forcibly, encouraged national unity and paved the way for the federal constitution drafted in 1853, which established a republic with a strong central government and autonomous provinces.

DEVELOPMENT AND DYSENTERY

The next two decades saw the forging of the new nation, as successive presidents worked to create a unified state. Democracy, even imperfectly administered, was an advance over the earlier despotism. Bartolomé Mitre, governor of Buenos Aires and the founder of *La Nación* newspaper, was succeeded by Domingo Faustino Sarmiento.

Despite further uprisings, the national army successfully defended the republic and were further battle-hardened during a pointless war with Paraguay which lasted from 1865 to 1870. The controversial 'Desert Campaign' of 1879, on the other hand, led by General Julio Roca was deemed a resounding success. The campaign resolved the long-running conflict with indigenous groups, and in the process opened up 605,000 square kilometres (233,500 square miles) of land for cattle farming.

Agricultural output was not restricted to livestock. Technological advances facilitated the country's first wheat exports in 1878, and the following year saw refrigerated meat shipments follow in their wake. Both developments would have a major economic impact in the decades to follow. The bulk of the profits went to the large landowners, however, or were spent on British imports. The British also reaped handsome rewards from the construction of the railways, which grew by 2,516 kilometres (1,563 miles) from 1862 to 1880.

Characteristically, the city benefited the most from these economic advances, developing a cosmopolitan look and feel. Nevertheless, the absence of water and sewage systems led to outbreaks of cholera in 1867 and yellow fever in 1871. The latter killed more than one-tenth of the city's population and encouraged its wealthiest inhabitants to relocate from the hard-hit southern sections to Barrio Norte.

In 1880 the city of Buenos Aires suffered its final assault at the hands of the provinces. Roca, like Rosas before him, used his slaughter of indigenous groups as a springboard for the presidency. Although backed by the provinces, he was resisted by Buenos Aires. The fighting that ensued killed more than 2,000, most of them *porteños*, before the national government was able to prevail. The city was then placed under central government control and separated from the province, which adopted as its capital La Plata, 60 kilometres (37 miles) to the east.

Roca was the figurehead for an oligarchy, represented by the Partido Autonomista Nacional (PAN), which held power for three decades. During this time immigration, especially from Spain and Italy, swelled the city's population from 90,000 in 1854 to 526,000 by 1890. By 1914 it was the largest city on the continent, with 1,575,000 inhabitants.

ROADS TO REGRESSION

Inspired by Haussmann's Parisian project, Buenos Aires was remodelled under Torcuato de Alvear, municipal chief from 1883 to 1887 and considered to be the father of the modern city. The grand public buildings, parks and plazas date mainly from this time. British companies built tramways and gas and electricity networks, and a modern sewage system was created. Meanwhile, Argentina established its place as the world's leading grain exporter and was second only to the US as a frozen meat exporter, creating a second boom for the port city.

'The growing urban working class enjoyed little protection from social and economic problems.'

But booms were fragile. A rise in British interest rates led the British Baring Brothers bank – which had funnelled vast sums into the republic – to cut off its cash supply and demand repayment. In 1890 Argentina was plunged into a sudden, massive economic crisis.

If emergency measures and the general conditions at the time – including devaluation and further credit from Britain – allowed Argentina to recover, the growing urban working class enjoyed little protection against social and economic problems. Discontent made them a ready audience for revolutionary ideas imported with European immigrants, and there was a series of strikes and armed uprisings. The government controlled these with police repression and the threat of deportation.

In 1912 Roque Sáenz Peña, leader of the PAN's liberal faction, enacted compulsory universal male suffrage. Electoral fraud had kept the party in government for three decades, but now the law signalled its demise. Hipólito Yrigoyen, leader of the newly formed Unión Cívica Radical (the Radicals), was elected president in 1916, marking the advent of popular politics after a century of elite rule.

The Radicals were to rule Argentina for the next 14 years. During this period, ten per cent of the rural population migrated to the cities, keen to join a vibrant, upwardly mobile middle class. Yrigoyen was equal to the party's promise of order, but did nothing to alter conservative political and economic structures. From 1914 international prices for Argentina's produce declined and growth was curtailed.

After initial conciliatory overtures to the unions, causing heated conservative protests, the government subsequently permitted their brutal repression. In Buenos Aires, the terror

Roca stared down criticisms of his bloody Desert Campaign against indigenous groups.

Hunting falcons

Heralded as the 'People's Car' when it was first conceived in 1947, the Ford Falcon, became the symbol of a briefly austere period in the US, when the motor industry came dangerously close to gorging itself to death on chrome and oil. Its success was assured and the car was produced around the world for decades to come. However, in Argentina the Falcon's image has taken on a much more sinister significance. Squads from the federal police and military often used bottle-green models to pick 'dissidents' off the cobbled streets of the capital during the Dirty War of the military dictatorship between 1976 and 1983, murdering an estimated 30,000 people. The cars, still ubiquitous on the streets of the capital today, became so representative of the dictatorship that some Argentinians still shudder at the sight of the many long-discontinued Falcons on the streets of BA.

Recently, alongside the graffitied portraits of Evita and el Che, stencilled renditions of the car have cemented its notoriety. The words 'Yesterday. Today. PFA (Policía Federal Argentina). Repression, Kidnapping, Torture, Murder' have been sprayed all over the city's walls and pavements alongside a picture of the car, many along Avenida de Mayo. Others

reached its height during *La Semana Trágica* (Tragic Week) in 1919, when the government put down a metalworkers' strike with the aid of gangs organised by the employers, who also attacked Jewish immigrants. The body count, although high, was never established.

Nevertheless Yrigoyen, in typical *caudillo* style, enjoyed almost reverential support as a populist demagogue who displayed a paternal interest in his supporters – especially students, for whom he opened up free university education. He also made nationalist gestures by creating the state-owned petroleum company Yacimientos Petrolíferas Fiscales to exploit the country's new oil wealth (oil had been discovered in 1907), and opposing US colonialism. But when Yrigoyen was re-elected in 1928, he was in his twilight years. The worldwide Great Depression, which started in 1929, limited his ability to buy support by dipping into the state coffers. His government was overthrown in 1930 by an army that he himself had helped to politicise, heralding a period of military intervention in state affairs after half a century in which the army had kept out of politics.

The coup was backed by the rural oligarchy, who were hardest hit by the global crisis and resented their removal from power in 1916. But it also owed much to the rise of fascist ideologies imported from Europe, which saw little use for democracy. General José Félix Uriburu's decision to dissolve Congress, censor the media and imprison political opponents in 1930 and the subsequent election of his military rival General Agustín Justo in 1931 inaugurated a period of what some termed 'patriotic fraud' – a populist ploy to prevent the Radicals from taking power.

Justo invested heavily in public works, including trunk roads from Buenos Aires to the provinces. Three new Subte (subway) lines – B, C and E – were inaugurated between 1930 and 1936, to supplement line A, the continent's oldest, which opened in 1913. Avenida 9 de Julio was also widened to its current size and the city's administration decided to broaden every third or fourth street between Avenidas Caseros and Santa Fe, replacing the narrow colonial streets with today's busy transport arteries.

Production flourished with the start of World War II, which stemmed the tide of European

Mayo. Others play on the police's motto: 'At the Service of Impunity' instead of 'Community'. This use of in-vogue stencil graffiti (*see p230*) is part of a wider wave of protest sparked by a series of recent high profile trials against those thought to have had links with the murderous junta.

And as local human rights groups, such as the Mothers of the Plaza de Mayo, pick up the momentum in their fight against impunity,

and even against former officers at Ford Argentina who they accuse of marking out trade unionists, these protests are only likely to proliferate.

But as Erel Pretrini, the secretary of the Mothers of the Plaza de Mayo, said about the notorious vehicles: 'The Falcon has become a symbol but we must remember they, and other cars, were merely an instrument to kidnap people. It's not the cars' fault.'

imports. Argentina stayed neutral until late in the war, but by 1943 the conservative government had lost much of its lustre and the army again intervened.

THE PEOPLE'S PARTY

The military was now installed as a de facto political party, running government for much of the rest of the century. But it had little idea what to do once in power. The issue was resolved with the emergence of another modern-day *caudillo*, army colonel Juan Domingo Perón, head of the then obscure labour department. He had a very keen understanding of the power of the masses, picked up during his time as a military attaché in late-1930s Italy, where he was impressed by Europe's burgeoning fascist movements.

Perón's genius was to recognise the growing importance of the Argentinian working class and win the support of the union movement, which remains under his spell to this day. He was soon named vice-president and war minister and eventually presidential candidate. With Argentina's produce fetching bonanza prices, the healthy state of the economy allowed

Perón considerable leeway with welfare projects, including housing and health schemes and the introduction of universal pensions.

Between 1936 and 1947 Buenos Aires' population swelled from 3,430,000 to 4,724,000. Most of the new inhabitants were poor migrants from the provinces – they increased from 12 to 29 per cent of the city's population – and they formed the bedrock of Perón's support. When the oligarchy decided, in 1945, that Perón had gone too far and arrested him, it was this underclass (known in Peronist lore as the *descamisados* or 'shirtless ones') that came to his rescue. On 17 October – still celebrated by Peronists as *Día de la Lealtad* (Loyalty Day) – workers massed in the Plaza de Mayo to defend Perón. When he appeared around midnight on the balcony of the Casa Rosada, to the cheers of 300,000 supporters, it became evident that he was too powerful to be stopped, at least for the time being.

In February 1946 Perón won the first democratic election since Yrigoyen, launching propaganda and state welfare campaigns that converted him and his young, ambitious wife,

Eva, into legends. While Perón fulfilled his duties, Eva dispensed the government's welfare budget, mixing easily with the poor, while enjoying her new wealth. She also took up the campaign that enacted women's suffrage in 1947.

Massive state intervention in the economy, however, was poorly handled. The railways, which were bought from the British to popular rejoicing, cost four times their official valuation. Mismanagement of the transport, gas and phone services damaged their efficiency. Nonetheless, in 1949 a new constitution was approved, guaranteeing social rights and allowing for Perón's re-election.

Perón was elected to a second term in 1951, but less than two months after retaking office, Eva died from cancer, aged 33. Although Perón remained a crucial figure until his death in 1974, the heart had gone from Peronism. Moreover, Argentina had exhausted most of its reserves of gold and foreign exchange, and two bad harvests exposed the fragility of his welfare drive. He promptly abandoned the more radical economic policies and passed a law protecting foreign investment. Yet even as the economy recovered, Perón inexplicably launched a series of barbed attacks on the church, which had previously backed him. The move fuelled a growing opposition. In 1955 the Plaza de

The misunderstood **Juan Domingo Perón**.

Mayo was bombed by naval planes during an attempted military uprising, killing more than 200 government supporters. In response, Peronists torched city churches. Argentina had begun to spin out of control.

A TIME OF TURMOIL

The next two decades saw a fragmentation of Argentinian society that gave rise to a period of unparalleled barbarism. In December 1955, Perón was overthrown by the military – with wide support from the upper and middle classes – and went into exile. His Partido Justicialista, or PJ, was banned and persecuted.

The Radicals split, too, and Arturo Frondizi, leader of their more combatative wing, was elected president in 1958. Once in power, however, Frondizi alienated those who had voted for him by reneging on campaign promises, though he won friends in the oligarchy with free-market policies. Angered by news that the president had held a secret meeting in Buenos Aires with Ernesto 'Che' Guevara, Argentinian-born hero of the Cuban revolution, the army forced Frondizi's resignation in 1962.

Arturo Illia, leader of the Radicals' more conservative wing, was elected president the following year, with just 25 per cent of the vote. Although his brief rule restored economic growth, the military was once again dissatisfied and retook power in 1966. The country continued its descent into chaos with the growth of guerrilla movements, led by the Montoneros, who had Peronist origins and, later, the Trotskyite People's Revolutionary Army (ERP).

Eventually even his opponents accepted that Perón was the only viable alternative to military rule, even though his movement was split between left-wing nationalists and conservatives. When Perón returned to Argentina in 1973, the tension erupted into bloodshed at a massive rally to welcome him. The violent conflict between the two factions left scores dead and the party split.

After his election as president the same year, Perón sided with the right, forcing the Montoneros to abandon the movement after haranguing them at the May Day rally in 1974. He died two months later at the age of 74, leaving the country in the incapable hands of his third wife, Isabel. She in turn was dominated by José López Rega, whom Perón had promoted to minister of social welfare. López Rega is famous as the founder of the Triple A, a shadowy paramilitary organisation dedicated to the murder of political opponents. As the violence spiralled and the economy collapsed, much of the population breathed a sigh of relief when Isabel was replaced in 1976 by a military junta, led by General Jorge Rafael Videla.

The satisfaction was short-lived. The *Proceso de Reorganización Nacional* (known as '*el Proceso*'), presided over by Videla, imposed order by eliminating the regime's opponents. Although the exact number of those killed during this time is still disputed, it may have been as great as 30,000, according to human rights groups. A minority had taken part in the armed struggle, but the majority were trade unionists, political activists, rebellious priests and student leaders. Most were kidnapped, taken to torture centres and then 'disappeared': buried in unmarked graves or heavily sedated and thrown from aircraft over the River Plate. In the face of such horrors, many Argentinians emigrated or were forced into exile – although many more stayed and feigned ignorance.

'Most were kidnapped, taken to torture centres and then "disappeared".'

The military government introduced radical free-market policies, reducing state intervention and allowing a flood of imports, much to the detriment of local industry. The deregulation of financial markets created a speculative boom, while spiralling national debt left a legacy from which Argentina has yet to recover. Inflation soared again and the regime sought ways to distract the population. The 1978 World Cup, staged in Argentina, was one such distraction.

But although Argentina eventually triumphed on the football field (after what many consider to be a rigged match against Peru), growing opposition off it encouraged political parties and the church to raise their voices. The greatest courage was displayed by human rights groups, particularly the Mothers of the Plaza de Mayo, who marched in front of the Casa Rosada on a weekly basis to demand information on their missing children.

On 2 April 1982, under the leadership of General Leopoldo Galtieri, the military made one last desperate attempt to flame popular support, invading the Falkland Islands/Islas Malvinas, occupied by the British since 1833. The action unleashed a flood of nationalist fervour, but the generals had misjudged the reactions of friends and enemies alike.

THE FALKLANDS/LAS MALVINAS

Britain had earlier shown little interest in preserving the Falklands, even downgrading the British citizenship of the islands' 1,800 inhabitants. But the British prime minister Margaret Thatcher's unpopularity at home meant a tide of patriotic passion was as much in her interests as the junta's. On 1 May,

a British submarine attacked and sank the Argentinian cruiser *General Belgrano*, killing almost 400 crew members. The ship was outside the 200-mile 'exclusion zone' that the British had imposed around the islands and was steaming away from them, although the Admiralty claimed that it might have intercepted British ships on their way to join the conflict. In retaliation, the Argentinians sank the British destroyer HMS *Sheffield* three days later, killing 20 of its crew.

A peaceful settlement was now impossible. Galtieri had trusted in US support, which never materialised; Washington eventually backed the British. The junta had an equally poor understanding of the military side of the conflict. After the sinking of the *Belgrano*, the navy sat out the rest of the conflict, and Argentinian forces, badly led and composed largely of ill-equipped conscripts, were no match for a professional British task force. The defeat was the final nail in the regime's coffin. It was also a huge shock to a society that had been convinced by its press that Argentina was winning the war until the very moment of surrender. Celebrated Argentinian writer/poet Jorge Luis Borges famously stated that the Falklands 'was a fight between two bald men over a comb'.

Defeat brought the population back to its senses, although the issue has by no means gone away. Most Argentinians believe that '*las Malvinas son argentinas*' and the 1994 constitution ratified Argentina's claim to the islands, specifying that the recovery of sovereignty is an unwaivable goal of the Argentinian people. The islands appear on all Argentinian maps as Argentinian territory.

BACK TO DEMOCRACY

Democracy returned in 1983 with the election of Radical leader Raúl Alfonsin, one of the few political leaders to have maintained his distance from the military and opposed the Falklands War. The momentous changes afoot were described at the time as '*una fiesta de democracia*' and a party atmosphere prevailed.

But the new president lacked a majority in Congress and faced a range of vested corporate interests. He also faced stiff military opposition to the investigation of abuses committed during *el Proceso* – although he was helped by the publication in 1984 of *Nunca Más* (*Never Again*), a harrowing report of human rights abuses during the military government, identifying 9,000 victims. In the ensuing public outcry, the three juntas that presided over the *Guerra Sucia* (Dirty War) were tried in 1985 and stiff sentences handed down, including life for Videla – one of very few cases of Latin

Heroes and villains

Argentina's history is littered with forceful, controversial individuals, and the line between saint and sinner is often a blurred one. One man's patriot is another's traitor, while that which some documenters have seen as brave progressiveness others have judged as either blind risk or criminal skulduggery. Here's an overview of some of the more prominent figures in the fabric of the republic – love 'em or hate 'em, but be aware that you could be on thin ice if you laud the wrong 'hero' in the wrong place.

José de San Martín 1778-1850
The Knight of the Andes. The Father of the Nation. El Libertador. Call him what you will, José de San Martín is one leader that modern Argentina is almost unanimous in its reverence for. Along with Simón Bolívar, the Corrientes-born San Martín successfully headed the revolutionary struggle against the Spanish grip on Latin America, most famously leading an army of 5,000 troops over the Andes to liberate Chile. He then brought an end to occupation in Peru, before a still mysterious contretemps with Bolívar saw him hang up his military braces. He spent time in Europe as both a young and old man and, ironically, was the son of Spanish officials.

General Julio Argentino Roca 1843-1914
Appearances can be deceptive. Julio Argentino Roca, the bearded oldie looking faintly sheepish on the back of today's 100-peso note, was in fact one of Argentina's steeliest leaders. Born into a prominent Tucumán family in the 1840s, he rose through military ranks and, as general,

introduced an 'extinguish, subdue or expel' policy towards indigenous inhabitants, particularly his controversial (genocidal?) Desert Campaign of 1879. The bloodshed and resulting territorial gains led to two terms as president, during which he oversaw the separation of church and state and brokered peace with Chile. Roca is still truly controversial – the frequent graffiti adorning his city centre statue tells its own story.

Juan Perón 1895-1974
Understanding the whys and wherefores of Peronism is about as straightforward as knitting sunshine, and the man behind the movement remains a truly divisive individual. The basic facts are simple enough – Perón enjoyed three terms as president over the course of 28 years, punctuated by a long period of exile – but that's pretty much where agreement ends. To his many followers, he revolutionised the lives of countless poor and dignified labour conditions; to his detractors, his legacy remains that of a dictatorial demagogue with Nazi sympathies. Second wife Eva also has her critics, but it's Perón who really splits opinion.

Leopoldo Galtieri 1926-2003
Leopoldo Galtieri sculpted out a remarkable career path for himself, rising from a working-class immigrant family to become a lieutenant general. Things weren't quite so admirable after that. He held a far-from-passive role in the merciless junta-led Dirty War, then claimed presidential office following a military coup in December 1981. Four months into power and with popularity low, he attempted

American military leaders being imprisoned for their crimes. But in the face of military pressure, the government passed the *Punto Final* (Full Stop) law in 1986, limiting the trials.

Another military uprising during Easter Week in 1987 was met by impressive public demonstrations in support of democracy. But after persuading the rebels to lay down their arms, Alfonsín then caved in to the military's demands, passing the *Obediencia Debida* (Due Obedience) law, which excused the vast majority of the accused officers on the grounds that they were only following orders.

Among the trade unions Alfonsín initially attracted hostility with a failed attempt to introduce new labour laws. But 13 general

strikes later, he capitulated and appointed a senior union leader as labour minister. He did little better with the economy. After initial economic stabilisation as a result of the Plan Austral in 1985, the government's nerve again failed when faced with serious restructuring.

PIZZA AND CHAMPAGNE YEARS
With the Peronist opposition gaining strength, Alfonsín finished his term in rout. His successor, Carlos Menem, was forced to take office five months early as the economy spun out of control, monthly inflation hit 197 per cent and looters raided supermarkets. Once in office, Menem abandoned his electoral promises and embraced neo-liberalism.

to curry favour by reclaiming the British-occupied Islas Malvinas (Falkland Islands) – initial public jubilation was short-lived, as young, under-trained troops fell in droves and retreat became enforced in under two months. Galtieri was held to trial on civil rights and mismanagement charges, and died in 2003 to little mourning.

Carlos Menem *1930-present*
Born into a Muslim family in La Rioja, Carlos Menem became governor of his home province before being imprisoned under the military dictatorship. The junta's downfall then see-sawed him to higher office, and he rose to president in 1989 (converting to Catholicism in the process). His decade-long tenure was marred by allegations of corruption and partisanship, although supporters point to the success of his free-market economic progress, detractors, and there are very many, see the 2001 crisis as essentially a legacy of his ruling and wince at the Ferrari-driving, champagne-supping president showing off while millions starved. His law *Punto Final* (Full Stop) was however the most controversial policy, effectively granting impunity to the leaders of the military dictatorship on the grounds of national reconciliation. Menem still faces questioning over tax fraud and embezzlement allegations (which he denies). It is, however, hard to label him a political dinosaur – in 2001 he took a

former Miss Universe, 35 years his junior, as his second wife.

Cristina Kirchner *1953-present*
To outsiders, it still looks decidedly improbable. Néstor Kirchner had spent four years as a popular if occasionally polemical president, but in 2007 declined to run for a second term, instead making way for his wife, Cristina. The glamorous porteña then won office at a canter and is now ensconced as Argentina's first elected female head of state. But she is no political ingénue – during her husband's years in the chair she gave backing to a number of populist agendas and drew plaudits for combative public speeches. Quite what the future holds for la *familia* Kirchner is the subject of warm speculation.

Under convertibility, introduced by finance minister Domingo Cavallo in 1991, the peso was pegged to the dollar at one-to-one. Privatisation resolved the problem of a bloated state sector, with handsome rewards for the business oligarchy. International capital was appreciative, too; the brisk opening of the economy left virtually all leading companies and financial institutions in foreign hands. After ten years of negative growth, Menem's decade in office saw total growth of around 35 per cent, and inflation was vanquished.

Menem ruled largely by decree and with little regard for constitutional niceties. But he finally dominated the military, and the mutiny by army rebels in December 1990 was the last of

its kind. Although he dismayed human rights campaigners by granting an amnesty to the jailed junta leaders, he also starved the armed forces of funds, leaving them operationally incapable of another coup. He negotiated a constitutional amendment allowing him to win re-election in 1995, although the opposition extracted some changes in return, including elected authorities for Buenos Aires city.

But Menem's second term could not sustain the impetus of his first. Local industry largely collapsed under foreign competition, turning the industrial belt around Buenos Aires into a wasteland, populated by an increasingly bitter and impoverished underclass. Real wages dropped and the gulf between the rich and poor

More handwringing from **Carlos Menem**.

steadily widened. Menem's flamboyant style and love of showbiz glitter – *la farándula*, as Argentinians call it – went hand in hand with numerous high-profile corruption scandals.

In the 1991 'Yomagate' or 'Narcogate' scandal, various Menem officials were accused of links to money laundering and the illegal drugs trade. Menem's association with Alfredo Yabrán (a shadowy businessman implicated in the murder of journalist José Luis Cabezas in 1997), and allegations that his Middle Eastern connections (he is of Syrian descent) had hampered official investigations into the terrorist attacks on the city's Jewish communities in 1992 and again in 1994, were sufficient to give Argentinians the impression that every injustice led back to the presidential palace.

'For Christmas 2001, Argentinians were gifted four presidents in just 11 days.'

Tired of such excesses, the population turned to Fernando de la Rúa, head of Buenos Aires's city council and self-styled antithesis of Menem. Running at the head of the Alliance, formed by the Radicals and Frepaso, a smaller left-wing party, de la Rúa was elected president in December 1999. For some, the rise of such an unexceptional man to the head of a coalition government marked the death of the *caudillo* and a new period in Argentinian politics. In retrospect, the de la Rúa years can be seen as little more than a period in which international financiers demanded payback for investing in Menem's chimerical new economy. Throughout his term, de la Rúa maintained an image of calm – soporific even – government, but the manner with which the Alliance led the country to economic meltdown was devastating.

SAY GOODBYE TO YOUR SAVINGS

The beginning of the end was a scandal over alleged vote-buying in the Senate, which dominated the media throughout the spring of 2000. The subsequent resignation of his popular vice president Carlos 'Chacho' Alvarez left de la Rúa weak and isolated. By this time, Brazil's decision to devalue its currency by 30 per cent the year before had caused Argentinian exports, still pegged to the dollar, to plummet. The ensuing crisis was met by severe austerity measures, but recession worsened and the beleaguered president turned, in early 2001, to former Peronist financial guru Domingo Cavallo to turn the economy round. But this time Cavallo was unable to rescue the country, and eight billion dollars of emergency aid was sought from the International Monetary Fund.

It was not enough. The economic situation atrophied as unemployment rose to 20 per cent in Buenos Aires and far higher levels in many provinces. Argentina's credit rating fell to a historic low, its national bonds designated as junk stock, and the dithering, quiet-mannered president was ill-equipped to reverse the inevitable economic disaster. In October 2001, the Peronist opposition took control of both houses and began to lead a takeover. On 19 December, protests segued into full-scale riots and looting, prompting heavy-handed police repression; de la Rúa declared a state of emergency. On 20 December, Cavallo resigned, followed next day by de la Rúa after massive rallies took to the streets and over 20 people were killed when riot police (and some shopkeepers) opened fire on looters, protesters and bystanders.

For Christmas 2001, Argentinians were gifted four presidents in just 11 days, the largest ever default in history – around US$150 billion – and the contempt of the IMF. When de la Rúa stood down, Ramón Puerta took over as caretaker between December 20 and 23; Adolfo Rodríguez Sáa ruled between December 23 and December 30 but was ousted by fellow Peronists when he made it clear that he wanted more than an interim role; Puerta became caretaker again for December 30 and Eduardo Camano stood in between December 31 and January 1.

The man then chosen by Congress to run Argentina until the next elections, Eduardo Duhalde, was a populist Peronist known for his opposition to neo-liberal ideology. A classic *caudillo* type, he had served as Menem's vice president. For 15 months he managed, with the aid of his appointed finance minister, Roberto Lavagna, to contain the crisis, further exacerbated by the January 2003 devaluation of the peso, and, slowly, a semblance of calm and order was restored in BA and across the country, although more than half of the population was left in poverty. Duhalde supported his successor, a modern and outgoing Néstor Kirchner.

MR & MRS PRESIDENT

When Néstor Kirchner took office on 25 May 2003, his presidency was welcomed as a change of atmosphere and a break with the Duhalde-Menem-Cavallo dynasty. But his mandate was by no means strong. Menem opted out of presidential run-offs when he looked likely to lose, allowing Kirchner to come to power with just 22 per cent of the vote.

Kirchner built and broadened his power base, co-opting the opposition parties' best talents and leaving those that remained glowering ineffectually from the sidelines. He took a bow for expanding the economy and consistently held high approval ratings until 2007, when he quietly stepped down from the presidential elections, passing the baton on to his wife, thus avoiding the 'two term' rule.

Cristina Fernández de Kirchner won the presidency with an astounding 45.29 per cent of the vote and a 22 per cent lead over her closest opponent. After decades of instability, the strong win was probably thanks to the desire for continuity, with Cristina promising to do what 'was necessary' to sustain a recovering economy. A Gucci-loving glamorous head of state – many criticise her for vanity – and, although she is the first wife in Argentinian history elected to succeed her husband, often compare her to Evita. Her future so far looks promising. Cristina is no dummy – previously a lawyer-turned-senator and active in the Peronist party since the 1970s, she is an excellent speaker and has put international relations at the top of her agenda. However, the task of maintaining a good rapport with both Hugo Chávez's oil-swollen Venezuela and the US powerhouse will be trying, especially as just weeks after her inauguration the US accused Venezuela of secretly funding her campaign (both Argentina and Venezuela officially stated this to be a fabricated scandal).

Will Mrs Kirchner become a beloved Cristin*ita* and is Mr Kirchner completely resigned to the role of house-husband – nothing more? We will have to wait and see.

Cristina Kirchner assumes power from her husband.

Key events

1516 Spanish settlers reach the River Plate and are killed by Querandí natives.
1536 First settlement of Buenos Aires.
1580 Lieutenant Juan de Garay returns to resettle the city.
1620 Diocese of Buenos Aires created.
1776 Spain creates the Viceroyalty of the River Plate.
1806-07 British troops fail after two attempts to occupy Buenos Aires.
1810 Argentinian-born leaders replace the Spanish viceroy with an elected junta.
1816 Argentina formally declares independence in Tucumán on 9 July.
1817 General José de San Martín defeats the Spanish at Chacabuco, Chile.
1820 Provincial forces defeat the central army at Cepeda outside Buenos Aires.
1826 Bernadino Rivadavia assumes the national presidency, declaring Buenos Aires the capital.
1835 Juan Manuel de Rosas becomes govenor of Buenos Aires.
1845 Britain and France join forces and blockade Buenos Aires in protest at Argentinian naval restrictions.
1851 Justo José de Urquiza defeats Rosas at Caseros on the outskirts of Buenos Aires.
1853 Federal constitution drafted.
1859 Provincial forces again defeat those from Buenos Aires at Cepeda, forcing the capital to accept the 1853 constitution.
1862 Bartolomé Mitre elected first president of the new Republic of Argentina.
1865 Argentina, Brazil and Uruguay unite in a bloody five-year war against Paraguay.
1871 Outbreak of yellow fever kills over 7,000 city residents, mostly in the south.
1879 General Julio Roca leads 'desert campaign' to exterminate the Indians.
1880 Buenos Aires becomes federal capital.
1890 Foundation of Socialist movement and the Civic Union, forerunner of the Radicals.
1907 Oil is discovered in the south of Argentina while drilling for water.
1912 President Roque Sáenz Peña enacts compulsary universal male suffrage.
1913 First South American underground railway – or Subte – is operated on Line A.
1916 Hipólito Yrigoyen, leader of the Radicals, elected president.
1919 During 'Tragic Week', gangs organised by employers help the government of Hipólito Yrigoyen brutally repress strikers.

1930 Yrigoyen government overthrown by an army coup.
1931 General Agustín P Justo elected president, heralding period of 'patriotic fraud'.
1943 Army overthrows conservative regime.
1945 Workers mass on 17 October to force liberation of Juan Domingo Perón.
1946 Perón wins presidential elections by 1,487,886 votes to 1,207,080.
1949 New constitution approved, guaranteeing social rights and allowing for Perón's re-election.
1951 Perón beats Radical leader Ricardo Balbín 2:1 in presidential elections.
1952 Perón's wife, Eva, dies aged 33.
1955 Perón is overthrown by a military coup.
1958 Radical Arturo Frondizi wins presidency with the support of the Peronists, who are banned from participating.
1962 Army forces Frondizi to resign.
1963 Another Radical, Arturo Illia, is electd president with just 25 per cent of the votes.
1966 Military retakes power.
1973 Perón elected president for a third term, defeating the Radical state of Balbín and Fernando de la Rúa by more than 2:1.
1974 Perón dies.
1976 General Jorge Rafael Videla leads military coup against Isabel Perón.
1982 The junta occupies the Falklands/Las Malvinas, but is defeated by the British.
1983 Radical leader Raúl Alfonsín democratically elected president.
1984 Argentine author Ernesto Sábato presents Nunca Más, a report detailing 9,000 'disappearances' carried out by the military government in the 1970s and 1980s.
1989 Peronist President Carlos Menem takes office five months early.
1994 Bomb attack on AMIA Jewish welfare centre kills 86 and wounds more than 250.
1995 Menem elected for second term.
1999 Fernando de la Rúa elected president for the Alliance.
2001 De la Rúa resigns when the economy collapses, prompting widespread rioting.
2002 Peronist Eduardo Duhalde is chosen as president by Congress on January 1.
2003 Peronist Néstor Kirchner elected president in run-offs with 22 per cent of vote.
2006 Kirchner settles Argentina's debts.
2007 Cristina Kirchner, Néstor's wife, wins presidential elections.

BA Today

Booming, stable, clean BA. And some other urban myths.

It would be unjust to suggest that all *porteños* are born pessimistic – some acquire the trait during childhood or adolescence. However, by their mid-twenties (give or take) most of the inhabitants of this gorgeous, enchanting city have deduced that their town – and usually, by extension, their country – has either gone to the dogs, is on its way to the dogs, or, at some point in the not-very-distant future, will be paying a visit to aforementioned canines. Never mind that the economy is thriving, the political scene stable, the inflation rate under control: like the Brit who stares at a cloudless blue sky and declares that rain must be on the way, *porteños* are resolute in their determination not to be 'fooled by appearances'.

Such, at any rate, is the stereotype. But how accurate is it? Answer: completely accurate – and wildly misleading. It all depends on how you interpret the evidence. Take, for example, the cited-ad-nauseum fact that Buenos Aires has more psychiatrists per capita than any other city on earth. This has led many to conclude that *porteños* must be more-than-averagely screwed-up. But it could just as easily mean that *porteños* are more-than-averagely analysed – and saner for it. And then there's tango, which many regard as the acme of

miserabilism; sad songs played on sad-sounding instruments by sad-looking people for sad people to shuffle around sadly to. But art is just as likely to distort life as it is to reflect it. Some of the most joyous music ever made has come out of the most benighted regions of Africa. Conversely, most of BA's canonical tangos were written during the city's belle époque, when grain was shipped out as fast as it could be harvested, and gold bars deposited in the country's bank vaults as fast as they could be stacked.

Since then dictatorship and democracy have danced their own *tango macabre*, as have those other terrible twins, boom and bust. But now, as the country approaches the bicentenary of its independence, in 2010, there are tentative signs that Argentina and its capital are entering an age of relative prosperity and – what is totally unprecedented – long-term stability. Just don't expect to hear this from a *porteño*…

NEIGHBOURHOOD WATCH

Buenos Aires is a city of barrios, some unofficial (if you ask someone where they're from and they reply with a number, you're probably talking to a shantytown, or *villa*, dweller), others, like Recoleta, long established and world-renowned. Most of the affluent and/or touristic barrios (poor but historically important neighbourhoods like La Boca attract busloads of tourists hunting that elusive quarry, the 'soul' of Buenos Aires) are largely concentrated in the eastern side of the city. This is the face of 21st century BA most people want to look at – reconstructive surgery and all. In the south, the Riachuelo river which flows, or rather oozes, into the Río de La Plata, and gives La Boca its distinctive stench, is finally, after many false starts and broken promises, earmarked for a clean-up. This septic tank masquerading as a waterway has long been a dumping ground for tanneries, abattoirs and small boys with nowhere else to pee, but thanks to a recent edict from the Supreme Court (itself subject to a much-needed purge in recent years) demanding an end to the effluence, Buenos Aires (or at least this small part of it) may finally begin to live up to its name.

A little further north is San Telmo, a barrio once famed for its cobblestone streets, crumbling stucco façades and overpriced tango venues but now increasingly known for its hip shops and restaurants, boutique guesthouses, gay nightlife (the Hotel Axel, a 'heterosexual-friendly' luxury hotel that is the first of its kind in South America, opened in San Telmo in 2007) and ever-more-overpriced tango venues.

> **'The efflorescence of "creative capitalism" in neighbourhoods like Palermo and San Telmo represents an important break with the past.'**

Such is the buzz around San Telmo, it has been dubbed the 'new Palermo Viejo'. Even if you've never been near Argentina, you've probably read about the latter barrio, a poster-child for creative, contemporary, cutting-edge (most locals would add 'costly') Buenos Aires, sardined with smart restaurants, quirky shops and many of the city's most noted design hotels. Unofficially divided into sub-barrios, with pretentious names such as 'Hollywood', 'Soho', and, for no apparent reason, 'Brooklyn', Palermo Viejo benefited enormously from the tourism boom that followed Argentina's economic crisis of 2001-02, and the subsequent currency devaluation. But it's not a tourist trap like, say, Montmartre in Paris. Locals as much as tourists come here to drink Manhattans, eat sushi, and buy Diesel. In one sense this is a logical continuation of the *porteño* narrative; a city built by immigrants importing cultures

and cuisines where once it imported farm workers and engineers. But in another sense the efflorescence of 'creative capitalism' in neighbourhoods like Palermo and San Telmo represents an important break with the past; a tacit acknowledgment that the days when the Argentinian economy meant outgoing steamboats laden with wheat and beef are long gone and never coming back.

Given this, it is perhaps fitting that the neighbourhood subjected to the most extreme makeover in recent years is the old dockside zone of Puerto Madero. Once busy and industrialised, then empty and rat-infested and now busy and service-oriented, this new barrio is Argentina in microcosm. The west side of the old docks (Puerto Madero Oeste), with its six converted redbrick warehouses, has been an important part of the city's commercial and social scene since 1996. The east side (Puerto Madero Este), however, was largely a wasteground until 2002, when the devaluation of the peso made the city a magnet for international property developers. Now Puerto Madero Este is the most valuable plot of residential real estate in Latin America, with prices averaging US$2,000 per square metre.

If you had to put a face to the Madero Este renaissance, it would be the handsome mug of beatnik-cum-businessman Alan Faena, owner of the Philippe Starck-designed Faena Hotel + Universe. Faena, something of a cross between Jay Gatsby and Donald Trump, and, depending on who you talk to, either a visionary or a snake-oil vendor, hopes to create a new kind of barrio in BA, one that reflects a city comfortable with its past and confident about its future. His latest venture is a huge multi-purpose venue designed by UK superstar architect Norman Foster, slated to be one of the centrepieces of the 2010 bicentenary fiesta.

SPORT AND POLITICS DON'T MIX?

In one form or another, all of the above passes through the in-tray of Mauricio Macri, who was elected mayor of Buenos Aires in December 2007. Macri has the perfect profile for an Argentinian politician: he's the scion of a wealthy family, he used to run a football club (Boca Juniors), he's on his third wife and he has a moustache. More surprisingly in a city that generally votes for left-leaning progressives, Macri and his party, PRO, are on the centre-right. Macri's support is largely drawn from the well-to-dos of barrios like Recoleta and Belgrano, and the just-about-getting-bys from less salubrious neighbourhoods in the west of the city. The issues that energise this coalition are the three Cs: crime, cleanliness and corruption. If Macri can make some headway

The art of memory

It took 25 years, hold-ups galore and the usual rounds of internecine wrangling, but Buenos Aires finally has a fitting memorial to the thousands of people who 'disappeared' – that is to say, were murdered – during the military dictatorship that ruled Argentina between 1976 and 1983. The **Monumento a las Víctimas del Terrorismo de Estado** (Monument to the Victims of State Terrorism) was unveiled by then president Néstor Kirchner in November 2007. It is now the centrepiece of the Parque de la Memoria, a sculpture park opened in 1998 located on a spit of reclaimed land in the north of the city fringed on three sides by the muddy waters of the Río de la Plata.

The rather nondescript location is inconvenient but appropriate. Of the perhaps 30,000 people who were tortured and killed in one or other of the junta's mini-gulags, many – either already dead, or drugged – were dumped into the river out of planes.

The names of those known to have died in this so-called 'dirty war' are engraved on a black granite monument which has been laid out so as to represent a scar in the earth: a twisted, running wound symbolising pain and a breach of natural law. It is a memorial that glorifies nothing; that in its jagged discontinuities suggests the absence of 'closure' for the families whose loved ones are buried in an unmarked grave they will never visit. Walking along the pathway that intersects the two sides of the monument takes the visitor to the edge of the river. Here, placed in the water but visible from a small viewing station, is the most moving sculpture in the park: a statue of Pablo Miguez, at 14 years old the youngest known victim of the junta.

Nine thousand names are inscribed on the walls of the monument, arranged chronologically. There is space for more. The names currently recorded are only of those whose disappearance and death have been officially confirmed; the fate of thousands of others is still under investigation, a process made difficult because those involved covered their tracks well, burning and shredding records as they went.

The park is still a work in progress. Nine more sculptures are due to be added to the four now standing. A cultural centre will contain a library, lecture hall and a multimedia archive. One task will probably never be completed: that of inscribing onto the wall every name of every victim that has a right to be there.

Parque de la Memoria

Avenida Costanera Norte Rafael Obligado, close to Ciudad Universitaria (4338 3000/ www.parquedelamemoria.org.ar). Bus 33, 42, 45, 160. **Open** Park 10am-7pm daily. Monument noon-4pm Wed, Thur; 10am-2pm Sat.

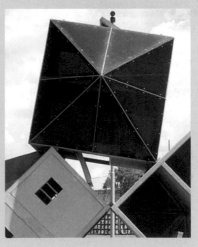

against these perennial blots on the *porteño* landscape, he'll be in good shape for what most presume is his ultimate goal: to successfully contest the Argentinian presidency in 2011. (Most people regard Macri as the de facto leader of the opposition to incumbent president Cristina Kirchner and the ruling Peronist party.)

It's too early to judge Macri. Like most Argentinian politicians, he divides without necessarily conquering. Half of his detractors will never forgive him for being rich, while the other half will always hate him for being the ex-president of Boca Juniors (politics may be important, but it ain't football). But this bland, even-tempered aristotechnocrat may turn out to be just the ticket for a citizenry fed up with would-be idealists, prophets, visionaries and saviours. Macri has already made a stab at

Makeshift home in **Barracas**

solving one of the country's most chronic malaises. In January 2008 he announced that, henceforth, cabinet ministers would be fined for arriving late at meetings, with fixed penalties of AR$50 for being 10 minutes tardy and AR$100 for any greater delay. 'A more punctual future' doesn't quite match up with 'the audacity of hope' or 'the great society' as a political slogan, but it's something.

REASONS TO BE FEARFUL

Despite the tourist boom (almost US$3 billion in tourism receipts in 2007, a rise of around 30 per cent on the 2004 figure), excellent GDP growth (well over five per cent per annum since 2003), falling unemployment (below 10 per cent in 2007 for the first time since 2001), the successful restructuring of the country's crippling debt to the IMF, a thriving export sector, and every sign that Argentina will field one of its best teams ever in the 2010 football world cup, the challenges still faced by BA and the country as a whole are daunting. And if the tangible problems weren't enough to be dealing with, there are a whole heap of imagined ones too. We've already noted that *porteños* tend towards gloominess and are generally highly receptive to any bad vibes in the air. This manifests itself in the so-called 'ten-year' rule. This theory, which you won't find in any economics

textbooks, states that every decade or so Argentina suffers some kind of cataclysmic snafu, either political (the ascension of a military dictatorship, for example), economic (hyperinflation and mass unemployment have been popular favourites over the years) or both.

So what needs crossing out on BA's to-do list in order that the ten-year anniversary of the December 2001 riots (in which more than 20 unarmed protesters were shot dead in the streets) passes without crash, crisis or coup? One of the top priorities is transport and infrastructure. A city in which many commuters travel to work on the outside of the train (often by choice so as to escape the suffocating conditions inside the carriages) and where children are sent home from school because the roof of the cafeteria has just collapsed, is obviously failing, regardless of the beauty of its buildings or the vibrancy of its cultural life. To give a specific example, what many people regard as the worst aspects of Argentinian society – institutionalised corruption, financial greed, a cavalier attitude towards rules and regulations – converged on 30 December 2004, when a fire sparked by a firework claimed the lives of 194 people in the overcrowded República Cromagnon disco, in the Once neighbourhood. The safety controls in place were found to be woefully inadequate and made worse by a culture in which bribery and kickbacks were commonplace. The tragedy cost then mayor Aníbal Ibarra his job and led to new and more stringent regulations for nightclubs and discos. The point, of course, is not the existence or otherwise of laws and standards – Buenos Aires has always had plenty of those – but whether or not they are enforced.

Much the same point can be made about crime. But here there is a further complication: Buenos Aires does not have its own police force. Law enforcement in the federal capital comes under the aegis of the federal government not mayor Macri. A referendum due to be held in 2008 may change this. If *porteños* vote 'yes' they will get their own police authority and, by extension, the chance to vote for local officials who not only have ideas on how to improve law and order in the capital but also have the power to put them into practice. The current statistics for crime in the federal capital paint a mixed picture. Compared to most Latin American cities of equivalent size, the city has a relatively low murder rate, with an average of 130 homicides per year. Crime against property is a much bigger problem, with around 135,000 reported incidents annually. Lack of confidence in the police means that the actual figure is certainly much higher.

You don't have to be a genius or a sociologist to figure out that the biggest challenge BA faces is the impoverishment of so many of its citizens. Many of the estimated 40 per cent of Argentinians thrust below the poverty line during the 2001-02 crisis got stuck there. Few salaries have kept pace with the country's recent economic growth, and the threat of runaway inflation – the price of butter is a serious political issue here – is an incubus as stubborn as it is scary. *Cartoneros* (collectors of cardboard and glass for recycling) are still an everyday spectacle, hauling their carts along the city's grand avenues as expensive imported cars flash past them, while street kids haunt the subways and trains, handing out astrology cards for '*una moneda*' (small change). Bear in mind that any *centavos* you give these artful dodgers are likely going straight into the pocket of a Fagin-type character waiting on the platform.

Poverty, poor housing, underfunded public hospitals, dilapidated public schools – these are all pressing issues in BA today. But even for the very poorest, it could be worse. In Buenos Aires, no one starves to death. In northern Argentina, particularly among the indigenous tribes of Chaco province, there have been recent cases of children dying as a direct result of malnourishment and starvation. Let's say that again. In Argentina, which exports all those lovely juicy steaks, grain and wine, children die from starvation.

MI BUENOS AIRES QUERIDO

Kvetch though they undoubtedly do, *porteños* love their city, and, in a manner that is hugely charming, want tourists to love it too. Unlike the stereotypical Parisian, who simply takes it for granted that he lives in a wonderful place and is colossally indifferent to outsiders who agree with him, *porteños* never seem to tire of hearing foreigners tell them how sensational their buildings/women/steaks/footballers are. One can stroke one's chin and impute this to insecurity, a need for validation, a bang on the head during childhood, or whatever. Or one can simply conclude that, despite all its problems, Buenos Aires was, is, and probably always will be one of the world's great cities.

We – surprise, surprise – lean towards the latter diagnosis. And we strongly suspect that, by the end of your stay, you will too. To adapt a non-tango standard, Buenos Aires gets under your skin and deep in the heart of you. And not necessarily for the reasons most people imagine. You can get a bad steak in Argentina and for every beautiful person, there are dozens who look like the author of this chapter. There are even people who can't play football. Do you want to know BA's secret? We do too.

BA by numbers

40 million population of Argentina in 2007.
12.5 million population of metropolitan BA in 2007 (3.1 million in the federal capital).
12th BA's ranking in list of world's biggest cities.
142nd BA's ranking (out of 144) in list of world's most expensive cities.
4th BA's ranking in list of world's noisiest cities (Corrientes and Madero is the loudest street corner).
1:30 ratio of psychoanalysts to population in Argentina.
1:100 same ratio in developed nations.
20 percentage of *porteños* who define themselves as 'unhappy'.
1 in 30 number of Argentinians who have undergone plastic surgery since 1970.
1 in 10 number of adolescent girls in Argentina suffering from an eating disorder.
40 percentage of Argentinian population living below the poverty line in 2005.
41 percentage of young Argentinians who say they would accept a bribe.
4 number of presidents since 1914 to complete a full term and hand power to elected successor.
7 number of Argentinian presidents since the 2001 crisis.
20 percentage of Argentinians who are practising Roman Catholics.
15 age of sexual consent in Argentina.
1986 year that divorce became legal in Argentina.
2003 year that same-sex civil union was legalised in Buenos Aires.
14,000 number of left-wing dissidents 'disappeared' under military rule from 1976 to 1983 according to official reports.
30,000 number of left-wing dissidents 'disappeared' according to most human rights groups.
1st Argentina's world ranking for soy meal and soy oil exports.
4th Argentina's world ranking for beef exports in 2007.
60kg amount of beef consumed per year per capita in Argentina.
7th Argentina's world ranking for wine consumption.
92 percentage of Argentinian households in which *mate* is drunk.
50,000 estimated number of tangos composed (and counting).
20 percentage of city streets still cobbled.

Spontaneous tango breaks out in bars and cafés across the capital.

Tango

The dance that still seduces.

Sex and death. Lust and frigidity. Rhythm and high-heeled shoes. *Mujeres y hombres.* Tango has always been about competing interests. Its flirtation with paradox is how, on one hand, it seduces us because it is ancient and timeless – in a world fixated with fads and fashions – and, on the other, it is rejuvenated, renovated and reimagined more often than Argentinian TV star Marcelo Tinelli's hairstyle (*see p41*).

Five years ago, Franco-Swiss-Argentinian outfit Gotan Project and their BA counterparts Bajofondo Tangoclub seemed to be the latest, coolest thing. Now the electrotango beat is as tired as yesterday's TV ident. Nonetheless, the 'boom' goes on, in a way. The Buenos Aires International Tango Festival (*see p212*) is in its tenth edition in 2008, and is firmly established as a major local event, as well as a key fixture on the international tourist calendar. Free tango classes build up to the week-long celebration, with hundreds of shows and tango-inspired events. The whole city jives to the rhythm of its native sound. In addition to gifted soloists, ageing veterans and emerging stars, the festival is increasingly a showcase for new *orquestas típicas.* These ten- to 12-piece bands, often fronted by four to six *bandoneón* (button accordion) players, fell by the wayside after the 1960s (probably because no one could pay that many people), but leading musicians such as Rodolfo Mederos and Leopoldo Federico have led the way in reforming groups and mixing old hands with young virtuosos to take the concert and ballroom tango into a new century.

In early 2008, the city government strategically changed the festival's dates from its February/March fixture to mid-August, so that attendees could continue tango-ing at the much less publicised Campeonato Mundial de Baile de Tango – in its sixth edition for 2008. This popular event is aimed primarily at dancers and voyeurs with a particular fetish for suspender belts and fishnet tights. That's to say, just about all voyeurs. It kicks off on the day the International Tango Fest ends, so you can do both in a single trip, for dates *see p212.*

November 2007 saw the first ever Queer Tango Festival, part of the city's campaign to become a major gay tourism capital and secure an inflow of pink pounds, pesos and dollars. With its fierce women and camp Gardel lookalikes, tango lends itself to easy queering, and no doubt the people behind the Axel Hotel (*see p235*) are already considering erecting a Gay Tango property alongside all the other tango-themed hotels that have appeared in the city. Tango tourism continues to grow, with the *milonga* scene particularly attractive as a point-of-entry for single American women. It might seem a long way to come for a firm hand on your back and a mere nod from some local stud, but it certainly beats internet dating.

Beyond the festival roster, impressive orchestras such as Sexteto Mayor, El Arranque, the Pablo Ziegler Trío, the Walter Rios Trio and solo performers such as Sandra Luna, Rodolfo Mederos (now fronting a large *orquesta típica*) and Juan Carlos Cáceres continue to play to full houses not only in Argentina, but in tango-loving cities around the world. You can catch a live quintet or a big band at venues such as the Torquato Tasso (*see p258*) or Salón Canning (*see p256*) clubs, and, if you are lucky, a superstar like Daniel Barenboim conducting grand tangos at the Colón theatre. Several orchestras also play live (usually free) at municipal theatres, cultural centres or even on the streets of San Telmo for the Sunday market.

'Few would deny that Buenos Aires and tango are inextricably linked.'

For all this, some think tango has had its day and is an anodyne fixation for a culture too slothful to enter a new, more relevant phase. Few would deny that Buenos Aires and tango are inextricably linked. That tango should be exploited by private and public sectors looking for the tourist coin is unsurprising, so to avoid a cheesy or merely dull night out, check the listings in the tango chapter before booking a show, searching for artists to see, or looking for your first lessons. There is a big difference between good and bad tango. Even if you're not moved to get into tango – and it's not the easiest of world music genres to penetrate – do brush up on the history and the broader culture of tango if you want to understand *porteños* and their rich culture better.

HISTORY FOR BEGINNERS

First appearing in the last quarter of the 19th century, the dance had its debut in Buenos Aires' outlying immigrant quarters, where Italians, Spaniards, blacks and urban *gaucho criollos* uprooted from the pampas brought together elements of *habanera*, polka, Spanish *contradanza* and Argentinian *milonga* (country songs) to create a new beat.

Responding to this hybrid sound, the local *compadritos* (small-time hoods) forged a lively, leg-twitching bop, which simulated the violent knife fights that characterised life in the *arrabales* (slums). Some tango historians believe the early dances were a send-up of those performed by black Africans, and links have been traced to 500-year-old dances in Angola.

It was in this context that *lunfardo* – BA's unique street slang – evolved, as the semi-literate *compadritos* modified the Spanish

language, mixing in Italian and Genovese words and, occasionally, the names of products or local businesses. Like young guns everywhere, they wanted to show that they belonged to a group, and a particularly cool one, at that; at the same time, the slang helped them to communicate without the authorities – police, jailers, even their parents – understanding what they were saying.

Some historians have over-emphasised tango's associations with whorehouses in these early years, but it's now generally agreed that the music served mainly as entertainment for those in the waiting room – a sort of live muzak for those about to undergo a more intimate and pleasurable check-up.

In the city's southern barrios of Pompeya, La Boca and Barracas, life moved to the rhythm of tango, and the romance of *El Sur* was given its first impulse. From humble beginnings in social and football clubs, tango moved to more central *boites* (salons), and the richer residents of Recoleta and Palermo began to take an interest in the new fashion. Between 1870 and 1910, the dance was transformed from a morally dubious jig of the underclasses into the latest craze of the *niños bien* (rich kids).

Dressed to impress.

Dames, daggers and drugs

It's easy to spin a tale about *tangueros* being a bit dodgy. Take Agustín Magaldi (1898-1938), one of the stars of BA tango between 1910 and 1920, and a rival of Carlos Gardel. In the musical *Evita* the crooner is portrayed as a wise guy who escorted 15-year-old Eva Duarte to BA in return for a quick tango. In reality, Magaldi was a clean-faced, married mummy's boy, known as the 'sentimental voice of Buenos Aires'. The clothes are also a red herring. Just because you wear a black pinstripe suit, patent leather shoes and spats, a cocked fedora-style hat and a greased-down 'tache, it doesn't mean you're a gangster. London lawyers are almost as dapper, after all. The same goes for suspenders, high stilettos and skirts split up to the waist. It's so easy to misconstrue. But the tangopolis has produced a few characters...

El Cachafaz *1885-1942*
Boedo-born Ovidio José Bianquet, nicknamed 'El Cachafaz' or 'the Rogue', was a legend of the dancefloor in the early 1900s. He was skinny, had a pockmarked mug, and wore black kid shoes with a military heel. One day he turned up at Palermo's Hansen club and, after blithely seducing one of the local women, was challenged by a rival dancer, 'El Pardo' Santillan. Cachafaz strutted his stuff, and was by far the best dancer. The two slicksters almost came to blows, but

Cachafaz's best friend, El Paisanito, was standing close by and gave everyone a flash of his knife to calm things down.

Celedonio Flores *1896-1947*
Songwriter and poet Flores was born and raised in Villa Crespo when it was still a *barrio* on the edge of the city and a meeting place for immigrant labourers, relocated gauchos, lowlifers and tango dancers. He wrote many classics, including 'Corrientes y Esmeralda' – a corner in the city known as Siberia because of all the snow that fell up people's noses – which alludes to tramps, whores, booze, drunks, prisoners and the pleasures of a *pris* or 'snort of coke'. The military coup of 1943 ushered in a period of strict censorship that lasted into the Perón years – Flores was one of the many great lyricists to be banned.

Aníbal Troilo *1911-1975*
'I live the night intensely, the small hours,' Aníbal 'Pichuco' Troilo (pictured above) told *Extra* magazine in 1965. Mention his name to anyone inside or outside the tango circuit and they will immediately associate the name with booze and nocturnal excess. But it was as a *palero* or cocaine-user – that Troilo excelled, and in films of his live shows, it's hard to tell if it's the music or the white stuff that is sending him into outer space. He wasn't just a fan of the marching powder

TANGO'S TRANSFORMATION

To become truly acceptable to the upper classes, though, tango had to be shown worthy of European culture. As early as 1906, tango scores had travelled to France, and the dance was consecrated in 1910 as the latest fad for the Paris bourgoisie. London and New York were quick to follow suit. This excursion overseas sealed it for Buenos Aires, and tango was no longer a scandalous, proletarian affair. By the time brothels were banned in 1919, tango was already as respectable as the waltz, but far more exciting and intimate.

Tango took a new musical turn with *tango canción* (tango song) when Carlos Gardel recorded *Mi Noche Triste* in 1917. Though

there were tango-like songs set to music before then, this is recognised as the first true sung tango in terms of its structure and Gardel's vocal style.

Of obscure roots, Gardel incarnates the *porteño* model of the working-class immigrant made good (a myth that often obscures his musical achievements), but for audiences in the 1920s it was his emotive tenor voice that made him a star. After establishing a name for himself as a *payador*, singing country songs to guitar accompaniment, he gradually moved to tango to become its leading exponent and ambassador. His life, musical career and the films he made in the US exemplify the social metamorphosis of tango. It developed from either: he loved bars, nightclubs, hanging out with the lads, gambling and, above all, las mujeres: 'women are probably the best thing that life has to offer,' he said.

Astor Piazzolla *1921-1992*
When Troilo met Piazzolla (pictured right) in the 1930s, he thought he was a bit wet to say the least – all that fancy finger work and classical training. But what particularly disappointed the veteran bandoneonist was that Piazzolla wasn't an all-night-partier. Piazzolla declared to journalist Bernardo Neustadt that 'the keyboard is the drug', and that he didn't even need whisky to compose. But Piazzolla was, like many geniuses, a moody, reckless, argumentative, often authoritarian maestro – and lived up to Troilo's assessment that 'you're the devil in person'.

Daniel Melingo *b. 1957*
The closest thing contemporary tango has to rock slummers such as Tom Waits or Lou Reed, Melingo has revitalised tango's talent for the grim and the gothic. The former Los Abuelos de la Nada saxophone player and Los Twist guitarist delivers his cheeky, *lunfardo*-laced lyrics in a dead-pan growl, and his 1998 album *Tangos Bajos* was peopled by likeable no-hopers sloping around in Buenos Aires's underworld of drugs, crime, corruption and cocaine.

Roberto Goyeneche *1926-1994*
Catulo Castillo's great tango about drunkenness, 'La Ultima Curda' – 'The Last Bender' – could have been written for Roberto 'Polaco' Goyeneche. Listen to the albums he made at the end of his career on the *Melopea* label, and you hear the slurring, blurring, occasionally barking voice of a blissfully semi-conscious artist who is beyond all hope. He got into such a state that In his later live shows, El Polaco kept a stash of charlie wrapped up in his pocket handkerchief, which he would surreptitiously take out between songs to nosebag from, while pretending to wipe the sweat off his brow.

Rosita Quiroga *1896-1984*
She was described by one journalist as 'the Piaf of the BA burbs'. A lisping, *lunfardo*-rapping lounge lizard from the La Boca district, Quiroga is unique in the annals of women tango artists for her liking of harsh language and the traditionally 'male' themes of dockside life. For many years she worked with writer Celedonio Flores, who wrote 'Muchacho, Beba and Audacia' for her ('If your old dear, the posh one, could lift her head up in the coffin and see you now... she'd die from indignation').

impromptu suburban bop into a cross-cultural, classless art form.

At the same time, the musical form moved on, trios becoming sextets to provide a richer sound for the dance halls. By the late 1930s, *orquestas típicas* – four *bandoneóns*, four violins, piano and double bass – were the darlings of the salon, and dozens of them played the circuit. Conservatory-trained Italians, such as Juan de Dios Filiberto and Julio de Caro, made tango more sophisticated, Filiberto in a traditional vein and De Caro exploring tango's potential as an evolving, experimental form. Just as the adoption of tango by the middle classes conveniently ignored its origins, so the importance of the dance's black roots was forgotten, as tango shed its folky origins and took on classical airs; even in contemporary histories, tango is presented as a very white, European affair.

From the 1920s on, tango was the 'in' thing in Buenos Aires, and the artists of this period – all those named above, as well as conductor Osvaldo Fresedo, lyricist Enrique Santos Discépolo and Francisco Canaro – make up the bulk of its most famous exponents.

Technological advancement in film, radio and the recording industry also helped its success. In the late 1930s and 1940s, new talents emerged, two giants among them: composer and *bandoneón* player extraordinaire Aníbal Troilo and composer Osvaldo Pugliese.

Troilo's orchestra was widely considered the best in town, and Pugliese shone as a key innovator, his ear-pleasing onomatopoeic compositions and staccato rhythm adored by dancers. Inspired by Gardel, Ada Falcón, Nelly Omar and Ignacio Orsini kept up the songs of *tango canción* for adoring audiences in BA and overseas.

FROM BOEDO TO BROADWAY

The young *bandoneón* player Astor Piazzolla worked with Troilo, but wanted to take tango even further – in a direction that would leave dancers cold, but thrill music-lovers. Exploring tango's affinity with jazz, he successfully fused the two forms and created *Nuevo Tango*. With poet Horacio Ferrer, he took tango into the modern world, attracting a new international audience and leaving traditionalists in BA to debate whether his highly lyrical, often frantic and explosive sound was tango at all.

'There's a *tanguero* nostalgia hanging in the air like musty French tobacco.'

In the 1970s and 1980s, Piazzolla spent time in Italy and toured the US and Japan, moving increasingly towards jazz fusion. Milongas continued to draw the tango faithful, and since young professional dancers still sought a challenge, an era of exportable shows set in. Dancer-choreographer Juan Carlos Copes' bestselling show *Tango Argentino*, which took off in Buenos Aires before repeating its success on Broadway in the 1980s, created a fresh international fashion in tango shows that has been re-imported into the capital by the burgeoning tourist industry. If it's through the great composers and lyricists that tango's history can be traced, then it's the dance that offers an opportunity to explore the roots of the *porteño* psyche.

Many commentators cite memorable, pithy expressions for tango – 'the vertical expression of a horizontal desire' – or wax excitedly about the dance's sensuality. But it has many shades, which can be read as an index of social, emotional and sexual traits: the playful suggestiveness, the decorous codes, the repressed hysteria, the absence of frivolity and let-it-all-go sexuality – in tango, there is nothing of the explosive, orgasmic energy of Brazilian rhythms. Moreover, the obvious machismo in the dance – it is the male who gives the nod to dance, who approaches, who leads – is reflected in the tango scene of mainly male composers, male singers and male DJs on the radio.

CITY OF TANGO

As well as being a visible, audible, danceable cultural expression, tango is also a set of myths, values, traditions and aspirations. Poet, librettist and songwriter Horacio Ferrer has coined the term 'tangopolis', alluding to an essential tango soul in BA and its residents.

At the obvious level, this would include the iconography of the songs – street lamps, corners, old bars, dancers in split skirts and suits strutting their stuff on familiar streets – but Ferrer believes tango is wired into the Argentinian psyche and embedded in the hidden archaeology of the city.

You can't avoid tango. Gardel's mug smiles from murals, shop windows, posters, CD covers and magazines. In the Chacarita cemetery, there's a bronze of his body and another one in Abasto – where Gardel's stamping ground, there are Gardel chemists, a Gardel Subte station and sections of the shopping mall named after his songs. Even the language is infected by icons: a great person is called 'Gardel'.

It's not all the main man though. Street corners, plazas and streets are dedicated to Enrique Santos Discépolo, Homero Manzi, Astor Piazzolla and, since 2005 – the anniversary of his birth – Osvaldo Pugliese. In barrios that have adopted tango – La Boca, San Telmo and Boedo all claim a key role in its genesis – there are bars and cafés named after tango stars. On Balcarce, between Avenida Belgrano and Estados Unidos, are the few blocks always chosen by many tango guides, with walks taking in Michelangelo, Bar Sur and El Viejo Almacén. Even when there are no shows, concerts or lone strummers, there's a *tanguero* nostalgia hanging in the air like musty tobacco.

If you're really passionate and serious about the dance, you can even study for a degree in tango at the Academia Nacional del Tango (*see p258*). Radio shows, including a tango-only service at Radio de la Ciudad (92.7 FM), and the Solo Tango cable TV channel, allow non-dancing fans to live and breathe the rhythms of the old port town while they drive taxis, do the ironing or get ready to go out. All major record shops have tango sections, and specialists such as Zival's (*see p207*) and Casa Piscatelli (San Martín 459, Microcentro, 4394 1992) have an amazing range.

Balancing on taxi dashboards and oddly displayed on garage walls, tango relics appear everywhere. To get your own souvenirs, there are numerous tango tack shops, with enough kitsch paraphernalia to keep any fan happy. Check out the market stalls on Plaza Dorrego and the shops around the square or the wacky tango diaries in city bookshops. There's even a news stand dedicated to tango at the corner of Avenida Corrientes and Paraná, with books and pamphlets on tango's history, lyrics and heroes, as well as CDs. For the more serious tangophile, specialist shops such as Chamuyo (Sarmiento 1562, Tribunales, 4381 1777) and Fattomano (Guatemala 4464, Palermo Viejo, 4823 3156) supply dancers with sultry stilettos and belle époque accoutrements.

If you want to see tango exhibits, there are several informative places to check out. The Academia Nacional del Tango (*see p258*) has a well put together Museo Mundial del Tango; the Casa del Teatro (Avenida Santa Fe 1243, 4813 5906) has a small Gardel room, open Tuesday and Thursday afternoons from 4pm to 6.30pm; and Bótica del Angel (Luis Sáenz Peña 541, Congreso, 4384 9396) is a 'living museum' of tango, but can only be visited via prearranged guided tours. Piazzolla Tango (*see p259*) downtown has a small museum and photo gallery, and the revamped Museo Casa Carlos Gardel (*see p254*), where the star was born, is worth visiting. Round the corner from the latter, on Zelaya, are murals venerating the Gardelian image. With Gardel in Chacarita cemetery is a whole pantheon dedicated to other tangueros including Pugliese, Goyeneche and Troilo.

But it's not all memorabilia and museums. Ferrer – a tangosopher and tanganalyst to his core – also hints at a more subtle tango play being performed on the city streets. What about the way *porteña* women walk? The way the sexes look each other up and down in the streets? Tangopolitans also include lonely bachelors, taxi drivers and caretakers, with radios as their only company, arguably the true bearers of the tango heritage – modern day versions of those immigrants who came up with the first tangos. Nationalist writer Raúl Scalabrini Ortiz wrote a novel infused with the tango spirit called *El hombre que está solo y espera* – the man who is alone and waits, meaning you don't necessarily need music, fancy clothes or even a partner to feel the rhythms and resonances of tango in Buenos Aires. Real tango is felt in daily existence.

Early in 2008, tango was given a new, potentially significant, renewal with the release of the film *Café de los Maestros*, directed by Miguel Kohan and with Gustavo Santaolalla (Bajofondo boss and Oscar-winning soundtrack composer) overseeing the music. Santaolalla has always insisted he did a Buena Vista Social Club long before Cooder and Wenders took their lucky flight to Havana – when he accompanied rock-folk star León Gieco on a town-hopping tour of Argentina for the recording of 1985's *De Ushuaia a La Quiaca* (an album and photo book). But if *Café* is a hit, it could do for tango what BVSC did for Cuban music – and then the so-called boom, which has so far been but a pale shadow of the tango booms of the first half of the 20th century, could take a new direction altogether.

Sex and sensuality on the streets of **San Telmo**.

River Plate take on Boca Juniors.

Football

Marvels and madness in Maradona's home city.

Moments after an Argentinian is born, crying and helpless, parents go through an important ritual: that of naming the baby's football team. A tiny jersey, probably fake, will then be ceremoniously placed on the child, thus colouring their lives blue and gold, red and white or claret and blue forever. At some point later the child will probably be named and baptised too, but as those who claim to know nothing about the beautiful game know, football in Argentina is more important than religion. Its influence even stretches into the afterlife. Have a look around Recoleta or Chacarita cemeteries where blue and gold flowers and trinkets signal the deceased's love for Boca Juniors. One BA funeral director actually makes coffins with the Boca logo on them (he refuses to make River ones).

It is a game that touches life perhaps more here than in any other city in the world. Walls are plastered with graffiti, memorabilia hangs from each rearview mirror, and every other person you pass wears a replica shirt.

'Which team do you support?' is basically an Argentinian greeting, unless of course they learn you're English, in which case Maradona's 'Mano de Dios' (hand of God) will be mentioned. But even those who confess to hate *fútbol* can't fail to get caught up in the passion *porteños* exude for it. Seeing a game is a highlight of any trip, just be careful which shirt you wear.

FEDORAS FOR GOALPOSTS

Like most of Argentina's culture and heritage, football came down the gangplank. It was British sailors in the 1860s who first introduced the game here, their shore leave kickabouts on the city's dusty plazas attracting first the attention and then the participation of locals. By the end of the 19th century amateur clubs had been founded in and around the city, and the game began its inexorable rise from fringe pastime to national pursuit.

So speedy was this process that, in 1930, Argentina reached the final of the first World Cup, losing to hosts Uruguay. The *selección* (as the Argentinian national team is known) gave an early demonstration of the two contrasting elements that always seem to define their play: brilliant skill and murky controversy. Unable to agree on which type of ball to use for the match, it was decided that an Argentinian brand would be used in the first half and a Uruguayan one in the second. At half-time Argentina were leading 2–1; by the end they had lost 4–2. Still muttering darkly about 'rigged balls', Argentinian footballers turned professional the following year.

Achievement and notoriety would continue to bless/dog Argentinian football. In the famously ill-tempered quarter-final between Argentina and England in the 1966 World Cup, Alf Ramsey's 'wingless wonders' beat the South

Americans 1–0. After Argentinian captain Antonio Rattin had been sent off for dissent, the match degenerated into a scrappy, dirty affair, and a rivalry was born that endures to this day.

Argentina finally got their hands on the World Cup trophy in 1978 when, playing on home turf, they beat the Netherlands 3–1. For the ruling military junta, it was a public relations coup to add to their military one of two years before. There were rumours that the Peruvian team was bribed to throw their group match against Argentina, allowing the latter to reach the final ahead of Brazil.

But 1986 in Mexico was a different ball game. The record states that Argentina won the World Cup by edging out West Germany 3–2 in the final. Far more memorable, however, was the quarter-final against England, illuminated by the divine talent and devilish opportunism of Diego Maradona. 'El Diez' (after his shirt number) scored one goal through pure skill – often cited as the best ever – and another through sheer cheek, knocking the ball past a floundering Peter Shilton with his hand – the infamous 'Hand of God' goal. It was sweet revenge for 1966; some – Maradona included – have also referred to the now legendary moment as payback for the Falklands/Malvinas debacle of 1982.

During the 2006 World Cup final, it wasn't only posturing *porteños* who saw their team as favourites, it was the rest of the world as well, with the possible exception of anyone in a yellow and green shirt. A 6–0 win over Serbia and Montenegro and a comfortable 2–1 win over the Ivory Coast may not have been against the toughest opponents, but Argentina did what they like to think they do best: play beautiful sweeping, selfish football. Not even a 0–0 draw against the Netherlands could dampen the spirits of those who saw them going all the way. But then the inexplicable happened, and Argentina's squad lost their mojo. After losing a quarter-final on penalties against Germany, the team did something else they are renowned for, and fought. It was an ugly display, and one Argentinians are keen to forget. Prospects for 2010, however, are much brighter, with pundits already proclaiming that the national selection is the best since 1986. And with the likes of Maradona's heir apparent, Lionel Messi, and fans' favourite Carlos Tévez, they could be right.

THE TEAMS

A strange thing happened at the end of the 2007. None of the 'big five' teams made it to the top of the table. Instead Club Atlético Lanús, a small team from the southern suburbs, won their first ever domestic tournament. Tigre, from the north of Buenos Aires, came in second, playing their first season in the *Primera*

División (first division) since 1980. Bronze went to Banfield, completing the most unlikely top three, since, well, ever.

Maradona's beloved Boca Juniors, are, of course, the most famous team from Argentina, unless you are a River Plate fan, in which case they are. A meeting between these eternal rivals is one of the most spectacular sporting events on the planet (*see p36* **Derby days**). Other big BA teams include San Lorenzo, the romantic's choice, whose profile is boosted by the support of Marcelo Tinelli, Argentina's top TV presenter; Racing Club and Independiente, both based in the poor southern neighbourhood of Avellaneda, and who share a mutual loathing to rival that of Boca and River; and, from the second division, Chacarita, whose *barra brava* is to other hooligan groups what the SAS is to the Boy Scouts.

SEASONS' GREETINGS

All professional football in Argentina comes under the aegis of the Argentinian Football Association (AFA). They don't believe in giving the players much of an off-season. The only significant hiatus in top-flight action comes during the summer months of December and January when the *Torneo de Verano* (Summer Tournament) is held. This is a chance for the bigger clubs to give their second-string players a run out; nonetheless, the matches, held in resort cities like Mar del Plata, still attract big crowds.

'Argentina's best footballers can still be seen playing every week in BA.'

For teams in the *Primera División*, the rest of the year is divided into two discrete seasons: the *Clausura* (Closing) tournament, from the end of January to May; and the *Apertura* (Opening), from August to December. If you're wondering why the Closing tournament comes at the beginning of the year, take a deep breath and then forget about it.

The system of relegation and promotion is an even harder nut to crack. Teams move between divisions in accordance with their average points score over a three-year period. Thus it's theoretically possible to win the *Primera* and be relegated from it on the same day. Cynics (that is to say, everyone bar AFA) believe this system was introduced to make it virtually impossible for the bigger teams to be relegated.

Argentina's top teams also qualify to play in the Libertadores Cup against championship winners from all over South America. It usually takes place at the beginning of the year. The Copa Sudamericana is later in the year.

Derby days

Football overwhelms other social and cultural activity perhaps like nowhere else in the world. And when two local teams clash, the true passion and fervour of Argentinian football fans comes to the fore in an electrifying show. Boca Juniors versus River Plate is, of course, the biggest derby, but other local games can be equally, if not more, intense. The biggest fights however, are often off the pitch when the fanatical and often, nay usually, violent *barra bravas* (hooligan gangs) clash, often grasping the following morning headlines over the game itself. However, with a little care – go to the *platea* – a visit to one of these encounters could be the highlight of any trip to Buenos Aires, and perfectly safe.

Boca Juniors vs River Plate

With the possible exception of a UFO landing on the Obelisco, there would be no other event that brings the city to a grinding halt like the *superclásico*. Taxi drivers pull up and poke their noses through packed café windows to watch TV, bus drivers pull over to listen intently to the crackly radio and all other manner of events are cancelled while the city watches the most fiercely fought football game in the world. Historically both teams emerged from the poor La Boca tenements around the port, until the 1920s when River Plate moved their stadium to the wealthy Núñez neighbourhood in the northern suburbs. And although both teams draw support from a cross-section of Argentinians, Boca Juniors fans like to think of themselves as being from the marginalised poorer areas, while Los Millonarios, as River Plate fans are also known, have upper class pretensions. Bloody brawls, and occasionally deaths, have marred these encounters in recent times, yet such is the restriction on the number of away fans the *superclásico* has lost some its previous intensity. It is nevertheless a great display of a quintessential part of Argentinian life.

Racing vs Independiente

Without a doubt the second biggest derby is *el clásico de Avellaneda*. Only a city block separates the Racing and Independiente stadiums in the poor Avellaneda neighbourhood just south of the city. Whereas absolutely everyone holds a preference for Boca or River, born and bred Racing and Independiente fans are probably the most

THE PLAYERS

Nothing whets the appetite of the Argentinian sports fan more than the emergence of a new football star. The current darling of the back pages is still Lionel Messi, the lank-haired, twinkle-toed centre forward at Barcelona, who famously scored a goal uncannily similar to Maradona's wondergoal against the English in 1986, swiftly followed by a goal with even more in common to Maradona's *other* goal a week later. Another rising star is Carlos Tévez, formerly of Boca Juniors, who has quickly become a favourite at Manchester United, as has Javier Mascherano at Liverpool. And while most of Argentina's top players ply their trade in Europe, the likes of Juan Román Riquelme,

Martín Palermo and Juan Sebastián Verón can be seen week in, week out, playing in Buenos Aires' ageing stadiums. These players, it would be fair to say, are in the twilight of their career, and when a young footballer (or rather his agent) says 'show me the money', it's more likely to be Real Madrid flashing the cash than River Plate. Interestingly, Argentinians don't seem to resent the fact that their idols play so far away from home. On the contrary, it's a source of national pride. In the same way that 19th-century Irish emigrants would proudly post money back to their families after making it good, the Argentinian soccer diaspora rewards its home following with goals and multi-million dollar transfer rumours.

die-hard loyal fans in BA. Match day in Avellaneda is an overwhelming affair, perhaps even more so than Boca versus River (shhh), especially in the cavernous Racing stadium which amplifies the fans' cries. Violence occasionally erupts, and at a 2006 game, such problems led the Argentinian Football Association to ban all away fans in all divisions for a few weeks.

San Lorenzo vs Huracán

Recently San Lorenzo, from the Almagro neighbourhood, have been consistently riding high in the league table, winning the 2007 season. Huracán however, have been loitering in the second division for a few seasons. But after they were promoted in 2007 the derby between these two could continue. The hatred between the Cuervos, (Crows) as San Lorenzo fans are known, and the Quemeros (Burners – after the rubbish incinerator on the site of Huracán's Parque Patricios stadium) is palpable in any encounter. A victory for Huracán over San Lorenzo is probably a sweeter moment for their fans than even winning the title.

Best of the rest

Although the smaller teams don't attract such a city-wide following, the fans are no less zealous and with Lanús, Tigre and Banfield finishing one, two and three in the 2007 Opening season, the clubs are gaining popularity and their fans, notoriety. *El clásico del sur* (the derby of the south) is between Lanús and Banfield, the only two teams from the southern suburbs in the Primera (first division), the cities separated by a single road. One of the most feared, or at least most raucous, *barra* support Nueva Chicago from the Mataderos neighbourhood, recently relegated to the Argentinian second division. The fans – who once lent their support to polo's number one Adolfo Cambiasso's team at a top flight chukka when he came out as a Nueva Chicago fan, to the horror of the polo glitterati – have enemies around the city, with Vélez Sársfield being particularly hated. Outside the capital, the Rosario derby between Central and Newell's Old Boys and in La Plata between Juan Sebastián Verón's Estudiantes and Gimnasia are also entertaining affairs.

MATCH DAY

To comprehend just how important football is to the average Argentinian, simply go to a game. To be a true football fan, follow the well-honed rituals of any football fan on match day. *A)* Wake up to the sound of non-stop football punditry on your radio, shower in team-branded soap and then pop on your retro 1972 top. *B)* Pick up a copy of the daily sporting paper *Olé* and head to a preordained bar for a Quilmes beer while deconstructing the team line up. *C)* Get to the stadium early to soak up the pre-match atmosphere. This usually involves chanting derogatory songs at any unsuspecting person wearing the wrong shirt, buying a *choripán* (hotdog) – possibly the most dangerous custom – and buying a fluffy, naff hat. *D)* After the *barra brava* have slipped past the police into the stadium, make your way through various friskings and walk up into the stand to the truly overwhelming sight of 30,000 or so bouncing and singing fans. *E)* Boo as the referee walks onto the pitch (it doesn't matter that he hasn't made a descision yet), and scream the worst word you know in Spanish as the opposition appear. And as your team walk out, throw the pile of ripped newspaper you were just handed into the air for a spectacular ticker-tape effect. *F)* Spend the next 90 minutes shouting yourself hoarse, enjoying what is usually a thrilling game and gaping at the unique spectacle that are the fans of Argentinian football.

A-Z BA Life

Find out what the taxi driver is harping on about with our handy A-Z guide to the idiosyncracies of life in the capital.

A is for after office

You don't have to work in an office to go to an 'after office' party – but you will need a lurid tie, a crisp white shirt, and your best David Brent/Michael Scott attitude. These self-explanatory events are hugely popular with the young white-collar set, lured in by 2-for-1 booze promotions, the chance to start the weekend on Wednesday, and an atmosphere in which pheromones seem to drift across the dancefloor like dry ice. Tempted? Check out **Dadá** or **La Cigale** (*see p167*).

B is for butt shots

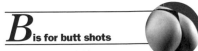

Argentinian publishing companies were a bit slow out of the gate when it came to the 'lads' mag' phenomenon of the 1990s, but no sooner had they caught up than they were sprinting ahead. Now the average *kiosco* groans with porn masquerading as periodicals, with titles ranging from international standards like *Maxim* to local efforts like *H*. The cover-art paradigm is pretty straightforward and usually integrates the following components: a scowling woman in her early twenties positioned as if she were being prepped for a gastrointestinal endoscopy; a large pair of fake boobs, nipples airbrushed (anything else would be in poor taste); and a good bad pun for the headline. Optional extras include handcuffs and another girl or two.

C is for Crónica TV

Launched in 1994 as Argentina's first 24-hour news channel, Crónica is like CNN…if CNN had no budget, was run from a lunatics' asylum, and devoted most of its afternoon programming to lottery results read by puppets (the iconic Carozo and Narizota). The format is crass, unchanging, and annoyingly addictive: punchy headlines in big white type on a red background set to the accompaniment of John Philip Sousa's military march *The Stars and Stripes Forever*. Specialising in car wrecks, domestic violence and lingering shots of leaky body bags, *Crónica* is, above all, political incorrectness incarnate and impossible to parody. Among celebrated headlines are: 'Three people and a Bolivian killed' and '90-year-old man gropes woman on her 100th birthday'. Charming.

D is for dog walkers

What could *porteños* possibly love more than their pet dogs and their easy access to cheap, cash-in-hand labour? The answer is, of course, professional dog walkers. These hulking hound-minders are a common sight around many of the city's swankier quarters, and the true pros in their ranks can walk a dozen or more dogs at the same time without breaking sweat. The going rate is AR\$5 per dog per three-hour walk. Some dog walkers actually walk their charges, though these types tend to be amateurs who quickly catch on. The more common practice is to tie one's dogs to a railing in a plaza while one kills a couple of hours shooting the breeze with other walkers. It's fair to say most walkers have a laissez-faire attitude towards their charges' poop and where to leave it.

E is for embracing

Tough guys not only dance in BA, they also smooch – or at the very least reward each other with Tony Soprano-style backslaps. This is a source of angst for many tourists, particularly

those who feel squeamish about sharing a lift with a stranger, let alone going cheek-to-cheek with him. Relax. The worse that can happen is that you end up feeling like a total fool. When greeting an older person, or in a formal setting, it's generally safer to offer a hand. If, by accident, you do something completely inappropriate, use your get-out-of-jail-free card and simply shrug: 'I'm a gringo, what do I know?'

F is for Fernet

Such is its popularity in Argentina, it's easy to forget that Fernet Branca is an Italian brand, a type of amaro liquor whose recipe, which incorporates more than 40 herbs and spices, is a closely guarded (aren't they all?) secret dating back to 1845. A member of that sadly mythical family of alcoholic drinks which 'don't give you a hangover', Fernet is usually 'enjoyed' either as a short, sharp shot or blended with cola to make a sweet, sickly and highly potent cocktail. Younger drinkers tend to enjoy Fernet via the latter method, and are highly appreciative of any foreigner brave enough to give this brew a go.

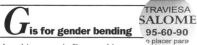

G is for gender bending

Anything goes in Buenos Aires – including the genitalia you were born with. While cross-dressing has always had a place in mainstream Argentinian culture, particularly in the popular satirical revues – imagine a collaboration between Benny Hill and Jon Stewart – that still dominate the major theatres, bona fide transsexuals were marginalised until the rise of the glamorous Florencia De La V, born Roberto Carlos Trinidad. Spotted on the club circuit by kingpin impresario Gerardo Sofovich, De La V hit the big-time in 2004 when she starred in *Los Roldán*, a dreadful soap opera that was – what a surprise – a huge hit across great swathes of South America.

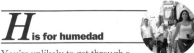

H is for humedad

You're unlikely to get through a holiday, or even a daytrip, in Buenos Aires without hearing plenty about the city's high levels of humidity, cause of the peculiarly dramatic *porteño* obsession with the *sensación térmica*. Humid conditions can make even moderate heat feel oppressive and the cold more cutting, so the so-called 'thermal sensation' measures the temperature your body feels rather than the actual temperature. Drama reaches fever pitch in high summer, when newsflashes regularly state the *sensación térmica* as being over 40°C; on such days, go local and chime in with exclamations such as '*es un horno!*' ('it's an oven!') and '*es un asco!*' ('it's disgusting!'), or why not go one step further and declare: '*es un infierno!*' ('it's hell!').

I is for ice-cream

For those still unpersuaded that BA is a great city, here is a typical exchange between two *porteños* that might tip you over: 'What shall we do?', 'I dunno, what do you reckon?', 'Well, I guess we could buy a kilo of ice-cream and just sit here and eat it.' 'Oh, OK'. That kilo of *helado* (from the Italian gelato) will comprise three or four flavours selected from a vast list of fruit, chocolate, and, of course, dulce de leche, based options. Almost every city block has an *heladería* (ice-cream shop). The best chains, open till late and drawing a post-supper, pre-club crowd, are Freddo, Persico, Chungo and Un'Altra Volta.

J is for Judaism

Buenos Aires has the largest Jewish community in Latin America. The neighourhood of Once is used to be the port of call for arriving Jewish immigrants and its streets were dotted with delicatessens where men would be seen reading Yiddish newspapers, sadly no longer in circulation. Today Jewish culture still thrives with activity centres, theatres, kosher ice-cream shops, restaurants – and the world's second kosher McDonald's (found in Abasto shopping centre). You can even do a Jewish tour of BA (*see p77*) if you fancy. The strength of the city's jewish culture speaks for itself, as there have been dark moments of antisemitism, not to mention the fact that Buenos Aires was also a refuge for Nazis and war criminials – an open-door policy many still dumbfoundedly shake their heads over.

K is for the Kirchners

First there was Néstor, then, in a slick transfer of power, came Cristina….

Kirchnerismo has been the dominant force in Argentinian politics since outspoken Patagonian Néstor Kirchner came into power in 2003, charged with the task of salvaging the economy from the rubble. Despite soaring approval ratings during his term, Néstor nominated his glamorous, globetrotting wife (already a senator) to run in the elections – for many a smart manoeuvre to elude the two-consecutive term limit and thus perpetuate Kirchnerist power. As we went to press, little had been clarified in the way of Cristina's policies, while the media appeared to be much more interested in frivolous chat about whether she has had hair extensions or Botox injections. Still, faced with an energy crisis, inflation and questions about her campaign funding, the *presidenta* will have no shortage of issues on which to prove her political mettle.

L is for love hotels

Sorry, The Supremes: you can hurry love. Known here as *albergues transitorios*, or by the *lunfardo* slang-term *telos* (backslang for 'hotel'), BA's many love hotels (look out for the fizzing neon sign and the clandestine car-ramp) are short-stop nests for lovebirds on the wing. Clients range from kids who can't do it at home because of their parents, to parents who can't do it at home because of their kids, to businessmen 'running through a PowerPoint presentation' with their secretaries. A *turno* gets you two hours' privacy, and costs around AR$50. The fancier *telos* have themed rooms, hot tubs, waterbeds, and access to a worryingly comprehensive range of carnal hardware.

M is for mullets

Kudos to the English football commentator who, on seeing the Argentinian team line up for a match in the 1990s, asked rhetorically: 'Is this a football match or a Michael Bolton look alike convention?'. Trends wax and wane in BA, but the male mullet is still a great way to make a style statement (that statement is: 'I've plenty of free time in the morning to preen my manly flowing locks – apologies for my lack of taste'). Perhaps the greatest Argentinian mullet of all time was that sported by footballer Claudio Caniggia. Wisdom has it that his nickname, 'The son of the wind', referred to his ability to ghost past defenders; but we actually prefer to believe it alluded to his breeze-buffeted blonde barnet.

N is for novelas

Telenovelas, to give them their full title, are the hugely popular soap operas that dominate Argentinian, and indeed South American, TV schedules. Every *novela* strives for originality in its setting and central conceit, but must incorporate the following components: sex; adultery; the cosmic struggle between good and evil; shockingly cheesy soundtrack; at least two pneumatic young actresses who can add value by appearing in the monthly glossies (preferably nude); and at least one housewives'-choice crumpet, a gruff lothario, known as the *galán*.

O is for Once

Tired of BA's 'Paris of South America' pretensions? Bored with all those sweeping, tree-lined boulevards? Then head for Once (pronounced 'ON-say'), the chaotic, congested barrio whose centre is the train station of the same name. Flush with outlets and stalls selling every kind of cheap knock-off you can imagine and packed with people haggling, playing reggaeton on unfeasibly old-looking tape recorders and having minor traffic accidents. Once has also become a byword for discounted and dodgy merchandise, as in: 'Your TV set has just burst into flames. Did you buy it in Once?'

P is for Punta

Geographically, Punta del Este is in Uruguay. Spiritually, it is part of Argentina. Each January this popular coastal resort becomes the mother lode of Latin hedonism for affluent party people, mostly from Buenos Aires. Expect polo tournaments, fashion shows, and the model-tastic Bikini Beach.

Q is for Quilmes

Argentina's national beer, decked out in the blue-and-white of the flag and sponsor to most of the country's major

sports teams, is, of course, Brazilian: it was bought by giant conglomerate AmBev in 2006, for an ice-cool US$2 billion. Never mind this technicality: the sight of a gaggle of youths sharing a one-litre bottle of Quilmes Cristal (this blonde, rather chemical-tasting brew is easily the most popular) sat outside a *kiosco* is a classic Argentinian urban tableau.

R is for Rollingas

Miguel, Carlos, Ronaldo and, er, Keith: the holy quartet of sixty-something rhythm 'n' blues and the absentee leaders of what is arguably the biggest fanclub-cum-tribe in Argentina. *Rollingas* don't just like the Rolling Stones; they live, breathe, and smoke the Stones. They can sing the first two lines of *Brown Sugar*. They see a red door and they want it painted black. They even think *Dirty Work* is a good album. Most are also fans of local outfit, the horrendously named Los Ratones Paranoicos, who look and sound like a crap version of the Stones.

S is for Susana

And the undisputed lightweight champion of Argentinian television is…Susana Giménez (the surname is in fact superfluous; Susana is Susana like Oprah is Oprah). Once a great beauty and a lousy actress, Susana handled the loss of the former by going under the scalpel and finessed the latter by becoming a talk-show host; her evening programme regularly tops the ratings. Like most notable 'dumb blondes', Susana isn't dumb at all. She was well educated and speaks good English. Paleontology – or the study of fossils – however, is not one of her specialities. Once, on live television, a fossil hunter informed her that he 'hunted dinosaurs'. Mouth agape, Susana expostulated: 'What? Alive?!'

T is for Tinelli

As well as being Argentina's most successful male television presenter, Marcelo Tinelli is also, like Diego Maradona, something of a sociocultural litmus test: you can learn a lot about an Argentinian from their opinion of Tinelli and his programme *Showmatch*. For some the show, with its blend of skits, tits, dancing with the stars and brazen product placement is a refreshingly unpretentious, zany chunk of escapism; for others it is cultural effluent, a fart in the face of the nation's collective IQ.

U is for Uruguay

Many locals – particularly the ones who divide their time between Buenos Aires and Miami – will tell you that Uruguay is 'just another province' of Argentina. You would expect Uruguayans to be annoyed by this kind of snarky chauvinism; as it is, they're so laid-back it doesn't seem to bother them. Everyone visiting the region should include a side trip to Uruguay in their itinerary. Options include: the Portuguese settlement of Colonia; the stunning coastline that runs all the way north to Brazil; and the underrated interior, with its green rolling hills, sleepy villages and real gauchos.

V is for villa

There are over 30 'official' *villa miserias*, or shantytowns, in Buenos Aires, along with many others that are neither large nor well-established enough to be given a number by the local government. *Villas* are poverty-stricken, crime-ridden slums; but, as in Brazil, they are also important incubators of cultural and sporting talent. Diego Maradona and, more recently, Carlos Tévez learned the tricks of their trade on the dusty *potreros* (improvised soccer pitches) that no *villa* is without. *Cumbia Villera*, a dance music genre that was spawned in the BA *villas*, and whose lyrics make Dr. Dre look like Dr. Hook, has been a crossover success in recent years and can now be heard both at high society wedding receptions and in some of BA's most influential underground clubs (*see p218*).

W is for waxing

Argentinian vanity knows no bounds, so it's not a surprise to learn that in Buenos Aires, hair removal, or *depilación*, is about more than mere necessity – it's a vocation in itself. *Depilators*, as they are known, are highly skilled, invariably female, and monomaniacal in their pursuit of the wayward strand of hair, or *pelito*. Leg, bikini line, armpits, face, back, and yes, even ass – in Argentina the wax goes on…and on. Useful phrases thus include: '*hasta ahí no más*' ('thus far and no further') and '*no quiero que me hagas el culo, gracias*' ('I don't want you to do my bottom, thanks awfully').

X is for Xeinezes

This is the polite, authorised nickname for Boca Juniors football club and its supporters. (The impolite, unauthorised nickname is *bosteros*, literally 'cowpat makers' – you get the idea.) The sobriquet is a nod to the sizable Genoese community that settled the La Boca barrio at the beginning of the 20th century. *Xeneizes* is actually a slight corruption of the Genoese dialect term *Zeneizes*. No one really knows how and why the 'X' came into play, though you won't hear any complaints from the compilers of A-Z guides.

Y is for yerba mate

Fancy slurping steeped dried holly leaves and twigs through a metal straw from a hollowed-out pumpkin? At first taste (during which foreigners usually report an overwhelming sensation that they are drinking grass), Argentina's national drink *mate* has all the hallmarks of that most euphemistic of denominations – an 'acquired taste'. Stay with it. Prepared in the right way (with hot, but never boiling, water), Argentina's time-honoured drink could have you hooked on its deep smoky flavour, the subtly energising effect and the attendant social rituals. Your starter kit should include a *mate* gourd, the leaves, a *bombilla* (metal straw-filter), a thermos and an open mind.

Z is for zapatos

For some an abundance of gorgeous shoes is worth crying in happiness over. If you're one of those people then the boutiques of Palermo and Recoleta are where to indulge in your fetish. Shoe shops display hand-crafted leather beauties that literally stop people in their tracks. Durable and stylish mens' shoes are equally alluring to even the scruffiest of men. And unlike BA's trendy threads – a bit of a squeeze if you're not size zero – the shoes actually come in sizes that fit people.

Where to Stay

Home Hotel. *See p63*.

Where to Stay

BA's burgeoning boutique options are easing the city's bed crisis. A bit.

From backpackers to hip thirtysomethings, from wealthy businessmen and their families to elderly adventure hunters, they are all heading to BA, lured by a devalued peso (it is still just about a bargain), a cosmopolitan attitude and rich cultural heritage. But the huge increase in tourism since 2001 took many by surprise, resulting in a lack of beds in the city, or at least nice ones with fluffy pillows and a view.

Fortunately the number of hotels is beginning to meet demand, especially in the small boutique sector, meaning that with a little forward planning you can find some of the best accomodation in the world, no matter what your budget or reasons for coming.

There are hotels for wannabe oenologists (**Miravida Soho**; *see p63*), tango aficionados (**Abasto Plaza**; *see p69*, and **Mansión Dandi Royal**; *see p53*), design geeks (**Tailor Made Hotel**; *see p69*, and **Home Hotel**; *see p63*), stylish gay hotels (**Axel**; *see p237*) and those wanting luxury (**Faena Hotel + Universe**; *see p55*, and the **Alvear Palace Hotel**; *see p57*).

Local design creativity, combined with international design investment and the Argentinian genius for hospitality, come together successfully in the boutique hotels that we have listed in this chapter, which by their nature tend to be small and book up quickly. Like many of Buenos Aires's great hotels they are often refurbished old houses, the best of them retaining some of their previous grandeur. Palermo and San Telmo are the best places to snuggle into a cosy retreat. Downtown and the exclusive Recoleta areas are dominated by larger hotels popular for their proximity to the business centre. It is also the best place for budget hotels.

South of the city, in the run-down areas of Constitución and Barracas are to be found dirt cheap lodgings that are mostly aimed at poor immigrant workers, known as Hoteles Familiares. Further afield and across Argentina, New Age Hotels (www.newage-hotels.com) has an impressive range of unique boutique hotels and estancias.

> ❶ Green numbers given in this chapter correspond to the location of each hotel as marked on the street maps. *See pp322-329.*

PRICES, BOOKINGS AND SERVICES

Our listings follow these categories: **Luxury** (over US$250/AR$750 for a double); **Expensive** (US$150-$250/AR$450-$750); **Moderate** (US$80-$150/AR$240-$450); **Budget** (under US$80/AR$240). We have given rates in US dollars; expect them to rise. Prices given in this chapter include 21 per cent VAT, and breakfast. If you want to rent – or even buy – a property, consider the following: **4 Rent** (www.4rentargentina.com), **El Cachafaz** (www.elcachafaz.com), **Living in Baires** (www.livinginbaires.com), **landinargentina** (www.landinargentina.com), **Room Argentina** (www.roomargentina.com), **BA House** (www.bahouse.com.ar), **Maison Buenos Aires** (www.maisonbuenosaires.com) and **Buenos Aires Habitat** (www.buenos aireshabitat.com), which offers the full gamut of real estate and rental services.

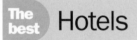

The best Hotels

For period drama
To glimpse BA's former grandeur book into the **Alvear Palace Hotel** (*see p57*) or **Park Hyatt Buenos Aires** (*see p57*).

For boutique bliss
Design students, bons vivants and Mac geeks need to see **Home Hotel** (*see p63*) and **Tailor Made Hotel** (*see p69*).

For peerless extravagance
Few are more opulent than the kitsch chic of **Faena Hotel + Universe** (*see p55*) or traditional **Marriott Plaza Hotel** (*see p47*).

For bargain hunters
The **Castelar Hotel** (*see p49*) or **Casa Alfaro** (*see p67*) best for budget seekers.

For urban escapes
Head to **Five** (*see p63*), **BoBo Hotel** (*see p61*) and **1555 Malabia House** (*see p61*) to hide away from the frenetic city life.

For sweet suites
Soho All Suites (*see p63*) and **Loft y Arte** (*see p51*) for independence.

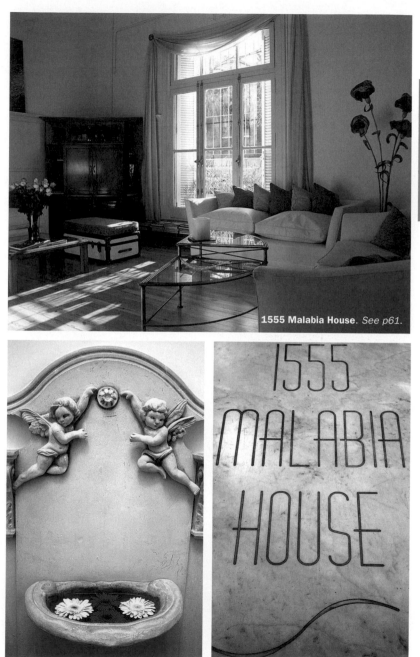

1555 Malabia House. *See p61*.

The Centre

Luxury

725 Buenos Aires

*Avenida Roque Sáenz Peña 725, y Perón (4131
8000/www.725buenosaireshotel.com). Subte C,
Diagonal Norte/28, 93, 152 bus.* **Rates** US$365-$460.
Rooms 192. **Credit** AmEx, DC, MC, V.
Map p325 F11 ❶
A tastefully decorated space located in the city's
bustling downtown area. Aimed at the cultivated
conference traveller, the rooms are slick, streamlined
and provide free wireless access for every guest. A
vast, airy restaurant called Centrino offers an
extensive menu of modern European fare, while
a small bar offering a choice selection of spirits
borders the heated swimming pool on the hotel's
stylish roof terrace.
*Bar. Business centre. Concierge. Disabled-adapted
rooms. Gym. No-smoking rooms/floors. Internet
(high-speed, wireless). Parking. Pool (outdoor).
Restaurant (2). Room service. Spa. TV: DVD.*
Other locations 562 Nogaro Buenos Aires,
Avenida Julio Argentino Roca 562 (4331 0091).

Marriott Plaza Hotel

*Florida 1005, y Marcelo T de Alvear, Retiro (4318
3069/www.marriottplaza.com.ar). Subte C, San
Martín/93, 130, 152 bus.* **Rates** US$240-$315. **Rooms**
320. **Credit** AmEx, DC, MC, V. **Map** p325 G11 ❷
For almost 100 years, this regal hotel (taken over by
Marriott in 1994) overlooking the verdant Plaza San
Martín has provided a white-gloved service fit for
royalty. Guests have a choice of three sumptuous
restaurants, including the Plaza Hotel Grill with its
Dutch porcelain tiles and fabulous open grill while
cascading chandeliers light the ballrooms.
*Bar. Business centre. Concierge. Disabled-adapted
rooms. Gym. No-smoking rooms/floors. Internet
(high-speed, wireless). Parking. Pool (outdoor).
Restaurants (3). Room service. Spa. TV: DVD.*

Sofitel Buenos Aires

*Arroyo 841, entre Suipacha y Esmerelda, Retiro
(4131 0000/www.sofitelbuenosaires.com.ar). Bus 92,
93, 152.* **Rates** US$425-$485. **Rooms** 144. **Credit**
AmEx, DC, MC, V. **Map** p325 H12 ❸
Housed in the flawlessly restored Torre Bencich (an
art deco tower built in the 1920s), the Sofitel was
opened in 2003 by French hotel group Accor. The
impressive glass-roofed lobby with its black and
white floor and huge chandelier sets the tone. Rooms
are quite small, though the upper floors offer views
of the river, and furnishings have a French twist.
The area around the property has a similarly
Parisian vibe, with smart cafés and hidden art
galleries. But you may prefer to eat in – the hotel has
one of the best French restaurants in the city, Le Sud.
*Bars (2). Business centre. Concierge. Disabled-
adapted rooms. Gym. No-smoking rooms/floors.
Internet (high-speed, wireless). Parking. Restaurant.
Room service. TV: DVD.*

Expensive

Claridge

*Tucumán 535, entre Florida y San Martín
Microcentro (4314 7700/www.claridge.com.ar).
Subte B, Florida/130, 152 bus.* **Rates** US$205-$395.
Rooms 152. **Credit** AmEx, DC, MC, V.
Map p325 F11 ❹
Close to the business and banking district, and some
of the city's main tourist attractions, stands the
Claridge Hotel. It's decorated throughout in either
mock-Tudor or classic-style design – the rooms are
comfortable but some are considerably smaller than
they look on the hotel's website. Business travellers
will enjoy the spacious meeting rooms, equipped
with state-of-the-art technology – though most deals
will be cut in the piano bar over cocktails and under
the doleful gaze of the wall-mounted moose head.
*Bar. Business centre. Concierge. Disabled-adapted
rooms. Gym. No-smoking rooms/floors. Internet
(high-speed). Parking. Pool (outdoor). Restaurants
(2). Room service. Spa. TV: DVD.*

Esplendor de Buenos Aires

*San Martín 780, entre Córdoba y Viamonte,
Microcentro (5256 8800/www.esplendorhotel.com.
ar). Subte B, Florida/93, 130, 152 bus.* **Rates**
US$205-$250. **Rooms** 51. **Credit** AmEx, DC, MC, V.
Map p325 G11 ❺

Faena Hotel + Universe. *See p55.*

The resplendent Esplendor wears its glistening Italianate façade on the intersection of Avenidas San Martín and Córdoba. Built in the 1900s as Hotel Phoenix, it was the first roof over the heads of many hopeful immigrants in the days when boats moored close to Avenida Córdoba. Monumental five-metre (16-foot) high ceilings, a total floor space of 4,000 square metres (13,100 square feet), and room doors seemingly as tall as skyscrapers, all give it a fairytale aura, and every century-old window and door has been restored to its former glory.

Bar. Business centre. Concierge. Disabled-adapted rooms. Gym. Internet (wireless). No-smoking rooms/floors. Restaurant. Room service. TV.

Intercontinental

Moreno 809, y Piedras, Monserrat (4340 7100/www.intercontinental.com). Subte C, Moreno/86, 100 bus. **Rates** US$200-$250. **Rooms** 319. **Credit** AmEx, DC, MC, V. **Map** p325 E10 ❻

The Intercontinental goes further than most to justify its five-star rating. The lavish interior design, with leather, wood and marble predominating, is accompanied by outstanding service and facilities. The hotel is well suited to the business traveller, with three meeting rooms and top-notch audio-visual equipment. The only problem could be the irresistible pull of the indoor heated pool, sun deck and health club. If you're a fan of the chain, you won't find much to disappoint you here.

Bar. Business centre. Concierge. Disabled-adapted rooms. Gym. Internet (US$15 high-speed, wireless). No-smoking rooms/floors. Parking (US$10). Pool (indoor). Restaurant. Room service. TV: DVD.

NH Lancaster

Córdoba 405, y Reconquista, Microcentro (4131 6464/www.nh-hotels.com). Subte B, San Martín/93, 152 bus. **Rates** US$195-$230. **Rooms** 115. **Credit** AmEx, DC, MC, V. **Map** p325 F11 ❼

First the plush holiday residence of a rich Russian and later an upscale hotel hosting the likes of Graham Greene, the once-grand Lancaster lost some of its lustre in recent years before it was acquired by the NH chain, owners of other hotels around the capital. Fourteen million dollars later, the original elegance of the Georgian-style structure has been restored, with interiors finished with a contemporary sensibility. Amply-sized suites and studios are especially sleek, but even the standard doubles in the 115-room hotel are a cut above. The location, though central, is perhaps best suited to business travellers.

Bar. Business centre. Concierge. Disabled-adapted rooms. Gym. Internet (high-speed, wireless). No-smoking rooms. Parking. Pool (outdoor). Restaurant. Room service. Spa. TV:DVD.

Other locations Throughout the city.

Panamericano Hotel & Resort

Carlos Pellegrini 551, entre Lavalle y Tucumán, Microcentro (4348 5000/www.panamericano buenosaires.com). Subte B, Carlos Pellegrini or D, 9 de Julio/24, 59, 67 bus. **Rates** US$280-$336. **Rooms** 440. **Credit** AmEx, DC, MC, V. **Map** p325 G10 ❽

The five-star Panamericano may not have the glitz of some of its counterparts, but its allure is its unpretentious dedication to service, not to mention some of the most breathtaking views of the city from its unique roof-top spa/pool/gym oasis on the 23rd floor. Keep an eye out for its many promotions: with its endless quantity of rooms it is often a good last-minute option. Another major draw is the notable Tomo I restaurant (*see p131*).

Bar. Business centre. Concierge. Disabled-adapted rooms. Gym. Internet (high-speed, wireless). No-smoking rooms. Parking. Pool. Restaurant. Room service. Spa. TV.

Pestana Buenos Aires

Carlos Pellegrini 877, entre Paraguay y Córdoba, Retiro (5239 1000/www.pestana.com). Subte B, Carlos Pellegrini/146, 152 bus. **Rates** US$220-$250. **Rooms** 133. **Credit** AmEx, DC, MC, V. **Map** p325 G11 ❾

The tinted glass exterior of Portuguese chain Pestana's Argentinian outpost houses 133 spacious rooms and towers over Avenida 9 de Julio. Although they aren't particularly exciting, its location close to the transportation hub of Retiro and a host of tourist sites (the Teatro Colón is opposite), provides comfort on prime real estate. The best executive suites have balconies providing dramatic views of the northern end of Avenida 9 de Julio.

Bar. Business centre. Concierge. Gym. Internet (high-speed). No-smoking rooms/floors. Pool (indoor). Restaurant. Spa. Room service. TV: DVD.

Sheraton Buenos Aires Hotel & Convention Centre

San Martín 1225, entre LN Alem y Madero, Retiro (4318 9000/www.sheraton-ba.com). Subte C, Retiro/93, 130, 152 bus. **Rates** US$230-$285. **Rooms** 742. **Credit** AmEx, DC, MC, V. **Map** p325 G12 ❿

Looking out onto Retiro, the Sheraton's top floors afford an awe-inspiring view of the River Plate. Newer and bigger than its sibling on Avenida Córdoba, the Retiro Sheraton has vast convention facilities and very little charm. Still, the 742 rooms are sizeable and the staff welcoming and efficient. Decent facilities include a gym, tennis court and two pools, indoor and outdoor. Popular with struggling boy bands and IMF bureaucrats.

Bar. Business centre. Concierge. Gym. Internet (high-speed, wireless). No-smoking rooms/floors. Parking. Pools (indoor & outdoor). Restaurants (2). Room service. TV: DVD.

Moderate

Castelar Hotel & Spa

Avenida de Mayo 1152, entre Salta y Cerrito, Congreso (4383 5000/www.castelarhotel.com.ar). Subte A, Lima/39, 64, 86 bus. **Rates** US$100. **Rooms** 151. **Credit** AmEx, DC, MC, V. **Map** p325 F9 ⓫

Halfway along Avenida de Mayo, this history-laden hotel was once home to Spanish poet and playwright Federico García Lorca for over a year; his room has

THE FIRST HOTEL WHERE YOU CAN DREAM DURING THE DAY.

LOISUITES CHAPELCO HOTEL, A SPECIAL DESIGNED HOTEL TO ENJOY THE THINGS, THAT YOU REALLY LIKE. THIS IS THE PLACE YOU WILL ALWAYS LIKE TO RETURN.

- Try your fly fishing technique.
- Horseback riding in exotics landscapes.
- Play golf in the first field co-design by Jack Nicklaus and Jack Nicklaus II in South America.
- Organize your corporate event with style.
- Ski in the steep mountains of Chapelco.

- 76 rooms, 5 lofts and 4 suites.
- Namasthé: exclusive spa.
- 2 Restaurants.
- Wine Cellar.
- 2 swimming pools.
- Meeting rooms with capacity for 220 people.

LOISUITES CHAPELCO HOTEL, RESERVATIONS (5411) 5777-8950

LOISUITES
CHAPELCO HOTEL
GOLF · RESORT · SPA

www.loisuites.com.ar

been restored and is now open to the public. Interior rooms are a tad melancholic – perfect for a self-exiled poet – but those of a less rarified sensibility may prefer one of the 44 rooms overlooking the tree-lined Avenida. But if you prefer a sense of history over mod cons, you'll enjoy the Castelar – the tangible sense of pride in the place displayed by the staff is infectious. A Turkish spa is hidden in the basement, with steam rooms, sauna and massage facilities. An evocative leftover from BA's golden past.
Bar. Concierge. Gym. Internet (high-speed, shared terminal). No-smoking rooms/floors. Parking. Restaurant. Room service. Spa. TV.

La Cayetana Historic House

México 1330, entre San José y Santiago del Estero, Monserrat (4383 2230/www.lacayetanahotel.com.ar). Subte E, Independencia/39, 103, 168 bus. **Rates** US$120-$180. **Rooms** 11. **Credit** AmEx, MC, V. **Map** p325 F9 ⓬
Opened in 2005 but harking back to a simpler age, La Cayetana has a refreshing lack of pretension. Peace and quiet in the town centre? Right here. The thoughtfully restored 1820s home is nestled away on a backstreet behind a plain wooden door, and a buzz-to-enter policy only adds to the sense of sanctuary. Inside, the 11 suites, set off an ivy-clad courtyard, are full of charm, with early 19th-century post-colonial stylings. Each boasts lovely interior design touches such as high, brick ceilings, original mosaic flooring and restored period furniture and furnishings, with just the right amount of mod cons.
Concierge. Internet (high-speed, wireless). Parking. Room service.

Loft y Arte

Hipólito Yrigoyen 1194, entre Lima y Salta (5411 4503/www.loftyarte.com.ar). Subte A, Lima/39, 60, 98 bus. **Rates** US$105-US$170. **Rooms** 26. **Credit** AmEx, MC, V. **Map** p325 F10 ⓭
This former short-term apartment hotel has been converted into a 26-room hotel. The advantage, of course, is that the rooms are normally twice the size of the standard hotel room, and also come with self-catering amenities. If anything, however, the 'arte' aspect of the enterprise is even more impressive than the 'loft' aspect. The building dates back to 1890 and has been carefully restored in the style of the period with marble stairwells, Italian porcelain and a sculpture garden with working fountains. Services and activities include tango classes, Ayurvedic massages, beauty treatments, city tours and – trust us on this one – transcendental meditation.
Internet (high-speed, wireless). Parking. Room service. TV.

Moreno 376

Moreno 376, entre Balcarce y Defensa, Monserrat (6091 2000/www.morenobuenosaires.com). Subte E, Bolívar/29, 56 bus. **Rates** US$95-$160. **Rooms** 39. **Credit** AmEx, DC, MC, V. **Map** p325 E10 ⓮
The interior of this seven-floor hotel is designed along starkly modern, minimalist lines; the only nostalgic flourishes are the 1920s art deco

trimmings, original stained-glass windows and wrought-iron elevators. The property, which previously housed one of BA's oldest publishing companies, has large spaces and an abundance of daylight. Rooms are vast, and the best have original artworks, whirlpool baths and either a balcony or views of the San Francisco church next door. All have dark wooden furnishings, plasma screens, king-size beds and watering can shower-heads. Breakfast is taken in the Sky Bar on the airy terrace, also used for al fresco *asados* in summer, while an open-air jacuzzi bubbles away. A 130-seat theatre and restaurant opened in early 2008.
Bar. Concierge. Gym. Internet (high-speed, wireless). No-smoking rooms. Parking. Pool (outdoor). Restaurant. Room service. TV: DVD.

Also recommended

Cambremon Suipacha 30, Microcentro (4345 0118/www.cambremonhotel.com.ar).

Budget

Gran Hotel Hispano

Avenida de Mayo 861, entre Piedras y Tacuarí, Monserrat (4345 2020/www.hhispano.com.ar). Subte A, Piedras or C, Avenida de Mayo/10, 17, 64 bus. **Rates** US$48 double. **Rooms** 60. **Credit** AmEx, DC, MC, V. **Map** p325 F10 ⓯
Since the 1950s, Gran Hotel Hispano has offered good value in the heart of BA's old Spanish barrio. The hotel shares the block with the legendary Café Tortoni (*see p167*). Those seeking silence should ask for an interior room away from the frequent, clamourous protests staged on Avenida de Mayo.
Bar. Internet (high-speed, wireless). No-smoking rooms/floors. Parking.

Hotel Bauen

Avenida Callao 360, entre Sarmiento y Corrientes, Congreso (4372 1932/www.bauenhotel.com.ar). Subte B, Callao/12, 37, 124 bus. **Rates** US$48. **Rooms** 120. **Credit** MC, V. **Map** p325 G9 ⓰
Originally built for the 1978 World Cup finals, the Bauen's rollercoaster history mirrors the trials and tribulations of modern Argentina. The hotel closed in 2001 under crushing debt. But the story has an interesting twist. Buoyed up by popular support, 30 or so former employees took matters into their own hands and broke back into the hotel. Ridding the hotel of rats and several years of dust has taken time, but well over half the original 224 rooms are available. So if you are into 1970s' architecture or want to raise a stiff two fingers at corporate arrogance, this could be the lodging for you.
Bar. Business centre. Gym. Internet (high-speed). Parking. Pool (indoor). Restaurant. Room service.

Also recommended

Hotel Facón Grande Reconquista 645, Microcentro (4312 6360/www.hotelfacongrande.com). **Ibis Buenos Aires** Hipólito Yrigoyen 1592, Microcentro (5300 555/www.accorhotels.com).

Sex in the city

Argentinians are an amorous bunch, never shy of a little plaza-side nookie, whatever their age or sexual preference. There is, nevertheless, a limit to what even liberal-minded *porteños* can stomach. So when the petting gets a little too hot and heavy, couples are often spied sneaking through a garishly lit doorway marked only with the words '*albergue transitorio*'.

These 'temporary lodging' hotels, known in *porteño* backslang as *telos*, exist for the sole but honourable purpose of clandestine copulation. Frequented by horny teenagers and illicit lovers with no shag shack of their own, *telos* offer rooms by the *turno* (around AR$50 for two hours).

Every neighbourhood will have several *telos*, but as anonymity is paramount, they are supposed to be tricky to spot. In reality, the giveaway signs – random bushes outside doorways, neon lights guiding cars to a hidden garage and a plastic Venus de Milo standing guard – are about as subtle as their names (Eros, Kiss Me, and the wonderful Pussu-Cats are just a few random examples). Once inside there is a choice between an often bewildering menu of room types. After selecting whatever takes you and your partner's fancy, a studiedly disinterested

(they've seen it all before) receptionist behind a smoked-glass window will throw some keys at you, and off you head through the dimly lit corridors.

Even the most basic rooms will have mirrored ceilings, a see-through shower and porn available on the telly; many also (somewhat bafflingly) advertise the option of live cable football. More exotic offerings will include water beds, medieval-looking 'sex chairs' and, occasionally, a covered outdoor garden. For the final preparations room service offer to bring up drinks, condoms and sex toys, all served through a sliding hole in the wall. Then – well, the rest is up to you.

If it all sounds a little seedy, it is. And that's all part of the fun. *Telos* are to Argentina what motels are to North America and the back of Ford Fiestas are to the UK. Nevertheless, an Argentinian who claims never to have visited one is either a man of the cloth, lying through his teeth, or both. The *telo* is an indispensable part of a culture where people often live at home with their parents until the day they marry, and quite often beyond. But they can also offer a precious moment of privacy for couples with kids, or couples without 'sex chairs'. Leaving the sprogs at the in-laws' with the statement 'we're going to the cinema' often implies a couple of hours' 'quality time' where the only movies will be from the low-budget Swedish collection. Another important thing to note about *telos* is that they're usually kept scrupulously clean – you've got more chance of, um, coming across a soiled sheet in a standard three-star than in a love hotel.

And if it's Swedish 'porn set' minimalism that you are after – or even an Arab-styled boudoir – the erotically titled **Rampa Car** (Angel J. Carranza 1347, Palermo Viejo, 4773 6964) is going to be a good bet. Don't forget to pick up the ultimate kitsch souvenirs from its 'gift' shop. Try **Torino** (Godoy Cruz 2409, 4773 8682) for a tamer (though, let's face it, it's all relative) Palermo Viejo option. If the urge should take you among the steel and glass erections of Retiro, walk through the subtle doors of **Monaco** (Ricardo Rojas 469, 4312 7301) or **Kansas City** (Talcahuano 844, 4813 6860) where couples wanting to experiment with a 'sex chair' should ask for the 'Especial' suite.

San Telmo & south of the centre

Moderate

1890 Boutique Hotel

Salta 1074, entre Carlos Calvo y Humberto Primo, San Telmo (4304 8798, www.1890hotel. com.ar).Subte C, Constitución/39, 133, 151 bus. **Rates** US$90-$180. **Rooms** 6. **No credit cards.** **Map** p325 E8 ⑰
A restored 19th-century house full of history and charm, whose owners like to think of it as a 'hotel with the spirit of a home'. And with a long wooden dining table in a kitchen, tall windows open for a jasmine breeze and relaxing patio garden, it does feel like an exquisite home . All six rooms contain original features as well as modern gadgets such as aircon and heating, stylish up-to-date bathrooms and soft new mattresses. Mother and daughter teamed up to design rooms with a sense of ease and comfort, their artistic flare displayed on the walls.
Internet (high-speed). TV.

Casa Bolívar

Finochietto 524, y Bolívar, San Telmo (4300 3619/www.casabolivar.com). Bus 36, 60, 168. **Rates** US$60-US$120. **Rooms** 14. **Credit** AmEx, V by Paypal only. **Map** p324 C8 ⑬
This charming French-owned hotel is situated among colonial-style buildings a few blocks away from San Telmo. Casa Bolívar is no different; the stunning building dominates the corner of the block and has succeeded in adapting to modern tastes and trends while maintaining a classic style. Each of the 14 lofts and studios, with kitchens, are well fitted and fall under themes including Industrial, Baroque and Art Deco. The friendly owners are often there to invite you for an *asado* on the terrace or arrange tango lessons. Free mobile phones are offered.
Internet (high-speed, wireless). Gym. TV: DVD.

Cocker

Avenida Juan de Garay 458, entre Defensa y Bolívar, San Telmo (4362 8451/www.thecocker.com). Bus 39, 93, 152. **Rates** US$90-$100. **Rooms** 5. **No credit cards.** **Map** p324 D9 ⑲
With a name paying homage to the owner's beloved pet spaniel Rocco, the Cocker was one of the first and is still one of the best boutique hotels in San Telmo. The design touches are exquisite; Egyptian linen, jasmine-entwined balconies, a grand piano in the front room, mosaic-tiled bathrooms, the list is long. Moreover the roof terrace boasts a verdant garden and striking views over San Telmo's chaotic skyline. But as much as a shrine to the art of good living and modern design, at a starting price of US$90 a night, the Cocker is a fantastic deal. As the amiable English owners stress, it's a classic case of quality over quantity. Another perk, pet-assisted therapy to lower blood pressure, is on the house.
Internet (high-speed, wireless). TV: DVD.

Mansión Dandi Royal

Piedras 922, entre Estados Unidos y Carlos Calvo, San Telmo (4307 7623/www.mansiondandiroyal. com). Bus 10, 24, 29. **Rates** US$150-$235. **Rooms** 30. **Credit** AmEx, DC, MC, V. **Map** p325 E9 ⑳
Tango and San Telmo go hand in hand and this self-styled 'Residential Tango Academy' – created by Héctor Villalba, globetrotting entrepreneur and tango teacher – fuses attentive service with the spirit of the sensual dance. The 30 rooms of this converted mansion are sumptuously appointed, with lush bedspreads and stately wooden furnishings. The tango theme is exploited throughout, with murals, paintings and ambient music. But it is all about the dancing. Classes in one of three salons are available daily, often led by an invited 'maestro', or sit back and watch one of their shows.
Bar. Concierge. Internet (high-speed, wireless). No-smoking rooms/floors. Parking. Pool (outdoor). Room service. TV: DVD.

Ribera Sur Hotel

Paseo Colón 1145, entre San Juan y Humberto I°, San Telmo (4361 7398/www.riberasurhotel.com.ar). Bus 93, 152. **Rates** US$130-$150. **Rooms** 16. **Credit** AmEx, MC, V. **Map** p324 D10 ㉑
True to its up-and-coming location, the Ribera Sur Hotel is a bona fide boutique hotel, built from the shell of a turn-of-the-century townhouse. The decor is a showcase for cool design, with some exquisite colour schemes. All the rooms have telltale boutique touches – pastel tones, fat pillows, wooden furnishings and colourful Mapuche rugs draped across the king-size beds. The rates beat most hotels of a similar class, and while Paseo Colón may not be the Riviera, the hotel is just a few blocks from the cobblestoned streets of San Telmo.
Bar. Internet (high-speed, wireless). Pool (outdoor). Restaurant. Room service. TV.

Budget

Boquitas Pintadas Hotel

Estados Unidos 1393, y San José, Constitución (4381 6064/www.boquitas-pintadas.com.ar). Subte E, San José/39, 53, 60, 102, 168 bus. **Rates** US$60-$100. **Rooms** 5. **Credit cards** AmEx, DC, MC, V. **Map** p325 E8 ㉒
This is a remarkable place. Owned by a German ex-bookseller, her prices unhiked for seven years, this self-proclaimed 'pop hotel' is no run-of-the-mill boutique. An eclectic in-house exhibition schedule means the decor changes on a monthly basis – even in the rooms – so the three floors might at any time brim with anything from shanty town art to abstract sculpture. Kooky outdoor patios, an unfussy atmosphere and enormous all-day breakfasts (in bed, if desired) help to lure a largely bohemian clientele. Truly a labour of love, but expect a unique experience rather than power showers. Keep an eye out for their parties too.
Bar. Internet (high-speed, wireless). No-smoking rooms/floors. TV.

Posada Gotan
Sánchez de Loria 1618, entre Pavón y Juan de Garay, Boedo (4912 3807/www.posadagotan.com). Subte E, Boedo/75, 126, 160 bus. **Rates** US$65-$85. **Rooms 11. No credit cards.**
BA's Italian immigrant roots are showing at this chic, off-the-beaten-path guesthouse. Built by current owner Gabriella's great-grandparents in 1890, the property has been impeccably restored to capture a *porteño* past while offering up-to-date comforts like wireless internet, air-conditioning and a home theatre outfitted with a large plasma screen (PlayStation for the kids). The proprietress and her French husband, Thibaud, clearly attend to the smallest of details – from the luxuriant white bed linens in each of the 11 suites to the flourishing plants on the patio, this charming hotel exudes old-time leisurely pace.
Bar. Internet (wireless). Restaurant. TV.

Posada de la Luna
Perú 565, entre Venezuela y México, San Telmo (4343 0911/www.posadaluna.com). Bus 26, 28, 86. **Rates** US$60-$70. **Rooms 5. No credit cards.** **Map** p325 E10 ㉔
This charming old colonial house sits on the cusp of San Telmo, just a ten minute walk from Plaza Dorrego. Wooden furniture and tropical plants have been scattered throughout to give the *posada* a relaxed and homey feel. The five rooms vary in size (two can sleep up to four) but they all showcase the creative, bohemian touch of the owner, Franco-Argentinian Nelida Reugger. There is a minimum reservation of two days.
Bar. Internet (high-speed). Room service. TV.

Also recommended
The Four Hotel Carlos Calvo 535, San Telmo (4362 1729/www.thefourhotel.com.ar).
Ibis Buenos Aires Hipólito Yrigoyen 1592, Microcentro (5300 5555/www.accorhotels.com).

Puerto Madero

Luxury

Faena Hotel + Universe
Martha Salotti 445, Dique 2, Madero Este, Puerto Madero (4010 9000/www.faenahotelanduniverse.com). Subte B, LN Alem/2, 130, 152 bus. **Rates** US$500-$550. **Rooms 105. Credit** AmEx, DC, MC, V. **Map** p324 D11 ㉕
There is simply no other hotel quite like Faena Hotel + Universe. Designed by French master Philippe Starck, this opulent, lavish and camp lodging is built in the shell of an eye-catching English-style red-brick silo. The mastermind behind the project, Alan Faena, is now expanding the brand around Puerto Madero with the 'Faena Art District', a series of redevelopments to build offices and arts spaces in Puerto Madero, with English architect Norman Foster. The hotel continues to house the famous and wealthy in the 105 gorgeous rooms, and the even

wealthier in the 83 privately owned apartments. One innovative idea is a personal 'experience manager' instead of a traditional desk-bound concierge. The 'Universe' part is a spacious complex that includes an incredible restaurant, El Bistro (*see p139*), an outdoor pool bar, slick cabaret and theatre, spa, boutique shop, and gourmet market, all open to mere mortals. Faena's self-consciously au courant vision is for his guests to experience an immersive lifestyle where 'dreams are transformed into reality...' *Photo p47.*
Bar. Business centre. Concierge. Disabled-adapted rooms. Gym. Internet (high-speed, wireless). No-smoking rooms/floors. Parking. Pool (outdoor). Restaurants (2). Room service. Spa. TV: DVD.

Hotel Madero
Rosario Vera Peñaloza 360, Dique 2, Madero Este, Puerto Madero (5776 7777/www.hotelmadero.com). Subte B, LN Alem/2, 130, 152 bus. **Rates** US$170-$350. **Rooms 197. Credit** AmEx, DC, MC, V. **Map** p324 D11 ㉖
Inconspicuously tagged on to the far end of Puerto Madero Este, Sofitel's latest BA venture breaks their traditional mould with this chic 197-room hotel. It is aimed at the discerning business traveller, although couples and families will be equally happy with the attractive features, which include a rooftop pool and the sensational open-plan Rëd Restó & Lounge restaurant. The inside wooden terrace is soothingly Zen-like and the upper floors afford stunning views of downtown BA. Rooms are fresh and tastefully decorated. Be sure to indulge in a cocktail or two in the stunning White Bar. They have also recently started more classes such as pilates in their spa.
Bar. Business centre. Concierge. Disabled-adapted rooms. Gym. Internet (high-speed, wireless). No-smoking rooms/floors. Parking. Pool (outdoor). Restaurant. Room service. TV: DVD.

Expensive

Hilton Buenos Aires
Avenida Macacha Güemes 351, Dique 3, Madero Este, Puerto Madero (4891 0000/www.hilton.com). Bus 130, 152. **Rates** US$200-$330. **Rooms 418. Credit** AmEx, DC, MC, V. **Map** p325 E12 ㉗
The Hilton was designed with prominent executives and affluent couples in mind. The vast glass-roofed atrium/lobby is embellished with chrome sofas, a marble reception and a pair of glass elevators at the back. The spacious, modern rooms have deluxe amenities and king-size bathrooms. This is a fine hotel in a coveted location, and boasts the killer advantage of having the best hotel pool in town.
Bar. Business centre. Concierge. Disabled-adapted rooms. Gym. Internet (high-speed, wireless). No-smoking rooms/floors. Parking. Pool (outdoor). Restaurants (2). Room service. TV: DVD.

Also recommended
Holiday Inn Express LN Alem 770, Puerto Madero (4311 5200/www.holidayinn.com).

Recoleta & Barrio Norte

Luxury

Alvear Palace Hotel

*Avenida Alvear 1891, entre Callao y Ayacucho,
Recoleta (4808 2100/www.alvearpalace.com). Bus 67,
93, 130.* **Rates** US$490-$580. **Rooms** 210. **Credit**
AmEx, DC, MC, V. **Map** p326 I11 ㉙
The clue is in the word 'palace' – not, in this
case, pretentious hyperbole. For the Alvear is more
than a mere hotel. It's also a source of civic pride, a
symbol of grandeur and an enduring reminder of
BA's golden, affluent era. Filling half a block of the
lavish Avenida Alvear (recently voted one of the five
most exclusive shopping areas in the world), it
shares a pavement with the likes of Armani, Ralph
Lauren and Cartier. The 210 rooms – 100 of which
are suites and among the largest in the city – are an
ocean of opulence: rich burgundies, antique French
furniture and Hermès bathroom goodies scattered
around the jacuzzis. Such resplendence is not with-
held completely from the hoi polloi, however; the bar
and restaurants are open to the public. The jewel in
the crown is La Bourgogne (*see p141*), overseen by
French chef Jean-Paul Bondoux. The L'Orangerie
(*see p140*) bar and terrace is the most exclusive
brunch and buffet venue in the city and the best way
for non-guests to soak up the hotel's ambience.
*Bars (2). Business centre. Concierge. Disabled-
adapted rooms. Gym. Internet (high-speed, wireless).
No-smoking rooms/floors. Parking. Pool (indoor).
Restaurants (2). Room service. Spa. TV: DVD.*

Caesar Park

*Posadas 1232, entre Montevideo y Libertador,
Recoleta (4819 1100/www.caesar-park.com). Bus 67,
93, 130.* **Rates** US$360-$440. **Rooms** 148. **Credit**
AmEx, DC, MC, V. **Map** p326 I11 ㉙
Directly behind the exclusive Patio Bullrich shopping centre, the 148 rooms (18 of which are suites)
of this sumptuous Recoleta hotel make ideal closets
for your latest acquisitions. Step inside the reception
and survey the marble floors, towering pillars and
gleaming stairways. Tapestries and paintings by
local artists line the corridors that lead to the suites,
which are decadently furnished with lavish gold
trimmings and dark wood. A communal lounge for
waltzing and schmaltzing has a resident pianist.
*Bar. Business centre. Concierge. Disabled-adapted
rooms. Gym. Internet (high-speed, wireless). No-
smoking rooms/floors. Parking. Pool (indoor).
Restaurant. Room service. TV: DVD.*

Four Seasons Hotel

*Posadas 1086, y Cerrito, Recoleta (4321 1200/
www.fourseasons.com). Bus 67, 130.* **Rates**
US$565-$630. **Rooms** 138. **Credit** AmEx, DC, MC, V.
Map p326 I11 ㉚
Frequently cited as the best hotel in Buenos Aires,
the Four Seasons is the lodging of choice for rock
stars, top executives and the occasional communist
icon (Fidel Castro has hung his fatigues here).

Towering over Posadas and Libertad streets, it's a
13-floor, 138-room masterpiece, with marble walls,
capacious rooms and well-chosen artworks in the
lobby and lining the corridors. Behind the tower lies
an attractive, if quite small, outdoor pool and a
seven-suite mansion with 24-hour butler service; it's
styled like a mini French château and is frequently
taken over by visiting celebs. It's rare to find an
establishment that orchestrates such a classy blend
of modern facilities and old-fashioned values.
*Bar. Business centre. Concierge. Disabled-adapted
rooms. Gym. Internet (high-speed, wireless). No-
smoking rooms/floors. Parking. Pool (outdoor).
Restaurant. Room service. Spa. TV: DVD.*

Park Hyatt Buenos Aires

*Avenida Alvear 1661, entre Montevideo y Rodríguez
Peña, Recoleta (5171 1234/www.buenosaires.park.
hyatt.com). Bus 93, 152.* **Rates** US$665-$1,230.
Rooms 165. **Credit** AmEx, DC, MC, V.
Map p326 I11 ㉛
Opulence and minimalism are the design imperatives
at the city's newest and most luxurious place of rest.
The hotel's palatial quarters, built in 1934 and once
home to the aristocratic Duhau family, are now joined
by an underground art gallery to a contemporary
building called the Posadas. In true belle époque style,
the entrance to the hotel is a portrait of neoclassical
columns, marble floors and cast-iron gates, while the
rooms themselves, simple and modern, speak of a
21st-century sensibility. Boasting a *vinoteca* with over
3,000 bottles of Argentinian wines, a cheese room
(yes, a cheese room) and three restaurants, the Hyatt
really is fit for a king – which might explain the
presence of the bulletproof Duhau Suite on the
penthouse floor. By day, succumb to the delights of
the Ahin Wellness Spa and its 25-metre swimming
pool. By night, enjoy a spot of al fresco dining on the
terraces, before retiring to the Oak Bar, where a
fireplace warms a room filled with leather armchairs.
*Bar. Business centre. Concierge. Disabled-adapted
rooms. Gym. Internet (high-speed, wireless). No-
smoking rooms/floors. Parking. Pool (indoor).
Restaurants (3). Room service. Spa. TV: DVD.*

Expensive

Blue Tree Hotel

*Laprida 1910, entre Pacheco de Melo y Peña,
Recoleta (5199 8391/www.bluetreehotel.br). Subte D,
Agüero/39, 60, 152 bus.* **Rates** US$180-$205.
Rooms 45. **Credit** AmEx, DC, MC, V.
Map p326 J10 ㉜
Situated in a quiet residential portion of the posh
Recoleta district, this hotel is one of two Argentinian
instalments in Japanese-born proprietor Cheiko
Aoki's Brazilian hotel empire. Beyond the discreet
exterior is a polished marble lobby integrated with
a small swanky restaurant featuring a carefully
styled bar that transforms into an 'American'
breakfast buffet complete with eggs, bacon and
sausage. The 45 rooms share a black and white
colour scheme consistent with the streamlined

Loft and Arte apart hotel offers the perfect blend of design, privacy and comfort.

Originally built in 1890, this boutique hotel maintains all its original architectural features with large windows, high ceilings, galleries, large interior spaces and even an indoor patio. It is strategically situated for both tourism and business, being nestled between Ave de Mayo and Ave 9 de Julio and just a stones throw away from the Obelisk, the theatres of Corrientes and the famous shopping street Florida. All of the 26 lofts (35m2 to 105m2) have been stylishly and eclectically decorated giving each room its unique charm. We have suites, duplexes and triplexes that are fully equipped with kitchens, living rooms, air-conditioning and balconies. Ideal for a long stay!

Hipólito Yrigoyen 1194, Buenos Aires
(054 11) 4115-1770
www.loftyarte.com.ar
reservas@loftyarte.com.ar

Categories: Junior/Executive/Superior
Capacity: SGL/DBL/TRL/CDPL

- Buffet breakfast, amenities
- NDD and IDD telephone
- Cable TV
- Cold-warm air-conditioning
- WI-FI internet in all areas of the hotel
- Safe boxes
- Kitchen with microwave and mini fridge
- Hairdryer
- Laundry and dry-cleaners
- Garden
- Parking
- Monitoring security

Loft&Arte

design of the rest of the establishment, and the suites on the eighth floor come with balconies.
Bar. Internet (high-speed, wireless). No-smoking rooms/floors. Parking. Restaurant. Room service. TV.

LoiSuites Recoleta Hotel

Vicente López 1955, entre Junín y Ayacucho, Recoleta (5777 8950/www.loisuites.com.ar). Bus 37, 59, 102. **Rates** US$250-$310. **Rooms** 112. **Credit** AmEx, DC, MC, V. **Map** p326 J11 ❸❸

Part of a small chain of well-run local hotels, this LoiSuites – in the bosom of Recoleta, close to the cemetery and the Village Recoleta cinema and shopping complex – is the flagship. The 112 decent-sized suites in the 13-floor building are chic and contemporary in style, with double glazing and soundproofed walls to muffle snuffles and grunts. Below in the spacious white lobby, large pastel sofas and potted plants sit in front of the *jardín de invierno* (winter garden), a two-tiered patio with a retractable roof and a Roman-style pool.
Bar. Business centre. Concierge. Gym. Internet (high-speed). No-smoking rooms/floors. Parking. Pool (indoor). Restaurant. Room service. Spa. TV.
Other locations LoiSuites Arenales, Arenales 855, Retiro (4324 9400); LoiSuites Esmeralda, Marcelo T de Alvear 842, Retiro (4131 6800).

Meliá Recoleta Plaza Boutique

Posadas 1557/59, y Ayacucho, Recoleta (5353 4000/www.solmelia.com). Bus 61, 67, 93. **Rates** US$220-$580. **Rooms** 57. **Credit** AmEx, DC, MC, V. **Map** p326 J11 ❸❹

Nestled among the plush properties of Recoleta, this jazz-themed hotel has a classic formal decor combined with modern touches that treats guests to an elegant and tranquil stay, managing to create a non-corporate atmosphere. Pass through polished surroundings or book yourself in for a massage at their top-floor spa. Rooms are stocked with all mod cons, including plasma screens and DVDs. But venture out of your room and you'll come across their lovely Piano Bar Jazz Voyeur (a lot less tacky than it sounds, trust us) and excellent Bistro restaurant. After indulging in one of the best hotel breakfasts in town, as a jazz pianist plinks away, you'll skip off humming 'What a Wonderful World'.
Bar. Business centre. Concierge. Gym. Internet (high-speed, wireless). No-smoking rooms/floors. Parking. Restaurant. Room service. Spa. TV: DVD.
Other locations Meliá Buenos Aires, Reconquista 945, Retiro (4891 3800); Tryp Buenos Aires, San Martín 474, Microcentro (5222 9600).

Ulises Recoleta Suites

Ayacucho 2016, entre Libertador y Posadas, Recoleta (4804 4571/www.ulisesrecoleta.com.ar). Bus 62, 93, 130. **Rates** US$225-$355. **Rooms** 26. **Credit** AmEx, DC, MC, V. **Map** pp326 J11 ❸❺

Positioned adjacent to what is arguably the most prestigious block of the city's most prestigious neighbourhood, this boutique hotel's prime selling point is indisputably its location. Ask for a room facing the street so you can look out at the regal

Alvear Palace Hotel and the neighbouring high-end designer stores in this pristine quarter of Recoleta, just a couple of blocks from the cultural centre and the shops. Freshly renovated, the elegant and comfortable rooms are equipped with kitchenettes and Wi-Fi. The duplexes have bathrooms on each level for extra privacy, and the penthouse suite features a large and lustrous living room topped off with a skylight. The privileged location is the key.
Business centre. Concierge. Gym. Internet (high-speed, wireless). No-smoking rooms/floors. Parking. Room service. TV.

Also recommended

Design Suites & Towers Marcelo T de Alvear 1683, Recoleta (4814 8700/www. designsuites.com).

Moderate

Onzé Trendy Hotel

Ecuador 1644, entre Beruti y Juncal, Recoleta (4821 2873/www.onzehotelboutique.com). Subte D, Pueyrredón/39, 152 bus. **Rates** US$120-$180. **Rooms** 11. **Credit** AmEx, DC, MC, V. **Map** p326 J10 ❸❻

Created by the award-winning team behind groundbreaking Palermo Viejo B&B Che Lulu (*see p65*), Onzé is a beautiful new boutique lodging with rates its competitors will find hard to match. From the L-shaped lounge-cum-breakfast room with its tall smoked mirrors and original artworks, to the spacious and cosy rooms, each fitted with a king-size bed and oodles of storage space, Onzé is dressed to impress. Authentic feng shui accents run throughout the property. It has also benefited from a recent expansion in amenities and services. From the moment you walk in you can expect a comfortable stay.
Bar. Business centre. Concierge. Internet (high-speed, wireless). Parking. Room service. TV.

Also recommended

Art Hotel Azcuénaga 1268, Recoleta (4821 4744/www.arthotel.com.ar).
Hotel Plaza Francia Eduardo Schiaffino 2189, Recoleta (4804 9631/www.hotelplazafrancia.com).

Budget

Guido Palace Hotel

Guido 1780, y Callao, Recoleta (4812 0674/www. guidopalace.com.ar). Bus 102, 124. **Rates** US$70-$115. **Rooms** 46. **Credit** AmEx, MC, V. **Map** p326 I11 ❸❼

Tucked deep in Recoleta, the quiet, spacious Guido Palace is a pleasant homey option in an upscale district. Rooms are simple but clean, well-lit and large; most of them are equipped with surprisingly spacious balconies. On the fourth floor there's a patio with seating – a perfect spot for a chilled beer.
Bar. Internet (high-speed). Room service. TV.

Palermo & Palermo Viejo

Expensive

1555 Malabia House

Malabia 1555, entre Gorriti y Honduras, Palermo Viejo (4833 2410/www.malabiahouse.com.ar). Bus 39, 55, 168. **Rates** US$145-$175. **Rooms** 15. **Credit** AmEx, DC, MC, V. **Map** p323 M5 ㊳

1555 is a pioneer among designer guesthouses in Palermo Viejo; it has been imitated, but hardly bettered. The interior design savvy of owner María is apparent throughout this converted convent, formerly the home of the San Vicente Ferrer ladies. The use of simple colours, natural light and three mini gardens come together to create a relaxed oasis. The warmth of the welcome is unsurpassed, and invites you to spend your days lounging on comfy living room sofas. All the rooms have queen-size beds. At the end of 2008 the team will open another 'house' in the barrio of Colegiales called 650 Freyre House (www.650freyrehouse.com.ar). *Photo p45.*
Internet (shared access). Room service. TV: DVD.

Bo Bo Hotel

Guatemala 4882, y Thames, Palermo Viejo (4774 0505/www.bobohotel.com). Subte D, Plaza Italia/36, 55, 60, 64, 93, 152 bus. **Rates** US$135-$170. **Rooms** 7. **Credit** AmEx, DC, MC, V. **Map** p323 M6 ㊴

Bo Bo stands for 'bohemian-bourgeois': it offers individuality alongside style and comfort. Each of the seven rooms in this popular, high-concept boutique hotel represents a 20th-century art or design movement. While some of these themes inevitably work better than others, a sense of affordable luxury runs throughout. The cool, friendly and efficient staff brings experience from five-star hotel chains, and there's a superb restaurant downstairs (*see p145*).
Bar. Internet (high-speed, wireless). Parking. Restaurant. Room service. TV: DVD.

Costa Petit Hotel

Costa Rica 5141, entre Godoy Cruz y Santa María de Oro, Palermo Viejo (4776 8296/ www.costapetithotel.com). Bus 39, 93, 168. **Rates** US$250-US$350. **Rooms** 4. **Credit** AmEx, DC, MC, V. **Map** p323 M5 ㊵

Petit indeed; there are only four suites in this discreet hotel. With almost everything you see, from light fittings to cutlery, sourced from estancias during two years of preparation and the rest hand-made by owner Diego, the Costa Petit prides itself on its attention to detail. Floor to ceiling windows in the central living room gives on to a grassy courtyard. In the two main suites everything is king-size – beds, Egyptian linen, marble baths, plasma screens – and all doors, mirrors, cupboards are handcrafted.
Internet (high-speed, wireless). Pool (outdoor). Room service. TV: DVD.

Get all boho at the **Bo Bo Hotel**.

Five (Cool Rooms Buenos Aires)

Honduras 4742, entre Armenia y Malabia, Palermo Viejo (5235 5555/www.fivebuenosaires.com). Bus 39, 93, 111. **Rates** US$130-$160. **Rooms** 17. **Credit** AmEx, MC, V. **Map** p323 M5 ㊶

As soon as it opened this striking 17-room venue quickly became one of the star residences in the Palermo boutique hotel scene. It has all the credentials: minimalist bare pine flooring, a Zen-like gravel and bamboo-shoots decor and a sizable rooftop terrace help make this the perfect Palermo Viejo base for trendy thirtysomethings. In addition to rooms with balconies and jacuzzi baths, you could splash out on a recently furnished suite. Keeping you cool in body and mind is the rooftop jacuzzi, new sauna and massage parlour.

Gym. Internet (high-speed, wireless). Parking. Room service. Spa. TV.

Home Hotel Buenos Aires

Honduras 5860, entre Carranza y Ravigniani, Palermo Viejo (4778 1008/www.homebuenos aires.com). Bus 39, 93, 111. **Rates** US$145-$190. **Rooms** 18. **Credit** AmEx, MC, V. **Map** p323 O5 ㊷

Aptly named, Home delivers an unforgettable accommodation experience. The brainchild of ex-record producer Tom and his wife Patricia, this 18-room hotel has become an instant classic, offering outstanding service and impressive added-value facilities. Each of the rooms has its own distinctive look, with vintage French wallpaper. It also has a new split level loft suite (for up to four people) with a terrace complete with *parrilla* for your own mini party. Two opposing Garden Suites, one with its own mini pool and roof terrace, are lovely relaxing spaces with their retro decor. But the real show stopper is the gorgeous secluded patio and garden out back, where guests can dip their feet in the infinity pool over drinks mixed by the highly competent bar staff – their early Friday night events, open to all, attract some of BA's top DJs and their eclectic record bags. Add on a fabulous spa and good well-priced lunches and brunches, you'll understand why so many are saying there's no place like Home.

Bar. Concierge. Internet (high-speed, wireless, shared terminal). Pool (outdoor). Room service. Restaurant. Spa. TV: DVD.

Krista Hotel Boutique

Bonpland 1665, entre Gorriti y Honduras, Palermo Viejo (4771 4697/www.kristahotel.com.ar). Bus 39, 93, 140. **Rates** US$135-$170. **Rooms** 10. **Credit** AmEx, MC, V. **Map** p323 N5 ㊸

While in terms of cutting-edge design this particular hotel may not reach the giddy heights of other B&Bs in the barrio, it offers a more down-to-earth service and, at a starting price of US$135 per night, a good deal. The bedrooms are large and comfortable, and despite the fact that eight of the ten rooms are on the ground floor, indoor patios ensure there is plenty of light. There is a massage salon and spa.

Concierge. Internet (high-speed, wireless). Room service. Spa. TV: DVD.

Mine Hotel Boutique

Gorriti 4770, entre Malabia y Armenia (4832 1100/www.minehotel.com). Bus 15, 55, 140, 168. **Rates** US$140-$180. **Rooms** 20. **Credit** AmEx, DC, MC, V. **Map** 323 M5 ㊹

It's no longer enough to throw an expensive rug on the floor, buy some kitsch furniture, decorate each room differently and put the word 'boutique' somewhere in the name. Thanks to BA's huge exposure in the press, today's visitors are more discerning than ever, especially when it comes to hotels. Mine Hotel, a late addition to the Palermo hotel frenzy, appears to go further in justifying its quality claim by offering a truly well-considered design and utmost professionalism. Every detail is designed to be harmonious, from the bedspreads to the lighting.

Bar. Concierge. Internet (high-speed, wireless, shared terminal). Pool (outdoor). Room service. TV: DVD.

Miravida Soho

Darregueyra 2050, entre Guatemala y Soler (4774 6433/15 6222 3547/www.miravidasoho.com). Bus 34, 55, 60, 93. **Rates** US$115-$218. **Rooms** 6. **Credit** AmEx, MC, V. **Map** 323 M6 ㊺

The owners of this hotel have opted for original features and old-fashioned charm over ultra-modern minimalism. Six high-ceilinged rooms all come with private balconies, and the rooftop jacuzzi provides a further suntrap. So far, so Palermo, but what marks this out from the rest is its wine bar and cellar, an atmospheric setting for sampling local and international wine, including often under-appreciated smaller *bodegas*. And if you overdo it on the grapes, soak up the hangover with a proper fry-up for breakfast the next morning.

Bar. Disabled-adapted rooms. Internet (high-speed, wireless). No-smoking rooms. Restaurant. Room service. TV: DVD.

Soho All Suites

Honduras 4762, entre Malabia y Armenia (4832 3000/www.sohoallsuites.com). Bus 39, 57, 168. **Rates** US$200-$410. **Rooms** 21. **Credit** AmEx, DC, MC, V. **Map** p323 M5 ㊻

No messing around with silly names here. Soho All Suites, quite simply, offers suites in the centre of Palermo Soho. The hotel's strength is its location, an area defined as much by its all-night bar and restaurant scene and cutting edge boutiques as by its tree-lined, cobblestoned streets. Each of the 21 amply sized suites is well-lit and well-equipped with a flat-screen TV, CD player, microwave and a breakfast bar. The superior suites can sleep up to four and have outward-facing balconies. The establishment is best described as a boutique hotel for people who are wary of boutique hotels: it's unpretentious and stylish without being over-stylised, and the staff are well-trained and happy to share their local knowledge. It's worth restating: the location couldn't be better.

Bar. Concierge. Disabled-adapted rooms. Internet (high-speed, wireless, shared terminal). Parking. Room service. Spa. TV.

Shooting stars

How exactly does a six-star hotel differ from a 'fiver'? Four you can be pretty sure is just a tired-looking place that looked quite fashionable in 1972. Three-star usually means nice-ish rooms with a crap breakfast. Two- and one-star? Who knows, but chances are if it were a one-star hotel they wouldn't advertise it: 'Welcome to the one-star Savoy: making mediocrity matter'.

There is no international standard to the starring system, meaning that five-star hotel in San Juan you've just booked for US$40 a night might not be quite the Alvear. So the announcement that the Mexican luxury hotel chain Mayan Resorts is to build a US$50 million six-star (count 'em) hotel in Puerto Madero has been met with mild scepticism.

Just what the US$1,000 a night Grand Mayan Buenos Aires will offer to add that extra star, we'll have to wait until 2011 to see. And along with the prospect of Jumeirah – owners of the iconic seven-star (!) sail-shaped Burj Al Arab in Dubai – opening their first Latin American project a few doors down (coinciding with new direct flights from UAE with Emirates Airlines), it at least demonstrates how tourism in Buenos Aires is heading in a new direction. The industry is deliberately moving its focus away from the 'How cheap is that for a steak!' crowd – mainly because already it is not quite the bargain it was – to the 'Get Jeeves to saddle up the polo pony' set.

There is certainly no shortage of monied types slumbering in unfeasibly fluffy dressing gowns and having in-room massages at the likes of Faena (*see p55*), Four Seasons, Park Hyatt (*see p57*) and Sofitel (*see p47*). And it is no coincidence that Axel Hotels opened its second five-star gay residence, after Madrid, in Buenos Aires (*see p237* **Thrills with frills**).

Ultra high-end lifestyle management concierge services and tour companies services such as Curiocity (*see p208*) and Quintessentially (www.quintessentially.com) are also proliferating, thanks to a stream of celebrities flocking to the country in search of *estancias* (Richard Gere), film locations (Francis Coppola) and love (Matt Damon).

It's difficult to predict just what the six-star luxury hotels will do to make guests' stays that much better. Maybe they'll invent a new, fancy breakfast – if five stars gets you poached, surely a six-star egg will have to be from a dodo. But whatever the extras, the new top end will introduce the delights of Buenos Aires to a whole new clientele.

Moderate

Posada Palermo

Salguero 1655, entre Soler y Paraguay, Palermo (4826 8792/www.posadapalermo.com.ar). Subte D, Bulnes/39 bus. **Rates** US$95-$115. **Rooms** 4. **No credit cards. Map** p322 L6 ⑰
After a visit to this B&B you won't be surprised to learn that it's owned and managed by an architect. The tasteful Italian-influenced design scheme preserves the aura of the building's former life as a lodging for Italian immigrants in the early 20th century. The four bedrooms, all with bathrooms en suite, boast careful attention to detail. Wind down in the hammock on the terrace or relax in the homely living room where Chungi, Marie and Laila, the three purring house cats, set the pace. A solid choice for those seeking a cosy retreat in the heart of Palermo. *Internet (high-speed, wireless).*

Budget

Che Lulu Trendy Hotel

Pasaje Emilio Zola 5185, entre María de Oro y Godoy Cruz, Palermo Viejo (4772 0289/www. luluguesthouse.com). Subte D, Palermo/39, 55, 111 bus. **Rates** US$40-$65. **Rooms** 8. **No credit cards. Map** p323 N6 ㊽
Hidden down an inconspicuous side street, Che Lulu is a pioneer of the Palermo Viejo guesthouse scene. Every bedroom is air-conditioned and benefits from abundant light. Extra colour by local artists and plentiful plant life keep this B&B bright and cheerful. The dining area has a TV and is a good spot to plan the day's activities; nearby excursions include Palermo parks, zoo and golf course. The team can also help with finding longer term accommodation in apartments around the city. *Bar. Internet (wireless). Room service. TV.*

Casa Alfaro

Gurruchaga 2155, entre Paraguay y Guatemala, Palermo Viejo (4831 0517/www.casaalfaro.com.ar). Subte D, Plaza Italia/29, 39 bus. **Rates** US$40-$80. **Rooms** 11. **Credit** AmEx, MC, V. **Map** p323 M6 ㊾
This colonial-style Palermo Viejo guesthouse is run by an approachable couple (and their multilingual staff) and is as warm and inviting as can be. Picture dark leather couches and heavy wood furniture, multicoloured woven rugs and a crackling open fire, and you'll get an idea why taking the complimentary continental breakfast here is so appealing. Guest rooms are simpler affairs with white bed linens; the family-sized suite and upstairs rooms overlooking the garden are more memorable. The hotel is almost television-free but in such a prime location guests aren't likely to want to watch the box anyway.
Internet (high speed, wireless). TV room.

Cypress In

Costa Rica 4828, entre Borges y Uriarte, Palermo Viejo (4833 5834/www.cypressin.com). Bus 34, 36, 39, 55, 93, 161. **Rates** US$65-$95. **Rooms** 13. **Credit** AmEx, MC, V. **Map** p323 M5 ㊿
The cypress trees that tower in the back garden inspired the name for this highly recommendable B&B. Located on an atmospheric cobbled street in the middle of Palermo Viejo, Cypress In has slickly designed rooms at bargain rates, especially considering its prime location just minutes from Plazoleta Cortázar. A delightful and mellow option.

Internet (high-speed, wireless, shared terminal). Pool (outdoor). Room service. TV: DVD.

Hotel Costa Rica

Costa Rica 4137/39, entre Gascón y Acuña de Figueroa, Palermo (4864 7390/www.hotelcostarica. com.ar). Bus 36, 110, 160, 188. **Rates** US$55-$95. **Rooms** 28. **No credit cards.** **Map** p322 L5 ㊿
Light and airy, Costa Rica is an affordable option for those wishing to get away from the headache of downtown traffic and noise. Rooms are basic but clean and if you don't mind sharing a bathroom, your gap-year budget might stretch that extra two days' worth of pizza. There's a rooftop terrace perfect for sunbathing, and drinking a glass or two of wine from the bar with other guests, however no wheelchair accessibility. The staff are unerringly friendly, and can arrange tours from visits to topflight football games to city tours. Breakfast is not included (US$3) but there are plenty of restaurants and cafés in the area.
Bar. Internet (high-speed, wireless). TV: DVD.

La Otra Orilla

Julián Alvarez 1779, entre Costa Rica y Soler, Palermo Viejo (4867 4070/www.otraorilla.com.ar). Subte D, Plaza Italia/39, 60, 152 bus. **Rates** US$35-$65. **No credit cards.** **Map** p322 L5 ㊿
During the 2001 banking restrictions, Cecilia and Agustina decided to put their money in a more secure financial institution: their own home. They went out and bought some stylish furniture and

Rooms tailored to your every need at **Tailor Made Hotel**. *See p69.*

reopened it as a comely, five-bedroom bed and breakfast. Two rooms have balconies overlooking a Palermo cobbled street. It's the suite, however, with a view of the garden that is the real catch. *Internet (high-speed). TV room.*

Las Cañitas

Expensive

Tailor Made Hotel

Arce 385, entre Chenaut y Arévalo (4774 9620/www.tailormadehotels.com.ar). Subte D, Ministro Carranza/15, 60, 152, 160 bus. **Rates** US$193-$290. **Rooms** 5. **Credit** AmEx, MC, V. **Map** p327 O9 ③
Absolutely everything from the bedclothes to the vase in your room has been custom made by some of the country's top designers. The team behind the five-room residence spent the last few years travelling around the world making copious notes about what they loved and loathed about hotels. With this information they have put together one of the best-equipped hotels in Buenos Aires. There is a Mac mini in every room, high definition TV, iPod dock and IP phones. Each also has a jacuzzi, private terrace or balcony. And if you liked any of their custom decorations, well you can also buy them. Another big attraction is that there is no annoying charges for many services. Wanna beer? No problem. Laundry? Sure. One day, all hotels will be so well equipped. An Asian deli is also planned to open in their ground-floor lobby early 2008. *Photo p67. Bar. Concierge. Disabled-adapted rooms. Internet (high-speed, wireless). Restaurant. Room service. TV: DVD.*

Moderate

Casa Bloody Mary

Volta 1867, entre Arce y Báez, (4777 7106/ www.casabloodymary.com). Bus 29, 59, 60. **Rates** US$85-$95. **Rooms** 5. **Credit** AmEx, MC, V. **Map** p327 P9 ③
The name alludes to England's Protestant-burning queen rather than the cocktail; the *casa* in question is a mock-Tudor residence down a pretty Las Cañitas side street. This B&B spans spacious, air-conditioned rooms in a great location – it's within walking distance of Báez street, the popular Las Cañitas bar and restaurant strip. *Bar. Internet (high-speed). Restaurant.*

Casa Las Cañitas

Huergo 283, entre Arévalo y Clay (47713878/www. casalascanitas.com). Subte D, Ministro Carranza/15, 60, 152, 160 bus. **Rates** US$110-$180 double; US$195 apartment. **Rooms** 9. **Credit** AmEx, MC, V. **Map** p327 O9 ③
This hotel in Palermo's most glam sub-district offers great value for money in a superb location. The stylish and well-equipped rooms all have queen-sized

beds, air-conditioning and Wi Fi. Just as good are the shared spaces which include a wine bar (open 24 hours), a lovely terrace and garden (with barbecue, natch) and a business centre. Their in-house services include private yoga and tango classes, massages and a babysitting service.
Bar. Internet (high-speed, wireless). No-smoking rooms/floors. Parking. Room service. TV.

Abasto

Luxury

Abasto Plaza Hotel

Avenida Corrientes 3190, y Anchorena (6311 4466/www.abastoplaza.com). Subte B, Carlos Gardel/24, 26, 124, 168 bus. **Rates** US$280-$370. **Rooms** 127. **Credit** AmEx, DC, MC, V. **Map** p322 I5 ③
The Abasto Plaza was the first hotel in Buenos Aires to capitalise on the tango tourism industry. Yet far from being some Las Vegas styled caricature, Abasto Plaza is a tasteful and subtle prospect aimed at tango aficionados. Residents enjoy a free daily tango class and a weekly show in the restaurant. The rooms are spacious and well equipped, and two suites have their own private dancefloor. It is also in the heart of Abasto, claimed by many to be the true home of BA's finest musical tradition.
Bar. Business centre. Concierge. Disabled-adapted rooms. Gym. Internet (high-speed). Parking. Pool (outdoor). Restaurant. Room service. Spa. TV.

Tango at **Abasto Plaza Hotel**.

Belgrano

Expensive

My BA Hotel

Zabala 1925, entre 11 de Septiembre y Arribeños (4787 5765/www.mybahotel.com). **Rates** US$140-$175. **Rooms** 9. **Credit** AmEx, DC, MC, V. **Map** p329 R8 ⑤⑦

Although there aren't many hotels dotting the leafy residential streets of Belgrano, My BA makes for a lovely way to draw your discerning dollar. A smart 1940s theme, in keeping with the hotel's history as a posh townhouse, means some lovely period and well restored pieces of furniture and fittings, mixed with brand new and very modern extras, but never out of place, while original art hangs from the walls. Five of the nine rooms have balconies (two and five are good bets) and there's further luxury in the fit-for-a-sultan beds. A fairly quiet location makes it well suited to those who have already seen the sights, or couples looking to lose themselves for a while in piles of pillows and big breakfasts, away from the bustle of downtown, but near enough to Palermo. Unveiled in late 2006, the hotel also offers free access to a nearby health club. Their restaurant is next door if you don't fancy heading in to Belgrano's hub.
Bar. Concierge. Internet (high-speed, wireless). Restaurant. Room service. Spa. TV.

San Isidro

Expensive

Hotel del Casco

Avenida del Libertador 16170 (4732 3993/www. hoteldelcasco.com.ar). Train from Retiro. **Rates** US$150-$170. **Rooms** 12. **Credit** AmEx, DC, MC, V.

One of the best lodging options in greater BA's most attractive suburb (an easy train ride from the federal capital). San Isidro has been home to the wealthy suburbanites since the 18th century and offers a relaxing escape from the rather less gracious pleasures of city life. The cathedral is the main landmark, but there are plenty of upmarket restaurants in the neighbourhood. This classic 1890s colonial house, with its whitewashed porticoes, pretty wrought-iron lanterns and striking interior glass-ceilinged patio, is as good to look at as it is to stay in. All the mod cons and extras that you'd expect from an upscale hotel perfectly complement the traditional vibe.
Bar. Disabled-adapted rooms. Internet (high-speed, wireless). Room service. TV.

Also recommended

Patio Inn Laberdén 466, San Isidro (4743 2981/www.patioinn.com.ar).
Posada San Isidro Maipú 66, San Isidro (4732 1221/www.posadasanisidro.com.ar).

History and grandeur at San Isidro's **Hotel del Casco**.

Youth hostels

About Baires Hostel

Viamonte 982, entre Suipacha y Carlos Pellegrini, Microcentro (4328 4616/www.aboutbaireshostel. com). Subte C, Lavalle/10, 99, 111 bus. **Rates** US$8 per person dorm; US$22 double. **No credit cards.** **Map** p325 G11 ⑱
About Baires Hostel is bang in the city centre. Decorated in a boutique style, it has four dorms and one double, and a comfy living room.

Casa Esmeralda

Honduras 5765, entre Bonpland y Carranza, Palermo Viejo (4772 2446/www.casaesmeralda. com.ar). Bus 39, 93, 111. **Rates** US$9 per person dorm; US$20-$25 double. **No credit cards.** **Map** p323 N5 ⑲
An unpretentious and comfy hostel run by amiable Franco-Argentinian Sebas. It has four doubles, two dormitories and a beautiful back garden.

La Casa Fitzroy

Fitz Roy 2461, entre Charcas y Santa Fe, Palermo Viejo (4777 3454/www.casafitzroy.com.ar). Bus 39, 93. **Rates** US$8-10 per person dorm; US$25-$30 single. **No credit cards. Map** p323 N6 ⑳
This big backpacker joint has a relaxed vibe – but it's also a slick operation. It's got 60 beds, a cosy TV room, a terrace and a large courtyard.

Casa Jardín

Charcas 4422, entre Uriarte y Thames, Palermo Viejo (4774 8783/www.casajardinba.com.ar). Subte D, Plaza Italia/39, 41, 60, 93 bus. **Rates** US$13 per person dorm; US$18 single; US$30 double. **No credit cards. Map** p323 M6 ㉑
This converted townhouse is packed with well-stocked bookcases and hosts art exhibitions.

Che Lagarto

Venezuela 857, entre Piedras y Tacuarí, Monserrat (4343 4845/www.chelagarto.com). Subte E, Belgrano/59, 67, 98 bus. **Rates** US$10-$13 per person dorm; US$32 single; US$26 double per person. **Credit** AmEx, DC, MC, V. **Map** p325 E9 ㉒
With some 30-odd beds, in dormitories, triple, double and single rooms, Che Legarto offers clean, cheap accommodation in a spacious, spruced up building.

Garden House

Avenida San Juan 1271, entre Salta y Santiago del Estero, Constitución (4304 1824/www.garden houseba.com.ar). Subte C, San Juan/29, 39, 59, 60, 102 bus. **Rates** US$9 per person dorm; US$20 double. **No credit cards. Map** p325 E8 ㉓
Despite its close proximity to one of BA's less reputable barrios, this hostel comes recommended.

Hostel Inn – Tango City

Piedras 680, entre Chile y México, San Telmo (4300 5764/www.hostel-inn.com). Subte E or C, Independencia/2, 17, 59 bus. **Rates** US$10-$12 per person dorm; US$40 double. **No credit cards.** **Map** p325 E9 ㉔

Hand-carved furnishings and diverse artwork are standout features of this boisterous joint, with capacity for 100 backpackers.

Milhouse

Hipólito Yrigoyen 959, entre Tacuarí y Irigoyen, Monserrat (4345 9604/4343 5038/www.milhouse hostel.com). Subte A, Piedras or C, Avenida de Mayo/39, 64, 86 bus. **Rates** US$11 per person dorm; US$45 double. **No credit cards. Map** p325 F10 ㉕
This three-tiered turn-of-the-century house is the city's liveliest hostel. Always buzzing, it also offers tango sessions, tours and barbecues.

Ostinatto Hostel

Chile 680, entre Perú y Chacabuco, San Telmo (4362 9639). Bus 2, 9, 10, 28, 29, 86. **Rates** US$10-$13 per person dorm; US$40-48 double. **No credit cards.** **Map** p325 E9 ㉖
The most impressive feature of this BA hostel is the modern design. There's a bar with leather couches, a piano for late-night knees-ups and an art gallery.

Palermo Soho Hostel

Nicaragua 4728, entre Borges y Gurruchaga, Palermo Viejo (4833 0151/www.palermosohohostel. com.ar). Bus 34, 55, 93. **Rates** US$12 per person dorm; US$30 double. **Credit** MC, V.
Map p323 M5 ㉗
Cut your lodging budget by staying at this cheap and trendy hostel, and blow what you've saved in the restaurants, boutiques and bars nearby.

Portal Del Sur

Hipólito Yrigoyen 855, entre Piedras y Tacuarí, Monserrat (4342 8788/www.portaldelsurba.com.ar). Subte A, Piedras or C, Avenida de Mayo/45, 56, 86 bus. **Rates** US$12-$13.50 per person dorm; US$20 single; US$30 double. **Credit** MC, V. **Map** p325 F10 ㉘
This hostel challenges travellers to name better backpacker digs in South America. Clean dormitories come with air-conditioning and telephone.

V&S

Viamonte 887, entre y Suipacha, Microcentro (4322 0994, www.hostelclub.com). Subte C, Lavalle/10, 99, 111 bus. **Rates** US$12 per person dorm; US$65 double. **No credit cards. Map** p325 G11 ㉙
An upmarket hostel for the bourgeois backpacker, what V&S lacks in party atmosphere it makes up for with a raft of added-value facilities including a giant TV. They can also arrange many activities.

Zentrum

Costa Rica 4520, entre Malabia y Armenia, Palermo Viejo (4833 9518/www.zentrumhostel.com.ar). Bus 15, 57, 110, 141, 160. **Rates** US$12 per person dorm; US$50-$60 double. **No credit cards.** **Map** p323 M5 ㉚
This new upscale hostel guarantees a good night's sleep with white starched sheets and great location directly across from Plaza Palermo Viejo. The highlight is the rooftop patio to watch the crowd below. Make sure you book well in advance.

Sightseeing

Introduction

Hit the ground strolling.

Stow the guidebook in your backpack and start walking. You won't have time to explore all of the 2,154 streets, avenues and motorways whose straight(ish) lines partition Buenos Aires into thousands of rectangular blocks; but since most of the landmarks of interest to the visitor are obligingly sited on the city's eastern side, in barrios such as San Telmo, Recoleta and Palermo, you can narrow down your target list.

But don't plan too far in advance or too assiduously. BA is a city that rewards the traveller whose approach to sightseeing values serendipity over a tick-off-the-statues checklist. The shopworn phrase 'you never know what might be around the next corner' might have been invented for the Argentinian capital.

As well as expecting the unexpected, you should prepare for the predictable: whimsical opening and closing times; a public transport system ill-equipped for the 21st century; dog walkers who have never heard of the gutter let alone a poop-scoop; police officers who are more likely to bum a cigarette off you than to give you accurate directions; and driving so bad and so dangerous as to be almost parodic.

Thankfully, BA's charms far outnumber its frustrations. Some of the magic is down to form – the seemingly endless *calles* perfumed with that unique amalgam of blossom and barbecue smoke; the glorious array of churches, palaces and public buildings that seems to run the gamut of every architectural style known to humankind (and some known only to *porteños*); the kooky little cobblestoned *pasajes* and alleyways with their Dickensian shops and crooked houses. But so much of what makes BA great is down to content – by which we mean the three million people who live, work and play in the federal capital. The extraordinary pleasure *porteños* derive from sharing the beauty of their hometown with foreigners is something most visitors will remember long after the canonical landmarks are forgotten. So don't just walk; talk.

GETTING AROUND

The city is largely laid out on the standard Spanish colonial-style grid pattern of wide *avenidas* and narrower *calles* in regular blocks – called *cuadras* or *manzanas* – with a regular numbering system that makes navigation relatively easy. Maps (ours included) are rarely oriented north, instead flipping the city to show the river to the south. In fact, Avenida 9 de Julio,

the city's main thoroughfare, runs north–south. Traffic is one-way; to orient yourself remember that on Avenidas Santa Fe and Corrientes traffic heads towards downtown, and away from it on Avenida Córdoba. The names of the north–south streets change at Avenida Rivadavia.

We've provided detailed street maps covering the barrios you'll spend most time in. Maps start on page 317 and the street index on page 330.

If you want a quick overall view of the city, take a *colectivo* (public bus); or if you're in a hurry, one of the guided air-con buses serving the hotels (ask your hotel concierge for details). Taxis are also affordable, and it's enjoyable to roll down the window and watch the city pass by. The Subte (subway) is ideal for central areas, but Buenos Aires only truly lays bare its soul to those prepared to go overground and on foot. In recognition of this, the local government (Gobierno de la Ciudad de Buenos Aires) has launched a free 'guided walks' service. For further details, go to the 'Recorridos' section on their website (www.bue.gov.ar). For more detailed information on all methods of transport, *see pp294-296.*

The best Sights

Groovy graveyards
Chacarita (*see p118*) and **Recoleta** (*see p106*) cemeteries.

Sensational sculptures
Canto al Trabajo (*see p96*); **Floralis Genérica** (*see p106*).

Brilliant buildings
El Abasto shopping centre (*see p116*); **Edificio Kavanagh** (*see p91*); **Palacio de Aguas Corrientes** (*see p115*); **Palacio Barolo** (*see p83*).

Peaceful parks and plazas
Jardín Japonés (*see p110*); **Parque Lezama** (*see p96*); **Plaza San Martín** (*see p89*); **Parque Tres de Febrero** (*see p109*).

Soccer shrines
La Bombonera (*see p101*); **Estadio Monumental** (*see p123*).

The Microcentro.

Argentina is only a click away.

Flying the skies of the world for more than half a century.

NZ

LV-BNZ

aerolineas.com

**AEROLINEAS
ARGENTINAS**

Note that many museums and government-run sights are closed on Monday. A lot of museums close for a break in the Austral summer (January and February) too, though market demand from the ever-increasing influx of tourists is shortening closed periods. Take cash when visiting museums: those that aren't free charge at most a few pesos, and rarely accept credit cards. You may be asked for some form of photo ID (a photocopy is sometimes acceptable) in certain public buildings. Most museums and historical sites offer scheduled guided tours in Spanish. If you phone ahead, many larger museums will try to arrange a guided visit with an English speaker – alternatively talk to a tour specialist (*see p79*).

Parque Tres de Febrero

Barrio guide

Not all *porteños* use the city government's barrio denominations, although you'll see them on many maps. For instance, Once is not technically speaking a barrio, but everyone uses the term for the commercial zone around Once de Septiembre train station. Hardly anyone uses the barrio names Balvanera or San Nicolás, preferring to highlight major buildings in those zones, such as the Abasto shopping mall and Congreso. In this chapter, and in our maps, we have tried to delineate the city in a way that acknowledges and incorporates both officialdom and common usage.

The Centre's focal point is Plaza de Mayo – the city's original main square and site of many important public buildings. Elegant Avenida de Mayo runs from the plaza across gaping Avenida 9 de Julio to the Plaza del Congreso, in the barrio of Congreso. Next door is Tribunales, the legal quarter, and to the north the railway terminal of Retiro. The Microcentro is the capital's downtown, a pullulating commercial and financial hub.

The **South of the Centre** chapter includes Monserrat, the historic district south of the Plaza de Mayo. San Telmo follows, drawing visitors to its antiques, tango and bustling Plaza Dorrego. Lying on the Riachuelo – the little river that empties into the River Plate – is La Boca, a working-class barrio famous for its football team and colourful street, Caminito. Run-down Constitución contains the railway terminal for the south.

North of the Centre, beyond Retiro, is Recoleta, where the rich live and the famous are buried. Its cemetery, plazas, shops and museums make it a tourist magnet. Barrio Norte is a neighbouring residential district. Further north is Palermo. It has three distinct sub-areas around the huge Parque Tres de Febrero: expansive Palermo proper, a middle-class residential area

with gardens, the zoo and well-kept plazas; opulent, tranquil Palermo Chico; and trendy Palermo Viejo (unofficially divided into sub-barrios Palermo Soho and Palermo Hollywood), full of hip restaurants and boutiques.

Just to the **West of the Centre** are Once and Abasto, rich in immigration, history, tango and commerce. Other western barrios for visitors willing to wander are Caballito, Villa Crespo and, slightly north, Chacarita.

Along the River is the Costanera Norte, north of the city airport, a popular place for weekend promenades. Next to the southern bank of the river is Puerto Madero – BA's yuppie dockland complex – and Costanera Sur, skirting the coastal eco-reserve.

Heading **Further Afield** to the north is Belgrano, with its plazas, museums and shops; nearby is Núñez. Further still, beyond the limits of the capital, are the wealthier suburbs of Zona Norte: Olivos, Martinez and San Isidro. On the city's western edge are Liniers and Mataderos, both associated with cowboys, cattle-dealing and meatpacking.

Sightseeing

Terrific tours

For the intellectual

5031 9916/www.eternautas.com
The 'Argentinian Labyrinth' documents the
city's political ups and downs from past to
present. This three-hour tour will cover any
questions you may have regarding politics,
history and culture. Guides are university
professors with a penchant for history and
foreign languages. Other tours include
'Images of Buenos Aires', 'Evita and
Peronism', 'Paris of South America' and,
if you're looking for an out-of-town experience,
'San Isidro and Tigre'.

For the BMX bandit

www.labicicletanaranja.com.ar
'The Orange Bicycle' is a popular tour
company for pedalheads of all ages. Choose
from four fun excursions: for a change of
scenery the Costanera Sur offers a pleasant
(and cheap) bike ride around the city's
ecological reserve. And remember, there's
nothing uncool about a horde of tourists on
orange bikes.

For the tango lover

Carlos Gardel is practically a saint in Buenos
Aires and with Caminos de Gardel visitors get
to retrace some of his favourite haunts, most
of which are in the neighbourhood of Abasto.
There's also a visit to Gardel's mausoleum in
Chacarita cemetery, Recoleta's poorer
cousin. Call Maria on 4931 0896.

For the couch potato

www.opcionsur.com.ar
If you're tired from the long flight over, Opcion
Sur is geared towards non-walkers and uses
audio-visuals. The tour bus is air-conditioned
and stops at all the city's must-sees, showing
passengers archive footage of the epoch-
defining events that took place in whatever
barrio the bus is passing through at the time.
It is a spoon-fed approach but no less
enjoyable for that.

For the loner

Make good use of your iPod before it
breaks down and download some MP3 city
tours. The best ones are available from either
www.mptours.com (for a fee) or the city
government's website at www.bue.gov.ar
(free, and in both Spanish and English).
Downloaded tours are a good option for those

who like to be discreet tourists, and also
allow you to explore the city at your own pace.

For a slice of Jewish life

www.traveljewish.com
Over the course of this half- or full-day tour,
you will learn about the struggles Argentinian
Jews have had to face, the history of
immigrants and Jewish lives today. The tour
centres in Once, a run-down but colourful
neighbourhood and home to one of the
largest Jewish communities in the city.

For the beatnik

www.cultour.com.ar
If you're looking for something out of the
ordinary, the The Buenos Aires Traces tour
attempts to explain the essence of Buenos
Aires by deconstructing iconic lives and
events. From political figures to graffiti,
intelligent guides (associated with the
University of Buenos Aires – UBA) will spark
your interest in the culture of modern-day
Buenos Aires.

For Mr & Mrs Goodtimes

www.whatsupbuenosaires.com/tourism
So you've learned about the City's turbulent
history and you've been to the Casa Rosada,
but now you want to experience BA's fun side
– it's real scene. With What's Up Buenos
Aires Tourism, you'll get local guides who are
in the know and on the pulse. On the Nightlife
Tour, Juan and his buddies will take you to
authentic pizza joints to fuel up for a night of
alternative bands, theatres and clubs. Don
your dancing shoes, line your stomach and
find out what it's like to party like a *porteño* –
and don't expect to go to bed until the sun is
half-way up the sky.

For art aficionados

www.galeriadearte5006.com.ar
If you're interested in checking out some of
Argentina's art scene, this tour gives visitors
a chance to see and talk to artists in their
workspaces. It is also an accessible way to
buy Argentinean art.

For the curious

www.bitchtours.blogspot.com
For a truly different perspective on the city,
visit Diva's popular blog and website. Read
her witty and often astringent takes on
porteño life and then book yourself on one of
her superb personalised tours.

The Centre

Obelisks, pyramids and a Big Ben lookalike? It can only be downtown BA.

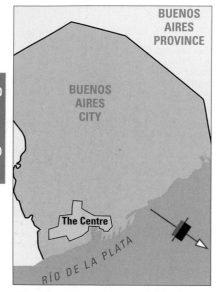

BUENOS
AIRES
PROVINCE

BUENOS
AIRES
CITY

The Centre

RÍO DE LA PLATA

BA's central districts have a reputation for urban dysfunction that is somewhat at odds with the reality – compared to many Latin American capitals, downtown BA is an oasis of tranquillity and sophistication. That said, the daily convergence of office workers, demonstrators, taxi drivers, tourists and pigeons on a zone that was designed to meet the needs of 19th-century commuters can be enough to make anyone reach for the Xanax. Top tip: the palaces and plazas will still be there at the weekend; the yuppies will not.

With or without the crowds, it's worth spending some time in 'el Centro'. The architectural diversity is astonishing: stroll around a single block and you might find a colonial-style tiled patio, a richly detailed Beaux-Arts façade, a soaring art deco apartment tower and a garish fast-food outlet. World famous thoroughfares such as Avenidas Corrientes, 9 de Julio, and de Mayo simultaneously evoke late-Victorian delusions of grandeur, mid-20th century planning cock-ups and the more environmentally conscious urban strategies (an ambitious tree planting programme is currently underway on Avenida 9 de Julio) of today.

The centre has also become the main stage for picketers' protests, and after dusk, hordes of *cartoneros* (cardboard collectors) descend, hauling their carts around before heading back to Retiro station or shantytown Villa 31. Just a stone's throw from such poverty is the affluence surrounding lush, stunning Plaza San Martín. Startling to outsiders, such contrasts are taken for granted by *porteños* accustomed to the centre's contending visions of past and present.

Plaza de Mayo

Map p325

Subte A, Plaza de Mayo or D, Catedral/bus 9, 10, 17, 39, 45, 93, 152.

Tradition and convention both dictate that if you want to do something big in Buenos Aires, you do it in **Plaza de Mayo**. Despite being shabby and overrun with pestiferous pigeons and tiresome souvenir hawkers, BA's central square remains the cockpit of Argentina's remarkable narrative. On its palm-bowered stage have strutted and fretted revolutionaries, reactionaries, human rights icons, rock stars, visionaries, lunatics, demagogues and Madonna.

The original *plaza mayor* (main square), was laid out by city founder Juan de Garay in the 1580s, shortly after the successful foundation of Buenos Aires. Garay still stands as a bronze statue in a tiny square just metres north-east of the plaza, beside an oak tree from his Basque motherland.

The colonial plaza became Plaza de Mayo to commemorate 25 May, 1810, when the masses assembled there to celebrate the deposition of the Spanish viceroy and the swearing in of the Primera Junta (First Council). Famously, it was the site of the great gatherings of the *descamisados* or 'shirtless ones' under Perón and was bombed by the military in 1955 (to oust the aforementioned general); bullet holes are still visible in the **Ministerio de Economía** building on Hipólito Yrigoyen next to Avenida Paseo Colón. Today, the Madres de Plaza de Mayo still march here every Thursday at 3.30pm to protest the 'disappearance' of their loved ones during the last military government, which itself announced the invasion of the Falklands/Malvinas islands (a last-ditch attempt to revive its flagging popularity) in early 1982 in front of vast crowds in the Plaza.

At the plaza's centre is the **Pirámide de Mayo**, an obelisk raised in 1811 for the anniversary of the May revolution. The Madres' internationally famous symbol – a white headscarf that alludes to motherhood and to the nappies of their lost children – is painted on the tiles circling the pyramid. To the east is a statue of independence patriot Manuel Belgrano – the only national hero to be honoured with a statue in the plaza.

Glowing like a psychedelic vermilion fantasy, especially at sunset, the **Casa Rosada** (Pink House) is the presidential palace (not the residence, which is out in the sticks in Olivos). Built between 1862 and 1885, it stands where Buenos Aires' 17th-century fort, later the viceroy's palace, used to be. The splendour of its European Renaissance-style façade came together in several stages. The emblematic rosy hue originated during Sarmiento's 1868-74 presidency: it was then common practice to add ox blood to whitewash to provide colour and thicken the mix. Today the front is pinker than the rest because a project to doll it up during the Menem years ran out of funds when only one side had been finished.

The central balcony has been the soapbox of diverse demagogues and dictators, although the Peróns used the lower balcony, to be 'closer to the people'. This was also used by Madonna in the filming of Alan Parker's *Evita*, despite protests by Peronists who felt the material girl was tarnishing the memory of Saint Evita.

Surrounding the Plaza de Mayo are a number of important buildings. On the corner of Avenida Rivadavia and 25 de Mayo is the **Banco de la Nación**, the country's state bank. The present building, constructed between 1940 and 1955, is topped by an enormous, neo-classical dome.

Heading west on Avenida Rivadavia is the neoclassical **Catedral Metropolitana** (*see below*). The Plaza's other main building, the **Cabildo**, was HQ of the city council from 1580 to 1821, and the place where revolutionaries took the first steps towards independence. Today it houses the **Museo Histórico Nacional del Cabildo y de la Revolución de Mayo** (*see p82*).

Catedral Metropolitana

Avenida Rivadavia, y San Martín (4331 2845). Subte A, Plaza de Mayo or D, Catedral or E, Bolivar/24, 64, 130 bus. **Open** 8am-7pm Mon-Fri; 9am-7.30pm Sat, Sun. **Admission** free. **Map** p325 E11.
On the west side of the plaza is this neo-classical cathedral, whose strictly-by-the-book columns and cornices look rather incongruous amid all this chaos. The cornerstone for the original church was laid by Juan de Garay in 1580 (perhaps he did a poor job of it as the structure has collapsed six times since then.)

The plan for the present cream-coloured building, the sixth cathedral on this site, was hatched in 1753; the first façade was blessed in 1791 and the final touches were added in 1910. The high baroque interior arches create a sombre atmosphere, while the rococo main altar and the organ (dating from 1822) stand out. The right-hand nave houses the mausoleum containing – since 1880 – the repatriated remains of the Liberator José de San Martín (who died in France in 1850). The most striking feature of the building's Greco-Roman exterior is the frontispiece, depicting the reunion of Jacob and his sons with Joseph in Egypt.

Museo de la Casa Rosada

Hipólito Yrigoyen 219, entre Balcarce y Paseo Colón (4344 3802/www.museo.gov.ar). Subte A, Plaza de Mayo or D, Catedral or E, Bolivar/24, 64, 130 bus. **Open** 10am-6pm Mon-Fri; 2-6pm Sun. **Guided tours** *Museum* (Spanish) 11am, 3pm Mon-Fri; 4pm Sun. *Casa Rosada* (Spanish) check website for details. **Admission** free. **Map** p325 E11.
Open to visitors again after extensive renovations in 2007, the Pink House museum displays portraits, hats, mate gourds, cigar boxes, military decorations and carriages that once belonged to Argentinian presidents, as well as some amusing – and often quite pointed – caricatures of said heads of state by the leading cartoonists of their era. There are some real curios too, including a black doll given to poor kids by Evita's charity. Tours of the Pink House itself were suspended at time of writing but should be running again by mid 2008.

Plaza de Mayo.

Culture clubs

Brimming with music, theatre, cinema, paintings, photography, conferences and classes, BA's cultural centres are, at their best, edifying islands of art, each with their own particular flavour. They act as cornerstones of artistic creation and dissemination. Some are state-funded and others run privately, but while politics play a part, most are surprisingly liberated from lobbying, choosing artists on the strength of their work. Part of the cultural centre concept is to spread knowledge across social lines, so admissions are usually free and tickets to events inexpensive. Descriptions below highlight the strong points of five of the most interesting centres, but are far from exhaustive. Nearly all of have broad and varied activities – check websites for a complete list.

Centro Cultural San Martín
www.ccgsm.gov.ar
A hub for BA cultural life over the past 30 years, the ten-storey Centro Cultural San Martín is a monolithic monument to good art and bad architecture. The main venue for several state-run theatres, the centre is known for having the city's best line-up of plays. It also houses at least two different photo exhibitions on the first floor and recondite cinema retrospectives at the tenth-floor Cine Lugones. Friday evening concerts of up-and-coming bands are the best place to get up close with new musical talent. Recent renovations have added chaos rather than charm to the severe 1970s design.

Centro Cultural la Cooperación
www.centrocultural.coop
Directly opposite Centro Cultural San Martín, Centro Cultural la Cooperación is its ultra-modern, politically left-leaning doppelganger. The centre hosts conferences and talks, with a particular emphasis on the so-called new Latin American left. Those who still think Hugo Chávez is a brand of aftershave will be

relieved to note that the line-up also includes a fair share of good music and theatre, in (relatively) state-of-the-art facilities.

Centro Cultural del Sur
www.ccdelsur.blogspot.com
This top cultural centre keeps the folk life of the Argentinian countryside alive in the big city, with the sounds of guitars, charangos and drums drifting across a patio complete with hitching posts and watering troughs for the horses. Outdoor shows attract renowned traditional folk musicians as well as new trailblazers in the genre such as Mariana Baraj. Weekday regulars are not averse to breaking out into handkerchief-waving folk dances, but Friday, Saturday and Sunday nights attract a more diverse programme.

Centro Cultural Borges
www.ccborges.org.ar
Named after the author Jorge Luis Borges and connected to shopping mall Galerías Pacíficas in the heart of BA's commercial district, Centro Cultural Borges is the city's glossy, highbrow outlet for art and experimental theatre. The AR$8 admission fee is scorned by purists who see it as exclusionary, but CC Borges clearly aims for a particular crowd, pulling in prestigious international artists from all genres.

Centro Cultural Recoleta
www.centroculturalrecoleta.org
Wedged in between the cemetery and Plaza Francia, the building housing Centro Cultural Recoleta forms part of an impressive complex tdating back to the 17th century. The long structure stretches out above the plaza, with numerous exhibition rooms broken up by courtyards dotted with orange trees. It's perfect to incorporate into a cemetery/cathedral/plaza stroll, and with up to 20 exhibitions running at once, you're bound to find at least something you like.

Museo Histórico Nacional del Cabildo y de la Revolución de Mayo
Bolívar 65, entre Avenida de Mayo y Hipólito Yrigoyen (4334 1782/4342 6729). Subte A, Plaza de Mayo or D, Catedral or E, Bolívar/28, 56, 105, 126 bus. **Open** 11.30am-6pm Tue-Fri; 2-6pm Sat, Sun. Admission AR$1. **Map** p325 E10.
The Cabildo was HQ of the city council between 1580 and 1821, and where the seeds of Argentina's

revolution were sown. Seemingly the oldest building on the plaza, it recovered its colonial style only in the 1940s, several decades after six of its original 11 arches were lopped off to make room for Avenida de Mayo and Avenida Julio A Roca. The museum comprises a number of austere rooms in which you'll find valuable items such as a magnificent gold and silver piece from Oruro (Bolivia); one of the country's first printing presses; and a number of items relating to the English invasions. Behind the building is a shaded colonial patio, the site of a handicrafts fair on Thursdays and Fridays.

Avenida de Mayo

Map p325
Subte A, Plaza de Mayo/bus 39, 60, 64, 168.

Opened in 1894, the grand **Avenida de Mayo**, its spacious pavements dotted with plane trees, is the most obvious example of Buenos Aires trying to emulate the wide boulevards of Paris. In reality, though, it's more closely associated with Spain, due to the large numbers of Spanish immigrants who settled in – and still live in – the neighbourhood.

Newly elected presidents make their way down this avenue to the Casa Rosada after being sworn in at the Palacio del Congreso. Common folk travel below, on Latin America's oldest underground railway, opened in 1913, just nine years after New York's subway started rolling. Although the Subte's *línea* A has lost much of its old lustre to modernisation, the retro posters and fittings at Perú station (Avenida de Mayo between Bolívar and Perú) recalls the Argentina that used to be.

Despite run-down sections, modern towers and some of the more faded-looking Spanish restaurants along and around its ten blocks, fine European-style buildings with exquisite architectural details still abound. The best example of art nouveau, richly decorated with elements from the natural world, is the **Hotel Chile**, on the corner of Santiago del Estero.

Heading west from Plaza de Mayo, the first highlight is the Gallic *La Prensa* newspaper building, from 1896, now the city government's **Casa de la Cultura** (*see below*).

The avenue's outstanding edifice and one of the city's notable buildings is the **Palacio Barolo** (*see below*). It was built as, and remains, office space, but you can enter its ground floor passageway with its gargoyles, Latin inscriptions and several kiosks that look like they were stolen from the set of *Brief Encounter*. Another stunning building marks the avenue's west end. With its two slender domes the **Edificio de la Inmobiliaria**, built in 1910 for an insurance company, is a nattily eclectic celebration of several styles including Italianate balconies and Eastern motifs. From here it's a few steps to the Plaza del Congreso.

Casa de la Cultura
Avenida de Mayo 575, entre Perú y Bolívar (4323 9669). Subte A, Perú or D, Catedral or E, Bolívar/24, 29, 64, 86, 105, 111 bus. **Open** *Feb-Dec* 8am-8pm Mon-Fri; by tour Sat, Sun. **Closed** Jan. **Admission** free. **Map** p325 F10.

Built in 1896, this was once the headquarters of the *La Prensa* newspaper but now belongs to the city government. This building's French feel goes beyond the façades – the impressive Salón Dorado, inspired by the Palace of Versailles, hosts chamber music concerts each Friday at 7pm (entry is free). A siren on top, sounded at crucial moments in the city's history, was last heard in 1983 when democracy was restored. (But curiously not in 1986 when Argentina won the World Cup) Guided tours also take in the city government headquarters on the Plaza de Mayo.

Palacio Barolo
Avenida de Mayo 1370, entre San José y Santiago del Estero. Subte A, Congreso/12, 37, 64, 86 bus. **Map** p325 F9.

One of the city's finest and most emblematic buildings, this 1923 construction is a neo-Gothic allegorical tribute to the 100 cantos of Dante's *Divine Comedy*. Hell is on the ground floor: Latin inscriptions taken from nine different literary works represent the nine infernal circles and are engraved on the entrance hall's nine vaults. Above, the first 14 floors comprise Purgatory (and if you get stuck in one of the picturesque but temperamental lifts, you'll know what it's like to be a soul in waiting) while Paradise can be found in the upper reaches.

Grandeur and colour on **Avenida de Mayo**.

At the very top is a domed lighthouse, representing God. It was built as, and remains as, office space but visitors can step inside the entrance hall to see the gargoyles. Ask at the desk about guided tours, some of which are led by English-speaking guides.

Congreso & Tribunales

Map p325

Subte A, Sáenz Peña or B, Uruguay/bus 60, 168, 180.

Plaza del Congreso is the popular name for the three squares filling the three blocks east of the Palacio del Congreso. Run down in recent years by protestors, vagrants and metal thieves who hijack commemorative plaques, all that's left of its once stately elegance are the shady jacarandas, *tipa* and *ceibo* trees (whose red blossom is the national flower) that colour the plaza in spring. It contains a version of Rodin's *Thinker* and a statue of Mariano Moreno, one of the May revolutionaries.

The western section of the plaza is dominated by the **Monumento a los Dos Congresos**, in remembrance of the first constitutional assembly held in 1813 and the Declaration of Independence three years later in Tucumán. The monument's centrepiece is the statue of the republic, propped up by a plough and waving a victorious laurel branch.

Like Argentina's federal constitution, which was inspired by the US model, the Greco-Roman **Palacio del Congreso** (*see p85*) is a dome-and-column affair resembling Washington's bicameral legislature. Finished in 1906, its extravagant interior can be visited with a guided tour (no access when in session).

On the corner to the right of the palace is a historical *confitería* (closed since 1996) where politicians used to sip their espressos between sessions. It's called **El Molino**, a reference to the windmill above its entrance. Currently under refurbishment, the small **Teatro Liceo**, on the corner of Rivadavia and Paraná, is one of the oldest playhouses in BA. It opened in 1876 and has been the stage for many of the country's greatest thespians. It's also where a struggling young actress named Eva Perón once performed.

To visit the rest of civic Buenos Aires, a good starting point is **Diagonal Norte**, running north-west from Plaza de Mayo. The avenue is a masterpiece of urban harmony; every building is ten storeys tall with a second-floor balcony, though a rigidly monumental style dominates many of its edifices. Empty on weekends, the Diagonal's finest architecture is on the corner of Florida where Bank Boston shows off its decorative façade and heavily decorated gilt ceiling of the inner hall (visible during bank opening hours only).

Diagonal Norte links the Plaza de Mayo with the barrio of Tribunales, where the law courts are surrounded by solicitors' offices, law firms and kiosks selling legal pamphlets. At the end of 2003 the block between Cerrito and Libertad was pedestrianised. The avenue's disappointing dead-end is the grubby-looking **Palacio de Justicia**, seat of the Supreme Court and another popular venue for public protest. Stretching out in front as far as Avenida Córdoba is the **Plaza Lavalle**, an attractive green spot rich in history and sprawling *ceibo* trees. Its focal point is a monument to Juan Lavalle, one of the military heroes who crossed the Andes with San Martín. Also look out for La Fuente de los Bailarines (Dancers' Fountain), a simple and touching memorial to two dancers from the Teatro Colón killed in a plane accident in 1971. Across the Plaza, and filling a whole block, is the **Teatro Colón** itself (*see p85*). With its regular lines and tempered classicism, it's a key landmark and an internationally renowned venue for opera and classical music. Or at least it was until the curtain came down for extensive renovation work in early 2007. Delays have ensued and regular service is not expected to be resumed until 2010 at the earliest.

On the corner of Avenida Córdoba and Libertad, is the **Teatro Cervantes** (*see p262*), the capital's grand old lyric theatre. Unveiled in 1921, its façade is a near replica of the university at Alcalá de Henares in Spain, where Don Quixote's creator was born. Equally impressive inside, the building also houses the **Museo Nacional del Teatro** (*see below*), a tribute to Argentina's thespian history.

It's just a short walk from here to the grand asphalt canyon of Avenida 9 de Julio and its iconic monument, the **Obelisco** (*see below*).

Museo Nacional del Teatro

Avenida Córdoba 1199, y Libertad (4816 7212). Subte D, Tribunales/23, 39, 109 bus. Open 10am-5.30pm Mon-Fri. **Admission** free. **Map p325 H11.**
Right next to the Teatro Cervantes, BA's Museum of Theatre offers the stage-struck visitor a fascinating insight into Argentina's thespian heritage, from the earliest colonial times up until the present day. Among the exhibits are costumes and personal effects, photographs of celebrated actors, writers and directors, programmes and documents.

El Obelisco

Avenida 9 de Julio, y Corrientes. Subte B, Carlos Pellegrini or C, Diagonal Norte/6, 7, 9, 10, 56, 67, 70, 100, 105 bus. **Map p325 G10.**
The Obelisco was built to mark four of the city's key historical events: the first and the final foundation of Buenos Aires; the 1880 declaration of the city as the country's federal capital; and to mark the site of the

Palacio del Congreso HQ of Argentina's not-universally-beloved governing class.

demolished church of San Nicolás where the national flag was first flown. When the 68-metre (223-foot) obelisk was completed in 1935, the critics went to town, describing it as an undignified, phallic, cement spike. Radical feminist groups suggested lopping it in half, and three years after its inauguration the city's parliament voted for its demolition. The decision was ignored and the Obelisco became, over time, the city's postcard emblem and a symbol of its self-conscious monumentalism.

Palacio del Congreso

Hipólito Yrigoyen 1849, entre Entre Ríos y Combate de los Pozos (4370 7100). Subte A, Congreso/12, 37, 60 bus. **Guided tours** call to arrange. **Closed** sometimes Jan. **Admission** free. **Map** p325 G9.
Argentina's constitution was inspired by its US equivalent. In a similar spirit of benign plagiarism, the Palacio del Congreso is a dome-and-column affair designed to resemble Washington's bicameral legislature. Depending on your architectural and/or political preferences, the Palace is either an awe-inspiring shrine to the democratic principle or an over-elaborate wedding cake. Completed in 1906, the Congress building's very extravagant interior, which includes an extensive network of basements and bunkers, can be visited by guided tour. (The advertised tour schedule is notoriously unreliable; call in advance if you want to arrange a guided visit.) Note that all 72 Senate seats have a button for direct calls to the cafeteria.

Teatro Colón

Cerrito 618, entre Tucumán y Viamonte, Tribunales (www.teatrocolon.org.ar). Subte D, Tribunales/29, 39, 59 bus. **Closed** until 2010. **Map** p325 G10.
There are few buildings in Buenos Aires that would merit a listing in this section despite being closed for renovation work, but this world-renowned opera house is one of them. With its regular lines and tempered classicism, the Colón is one of Buenos Aires' key architectural as well as cultural landmarks. Go peer through the scaffolding – and then come back in late 2008 to enjoy the experience.

Microcentro

Map p325

Subte B, Florida or D, Catedral/bus 4, 20, 56, 93, 152.

It's every claustrophobe's worst nightmare – weekdays during business hours the whole downtown district becomes a maelstrom of *porteños* shopping, working, running, shouting, flouting traffic laws, shouting some more, and generally fulfilling their big-city stereotype.

The district is nicknamed La City – and was once known as 'the 20 blocks that rule the country' – for its early association with British commerce. It has the largest concentration of financial institutions in the country, extending

almost the entire length of Florida, San Martín and Reconquista (named after the reconquest, when Buenos Aires repelled the English in 1806-07). Many of the banks were built during the first half of the 20th century, at a time when affluent Argentinians had money to deposit. A good example is the former **Banco Tornquist**, at Bartolomé Mitre 559, on the first section of street to be paved in BA. Scale models of what the district looked like during the 19th century are on display in the **Museo del Banco de la Provincia** (Sarmiento 362, 4331 1775). Another financially-themed museum is the excellent **Museo Numismático** (*see right*).

To see how affluent *porteños* lived during the economic boom of the late 19th century, step into the **Museo Mitre** (*see p89*) – home of former president and founder of *La Nación* newspaper, Bartolomé Mitre. It contains his rich library specialising in American history.

At the corner of Reconquista and Perón, protected by wonderful wrought-iron gates, is the 18th-century **Basílica Nuestra Señora de la Merced**, the richly decorative façade of which was restored in 1905. Next door, the **Convento de San Ramón**'s patio contains small attractive shops and a hidden lunchtime eaterie overlooking an attractive garden.

Along the west side of Avenida Leandro N Alem, more commonly called *el bajo* – meaning the low place – runs an almost uninterrupted arcade packed with banks, cafés, the stock exchange and, on its east side, the colossal **Correo Central**, located at Sarmiento 151. Inaugurated after 41 years of construction in 1928, the Central Post Office is one of BA's best examples of French-inspired classical architecture. Philatelists will want to check out the little museum inside. Diagonally opposite the post office's north-east corner is **Luna Park**, where Carlos Gardel's funeral was held in 1935 and where in 1944 Perón met Eva. It's now a music venue; *see p204*.

Though once an elegant thoroughfare, Florida, the only completely pedestrianised street in BA, is now unashamedly commercial. However, amid the cybercafé promo girls and money changers, you can still find traces of its refined past.

As Florida's old glamour wanes, more modern variations on retail sophistication spring up. **Galerías Pacífico** (*see p178*) is the city's most aesthetically inspired mall. In its south-east corner (with an entrance at the corner of Viamonte and San Martín) is the **Centro Cultural Borges** (*see p82* **Culture clubs**), built in memory of Argentina's greatest writer, and a thriving venue for the arts. Behind it on the corner of San Martín and Viamonte is the 18th-century church of **Santa Catalina**.

Lavalle, for pedestrians only between San Martín and Carlos Pellegrini, makes Florida look chic and classy. It's packed with blockbuster and B-movie cinemas, fast-food outlets, advertising boards, evangelical churches and subterranean girly bars.

Close by, but extending beyond the Microcentro, is Corrientes. Though it's been an *avenida* since 1936, people still fondly call it a *calle*. Until the 1970s it was the mecca for tango artists, BA's Broadway and a coffee-drinking, literature-loving nocturnal scene, where bohos would meet to talk revolution and rock 'n' roll.

Museo Histórico y Numismático del Banco de la Nación Argentina

First floor, Bartolomé Mitre 326, entre 25 de Mayo y Reconquista (4347 6277). Subte B, Florida/93, 109, 132 bus. **Open** 10am-3pm Mon-Fri. **Admission** free. **Map** p325 F11.

A real mouthful of a museum, mainly of interest to anthropologists and those who enjoy staring at money they'll never be able to spend, this financially themed centre was inaugurated in 1966 to mark the 75th anniversary of Argentina's central bank. It exhibits exotic early bank notes (from as far back as 1820) featuring dogs, goats, cows and even a kangaroo, as well as gold and silver coins.

Shop in style at **Galerías Pacífico**.

Museo Mitre

San Martín 336, entre Corrientes y Sarmiento (4394 7659/www.museomitre.gov.ar). Subte B, Florida/93, 99, 152 bus. **Open** 1-6pm Mon-Fri. **Admission** AR$1. **Map** p325 F11.

This gorgeous colonial mansion, dating from 1785, was, between 1860 and 1906, the home of former president and founder of *La Nación* newspaper, Bartolomé Mitre. The library is the main attraction; it holds some of the region's most important books as well as documents on Latin American history and some unique photographic exhibits.

Retiro

Map p325

Subte C, Retiro/bus 6, 20, 93, 152.

For centuries this area – a natural point on the river – was the northern edge of the town, and was once the refuge of a hermit known as 'la ermita de San Sebastián'. When a late-17th-century Spanish governor built a country house in the area for his retirement, and called it El Retiro – *retiro* means retreat – the district took

its name. Today the area's main attraction is its open space – the well-shaded green swath that is the lovely **Plaza San Martín**, the city's second most important plaza.

This natural bluff stretches down to three railway terminals, beyond which lie a jumble of official buildings and the docks. It's named after José de San Martín, who trained his troops here. The Liberator is still revered. According to protocol, all visiting dignitaries must lay a wreath at the **Monumento al Libertador General San Martín**, the city's most important monument. It's a heroic marble and bronze equestrian affair created in 1862 by French sculptor Louis Joseph Daumas.

Sun-worshipping office workers lunch in the plaza, while an inordinate number of couples locked in marathon kissing sessions loll underneath overhanging branches or lie exposed to the sun on the windy vantage point of the green slopes.

The first block of Florida leading off the plaza was called '*la manzana loca*' (the crazy block) in the 1960s for the avant-garde art

Sightseeing

Talk the talk

Like most big-city dwellers, *porteños* are fond of slang, but what means one thing in Madrid can mean quite another in Buenos Aires. To give an oft-cited example, if you *coger* a bus in Spain, you are simply catching it; if you *coger* a bus in Argentina, you'd be arrested for committing a lewd act with a road vehicle.

For more than a century the shoptalk of choice in BA has been *lunfardo*, often called the 'language of tango' because of its prevalence in that genre's song lyrics. This unique argot comprises thousands of slang words, phrases and idioms, some of which are ingenious mutations of standard terms (tango, for instance, can be turned back-to-front to become *gotan*), others pure neologisms of untraceable origin. To get a sense of the scope of this colourful lexicon, simply pick up a lunfardo dictionary (there are many) on your foot.

While many *lunfardo* terms have either fallen into disuse or been supplanted by Americanisms, some slang words are so common they barely qualify as colloquialisms at all. Here is our top 10.

Banana
An astute, street-wise guy; also a large, impressive penis

Boludo
Asshole; but also used affectionately by mates in '¡Che, boludo!' or 'hey, what's up?'

Cana
Pejorative term for a policeman/woman, translates as 'pig'

Chanta
An incorrigible bluffer, all talk and no walk

Guita
Cash

Mina
Young woman; sometimes translates as 'babe' but can be used pejoratively

Pibe
Kid

Pucho
Cigarette

Quilombo
Originally a term for a brothel, now meaning 'serious problem' or 'mess'

Telo
Backslang term for hotel; usually refers to a short-stay (two or three hours) 'love motel' or *albergue transitorio*

Edificio Kavanagh.

experiments held at the Instituto Di Tella at Florida 940 (now a multi-brand shop with a small art space). The district is still arty – with numerous galleries and regular gatherings among the creative set at trad cafés such as **Florida Garden** and funky bars like **Dadá** (*for both, see p167*).

Several impressive buildings surround Plaza San Martín. South-west is the gargantuan **Palacio Paz**, the largest private residence in the country and formerly the home of José C Paz, founder of the once important (but now derided) *La Prensa* newspaper. Since 1938, by which time the Paz empire had shrunk to insignificance, military officers have luxuriated in part of the palace renamed the **Círculo Militar** (to see inside, you have to join a 90-minute Spanish guided tour; 4311 1071, www.circulomilitar.org). One wing now houses the **Museo de Armas de la Nación** (*see p92*) which comprises a sizable collection of arms and military uniforms, some dating from medieval times, plus a room of ancient Oriental weapons.

At the edge of the plaza, the **Palacio San Martín** (Arenales 761, 4819 8092) – until recently home of the Argentinian foreign ministry – was built between 1909 and 1912 for the mega-rich Anchorena family. Nowadays, it's mostly used for official galas, although it opens for guided tours in Spanish most Thursdays and Fridays, which include a view of the garden containing a section of the Berlin Wall and an excellent collection of pre-Columbian Argentinian art.

On the opposite side of the plaza, the **Basílica del Santísimo Sacramento**, at San Martín 1039, regularly plays host to society weddings. Also built with Anchorena money (before they lost it all in the Depression) and consecrated in 1916, the Basílica's French exterior hides an inner sanctum combining Flemish and Italian handiwork with French and North African raw materials. Mercedes Castellanos de Anchorena, the woman who used some of her savings to build the church and lived at the Palacio San Martín, rests in expensive peace in an ornate marble vault in the crypt. The **Edificio Kavanagh** next door also points heavenward – at 120 metres (394 feet) it was South America's tallest building when completed in 1935, the project bankrolled by Irishwoman Corina Kavanagh. At the time of its construction, this apartment block was admired by rationalist architects all over the world and is still considered an art deco landmark. Next door the luxurious **Plaza Hotel** (now part of the Marriott chain; *see p47*) was built, in 1908, by Alfred Zucker, architect of Saint Patrick's Cathedral in New York.

Set your watch by the **Torre de los Ingleses**.

At the very foot of the plaza is a black marble cenotaph to those who fell in the Falklands/Malvinas War, watched over by two soldiers in traditional uniforms who perform a stiff changing of the guard several times a day.

Across the road from this sombre memorial, in an ironic twists of history, stands a Big Ben lookalike. The British-designed and built clock tower used to be known as the **Torre de los Ingleses** – it was presented as a gift to Argentina by local Anglo-Argentinians for the 1910 centennial celebrations. Since war with the UK in 1982, though, the authorities have insisted on using its official name, Torre Monumental, though most locals are too stubborn to hop on the patriotic bandwagon. Likewise, the land around it, formerly called the Plaza Británica, was renamed **Plaza Fuerza Aérea Argentina**. For a panoramic view of the plaza and the English-built railway stations, you can take a lift to the sixth floor – 35 metres (115 feet) up (though opening hours are irregular). There are occasional exhibits in the small photo gallery inside.

Shattering the peace is the endless din from horn-honking lorries on Avenida del Libertador

Estación Mitre.

leading to the railway stations. Though everyone says they are going 'to Retiro' to get a train or bus, there are, in fact, three separate train terminals plus a bus station along Avenida JM Ramos Mejia. The largest, English-built terminal, the **Mitre**, dates from 1915, and stands out as one of South America's best examples of Crystal Palace-inspired architecture. A plaque on an arch of its iron structure reads 'Francis Morton & Co Ltd – Liverpool'. Although recently renovated it still retains a hue of the golden age of railways in objects such as a tobacco-stained map of Argentina's once 45,000-kilometre (27,000-mile) network, by far the largest in South America.

Surrounding the terminals, food stands and market stalls add to the general noise and chaos, making for a colourful though stressful walk, especially in rush hours. The **Paseo del Retiro** handicrafts fair, created to give some life to the uninviting wasteland opposite the bus station, runs every weekend.

Just north of the bus terminal is Villa 31, the capital's best-known shantytown. The reason for the slum's notoriety is the community's refusal to move from this potentially prime real estate until the city offers them something better. Current mayor Mauricio Macri has made the clearance of Villa 31 one of the key policy aims of his administration; but short of sending in the bulldozers and the riot police it's hard to see how the issue will be resolved. The adjacent badlands consist of run-down military and other buildings. You should avoid this area, especially after dusk.

A couple of blocks up Libertador in an old railway building is the nostalgic **Museo**

Nacional Ferroviario (*see below*). Just a hop across the road and up the incline at Suipacha 1422 is one of BA's cultural gems, the **Museo de Arte Hispanoamericano Isaac Fernández Blanco** (*see below*) in a beautiful Peruvian-style mansion.

The **Plaza Embajada de Israel** lies on the corner of Suipacha and Arroyo streets. A bomb destroyed a previous Israeli embassy on this site in 1992. Each of the 29 trees represents a victim of the blast. At Suipacha 1333, Argentina's main English-language teaching organisation runs the **British Arts Centre** (BAC; *see below*).

British Arts Centre

Suipacha 1333, entre Juncal y Arroyo, Retiro (4393 6941/www.britishartscentre.org.ar). Bus 59, 61, 93, 130, 152. **Open** *Feb* 12.30-6.30pm Mon-Fri. *Mar-Dec* 3-9pm Mon-Fri. **Closed** Jan. **Admission** varies. **Map** p325 H11/H12.
A bit of Blighty in the heart of Buenos Aires, the BAC puts on loads of free events such as plays and films in English as well as jazz, Celtic and classical concerts, and photo and art exhibits and workshops.

Museo de Armas de la Nacíon

Avenida Santa Fe 750, entre Maipú y Esmeralda (4311 1071). Subte C, San Martin/10, 17, 152 bus. **Open** 1-7pm Mon-Fri. **Closed** Jan, Feb. Admission AR$5. **Map** p325 G11.
Founded by President Roca in 1904, this well-curated weapons museum moved to its current location in the Palacio Retiro in 1940. It houses a collection of arms and military uniforms, some dating from the 12th century, spread over 17 rooms.

Museo de Arte Hispanoamericano Isaac Fernández Blanco

Suipacha 1422, entre Arroyo y Libertador (4327 0228). Bus 93, 130, 152. **Open** 2-7pm Tue-Sun. **Admission** AR$1. **Map** p325 H12.
The white baroque building houses Spanish American paintings, religious objects and silverware. The ghost of a lady in white is said to inhabit the house. Classical music recitals are often held on Friday, Saturday and Sunday evenings at 7pm, usually featuring the museum's own baroque chamber orchestra. If you've time, wander about the mansion's peaceful, ivy-lined Andalucian courtyard.

Museo Nacional Ferroviario

Avenida del Libertador 405, y Suipacha (4318 3343). Subte C, Retiro/62, 93, 152 bus. **Open** 10.30am-4pm Mon-Fri. **Admission** free. **Map** p325 H12.
Housed in an ageing railway building, this tribute to trains covers two floors and comprises an intriguing hotchpotch of exhibits from a railway era that puts car-obsessed governments to shame. Alongside the museum is the cluttered workshop of Carlos Regazzoni, an internationally respected sculptor whose creations are made from the scrap he finds in the railway yards.

Sightseeing

South of the Centre

Long considered the mother lode of BA's song and soul, the mythical and slightly shabby *Sur* is on the up.

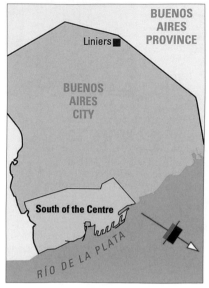

When people drone on about 'mythical' or 'romantic' or 'bohemian' Buenos Aires, more often than not they are referring to the southern barrios of the city – Monserrat, San Telmo and La Boca in particular. Tourists love these neighbourhoods and come to take in the tango murals, the cobblestoned calles, the colonial-style houses with their detailed – if often crumbling – stucco façades and sinuous wrought-iron balconets, and the eccentric street performers: a whiff (sometimes literally) of the past on every corner – or so it is easy to imagine. Locals, on the other hand, tend to look at the barrios south of Rivadavia street with a more ambivalent eye. In his short story 'El Sur', published in 1953, Jorge Luis Borges, a child of Palermo, wrote: 'Every Argentinian knows that the south begins at the other side of Rivadavia … whoever crosses this street enters a more ancient and sterner world.' While tourists are more likely to focus on the ancient part, *porteños*, less inclined to mythologise squalor or see the funny side of botched development projects, are struck more by the sternness.

But this may be changing. An unprecedented amount of investment is flowing into the south and an equally unprecedented number of development schemes are getting off the drawing board and on to the map. San Telmo, filling up with boutique hotels, fashion outlets, smart bars and restaurants, is looking to steal Palermo Viejo's crown as the city's hippest barrio. A plan to clean up La Boca's emblematic but disgusting Riachuelo river looks like it might actually happen. And tourists and locals alike are beginning to discover, or rediscover, historic but neglected barrios like Barracas. 'Timelessness' is for poets and *tangueros*; it isn't much of an urban strategy. The challenge for *El Sur* is to continue to evoke the past without becoming trapped in it.

Monserrat

Map p325

Subte A, Plaza de Mayo or E, Bolívar/bus 39, 60, 86, 105, 111, 126.

For those who are interested in Argentinian history (both the pre- and post-independence eras) or who simply enjoy mooching around in old churches, Monserrat is an education and a delight. While the barrio attracts fewer tourists than neighbouring San Telmo, its architecture and heritage are in a class of their own.

Bounded by Alsina, Bolívar, Moreno and Perú streets is a complex of historical buildings filling the whole city block and known as the **Manzana de las Luces** (Block of Enlightenment; *see p95*). The illumination moniker was coined in the early 19th century in allusion to the wisdom garnered by the leading lights who were educated here.

The block's **Iglesia de San Ignacio**, on the corner of Alsina and Bolívar, dates from 1734 and is the oldest church in the city. Hidden behind the church is the brick-walled patio of the **Procuraduría de las Misiones**, accessed on Avenida Julio A Roca (also known as Diagonal Sur), which cuts into the block, via a small handicrafts market. This was the HQ of the Jesuits who ran the New World conversion programme in the 18th century.

On the opposite corner of Alsina and Bolívar from the church is the **Librería de Avila** (4331 8989), the city's oldest bookshop, dating from 1785. There's another bookish haunt a few blocks south; the old Biblioteca Nacional building on Mexico 564, now a research centre

Sightseeing

for musicologists, is where Jorge Luis Borges served as library director for 17 years.

On the corner of Alsina and Defensa is the charming 1894 chemist La Estrella, whose mahogany interior has barely been touched. At lunchtime office workers file in to test its two-metre (seven-foot) Toledo, Ohio-made iron weighing scale, reputed to be the most accurate in the city. Directly above is the **Museo de la Ciudad** (*see below*).

Opposite the chemist's is the **Iglesia de San Francisco**, begun in 1730 by Jesuit architect Andrés Blanqui, who also worked on the Pilar church in Recoleta and the Cabildo. Inside, there is a startlingly gaudy 20th-century tapestry of St Francis by Argentinian artist Horacio Butler, evidently a fan of psychedelic flowers and cartoon animals.

Adjacent to this church is the smaller **Parroquia San Roque** (Roque parish church), built in the 1750s. Opposite, the **Plazoleta San Francisco** contains four statues, moved here from Plaza de Mayo in 1972. They depict geography, sailing, astronomy and industry – in short, all of the disciplines that have tested belief in the God worshipped across the road.

In the middle of all these Roman Catholic ramparts and monuments to post-colonial ambition, the **Museo Etnográfico** (*see below*) delivers a salutary reminder that before the arrival of the Europeans, Argentina had such a thing as an indigenous population.

The **Basílica de Santo Domingo** and the adjoining **Basílica Nuestra Señora del Rosario**, at Defensa and Belgrano, are two other important 18th-century centres of worship. One of the towers of the former was punctured by bullets during the English invasions of 1806-07. The flags seized from the vanquished invaders are on display in the far corner left of the altar and even the street name Defensa pays homage to this first popular local resistance against foreign forces.

Manzana de las Luces

Perú 272, entre Moreno y Alsina (4342 3964/www. manzanadelasluces.gov.ar). Subte A, Plaza de Mayo or D, Catedral or E, Bolívar/24, 29, 86, 126 bus. **Open** 3-8pm daily. *Tours* (Spanish) 3pm daily. **Admission** *Manzana* free. *Guided tours* AR$5; free under-6s. **No credit cards. Map** p325 E10.

The 'Block of Enlightenment' is a complex of historical buildings occupying an entire city block. The complex has been, *inter alia*, a Jesuit school and residence, a marketplace, a University library, and the representative chamber from where BA province was governed until 1880. You can take a tour of the semi-circular chamber, the patios, and a series of 18th-century tunnels that used to link the building to the coast. The block's Iglesia de San Ignacio dates from 1734.

Museo de la Ciudad

Defensa 219, entre Alsina y Moreno (4331 9855/ 4343 2123). Subte A, Plaza de Mayo or D, Catedral or E, Bolívar/24, 29, 64, 86, 152 bus. **Open** 11am-7pm daily. **Admission** AR$1; free under-12s. Free Wed. **No credit cards. Map** p325 E10.

Created as a labour of love by José María Peña, a leading authority on architecture in Buenos Aires, the objective of the museum is to conserve and investigate the physical structures and social customs of the city. Among the exhibits are photographs, blueprints, furniture, toys, magazines, and an interesting collection of door jambs with art nouveau detailings.

Museo Etnográfico

Moreno 350, entre Balcarce y Defensa (4331 7788/www.museoetnografico.filo.uba.ar). Subte A, Plaza de Mayo or D, Catedral or E, Bolívar/24, 29, 64, 152 bus. **Open** 3-7pm Wed-Sun. **Closed** Jan. **Admission** AR$2. **No credit cards. Map** p325 E10.

This museum's small but fascinating collection includes head-dresses, masks and cooking implements, as well as panels describing Argentina's indigenous tribes region by region. The moving stories of the Yamana tribe of Tierra del Fuego are part of the display, and include the astonishing tale of Jemmy Button, a young man kidnapped and forcibly transported to England in 1830 as a living

The illuminating **Manzana de las Luces**.

exemplar of what Rousseau had termed the 'noble savage'. A wood-carved Japanese Buddhist altarpiece is the museum's most valuable object.

San Telmo

Maps p324 & p325

Subte C, Independencia or San Juan/bus 20, 59, 67, 93, 98, 126, 152.

For visitors, San Telmo is enchanting: its cobblestoned streets and crumbling mansions echo European old quarters long since swept away by municipal clean-ups, Olympic-bid investments and the efforts Luftwaffe and Royal Air Force. Unfortunately, this somewhat romanticised vision is lost on locals; ask a *porteño* and they'll probably tell you that San Telmo is dirty, run-down and unsafe.

But San Telmo is changing. It is becoming more glamorous and less faded. A regeneration spurred by the arrival of antique dealers and restaurateurs – and more recently hostel owners and a thriving gay scene – has brought the area into the 20th century, if not yet the 21st.

Heading to San Telmo from the Plaza de Mayo, Defensa and Balcarce are the most pleasant streets to walk along. The former is full of antique shops and considered to be the main vein running through the barrio, while the latter is a quieter, cobblestoned street lined with tango venues (even though San Telmo is not historically linked to the dance) and tiny cafés. While walking you will pass by several of the tattered mansions and drooping balconies that give San Telmo its unmistakable appearance. Most were occupied by grand families until a mass exodus from cholera and yellow fever took place over a century ago.

Subsequently the old houses were turned into tenements – called *conventillos* – with poor immigrant families occupying what were formerly single rooms round the main patio. As these humble abodes are still very much lived in, no matter how open the doors look, the general public are not welcome. To see the inside of an 1880 house, visit the lovely **Pasaje de la Defensa** (at Defensa 1179), a refurbished two-storey building originally owned by the Ezeiza family, and now hectic with souvenir and bric-a-brac shops.

The adjacent streets are also of interest, with a myriad of bars and restaurants punctuating the houses. The quaint Pasaje San Lorenzo and Pasaje Giuffra – their cobbles harking back to a more attractive city from the 1930s and '40s – were formerly streams running down to the river where Avenida Paseo Colón now pullulates. San Lorenzo 380 is the location of the strikingly ultra-thin colonial house **Casa Mínima**, the narrowest house in the city at just

two metres (six feet) wide – but 50 metres (165 feet) long. According to local legend, the house was built by freed slaves in 1800 on a sliver of land bestowed by their master next door.

Casa Mínima is part of the same conservation initiative that rescued **El Zanjón de Granados** (*see p101*), a beautifully restored colonial mansion capturing three centuries of urban living, situated round the corner where San Lorenzo butts against Defensa.

Down on Avenida Paseo Colón is Rogelio Yrurtia's intriguing bronze monument **Canto al Trabajo** (Song to Work) on the plaza of the same name (at Avenida Independencia). The rest of Avenida Paseo Colón is dominated by a series of serious-looking public buildings, three of them – the army's **Edificio del Libertador**, the **Aduana** (headquarters of the customs service) and the **Secretaría de Agricultura** (Ministry of Agriculture) – built along French Academic lines. The Libertador is fronted by tanks, cannons and a Soviet-looking statue of an Unknown Soldier. The soldier has a hole in his chest, a symbol of those who died in the Falklands/Malvinas war, but, while not buried on the islands, left their hearts there.

The fourth public building is the University of Buenos Aires' **Facultad de Ingeniería** (Faculty of Engineering), a harsh classical building that originally housed the Fundación Eva Perón, the charity created by Evita. Far more attractive is the tall, slim red-brick **Iglesia Dinamarquesa** at Carlos Calvo 257. A Lutheran church built in 1931, its modern Gothic style is jovially at odds with everything else in San Telmo.

On Sundays, **Plaza Dorrego**, one of the few Spanish-style plazas in the city where you can drink beer and coffee in the open air, is taken over by traders, tango and tourists. Although it's a genuine, fully functional and ever-expanding antiques market, it also provides one of BA's most popular days out for visitors and locals alike, especially when the sun is shining.

For fashion victims only, there's an enjoyable small museum – **Museo del Traje** (*see p99*) – tracing Argentinian fads and fashions from 1850 to the present. Closed for extensive renovations at time of writing is the **Museo de Arte Moderno**, at Avenida San Juan 350. It's no Tate Modern or MOMA but it serves as a vital proving ground for contemporary Argentinian artists working in a variety of media. The museum, housed in a recycled tobacco warehouse, has no permanent exhibits. Instead it hosts excellent temporary shows, as well as various music and video events. The museum is slated to reopen in late 2008.

At the southern end of San Telmo, **Parque Lezama** is a dramatic patch of greenery on the

Walk on Origins of the city

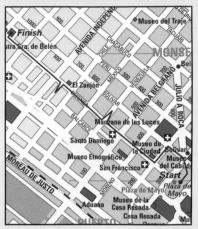

Start: Plaza de Mayo
Finish: Plaza Dorrego
Length: 1 mile
Buenos Aires has a tangled tale – evolving from smugglers' hive to trendy global metropolis in just a couple of centuries – and there's nowhere that matches **Plaza de Mayo** as a focal point for its unfolding story. Begin here, flanked by a through-the-ages palette of civic architecture. In the south-western corner, the whitewashed symmetry of the **Cabildo** has been reduced in size since colonial times, but it was here that mobs thronged in May 1810 to demand the resignation of the viceroy, triggering the onset of independence.

At the opposite end of the plaza, the salmon-pink **Casa Rosada** is no stranger to massed crowds of its own. Constructed in 1873, it sits on what was previously the site of a fortress and remains the official seat of government. Eva Perón's fabled public addresses took place from the balcony under the Arcadian windows in the centre of the left-hand façade – as did Madonna's controversial re-enactment.

In the centre of the square, the 67-metre (220-foot) **Piramide de Mayo** draws attention each Thursday at 3.30pm, when the Madres de la Plaza de Mayo make a humbling weekly protest march around the base looking for justice after their children were 'disappeared' during the military dictatorship of the 1970s.

Ground paintings of their iconic white headscarf symbol circle the obelisk. Exit the square along Bolívar. After a block you'll reach **San Ignacio**, the city's oldest standing church, constructed by Jesuits in the late 1600s. Facing it, **Avila Bookshop** dates back to 1785 and, as a key meeting place for intellectuals over 200 years, can claim to have helped shape generations of activists. Turning left down Adolfo Alsina, take time to enjoy a coffee from bow-tied waiters amid the old-world charm of **Bar La Puerto Rico** (Adolfo Alsina 416, 4331 2215).

On the corner of Alsina and Defensa, soothe any ailments at the extraordinary, and still prescribing, **Farmacia de la Estrella**, complete with frescoes, mosaic flooring and walnut panelling. There's a museum on the first floor. Opposite, the **Iglesia y Convento de San Francisco** warrants a guidebook of its own. Its bullet-riddled left tower is a reminder of 1807, when the church witnessed the luckless last stand of British invaders, while the charred ceiling is a legacy of Peronist arsonists. Don't miss the collection of 'trophy' pennants claimed from defeated armies, hung behind the shrine at the far end of the eastern side nave.

Continue along Defensa – named after its historical role as the city's main line of guard – before turning right onto Venezuela. At No. 469, the sturdy former home of Viceroy Liniers is one of BA's last remaining colonial houses. Across from its traditional barred windows, Italianate and art deco buildings complete an unlikely architectural threesome. Retrace your steps and continue down Defensa, before turning left onto Mexico. Pass the Old Mint on your right – now used as a military archive – then continue down leafy Balcarce. The street kinks to the left before crossing San Lorenzo, where distraction comes in the form of colourful *fileteado*-esque murals and, at No.380, the tiny **Casa Mínima** (immortalised in a Baldomero Fernández Moreno poem).

Back on Defensa street, the antique-market sprawl of **Pasaje la Defensa** at No.179 showcases what was once a traditional family home in the 1800s. Lastly, put your feet up in San Telmo's pre-independence heart, **Plaza Dorrego**, ideally over a sizeable *cerveza* in the earthy **Bar Plaza Dorrego** (No.1098; see also p169).

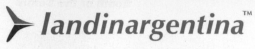

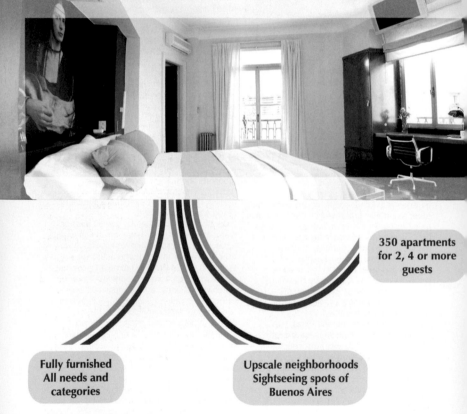

Leave your heart in **San Telmo**.

bluff of the old city, which, for many historians, is the location of the initial settlement of Buenos Aires. A monument at the Brasil and Defensa corner commemorates Pedro de Mendoza's hypothetical landfall at this spot in 1536 and on the south side is the **Monumento a la Confraternidad** (Monument to Brotherhood), expressed as a neo-industrial boat.

A beautiful terracotta-coloured colonial mansion houses the **Museo Histórico Nacional** (*see below*). Outside the museum, the park is a dramatic cliff covered in palms and yellow-flowered *tipa* trees. Musicians and market stalls fill the park at weekends and a wonderfully out-of-place **Iglesia Ortodoxa Rusa**, topped with blue onions in the Muscovite style, adds further colour to the scene.

Museo de la Caricatura 'Severo Vaccaro'

Lima 1037, entre Carlos Calvo y Humberto 1° (4304 6497/www.severovaccaro.sitio.net). Subte C, Independencia/28, 98, 195 bus. **Open** 3-8pm Thur, Fri (call ahead to arrange guided tour). **Admission** free. **Map** p325 E8.
In 1945 the chemist Vicente Vaccaro founded the first (and last) Museum of Caricature, in honour of his brother Severo who had built up a collection of humorous and satirical art dating back to the late 19th century. The museum comprises six permanent

exhibition areas in which you'll find most of the major heroes and villains of the 20th century mocked for posterity – Roosevelt, Churchill, Stalin, Hitler, Mussolini, Mother Teresa and Juan Domingo Perón, to name only a few. The museum's star exhibit is 'Mickey Gaucho', a cartoon of the world's most famous rodent decked out in cowboy garb, donated to the museum by Walt Disney during his visit to the country in 1941.

Museo Histórico Nacional

Defensa 1600, y Caseros (4307 2301). Bus 10, 24, 29, 39, 64, 130, 152. **Open** noon-6pm Tue-Sun. **Closed** Jan. **Guided tours** (Spanish) 3pm Sat, Sun. **Admission** AR$2. **No credit cards. Map** p324 C9.
This useful – if rather bland – introduction to the city's history includes exhibits from the pre-Columbian, conquest, and post-independence periods, plus countless photographs of military men with drooping moustaches who look like they might have played bass in the Allmann Brothers Band.

Museo del Traje

Chile 832, entre Tacuarí y Piedras (4343 8427/www.funmuseodeltraje.com.ar). Subte C, Independencia/59, 60, 126, 143 bus. **Open** 3-7pm Tue-Fri, Sun. **Guided tours** (Spanish) 5pm Sun. **Admission** free. **Map** p325 E9.
Fashionistas who've spent the morning twisting and twirling in front of three-way mirrors can take a quick post-lunch break – and appreciate some of

Sightseeing

BA's design history – at this small but entertaining museum. True, the bald, black-faced mannequins posed like cocktail partygoers are creepy, but the intricately crafted dresses they're wearing are gorgeous and perfectly preserved.

El Zanjón de Granados

Defensa 755, entre Chile y Independencia (4361 3002). Bus 24, 93, 130, 152. **Open** 11am-5pm Mon-Fri; noon-5.30pm Sun. **Tours** (English) Mon-Fri on the hr 11am-5pm. **Admission** AR$20; AR$13 Mon; AR$8 under-12s. **No credit cards.** **Map** p325 E10.
Part archaeological museum, part event space, El Zanjón is a beautifully restored residence encapsulating three centuries of urban living. Although the façade dates from 1830, traces from an earlier patrician home – an open-air cistern, a lookout tower and a 1740 seashell-mortared wall – have been excavated by amateur historian Jorge Eckstein, who started dredging the 166m (545ft) of tunnels beneath his property in 1985. Eckstein has unearthed a treasure trove of workaday but eclectic objects from the colonial era, including French tiles, African pipes, English china, and so on. An underground hit.

La Boca

Map p324
Bus 20, 25, 29, 53, 64, 152.
In both space and spirit, La Boca is as far south as Buenos Aires gets. Divided from the vast suburbs of greater BA by the dark and toxic gloop of the Riachuelo river, this working-class barrio was until the late 19th century the obligatory entry point to the city for both goods and immigrants – hence the name (literally 'the mouth'). But when the docks moved north decline set in, and today all that's left of the once bustling port are a few abandoned hulks and some crepuscular warehouses. The crime, unemployment and poor housing statistics have been trending upwards for decades: it's best not to go looking for the charismatic, dagger-swishing *compadrito* of yore, immortalised in countless tangos: you're more likely to bump into a furtive kid in a hoodie with his eyes glued to the floor. That said, those who cherish La Boca, whether for its history, its lack of Paris-of-South-America pretentiousness or its cheap rents, *really* cherish it. The barrio's waterfront in particular is enjoying a mini-renaissance, in part thanks to a booming tourist trade that has more and more people making the trek down to the tiny, multi-coloured Caminito.
The barrio stretches from the river right up to the roundabout where Avenida Paseo Colón becomes Avenida Martín García, and where a mast and a 3-D frieze announce that you are entering the 'República de la Boca'.
Set back from the river, on Brandsen, is the reason why people who have never been to BA have heard of La Boca. The port a thing of the past, the communal heart now beats at the Estadio Alberto J Armando, aka **La Bombonera**, where top-flight football team

An Italian job

Everyone knows that Italians do it better when it comes to fine arts and restoration (even the proudest *porteño* would agree, and not just because their grandparents were immigrants from Calabria). They proved their *savoir faire* in Buenos Aires in 1996, when a Milan-based architectural firm transformed a dilapidated mansion in La Boca into a sleek art venue, **Fundación Proa**, that quickly became one of the city's premier galleries. However, after ten years of hosting smart, thoughtfully curated contemporary shows, and sustaining a packed calendar of cultural events, Proa needed a facelift. The original architects were once again summoned from the old world in 2007, and the museum closed down while the Italians worked their magic.

After all, it's not easy staying competitive in BA's art world, especially when you're asking visitors to abandon the spiffy sidewalks of the Recoleta–Barrio Norte–Palermo Viejo circuit and trek across town to a bit of a dodgy neighbourhood. But Proa, in addition to its striking recycled design, boasts a few features that more than justify the trip south – Diego Rivera's rendering of sunflowers, for one, not to mention the expansive black and white tiled rooftop terrace overlooking the river. Thanks to last year's renovations, the gallery is also good to go technologically; from the moment the Marcel Duchamp show kicks off the 2008 reopening, the physical space will finally do justice to video installations and other contemporary media.

As if sponsoring Latin American film festivals and open-air musical performances isn't enough, Proa is also responsible for community art installations like Illuminación del Puente, the periodic beautification of the iconic Nicolás Avellaneda bridge. With so many innovative projects at hand and a massive restoration completed, Proa's the city's artistic frontrunner. Visit www.proa.org for the upcoming schedule.

Club Atlético Boca Juniors have held court for nearly a century. The blue and yellow of the team strip is ubiquitous on walls and balconies throughout the neighbourhood. The team's on-field exploits have fomented any number of off-field brand extensions, the most important of which is the **Museo de la Pasión Boquense**, located at the stadium's entrance (*see p103*).

From the museum's entrance a disused railway track runs down Garibaldi (where fugitive Nazi Adolf Eichmann lived for some years before Mossad caught up with him), which comes out two blocks later at the back end of **Caminito**, a short, banana-shaped pedestrianised theme street recognised as Argentina's only open-air museum (*see below*).

La Vuelta de Rocha, the road that follows the bend in the river at the opening to Caminito, is marked by a mast and rigging. A painting at the Museo Nacional de Bellas Artes in Recoleta bears the same name, and its stylised portrayal of this corner is an acknowledgement of the near-mythical status the area has for *porteños*.

However, it's not all nostalgia in La Boca. **Fundación Proa** (*see p101* **An Italian job**), due to reopen in late 2008 after extensive renovations, is one of the city's premier spaces for contemporary art and a great reason to visit the area. The area's other outstanding gallery is housed in the buildings donated to La Boca by painter Benito Quinquela Martín (1890-1977).

The **Museo de Bellas Artes de La Boca** (*see below*) contains works by Quinquela Martín and other Argentinian artists.

Three bridges at the northern end of Avenida Pedro de Mendoza connect the capital with the province. The oldest is the **Puente Trasbordador** (transporter bridge), a massive iron contraption not used since 1940.

Caminito
Bus 29, 53, 64, 152. Map p324 A8.
This street's name – literally 'little walkway' – comes from a 1926 tango by legendary composers Gabino Coria Peñaloza and Juan de Dios Filiberto, the lyrics of which are inscribed on a wall plaque. The corrugated zinc shacks stacked up on each side of the street owe their resplendent colours to the imaginative but impoverished locals who begged incoming ships for spare tins of paint. These days the street is thronged with tango dancers, small-time grifters and tourists, but Caminito's colour and chaos continue to charm.

Museo de Bellas Artes de La Boca Benito Quinquela Martín
Avenida Pedro de Mendoza 1835, entre Palos y Del Valle Iberlucea (4301 1080). Bus 29, 53, 64, 152. **Open** 10am-5pm Tue-Fri; 11am-5.30pm Sat, Sun. **Closed** Jan. **Admission** suggested contribution AR$2. **No credit cards**. **Map** p324 A9.
In the 1930s, over-excited local critics compared Martín's canvases, with their characteristic spatula marks, to those of Van Gogh. The artist's vibrant

Caminito.

collection is organised around three themes: fire (once a constant hazard for La Boca's wood-framed warehouses), port workers and ships' graveyards.

Museo de Cera

Del Valle Iberlucea 1261, entre Olavarría y Aráoz de la Madrid (4301 1497). Open 10am-6pm Mon-Fri; 11am-8pm Sat, Sun (opening times subject to change in Jan & Feb). **Admission** AR$3; free under-8s. **Map** p324 A8.

Argentina's only waxworks museum brings to life (well, sort of) some of the pioneers and personalities most closely associated with La Boca. Sculptor Domingo Tellechea founded the museum in 1980, adapting a colourful Italian-style mansion – which was incidentally one of the first cement constructions in the city – that dates back to 1904. As well as famous faces, there are tableaux scenes of cock fights, gaucho gatherings, and *compadritos* dancing tango in its earliest, earthiest form.

Museo de la Pasión Boquense

Brandsen 805, y la Via (4362 1100/www.museo boquense.com). Bus 29, 53, 64, 152. **Open** 10am-7pm daily (closed on match days). **Admission** AR$14 museum only; AR$22 museum & tour; 50% discount concessions. **Credit** AmEx, DC, MC, V. **Map** p324 B8.

For the real *pasión* you should visit the Bombonera on a match day; but for everything else Boca, this modern museum hits the back of the net. There are loads of audio-visual widgets and gizmos to twiddle with, mountains of facts and figures to absorb, and, naturally, tributes galore to Boca's greatest hero, Diego Maradona, including a bronze statue that is the museum's top photo-opportunity. In the gift shop you can buy your souvenirs in any colour you like – so long as they're blue and yellow.

Constitución & Barracas

Maps p324 & p325

Subte C, Constitución/bus 20, 37, 45, 148.

Constitución and Barracas are run-down barrios that most *porteños* prefer to avoid. But without the former's railway station and the latter's warehouses, BA would never have reached its late-19th-century economic zenith. Although close to the centre, these areas are rarely explored owing to their desolate streets and dodgy after-dark reputation. If you want to visit, go with a local or on an organised tour.

Dominating Plaza Constitución, the **Estación Constitución** is an imposing 1880s construction that has recently been restored. Built to shuttle the rich to the Atlantic resort of Mar del Plata, it now shuttles weary commuters southwards. The forecourt is a mad whirl of vagrants, vendors and commuters, with numerous bus lines terminating here too, just to add to the chaos. A full-scale riot here by fed-up commuters made the news headlines in 2007.

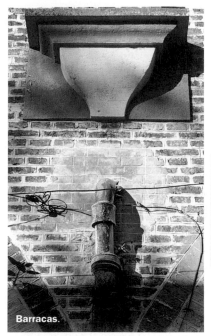

Barracas.

The name Barracas refers to the warehouses that clustered here from the late 18th century onwards; cheap housing and brothels completed the picture by the early 1900s. The barrio was once BA's ground zero for worker uprisings and their subsequent repression, but a fledgling gentrification effort is converting many of the crumbling warehouses and grand relics of capitalism into affordable housing and offices for young artists and professionals. An early anchor of the renewal is the **Centro Metropolitano de Diseño** (*see below*).

Among the artists breathing new life into Barracas is Marino Santa María. Since 2001, on the dead-end *calle* Lanín, Santa María has been spearheading an imaginative public-art project he calls the postmodern version of La Boca's Caminito. Every house on the curved two-block street is painted with colourful, abstract streaks resembling psychedelic tiger stripes. Santa María's studio can be visited at Lanín 33.

Centro Metropolitano de Diseño

Villarino 2498, y Santa María del Buen Ayre (4126 2950/www.cmd.org.ar). Train to Hipólito Yrigoyen/12, 93, 195 bus. **Open** 10am-5pm Mon-Fri. **Admission** free.

A city-run incubator for young designers that set up shop in 2001 in a remodelled facility that long ago housed the city's fish market.

Sightseeing

North of the Centre

For stately mansions and fashionable bars.

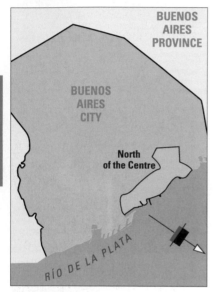

Sightseeing

BUENOS AIRES PROVINCE

BUENOS AIRES CITY

North of the Centre

RÍO DE LA PLATA

The streets of Recoleta, Barrio Norte and Palermo aren't exactly paved with gold, but a gratifying number of them are at least paved with smooth asphalt, which may lead you (correctly) to deduce that these northern barrios are where most of the federal capital's wealth is concentrated. It was to here that the *porteño* elite gravitated in 1871, fleeing the yellow fever epidemic then sweeping the city's southern zones. It was BA's first real estate boom. Now, with the exception of Puerto Madero, the northern neighbourhoods are the most exclusive and expensive of all BA's districts.

The area is bordered by Avenida Córdoba and a string of plazas and parks along busy Avenidas del Libertador and Figueroa Alcorta. The city is monumental and notably French in style in these parts, the wide boulevards and open spaces exploited as sites for statues honouring national heroes, immigrant communities and assorted international bigwigs. Many of Argentina's late greats are buried in the Cementerio de la Recoleta.

The greenery is in no small part due to the vision of French landscaper Charles Thays (1849-1934), who travelled to Argentina in the 1880s to study trees and ended up staying and designing the zoo, the Jardín Botánico, Parque Tres de Febrero and numerous private gardens.

Recoleta

Map p326
Bus 17, 60, 92, 93, 93.

It's BA's most exclusive patch of real estate – but nobody lives there. We refer of course to the **Cementerio de la Recoleta** (*see p106*), one of the world's great necropolises.

The plazas outside the cemetery walls were once on the banks of the river. Though barely a bump in its present landscaped form, the mount was of sufficient size to serve as a hiding place for bandits and other undesirables in the 17th century. Between 1716 and 1730, a French chapter of the Franciscans, known as the Padres Recoletos, chose the area to build a chapel and convent as a place of retreat. At the same time, the Jesuits, already established as missionaries and merchants in northern Argentina, Paraguay and Brazil, settled in the Recoleta. Building of

The best Museums

Famously owned
Museo Casa Carlos Gardel (*see p116*); **Museo Histórico Municipal Juan Martín de Pueyrredón** (*see p126*); **Museo Mitre** (*see p89*); **Villa Ocampo** (*see p126*).

Sportingly done
Museo de la Pasión Boquense (*see p103*); **Museo de Rugby** (*see p126*).

Perfectly preserved
Manzana de las Luces (*see p95*); **El Zanjón de Granados** (*see p101*).

Artistically outstanding
Malba: Colección Costantini (*see p111*); **Museo Nacional de Bellas Artes** (*see p108*); **Museo Xul Solar** (*see p109*); **Palais de Glace** (*see p106*).

Oddly engaging
Museo de la Deuda Externa (*see p116*).

their **Basílica Nuestra Señora del Pilar** (Junín 1904, 4803 6793) began in 1716 and the church site was consecrated in 1732.

The plain-looking façade, the whiteness barely interrupted but for the sky-blue Pas-de-Calais ceramic tiles that decorate its upper reaches, is reminiscent of many colonial churches found in remote northern provinces. Inside is a superlative baroque altar, featuring Incan and other pre-Hispanic motifs. The altar was brought along the mule trails from Peru, the heart of colonial South America, and given a wrought-silver frontal in Jujuy in north-west Argentina. You can visit the cloisters, with a mini museum of religious art, the crypt beneath the church and adjoining tunnels, thought to connect with tunnels in Monserrat, on regular guided tours.

To the north of the Pilar church, on the site of the Franciscan convent, is the **Centro Cultural Recoleta** (*see p229*). It promotes contemporary visual arts and contains several performance rooms. There is also a film projection room and an interactive science museum for kids (*see p216*). From the roof terrace, you can view the surrounding plazas and other sights.

It's not all high culture and high church, though: a specialised mall, **Buenos Aires Design** (*see p205*) has two floors showcasing the latest in designer furniture and interiors. The mall's terraces are lined with cafés and restaurants, and south-west of the cemetery

on Vicente López is the **Village Recoleta** shopping centre, completing the incongruous picture of a city of the dead encircled by outer suburbs of fun and frivolity.

In the attractive grassy spaces in front of the Centro Cultural stretching down to Avenida Libertador are three giant *gomero* trees that provide shade for strollers, loungers and dog walkers. **Plaza Francia**, directly north-east of the cultural centre, is commandeered on weekends and most public holidays by a handicraft fair, which draws tourists, stragglers and neo-hippies.

Across Posadas is the belle époque **Palais de Glace** (*see p106*), which was an ice-rink, a ballroom and an important tango salon in the 1920s, run by aristocrat Baron de Marchi. It was in this circular building that tango was officially embraced by the bourgeoisie.

In front of the Palais de Glace stands a monument to Carlos María de Alvear, an officer who founded the horse guards regiment in 1812 with San Martín, and was the first in a line of Alvears to play an important part in the city's history. Opposite are the monument and plaza dedicated to Carlos María's son, Torcuato de Alvear, the first governor of the city of Buenos Aires and an important urban planner.

The pedestrian walkway **RM Ortíz**, which runs from the corner of Junín and Vicente López to Avenida Quintana, is one of BA's most

Recoleta's **Plaza Francia**.

popular strips for the time-honoured evening stroll known as *el paseo* – though the new trend of restaurant staff pestering passers-by to come and eat is annoying. At the corner of Avenida Quintana is the classy and predictably overpriced café **La Biela**. Opposite the café, its tentacle-like bowers casting a great shadow over the outdoor terrace, is a magnificent rubber tree known as the Gran Gomero.

Cementerio de la Recoleta

Junín 1760, entre Guido y Vicente López (4803 1594). Bus 10, 17, 60, 67, 92, 110. **Open** 7am-5.45pm daily. **Admission** free (to the living). **Map** p326 J11.

Originally conceived by Bernardino Rivadavia and designed by Frenchman Prosper Catelin, the cemetery was opened in 1822. The narrow passages and high walls make comparisons with the real city outside inevitable. Entrance to the cemetery is through a Doric-columned portico designed in 1886 by Juan Buschiazzo, one of Argentina's most important architects. The cemetery is home to hundreds of illustrious corpses, laid out in a compact maze of granite, marble and bronze mausoleums – most of the materials came from Paris and Milan – and a slow walk down its avenues and alleyways is one of BA's undisputed delights. Originally a public cemetery on the fringes of the city – nearby Avenida Callao marked the limit of Buenos Aires until the 1880s – it is now even harder to move into than the posh flats that surround it. Seafarers and freed slaves were once given their final berths in Recoleta, but now ordinary folk can only get in alive. Many Argentinian presidents are entombed here, though most visitors come to see the resting place of María Eva Duarte de Perón, better known as Evita.

There are also impressive collective tombs (housing fallen soldiers), great pantheons and cenotaphs, inches away from one another. Assorted architectural styles are arranged side by side, from distinguished chemist Dr Pedro Arata's diminutive Egyptian pyramid to aristocrat Dorrego Ortíz Basualdo's monumental sepulchre, decorated with 'prudent virgins' and topped by a great candelabra. Among the patrician families here, residing in a style befitting one-time mansion dwellers, are the Alvears, the Estradas, the Balcarces and the Alzagas, together with members of the Paz clan.

Palais de Glace

Posadas 1725, y Schiaffino (4804 1163/www.palais deglace.org). Bus 17, 61, 67, 92, 93, 130. **Open** 2-8pm Tue-Sun. **Admission** free. **Map** p326 J11.

French speakers won't have to guess the original function of this elegant belle époque building: Palais de Glace, which opened its doors to skaters in 1910, means 'Ice Palace'. The grand circular structure also housed a landmark tango salon before being declared a national monument in 2004. Today, the palace hosts major exhibitions of fashion and the visual arts. The two-level space, complete with decorative reliefs and a huge dome, is suitably grand for the diverse roster of large-scale paintings, contemporary photography, engravings, sculpture and video installations. Free tours in English, held every Saturday and Sunday at 5pm and by appointment, are a welcome new feature.

Avenida del Libertador

Beyond the cluster of life, leisure and style that has sprung up around the necropolis, Recoleta has other public spaces and venues along Avenida del Libertador. At the centre of Plaza Francia, at Libertador and Pueyrredón, is a baroque marble monument to Liberty, which was presented to Argentina by France as part of the centenary celebrations in 1910.

Across the avenue from the Palais de Glace is the newest patch of urban landscaping, **Parque Carlos Thays**, which boasts a heroic bronze *Torso Masculino* by Colombian sculptor Fernando Botero. At Libertador and Callao is the **Museo de Arquitectura** (4800 1888), located in a former railway water tower dating from 1915. Exhibitions trace the evolution of Buenos Aires and general matters of design and architecture. It's open afternoons only from March to December; phone for more details.

Behind the museum, on Avenida Figueroa Alcorta, is the **Facultad de Derecho** (Law Faculty), thronged all year round by students. Plazas Urquiza, Uruguay and Naciones Unidas are plain public spaces. Eduardo Catalano's *Floralis Genérica* is a popular steel and aluminium sculpture, its six petals opening each day as the sun rises and closing at dusk.

Occasionally, a building or two gets in the way of the greenery – such as the Bauhaus-style, state-owned ATC Channel 7 TV studios, built in 1978 to broadcast the World Cup; but there are open spaces all the way to Palermo and beyond on the river side of Libertador.

Back across the road, the plazas don't last as long, but they are more dramatic. At the top of **Plaza Mitre**, a great red granite pedestal is adorned with lively allegorical and lyrical figures in marble, above which rides a stern bronze of Bartolomé Mitre, president from 1862 to 1888 and founder of *La Nación* newspaper .

The next patch of grass, the **Plaza Rubén Darío**, named after the Nicaraguan poet and philosopher, is brooded over by the jutting upper half of the functional-looking **Biblioteca Nacional** (*see below*), designed in the 1960s by three prominent architects, Clorindo Testa, Alicia Cazzaniga de Bullrich and Francisco Bullrich. Building dragged on for years, and the library only opened to the public in 1992.

Before the concrete block of the library was conceived, this was the land of the Unzué

Sainthood – the easy way

It doesn't take too much for someone to become 'sainted' in Argentina. First, of course, you have to die, hopefully prematurely and preferably in tragic and – better still – mysterious circumstances. Performing a miracle or two helps but it's not essential. Spending your entire adult life wandering around in lice-infested rags while talking to animals seems to be strictly optional. In recent years, for example, shrines have sprung up around Buenos Aires to popular *cuarteto* (a faster variety of cumbia that is popular in Córdoba province) singer Rodrigo, who died in a car crash just outside the city in 2000. Others popular saints, such as La Difunta Correa, were known as spiritual healers or selfless helpers and were always unlucky in love. And although not formally recognised by the Roman Catholic Church, they attract hundreds and thousands of people asking them to donate healing powers or simply a safe journey.

The prize for the most popular saint who isn't actually a saint, however, goes to Gauchito Gil. Red rags, red candles and red flags mark shrines around the city for this folk hero. Icons of the moustachioed gaucho are usually surrounded by offerings of wine, cigarettes, crucifixes and flour. (If you need incontrovertible proof of the Gauchito's supernatural powers, note that the wine and cigarette donations often miraculously 'disappear'.) And since Gauchito Gil is the adopted patron saint of travellers, rare is the truck or the taxi that doesn't have at least Gil's red ribbon hanging from the rear-view mirror.

Gauchito Gil is thought to have been a simple farmer born Antonio Mamerto Gil Nuñez in the north-eastern province of Corrientes around 1847. While the legend varies, Gil is thought to have had an affair with a wealthy widow. When her brothers found out, they told the head of police – also reputedly in love with the widow – and Gauchito scarpered to join the army, fighting in a civil war between the '*celestes*' and '*colorados*' political parties. Not being a particularly adept fighter he then went AWOL; some blame another woman; others say he received a revelation from a Guaraní god preaching peace. A fugitive, he became a kind of Argentinian Robin Hood, stealing from rich land owners and giving to the poor. Word also spread that Gauchito had received special powers from a Guaraní god. The authorities finally caught up with him, but before his execution, Gil reputedly said: 'When you get home tonight, you will find your son is gravely ill. You can pray for my intercession, you can ask me to save your child, because the blood of an innocent helps perform miracles.' Sure enough when the executioner returned home his son was ill, so he buried Gauchito and erected a cross covered in red ribbons. He prayed and the son survived.

These days more than 100,000 pilgrims descend on the Corrientes city of Mercedes to commemorate Gil's death on 8 January, asking for all manner of miracles and healing. Most of the devotees of the Gauchito and other 'grass roots' saints consider themselves Catholics and either fail to see or do not care about any doctrinal contradictions inherent in these kind of practices.

In Buenos Aires you can see a permanent shrine to the Gauchito at the corner of Atacalco and Honduras streets in Palermo Viejo. For a website so bizzare it defies description, go to www.gauchogil.com

Sightseeing

family, and for a time the site of the presidential residence, where the Peróns lived and Evita died at 8.25pm on 26 July 1952. The military tore down the mansion to erase the memory of Peronism, unswayed by the fact that Juan Domingo had risen from its very own ranks.

At the Palermo end of Recoleta, at Avenida del Libertador 1902, is the beautiful French-style mansion Palacio Errázuriz, which houses the **Museo de Arte Decorativo** (*see below*).

Of all the streets in the area, **Avenida Alvear** is the most palatial; rents here can hit New York levels (*see p112* **Walk on**).

Biblioteca Nacional

Agüero 2502, entre Libertador y Las Heras (4806 4721 ext 1140/www.bibnal.edu.ar). Bus 59, 60, 93, 102. **Open** 9am-9pm Mon-Fri; noon-8pm Sat, Sun. **Admission** free. **Map** p282 K11.
Most of the library's two million books and manuscripts are kept in the underground vaults, so there's not much to see except for occasional exhibits. Current and back issues of periodicals and newspapers are available, however: go to the Hemeroteca in the basement, with photo ID.

Museo Nacional de Arte Decorativo

Avenida del Libertador 1902, y Pereyra Lucena (4801 8248/www.mnad.org). Bus 10, 59, 60, 67, 130. **Open** 2-7pm daily. **Closed** 1st 2 wks Jan. **Admission** AR$8. free to all Tue. **Map** p326 K11.
This stunning building was converted into a museum in 1937, and its majestic ballrooms, bedrooms and hallways today display over 4,000 pieces of decorative art, plus works by well-known artists such as El Greco and Manet. The museum has a good bookshop in the basement.

Museo Nacional de Bellas Artes

Avenida del Libertador 1473, y Pueyrredón (4803 8814/4691/www.mnba.org.ar). Bus 17, 62, 67, 93, 130. **Open** 12.30-7.30pm Tue-Fri; 9.30am-7.30pm Sat, Sun. **Admission** free. Map p282 J11.
The MNBA has 32 rooms, several sculpture patios, a library and an auditorium. It houses the country's biggest collection of 19th- and 20th-century Argentinian artworks, which, after the property's extensive refurbishment in 2004/5, are now on permanent display. It includes outstanding works by Ernesto de la Cárcova and Cándido López. Twentieth-century pieces feature all the major names in Argentinian art, including Eduardo Sívori, Antonio Berni, Xul Solar and Guillermo Kuitca. The international collection on the ground floor includes works by El Greco, Rubens, Rembrandt and Goya, among others names. There is also a permanent display of indigenous art. Times of guided tours vary (check the section 'Visitas Guiadas' on the website).

Barrio Norte

Map p326

Subte D, Pueyrredón/bus 39, 64, 152, 188.
When alluding to the overcrowded, middle-class residential area between Avenida Las Heras and Avenida Córdoba, still officially Recoleta,

Barrio Norte.

most *porteños* use the term Barrio Norte. The nickname is often associated with the *chetos* (social-climbers) and *paquetes* (also poseurs, but with the confidence of older money) who live here. Evita, in one of her many fiery speeches to seduce the working classes, declared an ambition to 'bomb Barrio Norte'. The neighbourhood's main consumer corridor and a Barrio Norte symbol par excellence is **Avenida Santa Fe**, a gauntlet of big-name brand shops and boutiques.

If you take a stroll down this commercial thoroughfare, slip inside the converted cinema at no.1860 that now houses the **Ateneo** bookshop (*see p181*). Though the movie theatre closed, the bookshop is at least a nod to a continuing cultural presence in the area. Just few blocks from here, between Callao and Pueyrredón, is one of BA's most vibrant gay scenes.

Literary pilgrims should check out the **Museo Casa de Ricardo Rojas** (*see below*). Rojas (1882-1957) was an influential writer and one of Argentina's most important educators, teaching Argentinian literature at the state university before becoming its rector in 1926. Another cultural highlight in the area is the **Museo Xul Solar** (*see below*), two blocks from Avenida Santa Fe.

Museo Casa de Ricardo Rojas

Charcas 2837, entre Anchorena y Laprida (4824 4039). Subte D, Agüero/12, 39, 152 bus. **Open** 11am-5pm Tue-Fri. **Admission** (suggested) AR$1. **Map** p326 K9.

Rojas intended that his house, built in 1927 and donated to the state in 1957 by the writer's widow, should be a visual expression of the contending forces that have enriched and disfigured the Argentinian experience: civilization versus barbarism, South America versus Europe, city versus country, and so on. Consequently, the design of the building, by architect Angel Guido, is an attempt to harmonise a number of eclectic influences, including a Spanish-colonial façade (reminscent of buildings in Rojas' native province of Tucumán) and a patio that incorporates Incaic ornamental motifs. The interior is more ascetic, but preserves the original furnishings and household objects and more than 20,000 volumes from Rojas' personal library. A guide escorts you through the rooms of this quintessential writers' refuge.

Museo Xul Solar

Laprida 1212, entre Mansilla y Charcas (4824 3302/ www.xulsolar.org.ar). Subte D, Agüero/12, 39, 64, 152 bus. **Open** noon-7.30pm Tue-Fri; noon-7pm Sat. **Guided tours** 4.30pm Tue, Thur, Sat. **Admission** AR$6; AR$2 concessions. **Map** p326 J9.

This museum is installed in the house in which lived the city's most eccentric self-proclaimed visionary; sailor turned painter, astrologer, mathematician, writer and philologist Agustín Alejandro Schulz

Solari (1887-1963), or Xul Solar. Conceived by him in the late 1930s but only built in 1986, after his death, the museum exhibits 86 of his own self-selected works, alongside a collection of esoteric objects and weird instruments. Rightly acclaimed by friend Borges as 'one of the most singular occurrences of his time', Solar invented his own language (Pan) and lived in his own personal time zone (in Buenos Aires the latter is less of an eccentricity than it sounds). The main draw, though, is perhaps not Solar's art, but the building in which it is kept, his home having been completely remodelled to reflect his own peculiar 'cosmovision', resulting in an award-winning modern space.

Palermo

Sightseeing

Maps p326 & 327

Subte D, Plaza Italia/bus 15, 39, 55, 60, 93, 152.

As Walt Whitman might have said, Palermo is large; it contains multitudes. It's comfortably the biggest barrio in the city, and the famous parks, gardens and lakes make it also the greenest and most pleasant. There's there is space to jog, cycle, stroll and picnic; at times the air is almost fresh enough to breathe. The fact that the neighbourhood also contains a Japanese garden, a mosque and a cricket club – not to mention an airport that is knuckle-whiteningly close to all of the above – gives the impression that Palermo is a city within a city.

Helpfully – or perhaps confusingly – the neighbourhood contains a number of sub-divisions, some of which are semi-official, others so counter-intuitive they could only have been dreamed up by bureaucrats. Most people recognise three basic areas: tiny Palermo Chico (bordering Recoleta) for embassies and the filthy rich; atmospheric Palermo Viejo (comprising Palermo Hollywood and Palermo Soho) for global cuisine and funky boutiques; and plain Palermo for the rest, including all the greenery.

From the little street called Cavia to Monroe in Belgrano (the next barrio along), there's a patchwork of plazas and parks congregating round the **Parque Tres de Febrero**, formerly a flood plain drained in the late 16th century by the barrio's namesake, Italian farmer Giovanni Domenico Palermo. At the northern limit of the park is the **Hipódromo Argentino** racecourse (*see p250*), but walkers and cyclists can skirt this by heading towards the river and continue on to Nuñez and the River Plate football stadium.

Although you may stroll into Palermo as a continuation of your wanderings through Recoleta, the most usual point of access is **Plaza Italia**. The monument to Italian hero Giuseppe Garibaldi at the centre of the plaza is the only static figure in this hectic scene.

Jardín Japonés.

The **Jardín Botánico Carlos Thays** (*see below*) in between Avenida Santa Fe, Las Heras and Gurruchaga, is more peaceful. The **Jardín Zoológico** (*see p111*) is across the road.

South of the zoo, at the busy junction of Avenidas Sarmiento and del Libertador, is the bleached-white **Monumento de los Españoles**. A centenary gift from the Spanish, the four bronzes represent Argentina's four main geographical regions: the Pampas, the Andes, the Chaco and the River Plate.

Designed and overseen by Thays, the **Parque Tres de Febrero** – which locals call Parque Palermo or Los Bosques de Palermo (the Palermo Woods) – boasts well-kept lawns, beautiful jacarandas and palms, and a lake, as well as cafés and a good art gallery, the **Museo de Artes Plásticas Eduardo Sívori** (*see p111*). A particular highlight is the delightfully pretty **Rosedal** rose garden, accessible from Avenidas Iraola and Puerto Montt. After dusk this is the city's de facto red light district for tranvestite prostitutes, despite the strenuous efforts by many local residents to get them moved on. 'The function of oral sex in a public space is incompatible with the function of a historic rose garden', explained one city legislator. Less contentious spaces in the Parque include the Jardín de los Poetas, with its peaceful fountains surrounded by busts of literary giants, and a tiled Patio Andaluz. If you

prefer a lazy float on the lake, hire a pedalo. They're not remotely seaworthy, but the lake is shallow and life-jackets are available.

Along Avenida Figueroa Alcorta are a number of facilities, including **Paseo Alcorta** shopping centre (*see p178*). But the area's most important addition is a cultural space, paid for and stocked by art collector Eduardo Costantini, the Museo Latinoamericano de Buenos Aires (**Malba**; *see p111*).

Back on Libertador, on the way towards the centre, is the refurbished **Museo de Arte Popular José Hernández** (*see p114*), named after the author of Argentina's national epic, *Martín Fierro* (1873).

Heading back to Recoleta from the park, or vice versa, you can slip off Avenida del Libertador into **Palermo Chico** (aka Barrio Parque). This tiny, upmarket patch of suburbia is where TV stars like Susana Giménez and diplomats park their bulletproof jeeps. There are no shops or even *kioscos* to spoil the views, just plenty of grand architecture to admire. One exception: at the roundabout where Bustamante hits Rufino de Elizalde is the **Monumento San Martín Abuelo**, a rare effigy of the general without his horse. *Abuelo* means 'grandfather', and this likeable likeness of the Liberator shows him in his later years, dispensing advice to his granddaughters.

Jardín Botánico Carlos Thays
Avenida Santa Fe 3951 (4831 4527). Subte D, Plaza Italia/39, 93, 152 bus. **Open** *Nov-Mar* 8am-8pm; *Apr-Oct* 9am-6pm. **Admission** free. **Map** p327 M9.
Laid out by celebrated French landscaper Charles Thays and inaugurated in 1898, BA's botanical garden is a slightly shabby but nonetheless tranquil space, full of fascinating flora. Thousands of species flourish here, and fountains, orchids, cacti, ferns and spectacular trees makes this a paradise for anyone who likes to potter around a garden. Monuments include a Venus, Saturnalia and Romulus and Remus. Check out the old stagers playing cards and chess for money on the adjacent square. And if for any reason you need a dozen stray cats in a hurry, this is the place to come.

Jardín Japonés
Avenida Casares, y Berro (4804 4922/9141/www. jardinjapones.com.ar). Bus 37, 60, 93, 130. **Open** 10am-6pm daily. **Admission** AR$5; AR$2 6-10s, concessions; free under-6s. **Map** p327 M11.
Created in 1967 as a token of thanks from the local Japanese community, BA's Japanese garden is one of the largest in the world outside Japan. You'll find over 150 species of flora here, many brought specially from the mother country, and some on sale at the small shop next to the entrance. Once you've fed the ravenous ornamental carp (they can jump like Kobe Bryant), you can refresh yourself at the all-day tearoom which serves green teas and cakes. There's

also a highly regarded Japanese restaurant. The highlight of each day is the Ceremony of Tea, which takes place at 5pm and is open to all.

Jardín Zoológico

Avenida Santa Fe, y Las Heras (4011 9900/ www.zoobuenosaires.com.ar). Subte D, Plaza Italia/39, 93, 152 bus. **Open** 10am-6pm Tue-Sun. **Admission** AR$15; free under-12s. **Map** p327 M9.
BA's zoo is one of those interesting but somewhat discomfiting attractions many animal lovers will prefer to shun, although serious zoological and conservation work does go on here. Of more general interest are the buildings, constructed between 1888 and 1904, which ape the architecture of the animals' native countries, resulting in a landscape of scaled-down monumental follies that make the zoo look rather like 'Animal Town'. Of the beasts themselves, the polar bears are glum but stoic, the monkeys are loud and disquietingly horny, and a baby giraffe is the latest 'guest' to wow the crowds.

Malba: Colección Costantini

Avenida Figueroa Alcorta 3415, entre Salguero y San Martín de Tours (4808 6500/www.malba. org.ar). Bus 67, 102, 130. **Open** noon-8pm Mon, Thur-Sun; noon-9pm Wed. **Guided tours** (Spanish & English) by arrangement. **Admission** AR$14; AR$7 concessions; free to all Wed. **Map** p326 L11.

With almost 200,000 visitors in 2007 and consistent rave reviews in both the local and foreign media, Malba would be many people's pick for best museum in the city. Frida Kahlo and Diego Rivera, Tarsila do Amaral and other illustrious painters share the walls with wonderful Argentinian modern masters such as Antonio Berni and Jorge de la Vega, who are well respected but not well known internationally. There is also an excellent café and terrace restaurant, plus a small cinema specialising in cult and arthouse retrospectives. The building itself is smaller than Costantini originally wanted, and can house only 40 per cent of his collection. To solve this he has funded a three-year expansion project which will add several new exhibition areas in an underground space beneath Plaza República de Perú.

Museo de Artes Plásticas Eduardo Sívori

Avenida Infanta Isabel 555, y Libertador (4774 9452/www.museosivori.org.ar). Bus 34, 67, 130. **Open** noon-8pm Tue-Fri; 10am-8pm Sat, Sun. **Admission** AR$1; free under-12s, to all Wed. **Map** p327 N10.
Located in Parque Tres de Febrero, this excellent museum houses a major collection of Argentinian paintings and sculpture from the 19th century to the present day. If that doesn't appeal, at least have a coffee on the grass patio inside.

Palermo's **Parque Tres de Febrero**. *See p109.*

Walk on Palaces and polo shirts

Start: Plazoleta Carlos Pellegrini.
Finish: Plazoleta San Martín de Tours.
Length: 1 kilometre (0.6 miles).

Europe's belle époque ended in a nasty and brutish way in August 1914, when vast German and Franco-British armies clashed just a few miles from the city that had become a byword for splendour and sophistication: Paris. Buenos Aires, a city that would be the richest in the world were it given a dollar for every time it has been compared to the French capital, was, by contrast, untroubled by artillery fire and in the middle of a sustained economic boom. In fact, the gilding didn't start coming off the Argentinian golden age of crypto-aristocrats, cattle barons and celebrity émigrés until the end of World War II.

The city's grandest street then is the city's grandest street now, and to get a sense of just how much money was sloshing around Buenos Aires between, say, 1890 and 1940, you need only take a stroll along Avenida Alvear. Alongside and above the contemporary shrines to good living such as Ralph Lauren, Emporio Armani and Louis Vuitton, there are older, more interesting and – with any luck – more permanent statements of style, luxury and sheer in-your-face splashiness: the palaces, hotels and apartment blocks built for Argentina's old elite by some of the most talented architects ever to have worked in the city.

Start your walk in **Plazoleta Carlos Pellegrini** at the southern end of Avenida Alvear. This attractive square, inaugurated in 1914 just as the carnage was beginning in Europe, not only has one of the few

fountains in the city to consistently emit water, but is also surrounded by several of the area's stateliest piles. **The French embassy** (Cerrito 1399), its smooth domes and elaborate grillwork the design of French architect Pablo Pater, was opened as the Palacio Ortíz Basualdo in 1914 before becoming the embassy in 1939 – thus inadvertently marking the opening years of both world wars. Close by at Arroyo 1130/42 is another diplomatic HQ, this one waving the Brazilian flag. Originally known as the **Palacio Pereda**, and opened in 1917; the key features of the building are its Corinthian columns and the elaborate carvings around the doorways. At Cerrito 1433 is another neoclassical landmark, the **Palacio Alzaga Unzué** (1916).

Heading north up Avenida Alvear, you'll find something completely different at No.1402, an art deco residential block completed in 1937. Note the long, smooth curves and porthole windows, characteristic of the ocean liner-inspired streamline moderne style, then at its zenith. There are several other art deco buildings on the street, including no.1444 and the tower on the corner with Parera. This juxtaposition of

modernist structures designed to house 200 or so residents and neoclassical mansions designed to house one couple and their servants is one of the striking features of the Avenida.)

From here on, the mansions and palaces come at you thick, fast and, mostly, French. At no.1637 is the symmetrical **Nunciatura Apostólica**, dating from 1907 and the work of French architect Edouard Le Monnier. It once belonged to the mega-rich Anchorena family, and was used in the 1920s by president Marcelo T de Alvear. Since then, several popes have lodged here, including the late John Paul II in 1982 and 1987.

More secular living quarters are available at no.1661, where the stunning curved lines of the **Palacio Duhau** now front the Park Hyatt Hotel (*see p57*). The slightly jaundiced-looking Doric columns and imposing courtyard dominate the street, but this is all that remains of the original structure that was built in 1934 by French architect Leon Dourge. (If you're wondering how anything got built in France itself between the wars, you're probably not alone.) Next to the hotel is the spooky-looking **Residencia Maguire**, which looks like it should be backlit by chain lightning and inhabited by Boris Karloff. Its gloomy aspect has all sorts of incongruous

features, including some maritime touches like the boat prow over the door, and an art deco shell. Across the road, the **Casa Nacional de Cultura** (No.1690) has similar brickwork, but is much less scary.

Now whip out the credit card. At No.1750 is the Emporio Armani shop, a spruced-up mansion with floor-to-ceiling windows brightening up the traditional façade. Two doors down, the much more ornate Ralph Lauren store's best feature is the delightful baroque terrace.

Now that you've foolishly blown a month's salary on a seersucker sports coat or something similar, you can at least blend in with the crowd in the lobby of the Alvear Palace (No.1891; *see p57*), BA's most illustrious hotel. The *dernier cri* in interwar francophilia, the Alvear opened its doors to a well-heeled crowd in 1932, and hasn't looked back since. At the very least, take a peep inside its lush, chandeliered interior.

Our walk (and Avenida Alvear) ends at the Plazoleta San Martín de Tours, where several enormous *gomero* (rubber) trees offer shade to idling students, tourists and drunks. There are two sculptural tributes in the square: the *Monumento a Emilio Mitre* (1930) by Hernán Cullen, and the *Monumento al Coronel Ramón Falcon* (1918) by Alberto Lagos.

Museo de Arte Popular José Hernández

Avenida del Libertador 2373, entre San Martín de Tours y Coronel Díaz (4802 9967/4803 2384/www. museohernandez.org.ar). Bus 10, 37, 59, 60, 92, 102. **Open** 1-7pm Wed-Fri; 10am-8pm Sat, Sun. **Admission** AR$3; AR$1 residents; free under-12s, concessions, all free Sun. **Map** p326 L11.

The museum's main collection comprises gaucho motifs and other elements of Argentina's rural past. Two buildings off a patio are hung with *mate* gourds, spurs, weapons (especially knives) and other gaucho paraphernalia. There's also a reconstruction of a *pulpería*, the tavern-cum-grocer's shop that was the focal point of 19th-century country life. The museum also features exhibits inspired by matters of Argentinian history.

Museo Evita

Lafinur 2988, entre Gutiérrez y Las Heras (4807 9433/0306). Subte D, Plaza Italia/37, 59, 60, 102 bus. **Open** 1-7pm Tue-Sun. **Admission** AR$10; AR$5 residents. **Map** p283 M9.

Opened in 2001, this museum is housed in an aristocratic residence that Perón expropriated to convert into a women's shelter for his wife's welfare agency. It's worth a visit to see the range of myths she has inspired in Argentina. Paintings, posters and busts are displayed alongside fabulous outfits she wore on tours of Europe. The two star pieces are the dresses designed by Paco Jamandreu that she wore for her audiences with the Pope, and her *libreta cívica* (identity book) – No. 0.000.001. Arguably better than the museum itself is the newly refurbished restaurant and outdoor terrace.

Palermo Viejo

Away from the high-rises, open spaces and views of the river, Old Palermo clusters. Run down and romantic until the early 1990s, it has since been thoroughly brightened up by restaurants and fashion and design outlets. Most of the homes here are just one or two storeys high, and the town houses, many of them revamped into urban lofts, come with terraces or trees and long, crespuscular entrance ways. There's a literary/boho past here, as shown by the street called Borges and the Plazoleta Cortázar (at the junction of Borges and Honduras – sometimes referred to by its former name, Plaza Serrano), but thanks to the recent influx of nightclub and cocktail bars, these days there's more emphasis on high jinks than high culture.

East European and Armenian communities made Palermo Viejo their home in the early 20th century, and cuisines from all over the world are served in the area's many restaurants. For open air drinks, Plazoleta Cortázar is hugely popular, and those who find the pseudo-bohemian bars too expensive lounge beneath the lime trees with a beer.

Elsewhere in Palermo

Fringed by the polo ground and racecourse is a buzzing residential and dining district known as **Las Cañitas** (there were once sugar canes growing well here). It's a popular focal point for the monied socialites of Palermo and Belgrano, with little historical interest by day, though the **Cañitas Creativa** street fair on Fridays and Saturdays at 6pm brings in visitors. The area made the news big time when former president Carlos Menem gave the Saudis land on which to build BA's mega-mosque and religious centre, the **Centro Islámico Ray Fahd** at Avenidas Bullrich and del Libertador. For information on guided tours (Spanish only), call 4899 1144.

One of Palermo's most curious unofficial sub-barrios, just south of Plaza Italia, is called **Villa Freud**, in reference to the number of psychoanalysts working there. Sharing the area with the shrinks are several spiritual centres, including a Buddhist cemetery, a mosque and the **Basílica del Espíritu Santo** on Plaza Güemes (at the corner of Mansilla and Medrano). This sturdy church, built between 1901 and 1907, is known by locals as Guadalupe, after the 16th-century Mexican 'Virgin' who later became an icon of that country's independence struggle.

Palermo Viejo.

West of the Centre

West side stories? There's one for every street corner in BA's heartland.

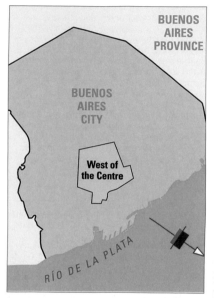

BUENOS AIRES PROVINCE

BUENOS AIRES CITY

West of the Centre

RÍO DE LA PLATA

If you're one of those visitors determined to find the *real* Buenos Aires – whatever that means – the western half of the city will suit you just fine. There are fewer architectural wonders and snazzy nightspots in these barrios than in, say, Recoleta – but there is also less pretension, a more easygoing atmosphere and an almost total absence of French poodles in bespoke velour jerkins. This is the Buenos Aires of pizza parlours, serious *milongas*, barbershops, rag-and-bone men, knife grinders, unsung parks and squares, avantgarde theatres, tilo-scented backstreets, and shops that sell 1980s videogame consoles new out of the box. It is, in short, where most *porteños* live, work, play and die.

Once & Abasto

Maps p322 & p326

Subte A, Plaza Miserere or C, Carlos Gardel/bus 24, 68, 88, 104, 168, 188, 194.

Once (pronounced 'ON-say'), about 20 blocks west along Avenida Corrientes from the Microcentro, is the city's most hectic commercial district, a warren of wholesale and retail outlets, the origin of whose wares it is best not to ask about. Visitors who have bought into the cliché of Buenos Aires being the 'Paris of South America' should take a detour here – Once has all the subtlety and sophistication of a Guatemalan bus station, but it's a heck of a lot more fun than the Champs-Elysées. Historically associated with the city's large Jewish population, it now has sizeable Korean and Peruvian communities.

The barrio is named after the ugly 11 (Once) de Septiembre railway station – which commemorates an 1852 battle between the provinces and the capital – on **Plaza Miserere** (usually called Plaza Once). The plaza, for years a rubbish-strewn hub for transport, the sex trade and preachers foretelling the apocalypse, is now also home to the monument to the dead of the Cromagnon nightclub fire (*see p27*). On the corner of Bartolomé Mitre and Ecuador is a blazing mural in their honour.

Avenidas Rivadavia and Pueyrredón are Once's main arteries, but the neighbourhood's pulse is found in the blocks to the south and west of their intersection. Here, Latin dance beats blast out from every store, and the selling of tack and trash spills onto the streets as visual pollution is taken to extremes. If you like sterile shopping malls, forget Once, though it certainly deserves a quick jaunt just to experience what local author Alvaro Abós calls a 'branch of hell'.

As for Jewish Once, the **Congregación Sefardi**, a Moorish-style Sephardic synagogue at Lavalle 2400, is worth a visit. Two blocks away, at Paso 400, is the elegant **Ashkenazi Templo de Paso**. The synagogues are best visited with a tour, as access has been restricted since the 1990s Jewish-targeted terrorist attacks. Victims of the 1994 car bomb attack on Once's AMIA Jewish Welfare Centre are remembered by the moving **Monumento de Homenaje y Recordación a las Víctimas del Atentado a la AMIA**, situated in the courtyard of the reconstructed building, at Pasteur 633. Tour agencies require 48 hours' notice to arrange visits here.

Once is, in fact, part of a barrio officially known as Balvanera, with its northern limit at Avenida Córdoba. At Córdoba 1950 is the striking **Palacio de Aguas Corrientes**

(Palace of Running Water), occupying a whole block. It's home to the capital's water works, which were run by private company Aguas Argentinas until the government intervened in 2006. Constructed between 1887 and 1895, this flamboyantly decorated building, with its vivid colours and jigsaw of architectural styles, is a real one-off among the city's civic piles.

Just up from Once, at Avenida Corrientes and Anchorena, is the beautiful **Mercado de Abasto** building, a startlingly curvaceous art deco masterpiece built between 1930 and 1934 as a central wholesale market for the city. It was neglected for decades, and the building's powerful, but empty, decaying presence became symbolic of the Abasto neighbourhood's own downward spiral into a seedy scene of blues, booze and cocaine.

In 1998 the market building was the first in the barrio to see rejuvenation, converted into a shopping mall known simply as **El Abasto** (*see p178*). Inside the mall is the **Museo de los Niños Abasto** (Abasto's Children's Museum – *see p216*), three floors of educationally minded displays about the commercial and industrial activities of Buenos Aires.

If one regards La Boca as the cradle of tango, Abasto can be thought of as its nursery. Seminal composers like Osvaldo Pugliese and Aníbal Troilo either lived or were born in the neighbourbood. But no *tanguero* is more closely associated with this barrio than the greatest of them all, '*el morocho*' Carlos Gardel, who lived here for most of his life. The small but neat **Museo Casa Carlos Gardel** (*see right*) offers a

peep into the domestic life of the legendary crooner. Tangophiles should also visit Pasaje Zelaja, a two-block street whose houses are adorned with six tango lyrics written by Alfredo Le Pera, and five colourful portraits of Gardel by the artist Marino Santa Maria.

Completion of the ambitious 'Cultura Abasto' initiative, currently underway, will see El Abasto's surrounding ten blocks benefit from a full 1930s style make-over, transporting the curious back to the barrio's heyday. Centre stage in Abasto's redevelopment plan is the multi-purpose **Ciudad Cultural Konex** (*see p264*), a vast arts complex at the intersection of Sarmiento and Jean Jaurès, which opened in 2005. The building's exterior echoes the geometric design of the Abasto's art deco style, and inside there's an opera house and a number of theatre spaces. Inspired by the Pompidou Centre in Paris, it's the nerve centre of the influential Fundación Konex .

Museo Casa Carlos Gardel

Jean Jaurès 735, entre Zelaya y Tucumán, Abasto (4964 2071). Subte B, Pueyrredón or Carlos Gardel/ 29, 99, 140 bus. **Open** 11am-6pm Mon, Wed-Fri; 10am-7pm Sat, Sun. **Guided tours** (Spanish) 3pm Mon, Wed-Fri; 1pm, 3pm, 5pm Sat, Sun. **Admission** AR\$2; free under-10s. to all Wed. **No credit cards**. **Map** p326 J8.

A long overdue tribute to one of the 20th century's greatest exponents of popular song, the Gardel museum is located in the house – a classic *casa chorizo* ('sausage house') in which all rooms open out onto a central patio – purchased by the singer in 1927. He lived here, in his beloved barrio, with his beloved mother, until 1933. The museum preserves and exhibits various items and memorabilia that either belonged to or were connected to the maestro. It's a reasonable, cost-effective tribute – but the artist who was to tango what Elvis Presley was to rock 'n' roll surely deserves better.

Museo de la Deuda Externa

Centro Cultural Ernesto Sábato, Facultad de Ciencias Económicas, Uriburu 763, entre Viamonte y Córdoba, Once (4370 6105). Subte D, Facultad de Medicina/39, 68, 152 bus. **Open** 3-8.30pm Tue-Fri; 11am-8pm Sat. **Admission** free. **Map** p326 I9.

A topical museum sounds like a contradiction in terms; but the Museum of Foreign Debt, run by the (itself permanently debt-stricken) University of Buenos Aires, harks back not only to the city's golden age but also to a very recent and far less glittering era – the economic crisis of 2001-02. Opened in 2005, the museum charts the course of the country's overdraft from the first default of 1827 to the chaos of December 2001. It all sounds pretty grim, but despite, or perhaps because of, the downbeat subject matter, the exhibits are suffused with the dark humour *porteños* are famous for. Probably best avoided if you work for the International Monetary Fund.

Pasaje Zelaja.

Boedo

Map p322

Subte E, Boedo/bus 75, 88, 97, 160.

Street corners hold a unique status in Buenos Aires life. According to tangos, illicit encounters and knife fights always happen on *esquinas*, and corner cafés are the settings for last coffees with lovers, or sorrowful binges. These days, plaques decorated in the traditional *fileteado* style appear on hundreds of corners around the city, commemorating anything from tango singers to long-gone bars. Nowhere is this more evident than in one of the bona fide barrios of tango, Boedo. Signs seem to hang from every corner around here; but one of these intersections is probably more famous than any other in the city: San Juan and Boedo.

When lyricist Homero Manzi scribbled his extraordinary ode to the city's poorer south, 'Sur', in 1948, he was already lamenting the loss of the neighbourhood's golden period as if it were a lover who'd just jilted him for another *tanguero*. 'Ancient San Juan and Boedo, lost sky ... Sorrow for the barrio that has changed/and bitterness for a dream that died'.

Were he alive today, Manzi would be aggrieved to discover that his beloved bar on this corner, where musicians and poets once gathered, is now a cheesy tango-for-tourists venue. He would have been more encouraged, however, to see a new crop of genuinely bohemian bars, art cafés and guesthouses springing up, prompting whispers that Boedo is becoming the 'new' Palermo. Whether this would be a desirable fate for the moody, old-school barrio, is a matter for debate.

In Boedo, as elsewhere, Avenida Rivadavia marks the boundary between the wealthier north and the poorer south. Heading south from here is **Avenida Boedo**, named after Dr Mariano Boedo, a brilliant lawyer born in 1782 who fervently supported the Argentinian drive for independence. A series of sculptures stretch down Avenida Boedo from Avenida Independencia – a classic example of how the artistic and political traditions of Buenos Aires are often so tightly interwoven.

At Boedo 745, only a plaque marks the location of the Café Dante. This 100-year-old bar, closed in 2003, was frequented by players and fans of Boedo's top-flight football team, San Lorenzo, whose red and blue stripes can be seen hanging from balconies around the barrio. Across the road is the compact **Museo Monte de Piedad** (*see right*).

A block further along is the formentioned Esquina de Homero Manzi. No longer a 'blacksmith's corner' scented with 'weeds and

alfalfa', this busy junction offers zero nostalgia. Better to head off Avenida Boedo to admire the many beautifully restored – or re-imagined – 18th- and 19th-century townhouses.

Museo Monte de Piedad

Avenida Boedo 870, entre Estados Unidos y Carlos Calvo (4932 4680). Subte E, Boedo/88, 97, 160 bus. **Open** 10am-5pm Mon-Fri (guided tours by prior arrangement). **Admission** free.

Essentially a history of how a municipal pawnbroker for immigrants became the city bank, this museum also provides a glimpse into the city at the turn of the 20th century. It includes a partly recreated Café Biarritz, which once stood on this spot and was the meeting place of the Boedo Literary Group, an assembly of socialist and anarchist writers, poets and playwrights active in the 1920s. Brutal, colloquial works by novelists such as Roberto Arlt, who influenced writers such as William Burroughs and Irvine Welsh, reflected their working-class roots.

Almagro, Caballito & Villa Crespo

Maps p322 & p323

Subte B, Angel Gallardo or Malabia/bus 24, 55, 160, 168.

West of Abasto, Almagro, Caballito and Villa Crespo are districts with particularly proud residents and a real neighbourhood air. **Parque Centenario**, in Caballito, serves as the sole park for these densely populated barrios, and fills up on weekends with market stalls and hordes of families. More gritty than green, it's currently being spruced up by the city government.

The main crowd-puller, and great for kids, is the **Museo Argentino de Ciencias Naturales Bernadino Rivadavia**, with plenty of fossils and botanical exhibits, as well as several enormous Patagonian dinosaurs.

Caballito is also a reminder of a gentler era in Buenos Aires, when the tram was king. Now, this is the only barrio that keeps the soothing clankety-clank alive, with a 25-minute service departing from Emilio Mitre and José Bonifacio every 15 minutes on Saturday afternoons and Sunday mornings and afternoons. For times, check the website of the **Asociación Amigos del Tranvía** (www.tranvia.org.ar).

Almagro and Villa Crespo are tranquil, traditional neighbourhoods, although the latter in particular is becoming increasingly gentrified, in large part due to its proximity to hip Palermo Viejo. Life in both revolves around the main *avenidas* Corrientes and Córdoba; off these traffic-choked thoroughfares you'll find quieter, often cobblestoned sidestreets where a number of small bars and restaurants offer good cheap drinks and meals.

Chacarita

Map p323
Subte B, Federico Lacroze/bus 39, 65, 93, 168.
Like many one-time outlying barrios, Chacarita – originally the location of an important Jesuit farming community, hence the name (*chacra* is Spanish for small farm) – developed around a railway station, Federico Lacroze. The terminus, opened in 1880, is now just a commuter hub. Far more interesting is the **Cementerio de la Chacarita** on the other side of Avenida Guzmán (*see below*). The cemetery was conceived as a resting place for the staggering numbers of dead from the yellow fever outbreak of 1871. A funeral train was set up that year, with an Englishman, Mr Allen, driving the steam engine.

The zone around Lacroze station is lively, bordering on chaotic, with numerous pizza parlours and primitive *parrillas* servicing the commuters, and plenty of pavement florists servicing tomb-bound mourners. Otherwise, Chacarita is quiet, pretty and solidly middle class – much as Palermo Viejo was before it became fashionable and expensive. The analogy has not been lost on local estate agents, who have begun to dub the barrio 'Palermo Dead' – either because they think an apartment within a stone's throw of a graveyard is automatically a des res, or because they just can't help themselves.

Cementerio de la Chacarita
Guzmán 630, y Federico Lacroze (4553 9034/9038/ tours 4553 0041). Subte B, Federico Lacroze/39, 93, 111 bus. **Open** 7am-6pm daily. **Admission** free. **Map** p323 O2/P2.
Now far more expansive than Recoleta's exclusive necropolis, with numbered streets and car access to its thousands of vaults, this cemetery is largely for ordinary folk. Still, a number of popular heroes have also wound up here, including Carlos Gardel, Alfonsina Storni and aviation pioneer Jorge Newbery. Until 1939, Chacarita also held the cemeteries of the Jewish, British and German communities. After the middle of the last century with Hitler affecting relations even in far-off Argentina, the Jews left for a new site west of the city, and the Brits and Germans built walls to separate their dead.

The densely populated but very quiet **Cementerio de la Chacarita**.

Along the River

Don't judge a brook by its colour.

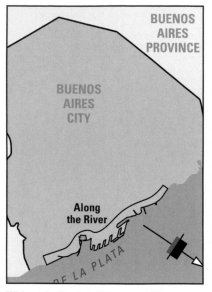

BUENOS AIRES PROVINCE

BUENOS AIRES CITY

Along the River

DE LA PLATA

Without the Río de la Plata – or as it's sometimes known in English, the River Plate – there would be no Buenos Aires. This vast, muddy waterway (technically the world's widest estuary: 200 kilometres – 137 miles – at its fattest point), fed from the north by the Paraná River and sheltered from the vagaries of the Atlantic weather systems, enabled Argentina to thrive commercially during the golden age of maritime trade. Beef and grain went out; manufactured goods and migrating workers came in. Long before the word 'globalisation' had been coined, Argentina's busy ports helped her win a place at the top table of the world's economies.

That was then. After the salad days came the locust years. The industrialised world found new, cheaper sources of wheat and meat, and BA's ports, along with the entire Argentinian economy, felt the pinch. For decades the city thumbed an ungrateful nose at the river that had made its fortune, leaving the port's warehouses and wharves to the rats. Over the past few years, however, in line with a trend that has seen the revitalisation of dockside neighbourhoods in cities like London and

Baltimore, a slew of ambitious development programmes around the old port and along the coastline has helped, as it were, to get the blood moving again in the city's erstwhile artery.

Puerto Madero & Costanera Sur

Maps p324 & p325
Subte B, LN Alem/bus 26, 61, 93, 152, 159, 195.

The appearance of Puerto Madero – the dockland area to the east of Plaza de Mayo, divided into two lengthy promenades on either side of the quay, Puerto Madero Oeste (west) and Puerto Madero Este (east) – is the embodiment of BA's self-image as a grand, European-style city. The red-brick port buildings and grain warehouses, built between 1889 and 1898, were the first view of BA seen by immigrants, and the city fathers wanted to impress them with a modern skyline.

Yet as early as 1911, a new harbour was being built, the narrow rectangular wharves having proved hopelessly inadequate. Puerto Nuevo, as it is known, is still loading up container ships north of Retiro. Meanwhile, Puerto Madero went into decline, and the dream docks became rat-infested husks. It was only in the late 1980s that the area began to get some love from the powers-that-be. The Puerto Madero Oeste development was officially unveiled in 1996, with a new-look quayside, flashy restaurants and high-rent flats. Only recently has the riverside zone gained some depth, with projects of a civic, cultural and commercial slant springing up along the promenades of BA's youngest barrio.

One of the most important of these is the long-awaited – six years and counting – opening of the **Fortabat Museum**, a glass and concrete structure shaped like a giant claw, located in front of Dique (dock) 4. Amalia Fortabat is Argentina's richest woman, and judging from the size and quality of her art collection, something of a Peggy Guggenheim *manquée*. The museum, scheduled to open some time in 2008 – but don't hold your breath – will be entirely consecrated to Argentinian art, with a single, very notable exception: a portrait of Fortabat by Andy Warhol, commissioned in the 1980s.

Sightseeing

The location of the museum couldn't be more appropriate. According to a recent survey, real estate prices in the Madero Este zone (developed later than the west side) are now among the highest in Latin America. This is a world created for the rich and beautiful. Although unabashed in celebrating the finer things in life, much of Puerto Madero is, curiously, also dedicated to struggle, as all its streets are named after women who fought for female emancipation in Argentina. Encarnación Ezcurra, wife of 19th-century *caudillo* Juan Manuel de Rosas, and Azucena Villaflor, founder of the Mothers of Plaza de Mayo, are among those honoured.

For evidence of the area's maritime history, visit the impeccable **Corbeta Uruguay**, moored further down on Dique 4 at Alicia Moreau de Justo and Corrientes. A museum vessel of Argentina's Naval Academy dating back to 1874, the *Uruguay* would apppear to have been above regular warfare, and instead distinguished itself in revolutions, expeditions and search-and-rescue missions. At Dique 3 is the even more impressive **Fragata Presidente Sarmiento** (*see p121*).

Stretching in front of the *Sarmiento* is the elegant **Puente de La Mujer**, a pedestrian bridge designed by the renowned Spanish engineer Santiago Calatrava. Opened to acclaim in December 2001, the bridge's US$6 million construction costs were covered by Alberto R González, late owner of much of Madero Este and its **Hilton Hotel** (*see p55*). The Hilton now faces competition from the **Faena Hotel + Universe**, a Phillipe Starck-designed hotel that opened in early 2005 (*see p55*).

Beyond Madero Este is an altogether earthier experience, the River Plate's other urban jungle: the **Reserva Ecológica Costanera Sur** (*see p121, and p122* **Special Reserve**), BA's biggest – free – wilderness on the edge of the city. The long esplanade skirting the reserve is one of the city's most pleasant spaces for walking, sunbathing and inhaling something other than sulphur dioxide. A lavish 1927 *bierkeller*, the **Cervecería Munich** houses the Centro de Museos, from where all the city's museums are administered. A guided tour of the picturesque pub gives an insight into how good life used to be for wealthy weekenders.

Slightly south, at the centre of a roundabout near the reserve's entrance (Avenida Tristán Achaval Rodríguez and Padre ML Migone), is an eye-catching fountain, executed in 1902 by Tucumán-born artist Lola Mora. The **Fuente de las Nereidas** is a marble allegory set in a clam shell, depicting fishily erotic female forms (if mermaids are your thing).

One block south is the **Museo de Calcos y Escultura Comparada** (*see p121*), an outpost of the city's main public art college, with a collection of replicas of ancient and Renaissance masterpieces. Around the museum, the land is occupied by cheap *parrillas* (most of them in the guise of small, technically mobile vans known as *carritos*), making this a popular weekend lunch spot.

Puerto Madero.

Buque Museo Fragata Presidente Sarmiento

Alicia Moreau de Justo 900, y Belgrano, Dique 3, Puerto Madero (4334 9336/9386). Subte B, LN Alem/4, 93, 152 bus. **Open** 9am-8pm daily. **Admission** AR$2; free under-5s. **Map** p325 E11.

This frigate, built in Birkenhead, was used as a training ship from 1897 to 1961. Its second life is as a wonderful museum, full of photos, maps and domestic objects, with the original cabins and dining rooms restored and intact. The vessel was a floating witness to numerous important occasions of state, including the coronations of Kings Edward VII and George V of Britain, the opening of the Panama Canal, and the 100th anniversary of Mexican independence. Photographs of these and other events are displayed on board.

Museo de Calcos y Esculturas Comparadas

Avenida Tristán Achaval Rodríguez 1701, Costanera Sur (4361 4419). Bus 2, 4. **Open** 9.30am-noon Tue-Fri; 11.30am-5pm Sat. **Admission** free. **Map** p324 C11.

This branch of the city's main public art college contains a collection of sculpted replicas of ancient, Gothic and Renaissance masterpieces. Among the notable knock-offs are Michelangelo's 'David' and the Venus de Milo. Guided tours are offered on request; Indeed, it's best to call ahead before visiting, since opening hours seem to be quite 'flexible'.

Reserva Ecológica Costanera Sur

Avenida Tristán Achaval Rodríguez 1550, entre Brasil y Estados Unidos (4893 1588/0800 444 5343 freephone). Bus 2, 4. **Open** Apr-Sept 8am-5.45pm Tue-Sun. Oct-Mar 8am-7pm Tue-Sun. **Admission** free. **Map** p324 C11.

Within this nature reserve's boundaries, four lakes, giant *cortaderas* (foxtail pampas grass), willows and shrubs provide nature habitats for more than 200 bird species, not to mention a bit of privacy for cruising men. Iguanas scuttle across the hard earth, but on weekends you're more likely to see joggers, cyclists and picnickers among the 15,000 or so visitors who descend on the reserve. Moonlight tours are organised one night per month, whenever the moon is fullest; phone ahead to book your place.

Costanera Norte

Maps p327 & p329

Bus 33, 37, 45, 130.

North of town, skirting the Aeroparque Jorge Newbery – the city airport that, rather scarily, runs the length of Palermo – is a traditional promenade. One of the few places where the mud-coloured river laps close to the land, the paved thoroughfare is lined with numerous restaurants and thronged on any given Sunday with anglers, walkers and *mate*-supping, picnic-eating day-trippers. Cyclists have to slalom

through the crowds, though a new bike path has eased congestion. The main road – Avenida Costanera Rafael Obligado – hums with traffic heading out of the city, and the airliners zooming overhead make the noise pollution almost comical. But it's dramatic in an urban jetsetter kind of way, and at least you can turn your head and watch yachts gliding across the water. The city's beach and sports clubs, where thousands of *porteño* families go to beat the heat during the sweltering summer months, dot the avenue.

At the southern end of the airport is the chalet-style Club de Pescadores, a private fishing club of which Carlos Gardel was once a member. The pier is for the club's anglers, but visitors can dine in the airy restaurant, accessed via the oak and marble entrance hall. North of the airport is wacky religious theme park **Tierra Santa** (*see below*), which has become one of BA's most popular attractions since opening at the turn of the millennium.

On the final northern curve of the Costanera Norte, close to the Ciudad Universitaria, is the **Parque de la Memoria** (*see also p25* **The art of memory**), which has been developed in remembrance of Argentinian victims of human rights abuses under the 1970s military dictatorship. The park's central work is the Monumento a las Victimas del Terrorismo de Estado, containing stone tablets bearing the names of Argentina's 'disappeared', many of whom were drugged and then thrown to their deaths from planes into the adjacent river. The Plaza de Acceso includes works by noted American sculptors Dennis Oppenheim and William Tucker.

For a boat trip along this part of the river, head to Puerto Madero's Dársena Norte, from where the *Galileo* (www.galileobuenos aires.com.ar) makes an hour-long tour on weekends; tickets start at AR$50.

Tierra Santa

Avenida Costanera Rafael Obligado 5790 (4784 9551/www.tierrasanta-bsas.com.ar). Bus 33, 37, 42, 160. **Open** May-Nov 9am-9pm Fri; noon-11pm Sat, Sun. Dec-Apr 4pm-midnight Fri-Sun. **Guided tours** (Spanish) every 20mins. **Admission** AR$20; AR$8 under-11s. **Credit** MC, V. **Map** p329 R11.

Modestly touted by its creators as 'a chance to visit Jerusalem all year round', Tierra Santa is the kind of project that might have been realised had Walt Disney and Billy Graham put their heads together. This Holy Land experience begins with a son-et-lumière extravaganza celebrating the Nativity. As the Angel of the Annunciation descends from a neon-lit sky, locals in Middle Eastern drag herd visitors into the 'world's largest manger'. But the pièce de résistance is the Resurrection – every half hour, on the quarter hour!

Special reserve

The genesis of Buenos Aires' **Reserva Ecológica** (*see p121*) is a testament to the miraculous rejuvenating powers of nature. Christened on reclaimed land in 1918, the Costanera Sur was the place to go when BA heated up. People sunbathed standing up in their heavy one-piece swimming suits, and waded in the silty waters of the Río de la Plata. But as the population grew, industrial and domestic waste began to choke the river out, and by the 1950s BA's urban development was turning its back on the brown, polluted estuary. When the last military dictatorship built the 25 de Mayo motorway at the end of the 1970s, they dumped the resultant rubble into the water where *porteño* bathers once swam. Among other (worse) things, the junta were indefatigable killjoys.

With the return of democracy, the practice was stopped, but plants had already taken root and animals had moved in. Local nature lovers starved for greenery and silence began to explore the area, discovering that a surprisingly diverse ecosystem had taken hold in just a few short years. The city council opened the gates on the unlikely ecological reserve in 1986 and it quickly became a refuge for joggers, cyclists, *mate* drinkers, picnickers, cruisers, families, couples and just about anyone looking to escape the glare and blare of the city. And with the recent explosion of adjacent Puerto Madero, the reserve and the entire Costanera Sur are having something of a rebirth in popularity, along with the threats of encroaching wealth. On the once-vacant lots across from the reserve, it's now a race to build the highest apartment tower. Land no one even wanted to walk across 15 years ago has now turned into some of the most expensive in Latin America, and the beeping of cranes drifts into the park, mixing with the chirping of birds.

But despite the nearby boom, the reserve is holding its own – and then some. In October 2007, a new 17-hectare (42-acre) sector was inaugurated, bringing the total area up to 370 hectares (914 acres). And while just metres away people are stacked 40 storeys high, sundry animal species have room to move about. Frogs, toads, turtles and lizards are part of a menagerie that includes nine species of amphibians, ten of mammals, 23 of reptiles and around 50 of butterflies. They share the area with a staggering number of bird species, the biggest draw for many visitors. Upwards of 250 varieties of our feathered friends bring the twitchers. Such a wealth of bird life so close to the ravaged urban environment of the city has given the area a sort of cult following among birders; but even without the novelty, the reserve provides good binocular candy. Shore birds and waterfowl abound, with multiple species of ducks, egrets, swans and herons, the latter including the regal rufescent tiger heron. There are colourful tyrants, a couple of cardinals, raptors and much more.

Impress your company by identifying these residents of the reserve. For the most rudimentary groups, an easy-to-identify bird is the black-necked swan, a massive white swan with, yes, a black head, that cruises the lagoons. Keep an eye high in the larger trees for the crested caracara, a large raptor easily identified by its black crest and white neck set off by a reddish-orange wattle around the base of the bill. Another easy ID is the spectacled tyrant, known locally as *pico de plata*, an all-black bird with a striking yellow circle around the eyes. But of course, nice as it is to randomly wander and gawp, the best way to do some birding is to take a tour. Check the website for schedules and show up ten minutes before tours start. Another option is to get in touch with the dedicated local ornithologists at **Aves Argentinas** (www.avesargentinas.org.ar).

Further Afield

Put your troubles behind you and get out of town.

Few tourists venture far off BA's well-beaten tourist circuit; but those that do are rewarded with some of the city's most distinctive and diverse sights and sounds. On the edges of the city, and just outside its limits, you'll find mansions and shantytowns within yards of one another, thriving commuter belts and shabby slums, gated communities reminiscent of Beverly Hills and warren-like barrios reminiscent of Mumbai.

A number of attractions draw visitors away from the usual haunts. The northern barrio of Belgrano hides historical and art museums, while Zona Norte offers you the chance to rub shoulders with BA high society; and out in the west by the cattle market, an urban rodeo draws in the tourists every weekend.

Belgrano & Núñez

Map p329
Subte D, Juramento/bus 60, 65, 152, 168.

From the north–south downtown axis, all roads initially lead west, but Avenidas Santa Fe, Córdoba and Corrientes eventually fan out

to the smarter north-western neighbourhoods in the conurbation of Belgrano. Those who live there rave about it, but it's essentially a residential and commercial district. Named after independence hero General Manuel Belgrano, it was originally a city in its own right, but its incorporation into the capital in 1887 turned the area into a des res option for affluent *porteños*. Though the Subte from the centre gets you there in a matter of minutes, it still feels like a separate town and its main thoroughfare, Avenida Cabildo, is as important and as horribly busy as any downtown.

The most attractive parts of Belgrano are a block from the commercial epicentre; the two museums on Plaza General Belgrano are definitely worth a visit. The **Museo de Arte Español** (*see p124*) is housed in a neo-colonial mansion that once belonged to wealthy Uruguayan exile Enrique Larreta. Across the road is the **Museo Histórico Sarmiento** (*see p124*), dedicated to one of America's greatest educators, Domingo Sarmiento.

Juramento Street runs north to the *barrancas* (cliffs) bordering the Belgrano C railway station (on the Mitre line from Retiro). On and around Arribeños, running parallel to the railway line, is BA's diminutive Chinatown, populated by mainland Chinese and especially Taiwanese immigrants, who arrived in several waves after World War II and own most of the restaurants and supermarkets in the area. At Chinese New Year (*see p210*), the community takes its celebrations on to the streets in style.

Avenida Cabildo runs on into Núñez, which borders BA province. Again, this is largely a residential district, with the smartest houses encircling the huge 100,000-spectator **Estadio Monumental** (*see p250*), home to River Plate Football Club and the venue for the 1978 World Cup final – which Argentina won amid rumours of bribery and protests about atrocities being committed under military dictator Videla. Nearby, at Avenida del Libertador 8000-8500, is the Escuela Mecánica de la Armada, the country's most notorious torture centre and death camp of the 1970s. ESMA, as it is known, has been transformed into a museum and is expected to start receiving visitors in 2008.

Flanking Núñez is Saavedra, where Parque Saavedra and Parque Sarmiento provide urban dwellers with cleaner air and greenery. The

Museo Histórico Cornelio de Saavedra

(*see below*) is located in the former residence of Luis María Saavedra (descendant of the museum's namesake who was one of the heroes of Argentinian independence).

Museo de Arte Español Enrique Larreta

Juramento 2291, y Vuelta de Obligado (4783 2640/ 4783 2640). Subte D, Juramento/55, 60, 65 bus. **Open** 2-8pm Mon-Fri; 10am-1pm, 3-8pm Sat, Sun. **Closed** Jan. **Admission** AR$1. **No credit cards.** **Map** p329 S8.

The varied collection here includes Renaissance and modern Spanish art, displayed among stunning furniture, tapestries and silverware. Equally eye-catching are the gardens, a riot of flowering and climbing plants skirting a large native *ombú* tree.

Museo Casa de Yrurtia

O'Higgins 2390, y Blanco Encalada (4781 0385). Bus 29, 59, 60, 152. **Open** 1-7pm Tue-Fri; 3-7pm Sun. **Admission** AR$1; free concessions. Free Tue. **No credit cards.** **Map** p325 O5.

This was the home of sculptor Rogelio Yrurtia (1879-1950) and is a joy to visit, as much for the beautiful white house and lush garden as for the small sculptures and casts of major works.

Museo Histórico Cornelio de Saavedra

Crisólogo Larralde 6309, y Constituyentes (4572 0746). Train to Villa Urquiza, then bus 176/28, 110, 111, 176 bus. **Open** Mar-Jan 9am-6pm Tue-Fri; 4-8pm Sat, Sun. **Closed** Feb. **Guided tours** (Spanish & English) by arrangement Sat, Sun. **Admission** AR$1; free under-12s. Free Wed. **No credit cards.**

In addition to 18th- and 19th-century furniture, silverware and arms, the museum records daily life, and highlights the fashions used in the old city.

Museo Histórico Sarmiento

Juramento 2180, entre Cuba y Arcos (4781 2989/ www.museosarmiento.gov.ar). Subte D, Juramento/60, 68, 152 bus. **Open** Apr-Nov 1-5.30pm Mon-Fri, Sun. Dec-Mar 1-5.30pm Mon-Fri. **Admission** AR$1. Free Thur. **No credit cards.** **Map** p329 R8.

Domingo Sarmiento was Argentinian president from 1868 to 1874. He was also a writer; his work, *Facundo*, was a treatise – somewhat reminiscent of Matthew Arnold's *Culture and Anarchy* – on the need for Argentinians to stop being gauchos. The museum, housed in a neoclassical building that once served as Belgrano's city hall, contains documents, old books and household objects.

Mataderos & Liniers

Bus 21, 28, 36, 141, 143.

In the far west, the barrios get noticeably poorer, with occasional shantytowns dotting the gloomscape of high-rise 'mono-blocks'. People tend to be friendlier and calmer in the outer

reaches, but some streets are dodgy and night strolls are not recommended. This is definitely the case at the outer city limits in the barrio of Mataderos, named after its slaughterhouses and formerly known as Nueva Chicago for the cattle carnage theme it shares with the Windy City.

On Sundays (Saturday evenings in summer), the place is brightened up by a rural-style fair, the **Feria de Mataderos** (*see below and p179*).

In nearby Liniers, another barrio linked closely with the meatpacking business, the country's second most important saint (after the Virgin of Luján) has his shrine. San Cayetano, a 15th-century Venetian priest, is the patron of bread and work, to whom proletarian pilgrims flock each month.

Feria de Mataderos

Lisandro de la Torre y Avenida de Los Corrales (information Mon-Fri 4374 9664/Sun 4687 5602/www.feriademataderos.com.ar). Bus 55, 80, 92, 126. **Open** Jan-Mar 6pm-1am Sat. Apr-Dec 1-7pm Sun. **Admission** free.

Every weekend (Saturday evenings in summer, Sunday afternoons the rest of the year) restaurants lay out tables under the arcade of the 100-year-old administration building of the Mercado Nacional de Hacienda, a massive livestock market where cows and sheep are corralled for auction. On the southern spoke of Lisandro de la Torre, brilliant horsemen take each other on at spearing the *sortija* – a small ring dangling on a ribbon – while standing high on criollo-breed horses.

Museo Criollo de los Corrales

Avenida de los Corrales 6436, y Lisandro de la Torre (4687 1949). Bus 55, 80, 92, 126. **Open** Mar-Dec noon-6.30pm Sun. **Closed** Jan, Feb. **Guided tours** (Spanish) by arrangement. **Admission** AR$2; free concessions. **No credit cards.**

The entrance to this excellent museum is beneath the same arcade as the market. Exhibits include farming implements and country artefacts, along with cartoons by Argentina's most famous painter of gaucho life, Florencio Molina Campos, and a reconstruction of a *pulpería* (rural bar/grocer's store). It's only open on Sundays.

Zona Norte

Tren de la Costa (various stations)/bus 60, 168.

Originally home to the grand *quintas* (or summer houses) of BA's 19th-century aristocracy, the riverside neighbourhoods of Zona Norte, stretching from Olivos to San Isidro, still exude exclusivity – elegant abodes, private country clubs and a wealthy minority renowned for its love of the 'upper-class' sports of rugby, windsurfing and yachting.

To lord it with the privileged or simply to enjoy the river life, take the **Tren de la Costa** (*see p216*), which skirts the River Plate all the

way up to Tigre. The train departs from Olivos'
Maipú station, and three blocks from here is La
Quinta Presidencial, the presidential residence.
The *quinta*'s main entrance is at the intersection
of Maipú and Libertador, but its grounds cover
nine blocks; it's so big that ex-President Carlos
Menem kept a private zoo here. Views of the
residence are obscured by tall perimeter walls.

For dramatic vistas head towards the river,
to **Puerto Olivos**, situated between Corrientes
and Alberdi streets. This private yacht club's
200-metre-long (656-foot) public pier offers a
stunning panorama spanning the River Plate
and BA's city skyline to the south.

Windsurfers and kiteboarders should hop
off at Barrancas Station – serving the barrios of
both Martínez and Acassuso – five minutes up
the line from Olivos. The **Perú Beach** complex
opposite the station (*see p251*) has numerous
wet and dry sports activities and along with
Club Social bar and restaurant next door are
popular places to hang out. These areas are
favourites with kite-flyers and rollerbladers too.

Far removed from nature, but perfect for
shopaholics, is Martínez's **Unicenter** shopping
mall (Paraná y Panamericana, Martínez, 4733
1130, www.unicenter.com.ar), Argentina's
biggest. For dining, check out the riverside bars
or Acassuso's strip on Avenida del Libertador,
between Roque Saénz Peña and Almafuerte.

Another eating strip is developing on Dardo
Rocha, which runs inland alongside the grassy
expanses of the **Hipódromo de San Isidro**
racetrack (*see p250*) and the Jockey Club. Funky
menswear boutique Etiqueta Negra (*see p195*)
is also upping this strip's hip factor.

Sticking to the coastal train, the next stop is
San Isidro, the most exclusive, and enchanting,
of all the riverside neighbourhoods. Highlights
are dotted around the main square, Plaza Mitre,
located in front of the station and home to an
artisans' fair every Sunday. At the square's far
end is the towering, neo-Gothic **Catedral de
San Isidro**, home to excellent programmes
of classical music (*see p240*). Situated opposite
are the area's tourist office and the **Museo del
Rugby** (*see p126*). Located on the same corner
is the **Museo Biblioteca y Archivo
Histórico Municipal** (*see p126*).

Beccar Varela, one of several cobbled streets
wending from Plaza Mitre, leads visitors to
the **Mirador de los Tres Ombúes**, which
offers breathtaking views across the Río de la
Plata to the lush islands of Tigre's delta.

Three blocks east is the **Museo Histórico
Municipal Juan Martín de Pueyrredón**
(*see p126*), the Spanish-colonial style *quinta* of
one of the heroes of Argentinian independence.
Another mansion where ghosts of the past
linger is the masterfully eclectic **Villa Ocampo**

All the fun of the **Feria de Mataderos**.

Sightseeing

(*see below*), former residence of literary luminary and arts patron Victoria Ocampo.

Museo Biblioteca y Archivo Histórico Municipal

Avenida del Libertador 16362, San Isidro (4575 4038). Train Mitre or de la Costa to San Isidro/ 60, 168 bus. **Open** *Museum* Mar-Dec 8am-noon Tue, Thur; 2-6pm Sat, Sun. Jan, Feb 8am-3pm Tue, Thur; 3-9pm Sat, Sun. *Library* Mar-Dec 10am-6pm Mon-Fri. Jan, Feb 10am-6pm Mon-Fri. **Admission** free.

Named a national monument in 2007, this colonial era building houses six exhibition areas dedicated to San Isidro's rich history and culture. As well as important documents, the exhibits include all kinds of odds and sods donated by important local families over the past couple of centuries – magazines, furniture, toys, paintings and so on. The library holds over 12,000 volumes and is open to both serious historians and the casual browser.

Museo Histórico Municipal Juan Martín de Pueyrredón

Rivera Indarte 45, y Roque Saéz Peña, San Isidro (4512 3131). Train Mitre or de la Costa to San Isidro/60, 168 bus. **Open** 2-6pm Tue, Thur, Sat, Sun. **Admission** free.

This Spanish colonial-style mansion was home to, and is named after, one of the heroes of Argentinian independence who lived here up until his death in 1850. It was here that Generals Pueyrredón and San Martín plotted the defeat of the Spanish while – as legend has it – sitting beneath a carob tree in the

glorious gardens. The building, with its white-washed brickwork and iron-grilled windows, has been lovingly preserved.

Museo del Rugby

Ituzaigó 608, y Libertador, San Isidro (information 4732 2547/www.museodelrugby.com). Train Mitre or de la Costa to San Isidro/60, 168 bus. **Open** 10am-6pm Tue-Sat; 10am-8pm Sun. **Admission** free.

Opened in 2003, this is a modern, interactive shrine to the oval ball. It's stacked with jerseys of famous players, narrative displays and memorabilia. Rugger buggers will love it of course; but even if you're not a fan, it's still worth a look. You might just be converted.

Villa Ocampo

Elortondo 1811, y Uriburu, San Isidro (4732 4988/www.villaocampo.org). Train Mitre or de la Costa to San Isidro/60, 168 bus. **Open** 3-7pm Sat, Sun. **Guided tours** every 30 mins. **Admission** AR\$12; free under-12s.

This is the former residence of socialite and arts patron Victoria Ocampo. The guest lists for the parties Ocampo threw here read like a roll-call of the 20th-century's most influential ink-slingers – Borges, Camus, Huxley, Greene, and many others. This important national monument was partially destroyed by fire in 2003 before being restored by UNESCO. The Franco-Victorian-style exterior has been repainted in its original colour, while the ground-floor rooms have been restored and filled with the things that survived the fire, including Ocampo's piano and some of her art collection.

It's not in Peru and it's not a beach – but **Perú Beach** is great fun for all the family.

Eat, Drink, Shop

Restaurants

Thrills, grills and belly ache. Buenos Aires comes of culinary age.

The government of Buenos Aires recently drew up a list of food they believed was of 'patrimonial' value; dishes that were either created in Argentina, or defined its cuisine. There were, briefly, a lot of swelled breasts and smug grins, while others scoffed at the audacity of the chosen plates. Undoubtedly the *milanesa* (breaded cutlet) is a dish omitted from the menu in only the most daring restaurants, but, as its name suggests, it hails from a certain north Italian city. Other inclusions also had rather dubiously non-Argentinian origins: *fugazzetta* (cheese and onion pizza), and even ice cream. Argentina can stake a good claim to *dulce de leche* (although the French claim *confiture de lait* dates back to the 14th century, but say that and expect to be lynched).

This was merely the latest move by the government to define what it is to be Argentinian and food is, if not the most important aspect, then certainly up there with football and politics. Cafés, restaurants and bars are constantly heaving with people until the early hours, enjoying the *sobre mesa*, the long lingering around the table after the meal.

The best Restaurants

For a sublime steak
La Brigada (*see p133*); La Cabrera (*see p143*); Don Julio (*see p143*).

For perfect pasta
Don Chicho (*see p163*); Filo (*see p131*); Lucky Luciano (*see p149*).

For exotic excellence
Empire Thai (*see p133*); Green Bamboo (*see p156*); Sudestada (*see p156*).

For a modern menu
La Vineria de Gualterio Bolivar (*see p135*); El Bistro (*see p139*).

For a fashionable feast
Casa Cruz (*see p145*); Gran Bar Danzón (*see p140*); Olsen (*see p155*).

For bargain bites
Eros (*see p143*); El Cuartito (*see p141*).

Until recently Buenos Aires was still a city where sauce on your steak would have been deemed avant-garde, with the main variation to the staple diet being admittedly excellent, pizza and pasta. A big buzz surrounds the influx of Peruvian food and *ceviche* (*see p157* **The new sushi?**). However, a more subtle movement, but one that may turn out to be more important, is the reassessment of local ingredients such as Andean potatoes and traditional cooking methods. **Restó** (*see right*) and **Bo Bo** (*see p145*) are experimenting, but these foods are finding themselves on more and more menus across the capital.

It is a good idea to look out for lunchtime set menus. They are generally well below the evening rate and are a good opportunity to try otherwise pricey cuisine. Look out for *menú del dia* or *menú ejecutivo* poster boards outside.

Service can be slow in this unrushed capital, although it usually compensates with warmth and character for what it lacks in speed and efficiency. A ten per cent *propina* (tip) will be greatly appreciated by underpaid staff.

Argentinians eat late and are unlikely to close their doors until the last customer has left. The closing times are usually the average time the restaurant locks its doors; however, if it is a quiet night don't expect it to remain open. As always, it's best to make sure up front that the restaurant's credit card facilities are in full working order.

ABOUT THE LISTINGS
The listings in this section give the range of prices for main courses, from the cheapest to generally what is the most expensive, although some restaurants have special dishes on their menus that can be much more pricey. It is well worth bearing in mind that inflation in Argentina is running at around 10-15 per cent, and restaurants are particularly sensitive to rises in costs, therefore prices may increase during the life of this guide. Prices given here do not include extras such as wine, starters, dessert or coffees.

❶ Purple numbers given in this chapter correspond to the location of each restaurant as marked on the street maps. *See pp322-329.*

El Bistro. *See p139.*

The Centre

Argentinian (traditional)

El Establo

Paraguay 489, y San Martín, Retiro (4311 1639). Subte C, San Martín/93, 132, 152 bus. **Open** 7am-2am daily. **Main courses** AR$25-$48. **Credit** AmEx, DC, MC, V. **Map** p325 G11 ❶
An Argentinian classic where happy locals mix with happier tourists from nearby hotels, cheered by the vast steaks that arrive flawlessly from the *parrilla*. There is a wide range of salads, fish and pasta too, not to mention classic Spanish tapas of *jamón*, peppers and tortilla. There is a cheerful crew of old-time waiters for company and banter.

El Federal

San Martín 1015, y Marcelo T de Alvear, Retiro (4313 1324). Subte C, San Martín/93, 152 bus. **Open** 11am-midnight Mon-Sat. **Main courses** AR$20-$30. **Credit** AmEx, V. **Map** p325 G11 ❷
Since chef-owner Paula Comparatore moved El Federal from Palermo it has successfully established a name for top quality lunchtime grub. They serve up some truly creative and delicious adaptations of classic Argentinian dishes. Paula's focus is on the flavours of the south and west of Argentina, and her passion for food shows through in every colourful plate.

Argentinian (modern)

Dadá

San Martín 941, entre Marcelo T de Alvear y Paraguay, Microcentro (4314 4787). Subte C, San Martín/93, 152 bus. **Open** noon-2am Mon-Sat. **Main courses** AR$20-$40. **Credit** AmEx, MC, V. **Map** p325 H12 ❸
It's rare we recommend a venue in both the restaurant and bar section (*see p167*) of this book, but Dadá slips so easily into both categories. Inside, owner and frontman Paulo manages to both entertain and feed clients with a menu that is as colourful and imaginative as the lighting and furnishings that adorn the restaurant. The chalkboard regularly features classics like Lomo Dadá, *ojo de bife* and grilled salmon, as well as shrimp salads, risottos, lamb and home-made chips the size of bananas.

Restó

Montevideo 938, entre Marcelo T de Alvear y Paraguay, Tribunales (4816 6711). Subte D, Callao/39, 152 bus. **Open** noon-3pm Mon-Fri; 8-11pm Thur, Fri. **Main courses** AR$22-$36 lunch. *Set menu* (dinner only) AR$40-$78. **No credit cards. Map** p325 H10 ❹
A disciple of the great Michel Bras, Francophile chef María Barrutia prepares reasonably priced but exquisite Latin American focused cuisine in this petite restaurant on the ground floor of the Central

GRAN BAR DANZON

RESTAURANT
WINE BAR & COCKTAILS

RESTAURANT - BAR - GREAT COLLECTION OF ARGENTINE WINES - SUSHI - HAPPY HOUR EVERY DAY
Chef Martín Arrieta

Open 7 days a week, we close late. Monday thru Friday from 7 pm / Saturday and Sunday from 8 pm

Libertad 1161 - Reservations: 48111108 / danzon@granbardanzon.com.ar / www.granbardanzon.com.ar

Architect's Society. The lunch menu offers two fish options and a choice of beef and chicken, though their preparation is altered daily. On Thursday and Friday nights, by reservation only, a choice of three thoughtfully combined set menus awaits. The wine list is short but superb.

Tomo I

Hotel Panamericano, Carlos Pellegrini 521, entre Lavalle y Tucumán, Microcentro (4326 6695/ www.tomo1.com.ar). Subte B, Carlos Pellegrini/10, 17, 29 bus. **Open** noon-3pm Mon-Fri; 7.30pm-1am Mon-Sat. **Main courses** AR$45-$78. *Set menu* AR$104-$129. **Credit** AmEx, DC, MC, V. **Map** p325 G10 ❺

Food fads and fashions come and go, and Ada and Eve Concaro continue to spurn them. Their philosophy is that great dishes comprising high quality and painstakingly sourced ingredients never go out of style. You can trust the menu in Tomo I: 'fresh fish' means fish delivered that morning; homemade ravioli means pasta mixed, rolled and filled on the premises, and so on. The menu changes with the seasons but the restaurant's legion of regular clients keep coming back whatever the weather. It's not cheap, but for food of this quality nor should it be.

French

Bouchon

Tucumán 400, entre Reconquista y San Martín, Microcentro (4313 3358). Subte B, Florida/22, 86, 93, 115, 102 bus. **Open** noon-4pm, 7.30-11.30pm Mon-Fri; 8pm-midnight Sat. **Main courses** AR$25-$50. **Credit** AmEx, MC, V. **Map** p325 F11 ❻

Bouchon is a relaxed bistro on a busy BA corner. The appealing atmosphere, however, is nothing compared with the stunning food, as attested to by the favourable scribblings around the walls from content customers. Their medallion of pork on a bed of black carrots in balsamic reduction and confit of onions can be cut with a spoon. The trout is also abundant and moist. Their lunchtime set menus are a real bargain for this location.

Italian

D'Oro

Peru 159, entre Hipólito Yrigoyen y Adolfo Alsina, Microcentro (4342 6959/www.doro-resto.com.ar). Subte A, Peru/22, 24 bus. **Open** 9am-12.30am Mon-Fri. **Main courses** AR$14-$35. **Credit** AmEx, DC, MC, V. **Map** p325 E10 ❼

If you have ever doubted the provenance of your food, this authentic Italian 'ristorante' should put your worried mind at ease. Watch the master chefs in the open kitchen, along one side of this skinny downtown restaurant and wine bar, turn out immaculately cooked Italian classics such as superb risottos and simple al dente raviolis, while their salads are big, imaginative and fresh. A good selection of wine can also accompany tasty snacks and pizza for long fun evenings with friends.

Filo

San Martín 975, entre Marcelo T de Alvear y Paraguay, Retiro (4311 0312/www.filo-ristorante.com). Subte C, San Martín/10, 93, 130, 152 bus. **Open** from noon daily. **Main courses** AR$22-$45. **Credit** AmEx, DC, MC, V. **Map** p325 G12 ❽

Just try snagging a table at this hip pizzeria at lunchtime: come 1pm, even the bar stools are occupied by financial advisers chowing down on focaccia chips and grilled vegetables. With a cool, urbane interior accented by splashes of red and yellow, a lengthy menu stocked with Italian pastas as well as over 100 gourmet pizzas, and a brick oven keeping the room toasty, Filo is a contender for the best place to grab a bite in the centre.

Peruvian

Chan Chan

Hipólito Yrigoyen 1390, entre San José y Santiago del Estero, Congreso (4382 8492). Subte A, Sáenz Peña/39, 60, 168 bus. **Open** noon-4pm, from 7.30pm Tue-Sun. **Main courses** AR$15-$25. **No credit cards.** **Map** 325 F9 ❾

Kitsch and colourful Chan Chan has already attracted a devoted fanbase with its lengthy menu of Andean classics – *ceviche* (raw marinated fish), *papas a la Huancaina* (spicy spuds slathered in a cream sauce), and so on. Wash it down with a pisco sour or a jug of chicha morada (fruit cordial). The bill is a real treat too.

Filo.

Eat, Drink, Shop

Crack the 'carta'

Basics

Menú/carta menu; **desayuno** breakfast; **almuerzo** lunch; **merienda** afternoon tea/snack (often *mate* and *medialunas*); **cena** dinner; **entrada** starter; **minutas** short orders; **plato principal** main course; **postre** dessert; **aceite y vinagre** oil and vinegar; **ajo** garlic; **casero** home-made; **pan** bread; **sopa** soup; **agua** water (**con gas** fizzy, **sin gas** still); **mate/yerba** local herb tea; **té** tea; **vino** wine (**tinto** red, **blanco** white, **de la casa** house).

Cooking styles & techniques

A la parrilla grilled; **al horno** baked; **al vapor** steamed; **asado** grilled; **frito** fried; **hervido** boiled; **picante** spicy/hot; **salteado** sautéed; **jugoso** rare; **a punto** medium rare; **bien cocido** medium to well done; **muy bien cocido** between well done and shoe leather.

Carne y aves (Meat & poultry)

Albóndigas meatballs; **asado** barbecue(d); **asado de tira** or **tira de asado** rack of ribs; **bife de chorizo** rump/sirloin; **bife de costilla** rib; **bife de lomo** tenderloin; **cerdo** pork; **chimichurri** spicy sauce for meat; **chivito** kid; **choripán** spicy sausage sandwich; **chorizo** sausage; **chinchulín** chitterling/intestine; **chuleta** chop; **conejo** rabbit; **cordero** lamb; **entraña** entrail; **hígado** liver; **jamón** ham (**cocido** boiled, **crudo** Parma-style); **lechón** suckling pig; **lengua** tongue; **lomo** tenderloin; **milanesa** breaded cutlet; **mondongo** tripe; **morcilla** blood sausage/black pudding; **molleja** sweetbread; **pancho** hotdog; **parrillada** small table grill; **pato** duck; **pollo** chicken; **riñones** kidneys; **ternera** veal; **vacio** flank.

Pescados y mariscos (Fish & seafood)

Anchoa anchovy; **almeja** clam; **atún** tuna; **calamar** squid; **camarón** prawn; **cangrejo** crab; **centolla** king crab; **langosta** lobster; **langostino** king prawn; **lenguado** sole; **mejillón** mussel; **merluza** hake; **ostra** oyster; **pulpo** octopus; **rabas** squid rings; **trucha** trout.

Verduras, arroz y legumbres (Vegetables, rice & pulses)

Apio celery; **arroz** rice; **arveja** green pea; **batata** sweet potato; **berenjena** aubergine/eggplant; **berro** watercress; **calabaza** pumpkin/squash; **cebolla** onion; **chaucha**

Sipan

Paraguay 624, y Florida, Microcentro (4315 0763/ www.sipan.com.ar). Subte C, San Martín/10, 45, 101, 132, bus. **Open** noon-midnight Mon-Sat. **Main courses** AR$18-$34. **Credit** AmEx, MC, V. **Map** p325 F11 ❿

This new Peruvian restaurant and pisco bar is named after a tomb uncovered in the north of Peru in 1987, one of the most important archaeological discoveries of recent times. Almost as hidden, in a gallery off Florida, Sipan is a gorgeously decorated little piece of Peru serving up some of the finest and most authentic Andean cuisine in the city. Mouthfuls of marinated octopus, beautifully presented on Japanese ceramic spoons, can be followed by exemplary spicy *ceviche*. Inspired interpretations of sushi and stir-fries, washed down with a tangy pisco sour makes for a lively lunch.

Status

Virrey Cevallos 178, entre Hipólito Yrigoyen y Alsina, Congreso (4382 8531/www.restaurantstatus.com.ar). Subte A, Sáenz Peña/37, 60, 168 bus. **Open** noon-5pm, 8pm-1am Mon-Thur; noon-1am Fri-Sun. **Main courses** AR$7-$30. **Credit** AmEx, MC, V. **Map** p325 G9 ⓫

Although Argentinians tend to shun most things indigenous to their own contintent, one day soon they're going to wake up to the potential of Peruvian cuisine. This simple but pleasant canteen owned by the friendly Valenzuela family from Trujillo serves abundant platters of ceviche and lamb, as well as spicy starters.

green beans; **choclo** corn; **espinaca** spinach; **garbanzo** chickpea; **humita** grated, cooked sweetcorn; **lechuga** lettuce; **lenteja** lentil; **palmito** palm heart; **palta** avocado; **papa** potato; **pepino** cucumber; **puerro** leek; **remolacha** beetroot; **repollo** cabbage; **soja** soya; **zanahoria** carrot; **zapallito** courgette/zucchini.

Fruta (Fruit)

Ananá pineapple; **cereza** cherry; **ciruela** plum; **durazno** peach; **frambuesa** raspberry; **frutilla** strawberry; **manzana** apple; **naranja** orange; **pera** pear; **pomelo** grapefruit, **pelón** nectarine.

Postres (Desserts)

Budín de pan bread pudding; **flan** crème caramel; **helado** ice-cream; **miel** honey; **queso** cheese.

Local specialities

Alfajor cornflower biscuits, filled with *dulce de leche*; **carbonada** thick stew of corn, meat, rice and veg; **dulce de leche** milk jam (tastes like caramel); **locro** stew of pork, beans, spices; **medialunas** sweet or salty croissants.

South-east Asian

Empire Thai

Tres Sargentos 427, entre San Martín y Reconquista, Retiro (4312 5706). Subte C, San Martín/26, 93, 152 bus. **Open** noon-midnight Mon-Fri; 7pm-1am Sat. **Main courses** AR$22-$40. **Credit** AmEx, MC, V. **Map** p325 G11 ⑫

Empire's fashionable interior is reason enough to swing by for chicken satays and green curry. Crossing a sleek New York sensibility with a more colourful Asian aesthetic, by night this eatery is a dimly lit space with mirror mosaics glittering on grass-green walls. You'll find mouth-burning authentic spices in the green curry and pad Thai. In summer it's worth heading to the paved terrace.

Spanish

Ávila

Avenida de Mayo 1384, entre Santiago del Estero y San José, Congreso (4383 6974). Subte A Sáenz Peña/29, 102, 86 bus. **Open** noon-4pm, 8pm-2am Mon-Sat. **Main courses** AR$22-$40. **No credit cards. Map** p325 G11 ⑲

Ávila is a dark, atmospheric set-up as quirky as owner Miguel, whose family have been on the premises since the 1940s. Once you're settled, a glass of jerez and steaming dishes of stew, paella, and squid and other seafood tapas, are delivered to your table. They keep coming until the flamenco troupe – of local gitanos – leap up clapping, stomping and strumming. Bag a table close to the stage, though you'll be invited to join in, especially the girls. When it's all over, Miguel strolls over and conjures up a price for the pleasure. Cheeky, perhaps, but considering the show and quantity consumed, spot on. Reservations are a must – the liveliest nights are Thursday to Saturdays.

Constitución

Argentinian (traditional)

Miramar

Avenida San Juan 1999 y Sarandí (4304 4261). Subte E, Entre Ríos/37, 53, 126 bus. **Open** 11am-4pm, from 8pm Mon-Wed, Sun. **Main courses** AR$8-$62. **Credit** AmEx, MC, V. **Map** p325 F7 ⑭

Beloved by its barrio, Miramar is an unpretentious eatery boasting a well-stocked wine cellar and super-amiable waiters. For lunch, try rabbit in white wine, a perfect Spanish tortilla, frogs' legs, Spanish-style oysters or shrimps in garlic while listening to the crackly tangos. The justly famed *rabo del toro* (oxtail stew) has a limb warming quality that's nigh on narcotic. You can also tuck into fresh *centolla* (king crab) and other deep-sea delicacies. One of the best times to go is on Sunday evenings, when *bandoneón* (accordion) maestro Julio Pane plays live.

San Telmo

Argentinian (traditional)

La Brigada ○

Estados Unidos 465, entre Bolívar y Defensa (4361 4685). Bus 22, 29, 126. **Open** noon-3pm, 8pm-midnight Sun, Tue-Thur; noon-4pm, 8pm-1am Fri, Sat. **Main courses** AR$22-$35. **Credit** AmEx, MC, V. **Map** p324 D10 ⑮

This San Telmo favourite is a refined version of the traditional *parrilla*, serving up excellent cuts of meat alongside spicy chorizo, grilled *provoleta* cheese, various salads, and crispy vegetable fritters. Regulars swear that their offal selection is among the best in the town, particularly their crispy kid *chinchulines* (chitterling). But also a good place to

Eat, Drink, Shop

try the excellent *molleja* (sweetbread). A good range of malbecs will bring a blush to your cheeks in the pleasantly snug dining room.
Other location Peña 2475, Recoleta (4800 1110).

El Desnivel 💥

Defensa 855, entre Independencia y Estados Unidos (4300 9081). Subte C, Independencia/24, 29 bus. **Open** noon-4.30pm, from 7.30pm Tue-Sat; noon-1am Sun. **Main courses** AR$12-$22. **No credit cards.** **Map** p324 D10 ⑯
High on the list of fun things to do in BA is a late-night steak blowout at this legendary San Telmo *parrilla*. Staffing the grill are bloody-apron-wearing, knife-wielding cooks (think Sweeney Todd meets Joe Pesci) and cheeky waiters. The equal mix of expatriates, tourists and locals makes for a boisterous and friendly scene. Make sure you get a table in the main restaurant to feel part of the action.

Lezama

Brasil 359, entre Defensa y Balcarce (4361 0114). Bus 33, 62, 64, 74, 143. **Open** noon-4pm, from 7.30pm Tue-Sat; noon-4pm Sun. **Main courses** AR$16-$30. **Credit** AmEx, MC, V. **Map** p324 C9 ⑰
Attracting everybody from neighbourhood families and arty couples to the odd well informed tourist and one Zinédine Zidane, this handsome San Telmo *bodegón* (traditional restaurant) is superb value and has the added boon of a view over Parque Lezama. Pick one of the classics – tortillas, salads, pastas, steaks – or ask for the waiter's advice.

Manolo

Bolívar 1299, y Cochabamba (4307 8743/www.restaurantmanolo.com.ar). Bus 10, 24, 29, 39. **Open** noon-1am Tue-Sun. **Main courses** AR$10-$32. **No credit cards.** **Map** p324 D9 ⑱
The late, great Manolo may not be overseeing operations any more, but his sons Gastón and Sebastián are holding down the fort at this friendly neighbourhood joint. Faithful local clientele feast on their meat and potatoes of choice – whether it be one of the usual *parrilla* specialities, or chicken prepared in a dozen different ways – from a menu that's as thick as a magazine. The football paraphernalia isn't exactly cutting-edge decor, but it's certainly atmospheric. **Photo** *p136.*

Argentinian (modern)

647 Dinner Club

Tacuari 647, entre México y Chile (4331 3026/ www.club647.com). Bus 59, 60, 168. **Open** from 8pm Mon-Sat. **Main courses** AR$25-$40. **Credit** AmEx, DC, MC, V. **Map** p325 E9 ⑲
Either stretch out on one of the enormous chaise longues and let one of the gorgeous staff bring you a crayfish salad perfumed with Bombay Sapphire, or try the duck breast with pear strudel and blueberry sauce over in the vintage chandelier-lit salon. Even enjoy your llama steak with feta cheese salad in one of the velvet booths. Head chef

Fernando Trump's modern Argentinian menu is mercifully free of annoying what-can-we-stuff-in-the-raviolis-today?-type clichés.

Los Loros

Estados Unidos 302, y Balcarce (4361 5539). Bus 10, 22, 24, 45. **Open** from noon Tue-Sun. **Main courses** AR$18-$32. **No credit cards.** **Map** p324 D10 ⑳
At last San Telmo is waking up to the fact there is more to Argentinian cuisine than a lump of beef and a portion of chips. Luckily on this cosy corner spot, you'll find nothing more than the picturesque façades of Bar Sur, and the latest culinary highlight to hit BA: Los Loros. It is an informal and classic-looking joint suitable for a lazy drink or enjoying an interesting selection of good grub. Choose from home-made houmous and a well-executed coriander and carrot soup, followed by German sausages with sauerkraut and mustard sauce, or maybe ribeye steak and penne in a cream and spinach sauce. The service is as impeccable as the food.

La Vineria de Gualterio Bolívar

Bolívar 865, entre Independencia y Estados Unidos (4361 4709). Subte C, Independencia/24, 29 bus. **Open** 12.30pm-midnight Tue-Sun. **Main courses** AR$15 for one tasting dish. **No credit cards.** **Map** p324 D10 ㉑
Among the endless *parrillas* and *pizzerias* of San Telmo is a completely new culinary prospect, not just for the area but also for the whole city. This diminutive white-washed restaurant is run by

Belly up at **647 Dinner Club**.

Alejandro Digilio, an Argentinian with Ferran Adriá's Spanish restaurant El Bulli on his CV. This hints at the direction of the food, but his preposition remains down to earth, with only minor touches of 'molecular gastronomy' such as foams of potatoes and olive oil salt. Their starters include a superb crunchy fish skin and dips of olive oil of pistachio and parma ham. The core of the cuisine is exceptionally well-cooked hard-to-find cuts of meat: their main dish is cooked for 12 hours and served only with a spoon, alongside plenty of little jewels of fascinating combinations, and ultra modern takes on latin staples. Each tasting plate costs AR$15 and three would easily suffice, they also have a very interesting wine list.

Basque

Burzako

México 345, entre Defensa y Balcarce (4334 0721). Bus 29, 93, 130, 152. **Open** noon-3pm, 8.30-11.30pm Mon-Thur; noon-3pm, 8.30pm-12.30am Fri, Sat. **Main courses** AR$18-$30. **Credit** AmEx, MC, V. **Map** p325 E10 ㉒
A lively bar-restaurant with touches of a traditional Spanish tavern, but which also tries to show that Basque cuisine can be young and cool. The fish specialities and tasty tapas are highlights, along with Basque classics like brazed oxtail in red wine. For dessert try the Turkish figs in a Basque wrap or the *natilla* (a Spanish crème caramel).

French

Brasserie Petanque

Defensa 596, y México (4342 7930/www. brasseriepetanque.com). Bus 29, 93, 130, 152. **Open** 12.30-3.30pm Mon; 12.30pm-1am Tue-Fri, Sun; from 8pm Sat. **Main courses** AR$22-$42. **Credit** AmEx, DC, MC, V. **Map** p325 E10 ㉓
Petanque is the quintessential French brasserie right down to the specially imported crème brûlée holders, and furniture made to comply with strict brasserie measurements. Everything you would expect from a French menu, designed by renowned chef Sébastien Fouillade, makes an appearance, including an exceptional boeuf bourguignon, steak tartare, and, of course, escargots.

Italian

Amici Miei

Defensa 1072, entre Humberto Primo y Carlos Calvo (4362 5562/www.amicimiei.com.ar). Bus 22, 29. **Open** 11am-midnight Tue-Sun. **Main courses** AR$25-$40. **Credit** AmEx, V. **Map** p324 D9 ㉓
Fed up with soggy noodles? Forget the oft-overcooked Argentinian pasta options and bite into something truly al dente at this spiffy new eatery. Considering its tourist-friendly location on a second floor overlooking Plaza Dorrego, the genteel Amici Miei décor and menu come as a bit of a surprise – from

Football and meat, a perfect Argentinian combination, at **Manolo**. *See p135.*

Show me the dough

In a country with such a deep fondness for the double entendre, it's only natural that in Argentina a ñoqui (gnocchi) refers to more than a potato dumpling from northern Italy.

Since the 1970s, *porteños* (and their Uruguayan neighbours) have used the word ñoqui – lump in Italian – to describe public sector employees who only bother to show up for work at the end of the month to collect their paychecks.

In a good-humoured bow to bureaucratic laziness, many *rioplatenses* (those from the River Plate region) extend their ridicule beyond their vocabulary and indulge in the custom of eating ñoquis on the 29th of each month. (Although some historians argue that

the tradition actually dates back to a feast commemorating San Pantoleón, an eighth-century Italian saint thought to be responsible for abundant harvests).

Whether for shiftless bureaucrats or generous saints, a good number of fun-loving *porteños* still enjoy the ritual at restaurants like Las Cortaderas (Charcas 3467, Palermo, 4825 2887) and Campo dei Fiori (Venezuela 1411, Montserrat, 4381 1800). If you happen to be in Buenos Aires on this date, you may also notice locals stuffing two peso bills under their plates after they've finished their pasta – a custom rumoured to conjure up financial prosperity for the coming month.

fresh salad tossed with grilled aubergine and brie, to the tagliatelle with shrimp and courgette.

Spanish

Café San Juan

San Juan 450, entre Bolívar y Defensa (4300 1112). Subte C, San Juan/24, 28, 29, 86 bus. **Open** noon-4pm, 8.30pm-midnight Tue-Sun. **Main courses** AR$25-$40. **No credit cards. Map** p324 D9 ㉕

It's a family affair at this enormously popular Spanish eaterie: chef Leandro Cristobal is busy fashioning inventive tapas from sun-dried tomatoes and brie, his mother pours wine while his small daughter, miniature Dachshund in tow, charms patrons who've come right across town for Café San Juan's fresh cuisine. Savoury tapas and generously sized pasta dishes are built around hand-picked seasonal vegetables – staples like cured ham with mushrooms or the courgette-rich fettuccine are for sharing.

Puerto Madero

Argentinian (traditional)

Cabaña Las Lilas

Alicia Moreau de Justo 516, Dique 4 (4313 1336/ www.laslilas.com.ar). Subte B, LN Alem/62, 93, 130, 152 bus. **Open** noon-3.30pm, 7.30pm-1am daily. **Main courses** AR$45-$70. **Credit** AmEx, V. **Map** p325 E11 ㉖

Eating steak at Cabaña Las Lilas is a little like taking tea at the Ritz. You know it's a tourist trap, you know you're being overcharged, but somehow you're still glad you came. The atmospheric dockside location helps, as does the exemplary service and jumbo wine list. But what really matters is the meat. Every chop, chump and *chorizo* is sourced from the company's own *estancias* and the award-winning thoroughbred cattle that graze there. And whatever ends up on the plate, from whatever part of the cow, will be cooked as requested and unforgettably tender. The bill is

memorable too. Sixty pesos for a *bife de chorizo*, while extortionate by local standards, is small change on an expenses account or a foreign credit card statement.

Spettus

Avenida Alicia Moreau de Justo 876, Dique 3 (4334 4126/www.spettusbuenosaires.com.ar). Subte B, LN Alem/93, 152 bus. **Open** noon-4pm, from 7.30pm daily. **Main courses** AR$25-$40. **Credit** AmEx, DC, MC, V. **Map** p325 E11 **㉗**
With a happy heifer guarding the front door, this has to be your classic Argentinian steakhouse, right? Wrong. While the meat served at Spettus is 100 per cent pride of the pampas, the chain is Brazilian, as is the method of serving the meat, a style known as *espeto corrido*. In brief: each table is provided with a card, one side of which is red, the other green. Flip it to green and a waiter will materialise with a skewer of grilled meat (over 20 cuts are available), which he will carve and slide onto your plate. Flip to red and the staff will hang five. As well as the usual range of red meats, fish and poultry are also available (the Pacific salmon is particularly good), and the buffet bar is one of the best in town.

Argentinian (modern)

El Bistro

Faena Hotel + Universe, Martha Salotti 445, Dique 2 (4010 9200/www.faenahotelanduniverse.com). Subte B, LN Alem/2, 130, 152 bus. **Open** 8pm-1am daily. **Main courses** AR$240 tasting menu. **Credit** AmEx, DC, MC, V. **Map** p324 D11 **㉘**
With the appointment of chef Mariano Cid de la Paza, another of BA's protégés of star Spanish chef Ferrán Adriá, in February 2007, Bistro's menu is now as singular the Philippe Starck-designed interior. Throughout the never-ending tasting menu (a regular menu is also available), molecular gastronomy techniques are evident: 'spherifications' of olives and 'foams' of lettuce appear. Yet there are touches in a resolutely Argentinian fare, albeit one that has been deconstructed, reworked and intensified. Yet with down-to-earth staff, the evening passes off as a surprisingly unfussy adventure that justifies its European prices. **Photo** *p129.*

I Fresh Market

Azucena Villafor, y Olga Cossettini, Dique 3, Puerto Madero Este (5775 0330/www.ifreshmarket.com.ar). Bus 2, 103, 152. **Open** from 8am daily. **Main courses** AR$29-$35. **Credit** AmEx, MC, V. **Map** p324 D11 **㉙**
Into its fourth year and still a favourite with the lunchtime suits, this modern New York style deli serves only the freshest of produce. Healthy breakfast and lunch items all feature and by dinner time the menu becomes a heartier affair with risotto and grilled peppers, courgette and aubergines with rice, and pink salmon with four citrus sauce and crunchy strips of potato making for solid meals. Service slows down a notch with the summer

lunchtime crowd, but you can browse luxury condiments at their deli counter and designer home accessories in their mini shop while you wait. **Other location** Pierina Dealessi y Macacha Guemes, Puerto Madero (5775 0330).

La Boca

Argentinian (traditional)

El Obrero   *IF IN LA BOCA !*

Agustín Caffarena 64, entre Ministro Brin y Caboto (4362 9912). Bus 25, 29, 68, 130. **Open** noon-4pm, from 8pm Mon-Sat. **Main courses** AR$16-$28. **No credit cards.** **Map** p324 B10 **㉚**
Everyone – from U2's Bono to Wim Wenders – has discovered this museum piece in the heart of the old port (best to come by taxi and with company). The decor is busy with boxing and soccer legends, the paint is peeling and the toilet is a glorified outhouse, but it's still a classic spot for long lunches or well-proportioned dinners with a gang of friends. Most people choose from the *parrilla* items listed on the chalkboard, but there are also fair pastas and fish dishes, and a selection of old-style desserts such as *sopa ingles* (like trifle). El Obrero is a BA institution.

Patagonia Sur

Rocha 803, y Pedro de Mendoza (4303 5917/ www.restaurantepatagoniasur.com). Bus 29, 33, 152. **Open** noon-4pm, 7.30pm-midnight Thur-Sat; noon-4pm Sun. **Main courses** Set menu AR$200. **Credit** AmEx, DC, MC, V. **Map** p324 A8 **㉛**
It sounds like the result of a late night bet. Open an exclusive restaurant in one of BA's most impoverished neighbourhoods; serve Argentinian comfort food like *choripánes* (sausage sandwiches) and *empanadas* at haute cuisine prices (AR$200 for a three-course set menu). It's owned by Argentina's most famous chef, the delightfully bohemian Francis Mallman who uses the very highest quality ingredients, in particular the meltingly tender braised Patagonian lamb.

Italian

Il Matterello

Martín Rodríguez 517, y Villafañe (4307 0529). Bus 29, 64, 86, 152. **Open** 12.30-3pm, 8.30pm-midnight Tue-Sat; 12.30-3pm Sun. **Closed** Jan. **Main courses** AR$18-$28. **Credit** AmEx, DC, MC, V. **Map** p324 B9 **㉜**
Is it by chance that the kitchen greets you as you roll into Il Matterello? Or is it a neat metaphor for the centrality that the food (the food!) takes in this crisp, clean, cantina-style La Boca eaterie? A mixed plate of warm and cold antipasti serves to liven the taste buds in preparation for al dente tagliatelle with a *putanesca* sauce and a truly sumptuous *fazzoletti alla carbonara*. Top service and unpretentious decor help to accompany, but not out-twinkle, the star: the food.

Eat, Drink, Shop

Argentinian (traditional)

Cumaná

Rodríguez Peña 1149, entre Santa Fe y Arenales, Barrio Norte (4813 9207). Bus 10, 37, 39, 101, 124, 152. **Open** noon-1am daily. **Main courses** AR$10-$18. **No credit cards. Map** p326 I10 ③

Cumaná is the kind of restaurant that makes you hungry as soon as you walk through the door, even if you only did so to use the bathroom. Surrender to the onslaught of tantalising aromas and settle at one of the rustic tables and order some *locro* (a thick Andean stew) and home-made empanadas.

L'Orangerie

Alvear Palace Hotel, Avenida Alvear 1891, entre Callao y Ayacucho, Recoleta (4808 2100/www. alvearpalace.com). Bus 67, 93, 130. **Open** for brunch 12.30-4pm Sun; lunch noon-3.30pm Mon-Sat; afternoon tea 4-7pm Mon-Sat, 5-7pm Sun. **Main courses** *Lunch* AR$115. *Brunch* AR$170. **Credit** AmEx, DC, MC, V. **Map** p326 I11 ③

Amid the truly palatial opulence of the Alvear Palace Hotel, L'Orangerie is the grandest brunch destination in the city: the Argentinian equivalent of tea at the Ritz. In their leafy Winter Garden, white-gloved waiters pour drinks while you serve yourself from their extensive buffet and sushi bar. Seasonal salads complement the cold cuts and smoked fish while the smell of hot dishes, such as duck magret with port wine, wafts through the atrium.

Argentinian (modern)

Gran Bar Danzón

Libertad 1161, entre Santa Fe y Arenales, Recoleta (4811 1108/www.granbardanzon.com.ar). Subte D, Tribunales/17, 39, 102, 152 bus. **Open** from 8pm daily. **Main courses** AR$20-$27. **Credit** AmEx, DC, MC, V. **Map** p326 I11 ③

The '*gran*' is fully merited – this is a great wine bar and restaurant, and a banquet for the senses from the moment you enter via the the candlelit and incense-scented stairwell. The main menu roams freely between Europe and Latin America, offering flawlessly executed fusion dishes like confit of duck served with a *ceviche* taco, and rack of Patagonian lamb in a brioche crust. A wine list of over 200 labels (many by the glass) make this a superb joint.

República Brasas Resto

First floor, Vicente López 1661, entre Rodríguez Peña y Montevideo, Recoleta (4816 7744). Bus 60, 110. **Open** noon-4pm, 8pm-midnight Tue-Sat; noon-4pm Sun. **Main courses** AR$35-$46. **Credit** AmEx, MC, V. **Map** p326 I11 ③

Cheaper (but still by no means cheap) sister restaurant of superb French restaurant Nectarine (*see right*), República goes easy on the foie gras and Piedmont truffles and heavy on superb grilled meats. In other words it's an upscale *parrilla*. Star dishes include the rack of beef ribs cooked twice (four hours in wine and then a quick stint on the grill), the home-smoked salmon, and one of the tastiest roast lamb dishes in town.

Gran Bar Danzón.

Eclectic

Casa SaltShaker

Address provided when you reserve, Barrio Norte (15 6132 4146/www.casasaltshaker.com). Subte D, Pueyrredón/10, 59, 60, 95, 101, 118 bus. **Open** from 9pm Fri, Sat. **Main courses** *five-course tasting menu* AR$75. **No credit cards.**
Among the various places in town that are not-so-well-kept secrets, Casa SaltShaker is one of the most intriguing. Hidden away in a rear garden apartment in Barrio Norte, it's one of the few 'communal table' dining spots in the city. The five-course tasting menus are planned around quirky themes based on random historical events: one night the theme may be the annual Night of the Radishes, on another English Renaissance. Certainly a night to remember.

French

La Bourgogne

Alvear Palace Hotel, Avenida Alvear 1891, entre Callao y Ayacucho, Recoleta (4808 2100/www. alvearpalace.com). Bus 67, 93, 130. **Open** noon-3.30pm, 7.30pm-midnight Mon-Fri. **Main courses** AR$80-$90. *Set menu* AR$115. **Credit** AmEx, DC, MC, V. **Map** p326 I11 ❸
La Bourgogne is considered to be one of the great restaurants of Buenos Aires and that is mainly down to the steering of French chef Jean Paul Bondoux. The sea bream with butter sauce and caviar is sublime and the truly Argentinian grilled veal with thyme flower is exquisite, as is the rabbit 'crunch' with mustard sauce. Among the stylings of the Alvear Palace Hotel, the setting couldn't be finer.

Nectarine

Vicente López 1661, entre Montevideo y Rodríguez Peña, Barrio Norte (4813 6993). Bus 10, 37, 59, 110, 124. **Open** noon-3pm, from 8pm-midnight Mon-Sat. **Main courses** AR$46-$56. **Credit** AmEx, MC, V. **Map** p326 I11 ❸
Nectarine is a peach of a destination for a special Buenos Aires evening. Hidden up a small pedestrian alley in the centre of the upmarket neighbourhood, the small interior is sophisticated without being formal, providing the ideal setting for a romantic tryst. Both the wine list and the menu are rich in options and flavours, and the well-trained staff will help you match the one with the other.

Sirop & Sirop Folie

Unit 11, Vicente López 1661, entre Montevideo y Rodríguez Peña (4813 5900). Bus 37, 124. **Open** Sirop noon-3.30pm, from 8pm Mon-Fri; from 8pm Sat. Sirop Folie 10am-close Tue-Sun. **Main courses** Sirop AR$32-$55. Sirop Folie *Weekend brunch* AR$65. **Credit** AmEx, MC, V. **Map** p326 I11 ❸
Sirop is a treasure nestled in the depths of Recoleta. The alley is very Parisian and is a fantastic place to eat outside on a warm spring day. So whether you choose to eat alfresco or inside, at lunch or at dinner, get your tastebuds ready for delicious

flavours, enjoy the sophisticated yet relaxed atmosphere, and be prepared to be spoiled. Across the passageway, Sirop Folie is a more relaxed version of sister Sirop. Beautifully decorated, with charming interior touches and plenty of light.

Italian

Sette Bacco

Agüero 2157, y Peña, Recoleta (4808 0021). Subte D, Agüero/93, 152 bus. **Open** 12.30-4pm, 8.30pm-midnight Mon-Fri; 8pm-midnight Sat. **Main courses** AR$14-$28. **Credit** AmEx, MC, V. **Map** p326 K10 ❹
Tucked away on a quiet tree-lined street in Recoleta is one of the city's most romantic restaurants, Sette Bacco. Owner-chef Daniel Hansen's paean-to-the-motherland menu is a journey through Italy's regional specialities that features familiar risotto and pasta true to an Italian formula, but also provides for the more gastronomically curious – try the eye-rollingly good *centolla* (king crab) and pasta main course. Wines are reasonably priced too.

Pizza

El Cuartito

Talcahuano 937, y Marcelo T de Alvear, Barrio Norte (4816 1758). Subte D, Tribunales/Bus 152, 111. **Open** from noon daily. **Main courses** ARS$16-$40; portions from AR$2. **No credit cards.** **Map** p325 H10 ❹
This pizza joint dates from 1934 and is still one of the best in town. The walls are covered with ancient framed photos of everyone from the ubiquitous Diego Maradona to a host of local boxing greats. Grab a table under Bruno versus Tyson or stand at the pizza bar and sprinkle your slice with the sundry dried toppings to hand.

Piola Pizzerie Italiane

Libertad 1078, y Santa Fe, Recoleta (4812 0690/www.piola.it). Bus 39, 152. **Open** noon-2am Mon-Wed, Fri; noon-3am Thur, Sat, Sun. **Main courses** AR$25-$40. **Credit** AmEx, MC, V. **Map** p325 H11 ❹
With locations scattered across both the Americas, this Treviso-born Italian pizzeria chain has got gourmet pie-tossing down to a science: roll the dough to make the thinnest crust possible, top it with the likes of smoked salmon and ricotta or rocket, chicken, and parmesan shavings, then serve it in a slick space lit by coloured lanterns.

Spanish

Oviedo

Beruti 2602, y Ecuador, Barrio Norte (4822 5415). Subte D, Pueyrredón/12, 64, 152 bus. **Open** noon-3.30pm, 8pm-1am daily. **Main courses** AR$30-$65. *Set menu* AR$59-$75. **Credit** AmEx, DC, MC, V. **Map** p326 J10 ❹

Eat, Drink, Shop

Outstanding *alta cocina* from the motherland, taking the standards of the Iberian kitchen – sole, sea bass, cod – and a netful of freshly caught seafood. Beef, rabbit and lamb appear too, the latter dressed in traditional *setas* (wild mushrooms). The wine list is one of the best in the city.

Palermo & Palermo Viejo

Argentinian (traditional)

La Cabrera ♻

Cabrera 5099, y Thames (4831 7002). Bus 39, 55. **Open** 8pm-1am Mon; 12.30-4pm, from 8pm Tue-Sun. **Main courses** AR$22-$32. **Credit** AmEx, DC, MC, V. **Map** p323 M5 ㊹

Undoubtedly one of the most popular restaurants in Buenos Aires right now, La Cabrera is set in an attractive former general store. Professional staff serve extra-large portions of expertly prepared beef, grilled with a few sprigs of rosemary or sage. The steak-size *mollejas* (sweetbreads) are the best we have tasted in the city and easily justify the price. Don't order too much; half portions will be fine for even the hungriest, especially as 10-12 interesting side plates land on your table. Its sister restaurant, La Cabrera Norte, half a block away, has helped to cut waiting times a little, but reservation need to be made several days in advance.

La Cupertina

Cabrera 5296, y Godoy Cruz (4777 3711). Bus 39, 55. **Open** 11.30am-3.30pm, 8-11.30pm Tue-Sun. **Main courses** AR$12-$18. **No credit cards.** **Map** p323 M5 ㊺

When it comes to making empanadas and *locro*, most Argentinians will tell you that grandma is in a class of her own. Battling for second place is Tucumán-born Cecilian Hermann, owner and cook at La Cupertina, a corner restaurant with the look and feel of a snug farmhouse kitchen. The menu is familiar in the truest sense of the word but also includes dishes like *guiso de lentejas con chocolate* (lentil stew with chocolate) and *chivitos*, the Uruguayan take on the transport caff sandwich.

Club Eros

Uriarte 1609, y Honduras (4832 1313). Bus 39, 55, 111. **Open** from noon daily. **Main courses** AR$8-$14. **No credit cards.** **Map** p323 M5 ㊻

Unless you get sexually aroused by laconic waiters in shabby tuxedos serving up fried food in a setting redolent of a 1970s union soup kitchen, Club Eros only half lives up to its name (the dining room is an adjunct to various indoor sports facilities). So why is this *cantina* crammed full with greedy punters lunch and supper? It's the economy, stupid. For around AR$10 they'll bring you steak, chips and a brimming tumbler (cork fragments and all) of Vasco Viejo, Argentina's most popular plonk.

Don Julio ✳

Guatemala 4691, y Gurruchaga (48[...] 35, 55, 93, 111, 161. **Open** noon-4[...] daily. **Main courses** AR$22-$30. C[...] MC, V. **Map** p323 M6 ㊼

It's very reassuring to know that certain bastions of familiarity remain in this fast-changing barrio; trends come and go, but Don Julio remains standing on the corner of a cobbled street, doing what it's always done and doing it well. The owner, Pablo, is a stickler for good meat and service: the beef is carefully selected and waiters are put through their paces at local wine schools. The menu doesn't veer far from the usual *parrilla* staples, but the quality is a cut above the average. Add to that an exemplary wine list and you understand why regulars swear it's the best *parrilla* in town.

Minga

Costa Rica 4528, entre Armenia y Malabia (4833 5775). Bus 39. **Open** 10am-1am Mon-Thur, Sun; 10am-3am Fri, Sat. **Main courses** AR$18-$30. **Credit** AmEx, MC, V. **Map** p323 M5 ㊽

The beige, glass, and unfinished wood furnishings don't give away the fact that Minga is in fact a *parrilla*, albeit a gourmet one – your *bife de lomo* (tenderloin) isn't just plopped down in front of you, but is presented on an elegant cutting board with tiny saucers of *chimichurri* and garlic. *Papas fritas* are available, sure, but they're hard to justify when grilled pumpkin and buttery sweet potatoes baked in foil are on the menu. But *parrilla* purists need not back away: despite some exotic ingredients, Minga's Argentinian staples are traditional and good.

El Trapiche

Paraguay 5099, y Humbolt (4772 7343). Subte D, Palermo/29, 60, 111, 152 bus. **Open** noon-4pm, 8pm-1am Mon-Thur, Sun; 8pm-2am Fri, Sat. **Main courses** AR$20-$35. **Credit** AmEx, DC, MC, V. **Map** p323 N6 ㊾

Surrounded on all sides by fashionable food haunts, El Trapiche is unstintingly Argentinian and always full. The grilled meat is magnificent, from the fillet steaks to what is probably the best pork flank (*matambrito de cerdo*) in town. Mountainous desserts include the classic Don Pedro (whisky and ice-cream) and hot *sambayón*.

Argentinian (modern)

Almanza

Godoy Cruz y Charcas (4771 2285). Bus 39, 93, 152. **Open** 8pm-1am Mon; noon-4pm, 8pm-1am Tue-Sat; 10am-5pm Sun. **Main courses** AR$25-$50. **Credit** AmEx, V. **Map** p323 N6 ㊿

Almanza specialises in dishes from the End of the World, aka Tierra del Fuego, Argentina's southernmost province. Fish and shellfish are brought daily from Ushuaia (the capital of Tierra del Fuego) and turned into simple but stylish dishes by chef Martin Baquero. King crab served with garlicky aïoli and the mussel spaghetti are stand-out choices.

Eat, Drink, Shop

Wine: a bluffer's guide

You've got all the basics down. You can deftly navigate a menu in a restaurant, ordering your way through a selection of fusion appetisers and a classic *parrilla*. Maybe you have mastered the basic eight steps of tango. But put you in front of the wine list and it might as well be a stone tablet scratched out in Aramaic. We're here to help out with the translation...

New arrivals

Anyone staying here for more than a couple of weeks knows they're going to end up with guests. Toast the new arrivals with a bottle of Escorihuela Gascon 'Pequeños Producciones' Brut Rosé – one of the best sparkling wines to come out of Argentina, setting you back a pricey, but not ridiculous AR$100. If your budget is a little more modest, or they're not such good friends, order the more economic Codorniú 'María' Extra Brut (AR$35-$40) and let them be amazed at your taste.

The parrilla

We all know that BA is about steak, steak, and more steak. With all those perfectly grilled innards and a selection of steaks, ribs and chicken, you need a versatile food friendly wine, with plenty of complexity and life. For a great inexpensive choice, the relatively new Bodega Lariviere Yturbe's Cuatro Estaciones (AR$20), is a delicious blend of cabernet, merlot and malbec. To stretch the budget, snap your fingers for Luigi Bosca Gala I, a whopper of a blend with malbec, petite verdot and tannat just pushing over the AR$100 mark.

Fish gotta swim

After a week, or a month, of carne, you'll probably be ready to dine out on some sea denizens – head to one of the delightful Mediterranean-style fish eateries and start looking for a top flight white. You don't have to drink white with fish, but the Carlos Pulenta La Flor de Pulenta sauvignon blanc (AR$35-40) has such lovely styling it could be a classic Sancerre. For a splurge, the same *bodega* produces a rich Tomero semillón, a grape not often seen alone, but we're thrilled they've made it an exception.

In the pink

If you're sitting on the balcony or the terrace and want to show off a bit, order a rosé. Anyone can order white or red and nine times out of ten do well – but not everyone can pull off a pink with aplomb. Topping our list is the Alamos malbec Maceración Atenuado, a dark pink quaff that nearly drinks like a classic red on ice, but is just a bit lighter and with more than enough acidity to take the cold and attract attention of anyone passing by. More traditional, with a faint pink colour that some folks call 'partridge eye', boutique producer Jose L Mounier has a malbec and cabernet blend called Finca Las Nubes that'll knock your socks off. Both around AR$40.

The club classic

Hey, you're in Argentina, you're supposed to drink malbec, right? But nobody says you're stuck with the usual suspects. Surprise everyone by diving into the lesser known sections of the list and ordering up something offbeat like the oddly named Bodega A Belgrano 10.640 – and don't forget to point out it is both organically certified and only cost you AR$20. If you're ready to spend a little more, plonk down around AR$150 and demand a bottle of the hard to find and elegant Valle Las Asequias 'Rosedal' from Luis Segundo Correas and if they don't have it, demand to know why.

Bar 6

Armenia 1676, entre El Salvador y Honduras (4833 6807). Bus 15, 39, 151, 168. **Open** from 8am Mon-Sat. **Main courses** AR$15-$29. *Set menu* (lunch only) AR$18. **Credit** AmEx, MC, V. **Map** p323 M5 🟠
Smartly designed, centrally located, and almost always packed with people, including the occasional celebrity, Bar 6 just keeps getting hotter. If you're able to acquire both a table and a waitress who'll notice your existence, then you're free to savour the cool Scandinavian interior, mood lighting and dark velvet couches. The fusion menu offers reliable crowd-pleasers like vegetable wok, coriander and chilli *quesadillas*, and more exotic fare like coconut vermicelli with clams and cuttlefish.

Bar Uriarte

Uriarte 1572, entre Honduras y Gorriti (4834 6004/www.baruriarte.com.ar). Bus 39, 55, 111, 166. **Open** noon-2.30am daily. **Main courses** AR$30-$40. **Credit** AmEx, DC, MC, V. **Map** p323 M5 🟠
These guys, it appears, can do no wrong. After the endlessly popular Belgrano restaurant Sucre and the wine bar Gran Bar Danzón, Bar Uriarte has the same modern industrial aesthetic, and is sort of the slinky, sexy sibling. Your senses are immediately drawn to the open kitchen that turns out food that could simply be termed classic. Superb pizzas come right out of that oven, there is great home-made *ñoqui* and perfectly cooked sweetbreads hot off the grill. **Photo** *p151.*

Bo Bo Restaurant

Guatemala 4882, entre Borges y Thames (4774 0505/www.bobohotel.com). Subte D, Plaza Italia/34, 55, 93, 161 bus. **Open** 8am-1am daily. **Main courses** AR$32-$40. **Credit** AmEx, MC, V. **Map** p323 M6 🟠
The menu speaks for itself really: carrot and thyme risotto with marinated rabbit; ribeye steak with red chorizo and corn cake and *criollo* sauce. Chef Adrián Sarkissian has taken Mediterranean elements and given them a wholly Argentinian flavour, using indigenous vegetables and herbs. The food looks gorgeous on the plate, but tastes even better in the mouth. The grand finale is a dessert cocktail. Try BoBo Cream, a heady mix of ice-cream, Baileys, strawberry liqueur and coulis of forest fruits.

Casa Cruz ✱ ? LAST NIGHT

Uriarte 1658, entre El Salvador y Honduras (4833 1112/www.casa-cruz.com). Bus 33, 55, 111. **Open** from 8.30pm Mon-Sat. **Main courses** AR$32-$55. **Credit** AmEx, MC, V. **Map** p323 M5 🟠
Forget Narnia and Turkish delight. For BA's most otherworldly dining experience, pass through a pair of 16ft brass doors and enter the magical land of Casa Cruz, the most daring and imaginative restaurant venture to hit the city since...well, ever. Glide (no walking – this is a classy joint) through to the spot-lit, redwood-panelled dining area then order what head chef Germán Martitegui calls 'modern urban Argentinian' cuisine.

Glide in to the very sexy **Casa Cruz.**

Cluny

*El Salvador 4618/22, entre Malabia y Armenia
(4831 7176/www.cluny.com.ar). Bus 15, 39, 55.*
Open 11am-2am Mon-Sat. **Main courses** AR$30-
$45. **Credit** AmEx, DC, MC, V. **Map** p323 M5 ⑮
Named after the Cluny Museum in Paris, Cluny is a
paean to the museum's star exhibit, the famed Lady
with Unicorn tapestries that celebrate six senses –
taste, smell, touch, sight, hearing and
understanding. With that goal in mind, you might
think you were in for some sort of overwhelming
temple of haute cuisine; instead, this a fashionable,
relaxed spot, with a kitchen that turns out simple
ideas with delicious touches – a spectacular salmon
tartare with delicate fresh herbs or a veal risotto
tinged with mushrooms and flavoured oil.

Crizia

*Gorriti 5143, entre Thames y Uriarte (4831
4979/www.crizia.com.ar). Bus 34, 55.* **Open** 7pm-
1am Tue-Sat; from 12.30pm Sun. **Main courses**
AR$26-$43. **Credit** AmEx, MC, V. **Map** p323 M5 ⑯
After three successful years in the Microcentro,
Crizia has uprooted and headed north to a larger
Palermo Soho location. Head chef Gabriel Oggero
will continue with his respected modern Argentinian
menu using fresh ingredients such as king crab. The
winelist too is equally comprehensive.

Dominga

*Honduras 5618, entre Bonpland y Fitz Roy (4771
4443/www.domingarestaurant.com). Bus 39, 93,
111.* **Open** 12.30-3.30pm, 8.30pm-1am Mon-Sat.
Main courses AR$25-$36. **Credit** AmEx, MC, V.
Map p323 N5 ⑰
Relaxed and intimate, the oriental influenced decor
of Dominga sets the perfect scene for a meal with
friends or an intimate date. Choose from either

expertly made sushi or well-presented modern
Argentinian dishes, including gnocchi and grilled
entraña. The star dessert is the baked torta de
chocolate – a delectable explosion of richness.

Freud y Fahler

*Gurruchaga 1750, entre El Salvador y Costa Rica
(4833 4306). Bus 39, 55.* **Open** noon-3.30pm,
8.30pm-midnight Mon-Fri; 12.30-4pm, 8.30pm-1am
Sat. **Main courses** AR$22-$60. **Credit** AmEx, MC,
V. **Map** p323 M5 ⑱
Portion sizes can be a tad 'nouvelle', and in some
dishes originality outstrips execution, but both the
traditional fare – fish, chicken, meat, pastas – and
the occasional excursions into exotica such as
Patagonian pheasant and quail are prepared with
care. Mediterranean ideas abound, especially in the
soups and pâtés.

Social Paraiso

*Honduras 5182, entre Thames y Uriarte (4831
4556). Bus 39, 55.* **Open** 12.30-3.30pm, 8.30pm-
midnight Tue-Sat; 12.30-4pm Sun. **Main courses**
AR$26-$40. **Credit** AmEx, V. **Map** p323 M5 ⑲
Youngsters and seniors, new world and old, all mix
in this sober, but attractive, high-ceilinged bistro
that helped pioneer the Palermo Viejo gourmet
explosion. Chef-owner Federico Simoes was raised
on Syrian-Lebanese cuisine and his changing menu
reflects his polyglot roots.

Standard

*Fitz Roy 2203, y Guatemala (4779 2774). Bus 39, 93,
161.* **Open** from 8pm Mon-Fri; noon-4pm, 8pm-1am
Sat. **Main courses** AR$28-$40. **Credit** AmEx, V.
Map p323 N6 ⑳
Standard is anything but. This is a thrilling
throwback, a painstakingly realised re-creation of a
typical 1950s diner, with tall windows and mirrors,

Eat, Drink, Shop

Cluny.

Foodies flock to **Standard**. *See p147.*

starched white table linen and slatted wall panels. The menu, too, harks back to old-school dinners, offering *porteño* favourites like *milanesa napolitana* (veal fried in breadcrumbs, topped with ham and melted cheese) and *raviolis de seso y espinaca* (raviolis of calves brain and spinach). Standard has style but without pretension; these are old-fashioned pleasures reinvented for a fashion-conscious crowd.

Brazilian

Maria Fulô
Cabrera 5065, entre Serrano y Thames (4831 0103/www.mariafuloresto.com.ar). Bus 39, 55. **Open** from 8pm Tue-Fri; from noon Sat, Sun. **Main courses** AR$30-$45. **Credit** AmEx, MC, V. **Map** p323 M5 ⑥①
No sweat, no samba, no 'Girl from Ipanema' – if you're not in the mood to party but want to sample authentic Brazilian cuisine, urbane Maria Fulô fits the bill. Each dish is a carnaval of flavours: fish, fruit and nuts combined with patriotic expertise by Sao Paulo chef Eduardo Pinheiro. Try a classic *moqueca* (stew) of sea bass and coconut, or the *feijoada* of black beans, meat and rice; a lively take on a classic.

Eastern European

La Casa Polaca
Jorge Luis Borges 2076, entre Soler y Guatemala (4899 0514/www.casapolaca.com.ar). Subte D, Plaza Italia/15, 39 bus. **Open** 8pm-12.30am Tue-Sat. **Closed** Jan. **Main courses** AR$18-$25. **Credit** AmEx, DC, MC, V. **Map** p323 M6 ⑥②
This basement restaurant in the Dom Polski cultural centre for Polish immigrants is poles apart from anything else in Palermo Viejo, but don't let the crusty decor put you off. Ultra-friendly, wildly camp chef Antos Yaskowiak and his trusty staff serve delicious rollmops, stews and goulash, each course punctuated by a sharp vodka and informative chat.

French Creole

Azema Exotic Bistró
Angel Carranza 1875, entre Costa Rica y El Salvador (4774 4191). Bus 39, 93, 111, 161. **Open** from 7.30pm Mon-Sat. **Main courses** AR$23-$36. **Credit** AmEx, DC, MC, V. **Map** p323 O5 ⑥③
Paul Jean Azema spent 15 years wandering around the Far East, and another ten saving up the cash, to open his own restaurant, but once he did it was an overnight success. His presence is apparent all over the restaurant, but it's in the kitchen that he is most appreciated, dressing up and dishing out great plates such as South Pacific rack of ribs, carpaccio of salmon with sake, *ceviche* marinated in lime and coriander, and *masala de cordero* (lamb curry). The white chocolate 'soup' with raspberries is a winning way to round things off. Azema is effortlessly fashionable and highly recommended.

Italian

Guido's Bar   MISS MARPLES

*República de la India 2843, entre Cabello y Gutiérrez
(4802 2391). Subte D, Plaza Italia/29, 39, 152 bus.*
Open from 11am Mon-Fri; 9am-3pm Sat. **Main
courses** AR$60-$80 set lunch. **No credit cards.**
Map p327 M10 ➓

This pea-sized trattoria is the kind of place one
always looks for but rarely finds in Italy. With every
inch of the letterbox-red walls plastered in movie
poster kitsch, featuring real Italians (Mastroanni and
Caruso) alongside honorary ones (John Lennon and
Sammy Davis Jr), Guido's is as much an evocation of
an era as it is a culture. But there's nothing tongue-
in-cheek about owner Carlos's passion for Italian food.

I Due Ladroni

*Fitz Roy 1955, entre Costa Rica y Nicaragua (4899
4060/www.idueladroni.com). Bus 39, 93, 161.* **Open**
from 8.30pm Tue-Sat. **Main courses** AR$40-$60.
Credit AmEx, MC, V. **Map** p323 N5 ➓

This is the place to recapture the wonderful simplicity of Italian food. The atmosphere is traditional: red and white check tablecloths, black and white
photos of Bergman's film stars and bits and bobs
any self-respecting Italian around the world should
have. And even though the open kitchen turns out
well-executed beef, chicken and fish dishes, the
pasta – imported from mother Italy – is, of course,
the reason this restaurant is always packed. Dried,
fresh or filled is the easy choice followed by the
trickier decision of which salsa. If we can help, the
two-meat bolognese is unforgettable, as is the mushroom sauce, especially mopped up with their bread.

Lucky Luciano   MISS MARPLES

*Cerviño 3943, entre República de la India y Lafinur
(4802 1262). Subte D, Plaza Italia/29, 39, 152, 188
bus.* **Open** from 8.30pm Mon-Sat. **Main courses**
AR$18-$35. **Credit** AmEx, MC, V. **Map** p327 M10 ➓

One of the reasons the Sosto brothers originally
opened Lucky Luciano's was to pick up the overflow
from dad Carlos's place (Guido's; see above) around
the corner, but they have since managed to stamp
this warm, busily decorated place with a distinctive
identity. The classy Italian menu majors in perfectly
executed pasta and pizza, but it's the sprinkling of
well-judged innovative details that really set
Lucky's apart from the pack: think *pain brioche* with
parmesan ice-cream and portobello mushrooms;
fantastically creamy *ravioles de humita* (corn ravioli)
with a sprinkling of smoked salmon; or *bife de
chorizo* a la pimienta with a watercress and lavender
salad. Linger over a super-moist chocolate and nut
cake with *torroncino* ice-cream and, with the help of
a bottle from the well selected wine list and the
award-winning cocktail maker, you could find
yourself lying horizontal by coffee time.

Japanese

Dashi

*Fitz Roy 1613, y Gorriti (4776 3500/www.dashi.com.
ar). Bus 93, 111.* **Open** 12.30-3pm, 8pm-12.30am
Mon-Fri; 8pm-1am Sat. **Main courses** AR$32-$50.
Credit AmEx, DC, MC, V. **Map** p323 N5 ➓

Sashimi and sushi plus sleek decor isn't an original
formula, especially in a city where Japanese fusion
restaurants are multiplying by the minute. Dashi
remains at the top of the heap, though, thanks to
Jorge, the charismatic world traveller who runs the
show. The sophisticated, light-filled interior is a
backdrop for superb sushi rolls crafted from red
porgy, octopus, and of course, salmon. The fine
dining comes at a comparatively hefty price, but
with a hands-on cooking school, Dashi is helping the
Japanese treats go down easily.

Other locations Salguero 2643, Palermo (4805
5575); Aguilar 2395, Palermo (4782 2666/3666);
Arribeños 2308, Belgrano (4783 1070).

Little Rose

*First floor, Armenia 1672, entre Honduras y El
Salvador (4833 9496). Bus 39, 93, 55, 168.* **Open**
12.30-4pm, 8.30pm-12.30am Mon-Sat. **Main courses**
AR$25-$42. **No credit cards. Map** p323 M5 ➓

It's a sushi restaurant, Jim, but not as we know it.
The space is decked out like a Transylvanian
gentlemans' club – lampshades, walls and plaster in
raven black and stylised photographs of deathly-
pale pre-pubescent blonde girls in pre-Raphaelite
garb. The sushi and tempura are both of a high

Modern Italian at **Lucky Luciano.**

Bar Uriarte. *See p145.*

standard, eschewing the tedious (but common to BA) 'a-thousand-ways-with-salmon' philosophy and instead offering a wide range of fresh fish.

Middle Eastern

El Manto
Costa Rica 5801, y Carranza (4774 2409/www. elmanto.com). Bus 34, 55, 93, 111. **Open** noon-1.30am daily **Main courses** AR$26-$35. **Credit** AmEx, DC, MC, V. **Map** p323 O5 ❻❾
Putting the chic into sheek kebabs, El Manto is easily the smartest and arguably the best Armenian restaurant in Buenos Aires. The interior is modelled on a typical Armenian convent from the year AD 301; think candles throwing shadows on terracotta walls and mock-Byzantine arches. As for the food, you'll find all your favourites, creatively crafted – houmous, kibbe, kefte, kebabs, pilaf, tabouleh and many more. El Manto claims to use traditional recipes that go back to before all the modern shortcuts and substitute ingredients came into play. The food is definitely different and better presented than your average Armenian joint. If it's sunny outside take your mezze or *kebab de cordero* (lamb) is out onto the terrace.

Bereber
Armenia 1880, entre Nicaragua y Costa Rica (4833 5662). Bus 39, 55. **Open** 12.30-4pm, from 8,30pm Mon-Thur, Sun; from 8.30pm Fri, Sat. **Main courses** AR$20-$35. **Credit** AmEx, DC, MC, V. **Map** p323 M6 ❼❶

The restaurant's location bang on Plaza Palermo Viejo and its modern North African cuisine make Bereber an ideal spot to line your stomach before hitting the bars. Besides a full range of fluffy couscous options with vegetable broth and fiery hot, traditional harissa chilli paste served on the side, there's a rich olive and chicken tagine, a sweet and savoury layered pastella, and lots of fresh *lavash* flatbread to keep you happily munching.

Peruvian

Ceviche
Costa Rica 5644, entre Bonpland y Fitz Roy (4776 7373). Bus 34, 55, 93, 111. **Open** noon-3pm, 8pm-1am Mon-Sat. **Main courses** AR$30-$40. **Credit** AmEx, MC, V. **Map** p323 N5 ❼❶
Although definitely not Argentinian, ceviche has got to be at the top of every traveller's 'to eat' list in BA. After all, it is the new sushi, you know. Perhaps out of homage to its succulence, Ceviche restaurant has adopted the name and mastered the art of preparing this emblematic Peruvian dish – raw fish 'cooked' in citrus juice. Polite waiters will direct you to other splendid Peruvian classics and excellent wines.

Peruvian-Japanese

Osaka
Soler 5608, y Fitz Roy (4775 6964/www.osaka. com.pe). Bus 21, 111, 161. **Open** 12.30-4pm, 8pm-1am Mon-Sat. **Main courses** AR$30-$45. **No credit cards. Map** p323 N5 ❼❷

Eat, Drink, Shop

The sweeter things in life

A product of Italian, Spanish, French, African, Arabic and indigenous influences, Argentinian desserts, like many Argentinians themselves, take sweetness to the extreme. The ubiquitous *dulce de leche* (milk caramel 'jam') stars in everything from cakes and ice-cream to bonbons, pastries, and crêpes. Although historical accounts, erm, differ, most *porteños* insist that the sugar-rich spread was invented in Argentina, when the poor maid of (the not very sweet) General Juan Manuel de Rosas, forgot a pot of sweetened milk on the stove and returned to discover it caramelised. Argue with this legend at your own risk.

Besides dulce de leche, meringue, *frutas en almíbar* (fruit in syrup) and ice-cream figure prominently in the Argentinian dessert repertoire, along with chocolate; however, since much of Latin America's best chocolate never makes it to Buenos Aires, many chocolate-based desserts might disappoint die-hard chocoholics.

Chocolate aside, if you're looking to journey into the sweet soul of Buenos Aires, the *panqueque de dulce de leche* (caramel-stuffed crêpe) is an excellent starting point. A fixture on most menus, the flambéed pancake often comes with bananas, berries or chocolate sauce. Sample it in its pure form at **Bendito** (Humboldt 1962, Villa Crespo, 4776 8732), a traditional-chic restaurant featuring a clay oven and a lovely outdoor terrace.

Another riff on the *dulce de leche* theme, the *torta rogel* (a cake with layers of crispy dough, *dulce de leche* and soft meringue), is sweet classic. Also known as mil *hojas de dulce de leche* – literally, a thousand layers of dulce de leche, the *rogel* supposedly originated in the province of Santa Fe, where industrial production of a cookie of a similar style began in 1853. **Como en Casa** (Laprida 1782, Recoleta, 4829 0624 and Céspedes 2647, Belgrano, 4788 2988), an upscale bakery-café that offers a heart-clogging range of cakes and *tortas*, makes an outstanding version of the *rogel*.

Popular since the mid-19th century (and now found all over the southern cone), *alfajores* (round biscuits sandwiched around a layer of *dulce de leche* or jam) arrived in Argentina via Spain by way of the Moors – the name *alfajor* comes from the Arabic for 'stuffed' or 'filled'. An extension of the national obsession with *dulce de leche*, ordinary *alfajores* are readily available at kioscos and supermarkets. For an extraordinary example, go to **Florencio** (*see p171*) or **Panadería Santa Teresa** (Arévalo 2882, Las Cañitas, 4777 3740).

Yet another vehicle for *dulce de leche*, for a change, *flan* or *flan casero* (homemade flan) plays a leading role in the *porteño* afters ensemble. Numerous restaurants, most notably the Italian-Argentinian **cantina Don Chicho** (*see p163*), serve a vanilla-based version of this custard-like confection with the option of, you've guessed it, *dulce de leche* or whipped cream on top.

Thanks to Italian immigrants who brought their gelato-making expertise to this side of the Atlantic in the mid-1800s, the local passion for *helado* (ice-cream) runs deep and wide. With flavours like *crema armenia* with figs and anise, *crema de canela* with cinnamon, and *coco quemado* (toasted coconut), **Scannapieco** (Córdoba 4826, Villa Crespo, 4773 1829) presents a good neighbourhood alternative.

On a quest for a traditional confection – but in need of a break from *dulce de leche*? Try the savoury-sweet *queso y dulce* (soft cheese paired with quince or sweet potato paste) after a good slice of pizza at **El Cuartito** (see p141). Not only was queso y dulce rumoured to be the preferred after-dinner treat of Jorge Luis Borges, it's also the official treat of Argentinian truck drivers and policemen who refer to it as *postre del vigilante* – the vigilante's pudding.

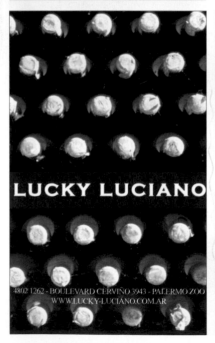

After hitting it big in Lima, the chain established residence in BA in 2005, and the expert kitchen staff has been winning *porteño* admirers ever since, with a fusion menu featuring truly eclectic creations like duck confit-stuffed samosas and deep-fried Peruvian-style fish in Japanese mushroom sauce. There is an ample wine list – though who wants an glass of torrontés when you could be sipping an exotic cocktail like the Thai Chi (a heady blend of sake, orange, cranberry, and cinnamon).

Patagonian

Divina Patagonia

Honduras 5710, y Bonpland (4771 6864/www.divina patagonia.com). Bus 39, 93. **Open** from 6pm Mon-Sat. **Main courses** AR$22-$35. **Credit** AmEx, MC, V. **Map** p323 N5 ⓻

Argentina's south is the source of many of the country's best ingredients, among them the rightly famed *cordero* (lamb), *centolla* (king crab), and all kinds of game and wild fruit and veg. All of this is on the menu at Divina Patagonia as main courses (for example, wild boar in a raspberry sauce) or tablas (platters) to mix and match. **Other location** Balcarce 958, San Telmo (4300 6454).

Scandinavian

Olsen

Gorriti 5870, entre Carranza y Ravignani (4776 7677). Bus 39, 93, 111. **Open** noon-1.30am Tue-Sat; from 10am Sun. **Main courses** AR$25-$42. *Sunday brunch* AR$21-$45. *Set lunch menu* AR$26. **Credit** AmEx, MC, V. **Map** p323 O5 ⓻

Some quandaries are more enjoyable than others. For example, how do you choose between 50 brands of vodka? Tackle this and other conundra at Olsen, German Martigui's hugely popular Scandinavian bar-restaurant where the atmosphere is as chilled as the drinks. It's hard to say which stands out more – the wooden sculptures and verdant garden or the fried oysters and wooden platters of exotic starter combos, which go down great with a sampler of ice-cold vodka and aquavit shots. Sunday brunch is the perfect way to wind down from an extended Saturday night. **Photo** *p156.*

Pizza

Angelín

Avenida Córdoba 5270, entre Godoy Cruz y Uriarte (4774 3836). Bus 34, 55, 140, 142, 151, 188. **Open** 8pm-midnight daily. **Main courses** AR$9-$30. **No credit cards.** **Map** p323 M4 ⓻

Eat, Drink, Shop

Chopsticks at the ready at **Moshi Moshi**. *See p157.*

A tiny pizza joint with a big reputation, in part thanks to the endorsement of actor and occasional BA resident Robert Duvall. Hollywood connections aside, this has been a barrio favourite since 1938, and the locals propping up the L-shaped counter look like they wouldn't bat an eyelid if Elvis dropped in. For the true pizza *al paso* (pizza on the go) experience, order a slice of *fugazzeta con queso* (cheese and onion stuffed crust pizza) with a shot of *cidra* (cider) and slouch around the front parlour.

South-east Asian

Green Bamboo
Costa Rica 5802, y Carranza (4775 7050). Bus 93, 111. **Open** 8.30pm-2.30am daily. **Main courses** AR$25-$35. **Credit** AmEx, MC, V. **Map** p323 O5 ⓻
It could easily be said that Vietnamese culture offers up a fascinating contrast between resonance and dissonance. The food: some of the most harmonious of the Asian cuisines, with a unique balance between sweetness, saltiness, sourness and spiciness. Green Bamboo offers up some of the best fried calamari you'll ever have – tentacles, not rings – with a trio of dipping sauces, a great five-spice pork, orange lacquered chicken and spot-on curries.

Sudestada
Guatemala 5602, y Fitz Roy (4776 3777). Bus 15, 55, 111. **Open** noon-3.30pm, 8pm-midnight Mon-Sat.

Olsen. *See p155.*

Main courses AR$24-$35 *Set menu* (lunch only) AR$23. **Credit** AmEx, V. **Map** p323 N6 ⓻
Don't be fooled by the cool and minimalist decor – Sudestada's dishes are hot enough to set your palate dancing. The food arrives brimming with ingredients and flavours that Vietnamese chef Tien Duic has drawn from Laos, Thailand, Burma and his homeland, like the unmissable *nem cua* (spicy minced crab and pork wrapped in lettuce) and the superb yellow curry of fresh fish and mussels. There's freshly squeezed lemonade, and for spice-phobes can choose from some of the milder menu options. Owners have recently repeated this success with a new branch... in Madrid.

Vegetarian

Artemisia
Cabrera 3877, entre F Acuña de Figueroa y Medrano (4863 4242/www.artemisiaresto.com.ar). Bus 36, 92, 106. **Open** from 8.30pm Tue-Sat. **Main courses** AR$14-$23. **No credit cards.** **Map** p326 K7 ⓻
With glass bottles of icy freshly squeezed lemonade on every table and soft olive loaves baking in the oven, Artemisia feels less like a popular Palermo dinner spot than a warm country kitchen. Proprietors Carolina Guryn and her husband Gabriel Gómez are hardly flipping buckwheat pancakes, but they embody the same earthy chic that characterises the restaurant's ambience and cuisine. The innovative organic menu includes polenta bruschetta topped with tomatoes and coriander, pear and rocket focaccia, and broccoli-laden mini-pizzas to more substantial home-made pastas, vegetable wok dishes, and tender pink salmon.

Bio
Humboldt 2199, y Guatemala (4774 3880/ www.biorestaurant.com.ar). Subte D, Palermo/93, 111 bus. **Open** 10.30am-5pm Mon; 10.30am-1am Tue-Sun. **Main courses** AR$18-$25. **Credit** AmEx, MC, V. **Map** p323 N6 ⓻
The menu of this utterly organic gourmet corner bistro reflects what is seasonally available. Vegetable tempura, goat's cheese and tomato couscous, and mushroom-topped bruschetta are just a few specialities of the house in summer, while in winter pumpkins are carved open and filled with sweetcorn stew. Vegetable juices and refreshing ginger lemonade are available throughout the year. Predictably great salads too.

Las Cañitas

Argentinian (traditional)

El Portugués
Báez 499, y Ortega (4771 8699). Bus 15, 29, 60, 64. **Open** 11am-4pm, from 7.30pm daily. **Main courses** AR$16-$26. **No credit cards.** **Map** p327 O9 ⓼

The new sushi?

It has been claimed that *ceviche* will be the new sushi. It's a bold declaration. But if the number of eateries serving up the Peruvian marinated fish dish in Buenos Aires counts for anything, and maybe it does, they might even be right.

The proliferation of Peruvian cuisine in the capital, in even the last year, has been an unexpected delight. Heck, on one week in late 2007, two upmarket *ceviche* restaurants opened on the same day, **Sipan** (*see p132*) and one that was actually called **Ceviche** (*see p151*). There are dozens of bargain outlets too, serving up cheap and tasty *ceviche* such as **Status** (*see p132*) and **Chan Chan** (*see p131*) not to mention all the trendsetting bars swiftly adding also adding *ceviche* to their menus.

So what is this dish that is poised to sweep the world in a whiff of fish, onion and chilli? At its simplest it is raw fish – usually sole, sea bass, or *toyo* (a small shark), but occasionally salmon – marinated or 'cooked' in citrus juices, usually limes or lemons, unlike Japanese sashimi which does not undergo this process. It is usually mixed with red onion and hot red chillies and served with corn-on-the-cob, sweet potato and white potatoes in a spicy sauce.

Occasionally they will give you a shot of the citric marinade called *leche de tigre* as an appetiser, if you are lucky, or unlucky depending on your taste. There are many endearing stories about the humble origins of this dish. Hernán Brennan, head chef of Sipan and Peru native, explained one of them. 'One anecdote is that a fisherman

was swept way out to sea in his little boat for several weeks. All he had on board was lemons, and he discovered he could preserve the fish with lemon juice. On his return, the idea took off.' The etymology of the word is also fascinating. One theory is that it came from the Quechua word *siwichi* or from the Spanish word *escabeche* meaning marinade. Whatever it's origins, one thng is certain: in Buenos Aires, *ceviche* is growing in popularity. And what's more, just like sushi became a blanket phrase used to describe all Japanese cuisine, *ceviche* too has turned into an all-encompassing, and equally inaccurate way to describe the amazing variety of Peruvian cuisine.

Before new cuisines hit Las Cañitas, Señor Merinho and family were well established as hosts of the barrio beefery. It might seem odd for the Portuguese to take on Argentina in the steak stakes, but this is a very popular *parrilla*, with two floors jammed with a noisy mix of families, television divas and the just plain hungry. Portions are enormous.

is a thriving, self-styled North American bistro that is bustling, smart and intimate enough for a candlelit smooch, all at the same time. The menu is modern Argentinian, with great peppered steaks, say, or booze-soaked sweetbreads. Its main strength lies in the simplicity of its menu, which transcends *parrilla* fare without being too exotic. Pastas here are also highly recommended. **Photo** *p159*.

Argentinian (modern)

Novecento

Báez 199, y Argüibel (4778 1900). Bus 5, 29, 59, 60, 64. **Open** 10am-12.30am Mon-Sat; 12.30pm-1.30am Sun. **Main courses** AR$18-$34. **Credit** AmEx, DC, MC, V. **Map** p327 O9 ③①
The flagship restaurant of a chain that has branches in Manhattan, Miami and Punta del Este, Novecento

Japanese

Moshi Moshi

First floor, Ortega y Gasset 1707, y Soldado de la Independencia (4772 2005/www.moshi-moshi.com.ar). Bus 29, 60, 64. **Open** from 8pm Tue-Sun. **Main courses** AR$24-$37. **Credit** AmEx, MC, V. **Map** p327 O9 ③②

Eat, Drink, Shop

DINNER CLUB

Not just a way to answer the phone, but an answer to your sushi craving. The high-standard sushi served here is a hit with the manicured Las Cañitas crowd and tourists alike. Practise your chopstick skills with beautifully presented sushi rolls and oriental dumplings, or throw them away and focus on the fancy finger foods, like the ebi no somen, an artistic combination of shrimp wrapped in fried noodles. The service matches the food's quality, yet perhaps the restaurant's best feature is the sake bar with smooth and strong cocktails. Try the yukata, a sake cocktail made with orange juice, berries and aniseed – it's sweet and silky, a geisha in a glass. **Photo** *p155.*

Vegetarian

Providencia
Cabrera 5995, y Arévalo (4772 8507). Bus 39, 93, 111, 161. **Open** noon-4pm Mon-Fri; noon-4pm Sat. **Main courses** AR$15-$20. **No credit cards.** **Map** p323 O4 ❸
Providencia is all about feeding people nourishing home-cooked food. The well-balanced plates are based around whole grains – Providencia is twinned with a bakery: Siete Panes, that makes wonderful chewy and seedy homemade bread, seven styles in fact. Indian stew, creamy pasta sauces and a divine apple, ginger and grape chutney.

Abasto & Caballito

Argentinian (modern)

Urondo Bar
Beauchef 1204, y Estrada, Parque Chacabuco (4922 9671/www.urondobar.com.ar). Subte E, Moreno/25, 126, 135 bus. **Open** 8pm-1am Tue-Sat. **Main courses** AR$18-$36. **No credit cards.**
Named for Francisco 'Paco' Urondo, one of Argentina's radical poets of the late 1960s and early 1970s before he tragically became one of the 'disappeared', this cosy corner spot is run by his grandson Javier and nephew Sebastián. The former turns out amazingly creative dishes that are a fusion of classic Argentinian with intense South-east Asian influences. Plate after plate delights the senses with unusual spices in incredible harmony. When they have it, the asparagus tart can't be beaten, and the *ossobuco* (veal) risotto with *gremolata* (garlic, parsley and lemon sauce) is out of this world.

Italian

Cantina Pierino
Lavalle 3499, y Billinghurst, Abasto (4864 5715). Subte B, Carlos Gardel/24, 26, 168 bus. **Open** 8pm-2am daily. **Main courses** AR$18-$30. **Credit** AmEx, V. **Map** p326 J8 ❸
Way off the tourist track, Pierino has been serving authentic Italian food since 1907. Tango

legends Astor Piazzolla and Aníbal Troilo (*see p30*) were regulars in the 1960s. Pedro, grandson of the original owners, is liable to suggest what he regards as best for you. Don't stress: the tasty starters – *fritata* (mozzarella tortillas) and *chiambotta* (baked aubergine with onion, courgettes and mushrooms) – and home-made pasta dishes lend credence to his telepathic skills.

Almagro, Once & Villa Crespo

Argentinian (traditional)

Cantina Los Amigos
Loyola 701, entre Malabia y Acevedo, Villa Crespo (4777 0402). Bus 55, 106, 109. **Open** from 7.30pm Mon; 12.30-3.30pm, from 7.30pm Tue-Sat; 12.30pm-4pm Sun. **Main courses** AR$15-$30. **Credit** V. **Map** p323 M4 ❻
Thrumming with that late-night good-time vibe for which Buenos Aires is famed, Cantina Los Amigos is a cracker of a traditional *porteño* eaterie. Packed every night with local families, TV stars, footballers, the dining area is decked out with football posters, tango tat and the odd stain from a stray meatball. Let the cocky waiters bring you a selection of starters and then go for one of the pasta specials or whatever's sizzling on the grill. If ever a restaurant could kick the blues it's this one.

Fabulous fare at **Novecento.** *See p157.*

Argentinian (modern)

Thymus
*Lerma 525, entre Malabia y Acevedo, Villa Crespo
(4772 1936). Bus 55, 106, 110.* **Open** 8.30pm-
12.30am Mon-Sat. **Main courses** AR$22-$38.
Credit AmEx, MC, V. **Map** p323 M4

As romantic as it is aromatic, Thymus deserves all
the rave reviews it gets from discriminating local
gourmets. Sculptor Martín Vegara's skilful copies of
classical antiquities decorate his former house and
studio, converted into a restaurant made for all five
senses. Chef Fernando Mayoral, who trained with
French masterchef Michel Bras, uses fresh garnishes
of rosemary, thyme and pineapple mint from a
rooftop garden to flavour fusion dishes like grilled
loin of pork in an orange mustard glaze served with
spicy pancakes and pak-choi, or Patagonian trout
with orange, green peppers and creamed potatoes.
If it is warm make sure you book a table on the patio,
or better on the terrace, and enjoy wafts of herbs and
wine from the 70-strong wine list.

Art and truly fine food at **Thymus**.

Middle Eastern

Sarkis
*Thames 1101, entre Jufré y Lerma, Villa Crespo
(4772 4911). Bus 34, 55, 106, 109, 168.* **Open**
noon-3pm, from 8pm daily. **Main courses** AR$10-
$20. **No credit cards**. **Map** p323 M4

The fluorescent-lit atmosphere is wanting and the
Monday night belly rippler could be your grandma,
but Sarkis's authentic Levantine cuisine means it's
packed at weekends (be prepared to wait unless you
turn up early). Choose tasty dips, snacks, soufflés,
raw mince and kebabs, or ask for a miscellany of
biggish starters and a couple of mains. A fun place
which is especially as the bill is often almost
embarrassingly cheap.

South-east Asian

Bi Won
*Junín 548, Once (4372 1146). Subte B, Pasteur or D,
Facultad de Medicina/24, 26, 60, 124 bus.* **Open**
noon-3pm, 7pm-midnight Mon-Sat. **Main courses**
AR$18-$28. **No credit cards**. **Map** p325 H9

Ignore the Korean tourist board posters and hammy
backing track at this authentic community restaurant down a dark Once street, because the food
is delightful and inexpensive. Two should share,
since meals come with eight tasty side dishes
including turnip, anchovies, corn, seaweed, spinach,
kimchi , cucumber and beans, most of them doused
in chilli and garlic.

Belgrano & Colegiales

Argentinian (traditional)

El Pobre Luis
*Arribeños 2393, y Blanco Encalada, Belgrano (4780
5847). Bus 29, 60,64, 113, 130.* **Open** from 8pm
Mon-Sat. **Main courses** AR$16-$24. **Credit** AmEx,
MC, V. **Map** p329 S9

Football and dining legend Diego Maradona cites this
as one of his favourite BA restaurants; the shirt of 'El
Diez' hangs on one of the walls. But it's meat, not
memorabilia, that maketh the *parrilla* and the steaks
here are in the premier league. Charismatic, ever-
present owner Luis Acuña is Uruguayan, so you'll
find novelties from over the River Plate like *pamplona
de cerdo* (pork flank stuffed with cheese and peppers)
on the menu. Offal lovers will rhapsodise over the
mollejas (sweetbreads), charred on the outside,
meltingly tender within. No reservations taken, so get
there early or be prepared to queue.

Argentinian (modern)

Sifones y Dragones
*Ciudad de la Paz 174, entre Santos Dumont y
Concepción Arenal, Colegiales (4413 9871/
www.sifonesydragones.com.ar). Bus 68, 152.*

Eat, Drink, Shop

Steak House
PUERTO MADERO

La . **mejor Carne Argentina**

CARNE CALIDAD
18
SPETTUS

www.spettusbuenosaires.com.ar ☎ 4334-4126

Open 9pm-2am Tue-Sat. **Main courses** AR$26-$36. **No credit cards. Map** p327 O8 ⑨

Lovely owners/chefs Mariana and Favio are quick to point out it is not a restaurant, but a kitchen with tables. The current courses coming out of the 'kitchen' include filet mignon in 'criolla' sauce with sweet potato tortilla, and salmon marinated in soy, lemon, coriander and mint. Desserts are suitably delectable and if you want to take a taste home, their 'shop' sells candy liquor, and even board games with edible pieces. Reservations are a must.

Sucre

Sucre 676, entre Figueroa Alcorta y Castañeda, Belgrano (4782 9082/www.sucrerestaurant. com.ar). Bus 37, 130. **Open** noon-4pm, 8pm-2am daily. **Main courses** AR$27-$40. **Credit** AmEx, DC, MC, V. **Map** p329 R10 ⑨

'Modern industrial' doesn't begin to capture the atmosphere at this cavernous, but thoughtfully appointed, space. Once seated, order anything at all, seriously, anything, off the nuevo-pan-Latino menu and you'll be happy. Plate after plate of delicious modern interpretations of *ceviche*, risotto, slow braised pork *bondiola* appear from the kitchen. The star chef, Fernando Trocca, has a penchant for touches of 'molecular gastronomy', so expect a foam or gel or powder here and there, but he's smart enough and talented enough to use them as touches, not as dishes. Sucre also offers up one of the best wine lists in the city.

Chinese

Palitos

Arribeños 2243, entre Mendoza y Olazábal, Belgrano (4786 8566). Bus 60, 130. **Open** 8pm-midnight

Mon; noon-3pm, 8pm-midnight Tu 8pm-midnight Sat, Sun. **Main cou No credit cards. Map** p329 S9

Muted red paper lanterns mea rosy in this stand-out Taiwanese Barrio Chino. Eager punters are prepared to qu for the sizzling fried whole shrimps and the sweet and sour chicken. And as long as you can wrench your mind away from Bambi, you'll find house speciality *ciervo salteado con verdeo* (sautéed venison with spring onions and ginger) a surprisngly successful dish, especially for the price.

Italian

Don Chicho

Plaza 1411, y Zarraga, Colegiales (4556 1463). Subte B, Tronador/21, 76, 87, 93, 127, 140 bus. **Open** 8pm-midnight Mon; noon-3pm, 8pm-midnight Tue-Sat; noon-3pm Sun. **Main courses** AR$10-$18. **No credit cards. Map** p329 R9 ⑨

Two pasta cooks quickly shuttle back and forth from the kitchen to two flour-covered worktables just inside Don Chicho's main entrance, rolling out, cutting, and hand forming some of the best pasta *al momento* in town. There's no menu, so take the recommendations off the daily board out front or whatever is recommended as the best of the day. The tables are packed with locals so expect some heads to turn when you walk through the door. But trust us, it's worth it.

Peruvian

Contigo Perú

Echeverria 1627, y Montañeses, Belgrano (4780 3960). Bus 64, 118. **Open** 11am-midnight Tue-Sun.

There are few sweeter dinner sports than **Sucre**.

Eat, Drink, Shop

..n courses AR$8-$18. **No credit cards.**
..ap p329 R9 **94**

Had enough of steak? Then let the technicolour-waistcoated waiters at this cool *cantina* bring you a short, sharp, citric shock in the shape of a plate of *ceviche* and a brace of Pisco Sours. Crowded with backpackers looking to relive Cuzco nights and Peruvian expats more interested in the taped soap operas on the telly than in actually ordering anything, Contigo Perú represents global cuisine at its most splendidly parochial. Great fun – and cheap.

Vegan

Verdellama

Jorge Newbery 3623, entre Charlone y Roseti, Colegiales (4554 7467/www.comidaconvida.com.ar). Subte B, Federico Lacroze/39, 65, 93 bus. **Open** 10am-6pm Mon-Wed; 10am-midnight Thur-Sat. **Main courses** AR$15-$25. **No credit cards.** Map p323 O4 **95**

Pizza made without cheese or flour? Spaghetti made entirely from courgette? Restaurateur Diego Castro is a practitioner of 'life food', a style of raw food preparation he picked up in New York. Diego's vegan innovations – walnut paté, coconut crêpes, cashew nut mousse, and cucumber-based nori – depend entirely on what his organic farming partners happen to be growing. The result is explosive flavours that bring out the vital energy in each ingredient. An all-organic wine list, wheat grass shots, fresh juices and smoothies (with optional *spirulina* or bee pollen) will satisfy those searching for a bit of Berkeley in Buenos Aires. Diego has also started 'Lifefood' classes where you can learn more than 20 ways to not cook soups, dressings, main courses, sauces, desserts and drinks.

Vegetarian

Masamadre es con M

Jorge Newbery 3623, entre Charlone y Roseti, Colegiales (4554 7467/www.comidaconvida.com.ar). Subte B, Federico Lacroze/39, 65, 93 bus. **Open** 10am-6pm Mon-Wed; 10am-midnight Thur-Sat. **Main courses** AR$15-$25. **No credit cards.** Map p323 O4 **96**

An anarchists' café with valet parking, this converted corner *almacén* (grocer's) also doles out some of the tastiest vegetarian food in town (and, oddly, some fairly hefty meat dishes). Justly famed for its home-made bread, Masamadre's main course options centre around a range of six or seven wholefood 'platters', organised by genre.

San Isidro

Argentinian (traditional)

O'Farrell

Avenida del Libertador 15274 (4742 4869/www. ofarrellrestaurant.com). Train from Retiro. **Open** 12.30-4pm, 7.30pm-1am Mon-Fri; 7.30pm-2am Sat. **Main courses** AR$35-$50. **Credit** AmEx, V.

It takes a special restaurant to be deemed exclusive in a neighbourhood as affluent as San Isidro, but O'Farrell is very special indeed and is regularly cited by critics as one of the best eateries in the country. Despite his Irish roots, Hubert O'Farrell's menu nods more towards Carcassonne than Cork, with star dishes including magret in a bitter chocolate jus, and haunch of lamb in a porcini reduction. The menu changes with the seasons, but freshness and quality is guaranteed. The wine list is sensational.

Make sure you phone ahead at **Masamadre es con M.**

Cafés, Bars & Pubs

Classy cocktails and cultural cafés.

The drinking scene in Buenos Aires is changing more quickly than the time it takes a Guinness to settle. Oops, sorry, Irish bars are so 2006. Let's try again. The drinking scene in Buenos Aires is changing more quickly than the time it takes for your mixologist to blend a dill martini.

As documented in a recent book *Mixology in Argentina* by Rodolfo Reich, Buenos Aires is experiencing the second coming of cocktail culture. Back between the 1930s and 1960s BA's bartenders travelled the world, bringing back awards, and generally being mooted as some of the best. Meanwhile in Argentina they became TV stars and hung out with presidents and tango legends. Inevitably the fall came during the dictatorship and it has taken until now to recover. Barmen and women are becoming

celebrities, as discerning drinkers follow their favourites from bar to bar. It's an ever altering scene, but in bars such as **878** *(see p173)*, **Casa Cruz** *(see p145)*, and **Gran Bar Danzón** *(see p171)* or hotels including **Hotel Madero** *(see p55)*, the **Alvear Palace** *(see p57)* and **Home Hotel** *(see p174)* a perfectly mixed cocktail is pretty much guaranteed. Even restaurants such as the Moroccan-styled **Bereber** *(see p151)* and the South-east asian **Green Bamboo** *(see p156)* are serving up mixes that fuse their culinary taste with a hefty whack of alcohol.

This may be surprising in a society that doesn't prize drunkenness, but it is a culture that prides quality over quantity, explaining how they can stay awake so damn late. Bars generally don't fill up until gone midnight, nightclubs get sweaty much later and the partying goes on until sunrise.

The best Bars

For a modern mix
878 *(see p173)*; **Casa Cruz** *(see p145)*; **Home Hotel** *(see p174)*.

For a winning wine
Gran Bar Danzón *(see p171)*; **Park Hyatt Hotel** *(see p57)*; **Limbo** *(see p174)*.

For a square meal
Bangalore *(see p174)*; **Mark's Deli** *(see p176)*; **Oui Oui** *(see p176)*.

For a history lesson
Café Tortoni *(see p167)*; **Bar Dorrego** *(see p169)*; **El Federal** *(see p169)*.

For a breath of fresh air
Carnal *(see p174)*; **Congo** *(see p174)*; **Olsen** *(see p155)*.

For a romantic liasion
647 Dinner Club *(see p135)*; **Bar Uriarte** *(see p145)*; **Pipí-Cucú** *(see p177)*.

For a downtown drink
Le Bar *(see p167)*; **Dadá** *(see p167)*; **Marriott Plaza Bar** *(see p169)*.

For a classy cuppa
Tea Connection *(see p171)*.

CAFFEINE KICKS

By day caffeine is the drug of choice. If the locals are not supping the tea infusion *mate*, they are knocking back their umpteenth coffee of the day. There are cafés on every block and all seem to be full. Most have a standard menu, papers strewn across the tables and a bleary-eyed waiter in a dicky bow who will reluctantly serve you. But it's all about taking your time.

Whether it's down to history, atmosphere or just bloody good coffee, many of the city's cafés are true classics, integral to the capital's cultural and social life. Little wonder, given BA's strong Italian heritage.

The most common caffeine kicks are a *café* (a single espresso) and a *cortado* (a single espresso with a 'cut' of hot milk). Other options include *café con leche*, *cappuccino* and the *lágrima* (warm milk with a 'teardrop' of coffee). These are usually accompanied with *medialunas* (croissants). A sweet speciality for winter is a *submarino*, a frothy glass of hot milk with a bar of chocolate submerged in it. For an early morning sugar rush, try one accompanied by *churros* (sticky, cigar-shaped doughnuts), often filled with the ubiquitous *dulce de leche*.

❶ Pink numbers given in this chapter correspond to the location of each café, bar and pub as marked on the street maps. *See pp322-329.*

Eat, Drink, Shop

The Centre

Le Bar

Tucumán 422, entre Reconquista y San Martín,
(5219 8580). Subte B, Florida/93, 152 bus. **Open**
noon-2am Mon-Sat. **Credit** AmEx, MC, V.
Map p325 F11 **❶**
This classy cocktail haunt is unflaggingly stylish,
with a cutting-edge interior design that contrasts
exquisitely with the colonial look. Worth it alone for
the impressive and witty art displays and their great
summer terrace which is playing host to a variety
of BA's hottest DJs. There is also an excellent range
of Mediterranean food.

Café Tortoni

Avenida de Mayo 829, entre Piedras y Tacuarí (4342
4328/www.cafetortoni.com.ar). Subte A, Piedras/17,
64, 86 bus. **Open** 8am-3am Mon-Sat; 9am-1am Sun.
Credit AmEx, MC, V. **Map** p325 F10 **❷**
Since it opened in 1858, the splendid Tortoni –
Argentina's oldest and most venerated traditional
café – has played host to a stellar cast, from the
depths of bohemia to the heights of the literati and
across the political spectrum. Today its reputation
attracts busloads of camera-swinging tourists, but
don't be put off – the Tortoni is one of a kind.

La Cigale

25 de Mayo 722, entre Viamonte y Córdoba (4312
8275). Subte B, LN Alem/93, 130, 152 bus. **Open**
from 6pm Mon-Fri; from 8pm Sat. **Credit** AmEx,
MC, V. **Map** p325 F11 **❸**
A huge bar counter, booth seating, fairy lights and
big moon lamps – this is not your classic French café.

Nevertheless, La Cigale, a forerunner among late-
night drinking dens, popular among French expats
and music-loving tourists, has an impressive roster
of DJs spinning anything from kitsch Rat Pack
classics to electropop and darkwave.

Dadá

San Martín 941, entre Marcelo T de Alvear y
Paraguay (4314 4787). Subte C, San Martín/
61, 93, 130, 152 bus. **Open** noon-3am Mon-Sat.
Credit AmEx, MC, V. **Map** p325 F11 **❹**
Drenched in colour with Mondrian glass, pop art
walls and a mosaic bar, Dadá is a bar-restaurant
with serious sex appeal. It draws an engaging mix
of intellectuals, artists and tourists with its classy
cocktails and modern bistro cuisine – classics like
the Lomo Dadá steak feature alongside more
adventurous options.

Deep Blue

Reconquista 920, entre Paraguay y Marcelo T de
Alvear (4312 3377). Subte C, San Martín/
93, 152 bus. **Open** 11am-4am Mon-Fri; 8pm-4am
Sat, Sun. **Credit** AmEx, MC, V. **Map** p325 G12 **❺**
Deep Blue is where fashion conscious poolheads
come to cross cues. Although the place is full of
helpful staff, some tables have a self-service beer tap.
Other locations Ayacucho 1204, Recoleta
(4827 4415).

Florida Garden

Florida 899, y Paraguay (4312 7902). Subte C, San
Martín/93, 130, 152 bus. **Open** 6.30am-midnight
Mon-Fri; 8am-11pm Sat, Sun. **Credit** AmEx, V.
Map p325 G11 **❻**

Art in the glass and on the walls at **Dadá**.

Eat, Drink, Shop

Take in San Telmo's chequered past in **Bar Plaza Dorrego**.

A leader in literary and artistic avant-gardism back in the 1960s (prominent local artists have been gathering here on Saturday mornings ever since), today this buzzy, two-tiered lunch spot is more geared towards business hounds than culture vultures. But if you can see past the suits, mobile phones and cable TV, the copper staircase leading to the mezzanine is a standout feature, and the long glass bar of cakes and pastries is a visual feast.

The Kilkenny

Marcelo T de Alvear 399, y Reconquista (4312 7291). Subte C, San Martín/26, 93, 152 bus. **Open** from 5.30pm Mon-Fri; from 8pm Sat, Sun. **Credit** AmEx, DC, MC, V. **Map** p325 G12 ❼

BA's Irish pubs are no longer prime movers of the city's drinking scene, yet the popularity of the Kilkenny is still amazing. The ultimate after-office hangout, droves of thirsty thirtysomethings stream in from the surrounding towers for some light drinking and heavy flirting. By Saturday it's all-out mayhem as the tourist set join in with the alcohol-fuelled game of sardines.

Marriott Plaza Bar

Basement, Florida 1005, y Santa Fe (4318 3000 ext 873). Subte C, San Martín/61, 130 bus. **Open** 11am-1am daily. **Credit** AmEx, DC, MC, V. **Map** p325 G12 ❽

You can easily imagine heads of government, captains of industry, or Argentina's literary greats slipping down to this beautifully conserved art deco bar for a sneaky gin and tonic or two. The flawless service jibes immaculately with the leather upholstery, background classical music and artwork reminiscent of the city's golden epoch. It's expensive in local terms though the quality of the cocktails helps justify the prices, as do the platters of canapés.

San Telmo

Bar Plaza Dorrego

Defensa 1098, y Humberto Primo (4361 0141). Bus 9, 10, 20, 126, 195. **Open** 8am-3am daily. **No credit cards. Map** p324 D9 ❾

With outdoor seating on Plaza Dorrego, this century-old watering hole embodies the *tanguero* spirit of San Telmo. Inside, a hue is cast over the dusty bottles and black-and-white images of Carlos Gardel, while tango crackles away. It's an ideal spot from which to watch the Sunday market goings-on; or, on a warm evening, to drain a frosty *chopp* (small glass of draught beer) while dismembering a few complimentary monkey nuts.

Bar Seddón

Defensa 695, y Chile (4342 3700). Bus 24, 29, 126, 130, 152. **Open** from 5pm Tue-Sun. **No credit cards. Map** p325 E10 ❿

Burning yellow candlesticks produce a face-flattering glow – and mesmerising waxy pools on the wooden tabletops – at this displaced institution. But Seddón has settled into its San Telmo skin,

attracting a mix of relaxed *porteños* and travellers who swing by for the house wine and live music on weekend evenings. The darkened interior and antique glass windows create an unassuming look-out point for watching the pavement traffic.

El Federal

Carlos Calvo 599, y Perú (4300 4313). Bus 10, 22, 24, 29, 86. **Open** 7.30am-2am Mon-Thur, Sun; 7.30am-4am Fri, Sat. **Credit** MC, V. **Map** p324 D9 ⓫

Built in 1864, El Federal is officially listed as BA's most historic bars. It's also one of the best-kept; check out the magnificent cash registers. It's pretty original too; bar staff work from a lowered floor while the bar itself is thigh high. There's a standard offering of beers and spirits and a long menu of sandwiches and other snacks. With the faded yellow lamps hanging overhead and the old advertising posters, it captures that elusive spirit of a bygone era.

Gibraltar

Perú 895, y Estados Unidos (4362 5310). Bus 24, 29, 86. **Open** 6pm-4am daily. **No credit cards. Map** p325 E9 ⓬

If you've been in town long enough to know that a pub – a *real* pub – is as rare a commodity in Buenos Aires as a stringless teabag, then pull up a stool in the Gibraltar and put your wandering feet to rest. This increasingly popular SanTelmo watering hole offers the precious combination of cheap beer in – gasp! – pint glasses, genuinely spicy curries, an exhaustive collection of whiskies and the friendliest bar-owners in the city. The place is packed to the gills most nights, especially from Wednesday to Saturday; get there early if you want to find a perch.

La Puerta Roja

Chacabuco 733, entre Independencia y Chile, (4362 5649/www.lapuertaroja.com.ar). Subte E, Belgrano/ 39, 60, 152 bus. **Open** from 6pm daily. **No credit cards. Map** p325 E9 ⓭

La Puerta Roja (The Red Door, which is all that marks the spot) is rare breed: a real bar. There isn't a cocktail umbrella in sight, the space is large, the music eclectic, and prices good, set to attract the backpacking fraternity and the large population of foreigners who live in the barrio. Happy hour on *cervezas artesanales* and certain spirits runs from 6pm to 10pm, there's a pool table with decent cue space, and the food has been designed to be cheap, tasty, and filling.

Territorio

Estados Unidos 500, y Bolívar (4307 0896). Bus 5, 22. **Open** 5pm-1am Mon, Tue; 10am-2am Wed-Sat. **No credit cards. Map** p324 D9 ⓮

With its dark wooden tables and tiny mosaic bar, Territorio typifies the ongoing transformation of this traditionally downbeat barrio. The very fact that such a sophisticated spot can thrive these days reflects this once gritty neighbourhood's changing demographic. Ponder on this with the aid of a fine cheese platter and plenty of wine.

Eat, Drink, Shop

DELI & COFFEE HOUSE

Monday to Saturday 8.30am to 9.30pm
Sundays and Public Holidays 10.30am to 9pm

El Salvador 4701 (Palermo Viejo) / (011) 48.32.62.44
info@markscoffee.com / www.markscoffee.com

Puerto Madero

Faena Hotel + Universe Bar

Martha Salotti 445, Dique 2, Madero Este, Puerto Madero (4010 9000/www.faenaexperience.com). Subte B, LN Alem/2, 130, 152 bus. **Open** from noon daily. **Credit** AmEx DC, MC, V. **Map** p324 D11 ⑮

This bar's cheeky homage to the gentleman's club, at once classic and couture, is an example of French wunderkind designer Philippe Starck's maverick approach. The cocktails are classic, and among the many delicious excesses on offer is Sevruga caviar at around US$170 for 50g.

Hotel Madero White Bar

Rosario Vera Peñaloza 360, Dique 2, Madero Este, Puerto Madero (5776 7777/www.hotelmadero.com). Subte B, LN Alem/2, 130, 152 bus. **Open** 7-10.30am, noon-4pm, 7pm-1am daily. **Credit** AmEx, DC, MC, V. **Map** p324 D11 ⑯

If you're on your way to a Madero Este club spot, try the chic and sophisticated White Bar for a pre-boogie beverage. Creative cocktails with exciting ingredients like lemongrass and jalapeños are the brainchild of master mixologist Sebastian Sulpizios.

Tea Connection

Loft 3, Olga Cossettini 1545, Dique 2, Puerto Madero (4312 7315/www.teaconnection.com.ar). Bus 105, 111, 129, 152. **Open** 8.30am-9.30pm Mon-Fri; 9.30am-9.30pm Sat; 10.30am-9pm Sun. **Credit** AmEx, DC, MC. **Map** p324 D11 ⑰

Having proved there is a strong market for healthy option tea houses, Tea Connection has opened the doors to a second beanch. 'Relaxing', 'energising', 'antioxidant packed' drinks are mixed freshly on the spot and can be bought in takeaway bottles. Delectable big and fresh salads, veggie sandwiches and rolls are available for pre-yoga takeaway, but the new premises is so sunny and chilled out, it's preferable to stay, eat and enjoy its friendly vibe. **Other location** Uriburu 1597, Recoleta (4805 0616).

Recoleta & Barrio Norte

Florencio

Francisco de Vittoria 2363, entre Guido y Agote, Barrio Norte (4807 6477). Bus 10, 37, 60, 102, 110. **Open** 9am-8pm Mon, Tue, Thur, Sat; 9am-1am Wed, Fri. **No credit cards. Map** p326 J11 ⑱

Among the affluent buildings in an exclusive Recoleta street is a diminutively sized patisserie with superlative pastries and cakes. Foodies will travel for miles to sink their teeth into a ricotta cake or cheesecake made by sometime TV celebrity chef María Laura. Should you be able to draw yourself away from the sweet counter, in favour of something savoury, sandwiches in home-made ciabatta or their pizza-of-the-day are superb options. It is a tiny establishment but the outdoor tables must be on one of the quietest streets in Buenos Aires. Dinner is served on Wednesday and Friday evenings.

Gran Bar Danzón

Libertad 1161, entre Santa Fe y Arenales, Recoleta (4811 1108/www.granbardanzon.com.ar). Subte D, Tribunales/39, 102, 152 bus. **Open** from 7pm Mon-Fri; from 8pm Sat, Sun. **Credit** AmEx, DC, MC, V. **Map** p325 H11 ⑲

Pull up a chair along with other cocktail lovers and wine aficionados at **Gran Bar Danzón**.

Eat, Drink, Shop

Gran Bar Danzón is undoubtedly one of the kings of the BA bar scene. Although its food is among the best in the city, cocktail quaffers will sup up their ingenious creations and wine aficionados will be scrambling to gawp at their vast wine list, many available by the glass. Crunchy chips arrive in a brown paper bag alongside huge club sandwiches, and the *ceviche* is really outstanding here. Recently inaugurated is their 'Ciclo V', a programme of DJs every Friday night from 11pm.

Milión

Paraná 1048, entre Marcelo T de Alvear y Santa Fe, Barrio Norte (4815 9925). Bus 29, 39, 102, 152. **Open** noon-2am Mon-Wed; noon-3am Thur; noon-4am Fri; 7.30pm-4am Sat; 8pm-2am Sun. **Credit** AmEx, V. **Map** p326 I10 ⓴

Milión's stunning transformation from stately townmansion to 21st-century 'it' bar has made it an emblem of cool in contemporary BA. While maintaining its original lavish form, the classic architecture is offset by cutting-edge art displays and projected visuals, bringing the space in line with its new, style-conscious clientele. Given its popularity, Milion's high-ceilinged rooms are often littered with reservation cards. But between the first floor terrace, picturesque garden and marble staircase you're bound to find a place to perch.

The Shamrock

Rodríguez Peña 1220, entre Juncal y Arenales, Barrio Norte (4812 3584). Bus 37, 39, 101, 124, 152. **Open** from 6pm Mon-Fri; from 8pm Sat, Sun. **Credit** AmEx, MC, V. **Map** p326 I10 ㉑

A genuine Irish bar – the owners hail from Cork – this BA institution sets itself apart with an open plan and modern vibe that is closer in spirit to the contemporary Celtic tiger than its shamrock and shillelagh Microcentro counterparts. It's good value, with a generous happy hour running from opening time until midnight. This and excellent music ensures that it's always jammed with hormonal hordes of twenty- and thirtysomethings. Heavy drapes lead down to the heaving Basement Club (*see p220*), open and always very busy from Thursday to Sunday thanks to its great DJs and beautiful crowd.

Palermo & Palermo Viejo

878

Thames 878, entre Loyla y Aguirre, Villa Crespo (4773 1098). Bus 34, 140, 151, 168. **Open** from 10pm daily. **No credit cards**. **Map** p323 M4 ㉒

Once a 'word of mouth' bar (in other words, a speakeasy), 878's now gone straight. Ring the bell at the unmarked door and you'll be invited into a slick, low-lit space with comfy couches and more than a few reminders of its early days as a carpentry workshop. It's a perfect spot for a sultry dinner-for-two or a hefty exploration of one of the best-stocked, coolest and least publicised bars in the city.

Acabar

Honduras 5733, entre Bonpland y Carranza (4772 0845/4776 3634). Bus 39, 93, 111. **Open** 8pm-4am daily. **Credit** MC, V. **Map** p323 O5 ㉓

Neon lighting, coloured corrugated iron sheets, mannequins and other odds and sods adorn every inch of wall space in Acabar. From these kitsch decorations it's clear that this bar is, to quote the Beach Boys, all about fun, fun, fun. Come here to share a *picada* (platter of meat and cheese cold cuts) or play a board game. Food here is average but this place is worth a visit if just to soak up its unique atmosphere.

Antares

Armenia 1447, entre Cabrera y Gorriti (4833 9611/www.cervezaantares.com). Bus 39, 57, 168. **Open** from 7pm daily. **No credit cards**. **Map** p323 M5 ㉔

Real ale. A yeasty brew. A 'proper' pint. The clever thing about Antares, a very popular venture that the brewery of the same name, is that it makes the argument moot through the simple virtue of appealing to everyone, from beer connoisseurs who will hold their porter up to the light, to sharply dressed lager louts who couldn't care less if their beer came out of a vat or an immersion heater.

Well-kept secret **878**.

The Bangalore Pub & Curry House

Humboldt 1416, entre Cabrera y Niceto Vega (4779 2621). Bus 93, 140, 168. **Open** *6pm-4am daily.* **No credit cards.** **Map** p323 N5

Think warm woods, soft chairs and ceiling fans and you've some idea what this classic colonial-style establishment has to offer. Another winner from the team that brought you Gibraltar (*see p169*), Bangalore is BA's first official pub and curry house and performs both functions with aplomb. Downstairs offers comfy seating and jugs of gin and tonic, while the upstairs dining area is an intimate hideaway in which to sample the subcontinental cuisine, including a *curry de calabaza* (pumpkin) that is so melt-in-the-mouth it'll probably have you speaking in tongues.

Carnal

Niceto Vega 5511, y Humbolt (4772 7582). Bus 39, 93, 184. **Open** *9pm-3am Tue, Wed; from 9pm Thur-Sat.* **No credit cards.** **Map** p323 N4

Thanks to its proximity to one of the coolest clubs in town, namely Niceto (*see p222*), and the Palermo Hollywood location, Carnal is one heck of a popular joint. During the summer, swarms of good-looking and flirtatious young *porteños* mill around until late, eventually heading out to hit the clubs until daylight. The eclectically decorated downstairs bar is well stocked and the cocktails well mixed. Beware,

though: it's a popular spot and the door policy has tightened up considerably. Make sure to book ahead or arrive before 10.30pm – it's not one to be missed.

Congo

Honduras 5329, entre Godoy Cruz y Juan B Justo (4833 5857). Bus 34, 55, 166. **Open** *8pm-3.30am Tue-Sun.* **Credit** *AmEx, V.* **Map** p323 M5

One of the bar kings of the Palermo Viejo jungle, this popular drinking hole has the same owners as the excellent Niceto Club (*see p222*). For all the laid-back charm of the cosy, brown and beige leather-clad interior, the true magic of Congo resides in its gorgeous, spot-lit summer garden, which ranks among the city's best outdoor drinking spaces. There's no better place to enjoy an icy Bossa Nova (rum, brandy, galliano, passion fruit and honey) as BA's sticky summer reaches boiling point. Lengthy queues form from midnight, and no wonder, it's probably the most happening bar in town.

Home Hotel

Honduras 5860, entre Carranza y Ravignani, (4778 1008/www.homebuenosaires.com). Bus 39, 93, 111. **Open** *9am-midnight.* **Credit** *AmEx, MC, V.* **Map** p323 O5

Apart from running one of the best hotels in BA, those clever folk at Home have also managed to draw a fair crowd to their lovely cocktail bar. It has more vodkas than a Russian Tsar and serves up tapas fit for one. The real draw is their summer patio (they give out mosquito repellent), perfect for lounging about before a big night out, especially with their happy hour prices. Friday nights are the most popular, when BA DJs spin an eclectic mix from a huge music catalogue, to a chilled international crowd.

Kim y Novak

Güemes 4900, y Godoy Cruz (4773 7521). Subte D, Plaza Italia/34, 55, 93 bus. **Open** *from 9.30pm Tue-Sun.* **No credit cards.** **Map** p323 N6

Aptly named after the demure 1950s Hollywood vixen, idolised for her platinum blonde hair and come-hither attitude, this funky space invites a hip, colourful and predominantly gay crowd. Down-stairs there's a lively dancefloor and Sundays are reserved for a gay party.

La Cava Jufré

Jufré 201, y Julián Alvarez (4775 7501). Bus 55, 140, 168. **Open** *10.30am-1.30pm, from 7pm Mon-Sat.* **Credit** *AmEx, V.* **Map** p322 L4

A genuine find for wine enthusiasts, this little corner of Villa Crespo has been taken over by Lito, an amateur wine enthusiast and photographer – and if you enjoy sitting around tasting and discussing interesting wines, you're in. There's a large and fairly priced range of wines on sale.

Limbo

Armenia 1820, entre Costa Rica y Nicaragua (4831 4040/www.limborestaurant.com). Bus 15, 39, 55. **Open** *9am-3am daily.* **Credit** *V, AmEx, MC.* **Map** p323 M5

Champagne and cocktails at **Congo**.

Literary ramblings

Start: Confitería Richmond, Florida 468
Finish: La Giralde, Corrientes 1453
Length: Two kilometres (1.2 miles)

You still see writers in cafés. There they are, hunched over their MacBooks, organic smoothies within reach, tapping away at their latest masterpiece. In the BG (Before Google) era, on the other hand, authors and artists used to *congregate* over coffee – and perhaps a nip of absinthe – to exchange views, draw up unrealisable manifestoes, and generally live up to their bohemian stereotypes. This was literary café culture, and BA had plenty of it.

Take our cultural café crawl to make the most of what remains – Starbucks is on its way. Order your first *café con leche* (skip the absinthe, it rots your teeth) in **Confitería Richmond**, at Florida 468. This Microcentro institution has a clubbish vibe and tends to attract a mix of well-fed tourists in shorts and blazered and brylcreemed local gents there to read the papers. Graham Greene liked it too: in *The Honorary Consul*, protagonist Eduardo Plarr's mother names the Richmond's *alfajores* (layered *dulce de leche* cookies) as the best in Buenos Aires.

You'll have several blocks to burn off the calories. Continue up Florida, crossing **Avenida Corrientes**, which, if no longer the favoured roost for culture vultures it once was, still has a host of theatres and second-hand bookstores. At the end of Florida turn left on Roque Sáenz Peña (better known as Diagonal Norte), take a quick orbit around **Plaza de Mayo**, and exit on Avenida de Mayo.

Your first pit stop on this history-heavy boulevard is **London City** at No.599. Propping up one of the avenue's most striking art nouveau buildings, the café is adjacent to the equally wonderful *La Prensa* building (now the city's Casa de Cultura), and in lunchtimes past used to serve the hacks from this once mighty newspaper with their *cortados* and sandwiches. But the most celebrated former patron of this lively coffeehouse was Julio Cortázar, who made it the setting for the opening chapter of his novel *Los Premios*.

From here it's only three blocks to Argentina's most famous café, the legendary Tortoni (see p167), founded in 1858. It's overpriced. It's a tourist trap. Service is sluggish. But the atmosphere makes it worthwhile. Entering the Tortoni is like walking into a film clip from the belle époque, set on loop. Héctor Negro's tango puts it best: 'The Tortoni of today, still living in the past/The stories that live in your silent walls!' The ghost list is stellar: Jorge Luis Borges, who preferred listening to talking; the more garrulous Roberto Arlt, who read his first short story aloud here; and the great Spanish philosopher José Ortega y Gasset, on the run from Franco's shock-troops in the 1930s.

Continuing along Avenida de Mayo and traversing the grand asphalt canyon of **9 de Julio** will lead you to the haunts of another great Iberian Republican partisan, playwright and poet Federico García Lorca. At No.1152 is the **Castelar Hotel**, where Lorca lived between 1933 and 1934. More relevant to the task at hand is **Café Los 36 Billares** at No.1317, where the author of *Yerma* used to tarry over coffee and croissants. To get the full flavour of this humongous bar, ignore the pleasant, but rather staid, dining room and slink into the back rooms, where sallow-cheeked and rosy-nosed old-timers hunch over their dominoes, and where the crack of billiard ball on billiard ball is unceasing.

Proceed along the Avenida until you see **Palacio Barolo** at No. 1370, modelled allegorically on Dante's *Divine Comedy*. Turn right on San José (it becomes Uruguay after one block) and continue until you hit Corrientes once more. Take a left, and finish the tour with a *submarino* (a chocolate bar submerged in hot milk at the table) and a brace of churros at **La Giralda** at No. 1453, a Corrientes classic and the kind of *sui generis* coffee bar no city should be without.

Eat, Drink, Shop

Mark's Deli: New York bagels BA style.

As unashamedly trendy as its customers, Limbo has just the right balance of style and substance. Out front a small patio (heated in winter) holds a handful of tables for those who want to be seen. The exposed concrete and steel entrance gives way inside to a comfortable bar replete with sofas, sculptures and paintings on the wall. The star attraction, however, is the rooftop terrace. Overlooking Plaza Palermo Viejo, this hidden sun trap is a perfect way to relax with one of more than 100 types of wine on offer.

Mark's Deli

El Salvador 4701, y Armenia (4832 6244). Bus 15, 39, 55. **Open** 8.30am-9.30pm Mon-Sat; 10.30am-9pm Sun. **No credit cards. Map** p323 M5 **②**
Mark's is modelled along the lines of a hip New York deli. This bright, orange-hued café is favoured by trendsetting Palermo folk. Take time out of your day to sip an icy lemonade and sink your teeth into a large smoked salmon sandwich, or munch on giant cookies and a café latte while watching the fashion identicats (mostly young, female and towards the top end of the beauty spectrum) play with their time.

Mundo Bizarro

Serrano 1222, y Córdoba (4773 1967/www.mundo bizarrobar.com). Bus 15, 55, 168. **Open** 8pm-3am Mon-Wed, Sun; 8pm-4am Thur; 8pm-5am Fri,Sat. **No credit cards. Map** p323 M4 **③**
In a city that loves late nights, Mundo Bizarro is on safe ground. Fascinating artwork hangs on the blood red walls, giving the whole place a hedonistic vibe that is carried through to their cocktail menu. They offer some food earlier on, but the joint really heats up after 1am. From then on it's a heady mix of music, really great cocktails and sociable people.

Oui Oui

Nicaragua 6068, entre Arévalo y Dorrego (4778 9614). Bus 39, 67, 152, 161. **Open** 8am-8pm Tue-Fri; 10am-8pm Sat, Sun. **No credit cards. Map** p323 O5 **④**
Until recently, most of BA's French eateries were expensive, formal bistros, more *7ème* than *5ème arrondissement*. Oui Oui, by contrast, offers honest, down-to-earth Gallic fare of the kind the French actually eat as opposed to simply write about. Francophile Rocio Garcia Orza does wonders with hot filled croissants, fresh baguettes, *vichysoisse* and *pain au chocolat*, in a colourful environment of dried flowers and rosewood tables. It's perfect for breakfasts, and weekend brunch. There are no reservations taken, so get in early.

Unico Bar Bistro

Fitz Roy 1892, y Honduras (4775 6693). Bus 39, 93, 111. **Open** 8.30am-6am Mon-Fri; 8.30pm-6am Sat, Sun. **Credit** MC. **Map** p323 N5 **⑤**
Unico is undoubtedly one of the most popular bars in Palermo Hollywood, mainly thanks to its relentless crusade in the cause of round-the-clock intoxication. The jumble of tourists, regulars and celebrity spotters creates a perpetual buzz, while frenzied staff navigate the inevitably packed bar wielding burgers,

beer and cocktails. It's the perfect spot for an early-evening nibble (and happy hour), a night of immorality, or a sneaky 6am top-up to propel you home.

Las Cañitas

Kandi

Báez 340, entre Arévalo y Chenaut (4772 2453). Bus 15, 29, 59, 60, 64. **Open** from 8.30pm Tue-Sun. **Admission** minimum spend AR$10 after midnight. **Credit** AmEx, MC, V. **Map** p327 O9 ③⑥
This happening two-floored cocktail bar shines, with its fluorescent panelling, slim waitresses and cool, young Cañitas crowd. Aloof and hip, it has two bars offering all manner of heady concoctions. A top spot to round off a classy binge.

Supersoul

Báez 252, entre Arévalo y Arguibel (4776 3905). Bus 15, 29, 59, 60, 64. **Open** from 6pm Mon-Fri, Sun; from 7pm Sat. **Credit** V. **Map** p327 O9 ③⑦
Although it has toned down a step or two, Supersoul retains its 1970s vibe: retro wallpaper and flashing disco lights. Sat at the bar, or in the booths opposite, are your typical Las Cañitas crowd (beautiful and a bit too skinny) sipping cocktails with saké pretty much thrown in everything. It has a retro-glam swagger that's guaranteed to get your mojo working and moving on long through the night.

Van Koning

Báez 325, entre Arévalo y Chenaut (4772 9909). Bus 15, 29, 59, 60, 64. **Open** from 8pm daily. **No credit cards. Map** p311 O9 ③⑧
If you've had enough sickly cocktails along the flashier and more pretentious Las Cañitas neighbours, duck through the door of this hugely popular (particularly with Dutch expats) bar for a pint from their very own superb microbrewery Otro Mundo (*see feature on p78*). There are three ales to choose from, including a great Red.

Belgrano

Pipí-Cucú

Ciudad de la Paz 557, entre Olleros y Maure (4551 9314). Bus 42, 59, 152. **Open** 9am-1am Mon-Sat. **Credit** AmEx, MC, V. **Map** p327 P8 ③⑨
Pipí-Cucú has entered the modern lexicon of the swankier Argentinian social strata to mean gorgeous, impeccable. It couldn't be a more perfect name for this intimate brasserie-styled restaurant and cocktail bar. Mismatched wine goblets, colourful chalkboard menu and chichi customers give off the vibe that Pipí-Cucú has been a firm Belgrano favourite for years. The cocktails are divine, especially head bartender Augustin Coconier's own creation Super Top (vodka, Cynar, grapefruit and lime). Fabulous Gallic food is served from morning to the early hours. The stuffed squid is a real highlight, but anything is guaranteed to be superb. *Tres* Pipí-Cucú.

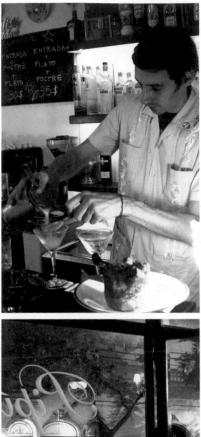

Life is peachy at **Pipí-Cucú**.

Eat, Drink, Shop

Shops & Services

Shopaholics of the world, unite – Buenos Aires has it all.

There are few visitors who don't rhapsodise about shopping in Buenos Aires. Boutiques are opening in Palermo Viejo at a frankly wallet-wincing rate, along with the reputation of creative Argentinian fashion designers on the world's catwalks. Those hunting for funky one-offs, custom-made leather goods or just a great bargain will never want to leave. And as UNESCO's first ever designated design city there are enough unique and beautiful homeware objects and gadgets in BA that even those who hate shopping (they are out there) will find something fascinating.

When you purchase Argentinian-made products worth at least AR$70 in a shop displaying a Global Refund/Tax Free Shopping sticker, don't forget to ask for the *factura* (bill) and the *cheque de reintegro*. When you leave the country, present both at Customs, which will send you to a *puesto de pago* where you will be given back the 21 per cent sales tax minus an administration fee.

Colourful crafts from **KENKO**. *See p191.*

General

Malls

Abasto de Buenos Aires
Avenida Corrientes 3247, entre Agüero y Anchorena, Abasto (4959 3400/www.abasto-shopping.com.ar). Subte B, Carlos Gardel/24, 26, 124, 146, 168 bus. **Open** 10am-10pm daily. **Credit** varies. **Map** p326 J8.
This spectacular building – formerly a market – in an old tango district houses more than 200 shops. It caters primarily to locals, with most of the main Argentinian chains represented, although some top brands have outlets here. The complex also has a large food court and a cinema.

Alto Palermo
Avenida Santa Fe 3253, entre Coronel Díaz y Bulnes, Palermo (5777 8000/www.altopalermo.com.ar). Subte D, Bulnes/12, 15, 39, 64, 152 bus. **Open** 10am-10pm daily. **Credit** varies. **Map** p326 K9.
One of the oldest and most representative of the 'shoppings', but with one of the youngest crowds. Popular with families and gaggles of giggling mall rats, it contains most of the Argentinian favourites, including Chocolate, María Vazquez and Rapsodia.

Galerías Pacífico
Florida 737, entre Viamonte y Córdoba, Microcentro (5555 5100/www.galeriaspacifico.com.ar). Subte B, Florida/6, 93, 130, 152 bus. **Open** 10am-9pm Mon-Sat; noon-9pm Sun. **Credit** varies. **Map** p325 G11.
The frescoes in this Florida street mall, housed in an elegant turn-of-the-century building, were painted by five Argentinian muralists. You'll find famous brand names such as Christian Dior and Ralph Lauren, as well as local stars Sibyl Vane and Vitamina.

Paseo Alcorta
Salguero 3172, y Figueroa Alcorta, Palermo (5777 6500). Bus 67, 130. **Open** 10am-10pm daily. **Credit** varies. **Map** p326 L11.
Paseo Alcorta, considered by shopping buffs to be the best mall in Buenos Aires, contains the gigantic Carrefour hypermarket and four cinema screens. It's also home to the latest Argentinian designer wears and wares, from children's shops Cheeky and Mimo & Co to womenswear stores Ayres and Awada. You'll also find well known brands such as Lacoste and Cacharel.

Patio Bullrich
Avenida del Libertador 750, entre Montevideo y Libertad, Recoleta (4814 7400/7500/www.shopping bullrich.com.ar). Bus 67, 92, 102, 130. **Open** *Shops* 10am-9pm daily. *Restaurants* 10am-midnight daily. **Credit** varies. **Map** p326 I12.

The oldest and most luxurious of all BA's malls (opened in 1988) was once the city's meat auction house. The elegance extends from the marble floors to the uniformed lift operators. Top-end boutiques include Trosman, Etiqueta Negra (menswear) and Jazmín Chebar, as well as Versace and Max Mara.

Markets

Feria de Mataderos
Lisandro de la Torre y Avenida de Los Corrales, Mataderos (www.feriademataderos.com.ar). Bus 55, 80, 92, 126. **Open** Jan-Mar 6pm-1am Sat. Apr-Dec 10am-9pm Sun. **No credit cards.**

At this rural-style fair located in the far west of the city, *gauchos* show off their skills with guitars and horses and day-trippers indulge in country food and browse through the *gaucho*-themed flea market. Folk bands perform on a small central stage and locals join in the *chacareras* (country dances). *See p206* **Urban gauchos.**

Feria Plaza Francia
Plaza Francia & Plaza Alvear, Avenida del Libertador, y Pueyrredón, Recoleta. Bus 17, 92, 110. **Open** 9am-7pm Sat, Sun. **Map** p326 J11.

Handbags, handcrafted kitchen utensils, *mate* gourds and mufflers – you name it, you can buy it at Feria Plaza Francia. All manner of arts and crafts are up for sale in this ever-expanding Recoleta fair.

Specialist

Books and magazines

Porteños are well read and Buenos Aires has more than 1,000 bookshops. Avenida Corrientes is home to a number of stores selling both new and second-hand books. Many of these outlets are open until midnight and central branches often have good cafés. Elsewhere, look out for the **Cuspide** and **Yenny** chains.

English language

Fedro San Telmo
Carlos Calvo 578, entre Bolívar y Perú, San Telmo (4300 7551/www.fedrosantelmo.com.ar). Bus 24, 29, 152. **Open** 11am-10pm Mon-Sat; 3-9pm Sun. **Credit** AmEx, V. **Map** p324 D9.

Just two blocks from Plaza Dorrego, this excellent store specialises in foreign language publications, stocking new books in English, French, Portuguese and Italian, as well as magazines and music CDs.

Where to shop

THE CENTRE
Florida is the main shopping thoroughfare and the only fully pedestrianised street in the city. Once an exclusive shopping zone complete with a Harrods (the premises is still empty) it is now full of tourist tat, 'discount' leather goods and all the usual high street shops. Up Corrientes, past the Obelisco, are many bookshops. On its cross streets there are secondhand photography and electronic shops and many jewellery oulets.

SAN TELMO
Antique buffs should head straight into San Telmo. Along Defensa there are beautiful shops selling furniture, jewellery and all sorts of interesting curios from Argentina's opulent past. Many cutting-edge designers are also opening shops in this area as well as in Palermo.

PUERTO MADERO
Along with the exclusive restaurants and hotels, several international brands are opening flagship stores around the docks, including Nike and La Martina polo brand.

LA BOCA
There are a swathe of tacky souvenir shops around the tourist centre Caminito, but if you want a football shirt head here – as long as it is in blue and gold.

RECOLETA & BARRIO NORTE
Recoleta's Avenida Alvear and the surrounding zone was recently named one of the five most exclusive shopping areas in the world with the usual Valentino and Cartier credentials as well as the best art galleries and Parisian-style cafOs. Design buffs should also check out **Buenos Aires Design**, a mall next to the Recoleta cemetery and weekend market.

PALERMO
This is without a doubt the best shopping area in Buenos Aires for designer clothes and objects. Every fashion designer of note has a boutique in Palermo Viejo. Nearby Las Cañitas should be visited too.

ONCE & ABASTO
These areas are the place to go for a bargain with hundreds of cheap discount stores blasting out cumbia.

ROSSI & CARUSO
ARGENTINA

branding: isoweb.com.ar

SINCE 1868

KEL Ediciones

Marcelo T de Alvear 1369, entre Uruguay y Talcahuano, Recoleta (4814 0143/www.kel-ediciones. com). Bus 39, 102, 111, 152. **Open** 9am-8pm Mon-Fri; 9.30am-1.30pm Sat. **Closed** Jan. **Credit** MC, V. **Map** p325 H10.

KEL stocks English-language fiction, non-fiction, travel books and teaching materials.
Other location Conde 1990, Belgrano (4555 4005).

Walrus Books

Honduras 5628, entre Fitz Roy y Bonpland, Palermo Viejo (4777 0632). Bus 39, 93, 151. **Open** 2-8pm Wed-Sun. **No credit cards. Map** p323 N5.

Run from home by photographer Geoffrey Hickman and his wife Josefina, this bohemian bookshop stocks an eclectic range of titles both new and second-hand. All books are in English.

General

Ateneo Grand Splendid

Avenida Santa Fe 1860, entre Callao y Riobamba, Barrio Norte (4811 6104/4813 6052). Subte D, Callao/12, 39, 152 bus. **Open** 9am-10pm Mon-Thur; 9am-midnight Fri, Sat; noon-10pm Sun. **Credit** AmEx, DC, MC, V. **Map** p326 I10.

This gloriously renovated theatre now contains the largest bookstore in South America. It includes an ample choice of English-language books and a café. The *Guardian* recently voted it the second most beautiful bookshop in the world.
Other location Florida 340, Microcentro (4325 6801).

Boutique del Libro

Thames 1762, entre El Salvador y Costa Rica, Palermo Viejo (4833 0068). Subte D, Plaza Italia/34, 55 bus. **Open** 10am-10pm Mon-Fri; 11am-11pm Sat; 2pm-9pm Sun. **Credit** AmEx, MC, V. **Map** p323 M5.

You'll find here an adequate selection of English-language literature as well as that newly released alternative CD you've been hankering for. Plenty of art and design books, quirky little souvenir editions, and a pleasant back-of-the-store café. One of the best bookshops in Palermo.

El Club del Comic

Marcelo T de Alvear 2002, y Ayacucho, Barrio Norte (4966 1748/www.clubdelcomic.com.ar). Subte D, Facultad de Medicina/39, 101, 111, 132, 152 bus. **Open** 10am-8.30pm Mon-Sat. **Credit** AmEx, DC, MC, V. **Map** p326 I10.

Comics and fanzines galore from Europe, the United States, Japan and Argentina. Rifle through deep stacks of rarities and limited editions. Most are in Spanish but there are some lovely things to be found included in the comic paraphenalia.
Other location Montevideo 355, Tribunales (4375 2323).

Gandhi Galerna

Avenida Corrientes 1743, entre Callao y Rodríguez Peña, Tribunales (4374 7501). Subte B, Callao/12,

Boutique del Libro.

24, 37, 60 bus. **Open** 10am-10pm Mon-Thur; 10am-midnight Fri, Sat; 4-10pm Sun. **Credit** AmEx, DC, MC, V. **Map** p325 G9.

Gandhi has long been the place where Buenos Aires' thinkers and talkers gather. It has a noteworthy music selection and an unrivalled choice of local journals and mags. Live music venue Notorious (*see p244*) is on the first floor.
Other locations throughout the city.

Used & antiquarian

Rigoletto Curioso

Paseo La Plaza, Local 10, Avenida Corrientes 1660, entre Montevideo y Rodriguez Peña, Tribunales (6320 5310/www.rigolettocurioso.com.ar). Subte B, Callao/12, 24, 37, 60 bus. **Open** 10am-10.30pm Mon-Thur; 10am-1am Fri; noon-1am Sat; 2-10.30pm Sun. No credit cards. Map p325 G9.

A real-life old curiosity shop piled high with rarities and out-of-print editions, from Italian anarchist tracts to gardening manuals. A treat for armchair generals, who are are sure to enjoy the antique lead soldiers.
Other location Soler 4501, Palermo Viejo (4831 3649).

Children

Owoko

El Salvador 4694, y Thames, Palermo Viejo (4831 1259/www.owoko.com.ar). Bus 15, 57, 151, 168. **Open** 11am-8pm Mon Sat; 3-7.30pm Sun. **Credit** AmEx, MC, V. **Map** p323 M5.

Eat, Drink, Shop

This bright and smiley kids' emporium makes shopping an interactive experience. With every purchase you get a free story about Planet Owoko.

Super Baby
Armenia 2302, y Charcas, Palermo Viejo (4833 6636). Subte D, Scalabrini Ortiz/39, 60, 152 bus. **Open** 10am-8pm Mon-Fri; 10am-2pm Sat. **Credit** AmEx, MC, V. **Map** p323 M6.
Shopping at Super Baby is a pleasurable experience for parents and brood alike. Owners Melina and Coco will show you through the collections as the little 'uns play with assorted puppets, puzzles and games. Designs come in high-quality cotton in a range of colours for babies and children.

Electronics & photography

There's a fast colour processing lab in every barrio in the city. For professional needs use **Buenos Aires Color** at Piedras 980, San Telmo (4361 4831), which provides a wide range of services from larger formats to black-and-white processing to digital imaging. For professional equipment go to **Cosentino** at Bartolomé Mitre 845 (4328 3290/www. opticacosentino.com.ar). It stocks a number of hard-to-find brands in excellent condition.

General

Frávega
Corrientes 756/60, entre Maipú y Esmeralda, Microcentro (4325 7863/www.fravega.com.ar). Subte B, Florida/22, 130, 152 bus. **Open** 9am-8.30pm Mon-Fri; 9am-8pm Sat. **Credit** AmEx, MC, V. **Map** p325 F11.
A huge chain selling all manner of electrodomestic products including MP3 players, laptops etc.

Specialist

Many hotels can offer mobile phone rental. **Altel** (First floor apartment 4, Avenida Córdoba 417, 4311 5000, www.altel.com.ar) also rents mobile phones. Local pay-as-you-go SIM cards can be bought in the very many mobile phone shops around the city. There is one on nearly every block. Service providers include **Movistar** (www.movistar.com.ar), **CTI Móvil** (www.cti.com.ar) and **Personal** (www. personal.com.ar).

For computer repairs try the professional **Funziona** (Fourth floor, office D, Callao 420, Microcentro, 5272 0300, www.funziona.com.ar). For problems with Apple Macs head to **LatinMac** (Fifth floor, office A, San Martin 910, Microcentro, 5219 9898).

Fashion

Many international designers have a strong presence in Buenos Aires, including Giorgio Armani, Louis Vuitton, Ralph Lauren, Hermès, Burberry and Versace – but imported luxury brands sell for top dollar prices. The fashion scene is very vibrant in Argentina and most of the designers mentioned below are recognised around the world.

Designer

Carolina Hansen
Pueyrredón 2501, Terrazas Buenos Aires Design, Recoleta (5777 6119/www.carolinahansen.com.ar). Bus 10, 17, 60, 92, 110. **Open** 10am-9pm daily. **Credit** AmEx, MC, V. **Map** p326 J11.
Weavers from the north-western province of Jujuy make the textiles and pass them to Hansen who designs unique feminine and charming garments.

Cecilia Gadea
Ugarteche 3330, entre Libertador y Juan F Segui, Palermo (4801 4163/www.ceciliagadea.com). Bus 60, 93, 108, 160. **Open** 11am-8pm Mon-Fri; 11am-4pm Sat. **Credit** AmEx, MC. V. **Map** p327 M10.
Always romantic and super feminine, Gadea's latest range is inspired by ocean waves. Ingenious dresses, skirts and cute coats made from strips of great quality cotton. These exquisite, painstakingly handmade clothes are simply amazing.

Mariana Dappiano
Gurruchaga 1755, entre Costa Rica y Nicaragua, Palermo Viejo (4833 4731/www.marianadappiano.

Great window shopping at **Cecilia Gadea**.

Eat, Drink, Shop

Made in Argentina

So you've got the tan, malbec stained teeth, photos of the Obelisco and your bag is just under that 23 kilograms weight limit. Is it possible to squeeze in a few extra souvenirs? But, of course. Below are some suggestions of authentically Argentinian mementos.

Mate set

You don't really like the stuff and would really just prefer a cuppa, yet Argentinians look so damn cool drinking it, and you want to show your friends back home how cultured you now are. So, for the inexperienced drinker: (1) Don't boil the water, it should be poured just before boiling point; (2) Don't move the *bombilla* (straw) around as if sucking up the last dregs of an iced cappuccino; (3) The server drinks first, refills, passes the *mate* to their left which is then returned back when finished; (4) If you say *gracias* to the server, that means you do not want any more; (5) Only wimps add sugar to *mate* but it can be done if you really can't stand its bitter taste. Oh, and it's pronounced 'ma-tay', not after your friend.

• Available from any market but for the one pictured (AR$18) go to **Estudio MW** (Cabrera 5187, Palermo, 4832 8407, www.webmw.com.ar).

Polo shirt

With the top ten polo players in the world being Argentinian, sporting a polo shirt is a nice way to support the country's unmatched talent and also a nice way to pretend to be posh. Originally imported by blueblood ranchers, the sport took off thanks to the horse happy pampas, healthy farm workers and its similarity to a traditional indigenous sport called Pato (*see p249* **Mounted and monied**). Player's positions are indicated by numbers one to four. Number one is an offensive position; two is a difficult position with an offensive, attack and defensive role; three is the leader and is usually the best player on the team (so buy a number three shirt); four is defence.

• Available from **La Martina** (*see p207*) along with all other polo gear.

Gaucho knife set

Let's face it, Argentinian men seem to exude manliness, with their carnivorous diet, dark wavy hair and confident demeanour. It makes the pasty tourist feel, well a bit inferior. What better way to dash such weakling thoughts than to own a bloody great big knife. A beautifully hand-crafted *gaucho* knife will not only banish that man complex but serve as a reminder of hidden machismo when you're back in the office. Remember to pack it in the check-in bag.

• Available from stalls at **Feria de Mataderos** (*see p179*).

Malbec

The pleasure in a soft fruity mouthful of malbec is unbeatable. Probably something the big man upstairs gave us to counteract the more unpleasant thinks in life, like a ride on a Buenos Aires bus. You may not be able to extend your ticket home, but you can make heaven linger a little longer by taking home a bottle of the ruby beauty. Wines from the Norton Bodega are powerful Argentinian staples that don't change their taste for a foreign market. Best drank with a traditional *asado*.

• Available from any supermarket (*see p201*) for a mere AR$12.

Dulce de leche

Argentinians have a real sweet tooth and tend to cater to that vice with dulce de leche, a caramel spread. From early in the morning and throughout the day, you can see people gobbling it down smeared across a bun or oozing out of a filled pastry. They claim it's an Argentinian invention – don't even try argue otherwise – although it's really just caramel and a clone of France's *confiture de lait*. A jar of the stuff would make an easy gift to any friends or family. There are many brands of dulce de leche, but one of the smoothest around is from La Salamandra.

• Available from all supermarkets (*see p201*).

Tango heels

The choice of designer shoes in Buenos Aires is overwhelming. They all seem to be as beautiful as the last pair and with the conversion rate, the tourist shopper's biggest bargain. **Comme il Faut** (*see p200*) have a gorgeous selection of heels originally designed for tango dancers and now enjoyed by stylish women all over the world.

Haircut

You've probably noticed a hefty proportion of young *porteños* walk around with some impressive haircuts, the most popular – and exhibited amongst top ranking footballers – is the mullet (*see p38*), also endearingly called a *camionero* (trucker cut). If you feel as if you haven't fulfilled an adventuresome urge, getting a haircut in Buenos Aires is the ultimate adrenaline rush. You never know what the final product will look like until it's done.

• See *p203* for hairdressers.

Mafalda comic book

Mafalda is a popular socio-political strip created by Argentinian cartoonist Quino in the 1960s and ran until 1973. Through the eyes of a little girl called Mafalda, we get to see insightful and extremely subtle satirical opinions about the world and humanity. Mafalda books are read to great acclaim throughout the world and offer an Argentinian point of view on the humorous side of the serious issues at the time. The books are also a wonderful way to practise your Spanish.

• Available from all good bookshops (*see p181*).

Eat, Drink, Shop

CHOCOLATE
www.chocolateargentina.com.ar

Mariana Dappiano

Gurruchaga 1755, entre Costa Rica y Nicaragua,
Palermo Viejo (4833 4731/www.marianadappiano.
com). Bus 34, 55, 161. **Open** 10.30am-8pm Mon-Sat.
Credit AmEx, MC, V. **Map** p323 M5.
In her new location, this auteur's shop is very
bohemian. Stripped of colour, Dappiano's look is
dominated by white billowing dresses which make
their impact through form.

Fiocca

Perú 599, y México, San Telmo (4331 4585/
www.ffiocca.com). Bus 39, 60, 152. **Open** 10.30am-
7.30pm Mon-Fri; 10.30am-3pm Sat. **Credit** AmEx,
MC, V. **Map** p325 E10.
Florencia Fiocca's work is a classic look using
simple colours but now swaying in to graphic design
territory. Playing with textures and organic forms,
Fiocca's garments are both adventurous and refined,
one of the reasons her clothes do well abroad.
Other location Cabello 3650, Palermo
(4806 5637).

María Cher

El Salvador 4714, entre Armenia y Gurruchaga,
Palermo Viejo (4832 3336/www.maria-cher.
com.ar). Bus 15, 39, 55, 151. **Open** 10am-8pm
Mon-Sat; 2-8pm Sun. **Credit** AmEx, DC, MC, V.
Map p323 M5.
Cher has quickly built up a solid reputation thanks
to her eclectic collections, which she sells to the
'feminine, independent and mature' woman. From
cocktail dresses to swimsuits, Cher can fit you out.
Other location Paseo Alcorta shopping centre,
Salguero 3172 (5777 6541).

María Martha Facchinelli

El Salvador 4741, entre Armenia y Gurruchaga,
Palermo Viejo (4831 8424/www.facchinelli.com). Bus
15, 39, 151, 168. **Open** 10.30am-8pm Mon-Sat.
Credit AmEx, MC, V. **Map** p323 M5.
The creations from this young designer exude a
refinement rare among her peers. The style is
romantic and ultra feminine, the cuts are impeccable
and the prices are accessible.

Mariano Toledo

Armenia 1564, entre Honduras y Gorriti, Palermo
Viejo (4371 5327/www.marianotoledo.com.ar). Bus
15, 55, 168. **Open** noon-7pm Mon-Sat. **Credit**
AmEx, MC, V. **Map** p323 M5.
Toledo is undoubtedly one of the most respected
designers in Argentina right now. Each collection is
high on concept: the 2007 collection was produced
with tech giants Philips.

Nadine Zlotogora

El Salvador 4638, entre Malabia y Armenia,
Palermo Viejo (4831 4203/www.nadinez.com). Bus
15, 39, 55. **Open** 11am-8pm Mon-Sat. **Credit**
AmEx, MC, V. **Map** p323 M5.
Zlotogora's idiosyncratic styling is an artful blend
of fantasy and romance. Her ethereal, other-worldly
clothes are distinctively feminine with satin,

macramé and embroidered pieces, each of which is
individually dyed to ensure its uniqueness.

Pablo Ramírez

Perú 587, entre Venezuela y México, San
Telmo (4342 7154/www.pabloramirez.com.ar).
Bus 12, 39, 102, 140. **Open** 10.30am-7.30pm.
Mon-Fri; 10.30am-3pm Sat. **No credit cards.**
Map p325 E10.
Pablo Ramírez is considered to be the king of
elegance. Famous for their black and white palette,
this designer's clothes are instantly recognisable –
a new menswear line continues the simple theme.

Tramando, Martín Churba

Rodríguez Peña 1973, entre Posadas y Alvear,
Recoleta (4811 0465/www.tramando.com). Bus 17,
61, 67, 92, 93. **Open** 10.30am-8.30pm Mon-Fri;
11am-7pm Sat. **Credit** AmEx, DC, MC, V.
Map p326 I11.
Always looking towards the fusion of the textile and
the visual, Martín Churba and his crew constantly
experiment with printing and weaving techniques
by applying plastic and paint to his clothes.
Homeware goods like rugs, bowls and chairs are
also manufactured from this peculiar and inventive
combination of pop and craft.

Rags and romance at **Nadine Zlotogora**.

"Indumentaria Masculina/ Men´s clothes"

Armenia 1735. Ph: (5411) 4833-2104.
Horario Lunes a Sábado de 11 a 21hs/ Domingo de 13 a 21hs

Trosman

*Patio Bullrich, Avenida del Libertador 750, entre
Montevideo y Libertad, Recoleta (4814 7411/
www.trosman.com). Bus 67, 92, 102, 130.* **Open**
10am-9pm daily. **Credit** AmEx, DC, MC, V.
Map p326 I12.

The rise and rise of Jessica Trosman has been lauded
in Taschen's prestigious book *Fashion Now*, and she
is without a doubt one of the international queens of
the new Argentinian fashion movement. Her
trademark is elaborate collections using innovative
materials like plastic and latex to create a chic look.
Other locations Armenia 1998, Palermo Viejo
(4833 3058); Paseo Alcorta shopping centre, Salguero
3172, Palermo (5777 6500).

Varanasi

*Costa Rica 4672, entre Gurruchaga y Armenia,
Palermo Viejo (4833 5147/www.varanasi-
online.com). Bus 15, 57, 140, 168.* **Open** 11am-8pm
Mon-Fri; 11am-6pm Sat. **Credit** AmEx, DC, MC, V.
Map p323 M5.

Mario Buraglio and Víctor Delgrosso, architects
turned designers, combine sophistication and daring
in overlayered materials, experimental shapes and
pairings of natural and synthetic fabrics. They also
designed this new two-floor flagship store.
Other location Libertad 1696, Recoleta (4815 4326).

Vero Ivaldi

*Gurruchaga 1585, entre Honduras y Gorriti,
Palermo Viejo (4832 6334/www.veroivaldi.com). Bus
34, 55, 110, 151.* **Open** 10am-8pm Mon-Sat. **Credit**
AmEx, MC, V. **Map** p323 M5.

Considered to be one of the most avant-garde
designers in Buenos Aires, Ivaldi turned to Magritte
for a recent collection, incorporating his character,
top hat and apple motifs in silk blouses, skirts and
dresses. We doth our cap to her creative mind.

Zitta

*Avenida Quintana 10, y Libertad, Recoleta (4811
2094/www.zittacostura.com). Bus 93, 152.* **Open**
11am-7pm Mon-Fri; 11am-2pm Sat. **Credit** AmEx,
DC, MC, V. **Map** p326 I11.

Zitta provides uptown clothes for uptown girls in an
uptown location. Using pure materials, they are
constantly pushing boundaries with their designs
for the female silhouette.

Mid-range

Adorhada Guillermina

*El Salvador 4872, entre Borges y Gurruchaga,
Palermo Viejo (4831 2553/www.adorhada
guillermina.com.ar). Bus 15, 57, 93, 161.* **Open**
10am-8.30pm Mon-Sat. **Credit** AmEx, MC, V.
Map p323 M5.

A lively and accessible range of everyday urban and
beach wear, with reasonably priced clobber for
professionals and frisky partygoers. The collections
have recently leant towards an early 1990s look,
with garish colours and skinny jeans.

Sweet clothes at **Chocolate**.

Other locations Avenida Santa Fe 1615, Barrio
Norte (4814 0053); La Pampa 2386, Belgrano
(4706 3196).

Chocolate

*Patio Bullrich shopping centre, Avenida del Libertador
750, entre Montevideo y Libertad, Recoleta (4815
9530/www.chocolateargentina.com.ar). Bus 102, 130.*
Open 10am-9pm daily. **Credit** AmEx, DC, MC, V.
Map p326 I12.

A pioneer in local high street fashion with branches
in the city's top shopping centres. Attracting discerning women shoppers since 1982, the chain has
remained cool with its diverse lines for all occasions
using high quality materials.
Other locations throughout the city.

DAM

*Honduras 4775, entre Malabia y Armenia, Palermo
Viejo (4833 3935/www.damboutique.com.ar). Bus
39, 55, 168.* **Open** 11.30am-8.30pm Mon-Sat. **Credit**
AmEx, MC, V. **Map** p323 M5.

It's always a fiesta at this wacky little boutique.
Opened in 1998, when Palermo Viejo had only a
handful of forward thinking boutiques, Carola
Besasso's project has taken much of its inspiration
from the Dutch aesthetic – she studied in
Amsterdam, hence her shop's name. Anyone could
find something of interest among her one-of-a-kind
items.

Eat, Drink, Shop

LEATHER WOMENSWEAR
SHOES
BAGS
TROUSERS
SKIRTS

Las Peros
FASHION BOUTIQUE

UNICENTER
LOCAL 1065

PASEO ALCORTA
LOCAL 1044 / 45

ALTO PALERMO
LOCAL 0001

AV. SANTA FE 1631
BUENOS AIRES
ARGENTINA

Dorina Vidoni

*Honduras 4384, entre Armenia y Gurruchaga,
Palermo Viejo (4833 4965/www.dorinavidoni.com).
Bus 15, 57, 110, 141, 160.* **Open** 11am-8pm Mon-
Sat. **Credit** AmEx, MC, V. **Map** p323 M5.
Dorina Vidoni brings us a new concept in dressing:
Each of her garments can be modified and combined
to create another new look. All in jersey cotton, these
versatile dresses, trousers and tops will make handy
additions to your wardrobe.

Jazmín Chebar

*El Salvador 4702, y Gurruchaga, Palermo Viejo
(4833 4242/www.jazminchebar.com.ar). Bus 34,
151, 168.* **Open** 10am-8pm Mon-Sat; 1-7pm Sun.
Credit AmEx, MC, V. **Map** p323 M5.
Young local designer Jazmín Chebar is Argentina's
very own Stella McCartney. Popular with mothers
and daughters alike – her jeans fit everyone. She
brings a fresh splash of fancy colour at her French-
style boutiques expanding across the city.
Other locations Paseo Alcorta, Palermo (5777
6770) and Patio Bullrich, Recoleta (4814 7424)
shopping centres.

KENKO

*Honduras 4832, entre Armenia y Gurruchaga,
Palermo Viejo (4832 8733/www.kenkosur.com). Bus
39, 55, 168.* **Open** noon-7pm Mon-Sat. **Credit**
AmEx, MC, V. **Map** p323 M5.
Who says Argentinian tradition is dead, or that
Andean-style woven ponchos are a fashion faux pas
in the big city? Certainly not Karina Johansen and
Selene Godoy, the energetic duo behind KENKO's
colourful line of clothing, handmade from cotton,
silk and wool and its funky bedspreads. *Photo p178.*

Kukla

*Bulnes 2677, entre Las Heras y Cabello, Palermo
(4807 2406/www.kuklaonline.com.ar). Bus 41, 60,
130.* **Open** 11am-8pm Mon-Sat; 3-7pm Sun. **Credit**
AmEx, MC, V. **Map** p326 L10.
This is a lovely locale for a brand that has been
going since 2002, founded by sisters Isabel and
Magdalena Palandjoglou. Their collections are
always cheerful affairs with innovative uses of
texture, cuts and colour in ultra-soft fabrics.

Lupe

*El Salvador 4657, entre Armenia y Malabia,
Palermo Viejo (4833 0730). Bus 15, 55, 151, 168.*
Open 11am-8pm Mon-Sat; 2-7pm Sun. **Credit**
AmEx, DC, MC, V. **Map** p323 M5.
This expanded Palermo boutique is worth a peep for
its casual designs at reasonable prices. In particular,
check out the glitzy belts and polka dot chemises.

Paula Cahen d'Anvers

*Avenida Santa Fe 1619, entre Montevideo y
Rodríguez Peña, Recoleta (4811 3176/www.
paulacahendanvers.com.ar). Bus 10, 37, 39, 152.*
Open 10am-8pm Mon-Sat. **Credit** AmEx, DC, MC,
V. **Map** p326 I10.
Come to this fabulous store for classic comfort rather
than avant-garde adventurism. Easy colours, latin

prints and oh-so-soft fabrics make this women's
clothing line a closet favourite. There is a new
children's line for little princes and princesses.
Other locations throughout the city.

Las Pepas

*Avenida Santa Fe 1631, entre Montevideo y
Rodríguez Peña, Recoleta (4811 7887/www.laspepas.
com.ar). Bus 10, 37, 39, 152.* **Open** 10am-9pm Mon-
Fri; 10am-8pm Sat. **Credit** AmEx, DC, MC, V.
Map p326 I10.
A busy on-the-button boutique for handbags,
satchels and shoes in bright colours, not to mention
a kaleidoscope of vintage-inspired leather jackets,
coats and skirts. Las Pepas has an adaptable range
which is very good for separates.
Other location Paseo Alcorta shopping centre,
Salguero 3172, Palermo (5777 6553).

Pesqueira

*Armenia 1493, y Gorriti, Palermo Viejo (4833
7218/www.pesqueiratm.com). Bus 15, 55, 151, 168.*
Open 11am-8pm Mon-Sat. **Credit** AmEx, MC, V.
Map p323 M5.
One of the new wave of Argentinian designers,
Valeria Pesqueira's trademarks to date are bold,
playful prints in modern cuts and fabrics. Her
Pesqueira store is home to a cute kawaii universe of
women's and kid's clothing, objects and decorations.
And to bring a smile to each person's face who walks
past you, wear one of her bear print T-shirts.

Seco

*Armenia 1646, entre El Salvador y Honduras,
Palermo Viejo (4833 1166/www.secorainwear.com).
Bus 39, 151, 168.* **Open** 11am-8pm Mon-Sat; 1-7pm
Sun. **Credit** AmEx, MC, V. **Map** p323 M5.
Seco – as in dry – is the place to run to when the city
gets wet. Fun, colourful wet-weather gear lines the
walls for the entire family. There is also an expanded
range of all-weather casualwear.

Vevú

*Honduras 4829, entre Armenia y Gurruchaga,
Palermo Viejo (4833 1973/www.vevu.com). Bus 15,
110, 151.* **Open** 11am-8.30pm Mon-Sat. **Credit**
AmEx, DC, MC, V. **Map** p323 M5.
At this elegant little boutique, you'll find all sorts of
ultra-feminine and vintage-inspired designs fit for
both mother and daughter. Find 1960s mini dresses,
jackets and skirts as well as plenty of flattering
floral garments. The retro-style shoes are
a real treasure.
Other location Arguibel 2898, Las Cañitas
(4772 4883).

Multi-brand boutiques

Un Lugar en el Mundo

*Defensa 891, entre Estados Unidos y Independencia,
San Telmo (4362 3836). Bus 20, 22, 24, 29.*
Open 10.30am-8pm daily. **Credit** DC, MC, V.
Map p324 D10.
Clothing and accessories for both sexes from young

Eat, Drink, Shop

cool. And before you get too excited about the original Pucci dresses, they're not for sale. *Photo p192.*

Salsipuedes

Honduras 4814, entre Armenia y Gurruchaga, Palermo Viejo (4831 8467). Bus 39, 55. **Open** 10.30am-9pm Mon-Fri; 10.30am-8pm Sat. **Credit** AmEx, MC, V. **Map** p323 M5.

Salsipuedes (meaning 'get out if you can') presents a compilation of each season's best collections from more than 30 designers. In addition, owner Mariana Szwarc has launched her own line of party dresses. Look for Posse's printed dresses and Orb's sexy strapless options.

Other location Libertad 1634, Recoleta (4831 8467), and General Paunero 1983, Martínez.

SoldBA

Costa Rica 4645, entre Gurruchaga y Armenia, Palermo Viejo (4833 7990). Bus 15, 39, 55. **Open** 2-8pm Mon-Fri; 2-9pm Sat; 3-8pm Sun. **Credit** AmEx, V. **Map** p323 M5.

This mini Camden Market in Palermo Viejo is constantly rotating its collections depending on what it believes is hot right now. Lots of very cool T-shirts, music and all sorts of other interesting items make this *multiespacio* well worth a look.

Tienda Porteña

Carlos Calvo 618, y Perú, San Telmo (4362 3340). Bus 60, 93, 152. **Open** 11am-8pm Tue-Sun. **Credit** AmEx, MC, V. **Map** p324 D9.

Un Lugar en el Mundo. See p191.

Owners Ana and Maria always offer a warm welcome to this fashion outlet-cum-cultural multispace, housed in a recycled early-20th-century mansion. Here they offer colourful clothes for colourful people. There are kids' and blokes' clothes.

Tienda Tres

Armenia 1655, entre Honduras y El Salvador, Palermo Viejo (4831 4193). Bus 5, 55, 151, 168. **Open** 11am-8pm daily. **Credit** AmEx, MC, V. **Map** p323 M5.

Three local designers – Verónica Alfie, María Lombardi and Flavia Martini – have grouped together to display their work at this Palermo boutique. Each has her own particular approach to fashion, but the general emphasis is on floaty prints and Argentinian cuts has made Tres exceedingly trendy right now.

Clubwear

AY Not Dead

Paseo Alcorta Shopping Centre, Salguero, y Avenida Figueroa Alcorta, Recoleta (5777 6655/www. aynotdead.com.ar). Bus 37, 67, 130. **Open** 11am-8.30pm Mon-Sat. **Credit** AmEx, DC, MC, V. **Map** p326 L11.

A 1980s London vibe is apparent upon walking into this new flagship store, as perhaps you'd expect from the St Martin's-trained Angie Chevalier and her sister Noel. The results are striking colours, surrealist tops and punk leather jackets that are glamorous and trendsetting.

Other locations Soler 4193, Palermo Viejo (4866 4855); Parera 175, Recoleta (4815 7954).

Charlotte Solnicki

Armenia 1577, entre Gorriti y Honduras, Palermo Viejo (4832 9277/www.charlottesolnicki.com). Bus 55, 110, 151. **Open** 10.30am-8pm Mon-Sat. **Credit** AmEx, MC. V. **Map** p323 M5.

Sexy and seductive, Charlotte Solnicki's designs now hang in London, New York, LA and Saint Tropez. Daring, provocative leather pieces, often seen on the city's dancefloors, feature heavily. The knitwear is always sexy and the accessories are fun.

Other location Cabildo 4193, Belgrano.

Fight for Your Right

Thames 1425, entre Cabrera y Gorriti, Palermo Viejo. Bus 34, 55, 168. **Open** 10am-8pm Mon-Sat. **Credit** AmEx, MC, V. **Map** p323 M5.

Customised dresses, printed T-shirts and a fun selection of retro baseball caps make this trendy boutique an emblem of streetwear-cool.

Jeans Makers

Soler 4202, entre Julián Alvarez y Aráoz, Palermo Viejo (4865 2420/www.jeansmakers.com). Subte D, Scalabrini Ortiz/39, 92, 110, 152 bus. **Open** 11am-9pm Mon-Sat. **Credit** AmEx, MC, V. **Map** p322 L6.

Customised denim dealer where you can pick your cut, choose your stitching and chew over the design choices, which range from diamanté studs to

Street style

Start: Jeans Makers, Soler 4202.
Finish: Standard, Fitz Roy 2203.
Length: 4 kilometres.

On sunny afternoons, the streets of Palermo Viejo are more like crowded catwalks where fashion-conscious porteños strut their stuff in voguish local designs. But don't just stand there with your mouth hanging open – join the promenade with this guided stroll through the stylish grounds of BA's beautiful people neighbourhood.

Kick off your design walk at the city's Holy Grail of denim, **Jeans Makers** (*see left*), located a few blocks east of Plaza Palermo Viejo. If you're used to unflattering back pockets and too-short trouser legs, get ready to air-kiss it all goodbye: you can choose every detail from cut to stitching to Swarovski crystal accents and come away with a perfectly customised pair of jeans.

Continue west along Soler, then hang a left onto Gurruchaga and check out the contemporary **Mariana Dappiano** at No. 1755 (*see p183*), line of form-focused knit tops and dresses. Turn the corner and walk east along El Salvador towards the whimsical **Juana de Arco** at No. 4762, where a collection of crocheted swimsuits, wispy sundresses, and colourful woven wraps was influenced by Argentinian artisan traditions. Head left on Armenia and take the load off your feet on a velvet couch at **Bar 6** at No.1676 (*see p145*), a cool bar designed by Argentinian virtuoso Horacio Gallo.

Head back down El Salvador and step through the glass doors of **Mishka** at No. 4673 (*see p200*), a boutique of ballet flats and granny-inspired boots that elevates shoe

design to high art. Pair your footwear with a textured piece from **Nadine Zlotogora** at No. 4638 (*see p187*) across the street, where romantic dresses and tulle-edged men's shirts comprise a rustic chic collection.

Continue exploring this jam-packed block by heading south along Malabia and turning right onto Honduras, then choose your own fashion adventure: one-piece terry cloth jumpsuits printed with Japanese cartoon characters are on offer at the wacky designer collective **DAM** at No. 4775 (*see p189*), lavish futuristic apparel by an award-winning Argentinian designer awaits at **Mariano Toledo** to your left on Armenia 1564 (*see p187*), and transparent polka-dotted raincoats and blush-red rubber boots are on display at the tiny **Seco** at No. 1646 (*see p191*), on your right.

Approaching the Honduras and Gurruchaga intersection, take a few steps towards Plaza Cortazar – where you can pick up a handmade paper journal stamped with Marilyn Monroe's face at **Papelera Palermo** (Honduras 4945; *see p206*) or stop at the popular **Calma Chicha** at No. 4925 (*see p205*), a home accessories shop whose cowhide banana chairs give a playful wink to gaucho tradition – or simply continue south along Gurruchaga. Peek into **Vero Ivaldi** at No. 1585 (*see p189*), on the left to see a Magritte-themed collection of jackets and trainers stamped with the Belgian artist's signature green apples and bowler hats. Stunning, cutting-edge leather goods can be found at **Qara** at No. 1548 (*see p199*), on your right.

Turn right onto Gorriti and forge on across the railway tracks, stopping on **Darwin** at No. 5656 if you happen to covet quirky high-tech illumination and home decor. Your eight-block journey will be well-rewarded with a vodka cocktail at the super-stylish **Olsen** at No. 5870 (*see p155*), a sleek Scandinavian bar and restaurant where even the placemats ooze sophistication.

Around the corner, near the intersection of Honduras and Ravignani, see for yourself why Wallpaper* magazine named **Home Hotel** at Honduras 5860 (*see p63*) the Best New Hotel of 2007. Finish your day of appreciating BA's finer things at the chic 1950s-inspired **Standard** (*see p147*). A few blocks north at the Fitz Roy and Guatemala intersection it's great for gourmet porteño cuisine and of ideally situated for people watching.

Eat, Drink, Shop

Swarovski crystals. They also stock a comprehensive range of off-the-peg jeans. Their new store in Alto Palermo shopping centre (*see p178*) even has a catwalk on which to strut your stuff.
Other locations throughout the city.

Kosiuko

Paseo Alcorta shopping centre, Salguero 3162, Recoleta (4717 3656/www.kosiuko.com). Bus 37, 39, 152. **Open** 10am-10pm daily. **Credit** AmEx, MC, V. **Map** p326 L10.
The trailblazer for hipster jeans poses only one question – how low can you go? Bold, vivacious, figure-hugging clothes for aspiring pop stars. Jeans feature heavily for her, particularly the Oxford style, but also T-shirts, cute cardigans and colourful shoes. For him, skinny jeans and red jackets.
Other locations throughout the city.

Kostüme

República de India 3139, entre Segui y Libertador, Palermo (4802 3136/www.kostume.net). Bus 10, 37, 67. **Open** 10.30am-8pm Mon-Fri; 10.30am-7pm Sat. **Credit** AmEx, MC, V. **Map** p327 M10.
From the creative hands of Camila Milesi and Emiliano Blanco, the racks of this Palermo store are unforgivably futuristic and underground. Outfits rendered in cotton spandex with three-quarter length jackets over bridge trousers are an attraction.

Ona Sáez

Avenida Santa Fe 1651, entre Montevideo y Rodríguez Peña, Recoleta (4813 2834/www.onasaez. com). Bus 10, 37, 39, 152. **Open** 10am-8.30pm Mon-Sat. **Credit** AmEx, DC, MC, V. **Map** p326 I10.
A trendsetting, seductive and provocative clothing store for him and her, particularly famed for its 'nice ass' jeans. They are always perfectly cut and come in so many varieties you'll get dizzy trying to choose a pair. The menswear line is very metrosexual.
Other locations throughout the city.

Menswear specialists

Balthazar

Gorriti 5131, entre Thames y Uriarte, Palermo Viejo (4834 6235/www.balthazarshop.com). Bus 34, 55, 166. **Open** 11am-8pm Mon-Sat. **Credit** AmEx, DC, MC, V. **Map** p323 M5.
Once you've finished admiring the beautiful Palermo townhouse or new San Telmo store, rifle through the racks of striking shirts in Italian textiles, perfect for urban dandies. *Photo p197.*
Other locations First Floor, Defensa 1008, San Telmo (4300 6926).

Bensimon

Avenida Quintana 4924, y Ayacucho, Recoleta (4807 5218/www.bensimon.com.ar). Bus 17, 101, 102. **Open** 10am-8.30pm daily. **Credit** AmEx, DC, MC, V. **Map** p326 I11.
Put together a great casual look, in bold colours and soft cotton. Bensimon kits out staff at some of the

city's funkiest bars and restaurants. It is a classic staple for young, wealthy Argentinian males.
Other locations throughout the city.

Bolivia

Gurruchaga 1581, entre Gorriti y Honduras, Palermo Viejo (4832 6284). Bus 39, 55, 151. **Open** 11am-8pm Mon-Sat; 3-8pm Sun. **Credit** AmEx, MC, V. **Map** p323 M5.
Eclectic, customised and packed with small but telling details, Bolivia balances the masculine and the feminine and has become one of the most innovative menswear shops in town.

El Cid

Gurruchaga 1732 entre El Salvador y Costa Rica, Palermo Viejo (4832 3339/www.el-cid.com.ar). Bus 34, 55, 93, 161. **Open** 11am-8pm Mon-Wed; 11am-8.30pm Thur-Sat. **Credit** AmEx, MC, V. **Map** p323 M5.
Actors, writers and other bohemians flock to El Cid in search of the classic white shirt, very Armani jackets and even a stylish little coat for your laptop.

La Dolfina

Martha Salotti 454, Dique 2, Puerto Madero Este (5787 5152/www.ladolfina.com). Bus 2. **Open** 10am-8pm Mon-Fri; 11am-7pm Sat, Sun. **Credit** AmEx, DC, MC, V. **Map** p324 D11.
La Dolfina, with star Adolfo Cambiaso, is probably the world's best polo team. Riding on the back of this success, the brand recently opened a new branch in Puerto Madero. You'll find a fine selection of cotton polo shirts, soft leather jackets, jumpers and quality leather accessories at surprisingly good prices.
Other locations Galerías Pacífico, locale 216 (5555 5216); Avenida Alvear 1315, Recoleta (4815 2698).

Etiqueta Negra

Dardo Rocha 1366, y Pringles, Martínez (4792 7373). Bus 60. **Open** 10am-8pm Mon-Sat. **Credit** AmEx, DC, MC, V.
After years of moving and shaking in BA's fashion scene, Federico Alvarez Castillo opened this bold shop in the northern suburbs to sell his super-chic but highly wearable menswear line. It's also worth the trip to drool over his collection of vintage sports cars and bikes parked in the store. It is now established as the city's leading menswear brand.
Other locations Patio Bullrich shopping centre, Libertador 750, Recoleta (4814 7430) and Paseo Alcorta shopping centre, Salguero 3172, (5777 6500).

Félix

Gurruchaga 1670, entre El Salvador y Pasaje Santa Rosa, Palermo Viejo (4832 2994/www.felixba. com.ar). Bus 15, 39, 55. **Open** 11am-8pm Mon-Sat; 3-8pm Sun. **Credit** AmEx, MC, V. **Map** p323 M5.
Félix is your preppie *porteño* classic. Details stand out but the price doesn't. Jeans, shirts, boxers, wallets, belts and scarves – the stock is all cool. To deck your kids out in the same look, pop round the corner to the children's branch at El Salvador 4742 (4833 3313).
Other location Libertad 1627, Recoleta (4815 4087).

Eat, Drink, Shop

Hermanos Estebecorena

El Salvador 5960, entre Ravignani y Arévalo, Palermo Viejo (4772 2145/www.hermanos estebecorena.com). Bus 39, 93, 111. **Open** 11am-9pm Mon-Sat. **Credit** AmEx, DC, MC, V. **Map** p323 O5.

These brothers are at the cutting edge of style, applying all the principles of industrial design to hip, comfy and functional items, from underwear and socks to all-weather coats. Their original range includes stylish shoes, shirts and trousers too. **Other location** Paseo Alcorta shopping centre, Palermo (5777 6687).

Key Biscayne

Armenia 1735, entre Costa Rica y El Salvador, Palermo Viejo (4833 2104/www.key-biscayne. com.ar). Bus 15, 110, 141, 160. **Open** 11am-10pm Mon-Sun. **Credit** AmEx, MC, V. **Map** p323 M5.

From the 'Philosophy' pop-up on their website to the ornamental interior patio at their Armenia street branch, it's clear that this growing Argentinian menswear chain is aimed squarely at the anti-corporate metrosexual. You'll find the outfits separated by colour, particularly lilac and lavender.

Mercer

El Salvador 4677, entre Malabia y Armenia, Palermo Viejo (4831 4891). Bus 15, 57, 110, 160. **Open** 11am-8pm Mon-Sat. **Credit** AmEx, MC, V. **Map** p323 M5.

The floor of this vast warehouse space is layered in rugs, Eastern-style lanterns and fans hanging from the roof, while the changing rooms feature old cabinets filled with oriental objects where you'll find a varied selection of good jeans, shirts and tops.

Spina

Gorriti 5887, entre Carranza y Ravignani, Palermo Viejo (4774 3574). Bus 39, 93, 111, 168. **Open** noon-8pm Mon-Sat. **Credit** AmEx, DC, MC, V. **Map** p323 O5.

Neither faddish nor retro, inspired by everything from Mexican cinema to contemporary Argentinian literature, Carla and Flavio's suits, jackets, shirts and accessories are sophisticated and wearable, rendered in their obsessively sourced quality fabrics.

Used & vintage

Galería 5ta Avenida

Avenida Santa Fe 1270, entre Libertad y Talcahuano, Recoleta (4816 0451/www.galeria5ta avenida.com.ar). Bus 10, 39, 59, 152. **Open** 10am-9pm Mon-Sat. **Credit** varies. **Map** p325 H11.

This arcade is lined with used clothing shops and tattoo parlours. It boasts bargains galore for the discerning shopper. For vintage eyewear, visit Hernán Vázquez at Optica Nahuel (4811 2837).

Gil Antigüedades

Humberto 1º 412, entre Defensa y Bolívar, San Telmo (4361 5019). Bus 24, 29, 126, 130, 152.

Open 11am-1pm, 3-7pm Tue-Sat; 11am-7pm Sun. **Credit** AmEx, DC, MC, V. **Map** p324 D9.

This is highly recommended in the antiques section but it is so popular for fashion that one Mr John Galliano visited to get some inspiration for his latest collection.

Hoy Como Ayer

Thames 1925, entre Nicaragua y Soler, Palermo Viejo (4771 1986). Bus 39, 55, 93, 168. **Open** 1-7.30pm Mon-Sat. **No credit cards. Map** p323 M5.

Passionate about all things retro, owner Sole Gotheil opened her first store in Miami. The BA version specialises in vintage garments from the 1920s to the 1980s, the most desirable items being the Pucci dresses and the 1960s YSL jackets. You'll also find mirrors, soda siphons and more accessories from yesteryear.

Keak

Costa Rica 5722, entre Bonpland y Carranza, Palermo Viejo (4772 2189). Bus 39, 93, 140. **Open** 11.30am-8.30pm Mon-Sat. **Credit** AmEx, V. **Map** p323 M5.

An incredible store where the clothes are vintage but, get this, unused. Siblings Alfonsina and Fausto own this retro store where potential buys include mint-condition Fred Perry tops, vintage Ray Bans, and some very French, very cool berets. A fantastic place for 1970s stompers. And very affordable.

Fashion accessories

Clothing hire

Last-minute bar mitzvah or wedding to attend and you haven't packed your handy tux? Not to worry, suit hire and sale is available at **London Tie** (Florida 769, 5555 5207, www.londontie. com) with full fitting service, located in the Galerías Pacífico. English is spoken.

Cleaning & repairs

If you need shoe repairs, **Fix Shoe** in Recoleta (Vicente López 1668, 4811 0226) can get most jobs finished in a day.

There are launderettes on almost every block most with dry-cleaning. A popular chain is Lava Ya. Try Esmeralda 577 (4861 5000).

General

Almacén de Belleza

Nicaragua 4835, entre Borges y Thames (4778 0050/www.almacendebelleza.com). Bus 34, 55, 93, 161. **Open** 11am-8pm Mon-Sat. **Credit** AmEx, MC, V. **Map** p323 M5.

This new shop is for women what Willy Wonka's Chocolate Factory was for kids. Everything you could imagine a lady would ever need: clothes (day and evening wear), accessories, bijoux, lingerie, home fittings, much of it designed for the Almacén.

Smart and sassy clothes at **Balthazar**. *See p195.*

could imagine a lady would ever need: clothes (day and evening wear), accessories, bijoux, lingerie, home fittings, much of it designed for the Almacén.

Anahi M
Uriarte 1490, entre Gorriti y Honduras, Palermo Viejo (4834 6005). Bus 34, 55. **Open** 10.30am-8pm Mon-Sat. **Credit** AmEx, DC, MC, V. **Map** p323 M5.
Without a doubt some of the most beautifully designed bags on the planet are on display here for your full ogle potential. They are all hand-stitched and inspired by natural elements.

Carla Di Sí
Gorriti 4660, entre Malabia y Scalabrini Ortiz, Palermo Viejo (4832 1655/www.carladisi.com.ar). Bus 15, 55, 151, 168. **Open** 11am-8pm Mon-Sat. **Credit** AmEx, DC, MC, V. **Map** p323 M5
For fans of vintage eyewear, this boutique is quite a spectacle. Carla's completely original collection of frames from the 1960s, 1970s and 1980s was sourced by her father, an optician. Carla's own line of Tupe sunglasses is a highlight.

Condimentos
Honduras 4874, entre Armenia y Gurruchaga, Palermo Viejo (4833 9403). Bus 39, 55. **Open** 10.30am-8.30pm Mon-Fri; 10.30am-8pm Sat. **Credit** AmEx, MC, V. **Map** p323 M5.
This boutique is in a converted garage, selling a come-hither range of handcrafted and designer accessories. Inside, owners Franca and Carolina will warmly show you around and explain the collections.

Fahoma
Libertad 1169, entre Santa Fe y Arenales, Recoleta (4813 5103). Bus 10, 39, 102, 152. **Open** 10am-8pm Mon-Fri; 10am-1.30pm Sat. **Credit** AmEx, DC, MC, V. **Map** p325 H11.
Women who know just how to accessorise shop for their striking jewellery and elegant handbags in this upmarket Recoleta store. The shop is nearly always crowded, in large part thanks to designer Julio Toledo's exclusive line of handbags.

Jewellery

925
Honduras 4806, y Armenia, Palermo Viejo (4843 5843/www.nueveveinticinco.com.ar). Bus 39, 55. **Open** 11am-8pm Mon-Sat. **Credit** AmEx, MC, V. **Map** p323 M5.
Ariel Paluch makes silver rings with semi-precious stones. Plata Textil also sell elegant silver bracelets. Around the corner (Cabrera 4937, 4833 5343), there is also an open gallery to browse.

Celedonio Lohidoy
Unit 39, Galería Promenade, Avenida Alvear 1883, entre Callao y Ayacucho, Recoleta (4809 0046/www.celedonio.net). Bus 61, 67, 93, 130. **Open** 10am-8pm Mon-Fri; 10am-2pm Sat. **Credit** AmEx, MC, V. **Map** p326 I12.
Celedonio Lohidoy's reputation for selling beautiful bijoux jewellery has spread around the world. The regular collection includes wonderfully baroque necklaces featuring pearls and semi-precious stones. There is an attractive line of romantic *objets d'art*, including lamps.

Metalistería
Borges 2021, entre Guatemala y Soler, Palermo Viejo (4833 7877/www.metalisteria.com.ar). Bus 34, 55, 93. **Open** 11am-8pm Mon-Sat. **Credit** AmEx, MC, V. **Map** p323 M6.
Contemporary jewellery with unconventional designs, incorporating flower petals, mesh, leather and paper for a unique way to accessorise. The company recently exhibited at New York's MOMA.

Plata Nativa
Unit 41, Galería del Sol, Florida 860, entre Córdoba y Paraguay, Retiro (4312 398/www.platanativa.com). Subte C, San Martín/6, 26, 93, 132, 152 bus.
Open 10am-7.30pm Mon-Fri; 10am-2pm Sat.

Eat, Drink, Shop

Credit AmEx, MC, V. **Map** p325 G11.
This small gallery is hard to find but well worth seeking out. The shop stocks a range os indigenous and Latin American art but also sells antique silver and contemporary ethnic accessories., which are unlike anything you're likely to find back home The necklaces woven in agate and turquoise, inspired by Mapuche jewellery, are in a class of their own.

Marcelo Toledo
Humberto Primo 462, entre Bolívar y Defensa (4362 0841/www.marcelotoledo.net). Subte C, San Juan/17, 59, 100, 126 bus. **Open** Sun-Fri 10.30am-6pm. **Credit** AmEx. **Map** p324 D9.
One of the most respected jewellers in BA is also one of the favourites of the King of Spain and has also made pieces for Prince Charles and his mum and, erm, Robbie Williams. A recent collection called 'Evita' featured more than 120 pieces including earrings, brooches and necklaces in silver and gold with precious stones, many of them replicas of pieces found in Eva Peron's wardrobe. Mostly working in silver, Toledo has become an icon and ambassador for Argentinian jewellery making.

Leather goods

Bag hags will be thrilled to know that thanks to Argentina's cheap and plentiful leather, bags, like shoes, are sold nearly everywhere. On and around Florida street has become the main leather zone, though you'll have to contend with an overly zealous sales approach. Or check out Murillo street in Villa Crespo, where the leather wholesalers are gathered.

Humawaca
El Salvador 4692, y Armenia, Palermo Viejo (4832 2662/www.humawaca.com). Bus 55, 151, 168.

Open 11am-8pm Mon-Sat; 3-8pm Sun. **Credit** AmEx, DC, MC, V. **Map** p323 M5.
An architect who has made the logical transition to fashion design, Ingrid Gudman works principally with leather to produce original bags, purses and wallets. Her trademark is multi-use items, like her reversible tote and her divisible bag. It is the perfect place to pick up a gift that uses local products and reflects the country's creativity.
Other location Posadas 1380, Recoleta (4811 5995).

Qara
Gurruchaga 1548, entre Honduras y Gorriti, Palermo Viejo (4834 6361/www.qara.com). Bus 39, 55, 168. **Open** 11am-9pm Mon-Sat; 4-8pm Sun. **Credit** AmEx, MC. V. **Map** p323 M5.
Young US designer and owner Amanda Knauer and her team of skilled artisans are breathing some fresh and funky life into BA's often (excuse us) hidebound leather goods market. All of the accessories on sale are made from the best available leather and aimed squarely at the contemporary urbanite who wants to carry things in style: note the BlackBerry and mobile phone-sized pouches in the bags. There is something for everyone who wants craftsmanship.

Rossi & Caruso
Posadas 1387, entre Rodríguez Peña y Montevideo, Recoleta (4800 1174/www.rossicaruso.com). Bus 67, 92, 93. **Open** 10am-8.30pm Mon-Fri; 10am-7pm Sat. **Credit** AmEx, DC, MC, V. **Map** p326 I11.
The old, tawny photos hanging on the walls say it all: Rossi & Caruso has been fashioning leather goods for more than six decades. They produce elegant handbags and traveller bags, men's and women's leather jackets, wallets and notebooks and skillfully fashioned saddles.
Other locations Avenida Santa Fé 1377, Barrio Norte (4814 4774); Galerias Pacífico, first floor, Microcentro (5555 5308).

Quality leather goods at **Qara**.

Lingerie & underwear

Beleidades

Galería Promenade, Avenida Alvear 1883, entre Callao y Ayacucho, Recoleta (4800 1275/www.beleidades.com). Bus 92, 93. **Open** 10am-8pm Mon-Fri; 10am-3pm Sat. **Credit** AmEx, MC, V. **Map** p326 I11.

There's a hint of the Moulin Rouge in the air at Beleidades, from this quirky local's interior design to the cabaret-inspired pieces on the racks and shelves. There are fun, cheeky, glamorous and very sexy collections in silk, muslin, satin and lace. **Other location** Pasaje Santa Rosa 4904, Palermo Soho (4137 6535).

Burdel

Gorostiaga 1559, second floor, entre Migueletes y Libertador, Recoleta (4776 3757/www.burdelsite.com). Bus 15, 29, 55, 60. **Open** Mon-Sat 3-8pm. **Credit** AmEx, MC, V. **Map** p327 P9.

Hot, hot, hot. French tunes, Picasso on the walls, Sartre on the bookshelf and erotic games are just some of the touches that make this shop sparkle. It's an intimate place where the owner personally greets you and revels in showing off some very sexy pieces.

Susila Tantrik

Marcelo T de Alvear 1477, entre Paraná y Uruguay, Recoleta (5811 0059/www.susilatantrik.com). Bus 39, 102, 111, 152. **Open** 10am-8pm Mon-Fri; 10am-4pm Sat. **Credit** AmEx, DC, MC, V. **Map** p325 H10.

Designer Giselle Schwerdfeger has put together a line that combines European fashions with Argentinian touches; colourful designs that range from sweet and pretty to sexy and naughty.

Luggage

Karpatos

Avenida Córdoba 834, y Suipacha, Microcentro (4328 3008/www.karpatos.com.ar). Subte C, San Martín/5, 10, 101, 111, 152 bus. **Open** Mon-Fri 9.30am-8pm. **Credit** AmEx, MC, V. **Map** p325 G11.

All your luggage needs can be easily met at this chain of superstores. Their own products are sturdy and hardwearing. Also the place for padlocks etc.

Shoes

28 Sport

Gurruchaga 1481, entre Cabrera y Gorriti, Palermo Viejo (4833 4287/www.28sport.com). Bus 93, 142. **Open** 11am-8pm Mon-Sat. **Credit** AmEx, MC, V. **Map** p323 M5.

As their marketing slogan roughly translates, when a shoe is well made, it's bleeding obvious. 28 Sport makes shoes as they used to be; with tight stitching, reinforced toes, and leather that smells like a cow. They specialise in the sporty bovver-boot look, and most of the designs hark back to the mid 1950s, a period when footwear was still made with TLC.

Comme Il Faut

Arenales 1239, Rue des Artisans, apartamento M, entre Libertad y Talcahuano, Recoleta (4815 5690) Bus 39, 101, 111, 152. **Open** 11am-7pm Mon-Fri, 11am-3m Sat. **Credit** MC, V. **Map** p325 H11.

Carrie Bradshaws of the world steer clear, your credit card is going to take a big hit. Handmade and designed by tango dancers for tango dancers, these are divine and durable heels.

Divia

Armenia 1489, entre Gorriti y Cabrera, Palermo Viejo (4833 9090/www.diviashoes.com). Bus 39, 93, 111, 161. **Open** 11am-8pm Mon-Sat. **Credit** AmEx, DC, MC, V. **Map** p327 M7.

The name Divia means 'something beautiful' and this can be applied to this lovely Bordeaux-painted boutique. Find your perfect pair of flirty heels, embellished with rhinestones or ankle charms to add sparkle to your step. Each pair is completely unique.

Huija

Armenia 1806, entre Nicaragua y Soler, Palermo Viejo (4833 9595/www.huijaonline.com.ar). Bus 15, 39, 111. **Open** 11.30am-8.30pm Mon-Fri; noon-9pm Sat; 3.30-7pm Sun. **Credit** AmEx, MC, V. **Map** p323 M5.

A fun and bright store stocked with fun and bright shoes. Funky flats, cool running shoes and shiny patent leather heels, take your pick. Chequered, polka dots and striped fabrics are playfully used in their collections, often spotted on local celebrities. **Other location** Libertador 14, 955, first floor, San Isidro (4798 9595).

Jackie Smith

Gurruchaga 1660, entre Honduras y El Salvador, Palermo Viejo (4115 6820/www.jackiesmith.com). Bus 15, 55, 140, 168. **Open** 11am-8pm Mon-Sat. **Credit** AmEx, DC, MC, V. **Map** p323 M5.

Jackie Smith opened her new shop with a classic, romantic and feminine touch in mind with eight very different lines of matching handbags, shoes and plenty of accessories such as wallets and purses.

Josefina Ferroni

Armenia 1471, entre Gorriti y Cabrera, Palermo Viejo (4831 4033). Bus 39, 55, 106, 109. **Open** 3-8pm Mon; 11am-8pm Tue-Sat. **Credit** AmEx, DC, MC, V. **Map** p323 M5.

Ferroni's immaculate handcrafted range of boots makes her the queen of stylish footwear; each design is extraordinary and precisely 15 pairs are made in each colour. The handbags and belts are also startlingly fresh and fashionable. *Photo p202.* **Other location** Arenales 1278 (5811 1951).

Mishka

El Salvador 4673, entre Armenia y Malabia, Palermo Viejo (4833 6566). Bus 39, 55. **Open** 11am-8.30pm Mon-Sat. **Credit** AmEx, DC, MC, V. **Map** p323 M5.

One of BA's best for shoes, Mishka can't be beaten on style or quality. The collection is small and

28 Sports.

chiefly designed for dainty feet, but it's happy days if you find your fit because these shoes are a guarantee of serious wow factor.

Ricky Sarkany

Paseo Alcorta, Salguero 3172, y Figueroa Alcorta, Palermo (4781 5629/www.rickysarkany.com). Bus 67, 102. **Open** 10am-10pm daily. **Credit** AmEx, DC, MC, V. **Map** p326 L11.

Glitz and glamour are all the rage at the busy store of headline-making local designer Ricky Sarkany. Ricky takes European trends and adapts them for the fashionable Argentinians.

Food & drink

Bakeries

There is certainly no shortage of carbohydrates in this city – you will find *panaderías* (bakeries) on every high street, selling sandwiches, freshly baked bread, *facturas* (sweet pastries) and cakes of all shapes and sizes (*porteños* are notoriously sweet-toothed). As Argentinian regional produce grows in popularity, delis are becoming more common too, although many stick to the cold cuts, cheese and olives formula. Two established chains, with cold meats (*fiambres*) and cheeses, are **La Casa del Queso** at Corrientes 3587, Abasto (4862 4794) and **Al Queso, Queso** at Uruguay 1276, Recoleta (4811 7113).

Dos Escudos

Montevideo 1690, entre Quintana y Guido, Recoleta (4812 2517/www.dosescudos.com.ar). Bus 17, 102. **Open** 7am-9pm daily. **Credit** AmEx, MC, V. **Map** p326 I11.

If you want to make an impression when invited to someone's house, buy a cake from Dos Escudos, an institution among old-school patisseries. **Other locations** Juncal 905, Retiro (4327 0135); Las Heras 3014, Recoleta (4805 4329).

Drinks

La Brigada Cava

Bolívar 1008, entre Carlos Calvo y Humberto I°, San Telmo (4362 2943/www.labrigada.com). Bus 24, 28, 29, 86. **Open** 9.30am-1.30pm, 4.30-9pm daily. **Credit** AmEx, MC, V. **Map** p324 D9.

With 32,000 bottles on sale, La Cava, an offshoot of the wonderful La Brigada steakhouse chain (*see p133*), stocks all the best local wines, with Catena Zapatas alongside the cheaper Weinert range.

La Cava de Vittorio

Arenales 2321, entre Uriburu y Azcuenaga (4824 0647). Bus 12, 39, 152. **Open** 10am-1.30pm, 5.30-8.30pm daily. **Credit** AmEx, MC, V. **Map** p326 J10.

This tardis-sized store in *Barrio Norte* stocks the finest wines from Argentina's smaller boutique bodegas, as well as the best from the usual larger suspects. Resident oenologist Eduardo Molteno can help you choose a wine for any occasion, maybe even let you try some. They are unassuming and will happily lead anyone through the cheaper options.

Ligier

Avenida Santa Fe 800, y Esmeralda, Retiro (4515 0126/www.ligier.com.ar). Subte C, San Martín/10, 111 bus. **Open** 9.30am-8pm Mon-Fri; 10am-2pm, 4-8pm Sat. **Credit** AmEx, MC, V. **Map** p325 G11.

Catering mostly to tourists and offering personalised attention, delivery and packaging, Ligier has cannily placed its branches close to many of the big hotels. **Other locations** throughout the city.

Bootylicious. **Josefina Ferroni**: heaven for shoe lovers. *See p200.*

General

There are plenty of major supermarkets all around the city. **Disco** (Rodriguez Peña 1430, Recoleta, 4807 3311) and **Coto** (Honduras 3862, Palermo) are probably the most common, with several in each neighbourhood. They usually stay open until 10pm. **Carrefour** and the discount supermarket **Dia** are also easily found. There are smaller minimarts on nearly every block in central areas. All accept credit cards but make sure the system is working.

Specialist

El Gato Negro

Avenida Corrientes 1669, entre Rodriguez Peña y Montevideo, Tribunales (4374 1730). Subte B, Callao/12, 24, 37, 60 bus. **Open** 9am-11pm Mon-Fri; 9am-1am Sat; 3-11pm Sun. **Credit** AmEx, MC, V. **Map** p325 G9.
A favourite of any cook keen on flavourings, the top-quality selection of herbs, spices and aromatic seeds here is unsurpassed in the city. The best way to appreciate the ambience is by taking tea at the in-house café, in the building dating back to 1928.

Kakao Maroa

Avenida Federico Lacroze 1660, entre Migueletes y Libertador, Belgrano (4775 3076). Subte D, Olleros/55, 60 bus. **Open** 9am-9pm Mon-Sat. **Credit** AmEx, DC, MC, V. **Map** p329 Q9.
If life's like a box of chocolates, we want ours to resemble the whimsical, artfully wrapped packages from this bombonería. The most fabulous of these gold-dusted confections is shaped like lips. You might feel reluctant to eat one but go ahead – sinking your teeth into the rich, buttery cocoa is worth it.

Tikal Chocolates

Honduras 4890, entre Gurruchaga y Armenia, Palermo Viejo (4831 2242/www.chocolatestikal.com). Bus 39, 55. **Open** 9am-9pm Mon-Sat. **Credit** AmEx, DC, MC, V. **Map** p323 M5.
This lovely chocolate shop uses Venezuelan cacao. The chocolate bonbons are dangerously delectable and you can eat-in or take them away.

Valenti Especialidades

Patio Bullrich, Avenida del Libertador 750, entre Montevideo y Libertad, Recoleta (4815 3090/3080). Bus 67, 92, 93, 130. **Open** 10am-9pm daily. **Credit** AmEx, DC, MC, V. **Map** p326 I12.
The best-quality cold cuts and cheeses from the Valenti family: salmon from Scotland, Greek feta and Spanish *jamón ibérico de bellota*.
Other location Soldado de la Independencia 1185, Belgrano (4775 2711).

Gifts & souvenirs

Airedelsur

9th floor, Arenales 1618, y Montevideo (5811 3640/www.airedelsur.com). Subte D, Callao/39, 60, 152 bus. **Open** by appointment only. **Credit** AmEx, DC, MC, V. **Map** p326 I10.
Marcelo Lucini, founder of and creative force behind airedelsur, sells a range of traditional Argentinian products – bowls, belts, wine decanters – all handcrafted by regional artisans from the finest materials. Call ahead to make an appointment.

Arandú

Paraguay 1259, entre Libertad y Talcahuano, Palermo Viejo (4816 3689/www.tal-arandu.com). Bus 55, 151, 168. **Open** 11am-8pm Mon-Sat. **Credit** AmEx, MC, V. **Map** p325 H10.
Under Arandú's roof you'll find all you ever need to kit yourself out as a hard-bitten *gaucho*, albeit an upmarket one. For equestrian fanatics check out the the saddle, the riding boots and the hats. For

everyone else there's always the trusty *mate* gourd and some other quality leather goods.
Other locations Ayacucho 1924, Recoleta (4800 1575); Talcahuano 949, Recoleta (4816 1281).

Pasión Argentina
Emilio Ravignani 1780, y El Salvador, Palermo Viejo (4777 7750/www.pasion-argentina.com.ar). Bus 39, 55, 152. **Open** 10am-7pm Mon-Fri. **Credit** AmEx, V. **Map** p323 O5.
Pasión Argentina was one of the first fair-trade companies to be founded in the country. Launched after training women from the northern provinces of Argentina in ethical, small-scale manufacturing, it now works with more than 50 families. The result is stylish leather and craft products. Look out for their sling-style leather bags and off-the-shoulder purses, and wooden tea caddies with weavings built into the lids.

Wayra
Patio Bullrich shopping centre, Avenida del Libertador 750, entre Montevideo y Libertad, Recoleta (4814 7544). Bus 67, 92, 102, 130. **Open** 10am-9pm Mon-Sun. **Credit** AmEx, DC, MC, V. **Map** p326 I12.
This classy, nature-themed shop stocks an exceptional collection of handmade goods, including jewellery, ceramics and rugs, produced by craftspeople from across Argentina.

Health & beauty

Complementary medicine

Aqua Vita Medical Spa
Arenales 1965, entre Riobamba y Ayacucho, Barrio Norte (4812 5989/www.aquavitamedicalspa.com). Bus 10, 12, 21, 29, 39, 132, 152. **Open** 9am-9pm Mon-Sat; 10am-7pm Sun. **Credit** AmEx, DC, MC, V. **Map** p326 I10.
Indulge in a range of delicious treatments – facial purification, aromatherapy massage or half-day head-to-toe programmes – in this aesthetically calming treatment centre.

Hairdressers & barbers

Cerini
Marcelo T de Alvear 1471, entre Paraná y Uruguay, Recoleta (4811 1652/www.cerini.net). Bus 39, 102, 111, 152. **Open** 8am-10pm Mon-Sat. **Credit** AmEx, DC, MC, V. **Map** p326 I10.
Cerini is a super-modern and incessantly bustling salon. Appointments are not essential, but if you arrive in the after-work period, you'll have to wait.

Club Creativo
Montevideo 1161, entre Marcelo T de Alvear y Santa Fe (4811 2202). Subte D, Callao/39, 152 bus. **Open** 10am-9pm Mon-Sat. **Credit** AmEx, DC, MC, V. **Map** p326 I10.

A glossy midsized salon decked out with neon lights and mirrors. Sneaker-clad stylists have a penchant for fringes and layers but will accommodate anyone wanting classic styles.

Opticians

Vision Express (freephone 0800 555 0182, www.visionexpress.com.ar) offers service in one hour; there are branches at Florida 713 (4314 4155) and in several of the shopping centres that will be able to complete most prescriptions without any problems. For vintage eyewear try Carla Di Si's emporium (*see p196*).

Exe Lens
Armenia 1636, entre Gurruchaga y Malabia, Palermo Viejo (4832 0373/www.exelens.com). Bus 57, 110, 142. **Open** 10am-9pm Mon; 11am-8pm Tue-Sat; 3-7pm Sun. **Credit** AmEx, MC, V. **Map** p323 M5.
As well as selling its own line of sunglasses and optical frames, Exe fills the racks with international brands like Tom Ford, Prada, Paul Frank, etc.

Infinit Boutique
Thames 1602, y Honduras, Palermo Viejo (4831 7070/www.infinitnit.la). Bus 39, 55. **Open** noon-8pm Mon; 11am-8pm Tue-Sat; 3-7pm Sun. **Credit** AmEx, MC, V. **Map** p323 M5.
This is the first manufacturer of sunglasses designed and made in Argentina to open up a shop. There's a great range of styles, and fine craftsmanship is assured. They have some great metal frames in gold, silver and bronze in the classic aviator style for the full 1970s look. Also check for the red-framed jackie O styles, and other accessories such as watches.

Pharmacies

FarmaCity
Florida 474, entre Corrientes y Lavalle, Microcentro (4322 6559/www.farmacity.com). Subte B, Florida/10, 59, 111 bus. **Open** 24hrs daily. **Credit** AmEx, DC, MC, V. **Map** p325 F11.
A mega-chain with dozens of well-stocked stores across the city – and growing. There's a good range of imported products, the pharmacists are skilled professionals, and staff are helpful. But remember that some prescriptions cannot be filled outside your home country. Most branches are open 24 hours and all offer delivery services.
Other locations throughout the city.

Spas & salons

Lulu of London
Rodríguez Peña 1057, entre Marcelo T de Alvear y Santa Fe, Recoleta (4815 8471/www.luluoflondon. com.ar). Subte D, Callao/39, 132, 152 bus. **Open** by appointment only. **No credit cards. Map** p326 I10.

An exclusive beauty salon run from the apartment of expat Jude O'Hara. Clients of all stripes turn up for expert skincare, massages, waxing and aromatherapy. Call in advance.

Nail Company
Arenales 1739, entre Rodríguez Peña y Callao, Barrio Norte (4815 2139). Bus 10, 12, 61, 110, 124. **Open** 9.30am-8.30pm Mon-Wed; 9.30am-9pm Thur, Fri; 10am-8.30pm Sat. **Credit** AmEx, MC, V. **Map** p326 I10.
Armed with the latest in technology, the Nail Company leaves your hands in tip-top condition.

Tattoos & piercings

Galería Bond Street
Avenida Santa Fe 1670, entre Montevideo y Rodríguez Peña, Recoleta. Subte D, Callao/37, 39, 111, 152 bus. **Open** 10am-10pm Mon-Sat. **Credit** varies. **Map** p326 I10.
There are plenty of places to get any type of tattoos and piercings imaginable, all clean and good quality. Goths invade at the weekends, but it's great for fresh local T-shirt designs too.

House & home

Antiques

San Telmo – particularly Defensa between Independencia and San Juan – has the biggest concentration of antiques dealers in the city. Serious collectors should go on weekdays, but for a casual browse go to Plaza Dorrego on Sundays between 10am and 5pm.

Feria San Pedro Telmo
Plaza Dorrego, San Telmo. Bus 9, 10, 29, 195. **Open** 10am-5pm Sun. **Map** p324 D9.
For a lighthearted browse go to the area's central square, Plaza Dorrego, on Sundays. Around 270 stalls sell antique dolls, soda siphons, jewellery, tango memorabilia and collectibles.

Gil Antigüedades
Humberto Primo 412, entre Defensa y Bolívar, San Telmo (4361 5019). Bus 24, 29, 126, 130, 152. **Open** 11am-1pm, 3-7pm Tue-Sat; 11am-7pm Sun. **Credit** AmEx, DC, MC, V. **Map** p324 D9.
The sheer volume of items here will dazzle vintage fashion victims. Check out the Victorian clothing and the German-made *mates* from 1880-90.

Guevara Art Gallery
Defensa 982, entre Carlos Calvo y Estados Unidos, San Telmo (4362 2418/www.guevaragallery.com). Bus 24, 29, 126, 130, 152. **Open** 11am-7pm Mon-Sat. **Credit** AmEx, MC, V. **Map** p324 D10.
For lovers of art deco and art nouveau, this gallery has around 2,000 WMF German tableware items from 1850-1930, as well as Daum and Lalique pieces.

HB Antiquedades
Defensa 1016, entre Humberto Primo y Carlos Calvo, San Telmo (4361 3325). Bus 24, 29, 152. **Open** 10am-7pm Mon-Fri; 11am-5pm Sun. **No credit cards. Map** p324 D9.
Stepping into this vast antiques emporium is like walking into a slightly over-furnished palace. It's worth a look if only to take in the imposing centrepiece, an Italian pink chandelier.

El Mercado de las Pulgas
Niceto Vega, y Dorrego, Palermo Viejo (no phone). Bus 140, 161, 168. **Open** 10am-5pm daily. **No credit cards. Map** p327 O7.
Those who just enjoy ferreting through heaps of unsorted curios should visit the Mercado de las Pulgas (Spanish for flea market). This chaotic warehouse is crammed full of second-hand furniture, junk and antiques. You'll find chandeliers and retro lamps, old signs, in fact pretty much anything.

General

For one-stop designer shopping for the home, head to **Buenos Aires Design** at Avenida Pueyrredón 2501, y Azcuénaga (5777 6000). Located next to the Centro Cultural Recoleta, it has more than 60 interior design shops.

Calma Chicha
Honduras 4925, entre Gurruchaga y Borges, Palermo Viejo (4831 1818). Bus 39, 151, 168. **Open** 10am-8pm Mon-Sat; 2-8pm Sun. **Credit** AmEx, DC, MC, V. **Map** p323 M5.
Argentinian-produced board games and *pinguinos* (penguin-shaped wine jugs) are among the witty items on sale here.
Other location Defensa 856, San Telmo.

Eat, Drink, Shop

Urban gauchos

Ox blood is said to have tinted pink the paint that washes the walls of the Mataderos slaughterhouses and cattle market. And it is under the shadow of these turn-of-the-century buildings that the Feria de Mataderos celebrates all things *gaucho*. At this country-style fair visiting folk artists from the country and even Bolivia plink away on stage to a multitude dancing the accordion-led *chamamé* or *chacarera* of the northwest before them.

Gauchos, and little *gauchitos*, show off their amazing horsemanship by spearing a small ring hanging from a ribbon at a thundering gallop, while stallholders hawk all manner of *gaucho* paraphernalia such as *boleadoras* (three leather bound rocks used to catch

L'ago
Defensa 919 and Defensa 970, entre Estados Unidos y Carlos Calvo, San Telmo (4362 3641/4362 4702/www.lagosantelmo.com). Bus 24, 29, 152, 10. **Open** 10am-8pm daily. **Credit** AmEx, MC, V. **Map** p324 D10.
L'ago offers an eclectic array of houseware, lighting fixtures, art, furniture, gifts and plenty more at its two San Telmo locations. A bizarre but delightful blend.

Materia Urbana
Defensa 707, entre Chile e Independencia, San Telmo (4361 5265/www.materiaurbana.com). Bus 24, 29, 126, 130, 152. **Open** 11am-7pm Tue-Sun. **Credit** AmEx, DC, MC, V. **Map** p325 E10.
Take an enjoyable meander through this spacious second-floor apartment displaying small-format art and designer objects from around 70 local artists, from leather briefcases to snazzy mugs. **Other location** Gorriti 4791, Palermo (4831 6317).

Picnic
Uriarte 1359 2b, entre Cabrera y Gorriti, Palermo, (4775 7503/www.picnicdecor.com). Bus 34, 55. **Open** 11am-7pm Mon-Fri. **No credit cards**. **Map** p323 M5.
It's always worth a look in here, where the city's most cutting-edge design duo Coty Larguia and Eugenia Troncoso show off an eclectic range of wallpaper, reversible pillows, plates, lamps, original fabrics and more. An imaginatively converted apartment is the showroom, where the bold stamp of wallpaper patterns such as 'Old Boy', inspired by Chan-Wook Park's 2003 cult film, provide objects with an attractive and surprising backdrop.

Ramos Generales
Ground Floor 'C', Cabello 3650, entre Scalabrini Ortiz y Ugarteche, Palermo (4804 3524). Bus 10, 15, 21, 37, 160. **Open** 10.30am-7.30pm Mon-Fri; 10.30am-1.30pm Sat. **Credit** AmEx, MC, V. **Map** p326 L10.

stray cattle) and *facóns* (large knives), *mates*, art works, country-style cheese and salami and the occasional bit of well-meaning tat – bring money, you can get all your gifts in one swoop.

During the week it is a fully working cattle auction, but come the weekend, the only cows to be seen are slowly cooking away on the expansive grills. Other stalls sell delightful northern foods such as tamales and humitas (stuffed corn-meal dough pasties steamed in husks), and there's even one that specialises in tasty food from Paraguay. All however, sell cheap and sweet *vino patero* (foot-trodden wine) that fuels any day there.

To learn a little more about the gaucho culture head under the haunches of the arcade surrounding the fair into the **Museo Criollo de los Corrales** (*see p124*). Here an old frontier wagon, painted in the colourful *fileteado* style, forms the centrepiece of a fascinating, if tired, exhibition charting the history of the cornerstone of the Argentinian economy, and its associated culture.

Feria de Mataderos
Lisandro de la Torre y Los Corrales, Mataderos (www.feriademataderos. com.ar). Bus 55, 80, 92, 126. **Open** Apr-Dec 11am-8pm Sun; Jan-Mar 6pm-1am Sat.

Luscious home linens in the very best fabrics and colours abound at Ramos Generales. The quality and selection is outstanding but it'll cost you.

La Serine
Malabia 1835, entre Costa Rica y Nicaragua, Palermo Viejo (4833 1316/www.laserinedeco.com). Subte D, Scalabrini Ortiz/15, 39, 110, 111 bus. **Open** 11am-8pm daily. **Credit** AmEx, MC, V. **Map** p323 M5.
This exquisite boutique specialises in design and decorative goodies. The stock ranges from French-inspired wallpaper to kitschy ornaments.

Specialist

Papelera Palermo
Honduras 4945, entre Gurruchaga y Borges, Palermo Viejo (4833 3081/www.papelerapalermo. com.ar). Bus 39, 55, 168. **Open** 10am-8pm Mon-Sat; 2-8pm Sun. **No credit cards. Map** p323 M5.
With handmade paper, binders, notebooks, boxes

and cards in all shapes, sizes and textures, this super stationer's is a joy to browse in.
Other location Arenales 1170, Recoleta (4811 7698).

Sabater Hermanos
Gurruchaga 1821, entre Costa Rica y Nicaragua, Palermo Viejo (4833 3004/www.shnos.com.ar). Bus 39, 55, 151. **Open** 10am-8pm Mon-Sat; 1-7pm Sun. **No credit cards. Map** p323 M5.
Run by the third generation of Sabater family soap makers, this funky shop/workshop is a soap version of a pick 'n' mix counter. Select from a huge range of smells and textures, plus plenty of whimsical coloured flakes, petals and hearts.

Wussmann
Venezuela 570, entre Bolívar y Perú, San Telmo (4343 4707/www.wussmann.com). Bus 9, 10, 24, 29, 86. **Open** 10.30am-8pm Mon-Fri; 10.30am-2pm Sat. **Credit** AmEx, V. **Map** p325 E10.
An exclusive paper shop, Wussmann offers beautiful leather journals, photo albums and handcrafted paper with ancient prints; all make excellent gifts. Also find antique books and curios.
Other location Wussman Gallery, Rodríguez Peña 1399, Recoleta (4811 2444).

Music & entertainment

CDs, records & DVDs

Musimundo
Avenida Santa Fe 1844, entre Callao y Riobamba, Barrio Norte (4814 0393/www.musimundo.com). Bus 10, 37, 39, 152. **Open** 10am-10pm Mon-Thur; 9.30am-10pm Fri, Sat; 11am-10pm Sun. **Credit** AmEx, DC, MC, V. **Map** p326 I10.
Argentina's own Musimundo has a good, mainstream selection of music from around the world and stocks all types of Argentinian music. Some branches sell audio and computer equipment.
Other locations throughout the city.

Zival's
Avenida Callao 395, y Corrientes, Tribunales (5128 7500/www.zivals.com). Subte B, Callao/12, 24, 37, 60 bus. **Open** 9.30am-10pm Mon-Sat. **Credit** AmEx, DC, MC, V. **Map** p325 H9.
Claiming to stock the widest selection of music in South America, Zival's has all genres, but specialises in classical, jazz, folk, tango and hard-to-find independent local recordings. It is also an excellent bookshop with travel guides, and books in English.
Other location Serrano 1445, Palermo Viejo.

Musical instruments
There is shop after shop selling all types of musical instruments, including native *bandoneones* and *charangos*, on Talcahuano, especially between Rivadavia and Corrientes downtown. **Daiam** (Talcahuano 139, 4374 6510, www.daiamnet.com.ar) has a large selection.

Sports & fitness

Depor Camping

Santa Fe 4830, entre Humbolt y Fitz Roy, Palermo Viejo (4772 0534/www.dporcamping.com.ar). Subte D, Palermo/34, 55, 111 bus. **Open** 9am-8.30pm Mon-Sat. **Credit** AmEx, MC, V. **Map** p327 N9.

A large store with adequate backpacking gear. Columbia, Salomon and Merrell are all represented. Sleeping bags, Swiss Army knives, and other camping equipment is available to replace any airport confiscations.

Other location Carlos Pellegrini 737, Microcentro (4328 6100).

La Martina

Paraguay 661, entre Florida y Maipú, Retiro (4576 0010/www.lamartina.com). Subte C, San Martín/7, 10, 17, 152 bus. **Open** 10am-8pm Mon-Fri; 10am-2pm Sat. **Credit** AmEx, DC, MC, V. **Map** p325 G11.

La Martina's flagship store feels like a polo museum, but it also has a collection of branded polo clothing and equipment, perfect for souvenirs.

Other locations Galerías Pacífico (5555 5234); Patio Bullrich shopping centres.

Tickets

Many music and sports venues, especially clubs, are unlikely to accept credit cards. Buy tickets using major credit cards at the following agencies: **Ticketek** (5237 7200, www.ticketek.com.ar, nine locations) and **EntradaPlus** (4000 1010, www.entradaplus.com.ar). Tickets can also be bought in person and in cash at Pago Fácil ticket servies at Perú 139, Microcentro. The booking fee is usually ten per cent.

Travellers' needs

Below is a list of recommended travel agents and tour operators. For city tours refer to the Sightseeing section (*see p77*).

Shipping goods to the UK, US and Europe can be a problem. **Correo Argentina** is not very reliable. See Directory *p298* for details of couriers. For computer repairs and phone rental *see p183*. For luggage *see p200*.

Tour operators

Curiocity

4th floor, Juncal 2021, entre Junín y Ayacucho, Recoleta (4803 1113/www.curiocitytravel.com). Bus 10, 39. **Open** 10am-6pm Mon-Fri. By appointment only. **Credit** AmEx, MC, V. **Map** p326 I10.

Specialising in high-end tailor-made holidays for the very wealthy and famous, Curiocity can sort out any trip anywhere in Argentina, Chile and Uruguay with no fuss, no matter how demanding the programme. Consulting fees start at US$100 an hour.

MAWA

Avenida Cordoba, Microcentro (4312 5111/www.mawatravel.com). Subte C, Lavalle/10, 17, 59 bus. **Open** 10am-7pm Mon-Fri. **Credit** varies (depending on itinerary). **Map** p325 G11.

A well established and slick operation that can arrange a wide range of tours and trips in the southern cone. They cater for backpackers as well as the more affluent traveller.

Other locations Malabia 1617, Palermo Viejo (4833 2900); Florida 737, Microcentro (4312 5111).

PlanBA.com

(4776 8267/www.planba.com/info@planba.com).

A reliable and imaginative concierge service for those keen to get the most out of their time in Buenos Aires. Among its services, PlanBA offers high-end city tours, VIP nights on the town, day trips and tickets to a range of matches, gigs, and events.

Robertson Wine Tours

(4772 5839/15 5715 0678 mobile/www.robertsonwinetours.com).

A British expat whose passion for selling, tasting and showcasing fine wines (and above all his passion for helping others share his passion) has taken him all over the world. Now based in Argentina they use expert guides and put clients up at fine hotels and wine lodges.

Say Hueque

Office 1, 6th floor, Viamonte 749, entre Esmeralda y Maipú, Microcentro (5199 2517/20/www.sayhueque.com). Subte C, Lavalle/10, 17, 59 bus. **Open** 10am-6.30pm Mon-Fri; 10am-1pm Sat. **Credit** varies (depending on itinerary). **Map** p325 G11.

Listed and recommended by all of the top travel guides, Say Hueque offers a full range of trips for discering travellers looking for good and chic accommodation, interesting unique tours around Argentina and Chile.

Special Buenos Aires

(15 4141 1776/www.specialbuenosaires.com.ar)

The ever cheerful founder Gustavo Santa Cruz and his team can offer a wide range of personalised city tours, trips out of town or to neighbouring countries or even a simple *asado* with a family to experience the more intimate details of life in Buenos Aires. Special Buenos Aires is a friendly, flexible and reliable operation.

Tangol

Unit 31, Ground floor, Florida 971, entre Paraguay y Marcelo T de Alvear, Microcentro (4312 7276/www.tangol.com). **Open** 10am-7pm Mon-Fri. **Credit** AmEx, MC, V. **Map** p325 G11.

Innovative and highly professional travel and tour agency offering a variety of activities both in and away from Buenos Aires. Their most popular services include BA city tours, football excursions, helicopter trips and a Patagonia Overland package.

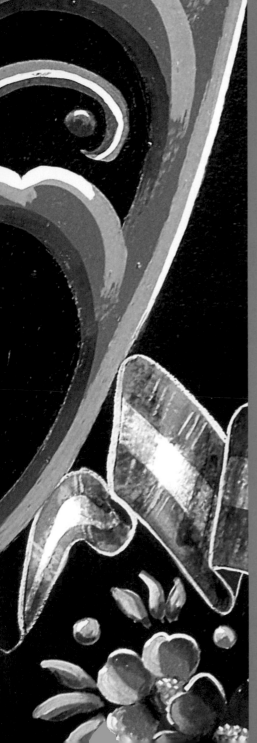

Arts & Entertainment

Features

Festivals & Events

From fine wine to home design, there's always something to celebrate in BA.

The party of all parties is coming to Buenos Aires in 2010, when Argentina celebrates 200 years of independence on 25 May. At the time of going to press plans are still to be finalised, but the festivities will undoubtedly involve some spectacular concerts, dazzling pyrotechnics, buckets of red wine and dancing in the streets.

The superb bilingual city government tourist website www.bue.gov.ar is a good port of call for information on local cultural events. Other useful guides are the hip and helpful www.whatsupbuenosaires.com, and www.letstango.com.ar, which has art and music listings as well as tango. Otherwise, newspapers (*Página 12* on Thursdays, *Clarín* on Fridays, the English-language *Buenos Aires Herald*) or tourist information points are your best sources.

January-March

Chinese New Year
Along Arribeños 2000-2200 blocks, Belgrano (Chinese Embassy 4541 5085). Bus 15, 29, 60, 64. **Map** p329 S9. **Date** Jan or Feb.
This small-scale day-long festival is an explosion of colour and clamour in Belgrano's tiny Chinatown, known locally as Barrio Chino. Local restaurants set up stalls on the streets and dole out dim sum.

Carnaval
Plazas & social clubs throughout Buenos Aires (www.buenosaires.gov.ar). **Date** Feb.
Don't expect Rio or New Orleans – here, festivities are on a smaller, albeit still enthusiastic scale, with local groups of *murga* drummers and dancers performing in plazas, and a parade down Avenida de Mayo. The best carnivals in the region are in the Uruguayan capital, Montevideo (*see p288*), while in Argentina the main action is in Gualeguaychú (pronounced Gwal-ay-gwah-CHOO) in Entre Ríos.

Abierto de Tenis de Buenos Aires
Buenos Aires Lawn Tenis Club, Olleros 1510, y Libertador, Palermo (4772 0983/www.copatelmex.com). Bus 15, 29, 59, 60. **Map** p329 Q9. **Date** Feb.
BA's annual Tennis Open gives locals the rare opportunity to watch their own players slug it out

▶ For more festivals, see our specialist **Arts & Entertainment** chapters. For a list of public holidays, *see p306*.

on the city's premier clay courts. Home-grown stars include David Nalbandian and Guillermo Cañas.

Opera Season
Teatro Colón, Libertad 621, entre Tucumán y Viamonte, Tribunales (box office 4378 7344/ www.teatrocolon.org.ar). Subte D, Tribunales/ 29, 39, 59, 109 bus. **Map** p325 G10. **Date** Mar-Dec.
The opera seasons have been thrown into disarray somewhat with the problems delaying the reopening of the stunning Teatro Colón (*see p240*). However, in all theatres the season officially opens its curtains in early March, with ballet, opera and classical concerts. Look out for brilliant pianist/conductor Daniel Barenboim's annual return.

South American Music Conference
Centro Costa Salguero, Avenida Rafael Obligado, y Salguero, Costanera Norte (www.samc.net). Bus 33. **Map** p326 L12. **Date** early Mar.
This world-class electronic music event, uniting DJs from around the globe, has helped establish BA as

Arts & Entertainment

the dance capital of South America. Expect seminars on trance and techno as well as a mammoth closing party that will leave your ears ringing for days.

Fashion Buenos Aires

Hilton Hotel, Avenida Macacha Güemes 351, Dique 3, Puerto Madero Este (4982 4074/ www.buenosairesmoda.com). Bus 130, 152. **Map** p325 E12. **Date** Mar & Sept.

The latest fads from local designers grace the catwalk in Buenos Aires' twice-yearly, five-day fashion week: the winter collection is presented in March, the summer one in September. Over 30 labels show off their wares to 13,000 guests per day. Pay around AR$10 to hang out with willowy beauties, catty *fashionistas* and other people who would happily spend a month's wages on a pair of sandals.

April-June

Festival Internacional de Cine Independiente

Hoyts Abasto & other cinemas (www.bafici.gov.ar). **Date** Mid-late Apr.

Hugely popular ten-day showcase for international non-Hollywood films, including the work of local directors. It attracts a couple of big-name filmmakers and high-profile actors usually seen only at the likes of the Cannes or Berlin film festivals.

Feria Internacional del Libro

Predio La Rural, Avenida Santa Fe 4201, y Avenida Sarmiento, Palermo (www.el-libro.org.ar). Subte D, Plaza Italia/29, 39, 60, 152 bus. **Map** p327 M9. **Date** mid Apr-May.

The annual BA Book Fair is a monster three weeks of readings, book signings and debates, some in English. Geared much more towards readers than publishers, the fair attracts an incredible 1.2m bookworms plus authors from all over the globe.

ArteBA

Predio La Rural, Avenida Santa Fe 4201, y Avenida Sarmiento, Palermo (www.arteba.com). Subte D, Plaza Italia/10, 29, 39, 60, 152 bus. **Map** p327 M9. **Date** mid May.

National and international galleries, specialist publishers, artists and collectors (not to mention 110,000 paying punters) descend on this week-long art fair, which has evolved into one of the best-attended and most-hyped cultural events in Latin America, displaying the works of hundreds of artists from Argentina and overseas.

Aniversario de la Revolución de Mayo

Plaza de Mayo (Museo del Cabildo 4334 1782). Subte A, Plaza de Mayo or D, Catedral or E, Bolívar/24, 29, 64, 86, 152 bus. **Map** p325 E11. **Date** 25 May.

The humble celebration of the 1810 revolution begins at midnight the day before, when people gather in front of the Cabildo for a lusty rendition of the (lengthy) national anthem. At 8pm on the 25th, the crowds mass again for another patriotic singalong.

July-September

Día de la Independencia

Across Argentina. **Date** 9 July.

Although the main events are held in freedom's birthplace in the north-western city of Tucumán, cafés along Avenida de Mayo serve up traditional hot chocolate with *churros* (doughnuts) and a solemn mass at the cathedral is attended by the president, who is forced to sit through a tongue-lashing homily delivered by the city's archbishop.

Carnaval. *See p210.*

Arts & Entertainment

Name the day

Every important historical figure in Argentina is commemorated with a *feriado* (public holiday), usually on the anniversary of their death. Aside from national heroes such as San Martín, Sarmiento and Belgrano – who frequently get streets named after them as well – days are set aside to celebrate the achievements of less illustrious, but no less worthy, workers, such as the Día del Obrero Fideero (Day of the Pasta Maker) on 22 May. The humble visitor also gets a chance to shine on 5 October's Día del Turista (Day of the Tourist). Even more bizarre are days dedicated to inanimate objects or abstract ideas. Below are a just a handful of the other 365 examples.

7 April Día del Acoplado y Semirremolque (Trailer and Breakdown Trucks Day)
8 May Día Nacional de la Prevención Sísmica (National Day for the Prevention of Earthquakes)
18 July Día del Riel (Day of the Rails – yes, as in train tracks)
20 July Día del Amigo (Friend's Day)
12 August Día del Jabonero (Day of the Soap Maker)
14 November Día del Amor (Day of Love)
11 December Día Nacional del Tango: Nacimiento de Juilo De Caro y Carlos Gardel (National Tango Day: Birthday of Juilo De Caro and Carlos Gardel)

La Rural
Predio La Rural, Avenida Santa Fe 4201, y Sarmiento, Palermo (www.exposicionrural.com.ar). Subte D, Plaza Italia/10, 29, 39, 60, 152 bus. **Map** p327 M9. **Date** end July-Aug.
The Exposición de Ganadería, Agricultura e Industria Internacional – known as La Rural – is the nation's supremely important two-week farm fair. Lambs, rams, pigs and other farm animals get a look-in, but it's the bulls who enjoy the most respect. The best events are the madly macho *gaucho* stunts. Also the time of year when BA's *peñas* (folklore nights; *see p246*) fill with genuine foot-stamping cowboys.

Buenos Aires Tango Festival
Various theatres & cultural centres (www.festivaldetango.com.ar). **Date** mid Aug.
This is the big one: it's the city's – and therefore the world's – most important tango festival, a nine-day extravaganza of concerts, shows, free classes, exhibitions, open-air *milongas* (Avenida Corrientes is closed for a massive dance off) and other tango-related festivities. If you're in town, don't miss it. If you're a tango fan, plan your trip around it.

World Tango Championships
Various theatres and cultural centres (www.tangodata.gov.ar). **Date** late Aug.
Prequalifying stages, strict rules and an eagle-eyed jury (Simon Cowell has nothing on these guys) are just a few of the hurdles awaiting those couples attempting to become the World Tango Champions. The prize money is small but the prestige is priceless, and those with two left feet can marvel at the leg flicking athleticism and passionate clinches on stage.

Feria de Vinos y Bodegas
Predio La Rural, Avenida Santa Fe 4201, y Sarmiento, Palermo (www.inasuvid.com.ar). Subte D, Plaza Italia/10, 29, 39, 60, 152 bus. **Map** p327 M9. **Date** early Sept.
Vineyards from around Argentina exhibit at the country's biggest wine fair, aimed at popularising home-grown brands. Grape connoisseurs can enjoy four glorious days of wine swilling with over 1,000 different labels to sample, as well as specialist tastings, seminars, and master chef demonstrations on what dishes to best accompany your *vino* with.

Festival Internacional de Teatro Buenos Aires
Teatro San Martín & other theatres (festivaldeteatro ba.gov.ar). **Date** every 2 years; next Sept 2009.
Buenos Aires' major performing arts festival, this is an impressive fortnight of Argentinian and international theatre, dance and performances.

October-December

Festival Martha Argerich
Teatro Colón, Libertad 621, entre Tucumán y Viamonte, Tribunales (box office 4378 7344/ www.teatrocolon.org.ar). Subte D, Tribunales/ 29, 39, 59, 109 bus. **Map** p325 G10. **Date** Oct.
Renowned Argentinian pianist Martha Argerich wows her legions of fans during this high-profile ten-day celebration of classical music, which includes Argerich's virtuoso solo performances as well as ensemble pieces with famous guests.

Alvear Fashion & Arts
Along Avenida Alvear, Recoleta (www.alvearfa.com.ar). Bus 17, 67, 93, 124, 130. **Map** p326 I11. **Date** Oct-Nov.
A one-week, red-carpet exhibition of local painters, sculptors and photographers held at the high-end boutiques and galleries on BA's swankiest avenue, recently voted among the top five shopping areas in the world. Also includes talks on issues in contemporary art and what rags we'll be wearing.

Casa Foa
Venue varies (www.casafoa.com). **Date** Oct-Nov.
Going strong for over two decades, this cutting-edge design fair presents new trends in the world

of architecture, garden and interior design, providing stylish inspiration on how best to personalise your home.

Código País

Venue varies (www.codigopais.com). **Date** Nov.
As well as showcasing the talents of innovative new artists, photographers and designers, Código País is dedicated to opening your eyes to new possibilities, through an eclectic programme of independent film screenings, live DJs, sustainable fashion workshops, avant-garde theatre and even an 'erotic space'.

Maratón de Buenos Aires

Information *www.maratondebuenosaires.com.*
Date Nov.
Roadrunners clog Avenida 9 de Julio in this annual marathon. The start and finish line is the Obelisco. As well as the international race there's a 'fun run' and a four-kilometre mini marathon for children.

Marcha del Orgullo Gay

Plaza de Mayo (www.marchadelorgullo.org.ar). Subte A, Plaza de Mayo or D, Catedral or E, Bolívar/24, 64, 86, 152 bus. **Map** p325 E11. **Date** 1st Sat in Nov.
BA's ever growing Gay Pride March gathers gays, lesbians, trannies and heteros for a serious protest parade through the city centre, and an even more serious party in the city's nightclubs afterwards. It might not be as big as its Sydney or Sao Paulo counterparts but it's seriously fun.

Creamfields

Autodrómo de Buenos Aires, Avenida General Paz y Avenida Roca (www.creamfields.com).
Date early Nov.
This one-day dance music festival has a relationship with rain similar to Glastonbury, but a bit of mud doesn't deter 60,000 party-loving *porteños* from stepping out in their finest for 15 hours of non-stop raving. International DJs such as Carl Cox and The Chemical Brothers get behind the decks, and a turn by local boy Hernán Cattáneo is pretty much a given.

Día de la Tradición

Feria de Mataderos, Lisandro de la Torre y Avenida de Los Corrales (www.feriademataderos.com.ar). Bus 55, 80, 92, 126. Also San Antonio de Areco, BA province (Tourist Office 02326 453165/www.san antoniodeareco.com). **Date** weekend nearest 12 Nov.
The annual *gaucho* day has regional food and music and impressive displays of horsemanship. The town of San Antonio de Areco (*see p276*), 113 kilometres (70 miles) north-west of the capital, or BA's Feria de Mataderos (*see p179*), are the places to be.

Gran Premio Nacional

Hipódromo Argentino de Palermo, Avenida del Libertador 4101, y Dorrego, Palermo (4778 2880/www.palermo.com.ar). Bus 10, 36, 160.
Map p327 O10. **Date** mid Nov.
First run in 1884, Argentina's top annual horse race attracts knowledgeable punters and social climbers alike. In recent years it's become a day-long event with

plenty of track-side entertainment and celebrity spotting. Dress appropriately – hats are not essential ladies, but for men, the jumper draped louchely over the shoulders is a must.

Abierto Argentino de Polo

Campo Argentino de Polo, Avenida del Libertador 4000 y Dorrego, Palermo (Asociación Argentina de Polo 4343 0972/www.aapolo.com). Bus 10, 64, 130, 160. **Map** p327 O9. **Date** mid Nov-mid Dec.
Argentina has long been polo's spiritual home, producing the world's top stars both on four legs and two. Held at Palermo's magnificent 16,000 capacity Campo Argentino de Polo, the Argentinian Polo Open is the sport's annual highlight.

Festival Buenos Aires Danza Contemporánea

Teatro San Martín & other theatres (www.buenos airesdanza.com.ar). **Date** held every 2 years in Dec; next in 2008.
For two weeks only, once every two years, tango takes a back seat and BA's sometimes overlooked modern dance scene twirls on to centre stage. Theatres around the city present the best in local as well as international talent.

Festival Buen Día

Venue varies (www.festivalbuendia.net).
Date mid Dec.
An ultra laid-back affair, this youth-oriented open-air party kicks off with a relaxed afternoon of browsing stylish fashion, music, photography and craft stalls, and climaxes with a host of live bands performing beneath the stars.

Día de la Tradición.

Children

Roaming around with the rugrats.

Argentinian families are often big families. Having five or six siblings is not a rarity here and tending to the little ones becomes second nature. Seats on public transport are consistently offered up to mum and child, store keepers tickle chins and grannies playfully jangle keys. It's a child-friendly atmosphere that often comes as a pleasant surprise to tourist parents. However, be prepared for some obstacles. This is not a city where pedestrians have the right-of-way, the traffic is choking and land mines in the form of dog poo are abundant. As you push your buggy along treacherous uneven pavements, you will come to understand the real meaning behind 'urban jungle'.

Yet despite all the noise and chaos that defines Buenos Aires, the children here are amazingly chilled out and well behaved. Temper tantrums in stores or screaming kids at restaurants are usually western imports and

Boating in **Parque Tres de Febrero**.

Argentinian toddlers seem to have better manners at the dinner table than a fiancé does at his in-laws.

Most restaurants are more than happy to cater to children and often have special menus. Popular with parents is **Cumaná** (Rodriguez Peña 1149, Barrio Norte, 4813 9207) where kids can draw on paper tablecloths with crayons.

Although the larger chain hotels are usually better equipped for children's needs, apart-hotels, which are popping up everywhere, make family holidays that much easier as they offer personal kitchenettes and extra beds. **Soho All Suites** (*see p63*) and **LoiSuites Recoleta Hotels** (*see p59*) are reliable options.

If you're at a loss for where to start to keep the kids occupied, a good point of reference is Revista Planetario (4554 8545, www.revista planetario.com.ar) a monthly magazine with a user-friendly website listing up-to-date children's events. Also have a browse on the Goverment of Buenos Aires' website (www.bue.gov.ar) for upcoming free activities. Throughout the summer, they put on a whole array of outdoor events and activities, many aimed at children. Arts are particularly well supported by the government and porteños, making open-air theatres, painting and workshops commonplace.

Outdoors

Believe it or not there is green space for Junior to practise his cartwheeling throughout the city. In fact, most parks have recently been revamped to attract families.

Parque Tres de Febrero (*see p109*) is frequented by lovebirds and powerwalkers alike – it's BA's version of Hyde Park. In the middle lies a lake (well, a large pond) where paddle and rowing boats can be rented for AR$20 per hour. Ducks and fish in the lake are also pretty to look at, not to mention the numerous different breeds of dogs being exercised in various zones of the park. Or, if your little one loves wheels, rollerblades at AR$12 and bicycles with child seats for AR$8 can be rented hourly. There is a paved cycle path around the lake that is probably the only constant smooth surface in the city.

If your kids are toddlers, the **Jardín Japonés** (*see p110*) has hide-and-seek-style

Ogling the elephants at the **Jardín Zoológico de Buenos Aires.**

gardens as well as mesmerising koi lurking around the pond lillies. Free exhibitions are put on during the summer, such as martial arts displays. Have a glance on their website (www.jardinjapones.org.ar) for ideas. **Reserva Ecológica** (*see p121*) is also a good option for fresh air. The reserve is made up of 865 acres and is home to mammals, many species of birds, reptiles and a butterflies. Guided tours are on Saturdays and Sundays from 10.30am to 3.30pm and are free to the general public, though it's worth turning in good time.

If you can manage a long bus ride/taxi fare, **Feria de Mataderos** (*see p179*) is a lively modern *gaucho* festival held every weekend. While making yourselves sick on toffee apples, you can watch traditional folk dancing, listen to live music and watch real *gauchos* gallop past displaying their horsemanship.

Perhaps the most amusing day out is a trip to **Tierra Santa** (*see p121*), a religious theme park where the story of Jesus is re-created in a dazzling laser light show. There is an educational element to it, but really the joy is in seeing a giant Jesus be resurrected every half hour, make sure to take your camera.

Jardín Zoológico de Buenos Aires

Avenidas Las Heras y Sarmiento, Palermo (4806 7412/www.zoobuenosaires.com.ar). Subte D, Plaza Italia/15, 36, 37, 60, 152 bus. **Open** *Jan, Feb* 10am-6pm daily. *Mar-Dec* 10am-5.30pm Tue-Sun. **Admission** AR$4-$8.50; free under-12s, reductions. **Credit** V. **Map** p327 M9.

All types of creepy crawlies and fuzzy things are housed here (350 to be exact). Educational activities such as cow milking and paper recycling will make good use of those wet wipes in mum's purse. Extremely busy at weekends.

Indoors

One advantage of visiting a large metropolis is the amount of indoor space to explore and air-conditioned oases, great for keeping overheated stroppiness at bay. The **Abasto** shopping centre (*see p178)* is an architectural beauty, but if a lecture on art deco's 1930s magnificence sets eyes rolling there's always a cinema, video arcade, amusement park and the **Museo de los Ninos**. For older kids, the **Malba** (*see p110*) and **Teatro Colón** (*see p240*) run great children's programmes, particularly during the summer holidays (Jan-March).

Arts & Entertainment

La Calle de los Títeres

Centro Cultural del Sur, Avenida Caseros 1750, y Baigorri, Constitución (4305 6653/4306 0301). Bus 45, 59, 67. **Open** Puppet shows *Mar-Dec* 3pm Sat; 3pm, 4pm Sun. **Closed** Jan, Feb. **Map** p325 E7

A real-life version of Punch and Judy takes place here, where free puppet shows and puppet-making classes magically keep youngsters engaged and occupied. Using puppets not only stimulates creativity and exercises the imagination, it is also a chance for your child to interact with local children in the picturesque patio of an old mansion.

Museo de los Niños

Level 2, Corrientes 3247, entre Agüero y Anchorena, Abasto (4861 2325/www.museoabasto.org.ar). Subte B, Carlos Gardel/24, 26, 124, 146, 168 bus. **Open** 1-8pm Tue-Sun. **Admission** AR$5; AR$12-$18 family ticket; free under-3s. **Credit** AmEx, DC, MC, V. **Map** p322 J5.

A centre for active minds where through play kids can develop skills to impress and outdo grown-ups. A good choice for children who are particularly creative and social.

Museo Participativo de Ciencias

1st Floor, Centro Cultural Recoleta, Junín 1930, y Quintana, Recoleta (4807 3260/4806 3456/www. mpc.org.ar). Bus 10, 17, 60, 67, 92, 110. **Open** *Jan, Feb* 3.30-7.30pm Tue-Sun. *Mar-Dec* 10am-5pm Tue-Fri; 3.30-7.30pm Sat, Sun. **Admission** AR$6; free under-4s. **No credit cards. Map** p326 J11.

'Prohibido no tocar' (it's forbidden not to touch) is the appealing motto of this science museum in the Recoleta Cultural Centre, where kids can investigate the mysteries of physics and have fun at the same time. It's best for children older than seven. Once the children have been worn out, parents can wander around in the art galleries housed in the same building. There is also plenty of green space outside to run around with all manner of distractions for the kids, especially at weekends.

Planetario de la Ciudad de Buenos Aires Galileo Galilei

Parque Tres de Febrero, Belisario Roldán y Avenida Sarmiento, Palermo (4772 9265/4771 6629/ www.revistaplanetario.com.ar). Subte D, Plaza Italia/37, 67, 130, 160 bus. **Open** *Museum* 10am-6pm Mon-Fri; 1-7.30pm Sat, Sun. *Shows* 3pm, 4.30pm, 6pm Sat, Sun. **Admission** *Museum* free. *Shows* AR$4; free under-5s, concessions. **No credit cards. Map** p327 M11.

Although the talks are given in Spanish, kids will always be fascinated with the solar system and for added appeal this planetarium is in the shape of a spaceship. Every Sunday night the public can test out telescopes and the website lists any celestially special nights of the year. Also keep your eyes peeled for their annual *Feria de los Chicos* (Children's Fair) held here in the second week of April; look under *'eventos'* on their website. Craft making, outdoor games, stalls and information for parents makes for a busy three days of fun and entertainment.

Outside Buenos Aires

Some of the best family outings to be found are outside the Capital Federal. Don't be afraid to explore the nearby countryside with big comfy buses and accessible trains. *Estancias (see p279)* are an excellent way to tire out children. They have pools, horses or bikes which offer endless hours of healthy outdoor fun. **Tigre** *(see p269)* is another good option whereby a surprisingly short train ride can get you to a Jurassic-looking world of streams and swampy islands. Wildlife park **Temaikèn** is a favourite and home to exotic animals including white tigers and a hippopotamus. Rest assured that compared to some other South American animal parks it has a more humane outlook, with large areas for the animals.

Parque de la Costa

Vivanco 1509, y Mitre, Tigre (4002 6000/www. parquedelacosta.com.ar). Tren de la Costa to Delta/ 60 bus. **Open** 11am-8pm Thur-Sun. **Admission** *Park* free. *Shows & rides* AR$20-$30; AR$9 3-12s; AR$6 concessions; free under-3s. **Credit** AmEx, DC, MC, V.

Next to the Delta train station in Tigre is a substantially sized amusement park (to find it just follow the screams). Rides, roller coasters, themed restaurants and a lake show should be enough to keep everyone happy for an action-packed day.

Parque Temaikén

Ruta Provincial 25, km 1, Escobar (03488 436900/www.temaiken.com.ar). **Open** 10am-7pm Tue-Sun. **Admission** AR$22; AR$12 3-10s, concessions. **Credit** AmEx, DC, MC, V.

This wonderful wildlife park is just 30 minutes from downtown Buenos Aires. Among the land mammals that roam its vast expanses are white tigers and pumas. In the aquarium, sharks, stingrays and other fish swim around in an overhead tank while outside the lovable hippopotamus can be viewed in a huge water tank.

Tren de la Costa

Avenida Maipú 2305, Olivos (4002 6000/www.trende lacosta.com.ar). From Retiro, Ramal 2 train on Mitre line to Olivos/59, 60, 71, 152 bus. **Open** 6.30am-11pm Mon-Fri; 8am-midnight Sat, Sun. **Return ticket** AR$16 non-residents; AR$10 residents; free under-3s. **Credit** AmEx, DC, MC, V.

On this delightful 25-minute train ride from Olivos to Tigre, you can get on and off at stations along the route, where there are cinemas, restaurants and shops. San Isidro station has the most options, including an arts fair on Saturdays and Sundays from 10am (www.artesanos-sanisidro.com.ar). Pack some sandwiches for a picnic or better yet, swimming costumes and splash about at **Perú Beach** (www.peru-beach.com.ar) where kayak and and windsuring rentals are available. There is some sand so castle building shouldn't be a problem.

Clubs

BA's latest clubbing revolution.

Buenos Aires has always had a (mostly deserved) reputation as Latin America's hottest clubbing destination. However, the BA club scene has seemingly changed little in the last few years; a sign of either success or stasis, depending on your point of view. The big river-side outpost of **Pacha** (*see p222*) had a reputation that crossed across the globe, as did the recently closed Mint. A clubber in Manchester may have thought Argentina was the capital of Brazil, but he may also have heard of BA's Pacha. Now, these clubs have been around for almost a decade, and nightclubs, like dogs, are considered elderly once they hit double figures. The same could be said of the average career span of a DJ, but that hasn't stopped people trumpeting Hernán Cattáneo as Argentina's top DJ since – or at least it feels like this – the invention of electricity. He's still a great DJ – but by the same token, Robert Plant is still a great singer. That said, currently keeping the monster club alive is Sunset (Roque Sáenz Peña 440, Olivos, 4794 8585, www.sunsetdisco.com) but you'll have to travel beyond the city limits.

But BA's *boliches* (nightclubs) are still among the best places in South America in which to dress up (not *too* much, this isn't Saint Tropez), flirt outrageously and dance till dawn. Regular visits from big-name foreign DJs, complemented by the talents of local mix masters, continue to feed the appetite for beats. Names to look out for on the dance, house and drum' n' bass scene include Javier Zuker, Cristóbal Paz, Elio Riso, Bad Boy Orange and Romina Cohn. Visit Surface Bookings (www.surfacebookings.com) for DJ biographies and upcoming parties. It has a surprisingly good English translation.

If you're one of those clubbers who is discerning about their music and would rather nod your head studiously to creative electronic beats than fling your limbs around randomly to cookie-cutter trance then we've got good news for you: BA has a vibrant avant-garde mash up scene, especially at places like Zizek at Niceto.

Fans of alternative electro should try to catch SoulFood producer Ezequiel Lodeiro in action (www.myspace.com/soulfoodnet). And, after years of following Europe's lead, hip beat makers (Villa Diamante, Chancha Via Circuito and G-Love) are creating a more local sound,

drawing inspiration from BA's own edgy neighbourhoods, *see p218* **Sound of the suburbs.** Less regular parties include the ultra-cool Fiesta Bubamara, where surreal gypsy tango meets electronic Balkan beats (www.fiestas-bubamara.com.ar), and the freakish discos thrown by Club Namunkura, where a mix of cross dressers, divas and rockers happily groove to funk, hip hop and tech house. (www.clubnamunkura.com.ar).

It's important to note that during the Argentinian summer (January and February) most of the city's bigger clubs move their operations to the Atlantic coast, particularly to Punta del Este in Uruguay. You should still pack your dancing shoes, however, since this gives smaller, underground venues the chance to flex their decks. But check the status of all the clubs listed here before rolling up, especially during the post-Christmas dash for the dunes.

CLUB CULTURE

When planning a night out, pace yourself and be prepared to travel. Venues are split between

Shamrock's Basement Club. See p220.

Sound of the suburbs

It may be premature to predict the demise of dance music in Buenos Aires, but few doubt it is a little moribund. Creamfields (see p213) may still attract tens of thousands of house-lovers in sunglasses, and young sexy types continue to pile into clubs like Pacha, for big-name international DJs, but the music hasn't really moved on since the days when Paul Oakenfold, Carl Cox, et al. praised the crowds of Buenos Aires. It was one of the most exciting places on the planet for dance music during the late 1990s. Ten years later, it all sounds a little bit tired.

Thankfully, a new generation of DJs and VJs, too young to remember the 'good old days', are slowly but surely piercing the Buenos Aires underground scene with a unique mix of music that takes inspiration from somewhere dance music has never looked before: Argentina.

Although cumbia originates from Colombia, where African rhythms mixed with indigenous music, the cumbia in Argentina is a separate genre. When the country's economy crashed in 2001 the 'cha, cha cha cha' beat that was resonant throughout the city's poorer quarters and on protest marches, became a soundtrack for the crisis. Cumbia sprang from the *Villas* (shanty towns), in particular *Cumbia Villera*, a notorious sound that glamorised the drug and gun culture rampant in the slums.

And now, cumbia, in much the same way as hip hop did in the US, is bridging the class divide, with the unmistakable lolloping beat starting to be heard at nights in the city's underground clubs.

One of the protagonists of this new cumbia electronica mash-up is Villa Diamante (*pictured*, www.diamantestyle.com.ar), who is one of the resident DJs at the Zizek party at Niceto (see p222). He says: 'cumbia has been around for many years in Argentina, but among the poorer people. Now people from all backgrounds are discovering it and beginning to experiment. There are a lot of people who are bored with house – which was, and still is, massive in BA, but people are going back to their roots.'

Meanwhile, bedroom producer Chancha Via Circuito (www.myspace.com/chanchavia circuito) is mixing coplas – traditional poems from the Jujuy province – with hip hop. Another laptop mixer, King Coya (www. myspace.com/kingcoya) is blending an even wider variety of indigenous beats and instruments. As his alter ego, Gaby Kerpel, King Coya put out the enthralling *Carnabalito* album in 2003, which looked to China and Africa for inspiration, while remaining in the soundscape of northwest Argentina folklore.

Are house music's days numbered? Log onto www.whatsupbuenosaires.com, hunt down a Cumbia party and decide for yourself. BA-based DJ Grant Dull, from the site, says: 'It is all informed from an urban culture that includes graffiti, street art, graphic design and all styles of music. It's all new and fresh. It's definitely the sounds of the streets now.'

central locations and the Costanera Norte along the river. Clubs don't open till at least midnight, get lively late (after 3am). Popular places, especially those with outside terraces like **Pacha**, rumble on past breakfast the next day, whereupon after-hours venues like **Caix** (*see p220*) and **Cocoliche** (*see p220*) offer wide-eyed clubbers an excuse to keep the party going until mid afternoon.

Though there is rarely a strict dress code in any club, *porteños'* slavery to fashion makes them militant about following the latest style commandments, and as dawn approaches, and usually well before, the (designer) sunglasses go on. Yet this posing reaps handsome visual rewards – BA's clubbers are a good-looking and flirtatious lot. The places that succeed are invariably packed with stylish, chatty people who never tire of foreign visitors. The welcoming, open attitude is not limited to the straight scene, gay clubs such as **Amerika** (*see right*) are now increasingly popular with heterosexuals. In general there's a friendly, non-aggressive vibe, partly owing, no doubt, to how little the locals drink. Dancefloor fisticuffs are mercifully rare, and anyone turning up steaming drunk or boisterous will be frowned upon by doormen and clubbers alike.

PRICES & INFORMATION

Though still affordable for tourists, entrance fees for many of the city's top nightspots have soared in the past year, though a foreign accent and a groomed appearance still help get you in pretty much anywhere. The admission price to smaller venues ranges from AR$5 to AR$25 (women usually pay less than men and sometimes get in for free), with larger clubs charging AR$20 to AR$60 depending on who's in the booth. As a rule, credit cards are not accepted, although if there's a restaurant you may be able to book a table before the music starts and pay for both your food and entrance on plastic. A drink, usually a beer, is often included with the cost of entrance: look out for *'con consumición'* or *'con trago'*. Many bars work on an annoying double queue system; pay for your drink at the cashier and get your receipt before you begin your fruitless attempts to make eye contact with the elusive bar staff. Best to stock up on receipts in one go.

For information about the latest happenings on the BA scene, and to purchase CDs of local DJs, check out www.buenosaliens.com. The best source of information for underground nights, interviews with DJs and links to myspace sites is www.whatsupbuenosaires.com, while the *noche urbana* (nightlife) recommendations at www.glamout.com are always worth a look. You can often email ahead to put yourself on a

queue-jumping guestlist and many of the clubs' websites have discount offers to print out. Keep an eye out for flyers (which also sometimes offer cheap admission) from **Galería Bond Street** (*see p203*) and various boutiques and bars dotted around Palermo Viejo.

WARNING!

BA's club scene has always been fickle, but it has become downright capricious since the Cromagnon nightclub blaze in December 2004, in which 194 young clubbers died, largely because the fire escapes had been bolted shut by greedy promoters trying to prevent non-paying customers sneaking in. Finally, club owners and the city council are taking their health and safety responsibilities seriously, but this new vigilance also means that venues are liable to be shut down overnight. While all the clubs listed below are up and running at time of going to press, it's more than possible that by the time you read this, some may be history. Check online or call up before venturing forth.

Venues

Amerika

Gascón 1040, entre Rocamora y Estado de Israel, Villa Crespo (4865 4416/www.ameri-k.com.ar). Subte B, Medrano/ 24, 55, 124 bus. **Open** from 1am Thur-Sun. **Map** p322 K5.
Three dance floors and a capacity of 2,000 makes this the largest gay disco in town in the city, but it is also one of the best parties in town with a very hetero-friendly vibe, particularly on Fridays when it attracts a mixed gay and straight crowd, who are perhaps curious to test out the dark rooms or eye up the regular live acts.

Asia de Cuba

Pierina Dialessi 750, y Macacha Güemes, Puerto Madero Este (4894 1328/www.asiadecuba.com.ar). Bus 2, 130, 152. **Open** *Restaurant* noon-3pm, from 9pm daily. *Club* from 10pm Tue-Sat. **Map** p325 E12.
At this flashy dockside spot (open at lunchtime as a bar-restaurant with comfortable loungers on the terrace) in posey Puerto Madero Este, you can dine on sushi, sweat it out on the dancefloor, or just enjoy the slightly mob-scented scenery while relishing a well-mixed drink.

Azúcar

Avenida Corrientes 3330, entre Agüero y Gallo, Abasto (4866 4439/www.azucarsalsa.com). Bus 24, 26, 124, 146, 168. **Open** from midnight Fri, Sat. **Map** p322 J5.
This small salsa venue verges on the tacky, with one wall painted with cartoon images of salsa's famous names, but it has energy to spare, an enthusiastic crowd and a cadre of resident – and impossibly cool – Cuban dance instructors. The dancefloor is small but there are plenty of places to sit and sup. There are dance classes most days in a variety of styles;

Bahrein

Lavalle 345, y Reconquista, Microcentre (4315 2403/www.bahreinba.com). Subte B, L.N. Alem/6, 22, 28, 93, 152 bus. **Open** *from 12.30am Tue, Wed, Fri, Sat.* **Map** *p325 F11.*

Since its birth in late 2004, Bahrein is one of the most happening clubs in the city. It draws a mixed crowd who flit between the swish top-floor restaurant and chillout area, the more commercial 'Funky Room' and the heavier grooves of the basement's 'XSS'. The owners have kept the features of this converted bank such as the original vaults and ornate chandeliers, adding a certain grandeur. Weekends are perpetually rammed, and come Tuesdays, it hosts to BA's most prominent drum and bass night – '+160' – fronted by the local talent Bad Boy Orange.

Basement Club

The Shamrock, Rodríguez Peña 1220, entre Juncal y Arenales, Recoleta (4812 3584). Bus 37, 39, 124, 152. **Open** *from 11pm Thur; from 1am Fri-Sun.* **Map** *p326 I10.*

Beyond the curtains to the basement of this popular Irish bar lies another world – fresh sounds, a giant glitter ball and disco floor lights. An ever changing roster of some of BA's best DJs, some well-known, some underground, keep this great little joint always full and fun. The crowd is a mix of locals, tourists and some of the hardest clubbers from the BA scene.

Big One

Adolfo Alsina 940, entre Bernardo de Irigoyen y Tacuarí, Monserrat (4331 1277/www.palacio buenosaires.com). Bus 10, 17, 59, 64, 86. **Open** *from 1.30am Fri, Sat, Sun.* **Map** *p325 F10.*

On Saturdays, Palacio Alsina hosts Big One, the capital's heaviest night of electronica. It's a vast venue that feels more like a cathedral than a disco. An upper balcony kitted out with tables and sofas allows a brief respite from the heaving mass of messy dancers below. Progressive house and banging techno are the orders of the night. International DJ sets are common on Saturdays, while Friday and Sunday nights are reserved for one of the city's best gay parties.

Caix

Centro Costa Salguero, Avenida Rafael Obligado y Salguero, Costanera Norte (4806 9749). Bus 37, 45. **Open** *from 1am Fri, Sat; 9am-3pm Sun.* **Map** *326 L12.*

Caix – situated close to a putting green, an evangelist temple, the city airport and the river's most polluted waters – is as surreal as the BA club scene gets. The place is at its most charged when the rest of the city is fully wound down. At 9am on Sunday morning, hundreds of indefatigable, sweat-sodden clubbers descend into a world of unrepentant hedonism, where most remain until the DJ pulls off his headphones sometime around 3pm. If the heat on the dancefloor becomes too much, try the airier second room, which looks out across the heads of a scattering of bewildered fishermen.

Club Aráoz

Aráoz 2424, entre Güemes y Santa Fe, Palermo (4833 7775). Subte D, Scalabrini Ortiz/36, 39, 106, 152 bus. **Open** *1.30-7am Fri, Sat.* **Map** *322 L6.*

Called 'Lost Clubbing' on Friday nights, Aráoz boasts an A-list roster of acclaimed home-grown spinners. Among the names who've dropped in for the night in Lost's booths are Martin Garcia and the ever popular Hernán Cattáneo, not to mention the mighty but ill-fated Grooverider. It's a smaller, more intimate and therefore more selective club than Pacha or Big One; so you can dive into the middle, flounder around, and come out still breathing. Thursdays are when BA's b-boys and girls come out to show off their breakdance tricks to a bouncy soundtrack of commercial hip hop.

Cocoliche

Rivadavia 878, entre Suipacha y Esmeralda, Microcentro (4331 6413/www.cocoliche.net). Subte A, Piedras/10, 64, 100 bus. **Open** *from 11pm Tue-Sun.* **Map** *p325 F10.*

This downtown club changes identity more times per week than a special agent. Get your groove on at BA's one-and-only breakbeat night every Tuesday, sing your heart out to classic Britpop at Thursday's *Les Inrockuptibles* indie-fest, and enjoy a kitsch mix of disco and pastries at Sunday evening's tea party. Weekend mornings from 8am sees a heaving afterparty.

Crobar

Paseo de la Infanta, Avenida del Libertador 3883, y Infanta Isabel, Palermo (47781500/www.crobar. com). Bus 10, 34, 36. **Open** *from 10pm Fri, Sat.* **Map** *p327 N10.*

Crobar – southern sister to the North American super clubs of the same name – is one of BA's biggest venues, drawing a regular crowd of dedicated party people. Stylishly industrial in design, it has a network of balconies, walkways and VIP areas which are cantilevered over the main dancefloor. Fridays are the see-and-be-seen nights for twenty to thirtysomethings, Saturdays tend to be quieter. Occasional visits from international DJs can push entry up to AR$60, but it's not enough to put off the hordes of wealthy young *porteños* and discerning tourists from their weekly pilgrimage to this classic party spot.

INK Buenos Aires

Niceto Vega 5635, entre Fitz Roy y Bonpland (4777 6242), Palermo Viejo. Bus 39, 93, 168. **Open** *from 10pm Thur-Sun.* **Map** *p323 N4.*

INK is a godsend for anyone craving access to the esoteric and exclusive fashion world. Arrive between 10pm and midnight to enjoy dinner and a show, invariably involving a catwalk of strutting *modelos*. Once the tables have been cleared (around 1am), it's time to dance and mingle with the beautiful. Expect plenty of pop on Fridays, followed by commercial house on Saturdays and Sundays. Getting into the club shouldn't be a problem; the real issue is how you make it upstairs to the VIP lounge.

Arts & Entertainment

Jacko's Club

*Cabrera 5569, entre Fitz Roy y Humboldt, Palermo
Viejo (4899 2337/www.jackos-club.com.ar). Bus 39,
93, 168.* **Open** from 10pm Thur-Sun. **Map** p323 N4.
Jacko's is actually better characterised as a DJ bar
than a bona fide nightclub, nonetheless the residents
are excellent. The guest DJs are up-and-coming and
enthusiastic rather than famous and bored-looking.

Jet

*Avenida Rafael Obligado 4801, Costanera Norte. Bus
37, 160 (no phone).* **Open** from 12.30am Thur-Sat.
Map p326 K12.
Another venture from the team behind the VIP area
at the now defunct Mint, Jet is considerably less
hectic than its better-known relative, with the focus
falling more on the people than the music. The
dancefloor is patrolled by cute young partygoers,
but the older and/or plainer won't feel awkward. In
any case, you can always retreat to a comfy booth,
sip a well-mixed (but pricey) cocktail and enjoy the
blend of mainstream indie and disco remixes.

Kika

*Honduras 5339, y Godoy Cruz, Palermo Viejo (4137
5311/www.kikaclub.com.ar). Bus 34, 55, 166.* **Open**
from 1.30am Fri, Sat. **Map** p323 N5.
If the young and cool Friday-night Crobar crowd
were saving themselves for Saturday, then Kika
would be their first port-of-call. The front room DJ
packs the dancefloor with a creative mix of classic
cheese, while his backroom counterpart spins
equally popular house. The club attracts its fair
share of BA's beautiful people, so the better you
look the more chance you have of queue-jumping.
The VIP section can fill up quickly, and the prices
are aimed at those who look down from its exclusive height on to the minions below.

Liquid

*Santa Fe 3651, y Scalabrini Ortiz, Palermo (4833
7748). Subte D, Scalabrini Ortiz/29, 39, 110, 152 bus.*
Open from 10pm Wed-Sat. **Map** p326 L9.
With its concoction of UV lighting, loud eighties
and nineties music and youthful crowd, Liquid may
well spark fresher's week flashbacks. Don't let this
completely put you off though, as it can be an
entertaining spot for a pre-club cocktail. Swing by
mid week to take advantage of the various drink
promotions and blag your way onto a comfy sofa
in the upstairs VIP area.

El Living

*Marcelo T de Alvear 1540, entre Montevideo y
Paraná, Tribunales (4811 4730/4815 6574/
www.living.com.ar). Bus 39, 152.* **Open** from 10pm
Thur-Sat. **Map** p325 H10.
Although the dance area of the relaxed El Living is
small, the music (think student disco circa 1992) has
enough verve to keep you bopping. There are three
bars – DJ, VJ and TV – the latter two fitted with big
screens and therefore perfect for those who prefer
watching to moving. Don't expect a wild crowd or
the beautiful set (again, think student disco circa
1992), but for a couple of drinks and a chance to
move your feet, it's spot on.

Maluco Beleza

*Sarmiento 1728, entre Rodriguez Peña y Callao,
Tribunales (4372 1737/www.malucobeleza.com.ar).
Bus 12, 24, 26, 60, 146.* **Open** from 10pm Wed,
Fri-Sun. **Map** p325 G9.
Maluco Beleza is a little slice of Brazil in Buenos
Aires. The music programming shows a typically
Brazilian disregard for genre (mixing Dire Straits
into samba), and the people an equally typical desire
to have a good time. Sunday nights gather a great

Getting busy at **Bahrein**. *See p220.*

Arts & Entertainment

crowd, but you're guaranteed some fun whenever you show up. The club gets going after 1am; before then there's a supper-show featuring saucy lambada moves and tasty Brazilian dishes such as *feijoada*.

Museum

Perú 535, entre Mexico y Venezuela, San Telmo (4771 9628/www.museumclub.com.ar). Bus 2, 9, 10, 22, 24, 29. **Open** 8pm-2am Wed; from 10pm Fri-Sun. **Map** p325 E10.

Wednesday's after-office parties, teeming with attractive thirtysomethings, are Museum's biggest – but wear a suit. Housed in a building designed by Gustave Eiffel (who also had a hand in some tower in Paris), it's a top venue for a night's boogying or prowling for members of the opposite sex. Girls get in free before 10pm. Fridays and Saturdays are heavy on house and techno and also bring in a crowd.

Niceto Club

Niceto Vega 5510, entre Humboldt y Fitz Roy, Palermo Viejo (4779 9396/www.nicetoclub.com). Bus 39, 93, 151, 168. **Open** from 12.30am Thur, Fri; from 1am Sat. **Map** p323 N4.

Niceto is undoubtedly still one of BA's trendsetting nightspots. Don't miss Wednesday's underground party Zizek (and occasionally SuperZizek on Saturdays), one of the best nights in town. Traditional South American styles and rhythms are mashed up with electronic beats, sparking a dancefloor frenzy. Weekend nights are harder to pin down, but at the monthly SoulFood Ezequiel Lodeiro serves up a delicious dose of alternative electro. Before 1.30am,

Niceto Club.

there's usually live music from local or international stars (Battles and Joanna Newsome recently played here), running the gamut from flamenco to electropop.

Pacha

Avenida Costanera Rafael Obligado, y La Pampa, Costanera Norte (4788 4280/www.pacha-ba.com). Bus 37, 160. **Open** *Mid Feb-Dec* from midnight Fri; from 2am Sat. **Map** p329 R11.

Saturday's Clubland@Pacha put BA on the global clubbing map, and it's still considered to be one of the best clubs in town and the best night to go. With several rooms, Pacha – pronounced Pachá by locals – is usually packed well into the morning – saying hello to the sun on the glorious riverside terrrace is standard, so bring your shades. Regular visits from key players such as the The Chemical Brothers keep it dominating the BA club scene, though the recent trend is to showcase the talents of the big local DJs.

Podestá Súper Club de Copas

Armenia 1740, entre El Salvador y Costa Rica, Palermo Viejo (4832 2776/www.elpodesta.com.ar). Bus 15, 39, 110, 140. **Open** from 11pm Fri, Sat. **Map** p323 M5.

Podestá retains a resolutely underground feel while attracting a loyal crowd of regulars. There's alternative rock in the lively ground-floor bar, while upstairs it's upbeat techno. While downstairs is gritty the second floor has benefited from a recent overhaul and now attracts an array of new punters, in addition to the diehard, art-student crowd. Still, it feels much more like a bar than club.

Roxy Club

Federico Lacroze y Alvarez Thomas, Colegiales (www.theroxybsas.com.ar). Subte B, Federico Lacroze/39, 93 bus. **Open** from 11pm Thur-Sat. **Map** p323 P4.

Home to one of BA's oldest and greatest parties, the splendidly notorious Club 69 (*photo p233*) is still the best way to pass a Thursday night in the city. Greeted by a fanfare of transvestite hostesses and a Rocky Horror-style stage show (from 3am), the more conservative may be forgiven for making a dash for the nearest exit. However, by 4am, the main room is rammed with clubbers, sweating it out to house and techno sets. Add some impressive visuals and a few licentious podium dancers and the recipe's complete.

Rumi

Avenida Figueroa Alcorta 6442, y La Pampa, Núñez (4782 1307/www.rumiba.com.ar). Bus 37, 130. **Open** *Restaurant* from 9pm Tue-Sat. *Club* from 1.30am Tue-Sat. **Map** p329 R10.

Rumi's strict door policy and queues from around 2am make it a good idea to turn up early; you can settle down to dinner before the club kicks off. Inside, you'll be privy to one of the most glamorous scenes in BA. Big names sometimes grace the DJ booth, but bigger names can be found on the dancefloor – a favourite haunt for many a model, celeb and young socialite. Fridays are 'Glamour Nights', while Saturdays are favoured by a younger crowd.

Arts & Entertainment

Film

Low-budget, high-impact cinema from home-grown directors.

Whether your tastes incline more towards a brooding single-shot Iranian masterpiece or Disney's latest cuddle fest, you'll have no problem finding something to watch in BA's abundance of cinemas. Those who've ventured beyond Spanish GCSE can enjoy original art-house fare in independent venues, while everyone else can munch popcorn in front of a blockbuster in a snazzy modern multiplex, wishing they'd turn down the air conditioning.

ARGENTINIAN CINEMA
The so-called 'new wave' of Argentinian cinema is in fact a marvellously messy bag of directors and styles, with little in common save an excess of creativity, a healthy contempt for parabolic plots and pat endings, and the gumption to make interesting features on a shoestring. *Upa! Una película argentina* (*Woah! An Argentinian Film*, 2007) takes an ironic swipe at the current obsession with obtaining European funding, and is an entertaining insight into the caffeine-fuelled paranoia of the BA film industry.

Two outstanding directors exploring human frailties are Daniel Burman and Lucrecia Martel. Burman's *Derecho de familia* (*Family Law*, 2006) is a sharp comedy-drama about a thirtysomething lawyer going through a premature mid-life crisis. Martel's gritty but moving *La niña santa* (*The Holy Girl*, 2004) shows the sexual awakening – and subsequent Catholic guilt – of a 16-year-old choir girl. Also favouring minimalist realism over expensive computer-enhanced wizardry is Carlos Sorín, whose whimsical and eloquent *Bombón, el perro* (Bombon The Dog, 2004) features a pure-bred, an endless Patagonian highway and a cheesy canine talent show.

In *El Pasado* (*The Past*, 2007) Hector Babenco delves deep into the *porteño* psyche, examining the three very different women who dominate one man's romantic life. Another must for those interested in BA's battle of the sexes is Hernán Gaffett's *Ciudad en celo* (*City in Heat*, 2007), a light-hearted look at love to a tango soundtrack.

Director **Daniel Burman** starts rolling on the streets of Buenos Aires.

Maradona, the documentary

Football fans were braced. It was coming out in 2006. And then it wasn't. But it was definitely in post-production. It would come out in early 2007. Then late 2007. Then 2007 came to a close. But Time Out Buenos Aires is here to proclaim that – although, um, we don't, ahem, have the exact date – Emir Kusturica's much-anticipated documentary about Diego Maradona is set to come out... sometime in 2008.

Much talk has gone on in the blogosphere that the reason for the delay in releasing the film is due to an apparent clash of titan egos. Diego's story has been told sundry times with varying results. But many, including Maradona himself, feel that Kusturica is the ideal man for the job. The internationally acclaimed director, famous for his farcical 1998 comedy *Black Cat, White Cat,* is an extrovert himself who has drummed up his own utopist commune in the hills of Serbia, challenged one of Milosevic's goons to a duel and made some of the most moving and quixotic films of the last 20 years. He seems perfectly suited for driving home Diego's wild-ride on the big screen.

After filming in key locations from the Maradona saga, Kusturica, whose directorial obsession borders on megalomania, insisted on a sit-down, one-on-one, face-to-face, man-to-man with Maradona. But 'El Diez' runs on his own time, and such a meeting wasn't as forthcoming as Kusturica expected. He has constantly referred to Maradona as 'the greatest football player ever' and has high praise for the Argentinian star, playing up the deified status handed to him (El Diez, Dios, Hand of God, Church of Maradona, etc...) by his devoted followers. The director has called modern football a 'video game' and regards Diego as the last great hero of the golden age of the beautiful game. In a memorable interview given to the *Guardian* newspaper at the beginning of filming, Kusturica said Maradona lifted people up to the 'level of the gods' and lamented those who discarded him on account of his drug problems, saying, 'there are always motherfuckers queuing up to pull you down to earth'.

But when Kusturica finally did get his interview in March 2007 after allegedly making three futile trips to Buenos Aires, he was disenchanted, telling a Belgrade newspaper that Maradona had 'no concept of time'. And with so much riding on the interview, one asks: What if Kusturica didn't get what he wanted? What if Maradona kept petulantly looking at his watch, the whole time wondering when the pizza will arrive? But these sorts of questions do little to dampen the desire to see what the Herculean filmmaker has done with the Atlas of the football world. On the contrary, they only increase anxiety for the film's release. So buck up, people. It's here, and coming out in 2008. We think.

Arts & Entertainment

FESTIVALS

For proof of the *porteño* passion for cinema, look no further than the booming **Festival Internacional de Cine Independiente** (*see p211*) which takes place in mid-April. For ten days of cinematic frenzy, the Hoyts Abasto multiplex and other city centre venues show 180 films from the most diverse reaches of the indie scene around the world. There's a fierce official competition and late-night screenings of bizarre cinema. Not to be outdone, the coastal city of Mar del Plata throws its own annual bash in November or December, the **Festival Internacional de Cine del Mar del Plata** (www.mardelplatafilmfest.com). As well as showcasing a variety of international flicks, the festival focuses on new movements in Latin American cinema, and takes a look at the particular issues facing local directors and screenwriters in a series of talks by industry insiders from all over the continent.

Cinemas

Independent but rather rundown downtown cinemas are congregated around Corrientes and Santa Fe; nowadays shiny new multiplexes in the suburbs attract most of the audiences. Smaller cinemas are fading at an alarming rate, but the cultural centres host regular *ciclos* (series) of specialist and art-house flicks, and in the summer open-air screenings abound.

INFORMATION, TIMINGS AND TICKETS

Nearly all films are shown in their original version with Spanish subtitles. Children's films are the only exception, and even then original versions are often shown at selected venues. Some cinemas have late-night showings (*trasnoches*) beginning around 1am, usually on weekends only. Tickets are around half-price Mondays to Wednesdays and during the day.

Check the *Espectáculos* sections of local papers for cinema listings. As English-language film titles are often translated and end up bearing no resemblance to the original, it helps to buy the *Buenos Aires Herald* for its English-language listings, and, in the Friday edition, capsule film reviews. Celluloid lovers who can read Spanish should pick up a copy of long-running film magazine *El Amante*. The website www.cinenacional.com is a superb Spanish-language resource on Argentinian cinema, with an exhaustive, searchable database. Free monthly listings mag *Llegás* (available in shops and bars) has trenchant reviews and excellent information on art-house screenings. If you have cable TV, tune in to Volver channel, with its classic reruns. I-SAT channel also shows hard-to-find classics and indie movies.

Argentina has four different rating categories: ATP (suitable for all ages); SAM13 (under-13s only if accompanied by an adult); SAM16 (no under-16s); and SAM18 (no under-18s).

City centre

Atlas Lavalle

Lavalle 869, entre Suipacha y Esmeralda, Microcentro (4328 6643/www.atlascines.com.ar). Subte C, Lavalle/10, 17, 70 bus. **Open** from noon daily. **Tickets** AR$13 Thur-Sun; AR$9 Mon-Wed. **No credit cards. Map** p325 G11.
This once-historical cinema has been split up into five smaller screens, but is still a bit of a relic. It mostly features Hollywood new releases.

Atlas Santa Fe

Avenida Santa Fe 2015, entre Ayacucho y Junín, Barrio Norte (4823 7878/www.atlascines.com.ar). Subte D, Callao/39, 60, 111, 124, 152 bus. **Open** from noon daily. **Tickets** AR$13 Thur-Sun; AR$10 Mon-Wed. **Credit** AmEx, V. **Map** p326 I10.
This ordinary Barrio Norte cinema, last renovated in the 1980s, shows a limited range of new releases on its two screens.

Espacio INCAA KM 0 – Gaumont Rivadavia

Rivadavia 1635, entre Rodríguez Peña y Montevideo, Congreso (4371 3050). Subte A, Congreso/12, 37, 102, 105, 151 bus. **Open** from noon daily. **Tickets** AR$4; AR$2 concessions. **No credit cards. Map** p325 G9.
This excellent and very cheap three-screen cinema, and the Complejo Tita Merello at Suipacha 442 (4322 1195), are supported by INCAA (the National Film Board). They only show new Argentinian releases (with no English subtitles).

Lorca

Avenida Corrientes 1428, entre Paraná y Uruguay, Tribunales (4371 5017). Subte B, Uruguay/24, 26, 102 bus. **Open** from 2pm daily. **Tickets** AR$13 Thur-Sun; AR$8 Mon-Wed. **No credit cards. Map** p325 G10.
One of the most traditional cinemas on Corrientes, Lorca is one of BA's best options for independent film, showing an excellent pick of local and foreign non-mainstream movies on its two screens.

Multiplexes

Arteplex

Avenida Cabildo 2829, entre Ugarte y Congreso, Belgrano (4781 6500). Subte D, Congreso de Tucumán/60, 68, 152 bus. **Open** from 1pm daily. **Tickets** AR$12 Thur-Sun; AR$8 Mon-Wed, concessions. **Credit** AmEx, V. **Map** p329 T8.
Formerly the Savoy (it will be a sad day when there are no cinemas called the Savoy left), Arteplex screens some of Hollywood's more inventive offerings – films by directors such as Scorsese.

Atlas Patio Bullrich

Patio Bullrich shopping centre, Avenida del Libertador 750, entre Montevideo y Libertad, Recoleta (4814 7400/www.atlascines.com.ar). Bus 67, 92, 102, 130. **Open** from 1pm daily. **Tickets** AR$16 Thur-Sun; AR$11 Mon-Wed; first showing Thur-Sun, concessions. **Credit** AmEx, MC, V. **Map** p326 I12.

After you've stocked up on imported designer gear at BA's most exclusive mall, take a break here to watch the latest Hollywood blockbusters. If it's well known enough, the occasional locally made flick also gets a chance to impress.

Cinemark 8

Alicia Moreau de Justo 1920, y San Juan, Puerto Madero (4315 5522/www.cinemark.com.ar). Bus 4, 64, 130, 152. **Open** from noon daily. **Tickets** AR$16 after 4pm; AR$11 Mon-Wed, before 4pm Thur-Sun, under-12s, concessions. **Credit** AmEx, MC, V. **Map** p324 D10.

This modern complex down in the docklands has eight screens and a restaurant. It shows a mixture of Hollywood and Latin American new releases. Another branch, with ten screens, is conveniently located near the Alto Palermo shopping centre. **Other locations** Cinemark 10, Beruti 3399, Palermo (4827 5700/4827 9500 information).

Hoyts Abasto Buenos Aires

Abasto de Buenos Aires shopping centre, Avenida Corrientes 3247, entre Agüero y Anchorena, Abasto (4319 2999/www.hgcc.com.ar). Subte B, Carlos Gardel/24, 26, 124, 146, 168 bus. **Open** from 11am daily. **Tickets** AR$17 before 3pm Thur-Sat,Sun; AR$11.50 Mon-Wed, before 3pm Thur-Sat. **Credit** AmEx, MC, V. **Map** p326 J8.

One of the best of the multiplexes, Hoyts Abasto has something of a split personality. During most of the year it shows Hollywood movies but transforms itself into an art-house venue during BA's excellent independent film festival, held each April.

Village Recoleta

Vicente López 2050, y Junín, Recoleta (0810 810 2463 credit card booking/www.villagecines.com). Bus 10, 130. **Open** from 11am daily. **Tickets** AR$17; AR$11.50 before 1pm and all day Wed, under-12s, concessions. **Credit** AmEx, DC, MC, V. **Map** p326 J11.

This huge complex near Recoleta Cemetery includes bars, restaurants, games arcade, bookshop and a record store. And if you've got any time left to watch a film, you're bound to find something that appeals in the 16-screen cinema spread over three floors.

Repertory & art-house

The **Malba** (*see p110*) hosts excellent cinema events: new indie releases, outstanding retrospectives with restored 35mm prints and lectures by international actors and filmmakers. Specialist series and home-grown films can be seen at the **British Arts Centre** (Suipacha

1333, 4393 6941, www.britishartscentre.org.ar) screens movies focused on British culture. A good place to go to if you're homesick for British humour. Classic sitcoms such as *Fawlty Towers* and *Blackadder* are sometimes shown. Opening hours vary so make sure to call ahead or check websites beforehand.

Alianza Francesa de Buenos Aires

Avenida Córdoba 946, entre Suipacha y Carlos Pellegrini, Microcentro (4322 0068/01/www.alianzafrancesa.org.ar). Subte C, Lavalle/59, 99, 106, 132 bus. **Open** movie showings from 8pm Tue. **Closed** Jan, Feb. **Tickets** free. **Map** p325 G11.

The respected French-language institution doubles up as a prestigious cultural centre, offering riveting cycles of good international cinema in its refined and comfortable auditorium.

Centro Cultural Ricardo Rojas

Avenida Corrientes 2038, entre Junín y Ayacucho, Once (4954 5521/www.rojas.uba.ar). Subte B,Callao/ 24, 26, 60, 124 bus. **Tickets** free-AR$6. **No credit cards. Map** p325 H9.

This lively cultural centre shows interesting art-house and experimental fare in its large film theatre. It's cheaper to see a movie here than to rent one from a video store.

Cine Club Eco

2nd floor, Avenida Corrientes 4940, entre Lavalleja y Julián Alvarez, Almagro (4854 4126). SubteB, Malabia/36, 92 bus. **Open** usually 8 or 9pm at week-ends; call ahead. **Tickets** AR$8. **No credit cards. Map** p322 L3.

If Bergman and Polanski retrospectives get your pulse racing, get your arty ass down to Cine Club Eco. The entrance price includes an invitation to a short post-screening coffee to discuss the movie.

Cosmos

Avenida Corrientes 2046, entre Ayacucho y Junín, Once (4953 5405/www.cinecosmos.com). Subte B, Callao/24, 26, 60 bus. **Tickets** AR$12 after 4pm Thur-Sun; AR$8 Mon-Wed, before 4pm Thur-Sun. **No credit cards. Map** p325 H9.

Not only a film buff's paradise but also an Avenida Corrientes landmark, the Cosmos 'cultural space' features the latest Argentinian releases as well as world cinema classic retrospectives and oddball auteur films.

Sala Leopoldo Lugones

10th Floor, Teatro San Martín, Avenida Corrientes 1530, entre Paraná y Montevideo, Tribunales (freephone 0800 333 5254/www.teatrosanmartin. com.ar). Subte B, Uruguay/24, 26, 60, 102 bus. **Tickets** AR$5. **No credit cards. Map** p325 G9.

Named after the Argentinian poet and cultural icon Leopoldo Lugones, this cinema is located within the San Martín theatre complex, and mostly screens left-field and hard-to-find art-house movies from all over the world as well as many national affairs. This is the place to check out first if you're into unconventional films and documentaries.

Galleries

No longer just framed in galleries, BA's art scene is reinventing itself.

Let's start with the bad news. For reasons geographical and economic, Buenos Aires is not on the major art exhibition circuit, which means that down here you won't catch that monster Matisse retrospective everyone's been raving about. Now for the good news. Buenos Aires is not on the major art exhibition circuit, which means you won't have to queue for hours to get into the city's hottest shows; nor will you need to be eight-feet tall to catch a glimpse of the works once you've finally got past security. The best news of all? Most *porteño* art lovers appear to be teetotallers, so that nice fellow hefting around a tray of champagne at the *inauguración* (opening) – ridiculously easy to blag your way into here – will gladly refresh your glass as often as you deem it necessary.

Hospitality aside, what you'll find at BA's expanding network of traditional museum-style venues and funky, independently run art spaces is the best in Argentinian art, from old masters such as Emilio Pettoruti and Antonio Berni to contemporary superstars like Guillermo Kuitca, not to mention the latest young turks who, as is the trend everywhere, increasingly create works in the form of video installations, digital art, and participatory 'happenings'. Of course, non Argentinian artistic heavyweights have their place in the city too: permanent collections feature crowd-formers such as Frida Kahlo and Diego Rivera, and the major galleries have a few Goyas and Picassos and so on.

The city's best known contemporary art space is businessman and philanthropist Eduardo Costantini's prestigious venture, the **Museo de Arte Latinoamericano de Buenos Aires**, (Malba; *see p110*), which has established itself as one of BA's most exciting cultural hotspots. Another superb modern gallery, La Boca's **Fundación Proa** (*see p101*), has reopened after a revamp in early 2008, to host the much anticipated first exhibition in Latin America of works by French thinker and artist Marcel Duchamp. These private ventures are successfully challenging the hegemony of traditional, state-managed – which often means mismanaged – institutions such as the **Museo Nacional de Bellas Artes** (*see p108*) and the **Museo de Arte Moderno** (*see p99*). Anyone too lazy to go to an actual gallery can check out an innovative virtual one: Red Galería at www.redgaleria.com.

INFORMATION
The websites www.ramona.org.ar, www.arte baires.com.ar and www.arsomnibus.com.ar provide listings, though none has an English translation. Better is the free, quarterly, pocket-sized guide **Mapa de las Artes**, which is bilingual and very well organised. For less mainstream events, flyers can be picked up in places as diverse as downtown bars and cafés and Palermo Viejo boutiques. To dig deeper into the lives of artists, join **Galería de Arte 5006** (www.galeriadearte5006.com.ar) for their Artists' Atelier Tour every Friday.

FESTIVALS
The flagship for the city's burgeoning art market is the annual **arteBA** fair (*see p211*), held every year in May since 1991. This week-long event has evolved into one of the best

Fantastic exhibitions at **arteBA**. See *p211*.

attended and most hyped cultural events in Latin America, regularly attracting more than 100,000 buyers and enthusiasts.

Galleries

Galleries do not charge admission or take credit cards unless otherwise stated. Many of them are closed during the summer months (January and February). Look out for the Gallery Nights programme (information at www.artealdia.com) that runs from March to November. Over 60 galleries open their doors (not to mention bottles of bubbly) to the public from 7pm to 11pm on the last Friday of every month.

Centre

Arroyo

Arroyo 830/834, entre Suipacha y Esmeralda, Retiro (4325 0947/www.galarroyo.com). Subte C, San Martín/1, 7, 59, 61, 67, 92 bus. **Open** 11am-9pm Mon-Fri; 11am-1pm, 4-9pm Sat, Sun. **Map** p325 H12.
Arroyo's real strong point is its monthly auctions. They offer a wide range of relatively affordable works by renowned local and international artists.

Autoría Bs As

Suipacha 1025, entre Santa Fe y Marcelo T de Alvear, Retiro (5252 2474/www.autoriabsas.com.ar). Subte C, San Martín/17, 59, 92, 152 bus. **Open** 10am-8pm Mon-Fri; 10am-2pm, 4-8pm Sat. **Map** p325 G11.
A hip downtown space dedicated to abstract photography, digitally-inspired painting and sculpture. It also stocks clothes and accessories.

Centro Cultural Borges

Galerías Pacífico, Viamonte, y San Martín, Microcentro (5555 5449/www.ccborges.org.ar). Subte C, San Martín/10, 17, 152 bus. **Open** 10am-9pm Mon-Sat; noon-9pm Sun. **Admission** AR$8; concessions AR$5. **Map** p325 G11.
It's not an art gallery per se (the eclectic programme includes independent cinema, tango spectacles and experimental theatre), but the Borges centre has hosted many must-see exhibitions.

Centro Cultural de España

Basement, Florida 943, entre Paraguay y Marcelo T de Alvear, Retiro (4312 3214/www.cceba.org.ar). Subte C, San Martín/10, 17, 152 bus. **Open** Mar-Dec 10am-8pm Mon-Fri. **Map** p325 G11.
This cultural centre promotes visual arts and media by Argentinian and Spanish artists, with a particular focus on digital and online art. There are also regular music events and poetry readings.

Fundación Federico Jorge Klemm

Basement, Marcelo T de Alvear 626, entre Maipú y Florida, Retiro (4312 4443/www.fundacionfjklemm.org). Subte C, San Martín/10, 17, 70, 152 bus. **Open** 11am-8pm Mon-Fri. Closed Jan. **Map** p325 G11.
This important gallery houses many key Argentinian works (including some Bernis) and an impressive international collection (Picasso, Dalí, Warhol, Mapplethorpe). At the back, founder Jorge Klemm's own creations (imagine an even more self-obsessed version of Andy Warhol) and his collection of 20th-century pop arcana – costumes worn by Nureyev and dresses owned by Evita – are on permanent display.

Pull up a pillow at **Centro Cultural Borges**.

Arts & Entertainment

Palatina

Arroyo 821, entre Suipacha y Esmeralda, Retiro (4327 0620/www.galeriapalatina.com.ar). Bus 93, 130, 152. **Open** 10am-8.30pm Mon-Fri; 10am-1pm Sat. **Closed** Feb. **Map** p325 H12.

In operation for 29 years (an aeon in BA art gallery terms), Palatina is one of the busiest galleries in town, promoting well established names such as painters Jorge Diciervo and Eduardo Faradje and sculptor Vivianne Duchini.

Ruth Benzacar

Florida 1000, y Marcelo T de Alvear, Retiro (4313 8480/www.ruthbenzacar.com). Subte C, San Martín/10, 17, 132, 152 bus. **Open** 11.30am-8pm Mon-Fri; 10.30am-1.30pm Sat. **Map** p325 G11.

Founded in 1965 by the late Ruth Benzacar and now run by her daughter Orly, this forceful gallery was the jewel in the crown of swinging 1960s BA. New artists are enthusiastically received, and it remains one of the leaders of the pack.

South of the centre

Appetite

Chacabuco 551, entre Venezuela y México, San Telmo (6112 9975/www.appetite.com.ar). Bus 20, 22, 25. **Open** 2-7pm Mon-Fri. **Map** p325 E10.

Given the thumbs up by the *New York Times* and *Rolling Stone*, Daniela Luna's hip San Telmo venue generates quite a buzz among young art types. Embracing the most provocative of contemporary art, the rising artist-run gallery takes an energetic pop-punk approach to showcasing new artists who work in all types of medium, including the likes of Victoria Musotto and Ariel Cusnir.

Espacio Ecléctico

Humberto Primo 730, entre Chacabuco y Piedras, San Telmo (4307 1966/www.espacioeclectico.com.ar). Bus 22, 25. **Open** 3-8pm Tue-Fri; 5-10pm Sat, Sun. Closed Jan, Feb. **Map** p324 D9.

Founded by six multidisciplinary artists, the self-dubbed 'Centre of diffusion of art' is an intimate space in the heart of San Telmo hosting theatre, music, and film in addition to the standard visual arts. The gallery's bi-monthly publication *Doble E* offers in-depth descriptions of current exhibitions, which range from traditional to unconventional.

Fundación Proa

Avenida Pedro de Mendoza 1929, y Del Valle Iberlucea, La Boca (4104 1000/www.proa.org). Bus 29, 64, 152. **Open** 11am-7pm Tue-Sun. **Admission** from AR$5. **Map** p324 A8.

Set on the La Boca riverfront, Proa has presented some of the most stimulating and insightfully curated shows in BA, and the roof terrace affords great views of the filthy, but nonetheless iconic, Riachuelo. The gallery reopened in early 2008 (*see p101;* **The Italian Job**) with a major show from the French surrealist Marcel Duchamp. There is also an impressive collection including Latin American artists such as Diego Rivera.

North of the centre

925 Galería

Cabrera 4937, entre Gurruchaga y Serrano, Palermo Viejo (4833 5985). Bus 39, 55. **Open** 11am-8pm Mon-Sat. **Map** p323 M5.

Argentina's only gallery devoted exclusively to the art of jewellery design, 925 Galería showcases a diverse range of pieces (earthy tribal-derived styles juxtaposed with feminine jewel-toned accessories) by top artisans. In the upstairs workshop you can create your own trinket in a personalised class. Visit the boutique on Honduras 4808 to browse gallery director Mario Paluch's own funky silver items.

Bacano

Armenia 1544, entre Honduras y Gorriti, Palermo Viejo (4831 3564/www.bacano.com.ar). Bus 39, 55, 111. **Open** 11am-8pm Mon-Fri; 11am-6pm Sat. **Map** p323 M5.

This hip art/design gallery is set in a 19th-century house with handsome wood furniture and recycled objects, alongside contemporary art created by well known painters and sculptors on the BA scene.

El Borde

Uriarte 1356, entre Niceto Vega y Cabrera, Palermo Viejo (4777 4573/www.el-borde.com.ar). Bus 34, 140, 151, 168. **Open** 3-8pm Tue-Sat. Closed Feb. **Map** p323 M4.

This neighbourhood metal shop turned art gallery is an attractive and original space in which to check out contemporary work from less commercial, up-and-coming BA artists.

Braga Menéndez Arte Contemporáneo

Humboldt 1574, entre Cabrera y Gorriti, Palermo Viejo (4775 5577/www.galeriabm.com). Bus 93, 140. **Open** 11am-8pm Mon-Fri; 11am-6pm Sat. **Closed** Jan, Feb. **Map** p323 N5.

Proudly independent and non-mainstream, this slick Palermo space houses contemporary works by artists who, in the words of founder Florencia Braga Menéndez, are 'from way down south'. Uniting the core group of 39 artists is a scornful contempt for the phony modishness that trend-defining tags such as 'Latin American art' are often freighted with.

Centro Cultural Recoleta

Junín 1930, y Quintana, Recoleta (4803 1040/www.centroculturalrecoleta.org). Bus 10, 17, 60, 67, 92, 110. **Open** 2-9pm Tue-Fri; 10am-9pm Sat, Sun. **Admission** free; suggested contribution AR$1. **Map** p326 J11.

The scope of CCR's 20 exhibition spaces ranges from children's drawings to work produced by psychiatric patients, as well as by established names. Its largest space, Cronopio, is used for major retrospectives and group shows, and has displayed artists as diverse as Yoko Ono, Liliana Porter and León Ferrari.

Don't say it – spray it

In early 2001, as the well-documented financial crisis was reaching boiling point, stencil art and graffiti, once thought to be the domain of punks with spray cans, suddenly became a middle class activity. Banks that had frozen accounts and government buildings were suddenly the target of politically motivated stencil art. Otherwise law-abiding citizens formed groups such as Grupo de Arte Callejero (Street Art Group) and swathed city walls as forms of public expression. Firstly, their politically motivated ideas and philosophies could be articulated in a simple, witty and eye catching way; and secondly, it was an activity that was understood as the reclaiming of the streets. They took their inspiration from internationally renowned stencil artists like the UK's hugely successful Banksy from Bristol, and especially the French stenciller Blek le Rat, who came to prominence in Paris in the 1980s.

The streets of Buenos Aires today are still colourful places, and such is the legacy of the recent explosion of street art, that many commentators recognise Buenos Aires as being at the forefront of the stencil art movement. Guido Indij, in the introduction to his book *1000 Stencil* (*La Marca Editora, 2008*), identifies the absence of state intervention as one of the reasons street art proliferated. Some of the finest stencil graffiti can be found along the principal protesting route of Avenida de Mayo, where anti-government, anti-police and anti-anything stencils are strewn across walls. Neighbourhoods such as San Telmo and Palermo are decorated with generally more intricate designs from world-renowned crews such as BsAs Stencil and Run Don't Walk.

Inherently, stencils are of a transient nature. However, one place where top quality stencil art is exhibited permanently is in Palermo's Hollywood in Cambodia (Thames 1885, www.hollywoodincambodia. com.ar), a gallery, bar and shop seling suitably trendy Tshirts, posters and prints, where crews often hold 'expression sessions' and repaint the whole place.

'They attempt to provoke a spontaneous reaction in the form of a smile, a reflection,' Indij concludes. 'After all, we have to remember the term 'stencil' has its origins in the Latin word 'scintilla', meaning spark.'

Dabbah Torrejón
Arte Contemporáneo

Sánchez de Bustamente 1187, entre Córdoba y Cabrera, Palermo (4963 2581/www.dabbahtorrejon. com.ar). Bus 99, 109. **Open** 3-8pm Tue-Fri; 11am-2pm Sat. Closed Sat in Jan, Feb. **Map** p322 K6.

Since September 2000, this cutting-edge gallery occupying a converted house near Abasto has promised to be 'a bridge between creativity and the public' – and it has kept its pledge. Exhibiting works by a stable of promising young artists – including the likes of Fabián Burgos, Alejandra Seeber, Sergio Avello and Mariana López – it is becoming accustomed to rave reviews.

Daniel Abate

Pasaje Bollini 2170, entre French y Peña, Recoleta (4804 8247/www.danielabategaleria.com.ar). Bus 10, 21, 37. **Open** noon-7pm Tue-Sat. **Map** p326 K10.

Daniel Abate's gallery is considered one of the best nurseries for young and original Argentinian artistic talent in a variety of media.

Daniel Maman Fine Arts

Avenida del Libertador 2475, entre Bulnes y Ruggieri, Palermo (4804 3700/www.danielmaman.com). Bus 10, 37, 59, 60, 102. **Open** 11am-7pm Mon-Fri; 11am-8pm Sat. **Map** p326 L10.

Openings at Daniel Maman's chic and good looking gallery attract a chic and good looking crowd. With an uncanny flair for selecting talented and charismatic artists, Maman's influential shows always make the headlines, and more often than not kick-start successful careers. **Other location:** Palacio Duhau, Avenida Alvear 1661 (5171 1984).

Dharma Fine Art

1st Floor, Door 1, Rue des Artisans, Arenales 1239, entre Libertad y Talcahuano, Recoleta (4814 4700/ www.dharmafinearts.com). Bus 17, 102. **Open** 2-8pm Mon-Fri. **Map** p325 H11.

A first-rate gallery and interactive space where artists and sponsors get together to create new projects. The thoughtful shows exhibit works by Argentinian masters, as well as the newest hot young things.

Espacio Fundación Telefónica

Arenales 1540, entre Montevideo y Paraná, Recoleta (4333 1300/www.fundacion.telefonica.com.ar). Bus 10, 37, 59. **Open** 2-8.30pm Tue-Sun. **Map** p325 H10.

Opened in late 2003, this two-floor contemporary centre has artistic and educational ambitions. Sophisticated multimedia technology is used to present the visual arts alongside social projects and research. There are media labs and educational activities as well as the exhibition space.

Fundación Alberto Elía/
Mario Robirosa

Ground Floor, Studio A, Azcuénaga 1739, entre Pacheco de Melo y Las Heras, Recoleta (4803 0496). Bus 10, 37, 41, 101, 102. **Open** Mar-Dec 2-10.30pm Mon-Fri. Closed Jan, Feb. **Map** p326 J10.

The owners of this small, smart space have a mind of their own and aren't afraid to show it. The place stages coherent exhibitions by contemporary artists from the *Who's Who* of the BA art world.

Galería Isabel Anchorena

Unit 'H', Arenales 1239, entre Libertad y Talcahuano, Recoleta (4811 5335/www.galeria isabelanchorena.sion.com). Bus 39, 152. **Open** 11am-8pm Mon-Fri; 11am-1pm Sat. **Map** p325 H11.

This superbly curated Recoleta gallery displays the works of around 30 contemporary artists.

Galería Thames

Thames 1776, entre El Salvador y Costa Rica, Palermo Viejo (4832 1968). Bus 39, 55, 93. **Open** 1-8pm Mon-Sat. **Map** p327 M8.

The focus of this chic gallery, which opened in 2007, is on the abstract and contemporary, but director Mabel Ibarra makes an effort to support prominent as well as lesser-known artists.

Praxis

Arenales 1311, y Talcahuano, Recoleta (4813 8639/ www.praxis-art.com). Bus 10, 152. **Open** 10.30am-8pm Mon-Fri; 10.30am-2pm Sat. **Map** p325 H11.

Praxis is one of the few galleries with international reach, with spaces in New York and Miami as well as BA. It's one of the driving forces in promoting Argentinian art abroad. **Other location:** Arroyo 858, Recoleta (4393 0803).

Rubbers

Avenida Alvear 1595, y Montevideo, Recoleta (4816 1864/1869/www.rubbers.com.ar). Bus 17, 61, 67, 92, 93. **Open** 11am-8pm Mon-Fri; 11am-1.30pm Sat. **Map** p326 I11.

Directed by Natalio Povarché, the name of this gallery has, paradoxically, always been synonymous with solidity in art. It displays a diverse range of contemporary Argentinian paintings and sculptures. **Other location:** 3rd Floor, Santa Fe 1860, Barrio Norte (4816 1782).

West of the centre

Arte x Arte

Lavalleja 1062, entre Córdoba y Lerma, Villa Crespo (4772 6754/4773 2738/www.artea.com.ar/artexarte). Bus 15, 92, 106, 109, 168. **Open** Apr-Dec 1-7pm Mon-Sat. Closed Jan-Mar. **Map** p322 L4.

At 1,800 square metres (19,355 square feet), Arte x Arte claims to be the largest South American gallery space. Dedicated to photography, video and digital art, it also has a spacious library and a bar.

ProyectArte

Castillo 540, y Malabia, Villa Crespo (4899 0444/www.proyectarte.org) Bus 55, 168. **Open** 11am-6pm Mon-Fri. **Map** p323 M4.

This innovative fine arts NGO rents out its sprawling studio space to artists of all levels for drawing and painting. Wander around with an empanada and enjoy the various pieces on display.

Gay & Lesbian

Join the fun in South America's biggest gay scene.

If you want to get all stereotypical about gay BA, then yes, it has the shopping, yes, it has the clubs and, and yes, its reputation for having some of the best looking men in the world still stands. Make no mistake, it is one of the buzziest, hottest and most stylish places on the planet. Yet all that glamour and charisma is not just surface deep; to really penetrate BA's vibe, you've got to involve yourself; taste its fruits, so to speak.

Superficialities aside, in a continent not renowned for its live-and-let-live attitude towards gay people, Argentina in particular has stood out as a beacon of hope. The established gay scene in BA lead the way for much of South America, with Buenos Aires the first city to legalise same-sex unions. The Gay Pride parade (www.marchadelor.gullo.org.ar), held in the third week of November, attracts thousands (25,000 at last count) to support gay rights and diversity, and the parties sandwiched around this time are hedonistic, to say the least. BA is also proud of the fact that in 2007 it hosted the world championships of the International Gay

and Lesbian Football Association (www.iglfa.org) – a groundbreaking move for Latin America, and the first international gay event in South America. Gay tourism is an accepted and successful trade here; bars, clubs, restaurants, hotels, you name it, are all well equipped for your needs and desires. In BA the service industry is always on standby, be it a perfectly mixed ginger martini or a self-indulgent 2am massage. When it comes to having a good time, Argentinians know what they're doing.

ORIENTATE YOURSELF

What draws many gay visitors here is not only the city's beauty and history, but its gay-friendly outlook. For an idea of just how vibrant the gay scene is, pick up a very helpful free listings guide called *Gmaps* (www.gmaps360. com), stocked at most bars and tourist points. With this, orientate yourself over fresh pastries and steaming coffee at **Oui Oui** (*see p176*) or **Pride Café** (Balcarce 869, San Telmo, 4300 6435). After a day's exploring, fortify your body

A warm welcome backstage at the celebrated **Club 69**. *See p238.*

with a steak at **La Brigada** (*see p133*) and head towards the beats of the nightlife.

Porteños – no matter what their sexual preference – are night owls. Nightlife is *the* life. The secret to staying up so late remains a mystery for visitors; perhaps remnants of the rave culture still linger, or it could just be the tanned, toned bodies of the bus boys that keep eyes popped open. To test your stamina, try **Amerika** (*see p236*) where world-renowned DJs are flown in once a month for a blow-out bash. For something more intimate, slip into a tango lesson at one of the gay *milongas*, **La Marshall** (*see p256*) or **Tango Entre Muchachos** in Lugar Gay (*see p236*), both excellent venues for 'queer tango' – a modern take on a traditionally heterosexual dance. Tight grips and cheeky dips result in flirtatious evenings, and with the abundance of tight buns and smoldering latino looks, resisting temptation is impossible.

SAFETY & INFORMATION

Safety guidelines are pretty straightforward, but do pay attention to a few potential pitfalls. Firstly, sex with anyone under the age of 18 is illegal (gay or straight). Secondly, street prostitution, though blatantly existent, is also illegal. Always bring condoms with you, as very few venues supply them. You'll be surprised how hard it is to find a condom vending machine at nightclubs. Further information about safety and health can be found through the organisations listed below. Basic English is often spoken by staff.

Resources

As well as the important gay and lesbian organisations listed below, **Lugar Gay de Buenos Aires** (*see p236*) is another useful source of information.

Comunidad Homosexual Argentina (CHA)

Tomás Liberti 1080, y Irala, La Boca (4361 6382/ www.cha.org.ar). Subte A, Loria/52, 86, 132, 151 bus. **Open** phone advice 1.30-8pm Mon-Fri; otherwise, call first. **Map** p324 B9.

Argentina's oldest and most politically influential queer organisation. Go here for advice, information and an exhaustive library of books, videos, films, newsreels and press clippings.

La Fulana

Avenida Rivadavia 3412, entre Sánchez de Bustamente y Billinghurst, Almagro (4867 2752/ www.lafulana.org.ar). Subte A, Loria/52, 86, 132, 151 bus. **Open** 6-10pm Tue-Sat. **Map** p322 I4.

The most useful and efficient community centre for lesbians and bisexual women in Argentina.

Sociedad de Integración Gay-Lésbica Argentina (SIGLA)

Pasaje del Progreso 949, y Salas, Parque Chacabuco (4922 3351/www.sigla.org.ar). Subte E Emilio Mitre/26, 86 bus. **Open** 3-6pm Mon, Wed, Fri; 5-10pm Sat.

SIGLA provides legal advice, health information, workshops and recreational activities for gays and lesbians. The website has listings of all the upcoming parties and events.

Where to stay

Many of the city's hotels are gay friendly, and while they may welcome gay visitors they often lack contact with the community. For more information on gay and gay-friendly hotels in BA, check out www.bestfriendlyhotels.com. Visitors looking for a longer stay should try **El Conventillo Tango Club** (4373 3995, www.conventillotango.com.ar) or get in touch wth **BAires Rental** (4829 1605, www.bairesgayrental.com.ar); both offer smart apartments close to the city centre. Otherwise, try these gay-owned hotels and bed and breakfasts.

Axel Buenos Aires

Venezuela 649, entre Chacabuco y Perú, San Telmo (4136 9393/www.axelhotels.com). Subte E, Belgrano/2, 10, 26, 29 bus. **Rates** US$248-$302 double. **Credit** AmEx, MC, V. **Map** p325 E10.

Step inside Axel's soothing surroundings – water cascading over glass walls – and appreciate modern tranquility. This new five-floor hotel offers comfortable, stylish rooms with the latest technological accessories. An upmarket restaurant, lounge and live DJ weekends complete the hotel's sleek ambience. *See p237* **Thrills with frills**.

Bayres B&B

Córdoba 5842, entre Carranza y Ravignani, Palermo Viejo (4772 3877/www.bayresbnb.com). Bus 39, 93, 111, 151, 168. **Rates** US$45-$65 double. **No credit cards**. **Map** p327 N7.

Located on the edge of Palermo Viejo, this cosy B&B is within walking distance of the best restaurants and shopping on the scene. Don't be fooled by its rather pedestrian exterior; upstairs and inside you'll find a beautifully restored example of art deco.

Big House

Bolívar 920, entre Estados Unidos y Carlos Calvo, San Telmo (4362 0701/www.bighousefriendly. com.ar). Bus 22, 28, 126. **Rates** US$36-$67 single; US$51-$85 double; US$73-$121 triple. **No credit cards**. **Map** p324 D9.

Gay-owned and operated, this San Telmo guesthouse invites you to make yourself at home. And it's hard not to, as the homely atmosphere drifts between seven rooms, a kitchen and a living room. Discounts are available for longer stays.

Arts & Entertainment

GLAM. *See p238.*

El Caldén Guest House

Reconquista 755, entre Córdoba y Paraguay,
Microcentro (4893 1060/www.caldenargentina.com).
Subte C, San Martín/5, 10, 17, 100, 140 bus. **Rates**
US$70-$90 double. **No credit cards.**
Map p325 G12.
The newest gay accomodation in El Caldén, and the
central location couldn't be better – between the
financial district and all the amenities and
restaurants of Puerto Madero. There are five rooms,
each named after Argentinian icons, and all simply
but tastefully decorated. There can be few hotels at
this price right in the middle of downtown BA.

Lugar Gay de Buenos Aires

Defensa 1120, entre Humberto 1º y San Juan, San
Telmo (4300 4747/www.lugargay.com.ar). Bus 24,
29, 126. **Rates** US$35-$65 single/double/triple.
Credit AmEx, MC,V. **Map** p324 D9.
A touch of Key West in the heart of picturesque San
Telmo, this is a racy men-only B&B where the host
isn't shy of greeting guests with a big Argentinian
man kiss. The cheeky atmosphere further manifests
·itself in a g-stringed mannequin at reception and a
jacuzzi and video salon. They also have a
programme of tango clases and *milongas*.

Palermo Viejo Bed & Breakfast.

Niceto Vega 4629, y Scalabrini Ortiz, Palermo Viejo
(4773 6012/www.palermoviejobb.com). Bus 39, 55,
168. **Rates** US$45-65 single; US$55-$75 double. **No**
credit cards. Map p323 M4.
This petite, excellently located B&B used to be a
factory, and with its handful of uniquely decorated
rooms it has bags of arty character. There's Wi-Fi
internet, air-conditioning and cable TV all available
at your fingertips, as well as a courtyard ideal for a
glass of wine or two in the evening.

Bars & clubs

Evening action doesn't get started until well into
the night. Midnight is considered premature and
clubs do not always fill until 3am, so take your
time preening yourself before prowling the
scene. Pad your pockets with enough cash to
cover entry charges and pricey cocktails. At the
door bars typically charge between AR$10-$20,
and clubs will certainly demand at least AR$20.
The gay bar and club scene in BA ranges from
the comfortably chaste to the outright lubricious.
For a fun young crowd, check out **Brandon**
Gay Day (www.brandongayday.com). To track
down the most happening spot, do a little
research on the web (www.gay-ba.com;
www.whatsupbuenosaires.com).

Alsina

Adolfo Alsina 940, entre Bernardo de Irigoyen y
Tacuarí, Monserrat (4331 1277/3231/www.alsina
buenosaires.com.ar). Subte C, Moreno/59, 64, 86 bus.
Open from 2am Fri, Sat; 10pm Sun. **Map** p325 F10.
This club throws a party to remember. From the
drag queen on the door to elevated gogo dancers,
all are here to let the good times roll. Friday
hosts the freshest of electronica beats, with guest
DJs from abroad.

Amerika

Gascón 1040, entre Rocamora y Estado de Israel,
Villa Crespo (4865 4416/www.ameri-k.com.ar). Subte
B, Medrano/24, 55, 124 bus. **Open** from 1am Thur-
Sun. **Map** p322 K5.
Three dancefloors and a capacity of 2,000 makes this
the largest gay disco in the city. It attracts an
increasingly mixed gay and straight crowd, who are
perhaps curious to test out the dark rooms or eye up
the regular live acts. The great music policy brings in
clubbers of all orientations from far and wide.

Bach Bar

Cabrera 4390, y Julián Alvarez, Palermo Viejo (15
5877 0919, www.bach-bar.com.ar). Bus 39, 151,
168. **Open** from 10pm Wed-Sun. **Map** p322 L5.
One of the few venues serving the BA lesbian scene.
Special themed nights are advertised on their website
and karaoke on Sundays draws fun-loving girls. The
music is predominantly cheerful, cheesy pop that
adds to the friendly flavour.

Thrills with frills

On first consideration, block 600 on Calle Venezuela is not the place where one would expect South America's first five-star gay hotel to be built, but there it is: a beacon of good taste between the gritty bus corridors of Perú and Chacabuco. It lies near San

Telmo, a scruffy, bohemian, arty area that is now receiving the lion's share of the city's pink pound.

Entering into Hotel Axel's open central lobby, the visitor is almost immediately soothed by water on all sides. A cascade descends the translucent walls from the fifth floor, finishing in a stone riverbed below your feet, visible through the glass catwalk floor. From almost everywhere on the hotel's five floors, the terrace pool creates a liquid roof that gives the building's interior a calming aquarium effect, as squiggles of watery light reflect throughout the glass-and-iron interior.

In the rooms, glass and glossy concrete are made cosy by fluffy duvets and crisp white linens. Bright splashes of rainbow colours catch your eye (a square mosaic theme, reminiscent of the rainbow-pride flag, runs through all the hotel's interior design). The shower is great for one or two, with pleasingly large rain-style showerheads (the same ones are used at the outdoor and rooftop pool).

Each level has its own lounge, complete with the latest flat-screen Macs (natch) and gay magazines and maps. Glass-and-iron staircases bisect the central open space at angles, giving the overall effect that the hotel is actually some sort of glass elevator shaft, underwater: sounds weird, looks cool. They didn't skimp in terms of the cuisine, either: traditional Argentinian dishes are joined by world fare in the posh restaurant, while the chillout lounge has fancy cocktails and live DJs at the weekends.

Arts & Entertainment

Bulnes Class

Bulnes 1250, entre Cabrera y Córdoba, Barrio Norte (4861 7492/www.bulnesclass.com.ar). Bus 26, 106, 109. **Open** from 11pm Thur-Sat. **Map** 326 K8.
This local hot spot attracts an older gay crowd. It has decent tunes and friendly flirtatious staff, and the usual attitude that comes with favoured watering holes is thankfully nowhere to be found. A good choice for pre-clubbing and casual encounters.

Club 69

Federico Lacroze 3455, y Alvarez Thomas, Colegiales (www.club69.com.ar). Bus 39, 63, 112 . **Open** from 11pm Thur. **Admission** free entry before midnight; AR$25 men, AR$20 women. **Map** p323 P4.
With a troupe of burlesque beauties, this carnivalesque show is like no other. Held in the Roxy Club every Thursday night, 69's high-camp mix of cigarettes and lipstick has won it a lot of fans. *Photo p233.*

Contramano

Rodríguez Peña 1082, entre Marcelo T de Alvear y Santa Fe, Recoleta (4811 0494/www.contramano. com). Bus 12, 39, 124. **Open** from midnight Wed-Sat; from 9pm Sun. **Admission** AR$10. **Map** p326 I10.
A pioneer of the Buenos Aires gay scene. For your musical delight, there's cheesy pop, golden oldies and Latin beats. Older gay men – and plenty of younger ones – have been getting it together here for over two decades now.

GLAM

Cabrera 3046, entre Laprida y Agüero, Barrio Norte (4963 2521/www.glambsas.com.ar). Bus 29, 109, 111. **Open** from 1am Thur-Sat. **Map** p326 J8.
This is one of the best gay bars in town, especially if you're cruising for a younger, livelier breed. Get frisky in the upstairs playroom, or dance your heart out all night long. Steamy, sweaty Saturdays and Sundays at full tilt make package-feeling practically a forced manoeuvre.

KM Zero

Santa Fe 2516, y Ecuador, Barrio Norte (4822 7530). Subte D, Pueyrredón/39, 41, 152 bus. **Open** from 11pm Tue, Wed, Fri, Sat. **Map** p326 J9.
Sing along to favourite show tunes and toss away your shame at this musical-themed drag show. Reserve a table if you can't hold back your inner Judy Garland.

Search

Azcuenaga 1007, y Marcelo T de Alvear, Barrio Norte (4824 0932/www.searchgaybar.com.ar). Bus 39, 111, 152. **Open** from 11.30pm daily; shows from 12.30am. **Admission** from AR$10. **Map** p326 J9.
Sweet and cuddly. Sugar and spice. Giant manly drag queens and muscled strippers. Salivate over washboard stomachs and chiseled arms: the strippers here give one of the best shows around. Music is latino pop, electronica, cheese and house spun by an ever-changing roster of DJs.

Sub Club

Córdoba 543, entre Florida y San Martín, Microcentro (www.thesub.com.ar). Subte C, San Martín/7, 20, 5 bus. **Open** from 1.30am Fri, Sat **Map** p325 G11.
A basement club for music buffs, a refreshing change from stereotypical gay 1980s disco. House, garage and techno are played in one room, while chill out, hip hop and funk are designated to another.

Verona

Hipólito Yrigoyen 968, entre Tacuarí y Pellegrini, Monserrat (www.veronadisco.com). Bus 59, 64, 86. **Open** 1am Fri, Sat. **Map** p325 F10.
Sexy ladies-only Saturdays please the dyke contingent at this effervescent club. Friday nights are a free-for-all when it comes to pick up time.

Gyms & saunas

Buenos Aires A Full

Viamonte 1770, entre Callao y Rodríguez Peña, Tribunales (4371 7263/www.afullspa.com). Subte D, Callao/12, 29, 37, 60 bus. **Open** noon-3am Mon-Thur; 24hrs Fri-Sun. **Admission** AR$35. **No credit cards. Map** p325 H10.
Frequented by a younger crowd and especially busy after 2am on weekends.

Carribean

Uriburu 1022, entre Marcelo T de Alvear y Santa Fe, Barrio Norte (4827 6643). Bus 39, 152. **Open** 7am-11pm Mon-Fri; 10am-6pm Sat. **Map** p326 I9.
Nice free weights and machines, but even nicer is the clientele, most of whom are toned city boys coming in from work nearby.

Energy Spa

Bravard 1105, y Angel Gallardo, Almagro (4854 5625/www.energy-spa.comar). Bus 55, 92. **Open** noon-midnight Mon-Sat. **Admission** AR$30. **No credit cards. Map** p322 L3.
A good option close to Parque Centenario. It includes a bar, gym, relaxation rooms, swimming pool, jacuzzis and the occasional live show.

Homo Sapiens

Gascón 956, entre Guardia Vieja y Rocamora, Almagro (4862 6519/www.h-sapiens.com). Subte B, Carlos Gardel/24, 92, 99, 160 bus. **Open** noon-midnight daily. **Admission** AR$12-$20. **No credit cards.**
This complex has private cabins, wet and dry saunas and even a smoker's area. An hour's massage will set you back AR$50.

Nagasaki Spa

Agüero 427, entre Valentín Gómez y Corrientes, Abasto (4866 6335/www.nagasaki.com.ar). Subte B, Medrano/24, 68, 101, 129, 151 bus. **Open** noon-midnight Mon-Thur; 24hrs Fri-Sun. **Admission** AR30. **No credit cards.**
Nagasaki has been a hit since it opened in early 2008. As well as the spas and sauna, there is also a sex bar, voyeur room, sling and dark cruising.

Music

Sound advice.

Classical & Opera

The arts scene in Buenos Aires really took off after Argentina won political independence from Spain in 1810, and by the turn of the century, this 'golden age' had left the city with no less than five opera houses. Today only two of these remain standing – the **Teatro Colón** and the **Teatro Coliseo** (Marcelo T de Alvear 1125, Tribunales, 4816 3789) – though only the former maintains a regular opera season. Normally, the Colón's season runs from March to December, with a limited summer programme. However, lengthy restoration work has meant this breathtaking venue has been covered in scaffolding with an empty stage since 2006 (*see p241* **The chronicle of Colón**).

Despite its status as the key classical music centre in South America, BA still doesn't have a venue devoted to symphonic concerts. Instead, these are performed across the city in places like the **Teatro Avenida** (*see p265*), **Museo Isaac Fernández Blanco** (*see p92*) and **Teatro Margarita Xirgú** (*see p240*), among others.

A large part of the classical music scene is in the highly capable hands of private professional and amateur groups, including important associations such as Mozarteum Argentino (www.mozarteumargentino.org) and Festivales Musicales (www.festivalesmusicales.org.ar). The Buenos Aires Philharmonic holds a sell-out season of around 20 concerts. There are also more modest, unsubsidised institutions – like **La Scala de San Telmo** (Pasaje Giuffra 371, 4362 1187, www.lascala.com.ar) – which open their doors to talented performers. For complete information on everything from classes to concerts, it's worth taking a look at www. musicaclasicaargentina.com. Also in San Telmo, the beautiful **Galería Wussmann** (*see p207*) hosts the odd classical concert (www.wussmann.com).

Classical music's status in Buenos Aires has been bolstered by keen critics, especially Marcelo Arce, whose lectures are attended by thousands of fans, plus specialist radio stations such as Radio Cultura Musical (100.3FM), Radio Cultura (97.9FM) and Radio Nacional Clásica (96.7FM). Social clubs, libraries, museums and cultural centres also occasionally screen ballet and opera

videos: try the **Círculo Italiano** (Libertad 1264, Recoleta, 4815 9693, www.circuloitaliano.com.ar).

If gala nights at the Colón (when it's open) are still occasions for tiaras and tuxes, interest in opera extends beyond BA's aristocracy. Performances also take place at more intimate, unusual venues like the former paper mill **Manufactura Papelera** (*see p240*) and welcome even the scruffiest bohemian.

Outside the capital, the most impressive venue is the **Teatro Argentino** (Calle 51, 0221 429 1746, www.teatroargentino.ic.gba.gov.ar) in La Plata (56 kilometres/35 miles from BA; buses from Callao 237, Tribunales, 4373 2636, AR$15 return). The **Teatro Roma** (Sarmiento 109, 4205 9646) in Avellaneda – just ten minutes from downtown – is a small opera house with good acoustics and an offbeat repertoire, featuring the likes of Verdi's *Corsario* or Bellini's *Capulets and Montagues*. Finally, in Zona Norte, try the first-rate Sacred Music series on Sunday

 **The best Venues**

Notorious
A daily dose of improvised live jazz comes courtesy of local and international legends. See p244.

La Peña del Colorado
If the wine doesn't make your head spin the frenetic folk dancing and fast-fingered guitar plucking will. See p246.

Teatro Gran Rex
Sit down, tune in and be dazzled by world-famous acts in this comfortable Corrientes institution. See p242.

Teatro Margarita Xirgú
Awesome acoustics and classical treats in this lovingly preserved theatre. See p240.

La Trastienda
Get ready to rock, Argentinian style, in this long-running San Telmo venue. See p243.

Vaca Profana
Get up close and personal to the latest indie and alternative stars. See p244.

afternoons at the **Catedral de San Isidro** (*see below*).

These are all places where opera fans can sate their appetite thanks to the efforts of Juventus Lyrica, Buenos Aires Lírica, Casa de la Opera, Peco o Peco and Opera del Buen Ayre. There are many locally trained, talented performers, directors and designers, including conductor/ pianist Daniel Barenboim (now an Israeli citizen) and pianist Martha Argerich (a festival named after her is held at the Colón; *see below*). Tenors José Cura and Marcelo Alvarez are also acclaimed at home and abroad.

Catedral de San Isidro

Avenida del Libertador 16199, y 9 de Julio, San Isidro (4743 0291). Train Mitre or de la Costa to San Isidro/60, 168 bus. **Open** 8am-8pm Mon, Fri; 8am-10pm Sun. **Admission** free. **Map** p324 C9.
Performances in this atmospheric venue usually begin at 4pm, from April to December; arrive well in advance to secure yourself a good seat.

La Manufactura Papelera

Bolívar 1582, entre Brasil y Caseros, San Telmo (4307 9167/www.papeleracultural.8m.com). Bus 24, 29, 39. **Shows** 6pm or 8.30pm Thur-Sun. **Closed** Jan. **Tickets** AR$7-$40. **No credit cards. Map** p324 C9.
Enjoy a more intimate operatic experience in this former paper factory, where talented groups stage a range of rarely performed works.

Teatro Colón

Cerrito, entre Tucumán y Viamonte, Tribunales (box office 4378 7344/tours 4378 7132/www.teatrocolon. org.ar). Subte D, Tribunales/29, 39, 59 bus. **Open**

El Teatro. *See p244.*

Box office 9am-5pm Mon-Fri. **Tickets** AR$5-$170. **Credit** AmEx, DC, MC, V. **Map** p325 G10.
Unquestionably BA's greatest cultural monument, at the time of going to press still closed for restoration work. Due to open in late 2008.

Teatro Margarita Xirgú

Chacabuco 875, y Estados Unidos, San Telmo (4300 8817/www.margaritaxirgu.com.ar). Bus 10, 17, 29, 59, 156. **Open** *Box office* 2-8pm Tue-Sun. **Tickets** AR$5-$40. **Credit** AmEx, DC, MC, V. **Map** p325 E9.
This stunning example of Catalonian architecture is a treat for your eyes as well as ears, boasting a carefully preserved interior and superb acoustics.

Rock, Folk & Jazz

Despite the continuing exchange-rate challenge, BA is beginning to make its presence felt on the international concert circuit. A number of well-known acts hit the capital recently, including the Police, Killers and the Artic Monkeys. Home-grown and Latin American acts also enjoy massive popularity, Spanish performers are particularly respected, and whatever genre of music you see, the enthusiastic crowd will be loud, appreciative and more than likely dancing in their seats and singing along to every word.

WE WILL ROCK YOU

Most people think tango when they think Buenos Aires, but, as you'll soon glean from the preponderance of power chords blaring out of taxi stereo systems, it seems that Argentina prefers to rock. Brazilians and Mexicans may disagree, but locals claim that Latin American rock was born in BA.

Argentina's *rock nacional* has had a tough trajectory. After gaining a toehold in the early 1970s, many rockers, labelled subversive by the military dictatorship, were censored or forced to leave the country in the 1970s and early 1980s. During the Malvinas/Falklands War, English-language music was banned, giving local talent the exposure it needed, and with the return of democracy, the scene took off, aided by Rock & Pop (95.9FM) radio station. Tours by the likes of Los Enanitos Verdes and Soda Stereo caused mass hysteria wherever they played.

Despite this love of Argentinian rock, most local hipsters still consider the Rolling Stones to be *the* definitive band. Fans of all ages, known as *rollingos* (*see p41*) continue to sport that lips logo on their T-shirts. An opposing fan group is (almost) as passionate about Los Beatles. Stones-inspired local bands include La 25, Intoxicados, and La Mancha de Rolando.

The chronicle of Colón

Since 2006, many visitors to BA have been disappointed to find the elegant doors of the Teatro Colón, once called 'the most beautiful of all theatres I know' by ballet dancer Mikhail Baryshnikov, firmly closed for renovations. But, to borrow a phrase from another man who knows a thing or two about theatre, 'what's past is prologue': after a lengthy delay, the Colón's velvet curtain is due to rise once again on May 25, 2008, exactly 100 years since the first note was sung on its stage. Whether this happens or not is another matter, since the restoration work has been plagued by resignations, redundancies and budget problems.

The theatre's history is as dramatic as its productions are. The original Italian architect died suddenly before the project was finished, his successor was murdered by a valet he'd recently fired, and a businessman whose deep pockets were funding the venture also checked out unexpectedly. Finally, a Belgian architect, Jules Dormal, took the helm, adding elements of French neo-classicism to a structure previously dominated by German and Italian Renaissance principles.

A rough start, yes, but the results are grand and gloriously eclectic: red velvet and gilded balconies, Venetian mosaics, Greek façades, white Portuguese marble, stained-glass windows depicting scenes from the Iliad, a glittering Salón Dorado reminiscent of Versailles, and a lavish auditorium seating 3,000. Richard Strauss, Igor Stravinsky and Aaron Copland have all waved their batons in the orchestra pit, while international ballet stars such as Margot Fonteyn and Rudolf Nureyev have pirouetted across its boards.

And that's just an example of what happens on stage. Real theatre fans should not miss the fascinating behind-the-scenes guided tour through the Colón's vast underbelly. Picture scenes from *Madame Butterfly* to *Aída* in the paint-splattered set design studio, marvel at the mechanical wizardry of the high-tech lighting department, and admire the vibrant, colourful costume store where hundreds of curly wigs perch on stands and 20,000 pairs of shoes await the dainty feet of divas and dancers. The Sala Nueve de Julio, a full-size replica of the theatre's main stage used for rehearsals, reminds visitors just how opulent the opera house really is – as if you could forget when a chandelier ablaze with 700 sparkling bulbs is hanging above your head.

Following the economic crisis of 2001, the Colón ran a Monday night concert programme called 'the Colón for Two Pesos', allowing a cash-poor but culture-hungry public in for the bargain price of, you guessed it, two pesos. The 'Master Plan', an ambitious US$25 million restoration effort, is a long overdue project to modernise and conserve this BA cultural monument. In addition to general repairs and cleaning, modern bathrooms and even air conditioning are being introduced, as well as a new outdoor stage in the spacious courtyard for summer performances beneath the stars. Well worth the long wait.

ALTERNATIVE RHYTHMS

An exciting deviation from the standard rock format are innovative groups such as Pequeño Orquesta Recincidentes (think a gypsy Arcade Fire with a tuba), the lively Me Darás Mil Hijos and Orquestra de Salón, led by the irresistible chain-smoking Pablo Ducal. These acts often play at the **Centro Cultural Torquato Tasso** (*see p258*). Another interesting band

going strong after a support slot with Coldplay is Brian Storming Orchestra, who can regularly be seen at **Thelonious** (*see p246*).

Punk and metal are still popular in BA, with all-girl group Estoy Konfundida updating the punk snarl for the 21-century. A host of ska and reggae nights are advertised around San Telmo, while swing, poodle metal (check out Whitesnake copyists Rata Blanca) and even

Arts & Entertainment

rockabilly have small but devoted followings.

Despite its macho reputation, BA boasts an impressive range of female singer-songwriters. Keep an eye out for concerts by Juana Molina, who samples and loops herself singing and playing during enthralling live shows, and Rosario Bleferi, BA's indie godmother, who delivers rowdy, high-energy rock sets. Waif-like folk singer Flopa's physical appearance belies her musical and emotional strength; her songs, like her guitar playing, are strong, clear and definitive. Rosal, fronted by the crystal clear tones of Maria Ezquiaga, offer an engaging line in melodic pop. And in Princesa Vale, a feisty reggaeton and cumbia influenced singer, BA has its own diminuitive rap queen. Many appear at the excellent Niceto club (*see p222*).

ALL THAT JAZZ

The local jazz scene numbers some outstanding artists, such as guitarist Valentino, bass player Javier Malosetti, trumpeter Fats Fernandez, pianist Adrian Iaies and bass quintet leader Alejandro Herrera. Visits from jazz heavies from across Latin America are on the rise, and living legends such as Wynton Marsalis sometimes make appearances. Jam sessions, usually advertised under the English nomenclature, are increasingly prominent and there's even a government initiative to promote live jazz, known as the Jazz Route (*see p244*).

GIGS & FESTIVALS

Buenos Aires boasts a huge number of live music venues. As with so many city spaces, they are often multifunctional – a place listed under 'Jazz' might have a folk night on Tuesday, tango class on Thursday and a mime performance on Friday. In this chapter we list places that have at least two shows a month; call ahead in January and February since some places put their agenda on ice over the summer. You can see gig listings at www.whatsupbuenosaires.com.

Many venues, especially clubs, are unlikely to accept credit cards. However, you can buy tickets using major credit cards at the following agencies: **Ticketek** (5237 7200, www.ticketek. com.ar, nine locations), and **Ticketmaster** (4321 9700, two locations). The booking fee is usually ten per cent of the ticket price.

Festivals include mobile phone company sponsored **Personalfest** in December, which in 2007 united acts as diverse as Snoop Dog, CocoRosie and Happy Mondays, as well as the most important local bands, in two busy beat-packed days. Also in December is the **Festival Buen Día** (*see p213*), held in front of Palermo's planetarium, a chilled out affair bringing together local bands and fashion designers. The city government (www.buenosaires.gov.ar)

often subsidises free outdoor concerts in places like the **Parque Tres de Febrero** (*see p109*). Keep an eye out also for posters advertising small, impromptu festivals.

Rock & folk venues

Major venues

Mega stars – whether local heroes like Los Piojos or international top dogs like U2 – play the city's football stadiums: River Plate, Vélez Sarsfield, Ferro Carril Oeste, and Boca's home turf La Bombonera. It's best (and cheaper) to buy a ticket for the main ground – *el campo* – rather than the stands, since the number of large screens is often limited. For details of sports stadiums, *see pp247-253*. Below is a list of other major venues, less monumental, but each with its own pros and cons.

Estadio Obras Sanitarias

Avenida del Libertador 7395, entre Núñez y Manuela Pedraza, Núñez (4702 3223/www.estadioobras. com.ar). Bus 15, 29, 130. **Box office** noon-8pm Mon-Fri. **Closed** Jan. **Tickets** AR$20-$65. **No credit cards**.
The so-called Temple of Rock, and a favourite with Argentinian rock fans, can hold 5,000 souls. Eric Clapton, James Brown, Megadeth and Manu Chao, along with BA's hottest bands, have all played here. Refurbished toilets and a very welcome new air-conditioning system have relieved the place of some of its former drawbacks.

Luna Park

Bouchard 465, entre Corrientes y Lavalle, Microcentro (4311 5100/4312 2135/www.lunapark.com.ar). Subte B, LN Alem/26, 93, 99, 152 bus. **Box office** 10am-8pm Mon-Sat; varies Sun. **Tickets** AR$15-$140. **Credit** AmEx, DC, MC, V. **Map** p325 F11.
Arctic Monkeys and Lily Allen are among the stars to have recently graced the stage of this boxing stadium (boxing can still be seen on a weekly basis, *see p248*). It's a good space that attracts enthusiastic audiences, but there are some negative aspects: thick columns can block views from the upper levels and the dodgy sound system has been known to make top acts sound like shambling amateurs. Ask whether the view is restricted when you book.

Teatro Gran Rex

Avenida Corrientes 857, entre Suipacha y Esmeralda, Microcentro (4322 8000). Subte B, Carlos Pellegrini or C, Diagonal Norte or D, 9 de Julio/10, 17, 24, 29, 70 bus. **Box office** 10am-10pm daily. **Tickets** AR$20-$75. **No credit cards**. **Map** p325 F10.
Ideal for artists who require the rapt attention of a comfortably seated audience; sell-out past performers include Bjork, Coldplay and local electronic beat masters Bajofondo. The Gran Rex holds 3,500 punters who can choose between the

stalls (*platea*), the mezzanine (*super pullman*) or the dress circle (*pullman* – cheaper seats, worse sound, and a pretty distant view). Also a venue for musicals and visiting ballet companies, it has its own car park and coffee shop.

Teatro Opera
Avenida Corrientes 860, entre Suipacha y Esmeralda, Microcentro (4326 1335). Subte B, Carlos Pellegrini or C, Diagonal Norte or D, 9 de Julio/10, 17, 24, 29, 70 bus. **Box office** 10am-8pm daily. **Tickets** AR$20-$60. **Credit** varies. **Map** p325 F10.

Situated opposite the Gran Rex, this is one of BA's classic art deco- and nouveau-style auditoriums. Since its opening in 1872 it's hosted dazzling concerts from the likes of tango stars Hugo del Carril and Edmundo Rivero, as well as international greats such as Louis Armstrong and Ella Fitzgerald.

La Trastienda
Balcarce 460, entre Belgrano y Venezuela, San Telmo (4342 7650/www.latrastienda.com). Subte A, Plaza de Mayo or D, Catedral, or E, Bolívar/24, 29, 126, 130 bus. **Box office** *Jan* 4-8pm daily. *Feb-Dec* noon-8pm Mon-Sat; 3pm-8pm Sun. **Tickets** AR$10-$60. **Credit** DC, MC, V. **Map** p325 E10.

In the ruins of an old mansion dating from 1895, the Trastienda holds 400 people seated at small tables and another 1,000 standing. A Mecca for serious musicians and discerning fans, it attracts cutting edge local bands, established Latin American talent and international groups such as Calexico.

Smaller venues

Mitos Argentinos
Humberto Primo 489, entre Bolívar y Defensa, San Telmo (4362 7810/www.mitosargentinos.com.ar). Bus 24, 29, 126, 130, 152. **Open** from 9.30pm Fri, Sat;

from 12.30pm Sun. **Tickets** AR$5 women Fri, Sat, all Sun; AR$8 men Fri; AR$10 men Sat. Free before 11pm. **Credit** AmEx, DC, MC, V. **Map** p324 D9.

Local rock and blues bands play in this old San Telmo house, and though most are barely known they're wisely selected, so it's worth the experience. Dinner is available on Fridays and Saturdays (10.30pm), while on Sundays lunch is served while tango shows and classes take place. After hours, dancing continues until the sun comes up.

ND/Ateneo
Paraguay 918, y Suipacha, Retiro (4328 2888/ www.ndateneo.com.ar). Subte C, San Martín/10, 59, 109, 152 bus. **Box office** *Feb-Dec* noon-8pm Mon-Sat. **Closed** Jan. **Tickets** AR$15-$40. **No credit cards.** **Map** p324 G11.

This traditional theatre is a key venue for all musical genres, from folklore and tango to rock and jazz. There are concerts most Thursdays to Sundays, mainly by talented Argentinian performers or other Latin American artists, as well as occasional film screenings, theatre performances and poetry recitals.

No Avestruz
Humboldt 1857, entre El Salvador y Costa Rica, Palermo Viejo (4771 1141/www.noavestruz.com.ar). Bus 39, 93, 111. **Open** *Jan, Feb* from 10pm Fri, Sat. *Mar-Dec* 8pm-1am Thur-Sat, 7-11pm Sun. **Tickets** AR$8-$15. **No credit cards.** **Map** p323 N5.

Once or twice a week, you can catch a concert from alternative local artists covering the spectrum from electronica to acoustic guitar in this creative cultural centre, which also hosts plays, photography exhibitions and clown classes. The comfy couches and chairs scattered about the spacious warehouse make for an informal atmosphere. This is one of the most vibrant *multiespacios* in the city and there is always something of interest here.

Live music at **Niceto**. *See p222.*

Arts & Entertainment

Sitio Plasma

Piedras 1853, entre Ituzaingo y Uspallata, San Telmo (4307 9171/www.sitioplasma.com.ar). Bus 10, 22, 28, 74, 126. **Open** from 8.30pm Wed-Sat. **Tickets** free-AR$10. **No credit cards. Map** p324 C8.

There's an eclectic mix of live music and visuals at this studenty venue, which showcases the talents of up-and-coming local acts, from young popstrels to soulful singer-songwriters. Check out Vibrato on Thursday nights for music on a more electronic tip, when the usual mosh pit is transformed into a heaving dancefloor.

Salón Pueyrredón

Avenida Sante Fe 4560, entre Godoy Cruz y Oro, Palermo Viejo (www.fotolog.com/spueyrredon). Subte D, Palermo/15, 29, 39, 95 bus. **Open** from 9pm Wed-Sun. **Tickets** AR$5-$20. **No credit cards. Map** p327 N9.

Dark, noisy and poorly painted, Salón Pueyrredón is the closest thing Buenos Aires has to a classic punk club, for people who don't actually like to be spat on. While the jerky strains of punk can often be heard, it's also a major testing ground for local rock and pop outfits, and most nights ironed jeans and designer T-shirts outnumber mohawks and studded dog-collars. The punk spirit is perhaps most notable at the bar, where heavy-handed bartenders fling out cheap, lethal drinks. DJs take over most nights after the live music, spinning a combination of punk, new wave and mod tunes.

El Teatro

Federico Lacroze 3455, y Alvarez Thomas, Colegiales (4555 1145). Bus 19, 39, 112, 168. **Open** from 9pm Wed-Sun. **Tickets** AR$10-$20. **No credit cards. Map** p323 P4.

El Teatro is spectacularly housed in a gorgeous old theatre. An unpretentious, decidedly long hair and leathers rock joint, they don't serve fancy cocktails or imported whisky, just beer and basic spirits. But great acoustics combine with a good atmosphere to make it a decent outing. Try to avoid new band nights, which tend to attract legions of homogeneous adolescents, in favour of checking out some more established rockers. *Photo p240.*

Vaca Profana

Lavalle 3683, y Bulnes, Abasto (4867 0934/ www.vacaprofana.com.ar). Bus 26, 168. **Open** from 9pm Tue-Sun. **Tickets** AR$7-$15. **No credit cards. Map** p322 K5.

Vaca Profana is quickly becoming a major stop-off point on the gigging circuit for quality local bands. Small and intimate, it's a prime place to relax in and get up close to the musicians, whether they be strumming a guitar, puffing on a tuba or improvising on a drum kit. A quirky, cult venue with a devoted following; there's bound to be someone interesting on the bill, wherever your musical tastes lie. Also doubles as an exhibition space and bar-café, offering good drinks and a menu of pizzas, cheese and meat platters and sandwiches.

Jazz & blues venues

Buenos Aires's jazz scene is gaining momentum, both in terms of musicians and venues. Look out for concerts at the **Teatro Coliseo** (Marcelo T de Alvear 1125, 4816 3789). Outside the capital, the October La Plata Jazz Festival attracts ever-increasing audiences keen to see local and international artists perform, while Bariloche's equivalent, in February, offers jazz in the open air. There's a first-class festival in Punta too.

More and more places in Buenos Aires are dedicated to jazz and blues, and as a result the city has organised and is promoting a specific jazz circuit called **La Ruta del Jazz** (the Jazz Route). Along the lines of the tango route, it's an attempt to bring together dozens of formal and informal joints – often bars and restaurants – where some kind of jazz, fusion, ethnic, R&B or Caribbean/Latin jazz takes place at least once a week. As well as places listed here, other Palermo Viejo venues on the Ruta where you can eat to a sax soundtrack are **Bar Abierto** (Borges 1613, 4833 7640), **Cala Bistro** (Soler 4065, 4823 0413) and **Las Cortaderas** (Charcas 3647, 4825 2887, www.cortaderas palermo.com.ar). If you're in San Telmo, try **El Perro Andaluz** (Bolívar 852, 4361 3501). For an up-to-date programme, have a look at the listings on www.rutadeljazz.com.ar.

Blues Special Club

Avenida Almirante Brown 102, y Pilcomayo, La Boca (4854 2338). Bus 29, 53, 64, 93, 168. **Open** from 10pm Fri-Sun. **Tickets** AR$5; international shows AR$15 (1wk in advance), AR$20 (on the door). **No credit cards. Map** p324 C9.

This soulful establishment is a classic for *porteño* blues fans. Affable owner Adrián regularly brings new artists over from the US. On Fridays, there are lawless '*zapadas*' (jam sessions).

Notorious

Avenida Callao 966, entre Marcelo T de Alvear y Paraguay, Barrio Norte (4816 2888/www. notorious.com.ar). Subte D, Callao/12, 39, 60, 111 bus. **Open** 8am-midnight Mon, Tue; 8am-1am Wed, Thur; 8am-3am Fri; 10am-3am Sat; 6pm-midnight Sun. **Tickets** AR$10-$20. **Credit cards** (restaurant only) AmEx, DC, MC, V. **Map** p325 H10.

Notorious has daily live shows by respected local jazzers such as Fats Fernandez and Adrian Iaies, as well as occasional new folk and world music acts. The tables are close to the stage, so you can catch every groan and moan during the improvs – but reserve ahead to be as near to the front as possible. The new branch – above bookstore Gandhi (*see p181*) – offers a similarly eclectic live programme and simple, decent food, but the view from the back tables is poor. There is an impressive range of jazz and world CDs. **Other locations:** First Floor, Gandhi, Corrientes 1743, Tribunales (4371 0370).

Nowt as queer as folk

Forget the beardy weirdy sensibility of folk clubs at home; in Argentina, folklore nights are wine-sloshing, foot-stomping, twirling and twisting shindigs, known as *peñas*. It is where the culture of the countryside collides with the grit of the city. Lively carnival tunes from the Andean north-west, such as *chacarera* and *zamba*, steamy accordion-led *chamamé* from the north-east and provincial pampas, as well as guitar-plucking *gaucho* laments of the milonga can all be heard (often on the same bill) at peñas around BA. Occasionally, there are even real life knife-sporting *gauchos* who, unlike their British Morris dancing counterparts, successfully manage to jig about with a handkerchief and retain their I-can-kill-a-cow-with-my-bare-hands mystique.

While each *peña* has a slightly different focus, the quality of musicianship is consistently high, and the mix usually means there is something interesting for everyone. Nor is it rare to catch a gig by a folk legend such as the *charango* maestro, Jamie Torres, *Jujeño* troubadour Tomas Lipan, or the internationally-renowned grande dame of folklore, Mercedes Sosa.

Musical distinctions are often blurry – quite possibly due to the cheap foot-trodden vino patero sold at these places – as *folklòrico* fuses sounds from pre-Colombia sources with the *criollo* syncretism of colonial and indigenous peoples. Instruments and rhythms from both traditions have been integrated into the melodies. Thus, European violins and guitars are played alongside the wood wind quena, the percussive *caja* (box) and the mandolin-like *charango* (often made from an armadillo shell) – which all hail from the Argentinian north, Bolivia, Peru and Chile – or the *kultrun*, a rhythm box from the south.

These long nights of guitar strumming and dizzying dancing are inevitably accompanied by copious amounts of red wine and the *gaucho* favourite Bols ginebra. They are also the perfect opportunity to sample Argentina's fine regional cuisine. Besides the staple meat and cheese filled *empanadas* (pasties), are tasty *tamales* and *humitas* (stuffed corn-meal dough pasties steamed in husks) and a warming stew of meat, corn and whatever is lying around (and we mean whatever) called *locro*. Argentina's national drink, *mate*, a herbal tea served in a gourd, may well also be passed around early on in the evening.

A good place to try the food, along with top quality acts, including the occasional tango (shhh), is **La Peña del Colorado** (Güemes 3657, Palermo, 4822 1038, www.del colorado.com.ar), which attracts a studenty crowd keen on making their own music after the show. Hidden behind a closed door on Uriarte is the relaxed **La Casa de los Chillado Biaus** (Uriarte 2426, Palermo) run by two talented brothers who always have a little tinkle before introducing their main act. If you are lucky enough to hit one of the monthly parties organised by **Los Cumpas** (various locations, see www.loscumpas.net) you're in for a happy hoedown, and almost certainly a hangover. Folklore is also often to be found squeezed in between tango and rock on the bill at **La Trastienda** (Balcarce 460, San Telmo, 4342 7650, www.latrastienda.com). Finally, **Los Cardones** (Borges 2180, Palermo, 4777 1112), is particularly popular when young *gauchos* descend on the city for the annual La Rural exhibition at the end of July, but is a great laugh all year round. At the end of the entertaining but often ramshackle performances, guitars are handed out for the partying to continue until early morning. Don't be surprised if you are asked to play a couple of folk tunes from home yourself – and no, Oasis and Led Zeppelin covers don't count.

To find out what's on take a look at www.folkloreclub.com.ar. Most record shops in the city sell plenty of Argentinian folklore, often at bargain prices. **Gandhi** (*see p181*) and **Zival's** (*see p207*) are known for their selections and stock the acts listed above.

Arts & Entertainment

Thelonious Bar

Salguero 1884, entre Güemes y Charcas, Palermo (4829 1562/www.theloniusclub.com.ar). Subte D, Bulnes/29, 39, 111, 152 bus. **Open** from 9pm Wed-Sun. **Tickets** from AR$8. **Credit** AmEx, MC, V. **Map** p326 L9.

Founded in 2000 by musicians Lucas and Ezequiel Cutaia and inspired by the sultry vibe of New York jazz clubs, Thelonious successfully combines the comforts of a bar with an impressive programme of live modern jazz and DJs. Order from an ample cocktail menu at the mammoth 13m long bar, or make yourself at home in a cosy cushioned booth. If you're after good local jazz, this is the place.

Other venues

Hotels, pubs & bars

If you want to cry into your beer to the melancholy strains of tango, or twirl a cocktail stick to a bossanova beat, BA has plenty of suitable venues. **El Teatro** at the very fancy Faena Hotel + Universe (*see p55*) attracts some of the city's top talent. It's expensive, AR$100 and upwards, but a beautiful venue, and you can get up close to legends like Nacha Guevarra, Fito Páez and Charly Garcia. In the city centre, **La Cigale** (*see p167*; free live shows on Mondays) is the place to enjoy well-prepared drinks while listening to the latest in electronic music, pop and retro rock or DJs spinning an eclectic range of tunes. **Bartolomeo** in Congreso (Bartolomé Mitre 1525, 4372 2843) has local bands playing (everything from jazz and blues to hip hop and latino) from Thursdays through to Saturdays, and theatre performances in the basement on Thursdays. Tickets cost AR$5-$8. **Milión** (*see p173*) in Barrio Norte uses a small part of its large mansion to provide an intimate setting for live music, often in conjunction with DJs on Friday nights, and there's live rock and cheap beer at the long-running Music is My Girlfriend night in the scruffy but extremely *buena onda* (good vibe) basement bar **Unione e Benevolenza** (Juan D Perón 1372) on Thursdays.

Peñas

Experience the typical folk sounds and taste the regional cuisines of Argentina's interior provinces at a *peña*. They are always fun affairs and any trip to Buenos Aires should include at least one night in the following three venues. For the lowdown on this scene, *see p245*, **Nowt as queer as folk**. Find out what's on at www.folkloreclub.com.ar.

Los Cardones

Jorge Luis Borges 2180, entre Paraguay y Guatemala, Palermo Viejo (4777 1112/www.cardones.com.ar). Subte D, Plaza Italia/34, 36, 55, 93, 161 bus. **Open** from 8.30pm Wed, Fri-Sun. **Tickets** AR$10. **No credit cards. Map** p323 M6.

An energetic and enthusiastic *peña* all year round, this spot becomes particularly popular at the end of July, when the young *gauchos* descend on Buenos Aires for the La Rural exhibition.

La Casa de los Chillado Biaus

Uriarte 2426, entre Santa Fe y Güemes, Palermo (4776 4320). Subte D, Plaza Italia/34, 57, 118, 160 bus. **Open** from 9pm Fri, Sat. **Tickets** AR$12-$15. **No credit cards. Map** p 327 M9.

Run by two musical brothers, who usually open proceedings before introducing the top quality acts, this *peña* is more of the sit-down-and-eat variety than a let's-go-crazy-on-the-dancefloor affair.

La Peña del Colorado

Güemes 3657, entre Vidt y Salguero, Palermo (4822 1038/www.delcolorado.com.ar). Subte D, Bulnes/15, 29, 39, 152, 160 bus. **Open** noon-2am Tue-Sat; 8pm-2am Sun. **Tickets** AR$10-$20. **No credit cards. Map** p326 L9.

A friendly *peña*, popular with students, with good acts and tasty food. There is usually an impressive amount of performers on any given evening and once the troubadours have finished, guitars are passed around for you to make your own music well into the night.

Thelonious Bar.

Sport & Fitness

Where to burn off all that meat and ice cream.

Something remarkable happened in October 2007. For a couple of weeks Argentina's rugby team, the Pumas, knocked the country's international and domestic football scene off the sports headlines en route to reaching the semi-finals of the World Cup (they lost to South Africa). Briefly the world turned oval, and the Pumas returned as national, almost-all-conquering heroes.

It couldn't last, of course. Football, not religion, is the opium of the Argentinian masses and it's not a habit they show any desire to kick. It doesn't hurt that some of the world's best players, including Lionel Messi and Carlos Tévez, wear the blue-and-white strip, but national pride is only one aspect of the sport's appeal. Like Brazil, Argentina has a huge underclass and little in the way of social mobility; the idea that a poor kid from a shantytown can win fame and fortune through talent alone is thus a powerful one; it is the Argentinian dream, lived out by, among others,

Diego Maradona, long past his prime but still one of the world's most recognisable sportsmen. And for many like 'El Diez', soccer still seems the only way out of poverty. (Incidentally, football *isn't* the official national sport. That honour belongs to *pato*, an equestrian game that used to be played with a live duck and that makes cheese-rolling look normal.)

Despite the current talent winning various golf, tennis, rugby, field hockey, polo, football and, phew, basketball tournaments, there still endures an overwhelming mood of nostalgia for past heroes. Walk down Lavalle street on any given day and you'll find scores of men gesticulating excitedly at televised replays of sporting events from years ago. Visually, the city is plastered with sporting memorabilia – on newsstands and in bars, in collector's emporia, and in the stadia themselves.

For shops selling sports clothes, goods and souvenirs, see p178. Most *kioskos* also have a plethora of Boca/River dashboard decorations.

Football starts at an early age in **La Boca**.

Spectator sports

Basketball

Argentinian basketball has steadily been attracting international attention in recent years. Eyebrows were raised around the world when they won the gold medal in the 2004 Athens Olympics. Next to Brazil, Argentina is one of the strongest South American teams, having won the South American Championships 11 times. In 2007, the men's team were ranked second by the International Basketball Federation (FIBA) in the Americas Championships and the women's team came a not too shabby fourth position.

Home-grown talent has produced NBA stars Carlos Delfino (Detroit Pistons), Emanuel 'Manu' Ginóbili (San Antonio Spurs), Andrés Nocioni (Chicago Bulls), and Fabricio Oberto (San Antonio Spurs). Next to football, basketball is the second most played sport on the streets. It is worth your time to catch a local league game; the best teams to watch are Boca Juniors and Obras Sanitarias. The national league (La Liga Nacional de Básquetbol) runs from October to June.

Estadio Luis Conde (La Bombonerita)

Arzobispo Espinoza 600, y Palos, La Boca (4309 4748/www.bocajuniors.com.ar). Bus 29, 33, 53, 64, 86, 93, 152, 168. **Tickets** AR$7-$15. **No credit cards.** Map p324 B9.

Club Atlético Obras Sanitarias de la Nación

Avenida del Libertador 7395, entre Crisólogo Larralde y Campos Salles, Núñez (4702 4655/4702 9467/www.clubosn.com.ar). Bus 15, 29, 130. **Tickets** AR$8-$15; free under-12s. **No credit cards.** Map p329 T9.

Boxing

Boxing was very much part of the local sporting calendar until the mid 1980s. **Luna Park** (*see p242*), BA's answer to Madison Square Garden, used to attract enormous crowds. Today, it's mostly used as a concert venue, attracting international names like the White Stripes and Oasis, though since early 2003 the red carpet has been rolled out every month or so for the slightly less glamorous ritual of the Saturday night fight.

Federación Argentina de Box

Castro Barros 75, y Rivadavia, Almagro (4981 8615). Subte A, Castro Barros/86, 128, 160 bus. **Closed** mid Dec-mid Jan. **Tickets** AR$10-$25. **No credit cards.** Map p322 J3.

The headquarters of Argentina's national governing body for boxing. Great place to watch local sportsmen duke it out. They can also recommend boxing instructors for lessons.

Football

Each club has its own stadium, and there are at least five top-flight matches to choose from at weekends. There are two annual league championships – the *Apertura* (Opening) from August to December and the *Clausura* (Closing) from February to July. Games for other regional championships, like the Copa Libertadores and the Copa Nissan Sudamericana, are also often played in Buenos Aires.

Seeing a match live, especially at Boca Juniors' Estadio Alberto J Armando, known as La Bombonera or 'Chocolate Box', is an unforgettable experience. Come kick-off, a cacophonous cocktail of fireworks and abuse greets players and ref alike, and the dancing and singing are a constant all the way through. Buy your ticket in advance and get a seat in the *platea* (seated area). Down in the terraced *popular*, it's more tribal. It's also worth noting that the better a team is doing, the higher the *platea* price; standard ticket prices are AR$24-$60, rising to AR$100.

Dress casually, don't carry valuables or potentially dangerous implements and keep your wits about you when leaving the stadium at night. You can buy tickets for Boca or River matches through **Ticketek** (5237 7200) or for any team at their ground (cash only). Go with a local fan or with one of the companies that escort tourists to matches (they guarantee good seats and transport for around US$50), such as **Tangol** (4312 7276). For more on BA's football culture, see our Football chapter (*p34*).

Estadio Alberto J Armando (La Bombonera)

Brandsen 805, y la Vía, La Boca (4309 4700/ www.bocajuniors.com.ar). Bus 10, 29, 53, 64. **Map** p324 B9.

Watching a game here is a unique and vertiginous experience: the concrete stands vibrate and at the higher levels you feel like a wrong move will tip you out on to the pitch itself. The *platea baja* in the stands area is your recommended vantage point. There's also a museum, plus guided tours of the grounds.

Estadio José Amalfitani

Avenida Juan B Justo 9200, y Jonte, Liniers (4641 5663/5763/www.velezsarsfield.com). Train from Once to Liniers/2, 52, 86, 106 bus.

Renovated for when Argentina hosted the 1978 World Cup and well maintained ever since, this comfortable stadium is the home ground of Vélez Sarsfield, the 1994 World Club Champions.

Arts & Entertainment

Mounted and monied

Long regarded as a sport for the elite, a means of trading hundreds of thousands of dollars worth of assets (AKA horses) and the breeding ground for royal love affairs, polo is not your average hobby.

It is, however, the world's oldest team sport and is thought to have originated in Persia around 6 BC. It later spread to India where British cavalry chaps licked it into shape with some formal rules and rather silly jargon, not to mention an equestrian version of the highway code; woe betide anyone who infringes the 'Right of Way' by 'Crossing the Line'. The sport of kings arrived in Argentina in the mid-19th century, and found its perfect natural playing field on the vast, flat expanses of the pampas. Locals took to it quickly, perhaps because it resembled the *gaucho* game of *pato* (duck), *see p250*, a kind of basketball on horseback where riders fought for possession of a ball (or, in early matches, a briefly distressed, but mostly dead, duck inside a basket).

Despite General Perón declaring *pato* Argentina's national sport in 1953, horseball, as it's known in english, lacked the brooding sex appeal and ostentatious flare needed to make it big in BA and it was polo that the country became famed for. The world's 27 best players are Argentinian, and the national team has been uninterrupted world champion since 1949. And it's not only the polistas (polo players) who dominate the game; locally bred pedigree horses are known for their intelligence, speed and agility, and can fetch a whopping US$250,000.

Most Argentinians, though, are about as familiar with a chukker as the average tourist, and the game remains the preserve of a monied minority. Trophies are generally contested between a few landed aristocrats; tournaments become a family affair when the seven brothers and cousins who make up the Heguy dynasty saddle up against each other. The Heguy sisters also compete professionally, proving that a woman's role needn't be restricted to aiming a stiletto at a divot, but in general polo players attract supermodels like British footballers attract girl groups, and the cream of BA's socialites and TV personalities can be seen cheering prettily in the VIP area at any match.

To quaff champagne with the rich and deeply beautiful, follow the heady aroma of cigars to the Argentinian Open, held at Palermo's magnificent 16,000 capacity Campo Argentino de Polo (*see p250*) in November/December. If you'd like to actually watch a game as well as spot celebrities, the basic concept is simple enough: teams of four bully off, then use mallets to whack the ball between the goal posts, over eight chukkers (seven-minute periods). So far, so straightforward, but it's easy to miss what's happening at the far end of a field the size of ten football pitches, and more confusing still what with the constant changing of exhausted ponies and swapping ends after each goal.

The other big tournaments making up the coveted Triple Crown are Tortugas (end of October at Tortugas Country Club) and Hurlingham (mid-November at Hurlingham Polo Club). Tickets are available from Ticketek (5237 7200, www.ticketek.com). If you're keen to have a go yourself, the very friendly folk at El Rincon de Polo Club and School (15 5228 9453, www.elrincondelpolo.com) offer a day of polo from US$200 that includes transport and lunch. Polo weekends are also provided by www.lamariposapolo.com.ar and www.elmetejon.com.ar.

Estadio Monumental

Avenida Figueroa Alcorta 7597, y Udaondo, Núñez (4789 1200/www.cariverplate.com.ar). Bus 12, 29, 42, 107, 130. **Map** p329 T10.

The Monumental – home to Club Atlético River Plate, eternal rivals of Boca Juniors – was the setting for the opening and the final of the 1978 World Cup. It's the largest stadium in the country and, thanks to its location in the swish, upper-class barrio of Núñez, probably the safest. Spend that extra few pesos on a ticket for the *platea* and avoid the *popular*, unless knife fighting and sweaty hooligans are your thing. It's also the only all-seater stadium in Buenos Aires that comes close to meeting FIFA standards. Big-name international musicians like U2 and Keane have also played at the Monumental to crowds of 60,000 and upwards.

Horse racing

Easily turf's most important venue, the elegant, palatial **Hipódromo Argentino** (which can squeeze in 100,000 spectators) is in Palermo. The biggest day on the racing calendar is the Gran Premio Nacional, held annually in November, although there are around ten regular meetings per month which are usually held on Mondays, Saturdays and Sundays and for which attendance is quite sparse. Betting is on the tote system and no alcohol can be purchased at the track. The other big race on the calendar is the Gran Premio Carlos Pellegrini, run in December at the very smart **Hipódromo de San Isidro** in Zona Norte, the only grass track in Argentina. It also hosts flat races on Wednesdays and on the weekends. Check their website in advance.

Hipódromo Argentino de Palermo

Avenida del Libertador 4101, y Dorrego, Palermo (4778 2800/www.palermo.com.ar). Bus 10, 37, 160. **Tickets** vary. **Map** p327 O10.

Under-18s must be accompanied by an adult. For guided tours of the Villa Hípica, telephone 4778 2820.

Hipódromo de San Isidro

Avenida Márquez 504, y Santa Fe, San Isidro (4743 4019/4743 4011/www.hipodromosanisidro.com.ar). Train from Retiro to San Isidro. **Tickets** AR$1-$5. **No credit cards.**

Motor racing

If you stare at 9 de Julio and Avenida de Mayo long enough (or any intersection for that matter) you'd probably think motor racing is the country's national sport. Speeding taxis, buses playing chicken and the stressed-out city commuter make the streets of Buenos Aires the most insanely dangerous in the world. Transfer that onto a race circuit and you've got yourself quite a hair-raising spectacle.

Autódromo de la Ciudad de Buenos Aires Oscar Gálvez

Avenida Roca 6700, y Ave Gral Paz, Villa Lugano (4605 3333/www.autodromoba.com.ar). Bus 21, 28, 114, 141. **Tickets** vary. **No credit cards.**

Races are held most Fridays, Saturdays and Sundays, and there is stock car racing some Fridays at 8.30pm.

Pato

Although *pato* is officially Argentina's national sport, most people in Buenos Aires have never seen it, let alone played it. The game is a bizarre cross between polo and a previously popular, but now extinct sport, *pelota al cesto*. Originally played with a dead duck wrapped in leather straps, a ball has now replaced the unfortunate fowl. If you can catch a match, it's a unique spectacle; the main tournament runs in November/December. The ground is 50 minutes outside town – entrance is usually free.

Campo Argentino de Pato

Ruta 8, at km 30, Campo de Mayo, San Miguel (information 4331 0222/www.fedpato.com.ar). Train from Federico Lacroze to Sargento Cabral. **Games** Sat, Sun.

Polo

Polo is played in Buenos Aires from September to November. The latter is the golden month when the venerable **Abierto Argentino de Palermo** (Argentinian Open – *see p213*) is contested. Beginners and experienced players can have polo lessons at several *estancias* in Buenos Aires province: **El Rincon de Polo Club and School** (*see p249*) is the best choice.

Campo Argentino de Polo de Palermo

Avenida del Libertador 4300, y Dorrego, Palermo (4778 2800/www.aapolo.com.ar). **Tickets** AR$12-$55; *Argentinian Open* AR$15-$60. **Map** p327 O9.

A first rate polo field, in the heart of the city, with capacity for 45,000. Tickets for all tournaments are available from Ticketek (5237 7200).

Rugby

The Argentinian rugby season runs from March to November. On the domestic scene, two teams from the affluent northern suburb of San Isidro dominate: Club Atlético de San Isidro (CASI) and the San Isidro Club (SIC).

Club Atlético de San Isidro

Roque Sáenz Peña 499, y 25 de Mayo, San Isidro (4743 4242/www.casi.org.ar). Bus 168/train from Retiro to San Isidro. **Tickets** AR$8; AR$4 13-18s; free under-13s. **No credit cards.**

San Isidro Club

Blanco Encalada 404, entre Sucre y Darregueira, San Isidro (4776 2030/4763 2039/www.sanisidro club.com.ar). Bus 60 (Panamericana line). **Tickets** AR$5; AR$2.50 7-15s; free under-7s. **No credit cards.**

Tennis

Tennis is taken pretty damn seriously, with 13 Argentinian players recently ranked in the world's top 20. In mid February Buenos Aires Lawn Tenis (sic) Club hosts the Copa Telmex, where, if you're lucky enough to score tickets (www.copatelmex.com/tickets), you may just have a chance to sniff the sweat off the determined David Nalbandian.

Buenos Aires Lawn Tenis Club

Olleros 1510, y Libertador, Palermo (4772 0983). Train to Lisandro de la Torre/59, 60 bus. **Tickets** AR$18-$100. **No credit cards. Map** p329 Q9.

Participation sports

Buenos Aires is a paradise for budding football stars. On any open space you'll find children, teenagers and adults playing on improvised pitches, shouting '*golaaaaaazo*' every time the ball slips through the posts. At weekends, the parks are full of people playing *picados*, as informal games are called. To play, just ask.

There are also a host of multi-sport venues (*centros deportivos*). Three with good locations and facilities are **Punta Carrasco** (Avenida Costanera Rafael Obligado, y Sarmiento, 4807 1010/www.puntacarrasco.com.ar) and **Parque Norte** (Avenida Cantilo, y Guiraldes, 4787 1382), located in Costanera Norte or, closer to the centre, **Club de Amigos** at Avenida Figueroa Alcorta 3885, Palermo (4801 1213/www.clubdeamigos.org.ar). All of the above have outdoor swimming pools, tennis courts and football pitches.

Not surprisingly, with a huge river lapping at its edges, Buenos Aires boasts lots of water-related sports – though you'll need to head out to the less polluted waters of Zona Norte. **Perú Beach** at Elcano 794, Acassuso (4793 8762/www.peru-beach.com.ar) is one of the best. As well as kitesurfing and windsurfing, it offers climbing, roller hockey and skateboarding. For the thirsty, the lazy or the indifferent, there's also a popular bar serving drinks and snacks.

Archery

Initiate that New Year's resolution of taking up archery at Palermo's **Artilaria** (Cabrera 4182, Palermo, 4866 5863, www.artilaria.com.ar).

Cycling

Buenos Aires is by no means a bicycle-friendly city, but there are decent guided tours organised by **Bike Tours** (4311 5199/www.biketours. com.ar) from US$30. They offer a choice of circuits, as well as bike hire. Another option is **La Bicicleta Naranja** (4362 1104/www. labicicletanaranja.com.ar) which organises both thematic and area tours (*see p79*). Alternatively, try the cycle paths in Palermo's Parque Tres de Febrero. The **Reserva Ecológica** is a great spot too, but you'll need your own wheels.

Fishing

There's stunning fly-fishing far from the city, in Patagonia and other regions, but fishing in the Río de la Plata is a dirty business. Along the Costanera Norte you'll see locals drinking *mate* and throwing lines out, but this is a fishing club for members only. You should head upriver, or deeper into the basin, for any action. Your best option is San Pedro, 150 kilometres (93 miles) up the coast where you can fish for two feisty local species – *dorados* and *surubíes*. **Daniel Beilinson** (4311 1222, dbeilinson@flyfishing caribe.com) is an experienced guide who can take you there on a day trip for US$550 for two adults, which includes tackle, transport and

This used to contain a duck for *Pato*. Really.

Arts & Entertainment

lunch with wine. **Deltasur Ecoturismo** (4553 8827/www.deltasurecoturismo.com.ar) offer *pejerrey* fishing around the delta for a very pleasant day out at US$70 per person for four hours and US$120 per person for 8 hours.

Football

If you want more than a kick around in the park look for the words *cancha de fútbol* (football pitch); there are hundreds of them. Pitch hire will set you back around AR$80-$120 per hour. Two of the bigger and better five-a-side centres are **El Parque Fútbol (**Facundo Quiroga y Libertador, 4807 8282/www.elparquefutbol. com) and **Madero Sport** (Moreau de Justo 989, 4342-6343/www.madero-sports.com.ar). Both are well maintained.

Golf

Campo de Golf de la Ciudad de Buenos Aires

Avenida Torquinst 6397, entre Olleros y Alsina, Palermo (4772 7261/7576). Bus 42, 107, 130. **Open** 7am-5pm daily. **Rates** AR$20-$30; AR$8-$10 under-18s. **No credit cards. Map** P329 Q10.
This well-located, though often water-logged, 18 holer is challenging in terms of length (6,585 yards) and bunker placements. Club hire costs AR$35 extra, carts are AR$5-$10, and you'll have to buy balls from the shop (AR$15 for 6). Information on other golf courses further afield in Argentina is available at www.aag.com.ar.

Perú Beach.

Golf Club José Jurado

Avenida Coronel Roca 5025, Villa Lugano (4605 4706). **Open** 7am-7pm Tue-Sun. **Rates** AR$50-$70. **No credit cards**.
Twenty minutes from the federal capital, this 18 hole course is a reasonably close option to tee off on. The course is par 72, including ten par four and three par five holes. The fairways are slightly narrow but good practice for all levels. There are plenty of trees and bunkers around each hole. AR$50 for club hire. Free parking is a bonus. Caddies and lessons are available. It is one of the most accessible courses for visitors.

Horseriding

Most of the *estancias* (ranches) in BA province offer day and weekend packages which include as much riding as your backside can stand. Two decent options are **Las Artes Endurance Country Club** and **Estancia Los Dos Hermanos**. For details on both, *see p280-281.* Alternatively, try one of the two centres below.

Club Alemán de Equitación

Avenida Dorrego 4045, y Lugones, Palermo (4778 7060/www.robertotagle.com). Bus 37, 130, 160. **Open** 9am-noon, 3-7pm Tue-Sun. **Rates** AR$40 per class for 45 mins. **No credit cards. Map** p327 O11.
This club offers instruction for all standards (including showjumping). Individual and group lessons offered, according to your level.

Club Hípico Buenos Aires

Avenida Figueroa Alcorta 7285, y Monroe, Palermo (4786 0262/www.clubhipicoargentino.org.ar). Bus 37, 130, 160. **Open** 8am-9pm Tue-Sun. **Rates** vary; AR$35 for 30 min consultation. **No credit cards. Map** p329 S10.
An expertly run school offering classes in showjumping, training, pony club, and, once a month, a full-day or night-time ride – call for details.

Karting

Circuito 9

Avenida Costanera R Obligado, y Salguero, Costanera Sur (5093 8210/www.circuito9.com.ar). Bus 33, 45. **Open** 4pm-1am Tue-Thur; 4pm-2am Fri, Sat; 4pm-midnight Sun. **Rates** AR$25-$45. **No credit cards. Map** p326 L12.
Up to ten drivers can compete in races of up to 25 laps, once the pecking order is established. The price includes all the extras – racing overalls with elbow and knee pads, gloves and helmet.

F1 Karting

Panamericana y Ruta 197 (4726 7888 www.f1karting.com.ar). **Open** 5pm-12.30am Mon-Fri; 4pm-1am Sat, Sun. **Rates** AR$50-$65. **No credit cards.**
Although outside the city centre, this course is the answer for any urge you may have to burn some rubber. Specially made mini-karts for kids available.

Racquet sports

The centros deportivos also have tennis and squash courts. If you are looking for lessons, Pablo Betelu (15 5809 5258/pablobetelu@ hotmail.com) is an experienced recommended pro with access to some excellent tennis courts. One hour classes cost between 60 to 100AR$.

Magic Center Club

Dorrego 2880, entre Luis Maria Campos y Huergo, Palermo (4772 3016/www.magiccentre.com.ar). Subte D, Carranza/12,29,39,60 bus. **Open** 8am-10pm Mon-Fri; 11am-8pm Sat; 11am-7pm Sun. **Rates** AR$30-$40. **No credit cards.**
A modern sports club with three well-lit clay tennis courts. You can also perfect your game with individual and group lessons, available for all levels.

Salguero Tenis

Salguero 3350, y Figueroa Alcorta, Palermo (4805 5144). Bus 37, 67, 102, 130. **Open** 8am-11pm Mon-Sat; 10am-9pm Sun. **Rates** *Tennis* AR$40-$48; *squash* AR$26-$33; *paddle* AR$26-$36. **No credit cards.** **Map** p326 L11.
Tennis (open-air clay courts), squash and paddle (a cross between the two) are on offer, plus free parking.

Running

The Palermo Parque **Tres de Febrero** and **Parque Thays** (*see p109*) are popular with joggers and runners. If you are downtown, the best bets are the flat promenades along Puerto Madero, down into the lovely, red-earth Reserva Ecológica (*see p122*).

Swimming

Splashing around in the Rio de la Plata is highly discouraged, unless typhoid's your thing. If you feel like going for a dip **Megatlón** (*see right*) clubs have pools. Alternatively, hotel pools are generally open to non-guests for a daily or monthly fee. The loveliest outdoor pool is at the **Hilton** (*see p55*; day use of pool and spa AR$180); for undercover swimming, head to the stunning Le Mirage pool and spa on the 23rd floor of the **Panamericano Buenos Aires** (*see p49*; day use of pool and spa AR$180). The **Marriott Plaza Hotel** boasts a small but pretty pool slap bang in the city centre overlooking leafy Plaza San Martin (day use of pool, gym and spa AR$120).

For outdoor pools try **Parque Norte** (Avenida Cantilo, y Guiraldes, 4787 1384), **Punta Carrasco** (Avenida Costanera Rafael Obligado, y Sarmiento, 4807 1010, www.punta carrasco.com.ar) or **Club de Amigos** (Avenida Figueroa Alcorta 3885, Palermo, 4801 1213, www.clubdeamigos.org.ar).

Watersports

Most of the aquatic and nautical activities on the River Plate are concentrated in Zona Norte, 45 minutes from downtown. In addition to **Perú Beach** (www.peru-beach.com.ar) there's **Renosto Nautica y Deportes** in San Fernando (Avenida del Libertador 2136, 4725 0260, www.wake-board.com.ar), where you can take lessons in waterskiing and wakeboarding. A 25-minute class, using their boats, costs AR$50. Add AR$40 to cover ski hire and additional equipment.

Fitness

Gyms & spas

Buenos Aires gyms are generally well-equipped. It's cheapest to go to one of the multi-sport complexes, though most of the larger hotels allow non-guests to use their health facilities for a fee. Alternatively, you can try one of these health clubs:

Megatlón

Rodriguez Peña 1062, entre Marcelo T de Alvear y Santa Fe, Recoleta (4816 7009/www.megatlon.com). Subte D, Callao/37, 39, 111, 152 bus. **Open** 24hrs from 7am Mon-8pm Sat; 10am-6pm Sun. **Rates** AR$20 per day; AR$80-$90 per mth. **Credit** AmEx, DC, MC, V. **Map** p326 I10.
Slick, clean and busy, the Megatlón chain has all the latest machines and and a wide range of classes from pilates to step.
Other locations: throughout the city.

Le Parc Gym & Spa

San Martin 645, entre Tucumán y Viamonte, Microcentro (4311 9191/www.leparc.com). Subte B, Florida/6, 93, 130, 152 bus. **Open** 7am-11pm Mon-Fri; 10am-8pm Sat. **Rates** AR$30 per day; AR$110 per week; AR$200 per mth. **Credit** AmEx, DC, MC, V. **Map** p325 F11.
One of the city's most exclusive health clubs, with computerised exercise contraptions, a swimming pool, squash courts and beauty treatments.

Yoga & pilates

All the city's main gyms offer yoga classes (*see above*). Otherwise go to major specialist centre **Fundación Hastinapura** (Venezuela 818, Monserrat, 4342 4250, www.hastinapura. org.ar). It teaches all levels, with variants of Hatha yoga on offer. Pilates has also become a somewhat trendy form of exercise, with flyers stuck on every lamppost in the city. For professional overseeing try **Pilates B.A** (Maipú 3144, Piso 1, Olivos, 4790 1008, www.pilatesbuenosaires.com.ar).

Arts & Entertainment

Tango

Anarchic punks, electro DJs and erotic dancers. This is 21st-century tango.

First it was for duffers and nostalgists, then it became a touristy rose-between-the-teeth, leg swinging dance, next the DJs mashed it up, but now tango is returning to its roots and in doing so discovering its relevance again in a new, troubled century. A host of nights have sprung up in grungy, dilapidated mansions, attracting an enthusiastic and bohemian crowd who are keen to learn the seductive steps of this difficult dance. Hugely passionate and talented new musicians are keeping alive traditional tango music and reinventing it for the iPod generation.

Exciting live shows by bands such as **Orquesta Típica Fernández Fierro** (*see p257*) capture the gritty rebel spirit of original tango, while groups like Bajofondo Tango Club add beats and scratching to create electronic anthems. One explanation for this revived interest in tango is that the effects of economic hardship have forced *porteños* to look inward to explore their cultural identity and reality. A less romantic theory is that tango satisfies the tourist image of the city. Whatever the reason, tango nostalgia permeates the very air, and you'll be able to hear the soulful strains of the *bandoneón* (button accordion) everywhere you walk.

THE TANGO CAPITAL

Tango boasts a set of myths and traditions born out of the iconography of the songs – fedora-wearing men waiting on lamplit corners at night and femme fatales in split skirts strutting their stuff on the cobbled streets. In barrios vying for the title of the birthplace of tango – La Boca, San Telmo and Abasto – bars and cafés named after tango stars attempt to re-create this look. You can even stay in a tango hotel, with all-inclusive packages of lessons, outings, *milongas* and shows – check out the **Mansión Dandi Royal** (*see p53*) and **Abasto Plaza** (*see p69*).

Carlos Gardel is to tango what Elvis Presley is to rock 'n' roll, so, unsurprisingly, his mug is ubiquitous, smiling down from murals around town. In the sprawling Chacarita cemetery, there's a bronze statue of his body; there are also Gardel pharmacies, a Gardel Subte station and sections of the Abasto shopping centre named after his songs. Besides the main man, plazas and streets are dedicated to Enrique Santos Discépolo, Homero Manzi and Astor Piazzolla.

If you want to see tango exhibits, there are a few places worth checking out. The **Casa del Teatro** (Avenida Santa Fe 1243, 4811 7678) has a small Gardel room, open Tuesday and Thursday afternoons 4-6pm, and **Botica del Angel** (Luis Sáenz Peña 541, Congreso, 4384 9396) is described as a 'living museum' of tango and folklore, but can only be visited via prearranged guided tours. **Piazzolla Tango** (*see p259*) has a small museum and gallery, and the adjacent and revamped **Museo Casa Carlos Gardel** (Jean Jaures 735, 4964 2015) where the star was born, offers an interesting glimpse of his early years. The **Academia Nacional del Tango** (*see p258*) houses a World Tango Museum, open 2-8pm on weekdays (Rivadavia 830) for those who want to delve into the history behind the moves.

After all the tombs and artefacts, you might even feel like dancing. The annual **Festival Buenos Aires Tango** (*see p212*) in February is the city's main tango extravaganza. Switch on Solo Tango cable TV channel for 24 hours of classics, or tune into radio station 2x4 (92.7 FM), dedicated exclusively to tangos past and present (www.la2x4.gov.ar). All major record shops have tango sections, but **Zival's** (*see p207*) and **Casa Piscitelli** (San Martín 450, Microcentro, 4394 1992) have the most impressive selections in the city.

The best Tango spots

For a modern milonga
La Viruta Tango (*see p256*); La Marshall (*see p256*); Soho Tango (*see p256*).

For showing off
Centro Región Leonesa (*see p256*); Tanguería El Beso (*see p256*).

For dangerous liaisons
La Calesita (*see p255*); Bar Sur (*see p259*).

For dancing till dawn
La Catedral (*see p256*); Tango Cool (*see p256*); Club Gricel (*see p256*).

For just enjoying the music
Centro Cultural Torquato Tasso (*see p258*); Club Atlético Orquesta Fernández Fierro (*see p258*).

INFORMATION

Navigating your way round the tango scene isn't easy, but there are plenty of free guides with listings of classes and *milongas*, most with English translations. You can pick them up in San Telmo bars, hostels and tourist information offices – some titles to look out for include *El Tangauta*, *La Milonga*, *Tango Map* and *Diostango*. BA Tango's comprehensive *Guía Trimestral* (quarterly, AR$2 from kiosks) includes just about everything related to tango. Government website www.tangodata.com.ar always has useful diary, and the bilingual www.todotango.com is an excellent site with news, essays and extensive links pages.

Where to dance tango

Tango tourists are easy to spot at the airport on their way home: pale, hobbling and weighed down by suitcases full of shoes. That's what a fortnight of dancing till dawn at *milongas* (tango nights which at best combine the neighbourliness of a social club with the faded elegance of a 1930s ballroom dance) can do to a person. But you don't have to be a tango fanatic to enjoy a half-drunken wobble around the dancefloor, and there are plenty of laid-back *milongas* that welcome novices, such as **Tango Cool**, **La Viruta**, **La Marshall** (*see p256*), **Confitería Ideal** (*see p258*) and **Lugar Gay** (Defensa 1120, 15 5458 3423, Sundays 5pm). Most of these have beginners' classes first; check the level for *nivel inicio* or *principiante*.

A *milonga* traditionally features three musical sets (*tandas*) separated into straight tangos, faster and more playful *milongas* (country songs) and formal waltzes. The music is usually piped in – which might sound cheesy but adds to the nostalgic atmosphere. Note that taking photos and filming are not always popular (that may, or may not, be his wife), besides you don't want to disturb the intimacy of the dancers.

If you want to leap straight into the BA tango scene without looking, book a tango tour with **Tango Focus** (www.tangofocus.com), a highly recommended BA-based travel operator that arranges lodging, classes for all levels (both group and one-to-one) as well as guided trips to the city's best *milongas*.

Traditional milongas

The venues listed in this chapter usually hold classes prior to the *milonga*. They mostly attract an older generation who prefer to dance *al suelo*; that is, feet pegged to the floor and legs discreetly doing tricks.

Seating is carefully organised and you'll be shown to the men's or women's side, or the places

for couples and groups. It sounds weird, but it signals who's available to dance. Finding a partner involves a bewildering code of *cabaceos* (nods) and subtle signs, the man leading the way. Basically girls watch for the eyebrow twitch, the twirly finger, the chin jutting, the no-messing glare or something that resembles a fish impersonation. Eye contact made, you move on to the floor. Darwin eat your socks: this is selection of the fittest and it's scary.

While the couple waits for the first few bars to be over before moving, they locate each other's hands as they make eye contact – anything more obvious is considered amateurish and unrefined. Don't be alarmed when you're grabbed inappropriately tight – what would is 'friendly' here might be considered hilariously inappropriate back home, it's all part of the fun, though.

Afternoon *milongas* tend to be more casual, just ordinary folk finding solace at the end of a hard day in a close embrace, a good dance and beautiful music – well, it beats going to the gym.

La Calesita

Comodoro Rivadavia 1350, Núñez (4743 3631). Bus 1, 28, 29, 130. **Open** *Milonga* 11pm Sat. *Class* 9pm Sat. **Admission** varies. **No credit cards.**
This little *milonga* is a summer gem, with a setting straight out of a fairytale. In between dances take a stroll out by the fountain to admire the stars, while the haunting strains of a tango lament float out on the night breeze. Worth the trip out to Núñez.

Esquina Homero Manzi. *See p259.*

Centro Región Leonesa

Humberto Primo 1462, y San José, Constitución (4147 8687/Wed, Fri 4704 6338/5620 5970/ Sat 5892 2056). Subte E, San José/39, 60, 102 bus. **Open** *Milonga* 8pm Mon; 6pm Wed, Fri, Sat; 10.30pm-4am Thur; 4pm Sun. *Classes* daily. **Admission** *Milonga* AR$10. **No credit cards.** **Map** p325 E8.

Excellent *milongas* in a superb hall boasting one of the best *pistas* (dancefloors) in town. Reservations are essential for the hugely popular Niño Bien event on Thursday nights, and the afternoon sessions on Wednesdays and Fridays are also well worth a look.

Club Gricel

La Rioja 1180, y San Juan, San Cristobal (4957 7157/8398). Subte E, Urquiza/20, 61, 118, 126 bus. **Open** *Milonga* 8.30pm Mon, Sun; 11pm Fri; 10.30pm Sat. **Admission** *Milonga* AR$12. *Classes* AR$12-$15. **No credit cards.**

You can't beat the atmosphere of Club Gricel for some serious tango enjoyment. A regular clientele rotate gracefully around the well-sprung dancefloor. Saturdays and Sundays are aimed more at couples.

Salón Canning

Scalabrini Ortiz 1331, entre Gorriti y Cabrera, Palermo Viejo (4832 6753). Bus 15, 39, 141. **Open** *Milonga* 11pm-4am Mon-Fri. *Classes* 8pm-11pm Tue; 8pm-10pm Sun. **Admission** *Milonga* AR$10-$20. **No credit cards.** **Map** p322 L5.

This large, traditional hall gets taken over by a variety of different *milongas*, including the long-running Monday and Tuesday night Parakultural events. Somewhat lacking in atmosphere at times, it is a good, if quiet, place to take a class.

Tanguería El Beso

1st Floor, Riobamba 416, entre Corrientes y Lavalle, Once (4953 2794). Subte B, Callao/37, 60, 124 bus. **Open** *Milonga* 11pm Tue, Wed, Sat, Sun. *Classes* 8.30pm Mon, Wed, Fri; 8pm Sun. **Admission** *Milonga* AR$7. *Classes* AR$12 per class; AR$48 for 8 classes. **No credit cards.** **Map** p325 H9.

A bijou setting for nightly dances, this attractive venue is also used by La Academia Tango Milonguero, part of Susana Miller's acclaimed academy, to host classes of a very high standard.

Modern milongas

At these relaxed venues anyone can get up and dance no matter what your level, and if there's any kind of code it's simply to have fun and enjoy yourself.

La Catedral

Sarmiento 4006, y Medrano, Almagro (5325 1630). Subte B, Medrano/24, 26, 268 bus. **Open** *Milonga* after classes. *Classes* from 8pm Mon, Tue, Fri; 6pm Wed, Thur; 7.30pm Sun. **Admission** AR$5-$15. **No credit cards.** **Map** p322 J4.

The atmosphere at this underground venue (now licensed) is pitched between post-punk/neo-goth and circus/music hall. Try to make the monthly Monday night party organised by Miguel Romero (4039 7105). The tangopolis doesn't get any cooler than this.

La Marshall

Maipú 444, y Corrientes, Microcentro (4912 9043/ mobile 15 5458 3423/www.lamarshall.com.ar). **Open** *Milonga* 11.30pm Wed. *Class* 10.30pm Wed. **Admission** varies. **No credit cards.** **Map** p325 F11.

Small, relaxed and very welcoming, this ultra modern *milonga* has no strict rules about who dances with who, and an open-minded musical programme featuring ethnic, contemporary and electronic tango as well as more traditional sounds.

Soho Tango

Cabrera 4849, entre Armenia y Gurruchaga, Palermo Viejo (4748 4490). **Open** *Milonga* 10pm Tue; 10.30pm Thur. *Classes* 8.30pm Tue; 9pm Thur. **Admission** AR$5. **No credit cards.** **Map** p323 M5.

A smart *milonga* that attracts a young, international crowd dancing 'new' tango. It has a smoking area upstairs but no lingering smells down below.

Tango Cool

Córdoba 5064, entre Thames y Serrano, Palermo Viejo (4383 7469/www.tangocool.com). **Open** *Milonga* 10pm Wed; 11pm Fri. *Classes* 8pm Wed, Fri. **Admission** AR$15. **No credit cards.** **Map** p323 M4.

A friendly and informal *milonga* with good beginners' classes in English. Start the night with a class, just turn up, and then dance away with an international crowd into the early hours. There are occasionally live music and shows at this relaxed tourist-friendly *milonga*. There is a tango-themed art space to browse.

La Viruta Tango

Armenia 1366, entre Cabrera y Niceto Vega, Palermo Viejo (4774 6357/www.lavirutatango.com). Bus 15, 55, 168. **Open** from 8pm Wed-Sun. *Milonga* midnight Fri-Sun. *Classes* varies; check website. **Admission** AR$7-$9; free after 3am. **No credit cards.** **Map** p327 M7.

Dancers of all ages come together for friendly *milongas* in this homely Armenian community centre. There's a sprinkling of salsa and even rock 'n' roll jiving should you start to tire of tango.

Classes and information

All the *milongas* in this chapter have resident teachers, and plenty of couples offer private, but considerably more expensive classes (look for adverts in the specialised magazines).

Estudio La Esquina (4th Floor, Sarmiento 722, 4394 9898) offers two-hour classes for all levels, with experienced (and patient) teachers. The **Confitería Ideal** (*see p258*), an historic and gorgeous – if somewhat dilapidated – old

Changing of the guard

Forget what you think you know about tango music. Banish any images of smoky dance halls and fishnet stockings. Tango is experiencing a thrilling evolution as the Golden Age maestros are passing the tradition to a younger, brasher generation. The *orquesta típica* (tango orchestra) is back in vogue, but the best young groups won't be playing 'La Cumparsita' for hordes of glassy-eyed tourists at gaudy spectacle shows. They'll be found holding court in clubs, *milongas* and warehouses in working-class barrios like Almagro and Abasto, playing for masses of equally hip and dedicated fans. These orchestras of the *Guardia Joven* (Young Guard) are generally divided into two camps: the *pura sangre* (pure blood) who dedicate themselves to the cause of preservation, and the rebels, who imbue the form with their own, often countercultural values. But no matter their allegiance, both sides disdain electrotango as irrelevant, agree that shows for export are, well, rubbish, and declare that now is the time to explore the modern acoustic tango scene.

For a taste of classic tango standards played with vibrancy and originality, check out **Orquesta El Arranque**, one of the first groups to make tango cool again for Generation X. These young virtuosos tour internationally, debunking any inkling that tango is stodgy or antiquated, even having been invited to New York by Wynton Marsalis to play with their counterparts of the jazz world – another group of young, not-so-bad musicians, the Lincoln Center Jazz Orchestra.

To watch the passing of the torch in motion, catch **Orquesta Escuela de Tango Emilio Balcarce** (www.musicaba.buenosaires.gov. ar). A unique training academy for aspiring professional tango musicians, under the baton of legendary bandoneonist Néstor Marconi and coached by the rising stars of the tango establishment, the OET was formed by Orquesta El Arranque's bandleader Ignacio Varchausky with the mission 'to pass the style and tradition of the Golden Age' to the next generation. They perform free regular shows at the Biblioteca Nacional and are the subject of American filmmaker Caroline Neal's documentary Si Sos Brujos.

On the other side of the spectrum and skirting the bleeding edge of the form are the experimental sextet **Astillero** (www.astillero tango.com.ar). Led by pianist Julián Peralta, they jam to a boldly contemporary set of percussive and jagged-edged originals against a surreal multimedia backdrop. More musically daring and athletic than any other orchestra around; these boys can chew the scenery, masticating in wild abandon at the air while writhing in place. Your mama's tango, this most certainly is not.

Finally, crawl into the underbelly of the tangopolis and behold the grungy and dreadlocked dark princes of tango, **Orquesta Típica Fernández Fierro** (www.fernandezfierro. com; see p258, pictured). Supported by a fierce cult following, this dirty dozen bang out a hard-rocking, angst-ridden set complete with disco ball, strobe light, and motorcycle helmet-wearing, cross-dressing vocalist Walter 'El Chino' Laborde. OTFF play both classic and original tangos in their deliciously distorted style of 1940s tango icon Osvaldo Pugliese as if he were hopped up on illicit narcotics and sporting wild facial hair. Take it from bassist Yuri Venturín when he says, 'It might be less subtle but it's more psychotic.' Proving that you don't need electronic beats to rock the house, this is tango music through a twisted carnival funhouse mirror, and remains one of the best kept secrets of BA.

café, holds afternoon tango classes for beginners. It's worth going on Tuesday and Friday nights for the Unitango Club events (11pm; live band and classes beforehand). There are well-taught, fairly formal daily evening classes at the **Mansión Dandi Royal** hotel (*see p53*), and one of the best-known tango dancers in BA, Mora Godoy, also has her own school, the **Mora Godoy Tango Escuela** (2nd Floor, Avenida Pueyrredón 1090, 4966 1225, www.moragodoy.com).

Argentina's very own 'university of tango', the **Academia Nacional del Tango** (1st Floor, Avenida de Mayo 833, 4345 6968, www.anacdeltango.org.ar) is an excellent source of information and tango lore, and also runs weekday classes from 6pm. Another good bet for classes is the **Tanguería El Beso** (*see p256*), a well-respected academy run by Susana Miller. Her schedule is complicated so call for details – and expect the style to be Salón tango, close and free from showy tics and pretentions.

To really master the moves you'll need the footwear. Slippery soled tango shoes are available in any number of outlets, but here are our top recommendations: **Comme il Faut** (*see p220*); and **Artesanías** (Avenida Juan de Garay 908, 4362 3939).

Where to hear tango

For the wooden-legged, there is, of course, tango music, to sit back, glass in hand, and simply enjoy. A classical tradition is kept up today by *bandoneón*-playing Piazzolla disciple Rodolfo Mederos and virtuoso pianists Pablo Ziegler and Sonia Possetti. Also look out for Julio Pane on *bandoneón* (you can often catch him on Sunday nights at the classic restaurant **Miramar**; *see p133*, and guitarist Juanjo Dominguez. Singer Adriana Varela's strong, sensual shows are exceptional, while Lidia Borda can pack a punch with her moody singing and strong French lilt.

Outside the ever-evolving mainstream, there's a new, more experimental scene led by Daniel Melingo, grumpy-voiced Omar Mollo and Latino fusioneers La Chicana. Several young orchestras are committed to keeping alive the rebel spirit of the original *tangueros*; *see p257* **Changing of the guard**. Adhering to the more traditional Salon sound are some talented smaller outfits, such as Sexteto Mayor and El Arranque.

La Trastienda (*see p243*) and **ND/Ateneo** (*see p243*) are both serious venues for hearing folk music and tango, along with rock and world music. Parakultural (5738 3850/www.para kultural.com.ar), a modern *milonga* rotating between Palermo's Salón Canning (*see p256*) on Tuesdays and Fridays and a Saturday San Telmo home (Perú 571) can be an interesting spot to people watch and hear good music.

Centro Cultural Torquato Tasso
Defensa 1575, entre Caseros y Brasil, San Telmo (4307 6506/www.torquatotasso.com.ar). Bus 24, 29, 39, 93, 130. **Open** from 4pm daily. *Milonga* 10pm Fri-Sun. **Admission** AR$5-$15. **No credit cards.** **Map** p324 C9.
This is a serious tango venue, with respected artists performing regularly. Friday's and Saturday's events have live music, including renowned orchestras as well as younger, up-and-coming outfits that stray further from traditional tango. The Sunday *milonga* is free and attracts a young crowd.

Club Atlético Fernández Fierro
Sánchez de Bustamante 764, entre Lavalle y Guardia Vieja, Abasto (www.fernandezfierro.com). Bus 26, 99. **Open** from 9pm Wed; 10.30pm Sat. *Milonga* 11pm Wed; midnight Sat. **Admission** AR$12. **No credit cards.** **Map** p326 J8.
The fantastic Orquesta Tipica Fernández Fierro have a twice-weekly residency here, filling the warehouse-like space with an enthusiastic crowd and their dramatic, thundering, rock-inspired tango. On Wednesdays there's a tango class at 9pm. Email ahead to reserve a table (caff@fernandezfierro.com). Without doubt, one of BA's tango highlights.

Confitería Ideal
Suipacha 382, 1st floor, y Corrientes, Microcentro (5265 8078/www.confiteriaideal.com). Subte C, Diagonal Norte/6, 10, 24, 70, 100 bus. **Open** *Milonga* 10.30pm-4am Tue-Sun. **Admission** AR$10-$15. **No credit cards.** **Map** p325 G10.
This busy tango spot has a full schedule of classes by day, but really comes alive at night with the *milonga* and live orchestra. Particularly good are the Thursday night bash thrown by Tangoideal (www. tangoideal.com.ar) and Unitango Club's Tuesday and Friday night affairs (www.unitango.com).

Italia Unita
Gral Juan Perón 2535, y Larrea, Once (4953 8700/www.saboratango.com.ar). Subte B, Pasteur, or A, Pasco/24, 101, 124 bus. **Open** from 9pm daily. *Show* 10.15pm. **Admission** AR$160-$480. **No credit cards.** **Map** p326 I8.
A glamorous setting for a tango show that features expert dancers, *gaucho* music and Argentinian folklore as well as a live orchestra. Go on Saturday to catch Italia Unita in full action.

Where to watch tango

Tango shows are rather artificial affairs focused on the tourist peso, but can be an entertaining, if slightly cheesy, introduction to the genre. Most include the option of a tasty dinner while you marvel at the quick footed manoeuvres on the dancefloor, and a live band belts out tango classics. For a large-scale dose of razzle and dazzle, try **Señor Tango** (Vieytes 1653, Barracas, 4303 0231, www.senortango.

Arts & Entertainment

com.ar). **Chiquín** (Perón 920, Microcentro, 4394 5004, www.chiquin.com) is a more atmospheric, intimate option, while venues offering a highly stylised – and hugely impressive – performance include **La Esquina Homero Manzi** (Avenida San Juan 3601, Boedo, 4957 8488, www.esquinahomeromanzi.com.ar); and **Sab or a Tango** (Perón 2535, Abasto, 5953 8700, www.saboratango.com.ar).

Bar Sur

Estados Unidos 299, y Balcarce, San Telmo (4362 6086/www.bar-sur.com.ar). Bus 29, 93, 130. **Open** 8pm-3am daily. **Show** every 2hrs. **Tickets** AR$80-$160. **Credit** AmEx, DC, MC, V. **Map** p325 D10.
The show is fairly fancy, but the intimate setting is romantic and fun. Used in films, the venue evokes the BA of cobbled streets and sharp-suited men.

Boca Tango

Brandsen 923, y Filiberto, La Boca (4302 0808/ www.bocatango.com.ar). Bus 10, 22, 33, 93, 152. **Open** *Dinner* 8.45 daily. *Show* 11pm. **Tickets** AR$168-$360. **Credit** AmEx, MC, V. **Map** p324 A8.
A tango-through-the-ages dinner cabaret, touristy but impressive nonetheless. Decent *asado* is followed by bawdy sketches (in Spanish) before a sensuous dance by *bandoneón*. The venue's rainbow shacks are fittingly located in Boca, the gritty birthplace of tango, directly across from La Bombonera.

Complejo Tango

Avenida Belgrano 2608, y Saavedra, Almagro (4941 1119/www.complejotango.com.ar). Subte A, Plaza Misere/56, 62, 101, 118 bus **Open** 8.30pm-12.30am

Rojo Tango.

daily. **Tickets** *Show* AR$165. *Dinner* AR$240-$420. **Credit** Amex, MC, V. **Map** p325 G7.
This classy and slick show takes place in a beautifully maintained mansion from 1850 and allows you to get up close to (and dance with) the talented performers. There's a free lesson at 7.30pm and dinner should you need sustenance and you can even bed down in one of eight comfortable rooms. Reservations can be made through their website.

La Esquina de Carlos Gardel

Pasaje Carlos Gardel 3200, y Anchorena, Abasto (4867 6363/www.esquinacarlosgardel.com.ar). Subte B, Carlos Gardel/24, 26, 124, 168 bus. **Open** 8.30pm-12.30am daily. **Tickets** AR$120-$350. **Credit** Amex, DC, MC, V. **Map** p326 J8.
OK, so it's a very touristy show. But the venue is grand, the dancers sexy and showbizzy, and the dinner involves big juicy steaks and blood-red wine. Leave your cynicism hanging in the cloakroom and enjoy – at least until they offer you a Gardel T-shirt.

Piazzolla Tango

Florida 165, entre Mitre y Perón, Microcentro (4344 8201/www.piazzollatango.com). Subte D, Catedral/ 10, 29, 64 bus. **Open** noon-midnight Mon-Sat; varies Sun. *Classes* 5pm, 8pm Mon-Sat. *Dinner* 8.30pm, *Show* 10.15pm Mon-Sat. **Tickets** *Classes* AR$12. *Show* AR$180-$430. **Credit** AmEx, DC, MC, V. **Map** p325 F10.
Theatre, gallery and museum, this new venue in one of the city's most gorgeous buildings – the Galería Güemes – is also a good place to take classes.

Rojo Tango

Faena Hotel + Universe, Martha Salotti 445, Puerto Madero Este (4010 9200/www.rojotango.com). Bus 2, 130, 152. **Open** 8pm-midnight daily. *Dinner* 8.30pm. *Show* 10pm. **Tickets** AR$370, with dinner AR$530. **Credit** AmEx, DC, MC, V. **Map** p324 D11.
Far from your average dinner show, you're first greeted with a bottomless glass of champagne prior to an excellent three-course meal and a sexy, intimate show. The orchestra traces the history of tango from its burdel roots to modern day groove, incuding tango's use in the *Moulin Rouge!* film, while extremely professional dancers and singers spring and slide around the venue. It doesn't break any rules but it is very polished, very flamboyant, very Faena.

El Viejo Almacén

Avenida Independencia 300, y Balcarce, San Telmo (4307 7388/4300 3388/www.viejoalmacen.com). Bus 29, 93, 130, 152. **Open** 2pm-2am daily. *Dinner* 8pm, *Show* 10pm daily. **Tickets** AR$110-$135. **Credit** AmEx, DC, MC, V. **Map** p324 D10.
A charming colonial venue and a tourist favourite on the corner of atmospheric Balcarce street. In 1968, singer Edmundo Rivero took over the building as a refuge for musicians, dancers and, as a plaque in the doorway states, ' for those who have lost their faith'. Today it offers the usual shows but more intimate than many larger productions.

Arts & Entertainment

Theatre & Dance

Buenos Aires proves great theatre can cross the boundaries of language.

Theatre

Buenos Aires loves theatre. Should the urge take you, you can sate your appetite for culture by seeing up to three *obras* (performances) in one night. You could kick things off in the early evening with a sinister take on traditional fairytales by a troupe of puppeteers, then move on to a Spanish language interpretation of Oscar Wilde, and wind up at midnight with an intensely expressive modern dance spectacle. Then grab a ritual post-show pizza along Avenida Corrientes and dissect the merits of the evening's entertainment.

Non-Spanish speakers (and non-culture vultures) shouldn't be put off; there is plenty of engaging physical theatre that abandons dialogue and verse in favour of wild movement and pounding soundtracks, and is accessible to all. Clowning, slapstick comedy based on mime, is hugely popular, and silly sketches involving people falling over or embarrassing themselves are universally hilarious. Thanks to the award-winning efforts of De La Guarda and Fuerzabruta (*see p265* **Dancing on air**),

dangling on wires is now an integral feature of many shows. Or get really back to basics with *teatro negro*, quite literally theatre in the dark, which employs the simple yet strikingly effective device of setting loose a team of fluorescent clad gymnasts beneath a UV light, in a kind of nu-rave contortionist's dream. Take a risk and catch a show: whatever you see, you're guaranteed an imaginative night out.

The traditional spotlight shines on Avenida Corrientes, the 'street that never sleeps'. Although several grand theatres have been sacrificed to make room for car parks, those that escaped the bulldozers continue to pull in hordes of avid theatregoers. The main attractions are glitzy, big-budget, Broadway style musicals, often Argentinian productions of foreign imports such as *Cabaret*, and the *Revista Porteña*, cabaret revue shows where you can marvel at the scantily-clad, high-kicking showgirls while sarcastic comedians viciously impersonate local politicians.

> ▶ For information on **tango shows** and **tango classes**, *see pp254-259* **Tango**.

For information on tango shows and tango classes, see pp254-259 Tango.

Street theatre in Barracas.

Arts & Entertainment

The alternative scene – known as Off-Corrientes and Off-Off-Corrientes – is mainly based in Abasto, although is now expanding geographically to other barrios such as San Telmo, Villa Crespo and even trendy Palermo Hollywood. Government subsidies for small playhouses and companies have allowed independent theatre to flourish, and hugely experimental crossover works achieve maximum impact in intimate, multipurpose spaces, which often double as dance schools or exhibition centres by day. Even further from the mainstream are tiny fringe performances in all kinds of improvised venues, from plazas to living rooms, even launderettes. In lieu of an entrance fee, a *gorra* (hat) is passed around, a sign of the current economic reality and the actors' burning desire to perform.

FESTIVALS

Although usually of the highest quality in terms of performance, theatre and dance festivals can be a bit disorganised. The most important is the biannual **Festival Internacional de Buenos Aires** (*see p212*), which swings through town in September 2009. The event attracts artists from around Latin America, but primarily showcases Argentinian actors, dancers and musicians. In alternate years in December, you can catch the **Festival Buenos Aires Danza** (*see p213*), which brings together the cream of local and international modern dance and choreography. Helping to keep alive the traumatic memory of Argentina's 'Dirty War' of the late 1970s is the sober and moving **Teatro por la Identidad** (Theatre for Identity, www.teatroxlaidentidad.net). This festival, which usually takes place in August, broaches the issue of the identity of children abducted from their 'disappeared' parents.

TICKETS AND INFORMATION

You can buy tickets at the *boletería* (box office) of the venue itself (often cash only) or, for major productions or venues, by phone through **Ticketek** (5237 7200, www.ticketek.com.ar) and **Ticketmaster** (4321 9700); local credit cards are accepted and booking fees apply. You can also pay in cash at the Ticketek office at Viamonte 560, Microcentro (10am-8pm Mon-Sat). Discounted tickets – 30 to 50 per cent off – for plays, musicals, supper shows and films are available at **Cartelera Lavalle** (Lavalle 742, Microcentro, 4322 1559, www.123info.com.ar); **Cartelera Baires** at (Unit 24, Avenida Corrientes 1382, Tribunales, 4372 5058, www.cartelera-net.com.ar); and **Unica Cartelera** (Unit 27, Lavalle 835, Microcentro, 4370 5319, www.unica-cartelera.com.ar). You can reserve seats by phone but must pay in cash when you go to collect the tickets.

Venues

Major theatres

There are two main theatre centres funded by the national government. The 80-year-old **Teatro Cervantes** seats 1,000 people in two auditoriums; and five separate venues are grouped together to form the **Complejo Teatral de Buenos Aires**. The complex includes the centrally located Alvear, Regio and Sarmiento theatres, as well as the picturesque Teatro de la Ribera in La Boca, plus the flagship is the **Teatro San Martín** on Avenida Corrientes. Come here to pick up a programme for all five theatres. You can buy tickets in person, or at www.teatrosanmartin.com.ar.

Well worth checking out are the cultural centres such as the **Ricardo Rojas** (*see p262*), **Ciudad Cultural Konex** (*see p264*) and **Centro Cultural Borges** (*see p265*), which host a wide-ranging and unusual programme of multimedia spectacles, as well as running workshops and classes across the performing arts. Also on Avenida Corrientes are the venerable **Teatro Opera** (*see p243*) and **Gran Rex** (*see p242*), used mainly for concerts.

Belisario Club de Cultura

Avenida Corrientes 1624, entre Rodríguez Peña y Montevideo, Tribunales (4373 3465/www.belisario teatro.com.ar). Subte B, Callao/24, 26, 60, 102 bus. **Box office** *Jan, Feb* 4-9pm Wed-Sat. *Mar-Dec* 4-9pm Thur-Sun. **Shows** *Jan, Feb* Fri, Sat. *Mar-Dec* Thur-Sun. **Tickets** AR$10-$20. **No credit cards. Map** p325 G9.

A small but interesting venue, home to some of the best experimental theatre around, including improv shows where actors take their cue from audience requests, and circus-influenced antics.

Centro Cultural Ricardo Rojas

Avenida Corrientes 2038, entre Junín y Ayucucho, Once (4954 5521/www.rojas.uba.ar). Subte B, Callao/24, 26 bus. **Box office** 3-8pm daily. Wed-Sat. **Tickets** AR$10-20. **No credit cards. Map** p325 H9.

Part of the University of Buenos Aires, this cultural centre puts on challenging new productions with a twist. If what you see tempts you to tread the boards, they hold public classes running the gamut from acting to screenwriting and Arabic dance.

Multiteatro

Avenida Corrientes 1283, y Talcahuano, Tribunales (4382 9140/www.multiteatro.com.ar). Subte B, Uruguay/26, 60, 102 bus. **Box office** 10am-10pm daily. **Shows** 9pm Wed-Sun. **Tickets** AR$25-$30. **No credit cards. Map** p325 G10.

In its three smallish auditoriums, Multiteatro regularly stages provocative one-person shows as well as local adaptations of contemporary classics.

Arts & Entertainment

Carnival kicks

Summer in the city and there's not a breath to be had. Through the stillness, though, soft 'tum-tums' ripple the air, rising to a pulsating, sense-tingling cocktail of bass drums and cymbals, leaps and kicks, tails and top hats: the neighbourhood *murga* (carnival group) is winding it up for February, carnival month.

The predecessor of what today is known as *murga* (possibly a form of the word 'music') reached Buenos Aires through Uruguay,

Teatro Astral

Avenida Corrientes 1639, entre Montevideo y Rodríguez Peña, Tribunales (4374 5707/9964). Subte B, Callao/12, 24, 37, 60 bus. **Box office** 10am-10pm daily. **Tickets** AR$35-$160. **Credit** AmEx, DC, MC, V. **Map** p325 G9.

Argentina's most famous feather-clad showgirls have swayed their hips on the stage of the Astral, the main revue theatre on Corrientes, which recently hosted a sizzling-hot production of *Cabaret*.

Teatro Liceo

Avenida Rivadavia 1494, y Paraná, Congreso (4381 5745/www.multiteatro.com.ar). Subte A, Sáenz Peña/86, 102, 168 bus. **Box office** 10am-8pm Mon; 10am-11pm Tue-Sun. **Tickets** AR$15-$40. **No credit cards.** **Map** p325 G9.

Part of the same theatre group as Multiteatro, this 700-seater, 140-year-old venue is the oldest in the city and still going strong. It focuses largely on Spanish language productions.

Teatro Cervantes

Córdoba 1155, y Paraguay, Tribunales (4816 4224/www.teatrocervantes.gov.ar). Subte D, Tribunales/29, 39, 109 bus. **Box office** 10am-9pm Wed-Sun. Closed Jan. **Tickets** AR$10-$15. **No credit cards.** **Map** p325 G10.

The packed programme at the Cervantes includes Latin American and Spanish plays, regular film cycles of mainly Argentinian classics, as well as some hard-to-find tango. The buiding is a work of art in its own right.

Teatro del Pueblo

Avenida Roque Sáenz Peña 943, entre Carlos Pellegrini y Suipacha, Microcentro (4326 3606/ www.teatrodelpueblo.org.ar). Subte B, Carlos Pellegrini or C, Diagonal Norte or D, 9 de Julio/17, 24, 59, 67 bus. **Box office** 3.30-8pm Wed-Sun. **Shows** from 8.30pm Fri-Sun. **Tickets** from AR$15. **No credit cards.** **Map** p325 G10.

where, in the early 1900s, a group of *zarzuela* (light Spanish opera) singers, La Gaditana, took to Montevideo's streets when their stage performances failed to draw crowds. The following year, local lads parodied their escapades, and a long lasting tradition was born.

With the cultural lives of the sister River Plate cities being closely linked, it wasn't long before Buenos Aires also boasted its own *murgas*. As the city expanded in the 1920's, new *barrios* (neighbourhoods) grew out of previously ethnic-based areas, and *barrio* boys would parade the streets during the carnival season singing picaresque songs accom-panied by homemade instruments.

But *murga* had some way to go to develop into the colourful, pulsating display that we see today. Along the way, several elements considered characteristic in the present *murga* were incorporated: the parade, a parody of marching or military bands, components of Afro-American dance culture and the boom of the big bass drum. The lyrics, less prominent in *porteño murga* than the stage-based Uruguayan version, also evolved to include socio-political commentary based on popular songs, and the music resonated more and more with Afro-American inspired rhythms such as *candombe* and *rumba*. The costumes, too, with their sequinned tails, white gloves and top hats, constitute a burlesque of the used clothes handed down to the early practitioners by

their 'masters'. Add to these, influences from the Venetian carnival and the *commedia dell'arte*, and the result is a stirring, stomping mixture as varied as the city that hosts it.

The fortunes of *murga*, however, have been as chequered and sometimes as tight as a harlequin's tights. After the initial growth in the barrios, and the naming of the Monday and Tuesday of carnival as holidays, this privilege was taken away in a decree just months after the 1976 coup d'état. The military made life difficult for many *murga* groups – the community-based nature of the activity and the strong socio-political content of the songs meant it wasn't really the Junta's cup of tea.

In more recent years the outlook has changed, and there has been a definite resurgence. David Robles of the 'Usual Suspects of San Cristobal' *murga*, said: 'In 1997, when the city's Carnival Commission started to register groups, just 32 *murgas* submitted their names. In 2007, there were 106 *murgas* that participated in 36 *corsos*, or parades, around the city'. In total, over 15,000 *murgeros* huffed, puffed, danced and pranced down the streets of the city, watched by an estimated one million spectators, most of them seemingly utterly delighted to be doused in shaving foam.

The future, then, looks colourful, so keep an eye out in plazas around the city, especially in February, and *murga* forth to the sound of the cymbals and the big bass drum.

Founded in 1930, this was one of the very first independent theatres in Latin America. Dedicated to bringing national theatre to the public, it only stages works by Argentinian playwrights, past and present, and organises a busy programme of acting workshops and courses.

Teatro San Martín

Avenida Corrientes 1530, entre Paraná y Montevideo, Tribunales (freephone 0800 3335254/www.teatro sanmartin.com.ar). Subte B, Uruguay/24, 60, 102 bus. **Box office** 10am-10pm daily. **Tickets** AR$4-$10 children's shows; from AR$10-20 adult shows. Half-price Wed. **Credit** AmEx, MC, V. **Map** p325 G9. Renowned for the quality and eclecticism of its programmes, ranging from cast-iron classics to avant-garde experiments, the Teatro San Martín incorporates three auditoriums with a combined capacity of 1,700, in a building that is a testament to 1970s design. Check the website for news on regular film screenings of independent gems.

Off-Corrientes

Most of the alternative venues are based on quiet sidestreets around the mainly residential Abasto area, a world away from the razzmatazz and neon billboards of Corrientes. For complete and up-to-date listings of independent theatre, go to www.alternativateatral.com. The site is in Spanish, but easy to navigate. As many performance spaces are small and places limited, it's best to phone ahead to reserve your seat (in the loosest sense of the word: you may well find yourself perched on plastic garden chairs or ensconced in a beanbag), then arrive half an hour before curtain up to pay in cash. Don't fret if you're running late, punctual start times in these laid back venues are rare.

Some exciting playwright/directors whose work you should look out for are Rafael Spregelburd, Javier Daúlte, Federico León

Arts & Entertainment

and Alejandro Tantanián. Quality innovators, they've helped raise a generation of young, multi-talented thespians such as Santiago Gobernori, Mariana Chaud, Lola Arias and Matias Feldman.

The Actors Studio

Avenida Díaz Vélez 3842, entre Medrano y Jerónimo Salguero, Abasto (4958 8268/www.actorsstudio.org). Subte A, Castro Barros/19, 128, 180 bus. **Box office** 5-8pm Mon-Thur, 6-9.30pm Sat, 6-8pm Sun. **Shows** Fri-Sun. **Tickets** AR$15-$20. **No credit cards.**
Varied programme featuring new versions of classics and a diverse selection of outrageous original works.

El Camarín de las Musas

Mario Bravo 960, y Córdoba, Abasto (4862 0655/www.elcamarindelasmusas.com.ar). Subte B, Medrano/26, 36, 128 bus. **Box office** 5-8pm Mon-Thur; 6-9.30pm Sat; 6-8pm Sun. **Shows** Fri-Sun. **Tickets** AR$15-$20. **No credit cards.** **Map** p326 K8.
A sophisticated, multipurpose venue that gets rave reviews for its highbrow productions. Enjoy a meal or a drink in the arty restaurant before moving to the stripped-down space to watch a show.

Ciudad Cultural Konex

Avenida Sarmiento 3131, entre Jean Jaurés y T M de Anchorena, Abasto (4864 3200/www.ciudad culturalkonex.org). Subte B, Carlos Gardel/26, 168, 180 bus. **Box office** 6-10pm Mon; 6-9pmTues-Thur; 6-11pm Fri,Sat; 6-8pm Sun. **Shows** Jan, Feb Fri, Sat. Mar-Dec Mon, Wed, Fri, Sat. **Tickets** AR$7-$15. **No credit cards.** **Map** p326 I5.
This trendy complex, based in a former factory, provides a gritty industrial backdrop to a wide array of original events, pulling in a young, bohemian (and often dreadlocked) crowd.

Espacio Callejón

Humahuaca 3759, entre Bulnes y Mario Bravo, Abasto (4862 1167/www.callejonteatro.com.ar). Subte B, Medrano/19, 127, 160 bus. **Box office** email espaciocallejon@speedy.com.ar at least 24 hours ahead. **Shows** Mon, Wed-Sun. **Tickets** AR$15-$20. **No credit cards.** **Map** p326 J7.
One of the best BA showplaces for gutsy and unusual new productions, this quirky theatre also offers evening classes in clowning and theatre, for those who want to get a little more involved.

El Pórton de Sánchez

Sánchez de Bustamante 1034, entre Córdoba y San Luis, Abasto (4863 2848). Bus 29, 106, 140. **Box office** from 5pm Thur-Sun, reservations by phone 10am-8pm Mon-Fri. **Shows** Thur-Sun. **Tickets** AR$15-$30. **No credit cards.** **Map** p326 J8.
One of the bigger alternative venues. A dance studio by day, the Pórton's agenda is heavy on contemporary dance from troupes such as the physically extreme Grupo Krapp, but it also features more polished plays.

Dance

Although tango tends to dominate the dance scene in Buenos Aires, there's a strong classical tradition dating back to the 1920s, when South America's first academic ballet company was founded in the Teatro Colón. The world of tutus and pointe shoes remained the reserve of the elite until Julio Bocca arrived in 1985 and brought it to the masses, staging hugely successful performances in non-conventional arenas such as the Boca Juniors stadium. His choreography to Astor Piazzolla's tango music was equally audacious. In 1990, Bocca founded the **Ballet Argentino** (www.granballetargentino.com), and in 2007 he danced for the last time in a star-studded outdoor show that blocked off Avenida 9 de Julio. Nowadays, Argentinian ballet dancers such as Paloma Herrera, Iñaki Urlezaga and Hernán Cornejo have become, in their field, as famous as football stars. Another world-renowned homegrown company to look out for is Maximiliano Guerra's **Ballet del Mercosur** (www.maximilianoguerra.net).

Modern dance isn't as popular as classical, but **Teatro San Martín**'s (*see p263*) acclaimed resident ensemble, the Ballet Contemporáneo, is ideal for those who feel they've seen one *Swan Lake* too many. The Resident Ballet of the **Teatro Argentino** (www.teatroargentino.ic.gba.gov.ar) in La Plata, under the aegis of choreographer Oscar Aráiz, dabbles in classical and modern dance. Keep an eye open for the work of **Tangokinesis** (www.tangokinesis.com) and Roxana Grinstein's **El Escote**, two avant-garde companies renowned for their absurdist take on tango. Stars of the alternative scene include Gerado Litvek, a director who has taken his experimental works all over the world, in between teaching at the Ricardo Rojas cultural centre, and Gabriela Prada, a highly acclaimed dancer who choreographs and interprets her own futuristic spectacles.

Traditional styles of dance, such as the foot-stomping *zamba* and *chacarera*, both solidified in their present form in the province of Salta in the north-west of the country, can be seen and practised at *peñas* (folk music venues; see *p246*). Murgas, neighbourhood groups that combine energetic, semi-tribal dance moves with a steady drum beat (*see p262* **Carnival kicks**), perform in plazas and parks around the city, especially in the run up to, and during, the carnival season in February and March; but the *murga* troupes can often be seen practising in parks and plazas across Buenos Aires.

Venues

Argentina's best contemporary dance troupes perform at the Teatro San Martín (see p263). Another good venue for modern dance is the Alvear (part of the Complejo Teatral de Buenos Aires, see p263). Alternative venues include Espacio Callejón (see p264), the tiny Teatro del Sur at Venezuela 2255, San Cristóbal (4941 1951) and El Ombligo de la Luna at Anchorena 364, Abasto, (4867 6578). Fans of Flamenco and Spanish dance should check the listings for the Teatro Astral (see p263) and the Teatro Avenida (Avenida de Mayo 1222, Congreso, 4381 0662). It's also worth looking out for tablaos (Flamenco) at Spanish restaurants.

Centro Cultural Borges

Viamonte y San Martín, Microcentro (5555 5359/www.ccborges.org.ar). Subte B, Florida/7, 62, 109 bus. **Box office** 10am-9pm Mon-Sat, noon-9pm Sun. **Shows** Fri-Mon. **Tickets** AR$15-$35. **No credit cards. Map** p326 G11. Oddly situated in the throbbing heart of the Galerias Pacifico shopping complex, this cultural centre organises a diverse programme of flamenco, ballet and postmodern tango and art exhibitions.

Teatro Colón

Cerrito 618, Tribunales (4378 7344/www.teatro colon.org.ar). Subte D, Tribunales/7,10,100 bus. **Box office** 9am-5pm Mon-Fri. **Map** p326 G10.

This stunning opera house closed for a major facelift in 2006, and an elaborate opening ceremony was scheduled for 25 May 2008 to mark its centenary. In the event of renovation delays check their website www.teatrocolon.org.ar for details.

Dance schools

Dance classes are very popular, and there are plenty of schools. If your Spanish is up to it, the cultural centres are the most accessible. The **Centro Cultural Ricardo Rojas** (*see p262*) and **Centro Cultural Borges** (*see left*) both offer classes in every type of dance and for all levels. *Talleres* (courses) tend to start in March.

Danzario Americano (Guardia Vieja 3559, Abasto, 4863 8401) teach native dance styles, from salsa and lambada to Afro-Caribbean and tango. Arabic dancing is also popular, thanks largely to Shakira's music videos. For modern and classical dance, as well as musical theatre, check out the schools run by Noemí Coelho and Rodolfo Olguín at Montevideo 787, Tribunales, (4812 5483,www.coelholguin.com.ar) and Blanco Encalada 2126, Belgrano (4781 0130).

If you're tempted to follow in De La Guarda's steps (*see below* **Dancing on air***)* and get airborne, you can learn a few trapeze tricks at Brenda Angiel's aerial dance school (4983 6980, www.danzaaerea.com.ar).

For details about tango classes and schools see the **Tango** (*see pp254-259*).

Dancing on air

For around two centuries, Argentinian cows have shared the *pampas* with another species of migrant animal – circus performers. These nomadic shows – known as *circo criollo* – feature acrobats, clowns, jugglers, freaks and the gravity-defying feats of trapeze artists. This obscure, low-budget tradition spawned an urban, high-concept genre: impact theatre.

Argentinian aerialism hit the mainstream when Diqui James and Pichón Baldinú set up the now world-renowned *De La Guarda* in 1992. To elaborate sets – towers, pulleys, stages on wheels, paper ceilings that fell like confetti – they added dazzling lights, water and fire, plus a soundtrack of live, primal drumming textured by electronic music.

By 1995 the duo's vision had taken them to New York; their electrifying show *Villa Villa* ran off-Broadway for six years, attracting over a million spectators. Chiming with the rave culture hedonism of the 1990s, their mission statement read: 'language is not intellectual, it goes straight to the body, straight to the senses, straight to the soul.'

In 2005 James launched his solo career with an act called *Fuerzabruta*. To the industrial acrobatics, he added electronic music and a heavy dose of carnival sounds. A resounding success, the show was the high energy star of the 2007 Edinburgh Festival.

Now everyone's doing it. BA television audiences have been captivated by *El Circo de las Estrellas*, a reality show in which a motley assortment of models, pop stars and former footballers juggle vertigo with the need for column inches, learning how to negotiate the high wire and dangle gracefully from the trapeze while competing against each other for viewers' votes.

For more information on the shows, and to find out where they are playing, go online check out www.delaguarda.com and www.fuerzabruta.net.

Trips Out of Town

Getting Started

Even the best cities have their limits.

When the sun is out, beautiful people are on the street, the parks are alive, the restaurants and bars are brimming, Buenos Aires becomes one of the greatest cities in the world. Nobody, however, can take cities like this forever. When you get to the stage of wanting to confront a taxi driver about speeding, you feel like hurling dog walkers who don't pick up poop in front of said taxi, and you start formulating a strongly worded letter to the government about cutting pollution, it's time to get the hell out.

For a metropolis that appears on maps to be a citadel hemmed in between a latte-coloured river and endless shrubland there are surprisingly beautiful areas to explore within just an hour or two of downtown.

Depending on the season and your interests, BA serves as a great hub for seeking out sun, sand, history and horses. We've divided Argentinian trips thematically into different physical environments – **Upriver** for short distance destinations, up to the **Cataratas de Iguazú**; **Country** for *gaucho*-inspired retreats; and **Beaches** for the Atlantic Coast in the southern Buenos Aires province. You can also head to some of the loveliest places in Latin America across the Rio de la Plata in neighbouring **Uruguay**.

An hour's train ride from Retiro is **Tigre**, a tranquil river town, worth a trip in itself, and also the gateway to another world: the vast islands and waterways that make up the **Delta** and its UNESCO Biosphere Reserve. Cruising its rivers is a spectacular experience. Further away than the typical day out destination, but eminently accessible from Buenos Aires, are the thrilling **Cataratas de Iguazú**, a network of stunning waterfalls in the jungle border region of Argentina and Brazil.

If you prefer to head inland to enjoy the wide open spaces of the country, nearby and picturesque **San Antonio de Areco** is where you can pick up the trail of Argentina's legendary *gauchos*. Throughout the province of Buenos Aires you can explore the pampas on horseback, or just kick back and let someone else do the hard work of stoking the barbecue at one of the region's beautiful, historical *estancias*, as ranches are known.

Of course, you may simply want to hit the beach. If you are visiting between November and April, the chances are you'll get enough sunshine to yearn for some sand between your toes. If you can't bear border crossings, you need to go south to the Atlantic Coast. **Mar del Plata**, **Pinamar** or **Mar de las Pampas** and **Mar Azul** all offer varying degrees of sun-soaked action among the crowds or soporific summer solitude.

Just a short one-hour ferry ride across 'the puddle', as the River Plate is affectionately known, will get you to Uruguay. Popular **Colonia de Sacramento** is a World Heritage Site that marries time travel with tranquillity, and further north is the even more secluded tiny town of **Carmelo**. Uruguay feels like an oversized *pueblo* and even its capital, **Montevideo**, exudes a small-town vibe. Once you slip into its mellow groove though, you'll be pleasantly surprised by its diversity and sophistication. Throughout Uruguay, small beaches line the shore from Colonia to Montevideo and beyond, but it is **Punta del Este**, one of Latin America's favourite and most fashionable summer retreats, that gets the buzz, the attention and the stars.

Information

The local tourist office for each destination is given at the end of each relevant section.

Administración de Parques Nacionales
Avenida Santa Fe 690, entre Maipú y Marcelo T de Alvear, Retiro (4515 1365/www.parques nacionales.gov.ar). Subte C, San Martín/10, 17, 59, 152 bus. **Open** 10am-5pm Mon-Fri. **Map** p325 G9.

Provincia de Buenos Aires
Casa de la Provincia de Buenos Aires, Avenida Callao 237, entre Perón y Sarmiento, Tribunales (4371 7045/3587/www.casaprov.gba.gov.ar). Subte B, Callao/12, 24, 26, 60 bus. **Open** 9.30am-7pm Mon-Fri. **Map** p325 G11.

Provincia de Misiones
Casa de la Provincia de Misiones, Avenida Santa Fe 989, entre Carlos Pellegrini y Suipacha, Retiro (4322 0677/www.misiones.gov.ar). Subte C, San Martín/10, 17, 59, 152 bus. **Open** *Jan, Feb* 9am-6pm Mon-Fri. *Mar-Dec* 9am-5pm Mon-Fri. **Map** p325 G11.

Uruguay Tourist Information
Embajada de Uruguay, Avenida Las Heras 1907, Recoleta (4807 3040/www.embajadadeluruguay. com.ar). Bus 10, 37, 60, 101. **Open** 9.30am-5.30pm Mon-Fri. **Map** p326 J11.

Upriver

Whatever floats your boat, the Delta is the perfect antidote to city smog.

Tigre

Less than an hour north of BA, this riverside town is the ideal spot for a lazy lunch and a welcome breath of fresh air. Appealing to locals and foreigners alike, Tigre's vividly-coloured colonial edifices, densely humid micro-climate and blood-orange sunsets are reminiscent of more tropical zones, and have won the town a somewhat exotic reputation; it's easy to forget, when strolling along palm-lined streets, that this is as much a working community as a daytripper destination. It's also the gateway to the islands and waterways that make up the **Delta** (*see p272*).

The town retains the charm of a well-kept colonial port, having flourished at the end of the nineteenth century, when BA's high society used it as a summer playground, hosting extravagant galas and balls. Soon after, though, improved transport and white sands lured the aristocrats south to the beaches of Mar del Plata, and all that remained of the party were magnificent buildings such as the **Buenos Aires Rowing**

Club. Over a century later, Tigre is enjoying something of a revival, and around 80,000 visitors now crowd in each weekend.

The **Mercado de Frutos** (Sarmiento y Perú) is a thriving daily market where you'll find local honey, handicrafts, wicker furniture, jewellery and, of course, fruit. Head to the **Museo Naval de la Nación** (Paseo Victorica 602, 4749 0608) for an insight into the maritime history of Argentina and an amazing collection of model boats. Housed in a painstakingly restored 1910 belle époque building is Tigre's finest cultural offering: the **Museo de Arte Tigre** (Paseo Victorica 972, 4512 4528). The museum displays Argentinian figurative art from the late nineteenth and early twentieth centuries. At the informative **Museo de la Reconquista** (Padre Castañeda 470, 4512 4496), find out how General Liniers won Buenos Aires back from the British. Need more thrills? Follow the screams to the **Parque de la Costa** amusement park (*see p216*) for all the fun of the fair, or head to the **Nuevo Trilenium Casino** (Perú 1385, 4731 7000), where three floors of slot

Museo de Arte Tigre.

machines twinkle and chime. Big betters can step up to the roulette tables in the VIP room.

Where to eat & drink

The **Mercado de Frutos** (*see p269*) has plenty of food stalls offering quick, cheap snacks and good smoothies. For something more substantial than a waffle or greasy *choripán* (chorizo sandwich), try **Vuelta & Victorica** (Paseo Victorica 50, 4749 2138, main courses AR$20-$37). This popular restaurant has a large deck overlooking the riverside promenade, and serves an array of traditional Argentinian dishes and seafood.

Further along the main restaurant drag of Paseo Victorica (overwhelmingly *parrillas*) is the excellent **La Terraza** (Paseo Victorica 134, 4731 2916, www.laterrazatigre.com.ar, main courses AR$18-$25). Book in advance to get a table on their terrace.

Slightly more expensive is **Il Novo María Luján de Tigre** (Paseo Victorica 611, y Vito Dumas, 4731 9613, www.ilnovomariadellujan. com, main courses AR$25-$45). Located in a grand old colonial house, with a terrace overhanging the Río Luján, it's worth the extra pesos for its lovely setting as much as the tasty home-made pasta.

Island kids having fun on the riverbank.

Where to stay

Built in 1893, the Italian-style **Casona La Ruchi** (Lavalle 557, 4749 2499, www.casona laruchi.com.ar, doubles US$47) is a charming little hotel close to the main bridge. Its 'home from home' feel is complemented by an exquisite rustic decor, a secluded garden containing a swimming pool and a *parrilla* (grill) for those outdoor summer *asados* (barbecues). It has four double rooms and one triple, some with either a lovely river or garden view.

Tigre Hostel (Avenida San Martín 190, 4749 4034, www.tigrehostel.com.ar, US$12 dorm, US$30 double), housed in a stylishly restored 1860 *posada*, has high-ceilinged dorm rooms and doubles, although the latter face the main road and can be noisy. Friendly staff, a huge kitchen, cosy communal areas and the tree-filled garden make it a good spot at which to chill out. Breakfast and Wi-Fi are included. A more upmarket option is the elegant **Villa Julia** (Paseo Victorica 800, 4749 0242,www. villajulia.com.ar, doubles US$155-$175). This delightfully converted mansion dates from 1913, and is the perfect place to dine, sleep and unwind in style. In summer you can relax on the lawn among the shady palms or take a dip in the pool, and there's also a library and reading room if it's nippy out. Their Acacia restaurant, open to non-guests, serves superb gourmet dinners, reasonably priced lunches and afternoon teas. For more options, enquire at the tourist information centre (*see below*). Another option is to jump on a river boat and head into the Delta (*see p272*). These tend to be pricier options and are often resorts in themselves. They also offer a variety of activities such as kayaking and horse riding.

Getting there

By bus

The *colectivo* 60 from BA takes between 1hr 15mins and 1hr 45mins, depending on traffic, and costs AR$1.35 one way.

By train

Tigre is a 50min train ride from Retiro (a return ticket costs AR$1.90). Trains run every 15mins from 4am-1.30am. For a more scenic route, you can take the **Tren de la Costa** (*see p216*) from Olivos.

Tourist information

Ente Municipal de Turismo de Tigre

Estación Fluvial de Tigre, Mitre 305 (4512 4497/www.tigre.gov.ar). **Open** 9am-5pm daily. As well as providing information about Tigre, staff here will be able to advise you on the different boat services that cruise the Delta.

Trade and commerce **Delta** style. *See p272.*

Trips Out of Town

The Delta

On a sunny day, your best bet is to get out onto the Delta rather than hang about in Tigre. This network of waterways and islands extends over approximately 14,000 square kilometres (5,405 square miles) and offers a wealth of recreational and gastronomic possibilities. It is broken into three sections, the first (*primera sección*) being closest to Tigre. Further away, rare flora and fauna are protected in a jungle-like UNESCO Biosphere Reserve.

River excursions

To explore the less travelled waterways, sign up for a boat tour or fishing trip. All of the following operators speak English and offer on-board food and drinks. Prices vary according to the number of passengers and length of the excursion. Santiago Bengolea, captain of the *Barba*, has many a Delta tale to tell. His fully equipped 27-foot six-berth cruiser can be chartered for tailor-made trips: **Barba charters Nautical Tours & Fishing** (4824 3366, mobile 15 4403 2829,www.barbacharters. com.ar). Leading the way in the eco tourism sector, **DeltaSur Ecoturismo** (4553 8827, mobile 15 6294 9063, www.deltasureco turismo.com.ar) offers more than simply watching the river flow past. Their guides' knowledge of the Biosphere Reserve, hidden deep in the Delta, is unsurpassed, and a visit to a cultural centre is a fascinating insight into the lives of the 'islanders'. Another good option is **Navegando por el Delta** (4816 5010, mobile 15 5001 1324, www.navegandoporeldelta. com.ar), which organises half-day, full-day or – their speciality – night trips. *Bruma*, a spacious wooden sailing boat piloted by 'Chuck' Serantes. is a stylish way to cruise the waterways, boasting two dining areas (one below deck, one above with barbecue), a solarium and a library.

Where to eat & drink

Ask at the **Estación Fluvial de Tigre** (*see p270*) which boat service is best for getting to each of these riverside restaurants. **Beixa Flor** (Arroyo Abra Vieja 148, 4728 2397, www.beixaflor.com.ar, main courses AR$17-$35) is a bohemian hangout with very good, if a little overpriced, home-made food. Funky tunes, a huge open stove, private beach and verdant gardens, make it a perfect summer stop-off. One of the biggest eateries on the Delta, and popular with families, is the sophisticated **El Gato Blanco** (Río Capitán 80, 4728 0390, www. gato-blanco.com, main courses AR$20-$35). Depending on the weather, you can choose to eat indoors or outside on the deck, prop yourself up at the bar or sip coffee in the tea room. There's even a children's playground. **Lima Limó** (Canal del Este y Arroyo Tres Sargentos, 4728 0785, main courses AR$25-$35) is where the smart set head after their wakeboarding classes or sunset sails. Open from October to March, Thursday to Sunday, it keeps a crowd of trendy young things happy with beer, cocktails and good music. Food on offer includes sushi and pizza, but the menu's highlight is chef and owner Pablo Sabelli's superb giant beef burger with quail eggs. Arrive early to grab a sunbed or table on the attractive eucalyptus-lined deck.

Where to stay

There are some highly atmospheric places to stay at, tucked away amid the verdant vegetation of the Delta. Fifty minutes from Tigre lies **Bonanza Deltaventura** (Río Carapachay, 4728 1674, 15 5603 7176, www.deltaventura.com, doubles US$75). The simple rooms are warmed with a crackling fire on colder nights, and are good value. Bilingual owner Rosana offers action-packed days of horseriding, kayaking in a nearby lagoon or birdspotting in the marshes. Or you can simply snooze in a hammock until it's time for a scrumptious meal made from local products. Hidden under thick foliage, **La Pascuala Delta Lodge** (Arroyo Las Cañas, 4728 0982, www.lapascuala.com.ar, doubles US$150 per person all inclusive) – built entirely from wood from its own island – includes 15 luxury cabins, a pool and a self-service cocktail bar. The deal inclues food from the gourmet restaurant, booze and the use of all recreational equipment. Another good all-inclusive deal is **Rumbo 90 Delta Lodge & Spa** (Canal Del Este, 15 5006 4341, www.rumbo90.com.ar, doubles US$235-$360 all inclusive), a stunning riverside lodge with six exquisite suites, natural spa and swimming pool. You can take canoes out on the river, sign up for fishing excursions, explore the forest on marked footpaths or befriend the animals on the small farm. Do as much or as little as you like, but it all makes for an interesting stay. Prices drop mid-week and in between May and September.

Getting there

By boat

Lanchas colectivos (public river buses) depart regularly from the boat terminal (Estación Fluvial de Tigre, Mitre 305). Three companies serve different sections of the Delta. Ask in the ticket office for the service you need. Prices depend on the journey. AR$11 for a return journey of up to 30 mins.

Fantasy islands

If you've ever harboured *Heart of Darkness* pretensions while silently weaving your way through swampy undergrowth, or simply need a quick break from the big smoke, the vast Delta, starting a mere hour north of Buenos Aires capital, can, with a little imagination, fulfil many a fantasy.

The Paraná Delta is a network of waterways, runnels and islands, which extend up to the cities of Santa Fe and Rosario. Hidden among the islands are restaurants, luxury lodges, aquatic sporting centres, bars, houses and cottages. However, perhaps one of the more interesting aspects of the Delta is seeing the lives of the 3,600 'islanders' who make their living from the natural resources, such as small-scale logging and growing fruit. To see this life you have to travel beyond the clamorous first part of the Delta that begins in the town of Tigre (*see p269*), hunker down, spray on some insect repellent and float up to the second and third parts, deep amid the sub tropical environment of the UNESCO-declared Biosphere Reserve of the Paraná Delta.

This unique and otherwordly area is a sanctuary for wildlife such as marsh deer, capybara (a large tail-less rat with hooves – presumably created the same day as the duck-billed platypus), otters and the occasional jaguar. Bird spotters will also keep busy with the vast array of bird species, including grebes and limpkins, which thrive in these flood plains; binoculars are a must.

These fertile swamplands are a mosaic of floral life. Living fossils of ancient plants that may have brushed the legs of dinosaurs happily bloom and grow on the banks. Indigenous willows bend and weave to the marshy breeze. The further into the Delta you go, the thicker the vegetation becomes, leaving you in an environment far removed from cement and skyscrapers. It is a wetland teeming with life, perfect for sightseeing, as well as an essential natural ecosystem which, like a dirty cook's hairnet, filters the water by catching pollutants.

The balancing act played between humans and nature is closely kept under watch. Core protected areas cover 106 square kilometres and the inhabitants deep in these parts live their lives lightly, with respect for this environment. Camouflaged within the forests, you'll see ramshackle cottages. Awareness of islanders' needs and unique living conditions is supported by the government, and you can visit their newly opened cultural centre. The people of the Upper Delta do all their trade by boat, making heavily laden longboats chugging along a common sight. Like a nautical version of *The Little Engine That Could*, everything from building materials to consumables is piled on, including fresh beef: even without roads, an Argentinian must get his *carne*.

Venturing into the Delta is an eye-opener to a different way a of life, as well as a chance to see some greenery during your stay in the city. This fluvial labyrinth is a fascinating environment in which to fulfil your anthropological yearnings or just simply kick back and relax.

Trips Out of Town

Cataratas de Iguazú

One of the true wonders of the natural world, the Cataratas de Iguazú is a goose-pimple-inducing sight of 23 kilometres (14 miles) of foaming waterfalls thundering into a 70-metre (230-foot) high river canyon, studded with rainbows, and speckled with darting grey-rumped swifts and butterflies. This jewel of the jungle is just an hour and a half's flight from Buenos Aires; if you only have time for one weekend getaway, make sure you see this.

The falls lie in the lush **Parque Nacional Iguazú** (www.iguazuargentina.com), at the northern tip of the province of Misiones on Argentina's frontier with Brazil and Paraguay. The sleepy town of Puerto Iguazú on the Argentinian side, with a population of just 5,000, is the best place to stay at for a two or three-day visit. There are bus services every half hour (AR$15 return) to the park gates, 15 minutes away, where you pay AR$40 admission per day.

Once inside you're free to explore along well-marked paths, or visit an impressive information centre charting the cultural history of the native people as well as the abundant flora and fauna. There's a variety of ways to see the different aspects of the falls. Most visitors head straight to the main precipice, the thundering Garganta del Diablo, a horseshoe-shaped 'Devil's Throat' that receives around 70 per cent of the tumbling Río Iguazú. This is reached by a propane-fuelled train that takes visitors from the reception area to a station, with a 15-minute walk from the Garganta del Diablo. It's a pleasant stroll when it's not too hot. Alternatively, there are quieter routes (there's always a lot of people) that offer better views, either from above or below the falls; and keep in mind that there are 250 separate cascades that make up the Cataratas de Iguazú.

Throughout the park, lemur-like coatis abound, and higher up, capuchin and squirrel monkeys inhabit the forest's canopy. Caimans feed in the Río Iguazú, but you're more likely to see lizards such as the large *tegu*. At night, jaguars stalk the undergrowth, and when the moon is full, park rangers run night walks (organised via the visitors centre; US$8-$15).

Iguazú Jungle Explorer will take you practically under the waterfall in their Gran Aventura speed boat tour (AR$100), and **Explorador Expediciones** (421632), offers a two-hour overland photo trail (AR$50) that can be extended to a four-hour birdwatching tour.

Where to eat & drink

Inside the park there are three basic snack bars. Back in Puerto Iguazú for the evening, try **La Rueda** (Av. Córdoba 28, 422531, main courses

AR$15-$40) or **El Charo** (Av. Córdoba 106, 421529, main courses AR$14-$38), where you can have grilled surubí, a local river fish. For international fare in a fancy setting, head to the **Iguazú Grand** (www.casinoiguazu.com, main courses AR$26-$55). If you don't get lucky in the casino, there are several beer-and-pizza joints with terraces on Avenida Victoria Aguirre near the plaza.

Where to stay

Numerous travel agencies in Buenos Aires offer package tours to Iguazú. Expect to pay US$400-$600 for a three-day/two-night deal. The only hotel in the park, the luxurious **Sheraton Iguazú** (491800, www.starwoodhotels.com/sheraton, doubles from US$381), has five-star comforts and a spa. In Puerto Iguazú a good three-star option with a pool is the **Hotel Saint George** (Av. Córdoba 148, 420633, www.hotelsaintgeorge.com, doubles US$95-$125). On the edge of town, the lovely **Iguazú Jungle Lodge** (Hipólito Irigoyen, 420600, www.iguazujunglelodge.com, doubles US$80) has stunning jungle views from the balconies of its seven well-equipped bungalows, arranged around an inviting pool. They sleep seven and are great value if you fill them up. Budget travellers can try the **Hostería Los Helechos** (Paulino Amarante 76, 420829, www.hosterialoshelechos.com.ar, US$25-$30).

When to go

The average temperature in Iguazú is a pleasant 23°C (73°F), although extremes can range from zero in July to 40°C (103°F) in January. The all-pervading spray from the falls helps, but don't forget high-factor suncream.

Tourist information

Secretaria de Turismo

Avenida Victoria Aguirre 311, y Brañas, Puerto Iguazú (03757 420800). **Open** 8am-midnight daily.

Getting there

By air

There are several direct daily flights with Aerolineas Argentinas to Puerto Iguazú from Buenos Aires' Jorge Newbery airport. The flight takes 1hr 30mins and costs about US$250 return.

By road

From Posadas, the provincial capital of Misiones, Iguazú can be reached via Rutas Nacionales 12 and 9. Buses leaving Retiro bus station in BA take a whopping 21hrs to get to Puerto Iguazú (various operators; from AR$100 one way).

Cataratas de Iguazú, one of the natural wonders of the world.

Country

Embrace your inner gaucho and saddle up in the Argentinian pampas.

San Antonio de Areco

San Antonio de Areco is at the epicentre of *gaucho* lore, not simply because walking around the cobbled streets you are as likely to pass a cowboy trotting on horseback as a child pedalling a bicycle, but also because this was the home of author Ricardo Güiraldes and his semi-mythical *gaucho* hero, Don Segundo Sombra. Around 113 kilometres (70 miles) from Buenos Aires, with a population of 20,000, this popular weekend tourist destination is a mass of one-storey, century-old buildings surrounded by seemingly limitless grassy plains. Perfect for brushing up on half-forgotten horse riding skills in the company of a few of these genuine Latin cowboys.

Begin your tour with a stroll along the town's main drag, Alsina, through to the town's centre and the charming square **Plaza Ruiz de Arellano**. This central plaza is overlooked by the Iglesia Parroquial, built in 1728 by the town's original settlers in honour of San Antonio de Padua, thanking him for protecting them from attacks by local tribes. Directly opposite the church, in the centre of the plaza, is a statue of Vieytes, commemorating a visit from former Irish president Mary Robinson and the Sociedad Argentino Irlandesa of San Antonio de Areco. It's ironic that, in an area central to the *gaucho* mystique, an Irish community predating Güiraldes's novel by over a century should have been so pivotal to the evolution of a town so important to Argentinian identity.

One thing that strikes you as you walk through San Antonio de Areco is the separation of town and country, sharply divided by the Areco River that marks a border between the stone streets and the pampas. The easiest way to cross this divide is via **Puento Viejo**, one of the country's first toll bridges and the unofficial symbol of the town. Passing over the bridge to the north of the town you will arrive at the **Parque Criollo** and the **Museo Gauchesco Ricardo Güiraldes**. The 90 hectares of green park land contain a stud farm and the atmospheric **Pulpería La Blanqueada**, a rustic tavern-cum-general store that featured in Güiraldes's novel. The museum, which opened in 1938, is a homage to Güiraldes himself, exhibiting early editions of Don Segundo Sombra, photographs of the real-life characters

of the book and random curiosities such as an old and regal safety deposit box and a bed that once belonged to General Rosas. To the east of the museum, on A Pazzaglia street, you can get a real feel for the *gaucho* lifestyle with horses for hire by the hour (around US$10). Thankfully the owners (but probably not the horses) are more than happy to chaperone those who've spent more time in bars than barns.

Tradition is everywhere in San Antonio de Areco and many of the structures remain exactly as they were a century ago, albeit a little worse for wear. One must-see building is the **Los Principios** grocery store, located to the west of the town centre at Bartolomé Mitre 151. The dusty, old, dark-wood store is a throwback to 1922, the year it opened, and the present owner, Américo Fernandez, has been selling his wares there for over 60 years. Sweets and confectionary of all kind are weighed out on ancient metal scales and the rolling ladder is still the only way to reach the paint thinners and spirits that line the very highest shelves.

The town is small enough to get around on foot, though most of the locals travel by moped or bicycle (available for hire, AR$30 per day). If you want to save time or are heading straight to an *estancia*, your best bet is a car service. Remis Zerboni (453288) operates 24 hours a day.

If this quiet town has a high season it's in November, when a buzz of rural activities lead up to the spirited *gaucho* festivities of the annual **Día de la Tradición** (*see p213*). Exhibitions of the traditional *gato* (cat) dance and performances by *folklore* bands are coupled with feats of country skills and horsemanship, in a busy programme spread out over two weeks. The celebrations culminate in the Día de la Tradición itself and a procession of *gauchos* in full regalia, riding horses adorned with silver and gold. If you want to be a part of the festivities, book hotel rooms early to avoid disappointment.

Parque Criollo & Museo Gauchesco Ricardo Güiraldes

Camino al Ricardo Güiraldes, y Camino al Parque (02326 455839). **Open** 11am-5pm Mon, Wed-Sun. **Admission** AR$3; free under-12s. **No credit cards.** This small museum re-creates an 18th century ranch, each room in a different style. There is the *gaucho* room, rancher room and two dedicated to Güiraldes.

Rolling over the ranch

If Carlos Gardel is the popular – as well as the homoerotic – icon of Argentina's urban masses, then the *gaucho* is his country counterpart. This local hero is a variation on the solitary ranching type that is found right across the American continent, his roots to be found in the days of the 19th century 'frontier' when city gents dumped their tenants on the fringes of 'civilisation' as a first buffer against raiding Indians.

The archetypal Argentinian *gaucho* is as gifted a horseman as any Mongolian, as unhurried as Clint Eastwood and as macho as a very big stallion driving a tank into a brothel. His clothes are distinctive – especially his Arabian pantaloons, which may hint at some vague Andalusian connection – but, in essence, he's just a cowboy.

You will – and should – want to explore further, because the world of the *gaucho* is one of the best exits out of modernity Argentina offers. Book into one of the *estancias* (ranches) that litter the pampas close to Buenos Aires – you can go for the day or, far better, for a long weekend. The best ones boast well-stocked libraries, and you can browse through no end of coffee-table photographic guides or dig deeper and read classics of rural life such as Don Segundo Sombra, Martin Fierro or the nature stories of Horacio Quiroga.

But you're not only here to study. *Estancias* offer a wide range of activities aimed at giving visitors a healthy induction into *la vida rural*. Horse riding, birding, nature trails and long, lovely *asados* under the ombú tree are par for the course. Some *estancia* owners will recount anecdotes around the communal dinner table of an evening, while others will actually organise storytelling.

Slightly livelier are the rural dances, which change according to the region and tastes of the *estancia* owners and resident *gaucho*s. You will be able to watch, or practise, country dances such as the foot-stamping *chacarera*, the playful *gato* and the amorous *zamba*. On working farms it is possible to get involved with anything from herding and watching over the cattle or sheep to helping with the shearing – usually a guest will just hold the animal while an expert does the clipping. At the luxury end of the market, there are also *estancias* that offer golf courses, balloon rides, fishing trips and hunting excursions.

But how about following the lead of the best known expat *estanciero* to hang out on the pampas – William Henry Hudson. As well being as a brilliant birdwatcher, forward-looking eco-thinker and innate mystic, Hudson was a genius at idling, chilling, wasting time and just being there. The *estancia*, according to this philosophy, is best treated as a sort of antidote to the city. BA is vertical, claustrophobic, pretentious and everyone is always dashing off to an English lesson, a shrink or some other self-improvement rendezvous. The *campo* – or countryside – is the opposite: flat, empty and raw. Most importantly of all, there is absolutely nada that you are obliged to do. Just grab a hammock and sip that *mate*.

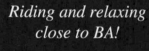

Where to eat & drink

The pick of the town's restaurants is **Almacén de Ramos Generales** (Zapiola 143, 456376, main courses AR$15-$24), a popular *parrilla* serving traditional fare made from locally sourced ingredients, decorated in the style of an old general store, or *almacén*. For modern dishes in a stylish contemporary setting, try **Zarza** (San Martín 361, 453948, main courses AR$14-$24). If you're after something a bit more local, 'follow the goat' to the deliciously named **Siga al Chivo** (Zerboni 278, 455238, main courses AR$12-$16). **Puesto la Lechuza** (Sdo. Sombra y Bolivar, 454542, main courses AR$12-$20), a covered-terrace restaurant serving traditional country fare with regular *folklore* shows. If you're just in need of a drink, **Barril** (San Martín 381) is a typical downtown pub, with outdoor seating. The cosy **La Vieja Sodería** (Bolivar 196) serves coffee and cake during the day, and gin and tonics at night.

Where to stay

The first boutique lodging in San Antonio de Areco, **Patio de Moreno** (Moreno 251, 455197, www.patiodemoreno.com, doubles US$145-$180) raises the bar dramatically in this unsophisticated town where the available accommodation is dominated by humble guesthouses. New Age Hotel's latest venture occupies a former workshop, which has been carefully modernised while maintaining its original charm – dark hardwood floors and high beamed ceilings frame antique wall clocks, while skylights, a wine bar, and abstract art keep the place firmly grounded in the 21st century. The six spacious rooms are the ultimate in *gaucho* chic – think jet-black cow hides and fluffy white towels – and the gorgeous garden has a small pool.

Nothing else in San Antonio quite matches this standard, but two other hotels situated in converted colonial buildings are **Paradores Draghi** (Lavalle 387, 455583, doubles AR$150), which also showcases locally made silverware, and **Antigua Casona** (Segundo Sombra 495, 456600, www.antiguacasona.com, doubles AR$133). Typical, but not particularly special, country hotels include **Hostal de Areco** (Zapiola 25, 456118, www.hostaldeareco.com.ar, doubles AR$140) and **Hotel Los Abuelos** (Zerboni y Zapiola, 4563900, doubles AR$120), which has motel-like rooms, with ceiling fans, cable TV and a pool that's just about big enough for a duck under water. (The fact that its name translates as the Grandparents' Hotel tells you most of what you need to know.) Directly opposite, **Hotel San Carlos** (453106,

www.hotel-sancarlos.com.ar, doubles AR$133) has smaller rooms and the option of six-person apartments with air-conditioning.

Shopping

You'll be able to pick up a cowboy hat and poncho at any of the *gaucho* themed souvenir shops, but, for a more unique memento, visit the workshop of esteemed Argentinian jewellery designer **Marina Massone** (Azcuénaga 336, mobile 15 5248 9744, www.massonepiniquerio.com.ar) to see her covetable contemporary pieces; her jewellery is also available at Patio de Moreno (*see left*). **Las Nativas** (Arellano 121, 456927), on Plaza Arellano, sells high-quality rugs and blankets, as well as local leather and silver goods.

Tourist information

Dirección de Turismo de la Municipalidad

Boulevard Zervoni, y Arellano (02326 453165/ www.arecogaucho.com.ar). **Open** 8.30am-7pm Mon-Fri; 8am-8pm Sat, Sun.
The English-speaking staff will provide you with brochures and maps pointing out the town's historic sites. They can also organise a three-hour tour of the town in English for AR$100.

Getting there

By road

San Antonio de Areco is 1hr 30mins from BA on Ruta Nacional 8. A taxi from BA will cost around AR$240. If you're travelling by bus, Chevallier (4314 3639) offers the most frequent daily service, about once an hour, AR$23 each way, from Retiro bus terminal. The journey takes about 2hrs. Upon arrival in San Antonio, ask at the bus station (located on the edge of town, a 15-min walk from the main square) for the departure schedule.

Estancias

In the 19th century, European immigrants flocked to Argentina to take advantage of a vast, fertile, untapped territory, building *estancias* (ranches) throughout the countryside. Many of these rural estates have been in the same family for generations, and some still raise cattle and crops. In the past decade, more and more of these homes have opened to the public as agro-industry replaced the family farm and owners faced the choice of shuttering large homes that were too expensive to run or opening them as upmarket B&Bs.

Buenos Aires province has the highest concentration of these ranches, ranging in style

Trips Out of Town

from Tudor castles to Italian villas. Offering everything from al fresco *asados* (barbecues) to polo lessons, they allow travellers to live out their *gaucho* fantasies – chaps and all. A *Día de Campo* (day in the country) package includes plenty of galloping (or trotting, depending on how terrified you are), so much steak that you'll need to take a hammock siesta after lunch, and often a folk music or *gaucho* show. You could also choose to stay for a weekend or longer. Many *estancias* host corporate events or weddings, so check first to avoid your tranquillity being breached by smiling salesmen or drunken relatives. It may look expensive at first, but horse riding and all your food (which is usually excellent) are included – though some drinks and activities may be extra – and children generally pay half-price. Many also offer rides in horse-drawn carriages and some have pools. They will cater for vegetarians, but tell them in advance. Bring insect repellent in summer to ward off the area's voracious bugs and mosquitos.

Owing to its popularity as a tourist destination, many of the *estancias* we've listed below are located near San Antonio de Areco. Most of the rest are within 125 kilometres (78 miles) of Buenos Aires. Reservations are a must:

call the *estancia* direct or book through knowledgeable BA-based travel agents **José de Santís** (Office 313, Avenida Roque Sáenz Peña 616, Microcentro, 4343 2366, www.estanciasargentinas.com) or **Estancia Travel** (14th Floor, Office H, Florida 868, Retiro, 4748 4440, www.estanciastravel.com). If driving, ask for directions when you book.

Las Artes Endurance Country Club
Mercedes (in BA 4811 6024/www.lasartes endurance.com). **Rates** per person US$120 full-day programme for riders; US$60 (non-riders). **No credit cards**.
A day at Las Artes gives riders the chance to see the pampas from atop a competition-standard Arabian horse. Friendly, multi-lingual owners Reinhard and Cristina host full-day programmes for small groups (up to a maximum of six) and welcome non-riders, who can lounge by the pool. The cost includes all rides, food and drink.

La Bamba
San Antonio de Areco (in BA 4732 1269/02326 456293/www.la-bamba.com.ar). **Rates** US$300 double; US$60 Dia de Campo. **Rooms** 12. **Credit** AmEx, MC.
La Bamba is one of the region's most traditional *estancias*, offering an window into the country's

La Oriental. *See p281.*

criollo past. Built in 1830, it has been declared a place of historical importance and numbers tango star Carlos Gardel among its former guests.

La Candelaria

Lobos (02227 424404/www.estanciacandelaria.com). **Rates** per person US$80-$100 double; US$40 Dia de Campo. **Rooms** 10. **Credit** MC, V.

The most regal looking of all the Argentinian *estancias*, La Candelaria's magnificent castle is straight out of a period drama, and is perfectly complemented by the vast gardens, designed by Englishman Charles Thays, who also laid out BA's botanical gardens. Depending on your fantasy, you can either act the part of a polo millionaire or a hard-up aristocrat as you stroll serenely over these ancestral lawns, glass of malbec in hand.

Los Dos Hermanos

Zárate (in BA 4765 4320/03487 438903/ www.estancialosdoshermanos.com). **Rates** per person US$120 double; US$65 Dia de Campo. **Rooms** *main house* 3; *cabins* 5. **No credit cards**.

No touristy gimmicks or hokey *gaucho* costumes distract from the equestrian merriment at this delightful ranch. Down-to-earth owners Ana and Pancho Peña and their easy going, professional staff get the details right, from the appetising *asado* and lengthy trail rides to the buttery *tortas fritas* (pastries) served before sunset. Just an hour's drive from BA, Los Dos Hermanos is a consistently well-liked option for either a day trip or an overnight stay.

Juan Gerónimo

Verónica (in BA 15 4937 4326/www.juangeronimo. com.ar). **Rates** per person US$120 double. **Rooms** 11. **No credit cards**.

This *estancia* is one of the largest, most prominent and important south of Buenos Aires, comprising 10,000 acres of land stretching up to where the Rio de la Plata meets the Atlantic. Offering well-trained horses and a UNESCO Biosphere Reserve to test them on, it's an excellent break from the city smog. The main house situated in front of the lake has a typical English feel, and expect a warm greeting (along with crackling log fire in winter). The hearty meals include delicious desserts you'll want to get the recipe for.

Hotelito de Colores

General Rodríguez (11 5756 6354/www. hotelitodecolores.com). **Rates** US$150-$220 per person per day. **Rooms** 4. **No credit cards**.

The equation is simple: hustle, bustle, fuss and tussle + 50 minute car journey = peace, quiet, chirping birds and organic diet including home-made jams, cheeses and pastries. A handful of diminutives (*hotelito*, *asadito*, etc.) in a cartload of superlatives (great service, profound quiet, etc.) are the signatures of this four-bedroom ranch set in neat, but not overly fussy, grounds outside of the town of General Rodríguez. The horse ride will leave you at the door of cooking and art lessons, there's polo next door on order, and finally massages beside the (shallow) swimming pool to ease the saddle sore. All

capped by that Holy Grail of tourism: there-but-not-there, friendly but discreet service. The hotel is open from September until the middle of June.

La Martina

Vicente Casares (02226 430777/www.lamartina polo.com.ar). **Rates** per person US$350 for polo-playing guests; US$170 for non-polo-playing guests; US$80 Dia de Campo. **Rooms** 15. **No credit cards**.

Adolfo Cambiaso – one of the world's leading players – runs a top-flight polo school for foreigners out of this century-old *estancia* just 45 minutes from Buenos Aires.

Mestiza Pampa Lodge

Ruta 4, km5, Alto Los Cardales (15 4474 5899, 02322-493715/www.mestiza.com.ar). **Rates** US$75-$100 per person. **Rooms** 3. **No credit cards**.

Among 15 hectares of open pampa, the distinctive Mestiza Pampa Lodge offers a different experience than the usual eat *asado*, drink *mate*, go for a trot formula of many estancias. There are only three well-equipped rustic bedrooms (that's rustic as in designer), each with a living room and private terrace. Every element has been thoughtfully considered to ensure the ultimate in relaxation. For the restless, there are horse rides, hot air balloon trips and a photography safari on offer at perfectly reasonable rates.

La Oriental

Junín (in BA 4801 4876/02362 15 640866/ www.estancia-laoriental.com). **Rates** per person US$130-$165; US$60 Dia de Campo. **Rooms** 9. **Credit** AmEx.

From the moment you head down the long Eucalyptus-lined drive towards La Oriental you are transported to an altogether more elegant era. The principal house of the *estancia*, built in 1890, is a vast, opulent affair. Seven metre high ceilings protect early 1900s French furniture, a library, family portraits and a billiard table. This still fully working *estancia* has been in Rafael and Estella's family for more than 80 years and nine suites are open for guests. Saddle up for a horse ride or take a stroll through 2,500 acres of pampas, go fly fishing by the lake or enjoy a refreshing dip in the pool. Included are home-baked organic meals, excellent *asados* and a hearty breakfast. Pure countryside relaxation.

Villa María

Máximo Paz (in BA 6091 2066/www.estanciavilla maria.com). **Rates** US$300 double all inclusive; US$100 Dia de Campo. **Rooms** 15. **No credit cards**.

Argentinian architect Alejandro Bustillo, also responsible for Buenos Aires' Banco Nación, built this monumental Tudor mansion in 1925 for beef baron Celedonio Pereda. Fifteen bright, elegant rooms look over an impressive artificial lake and immaculate grounds. A huge spa, offering a range of pampering beauty treatments and massages, as well as a professional equestrian centre, 18-hole golf course, tennis club, not to mention restaurant, wine cellar and bar speak for themselves.

Trips Out of Town

Beach

Seaside city resort or peaceful pine-fringed sands - the choice is yours.

Mar del Plata

A city by the sea, Mar del Plata is big, brash, tacky and extremely popular, attracting huge crowds year after year. During the summer, when most of Buenos Aires life – from theatre to TV productions and football matches – ups sticks and heads to the coast, you'll be hard pushed to find a place to lay your towel.

The city – 400 kilometres (250 miles) south of Buenos Aires, with a year-round population of 650,000, swelling to over a million in summer – was founded in 1874. It was once a refuge for the *porteño* aristocracy; now it's the Argentinian middle-class tourist destination of choice, while the wealthy head to the warmer shores of Punta del Este in Uruguay and further afield.

To the south, 20 kilometres (12 miles) beyond the lighthouse, lie the most exclusive beaches: **La Reserva**, **Del Balcón** and **La Caseta**. Continuing south on Ruta 11 brings you to Miramar, with magnificent views, woodland and 20-metre (65-foot) high cliffs running down to the ocean. This is the best spot for surfing; for more information, see www.elsurfero.com.

The seafront boardwalk, **La Rambla** – constructed in 1940 by architect Alejandro Bustillo, who also built the casino – and the San Martín pedestrian area are the most popular walkways. The *puerto* (port) is full of pervasive odours from the fishmeal factories and old, rusting yellow boats. In the south docks there's a large colony of sea lions (the symbol of Mar del Plata), and you can take a one-hour boat trip to view the main beaches from the sea.

For a blast of Mardel's past, walk through the barrios of Stella Maris, Playa Grande, Los Troncos and Divino Rostro. There you'll find the **Centro Cultural Victoria Ocampo** (Matheu 1851, 0223 4920569), open 10am-5pm on weekdays and 1-6pm at the weekend. It's an English-style mansion once home to writer and literary patron Victoria Ocampo.

Where to eat

The all-you-can-eat *tenedor libres* tend to be concentrated in the San Martín area and are extremely cheap, sometimes with queues out the door. **Montecatini Alpe** (Belgrano 2350, 0223 4943446, main courses AR$14-$24) has decent, cheap nosh featuring fish, pasta and superb *sorrentinos gratinados*. In the port, check out **Chichilo** (Centro Comercial Puerto Unit 17, 0223 4896317, main courses AR$16-$30), where the *calamares a la provenzal* (squid in garlic sauce) are highly recommended. But if you only have time to try one seafood restaurant in Mar del Plata, head straight to **Viento en Popa** (Avenida Martínez de Hoz 257, 0223 4890220, main courses AR$22-$36) which serves simple but exquisite cuisine.

Where to stay

Mar del Plata boasts an enormous variety of accommodation options. Opposite Playa Grande is the five-star **Hotel Costa Galana** (Boulevard Marítimo Patricio Peralta Ramos 5725, 0223 4105000, www.hotelcostagalana.com, doubles US$200-$350). The slightly cheaper **Hotel Amsterdam** (Boulevard Marítimo Patricio Peralta Ramos 4799, 0223 4515137, www.hotelamsterdam.com.ar, doubles US$120-$135) is housed in a 1920s family home and comes with spacious, well-equipped rooms. For something cheaper still, try the lovely and, of course, sea-facing **Hotel Guerrero** (Diagonal Juan B Alberdi 2288, 0223 4958885, www.hotelguerrero.com.ar, doubles US$95-$125); their out-of-season promotions are fantastic value.

Getting there

By air

Mar del Plata is served by daily flights from Buenos Aires (55 mins). The city's **Aeropuerto Brigadier Gral. Bme. de la Colina** (Ruta 2, km.386, 478 5811) is 40 minutes from the city centre.

By road

Numerous hourly services make the 5hr trip from BA's Retiro station to Mar del Plata's main terminal (Alberti 1600, 451 5406). Buses also run from Retiro to Pinamar (5hrs) and other resorts along the coast. Those driving to Mar del Plata from BA (4hrs), should take the RN2. Up to four people can take a taxi for around AR$400 one way.

Tourist information

Centro Información Turística

Boulevard Marítimo Patricio Ramos 2270 (0223 495 1777/www.mardelplata.com). **Open** 8am-8pm daily.

Trips Out of Town

Pinamar, Cariló & Ostende

Pinamar, located 340 kilometres (211 miles) south of BA, is surrounded by golden dunes and wonderfully fragrant pine forests. It clings to a reputation as the trendiest beach resort in Argentina, so don't expect peace: the resident population of 22,000 explodes to 600,000 during the summer months of January and February.

A couple of kilometres from Pinamar is the very exclusive resort of **Cariló**. It's a separate and far more peaceful world of red brick houses set among woodland. Eight kilometres (five miles) from Pinamar is **Ostende**, a small resort with one of the best beaches in the area. It was founded at the beginning of the 20th century by a group of homesick Belgians.

Where to eat

In Pinamar, **Green Mango** (Quintana 56, 02254 407990, main courses AR$18-$30) is a good bet for classy drinks and delicacies plucked from the sea. Pinamar is renowned for good fish; local classic **El Viejo Lobo** (Avenida del Mar y Bunge, 02254 483218, main courses AR$22-$35) also has a good wine list.

Where to stay

In Cariló, the **Hotel Marcin** (Laurel y el Mar, 02254 570888, www.hotelmarcin.com.ar, doubles US$120-$225) is ideally situated on the beach-front. **Cariló Village** (Carpintero y Divisadero,

02254 470244, www.carilovillage.com, doubles US$120-$183 all inclusive) has 59 bungalows that can sleep up to eight. In the centre of Pinamar is one of the coolest options in the area: **Hotel Las Calas** (Bunge 560, 02254 405999, www.lascalashotel.com.ar, doubles US$95-$125). The fully equipped boutique suites can sleep up to four. In Ostende, the attractive **Viejo Hotel Ostende** (Biarritz y El Cairo, 02254 4860810, www.hotelostende.com.ar, US$65-$140 per person) has a programme of live music and art.

Tourist information

Secretaría de Turismo

Avenida Bunge 654, entre Marco Polo y Libertador, Pinamar (02254 491680/www.pinamar.gov.ar). **Open** *Jan, Feb* 8am-10pm daily. *Mar, Dec* 8am-8pm daily. *Apr-Nov* 8am-8pm Mon-Sat; 10am-6pm Sun.

Getting there

To reach Cariló and Ostende, most people take a taxi or a minicab from Pinamar.

By bus

Buses for Pinamar depart daily from BA's Retiro (around AR$50 one-way, AR$90 return); companies include **Río de la Plata** (4305 1405) and **Plusmar** (4287 2000). The trip takes 5hrs.

By car

For Pinamar, take Ruta 2 to Dolores, Ruta 63 to Esquina de Croto, Ruta 11 to General Consesa, Ruta 56

Mar del Plata.

to Madariaga, then Ruta 74 to Pinamar. A taxi for up to four people costs around AR$300 one-way.

Mar de las Pampas & Mar Azul

Emerging out of the thick pine forests bordering the coast, **Mar de las Pampas** is how Pinamar was 25 years ago: quiet and beautiful. Cul-de-sacs and sandy roads limit the speed of passing vehicles and strict building laws keep the pine trees standing, although it's hard to believe that in 1957 there wasn't a tree to be seen – these were planted by developers who bought the land at an auction. It is now home to willows, acacias and eucalyptus harbouring all manner of creepy crawlies and, according to local lore, little elves.

The village is neatly split into three zones: commercial, residential and hotel. On the beach, **El Soleado** is where people come to buy refreshments, relax and shelter from the winds.

Mar Azul is even smaller, even quieter and equally paradisiacal. The village is little more than a clutch of sandy roads centred on cabin-style lodgings, a hotel and a supermarket.

Where to eat

In Mar de las Pampas, **Amorinda Tutto Pasta** (Avenida Gerchunoff y El Lucero, 02255 479750, main courses AR$14-$22) is a village classic. **Cabaña Huinca** (Querandíes, entre Avenida El Lucero y El Ceibo, 02255 479718, main courses AR$28-$34, closed weekdays in winter) serves up delightful culinary treats, though Osvaldo, the owner, is proudest of his home-made beer.

Tiny Mar Azul has fewer dining options but boasts an excellent sushi restaurant – **Apart Heiwa** on Calle 34 (02255 453674, main courses AR$30-$45). For meat, try **El Rodeo** (Calle 35 y Mar Azul, main courses AR$20-$28).

Where to stay

In Mar de las Pampas, metres from the beach, are the *cabañas* of **Rincón del Duende** (Virazón y Cuyo, 02255 479866, www.rincondelduende.com, rental for four people US$1,000 per week). As well as a fine restaurant, the complex boasts a swimming pool and tennis court. The apartments at plush **Miradores del Bosque** (JA Roca y Hudson, 02255 452147,www.miradoresdelbosque.com) don't quite blend in with the sylvan style of the village but are suitably luxurious and include a spa. Rates are US$850-$1200 per week for 2-6 people, 40 per cent less out of season.

Just off the crossroads in Mar Azul, and 100 metres from the beach, are the *cabañas* of **Puerto de Palos** (Calle 35 y Mar del Plata, 02255 470311, www.puertodepalosweb.com.ar, US$45-$125 per day). A mini complex of log cabins set in the woods, with a pool, this is the best value option in the area. For a seafront location, check out the luxurious **Rincón del Mar** (Calle 30 y La Playa, 02255 456003, www.rincondelmar.com.ar). A two-person studio costs US$800 per week in high season.

Tourist information

In Mar de las Pampas: *Avenida 3, y Rotunda (02255 470324/www.mardelaspampas.com.ar).* **Open** *Jan-Mar, Dec* 10am-6pm.

Getting there

There are regular coaches from Buenos Aires to **Villa Gesell** with **Plusmar** (5hrs, AR$56 one-way). The closest town to Mar de las Pampas, it's just 10km (6 miles) away and AR$20-$25 by taxi. Add another AR$10 by taxi to Mar Azul, 5km (3 miles) further on. There's a local bus service running from Villa Gesell to Mar de las Pampas and Mar Azul (AR$3 one-way).

The forest meets shore at **Mar de las Pampas**.

Uruguay

Secluded sands plus colonial charm equal ultimate relaxation.

Colonia del Sacramento

Ah, Colonia del Sacramento. A city by name, a sleepy world of cobbled streets, verdant foliage and birdsong by nature. Its origins as a Portuguese settlement date back to 1680, but a battle-heavy past belies the fact that the only damage you're in danger of sustaining these days is through overindulging in lazy lie-ins and *vino tinto*. Now a UNESCO World Heritage Site, the leafy town acts as a soothing antidote to the pacy onslaught of Buenos Aires. For serious downtime, it's ideal.

The charming **Barrio Histórico** (old town), surrounded on three sides by the waters of the Río de la Plata, is where most of the sights are found. Arriving by boat, you're just a ten-minute stroll away, and it's on foot that the area is best explored. Stroll along the **Calle de los Suspiros** (Street of Sighs), with its knock-kneed cobbles and typical colonial architecture; take in the view from the active lighthouse, amid the ruins of the 17th-century Convento de San Francisco; or enjoy a leisurely amble beside the walls of the old town's fortification.

Naturally, day-tripping tour groups have also discovered Colonia, although the only real detriment comes via hiked café prices in and around the centre. To fully unwind, it's well worth bedding down for a night or two. Faded paintwork and vintage cars make the city a joy for photographers, and the long coastal road west of town leads to some great beaches and countryside; mopeds, bicycles and even golf carts are widely available for hire. A word to the wise sunbathers: summer temperatures can be relentlessly high.

Finally, near the swish, new, out-of-town Sheraton resort, keep an eye out for one of the oddest sights in Uruguay; a vast and long-defunct Moorish-style bull ring, now decaying quietly. Horses can still be heard thundering around the neighbouring track.

Where to eat

Colonia has plenty of costly, average places to eat (like Buenos Aires, it can be tough to escape *parrilla* and pizza) although there are a number of exceptions. In the old town, **El Drugstore** (Portugal 174, 00 598 52 25241, main courses US$4-$13) provides a colourful variety of tapas, salads and mains in jaunty surroundings; you can even take a table in a vintage car outside. Nearby, the wacky-waitered **Viejo Barrio** (Vasconcellos 169, 00 598 52 25399, main courses US$4-$7) serves up hearty local fare, including good pasta. It's closed on Tuesday and Wednesday evenings. The restaurant of the discreet **Club de Yachting y Pesca** (Puerto de Yates, 00 598 52 31354, main courses US$11-$25) offers fresh seafood and more or less exclusive harbour views. **La Bodeguita** (Del Comercio 167, 00 598 52 25329, main courses US$3-$7) has good pizzas, and an even better terrace from which to watch the sunset.

Where to stay

The finest lodging in the old town is at the **Posada Plaza Mayor** (Calle del Comercio 111, 00 598 52 23193, www.posadaplazamayor.com, doubles US$85-US$150), a historic house with well appointed rooms, a lovely patio and a small garden near the river. Another classy option is

Colonia's landmark lighthouse.

The grape escape

Bordeaux? Too snooty. Napa Valley? Too American. Mendoza? A 12-hour bus ride. Uruguay? Bet you never considered Uruguay as a wine country before. In fact, it is often met with a similar facial expression as when being offered a warm glass of Lambrini. But before you scoff at the thought, this Belgium-sized country has unique varieties of grape, generations-old vineyards, and it produces some world-renowned wines.

the **Manuel de Lobo** (Ituzaingó 160, 00 598 52 22463, US$70-$100), furnished with funky artwork and Hispanic touches. It's worth paying the extra for the superior rooms. Elsewhere, **El Mirador** (Avennida Roosevelt 381, 00 598 52 22552, www.hotelelmirador.com, US$130) is a large, four-star hotel with two great pools and tennis courts. The **Radisson** (W Barbot 283, 00 598 52 30460, doubles from US$94) is a clean, tasteful chain hotel. For cheap stays, try the cheery **El Viajero** (W Barbot 164, 00 598 52 30347, US$11 per person dorm).

Getting there

By boat

From its Puerto Madero terminal in Buenos Aires, **Buquebus** (www.buquebus.com) has at least two fast crossings per day to Colonia (1hr, from US$70 return)

on a comfy hydrofoil, and two slow ferries (3hrs, from US$50 return), both with room for cars. An often cheaper, and comfier, option is **Colonia Express** (www.coloniaexpress.com) whose hydrofoils reach Uruguay in 50 minutes. Rates for returns vary between US$40 (weekdays) and US$60 (weekends). It leaves from the cruise liner terminal on the corner of Avenida de los Inmigrantes and Castillo in Retiro.

Tourist information

Oficina de Turismo General

General Flores y Rivera, Colonia (00 598 52 23700). **Open** 8am-8pm daily.

Carmelo

Just 40 kilometres (25 miles) north-east across the river and 77 kilometres (48 miles) along the coast from Colonia, the sleepy backwater town

Uruguay isn't a big league producer – around 95 million litres per year, about the same amount a large Chilean company makes – but quality over quantity is revered by this forgotten nation of wine lovers. Uruguay's sacred variety of grape is tannat. Similar to Argentina's malbec, the grape was brought over from France, and from the moment the seed touched the soil, perfection was sown. Although it has been derided for its tongue-clogging tannins (the name derives from 'tannin'), with fine quality control and imaginative blends, its strong fruity flavour has been winning medals around the world.

Uruguay's success is partly due to its ideal climate and soil. No irrigation is needed, thanks to arable land, and the grapes grow full of sugar in the strong sun. In addition to the fertile environment, respect for the noble grape is ingrained in the people. Romantic tales of European immigrants setting up camp 200 years ago are often recalled as their great-great-grandchildren swill, smell and swallow. And now, an association of 15 Uruguayan family-owned wine growers has been working hard to promote their products with a thoroughly enjoyable tour of their wineries called Wine Roads (www.uruguay winetours.com).

At each *bodega*, visitors are given an insightful tour of the property and wine-making process, and then invited to sit down to enjoy a selection of *picadas* (snacks) of fresh bread and cheeses, carefully matched to your tasting session. The appeal of Wine Roads is the genuine love that goes into producing the wine, the continuing tradition and the friendly family atmosphere. All the owners are directly involved, and the smiles on their faces are clear proof of the pride they have in their wines.

From the beautiful Los Cerros de San Juan (*see below*) to the small grappa-producing Bernardi (www.bodegabernardi.com) near Colonia, onwards to Montevideo and the Canelones province and stretching up to Rivera, each *bodega* offers drinks so delicious you wish you could be as fly and drown in the stuff. The surrounding countryside enhances the natural, earthy quality: from rolling hills at *bodega* Alto de la Ballena (www.altodelaballena.com) in Maldonado to the Midas-touched sunsets at Viñedo de los Vientos (www.vinedodelos vientos.com) outside Atlántida, the views in Uruguay are breathtaking. And although new blends of grape and high-tech machinery may be used, the final product and contentment in the sound of opening a bottle never changes.

Other vineyards near Montevideo with welcoming visitors' centres include Carrau (www.bodegascarrau.com), De Lucca (www.deluccawines.com), Castillo Viejo (www.castilloviejo.com), the large Juanicó bodega (www.jaunico.com), Filgueria (www.bodegafilgueira.com) Santa Rosa (www.bodegasantarosa.com.uy) and the boutique Bouza (www.bouzawines.com).

of Carmelo is situated where the River Uruguay broadens to become the River Plate.

Between Carmelo and Colonia Carmelo, on the R21 between Colonia and Carmelo, is **Los Cerros de San Juan** (00 598 481 7200, www.loscerrosdesanjuan.com.uy), the country's oldest *bodega*. Founded in 1854, it still stores its wines in a century-old stone warehouse. After a visit – by appointment – there's a sampling of local delicacies served with a glass of tannat.

In this oasis of tranquillity, and nestled in a pine forest outside town on Ruta 21, is the stunning **Four Seasons Carmelo Resort** (in BA 4321 1711, 00 598 542 9000, www.four seasons.com/carmelo, doubles US$330-$520), Carmelo's budget-busting big draw. With 20 Zen-inspired bungalows around a gigantic pool, plus deluxe spa and golf course, it's the nearest thing to Bali on the River Plate. For something less flash, stay in town at the **Hotel-Casino Carmelo** on Rodó street (00 598 542 2314/2333, doubles US$50). From there, it's a short walk across the swing bridge – built in 1912 – to the golden beaches that earn Carmelo's fame, the main draw for any visit to this sleepy town.

Close by, a few minutes towards Nueva Palmira, is the delightful **Finca Narbona** (Ruta 21, km 267, 00 598 540 4778; www.fincaygranja narbona.com), a restaurant, cheese factory and bakery in a converted 1909 general store.

Tourist information

Dirección de Turismo

Casa de Cultura, 19 de Abril, y Rodríguez (00 598 542 2001). **Open** *Jan, Feb* 10am-noon, 5-9pm Mon-Thu; 9am-9pm Fri-Sun. *Mar-Dec* 8am-6pm Mon-Thur; 9am-3pm Fri Sun.

Trips Out of Town

History, food and architecture in **Montevideo**.

Montevideo

Montevideo is barely more than a river breeze away from Buenos Aires, and the proximity of the two cities makes constant comparison inevitable. However, if you're expecting the Uruguayan capital to be a near-mirror image of its trendy neighbour, think again. It might offer the same strain of faded colonial glamour, but it's altogether quieter, smaller and less frenetic. Many visitors love it for its slower pace, sandy beaches and measured friendliness; others find it, well, ho-hum.

Montevideo has genuine points of interest. There's plenty of ebbing grandeur in the **Ciudad Vieja** (old town), where wrought iron balconies and stucco facades give on to pleasant green plazas. The largest civic space, Plaza Independencia, is overlooked by the cupola-crazed whimsy of **Palacio Salvo**; built in 1928, this was for decades the highest structure in South America. In the square itself, you can head below the statue of independence hero José Artigas to see his singular final resting place.

The city is home to several notable museums. The **Museo Romántico** (25 de Mayo 428) showcases the impeccably preserved belongings of the local 19th-century elite, and the impressive **Museo del Azulejo** (Calle Cavia, Pocitos) houses more than 2,000 French tiles –

Montevideo was once the world's largest importer. There are two strong art galleries: **Museo Joaquín Torres García** (Sarandí 683), dedicated to Uruguay's favourite painter son, and the new **Museo Gurvich** (Ituzaingó 1377), displaying the eclectic work of José Gurvich, himself a protegé of Torres García. If you're pushed for time, the latter is the more rewarding.

The town centre makes for a calm, unhurried saunter (with regular pitstops at the genial local cafés, naturally), but heading into the residential suburbs is also an interesting diversion. Follow the coastal path and you'll eventually be rewarded by miles of city-front beaches and a fresh take on urban Uruguay. The city's youth hostels are the best option for bike hire.

Montevideo is one of the spiritual homes of international football, and for anyone who's ever harboured dreams of goal-scoring glory (go on, admit it), a trip to the **Estadio Centenario**, which hosted the first World Cup Final in 1930, is more or less obligatory. It's a slight slog from the centre, but the large **Museo del Fútbol**, displaying two Jules Rimet trophies among a host of other memorabilia, is incentive enough.

Finally, if you're in town on a Sunday, don't miss the **Feria Tristán Narvaja** (Tristán Narvaja y 18 de Julio), one of the world's great outdoor markets. Every Sunday, from 9am to

2pm, seven blocks of Tristán Narvaja Street are packed with antique dealers touting all manner of curious trinkets and furniture.

Where to eat & drink

Montevideo's attractions include its many photogenic bars and cafés. Highlights include the magically old-fashioned **Bar Hispano** (San José 1050) and **Baar Fun Fun** (Ciudadela 1229, 00 598 2 915 8005), whose house shot, the sugary sweet Uvita, was immortalised in a tango by patron Carlos Gardel. The bar fills up from Wednesday to Saturday, when bands play. For the most atmospheric lunch in town, head to the wonderful **Mercado del Puerto**. It's possible to take a lively ringside seat at most of the gut-busting indoor *parrillas*, and for special occasions **El Palenque** (Pérez de Castellano 1550, 00 598 2 915 4704, www.elpalenque.com.uy, main courses US$13-$40) pulls in international celebs and local politicians. Come hungry. For upmarket but still relaxed dining, there's a growing bar and restaurant scene surrounding the one-block pedestrianised street Bacacay, in the old town.

From Thursday until Sunday, the five dancefloors of the beachfront **W Lounge** (00 598 2 712 5287) are where much of the nightlife scene is concentrated. Just below the Montevideo World Trade Center, **Lotus** (Luis A de Herrera y 26 de Marzo, 00 598 2 628 1379) is a popular late-night hipster hangout.

Where to stay

For luxury, **Belmont House** (Avenida Rivera 6512, 00 598 2 600 0430, www.belmonthouse.com.uy, doubles US$220), in the stylish Carrasco barrio, is an elegant B&B full of antiques. **Posada al Sur** (Perez Castellano 1424, 00 598 2 916 5287, www.posadaalsur.com.uy, private rooms US$30) is a comfortable, friendly option with a strong sustainable tourism philosophy. The imaginatively refurbished **Plaza Fuerte Hotel** (Bartolomé Mitre 1361, 00 598 2 915 6651, www.plazafuerte.com, US$83-$115) includes all the lovely original details of this stunning building, but with thoroughly modern components. The **NH Columbia** (Rambla Gran Bretaña 473, 00 598 2 916 0001, www.nh-hoteles.es, doubles US$100) is in a modernist building with attractive rooms and river views.

Getting there

By air

Aerolíneas Argentinas and Uruguayan airline **Pluna** fly several times a day to from BA to Montevideo (40mins). Flights depart from BA's **Aeropuerto Jorge Newbery** and arrive at Montevideo's **Carrasco** airport (604 0272), 10km (6 miles) from the city centre.

By boat

From its Puerto Madero terminal (Av. Cordoba y Madero, www.buquebus.com) in BA, **Buquebus** has at least two fast boats a day direct to Montevideo (3hrs, from US$69 one way).

Tourist information

Centro de Información Turística

Explanada Palacio Municipal, Avenida 18 de Julio, y Ejido (00 598 2 1950 1830). **Open** 10am-6pm Mon-Fri; 9am-5pm Sat, Sun.

Punta del Este

Brazen, cool, and shamelessly obsessed with aesthetics, this glamorous resort is one of the world's most exclusive. Concrete and crowded, the **Punta** of today has come a long way from the time when 1950s starlets such as Rita Hayworth graced its shores, but it remains a staggeringly expensive luxury destination for American and European tourists, as well as Argentinian and Brazilian regulars, all lured by its combination of fashionable beaches, superb restaurants and hordes of clubs where you can greet the dawn dancing away, cocktail in hand.

The mixed demographic features a fascinating cast of millionaire yacht owners, 18-year-old models with their 49-year-old beaus, divorced lawyers specialising in divorce, surgeons and plastic surgeons, successful and disgraced former footballers, and teenage surfers with their families. But it's this dynamic clash of cultures that gives Punta its unique, indefinable charm, creating a magic that transcends the ephemeral and frivolous summer season.

As you travel north out of the peninsular, the white sands empty and the high rises are replaced by mansions. After about ten kilometres (six miles) you hit Punta's most happening patch: **La Barra**. In recent years the town has mushroomed from scarcely a village to the stylish summer residence of the international fashion set, who've fled the uncouth masses crowding into Punta. During January it's the throbbing heart of the Este scene, as every brand manager worth his budget knows. It's also the gastronomic capital of the area, and the best place in which to enjoy an ice-cream, take in an exhibition at one of the many museums or galleries, or simply frolic on the beautiful beaches – **Bikini** is the focal point for the catwalk show of sunbathers. But the indisputable draw here is the nightlife, when the streets heave with traffic (peak rush hour is 3am) and the clubs are full to bursting.

Where to eat & drink

Food lovers will salivate over Punta's thriving gastronomic scene. For sublime fish and seafood with Mediterranean flourishes, try the upmarket **Lo de Charlie** (Calle 12, 819, y 9, 00 598 42 444183, main courses US$10-$15). Even fancier is **Don Polidoro** (Pedragosa Sierra y La Paloma, 00 598 42 480898, main courses US$15-$22), perhaps Punta's best *parrilla*, offering unusual salads, rarely seen meat dishes (pork with grilled pineapple) and seemingly infinite varieties of offal, all in tasting-sized portions. If you make it to dessert, the grilled spiced nectarines are highly recommended. **Citrus** (Rambla Circunvalación, Complejo el Mejillón, 00 598 42 447006, www.citrus.com.uy, main courses US$11-$16) has a winning combination of minimalist cuisine and impressive views of Isla Gorriti from its large circular windows. Remember that during the busy summer months, restaurant reservations are a must everywhere.

Patxi (Dodera 944, Maldonado, 00 598 42 238393, main courses US$5-$12) lures in diners with its Basque seafood dishes and well stocked wine cellar, and the exclusive Italian chain restaurant **Piegari** (Boulevard de las Palmeras 668, Calle 11 e/10 y 12, 00 598 42 449752, main courses US$11-$18) is the ideal spot for special occasions. Regulars rave about the *pulpo a la gallega* (Galician octopus) and seafood risotto. For a superb example of a classic Uruguayan *parrilla*, try **Lo de Rubén** (Santa Teresa 846 y Avenida Aigua, Maldonado, 00 598 42 223059, main courses US$7-$9), which boasts the tastiest *pamplonas* (traditional meat dish) you'll find this side of the River Plate.

Substance over style is the order of the day at **El Viejo Marino** (Calle 11, No 739, 00 598 42 443565, www.viejomarino.com, main courses US$6-$10). Ignore the tacky decor and the over-fussy service, and focus instead on the huge portions and wonderfully fresh seafood. The large platter of diced *chipirones* (baby squid) and fried onions are an absolute must, as is the flaky, melt-in-your-mouth *lomo de mahi-mahi*, a deep sea water fish. And no visit to Uruguay is complete without a trip to **La Pasiva** (Gorleo y Calle 28, 00 598 42 441316); their *panchos* (hotdogs), bathed in exquisite mustard, make the perfect cheap snack.

Feeling queasy after boat across? Head to **Moby Dick Bar** (Rambla General Artigas 650, 00 598 42 441240) for a restorative tonic. Whiling away the afternoons in this popular sailors' haunt are captains of incredible yachts, rugby players on tour, and a multitude of monied American and British tourists. Another pleasant place at which to enjoy an evening cocktail is **Company Bar** (Calle 29, entre 18 y 20, 00 598 42 440130).

In La Barra, an established bistro in the centre is the Este branch of **Novecento**, the preferred meeting place of the young and wealthy (Ruta 10, esquina Las Sirenas, 00 598 42 772363, www.bistronovecento.com, main courses US$9-$12). A cheaper and more relaxed option is **Rex** (Ruta 10, 00 598 42 771504, main courses US$3-$6), serving up tasty *chivito* and refreshing *licuados* (fruit smoothies) off the main strip. It's also worth the short but vertiginous climb from the beach to visit **Baby Gouda** (Ruta 10, esquina Los Romances, 00 598 42 771874, main courses US$8-$10), a kitsch and colourful deli with a Moroccan twist.

In Manantiales, overlooking model-packed Bikini beach, **Cactus y Pescados** (00 598 42 774782, main courses US$7-$9) is perfect for a late, post-beach lunch. The snug and charming **O'Farrell** (Calle Punta del Este, almost Ruta 10, 00 598 42 774331, main courses US$16-$25) is one of the highlights of the local restaurant scene: think duck foie gras with caramelised pear and Valrhona chocolate cake with passion fruit sorbet. If you're in the mood for good old-fashioned plain food that won't burn a hole in your wallet, the unpretentious **Las Dos Hermanas** (Manantiales, 00 598 42 774743, main courses US$3-$5) is the place for you.

Punta del Este is unique: as well as having one of the shortest high seasons anywhere in the world (Christmas to mid January), it also has the odd reputation of being the resort of choice for Argentinian retail brands to open bars. **KSK Rock Bar** on Barra's Ruta 10 comes courtesy of Kosiuko, famous for its saucy, figure-hugging garb. Up for grabs you'll find a heady mix of cocktails, sushi, international DJs and limited edition clothing ranging from a cool US$250 to $1000. Two grungy options for surfers and wannabe surfers are **No Me Olvides** (Ruta 10, Manantiales, 00 598 42 775531) and the always packed **Pico Alto** (Ruta 10, km 160.6, 00 598 42 770436), where you can discuss the day's waves over a chilled beer and a slice of pizza.

Where to stay

Lodging in Punta is expensive, but becomes considerably cheaper if you buy a package through ferry operator Buquebus (*see p286*). **Conrad Resort & Casino** (Parada 4, Playa Mansa, 00 598 42 472065, www.conrad.com.uy, doubles US$180-$7500), best known for its bikini fashion shows and cavernous casino, became the peninsula's first five-star hotel on opening its doors in 1997. A lesser known option is the peaceful **La Capilla** (Viña del

Join the yachting set in **Punta del Este**.

Mar y Valparaíso, San Rafael, 00 598 42 484059, suite from US$210) where celebrities as diverse as Pelé and Jorge Luis Borges have sought rest. Run by a family of inveterate travellers, boutique art-hotel **Las Cumbres** (Ruta 12, km 3.5, Laguna del Sauce, 00 598 42 578689, www.cumbres.com.uy, doubles US$138-$826) is a visual feast containing a fascinating collection of objets d'art from around the world. The eclectic interior design features high-tech gadgets and plasma TV screens. **Posada Aldila** has great sea views and the distinction of being the first (and so far only) expressly gay-friendly guesthouse in Este (km 120, Punta Ballena, 00 598 42 579202,www.posadaaldila. com, doubles US$250-$370).

For a relaxed, and informal stay in La Barra, **Hotel La Bluette** (Ruta 10, Parada 49, 00 598 42 770947, www.hotellabluette.com, doubles US$60-$450) is a delightfully decorated 12-room guest house. The impromptu *parrillas* in the summer and roaring fires in the winter pull together guests for wine and plenty of spirited chat. If cash is running thin, take refuge in the tiny **La Ballenera** (Ruta 10, km 162, 00 598 42 771079, www.laballenera.net, doubles US$70-$160), a prairie-style wooden abode close to the beach. Real high-rollers and fashionistas stay in luxury at the **Mantra Resort & Casino** (Ruta 10, Parada 48, 00 598 42 771100,

www.mantraresort.com, doubles from US$600-$6500), which has its own spa. At the peak of high season it seems that most of Barra stops in at **Le Club** (Av. de los Cangrejos y Calle del Mar, 00 598 42 772082, www.leclubposada.com, doubles from US$100) for a sunset cocktail. This chic hotel-cum-bar-cum- restaurant dedicates itself to the fine art of good living. Facing the rolling waves, Miami Vice-inspired **Esturion de Montoya** (Playa Montoya, 00 598 42 772116, www.esturiondemontoya. com.uy, doubles US$330-$1300) regularly hosts post-catwalk parties.

José Ignacio

Leave behind the high-rise towers of Punta del Este to visit the seemingly sleepy fishing village of José Ignacio. Just 40 kilometres (25 miles) northwest of Punta, José Ignacio is a small, stubby peninsula of tidy, single-family houses with thatched roofs. A slight hill makes sure the ocean is omnipresent for the lucky 300 or so inhabitants.

But don't let its apparent sleepiness fool you. Those quaint thatched roofs have sheltered many a model, photographer, tycoon, writer with bad teeth, ageing pop-star with highlights....Residents and visitors have included: Naomi Campbell, Gisele Bündchen,

Trips Out of Town

Mario Testino, Ralph Lauren, Michael Eisner, Martin Amis and Simon Le Bon. Owing to the march of big names in high season (Christmas to January), mere mortals may have to wait three hours for a table at José Ignacio's famous, beachside fish shack **Parador La Huella** (*see below*).

First, to find your bearings, head to the lighthouse. On a rocky promontory jutting out to sea, the 130-year-old, iconic **Faro de José Ignacio** is one of the only structures on the peninsula that's over two storeys tall. You really can't miss it. Climb up any time between 10am and sunset to get the lie of the land.

From the lighthouse, facing the water, Playa Brava (with rougher surf) is on your left and Playa Mansa (the gentler one) on your right. Playa Mansa, next to **Laguna José Ignacio**, is a top fishing spot. Playa Brava, heading out towards the kitesurfers' favoured Laguna Garzón, is the best place to eat fish – which is probably higher up on most holidaymakers' to-do lists.

Where to eat & drink

On the Brava beach, we have to talk about **Parador La Huella** (Los Cisnes at the beach, 00 598 48 62279, www.paradorlahuella.com, main courses US$15-$25). Besides offering delicious grilled fish and sushi, La Huella is the place to see and be seen. And, yes, there's all the hassle that goes with that. Reserve a table for lunch or dinner – preferably out on the porch – as soon as you can.

Off the beach, near the plaza, there's the more low-key **Lucy** (Las Garzas and Las Golondrinas, 00 598 48 62090, main courses US$10-$15). This is a tea house and casual spot for a quick bite. Foody visitors looking for Francis Mallman's famous Los Negros will be disappointed this year: the seaside spot was shuttered to make way for a private residence. If you want what Los Negros used to offer, head 45 minutes inland to the tiny town of Garzón, where Mallman has opened a restaurant and hotel called **Garzón** (Garzón's central plaza, 00 598 41 02811, www.garzon.com.uy, main courses US$30-$50).

Where to sleep

If you think it's tough finding a table in José Ignacio, good luck finding a bed. With strict zoning laws limiting hotel operations, there are only a few dozen rooms on the entire peninsula. What to do? Well, you could rent a house for thousands (see local real estate listings) or just come in for day trips. But if you can book in

advance, try **La Posada del Faro** (Calle de la Bahía, 00 598 48 62110, www.posadadelfaro.com, doubles US$170-$550), the peninsula's top spot. La Posada del Faro is unfailingly chic, even though it's showing its age slightly. Bonus: there's a wet bar in the swimming pool – a trick that never fails to please.

Just off the peninsula, about three minutes down Route 10 towards Laguna Garzón, there's also the super-chichi **Casa Suaya** (Route 10, km 186.5, 00 598 46 80200, www.casasuaya.com, doubles US$300-$600). It's an estate billed as an 'exclusive home resort', created by Adolfo Suaya, the Argentinian impresario behind buzzy restaurants in Beverly Hills (the Lodge) and Hollywood (Geisha House).

Shopping

If the prices of accommodation don't leave you feeling too poor, stroll through the local art gallery **Galería de las Misiones** (Las Garzas y Los Tordos, 00 598 48 62645, www.galeria misiones.com), the Uruguayan-designer clothing stores, **Bajo el Alma** (Las Garzas y Las Golondrinas, 00 598 486 2098) and **El Canuto** (Los Cisnes and Los Horneros, 00 598 48 62028) and the wine, art and book emporium **Tierra y Vino** (Las Garzas and Los Tordos, 00 598 48 62550). Note that most shops are closed in the off-season.

Resources

Centro Información Turística

Parada 1, Calle 31, La Mansa (00 598 42 440514). **Open** *Dec-Feb* 8am-10pm daily. *Mar-Nov* 10am-6pm daily.

Getting there

By air

Aerolíneas Argentinas and Uruguayan airline **Pluna** fly several times daily from BA to Punta (50 mins). Flights depart from BA's Aeropuerto Jorge Newbery and arrive at Punta's **Laguna del Sauce** airport, 16km (10 miles) outside the city centre.

By boat & road

From its Puerto Madero terminal (Av. Cordoba y Madero, www.buquebus.com) in Buenos Aires, Buquebus runs at least two boats a day to Colonia (3hrs) and Montevideo (3hrs). Buses then take you to Punta, four hours from Colonia and two from Montevideo. Boat and bus one way costs US$47-$92 to Colonia and US$82-$112 to Montevideo. **Colonia Express** (www.coloniaexpress.com) can also link Colonia with Punta del Este and José Ignacio. Hydrofoils reach Uruguay in 50 minutes; you can then a transfer by bus to Punta del Este. One-way rates are US$55.

Directory

Features

Directory

Getting Around

Arriving & leaving

By air

Ezeiza (Aeropuerto Ministro Pistarini)

Ezeiza, Buenos Aires, 35km (22 miles) from city centre. Recorded flight information or operator, plus listings of airline telephone numbers 5480 6111 (English & Spanish)/ www.aa2000.com.ar.
The official name of Buenos Aires' international airport is Aeropuerto Ministro Pistarini, although it is more commonly known as Ezeiza. All international flights arrive and depart from here, except those between Buenos Aires and Uruguay (*see below* **Aeroparque Jorge Newbery**). The airport has two interlinked terminals, A and B, in close proximity. Aerolíneas Argentinas uses Terminal B, while all other airlines operate out of Terminal A.

During rush hour allow 1 hour 20 minutes for travel between downtown BA and Ezeiza. At all other times, plan for 30-40 minutes.

Arriving at Ezeiza used to be a terrifying experience, when hordes of 'independent' taxi drivers would pounce on nervous tourists fresh off the plane. Thankfully the system has been cleaned up and is now much more straightforward; on arrival, go to the taxi desk in the arrivals hall and pre-pay a set fare of AR$80-$100 to city centre destinations. Approved and reliable operating companies include **Manuel Tienda León** (4314 3636/www.tiendaleon.com) and **Transfer Express** (4312 8883), who also both offer *remise* (minicab) services. Fares are one-way to the centre and include road tolls. Several other *remise* companies accept advance calls on airport pick-ups and drop-offs. Alternatively, call on arrival and they will send a driver within about 15 minutes. Check they include road tolls. Try **Le Coq** (4964 2000) or **Recoleta VIP** (4983 0544).

Manuel Tiendo León also operate a shuttle bus service to/from the airport – with one stand in the arrivals hall and one outside the terminals – and its downtown office (Avenida Eduardo Madero s/n, Retiro). Buses leave every 30 minutes from the city centre, from 4am to 10.30pm. From the airport there is a 24-hour service, with buses every 30 minutes. Fares per person: AR$38 one way, AR$69 return. There's free pick-up and drop-off at hotels, offices or homes in a defined area of the city centre; otherwise, journeys start and finish at the firm's office on Avenida Eduardo Madero.

If you have more time than cash on your hands, you can take a *colectivo* (city bus) for just AR$1.50, but allow at least two hours. Bus 86 (make sure you take one that says Aeropuerto Ezeiza) runs to/from La Boca and Avenida de Mayo.

International airlines
In addition to these airlines, all the major Latin American airlines have services to Buenos Aires.
Aerolíneas Argentinas
0810 222 86527/4139 3000/ www.aerolineas.com.ar.
Air Canada
4327 3640/www.aircanada.com.
Air France
0800 222 2600/4317 4700/ www.airfrance.com/ar
Alitalia
4310 9999/www.alitalia.com.ar.
American Airlines
4318 1111/www.aa.com.
British Airways
4320 6600/www.britishairways.com.
Iberia
4131 1000/01/www.iberia.com.
KLM
4326 8422/www.klm.com.
Lufthansa
4319 0600/www.lufthansa.com.
Swiss
4319 0000/www.swiss.com.
United Airlines
4316 0777/www.united.com.ar

Aeroparque Jorge Newbery
Avenida Costanera Rafael Obligado, entre La Pampa y Sarmiento, Costanera Norte. Recorded flight information or operator, plus listings of airline telephone numbers 5480 6111 (English & Spanish)/ www.aa2000.com.ar. **Map** p327 P12.
Aeroparque Jorge Newbery, more commonly known as simply Aeroparque, is the arrival and departure point for all domestic flights, as well as those to and from the Uruguayan cities of Montevideo and Punta del Este. It's conveniently located on the Costanera Norte, beside Palermo park, just 15 minutes from the city centre. **Manuel Tienda León** (4314 3636/www. tiendaleon.com) has a shuttle bus service to/from Aeroparque every 30 minutes (AR$14 one way), as well as *remise* services. **Transfer Express** (4312 8883), operating from the airport, also has *remise* services to the city centre. *Remises* cost AR$25-$30. Several city buses also serve the airport; the fare is AR90¢. The most useful is the No.33 (make sure it says Aeroparque on the front), from Plaza de Mayo. There is also a taxi rank at the airport entrance. A taxi to a downtown hotel costs AR$15-$20.

Domestic airlines
Several of these airlines also offer international routes to neighbouring countries, particularly to Uruguay. Note that non-Argentinian residents pay significantly higher prices for internal flights in Argentina.
Aerolíneas Argentinas
0810 222 86527/4139 3000/ www.aerolineas.com.ar.
Lade
0810 810 5233/5129 9000/ www.lade.com.ar
LAN Chile
0810 999 9526 option 7/ www.lan.com.

By road

Estación Terminal de Omnibus
Avenida Ramos Mejía 1680, Retiro. Passenger information 4310 0700. Subte C, Retiro/6, 93, 130, 152 bus.
Buenos Aires's bus station is in Retiro, next to the train station (see Map p325 H12). There are left-luggage lockers in the station (AR$3) but they are not completely secure. Be wary of pickpockets in and around the terminal, there are frequent reports of bag snatching.

More than 80 long-distance buses operate out of Retiro. Don't panic: they are grouped together by region (i.e. North-west or Patagonia), so it's easy to compare prices and times. There are services to every major destination in Argentina, and also to neighbouring countries.

For most destinations there are two levels of service, known respectively as *común* and *diferencial* or *ejecutiva* The latter has hosts or hostesses, includes food, and has different types of seat – the most comfortable is the *coche cama*: larger, almost fully reclining 'bed seats'. Tickets to all destinations must be purchased at the bus station. In high season (December to February, Easter week and July) it is worth buying your ticket in advance.

By sea

Unless you are arriving from Uruguay, across the River Plate, or stopping off on a cruise, it is unlikely that you will arrive in BA by boat. Regular boat services run between BA and Colonia and Montevideo in Uruguay (*see pp285-292*), docking at the passenger port in **Dársena Norte**, a few blocks from the city centre at Avenida Córdoba and Avenida Alicia Moreau de Justo. Cruise ships dock at the new **Terminal Benito Quinquela Martín** (4317 0671) at Avenida de los Inmigrantes and Castillo.

Public transport

Getting around Buenos Aires is relatively easy and cheap. *Colectivos* (city buses) run frequently, cover the whole capital and offer 24-hour service, while the Subte – the small but reliable underground network – is a fast alternative.

Buses

City buses are known as *colectivos*. There are 140 bus lines along a variety of routes (*ramales*) through every city *barrio* (neighbourhood). Service during the day is frequent, and companies are also obliged to provide an all-night service, with at least one bus every half hour, although not every line complies.

Bus fares are AR90¢ for journeys within the capital, AR$1 for journeys of more than 12 kilometres. Just say *noventa* (ninety) when you get on, then pay the fare into the machine behind the driver – make sure you have coins, notes are not accepted. Be warned that the average bus driver imagines himself (it usually is a he) as the reincarnation of Ayrton Senna: very few come to a complete halt to let pasengers on and off, except by mistake. You need to be agile, hold on tight while on board, and be ready to yell if it moves off while you're hanging out of the door.

Pick up a *Guía T*, a handy guide to bus routes, for AR$6 from most newspaper stands. For complaints or information, call freephone 0800 333 0300. For lost property *see p301*.

Underground

Buenos Aires's underground train network, operating since 1912, is called the Subte. It's the quickest, cheapest and easiest way to get around the city during the day, though it can be very crowded during morning and evening peak hours. The service runs from 5am to 10.45pm (8am to 10pm on Sundays). Large parts of the city are not served by the network, including some fashionable tourist areas such as Recoleta and Palermo Viejo. A single journey, *un viaje*, to anywhere on the network costs just AR90¢. Magnetic card tickets, for anything between one and thirty Subte journeys, can be bought at the *boleterías* (ticket offices), located inside the stations.

For complaints or suggestions, call Metrovías on 0800 555 1616. The website www.metrovias.com.ar has a useful English version, and also has regular updates about the service. LCD screens above entrances give information about connections. For lost property, *see p301*.

Trains

Trains connecting the northern suburbs with the city centre are modern and air-conditioned, while those serving the south are more run-down. Trains linking the capital with destinations in Buenos Aires province are not in great nick either, but they do have three classes: *turista* (wooden seats); *primera* (soft seats); and *pullman* (even better seats and air-conditioning).

There are several different private companies running the trains, which can make it difficult to get the times, prices and information you need. For lost property *see p301*.

These are the main stations:

Constitución

General Hornos 11, Constitución. **Map** p324 D8.
Trains from Constitución go south. **Metropolitano** (passenger information freephone 0800 122 358736/4018 0719) runs services on the Roca line to Buenos Aires province, to La Plata, Glew, Ezeiza (20 minutes from the airport by a connecting bus) and Temperley. **Ferrobaires** (passenger information 4306 7919) runs a long-distance service to the BA province coastal destinations of Mar del Plata, Tandil and Bahía Blanca.

Retiro

Avenida Ramos Mejía 1508, Retiro. **Map** p325 H12.
Trains run north and west from Retiro, actually three stations in one,

known by their old names: Mitre, Belgrano and San Martín.

From Mitre, **Trenes de Buenos Aires** (TBA – passenger information 4317 4407/4445) runs services to Tigre, with connections to Capilla del Señor, José León Suárez and Bartolomé Mitre (in Olivos). There is a weekly service to Rosario in Santa Fe province. From Belgrano, **Ferrovías** (passenger information 4511 8833) runs trains to Villa Rosa. From San Martín, **Transportes Metropolitanos** (passenger information 4011 5826) goes to Pilar.

Taxis & *remises*

Taxis in Buenos Aires are reasonably priced and plentiful (except in rainy rush hours). However, visitors need to be wary of being taken for a long ride, or worst of all, being robbed by an unlicensed driver. For this reason, it is recommended that you use only a radio taxi or a *remise* (licensed minicab). Both will come to any destination in the city. You will need at least a few words of Spanish to book a cab by phone, though staff in hotels and restaurants will usually be happy to help. If you're in a rush and need to hail a cab in the street, try to stop a radio taxi (look for 'radio taxi' and the company name and phone number written on the doors).

Taxis run on meters: the initial fare is AR$3.10, plus AR31¢ for every 200 metres or one minute of waiting time. You are not expected to tip taxi drivers and they should give you change to the nearest AR10¢. Change is the perennial problem with taxis. Anything larger than a AR$10 bill is guaranteed to produce a sigh, and most taxi drivers would rather gargle battery acid than change a AR$100 note. Many radio taxis have a minimum charge of AR$3.50, and a few charge an extra fee for a pick-up (*adicionales*). Check first.

Taxis are black and yellow (radio cabs included), with a red *libre* (free) light in the front window. *Remises* look like other private cars and do not run on meters. You should agree a price before setting off. Also, bear in mind that *remises* are often less punctual than radio taxis. It's a good idea to make a second call, ten minutes before pick-up time, to check the *remise* is on its way. For lost property *see p301*.

Radio taxis

Pidalo *4956 1200.*
Radio Taxi Premium *4374 6666.*

Remises

Remises Blue *4777 8888.*
Remises Recoleta Vip *4804 6655.*

Driving

Driving in Buenos Aires is the surest way to raise your blood pressure. Chaos rules as buses, taxis and private cars fight it out on the roads. People drive at very high speeds, change lanes with dizzying frequency, and generally bring out the Mr Hyde aspect of their personality while behind the wheel. Setting off slowly at a green light is considered an unpardonable sin by many drivers, who will proceed to honk their horns and run through their full repertoire of hand gesticulations.

Despite the apparent anarchy, there are a few basic rules:
• You have to be 17 to drive (16 with a parent or guardian's permission).
• Front seatbelts are compulsory.
• Under-10s must sit in the back.
• Priority is given to cars crossing other streets from the right. Cars fly out of nowhere on cross streets, so be warned.
• Overtake on the left – that's the principle, anyway. No one respects this rule, and even the law bends a little to say that if the left-hand lane is moving slower than the right-hand one, you can overtake on the right instead.
• On streets (*calles*), the maximum speed is 40kmh; avenues (*avenidas*), maximum 60kmh; semi-motorways (*semiautopistas*), maximum 80kmh; and on motorways (*autopistas*), maximum 100kmh. On main national roads (*rutas nacionales*), signs on different stretches of road indicate minimum and maximum speeds, but the max never exceeds 130kmh.

Car hire

You need to be over 21, with a driver's licence, passport and credit card to hire a car in Buenos Aires. Prices vary greatly – a rough guide is AR$150-$200 per day, depending on mileage. Major car rental companies will allow you to take the car out of the country if you sign a contract in front of a public notary, which will set you back around AR$180. You can often return the car to a different office within Argentina. You must have at least third party insurance (*seguro de responsabilidad civil*), but it makes sense to take out fully comprehensive insurance.

Avis

Cerrito 1527, y Posadas, Retiro (4326 5542/www.avis.com.ar). Bus 17, 59, 67, 75, 102. **Open** 8am-8pm Mon-Sat, 9am-6pm Sun. **Credit** AmEx, DC, MC, V. **Map** p326 I11.

Baires Rent a Car

4822 7361/www.bairesrentacar.com.ar). **Credit** AmEx, MC, V.

Hertz Annie Millet

Paraguay 1138, entre Cerrito y Libertad, Tribunales (4816 8001/www.milletrentacar.com.ar). Subte D, Tribunales/10, 17, 59, 132, 152 bus. **Open** 8am-8pm daily. **Credit** AmEx, DC, MC, V. **Map** p325 H11.

Breakdown services

Only members of automobile associations or touring clubs with reciprocal agreements with other regions (FiA in Europe and FITAC in the Americas) can use the breakdown services of the **Automóvil Club Argentino** (ACA, www.aca.org.ar). This includes members of the British AA and RAC. You can use this facility in Argentina for up to 30 days. You will have to present the membership credentials of your local club, showing the FITAC or FiA logo, to the mechanic.

Various companies offer emergency assistance to drivers. The basic call-out price is AR$50-$70. Try **ABA** (4572 6802), **Estrella** (4922 9095) or **Mecánica Móvil** (4925 6000).

Automóvil Club Argentino (ACA)

Information 4808 6200/breakdown service 4803 3333/www.aca.org.ar. FITAC members also get special deals on hotels and car rental.

Parking

Parking restrictions are indicated on street signs, but in general there is no parking in the Microcentro area downtown during working hours (and on some streets, there's no parking at any time). Parking is prohibited in the left lane on streets and avenues throughout the city, unless otherwise indicated.

The easiest option is a private garage (*estacionamiento privado* or *garaje*), signalled by a large blue sign with a white letter 'E' in the middle, costing around AR$3.50 per hour. Some barrios still have free on-street parking, though you'll probably be approached by an unofficial *guardacoche* (car-keeper, possibly a child), offering to look after your car while you're gone. You will be expected to pay a couple of pesos on your return. If you're not happy with this arrangement, find somewhere else to park.

Always take all valuables out of your car (stereo included, if possible), close windows and lock all doors.

Cycling

This ain't Holland. Cycling in Buenos Aires can be a hazardous undertaking, thanks to potholes, sociopathic drivers, pollution and a lack of respect for cycle lanes. However, there are pleasant cycling areas in Palermo, the Reserva Ecológica and the riverside neighbourhoods.

There are bicycle hire stands (open at weekends during daylight hours, and on some weekdays) around the entrance to major parks, including Parque Tres de Febrero and the Reserva Ecológica, the most cycle-friendly areas. A word of warning: think twice before locking up your bike up anywhere. For more on circuits and bike hire, *see p77*.

Walking

Despite frustrations such as broken pavements and ongoing street repairs, when the weather is good and the sun is shining – which, let's face it, is a significant amount of the time – walking in Buenos Aires is a great pleasure, and one of the best ways to get to know the city. The terrain is flat, the block system makes it easy to navigate and if you get lost you can always have the fallback of hopping in a cab. A useful city map is the *Guia T*, available from most newspaper stands for AR$6.

Green spaces in Palermo and Recoleta make these ideal *barrios* for a stroll. San Telmo is also a delightful area to explore on foot. See the walking boxes in Bars, Sightseeing and Shops & services chapters for tours.

Resources A-Z

Addresses

Addresses begin with the street name, then the house or building number, followed by the apartment number. For directions the cross street or the two streets either side of the building are given. Postal addresses should be written as follows:

Mickey MOUSE
Honduras 2738
Piso (floor) 2, Dept (flat) 34
1414 Buenos Aires
ARGENTINA

Age restrictions

The law says that to buy alcohol or have sex you must be at least 18; to buy cigarettes you need to be at least 16; and you have to be at least 17 (16 with parental consent) to drive. In general, the law (or at least in the first three of those four cases), is broken.

Attitude & etiquette

Meeting people

Argentinians are gregarious, friendly and usually interested in meeting foreigners. Tactile and physically demonstrative, most exchange a single right cheek-to-cheek kiss on first meeting – men as well as women. If you're meeting someone in a formal or business context, it's safer to shake hands.

Personal contacts are highly valued. In business, if someone is proving difficult to get hold of, a quick name-drop can help; or, better still, use a third party for an introduction. It does no harm, and often a lot of good, to lean on the foreign side of your business background.

It's best to start most conversations with a *buen día* (before noon) or *buenas tardes* (afternoon) and a brief exchange of pleasantries, if your Spanish is up to it. You will find that most business people speak – and are happy to use – at least some English. Any kind of attempt to speak in Spanish tends to be very much appreciated.

Punctuality for meetings is a phenomenon that barely exists. Out of politeness, as the foreigner, it is better if you are on time, but expect to be kept waiting, always.

Dress & manners

Argentinians are usually well presented. The dress code is best classified as smart casual and applies from the boardroom to the bedroom.

Argentina's contradictory quality is never more apparent than in the behaviour of its citizens. On the one hand, they are champions of door opening, friendly salutations and good manners; on the other, they are among the world's greatest perpetrators of shoulder barging and shameless queue jumping.

Business

When considering doing business in Argentina, you should first contact the commercial department of your embassy. It's also worth contacting the **Cámara Argentina de Comercio** (Argentinian Chamber of Commerce, Avenida Leandro N Alem 36, 5300 9000).

Conventions & conferences

Many of Buenos Aires' major hotels offer comprehensive convention and conference facilities. The long established **Sheraton** in Retiro (*see p49*) can accommodate up to 9,000 people in its 15 event rooms. A stone's throw from the Obelisco, the **Panamericano** (*see p49*) has 16 rooms for between six and 1,000 participants, while the **Hilton** in Puerto Madero (*see p55*) has extensive facilities for up to 2,000 delegates.

For smaller meetings, many restaurants – particularly those in Puerto Madero – offer a private room. Most do not charge for room hire if you are hosting a meal there.

Travel advice

For up-to-date information on travel to a specific country – including the latest news on safety and security, health issues, local laws and customs – contact your home country government's department of foreign affairs. Most of them have websites packed with useful advice for would-be travellers.

Australia
www.smartraveller.gov.au

Canada
www.voyage.gc.ca

New Zealand
www.mfat.govt.nz/travel

Republic of Ireland
http://foreignaffairs.gov.ie

UK
www.fco.gov.uk/travel

USA
http://travel.state.gov

Couriers & shippers

DHL

*Avenida Córdoba 783, entre
Esmeralda y Maipú, Microcentro
(4314 2996/freephone 0800 222
2345/www.dhl.com.ar). Subte B,
Florida/6, 26, 93, 130, 152 bus.*
Open 9am-7pm Mon-Fri; 9am-noon
Sat. **Credit** AmEx, DC, MC, V.
Map p325 G11.
Call two hours ahead to arrange pick-
up from your premises at no extra
charge, between 9am and 6pm.

FedEx

*Maipú 753, entre Córdoba y
Viamonte, Microcentro (4393 6139/
customer service 4630 0300/www.
fedex.com/ar). Subte B, Florida/6,
26, 93, 130, 152 bus.* **Open** 9am-
7pm Mon-Fri; 9am-1pm Sat. **Credit**
AmEx, MC, V. **Map** p325 G11.
International door-to-door express
delivery. Home, office or hotel pick-
ups costs US$3 extra.

UPS

*Bernardo de Irigoyen 974, entre
Estados Unidos y Carlos Calvo,
San Telmo (freephone 0800 222
2877/www.ups.com/ar). Subte E, San
José/39, 96, 126 bus.* **Open** 9am-
7pm Mon-Fri. **Credit** AmEx, DC,
MC, V. **Map** p325 E9.
International delivery for packages
from 0.5-50kg. Free home pick-up.

Office hire &
business centres

If you need use of a telephone,
fax or internet, your best bet is
one of the many *locutorios* (call
centres) situated all across
town (*see p305* **Telephones**).
Charges are from AR$1.50 a
page for sending and receiving
faxes and around AR$2 for an
hour's internet use.

Most hotels, of course, have
business centres although
the standard and amount of
computers vary widely.

If you need something more
permanent (or to give that
impression), there are several
temporary offices. Options
range from upmarket and
expensive outfits such
as **Regus** (4590 2227,
www.regus.com), to these
local choices:

Cerrito Rent-An-Office

*2nd Floor, Cerrito 1070, entre Santa
Fe y Marcelo T de Alvear, Recoleta
(4811 4000/www.rent-an-office.
com.ar). Bus 10, 59, 101, 152.* **Open**
8am-8pm Mon-Fri. **Credit** AmEx, V.
Map p325 H11.
Office and meeting room hire by the
day, week or month. Monthly rates
from AR$700-$2,500. Translators,
secretaries, lawyers, accountants and
architects available at extra charge.

SG Oficinas

*6th Floor, Maipú 267, entre
Sarmiento y Perón, Microcentro
(4328 3939/www.sgoficina.com.ar).
Subte B, Florida/6, 10, 17, 24, 29
bus.* **Open** 9am-7pm Mon-Fri.
No credit cards. Map p325 F10.
Serviced offices from AR$800 per
month or from AR$85 per day.

Translators &
interpreters

Aleph Translations

*6th Floor, Office C, Godoy Cruz
2915, y Juncal, Palermo (4779 0305/
www.alephtranslations.com). Bus 15,
39, 152.* **Open** 9am-5pm Mon-Fri.
No credit cards. Map p327 N9.
General, technical and legal
translations, with an online
express service.

Estudio Laura
Rosenzwaig

*3rd Floor, Apartment C, Billinghurst
2467, entre Las Heras y Pacheco
de Melo, Recoleta (4801 4536). Subte
D, Bulnes/10, 37, 59, 60, 102 bus.*
Open 9am-7pm Mon-Fri. **No credit
cards. Map** p326 K10.
Simultaneous translation for
conferences and written translation
work via fax or email.

Interhotel

*1st Floor, Office M, Esmeralda
1056, entre Santa Fe y Arenales,
Retiro (4311 1615/www.inter-
hotel.com.ar). Subte C, San
Martín/45, 106, 152 bus.* **Open**
9am-6pm Mon-Fri. **No credit cards.**
Map p325 H11.
Scientific and public translations.

Useful organisations

Ministerio de
Relaciones
Exteriores, Comercio,
Internacional y Culto

*Esmeralda 1212, y Arenales, Retiro
(4829 7504/www.mrecic.gov.ar).
Subte C, San Martín/10, 17, 152 bus.*
Open 9am-6pm Mon-Fri.
Map p325 H11.

The public face of the government
arm responsible for international
business relations.

Dirección Nacional
de Migraciones

*Avenida Antártida Argentina 1355,
Dársena Norte, Retiro (4317 0200/
www.mininterior.gov.ar). Subte C,
Retiro/7, 9, 92, 100 bus.* **Open**
7.30am-1.30pm Mon-Fri.
Map p325 G12.
For entry visas, student permits and
work permits. Three-month business
visas are also issued here.

Consumer

Dirección General de
Defensa y Protección
al Consumidor

*Esmeralda 340, entre Corrientes y
Sarmiento, Microcentro (5382 6234/
www.buenosaires.gov.ar). Subte B,
Florida/6, 26, 93, 130, 152 bus.*
Open 9am-5pm Mon-Fri; 9am-1pm
Sat. **Map** p325 F10.
Receives and investigates consumer
complaints and gives advice on what
rights and actions are available to
consumers (including tourists).

Customs

Entering Argentina from
overseas you can bring in
the following without paying
import duties: 2 litres of
alcoholic drinks, 400
cigarettes, 5kg of foodstuffs,
100ml of perfume. If entering
from a neighbouring country,
these quantities are halved.

If travelling to the United
Kingdom, you're allowed to
bring back 200 cigarettes,
2 litres of wine, 1 litre of spirits
and 60ml of perfume free of
charge. Goods totalling up to
US$800 are duty-free are
allowed to the US.

Disabled

Getting around

BA is not an easy city for those
with mobility problems to get
around. Pavements are in bad
condition and there are often
no drop-kerbs – or if there are,
people will have parked in
front of them. Using the Subte
is practically impossible, as

few stations have lift access. An increasing number of *colectivos* (city buses) are *super-bajo* (ultra-low), and just about accessible for accompanied wheelchair users. Radio taxis and *remises* do what they can but are not specially equipped, and many lack the space to stash a wheelchair. There are several companies that specialise in transport and trips for disabled passengers.

Movidisc

4328 6921/15 5247 6571 mobile/www.movidisc-web.com.ar. Specially adapted vans for wheelchair users. City tours also available with advance booking.

QRV – Transportes Especiales

4306 6635/mobile 15 5248 4423. Adapted minibuses for wheelchair users, with microphones and guides. AR$25 for a standard journey within the capital; call to check prices for city tours. Book 24 hours ahead.

Useful contacts

Red de Discapacidad (REDI)

4706 2769/www.rumbos.org.ar. Eduardo Joly, a sociologist who has also studied tourism, is a wheelchair user and director of this disabled persons' network, which can provide advice and information in Spanish.

Drugs

Penalties for drug offences, even possession of small amounts, are severe in Argentina, and include lengthy imprisonment in local jails.

Electricity

Electricity in Argentina runs on 220 volts. Sockets take either two- or three-pronged European-style plugs. To use US electrical appliances, you'll need a transformer (*transformador*) and an adaptor (*adaptador*); for UK appliances an adaptor only is required. Both can be purchased in hardware stores (*ferreterías*) all over town. Power cuts are occasional.

Embassies & consulates

Australian Embassy & Consulate

Villanueva 1400, entre Zabala y Teodoro García, Palermo (4779 3500/www.argentina.embassy. gov.au). Bus 59, 63, 67, 152, 194. **Open** 8.30am-12.30pm, 1.30-5.30pm Mon-Thur; 8.30am-1.30pm Fri. **Map** p329 Q8.

British Embassy & Consulate

Luis Agote 2412, entre Libertador y Las Heras, Recoleta (4808 2200/ www.britain.org.ar). Bus 37, 60, 102. **Open** *Jan, Feb* 8.45am-2.30pm Mon-Thur; 8.45am-2pm Fri. *Mar-Dec* 8.45am-5.30pm Mon-Thur; 8.45am-2pm Fri. **Map** p326 J11.

Canadian Embassy & Consulate

Tagle 2828, entre Figueroa Alcorta y Juez Tedín, Recoleta (4808 1000/ www.international.gc.ca/argentina). Bus 67, 130. **Open** 8.30am-12.30pm, 1.30-5.30pm Mon-Thur; 8.30am-2pm Fri. **Map** p326 K11.

Irish Embassy

6th Floor, Avenida del Libertador 1068, entre Ayachucho y Callao, Recoleta (5787 0801). Bus 61, 62, 93. **Open** 9.30am-1pm Mon-Fri. **Map** p326 I12.

New Zealand Embassy & Consulate

5th Floor, Carlos Pellegrini 1427, entre Arroyo y Posadas, Retiro (4328 0747/www.nzembassy.com). Subte C, Retiro/10, 59, 130 bus. **Open** 9am-1pm, 2-5.30pm Mon-Thur; 9am-1pm Fri. **Map** p325 H11.

United States Embassy & Consulate

Avenida Colombia 4300, entre Sarmiento y Cerviño, Palermo (5777 4533/http://buenosaires. usembassy.gov). Subte D, Plaza Italia/37, 67, 130 bus. **Open** *Visas* 7.30am-12.30pm Mon-Fri by appointment only. *Information* 8am-noon Mon-Fri. **Map** p327 M10.

Emergencies

All available 24 hours daily.

Fire

100. For the fire brigade you can also call 4383 2222, 4304 2222 and 4381 2222.

Police

101. Also 4370 5911 in an emergency. For tourist crime *see p303.*

Defensa Civil

103 or 4956 2110. For gas leaks, power cuts, floods and other major catastrophes.

Medical emergencies

107. To call an ambulance. For non-emergencies *see below,* **Health,** and for information on **Hospitals** and **Helplines,** *see p300.*

Emergencies at sea

106.

Gay & lesbian

For more information on advisory and cultural centres, as well as gay accommodation options, *see pp217-22* **Gay & Lesbian.** For HIV/AIDS advice and info, *see below* **Health.** The **Centro Cultural Ricardo Rojas** has a library and archive devoted to gay issues; *see p262.*

Grupo Nexo

4374 4484/www.nexo.org. Useful multifaceted cultural centre, offering counselling, information and free HIV tests.

Health

No vaccinations are required for BA and the city's tap water is drinkable. Argentina doesn't have reciprocal healthcare agreements with any other countries, so take out your own medical insurance policy.

Accident & emergency

In case of poisoning, call the **Centro de Intoxicaciones del Hospital Ricardo Gutierrez** on 4962 6666.

Ambulances are provided by **SAME** (Sistema de Atención Médica de Emergencia) – call 4923 1051 or 107. The specialist burns hospital, the **Hospital de Quemadas,** is at Avenida Pedro Goyena No.369, Caballito (4923 3022 or emergencies 4923 4082).

Directory

Hospital Británico

*Pedriel 74, entre Finnochietto y
Caseros, Barracas (4309 6400/6500).
Bus 59, 67, 100.* **Map** p324 D7.
Your best bet as an English speaker
is this private, modern hospital. An
appointment can be made to see an
English-speaking doctor at a cost of
AR$45. The hospital has several
locations; the most central is in
Barrio Norte at Marcelo T de Alvear
1573 (4812 0048/49).

Hospital de Clínicas
José de San Martín

*Avenida Córdoba 2351, entre
Uriburu y Azcuénaga, Barrio Norte
(5950 8000). Bus 29, 61, 101, 111.*
Map p326 I9.
Buenos Aires' largest, most
centrally located public hospital.
It has departments for all specialities
and the city's main accident and
emergency unit. If you don't have
insurance, come here.

Hospital de Niños Dr
Ricardo Gutiérrez

*Sánchez de Bustamante 1330,
y Paraguay, Barrio Norte (4962
9232/9229). Bus 29, 92, 111,
128.* **Map** p326 K9.
Public paediatric hospital.

Contraception &
abortion

Public hospitals will supply
the contraceptive pill after an
appointment with a doctor.
Alternatively, condom
machines are found in the
toilets of most bars, clubs
and restaurants and are
available over the counter
in pharmacies. Abortion is
illegal in Argentina.

Dentists

For emergency dental
treatment, call the Servicio
de Urgencias at 4964 1259.

Drs Gustavo &
Marisol Telo

*12th floor, Office G, Santa Fe 2227
(4828 0821/mobile 15 5400 5999
/www.dental-argentina.com.ar). Subte
D, Pueyrredón/39, 152 bus.* **Open**
10am-5pm Mon, Tue, Thur, Fri. **No
credit cards.**
Excellent surgery close to the city
centre. Services include cleaning,
cosmetic treatment, emergency care,
dental implants, crown and bridges –
all at reasonable rates. English spoken.

Hospital Municipal de
Odontología Infantil

*Pedro de Mendoza 1795, entre
Palos y M Rodríguez, La Boca (4301
4834). Bus 29, 53, 64, 152.*
Map p324 A9.
24-hour dental attention for children.

Dr José Zysmilich

*1st Floor, Apt C, Salguero 1108,
entre Córdoba y Cabrera, Palermo
Viejo (4865 2322). Bus 26, 36, 92,
128.* **Open** 3-7pm Mon, Wed, Fri.
Map p322 K5.
English-speaking private dentist:
a member of the American
Dental Association.

Servicio de Urgencias

*Marcelo T de Alvear 2146, entre
Junín y Uriburu, Barrio Norte
(4964 1259). Subte D, Facultad de
Medicina/12, 39, 60, 111, 152 bus.*
Map p326 I9.
Foreigners are welcome at this
university dental faculty but are
usually asked to pay a small fee of
between AR$8 and AR$15.

Hospitals

For general medical needs,
you can see a doctor at the
hospitals listed in **Accident
& emergency,** *p299.*

Opticians

For a list of opticians, *see
p203,* **Shops & services.**

Pharmacies

There are always some
pharmacies open all night.
Go to the nearest; if it's not
open, it will post details of
the nearest *farmacia de turno.*
Mega-pharmacy Farmacity has
24-hour branches across the
city – for details, *see p203.*

STDs, HIV & AIDS

Gay information service **Nexo**
(*see p299*) offer free HIV tests
and a phoneline for people who
are HIV-positive: Línea Positiva
4374 4484.

Pregunte Sida

0800 333 3444. **Open** 9am-10pm
Mon-Fri; 9am-4pm Sat, Sun.
Free HIV/AIDS helpline. Also advice
on general sexual health issues and
where to go for testing or treatment.

Helplines

Although few helplines have
English-speaking staff, most
will find someone with at least
a few words – be ready with
your phone number in Spanish
in case they need to call back.

Alcohólicos Anónimos

4788 6646.
English-speaking groups meet
Monday to Friday at 7pm in the
Evangelical Methodist Church,
Corrientes 718, Microcentro.

Centro de Orientación
a la Víctima

4801 4444/8146.
Victim support.

Comunidad
Terapéutica El Reparo

4664 6641/www.elreparo.org.ar.
24-hour support for the drug
dependent. Some English spoken.

Teleamigo

4304 0061.
Phone support for people in crisis.

ID

By law everyone must carry
photo ID. Checks are rare, but
if you do get pulled over, you
will be expected to show at
least a copy of your passport
or (photo) driving licence.
Depending on how youthful
you look, you may also be
asked to produce ID to get into
some bars and clubs.

Insurance

Argentina is not covered by
any reciprocal health insurance
schemes, so visitors from all
countries are advised to buy
comprehensive private
insurance before they travel.

Internet

Downtown and in the more
affluent neighbourhoods you'll
rarely be more than a block
away from an internet café.
Most have high-speed
connections for about AR$2.50
an hour. *Locutorios* (call
centres) also offer internet, but

Directory

at a slightly higher rate. Wireless access is popular in BA, and you'll be able to connect for free in most hotels as well as many cafés and bars; look for the Wi-Fi signs.

For useful websites, *see p309*, **Further Reference**.

Language

Spanish is spoken in Buenos Aires, though it differs from the language you'll hear in Spain in a few key aspects. For the basics *see p307*, and if you're interested in taking classes *see p304*, **Study**.

Legal help

For legal help, contact your consulate or embassy (*see p299*) in the first instance.

Libraries

Buenos Aires has no major English-language lending library, but the **Biblioteca Nacional** (National Library) has a reasonable reference section and the Hemeroteca in the basement is a good resource for newspapers, magazines and leaflets.

Lost property

Keep a close eye on your belongings at all times. In general, if you've lost it, forget about it. Inside the airports, try contacting the National Aeronautical Police to see if some honest soul has handed in your property: Ezeiza, 4480 2327/4314 6984, Aeroparque, 4514 1541. If you've lost something on public transport, call the operator (*see p295*), who should store lost property – but don't hold your breath.

This is another good reason to take radio taxis, as you can call the company if you leave something in a cab. It's always worth trying to make a mental note of your cab number for just such an eventuality.

Media

Magazines

El Amante del Cine
Reviews of international films and interviews with local filmmakers.

Gente
The bestselling weekly guide to the BA *beau monde*, with a straight-faced, almost reverential take on celebrity and media culture.

Los Inrockuptibles
Funky monthly mag with the word on BA's music scene and gig listings.

Noticias
Popular news weekly, juxtaposing provocative investigative specials and society nonsense.

Time Out Buenos Aires for Visitors
You've bought the book so, ahem, why not pick up the magazine as well? Published December and July and available in all good bookshops and downtown *kioscos*.

Veintitres
Local loudmouth celeb journo Jorge Lanata's anti-establishment organ.

Newspapers

Buenos Aires Herald
English-language daily, read by expats and Argentinians. Sunday edition includes articles from the *New York Times*. The classifieds are a good resource for finding private Spanish teachers.

Clarín
Mass-market daily that's fat with both local and international news. Somehow manages to be high-, middle- and low-brow at the same time and so sells loads.

La Nación
BA's grand old daily, beloved of the safe middle classes and conservative on culture, art and lifestyle. Better than *Clarín* for international news. Buy it on Friday for the *Ticket* entertainment listings supplement.

Página 12
Here the word on every article is '*opina*', as every leftie in the city gives his or her opinion on every subject, squeezing in a bit of news here and there. The Sunday cultural supplement *Rádar* is among the best. Also pick it up on a Thursdays for a comprehensive guide to the weekend.

Radio

FM de la Ciudad
92.7FM
Municipal service started in 1990 to ensure that tango, the essential soundtrack to Buenos Aires life, is available all day and all night.

La Radio del Folklore
105.7FM
Get your fix of folky strumming and *gaucho* choirs to help you slow down in the big brash city.

Mega – Puro Rock Nacional
98.3FM
No chat, only music, and *rock nacional* at that. One of the most listened-to stations by young people.

Metrodance
95.1FM
By day, hip variety shows and news; by night and on weekends, even hipper dance and electronic music.

Rock & Pop
95.9FM
Brought *rock nacional* and rock culture in general to the fore. Mario Pergolini's morning show is the soundtrack young office workers wake up to city-wide.

Television

These are the free-to-air channels available in Argentina; most hotels and homes also have cable and satellite channels.

América TV
Shows live football from the Argentinian *primera*, plus soaps and countless late-night talk shows.

Canal 7
The only state-run TV channel, and thus the one that can afford not to play the ratings game. Programming is big on local culture and music.

Canal 9
Sex, scandals, sex, alien abductions and more sex are the hallmarks of BA's lowest of low-brow channels.

Canal 13
The most watched channel with the best series. Good nightly news.

Telefe – Canal 11
Big channel, fronted by big personalities like national treasure Susana Giménez. Also soaps and imports such as *The Simpsons*.

Directory

Money

The Argentinian currency is the peso. After the old system which pegged the peso to the US dollar at 1:1 was abandoned in January 2002, the currency was allowed to float freely and consequently devalue. Its value has since remained largely stable, at AR$3-$3.15 to one US dollar, and AR$6-AR$6.15 to one UK pound. At time of going to press the headline inflation rate stands at a worrying, but hardly cataclysmic, ten per cent per annum.

The peso is divided into centavos. Coins are the silver and yellow-gold one-peso coin, 50, 25, ten and five centavos. Newer 25-centavo coins are silver. Notes come in denominations of 100 (purple), 50 (dark grey), 20 (red), ten (brown), five (green) and two (blue) pesos, and in every kind of condition.

Beware of counterfeit money. There are many fake notes and coins in circulation, so check your change, especially in cabs. False bills are generally easy to detect, as the colours tend to lack the precision of authentic notes and the texture is plasticky. Fake coins (predominantly 50 centavos) are commonplace; they're lighter in both colour and weight than legal tender.

Also avoid the illegal money changers (known as *arbolitos*, or little trees) lining Florida. They are the ones most likely to sting you with fake pesos and a low exchange rate.

ATMs

Most banks have 24-hour ATMs, signalled by a 'Banelco' or 'Link' sign. They distribute pesos only and usually charge a fee (US$1-$5). Some are only for clients of the bank in question, so look for a machine showing the symbol of your card company. If withdrawing large sums, do so discreetly and be careful picking a cab. Also, some banks only allow you to withdraw AR$320 per transaction.

Banks

It's extremely difficult to open an Argentinian bank account if you are a foreigner. Banks ask for endless paperwork, including wage slips and a local ID. To compound the situation, most won't accept a transfer unless you have an account. To receive money, use Forexcambio, who can also cash foreign cheques or bankers' drafts, or Western Union. Charges vary according to the state of the market and the transfer amount, but average around US$50.

Forexcambio

Marcelo T de Alvear 540, entre Florida y San Martín, Retiro (4010 2000/www.forexar.com.ar). Subte C, San Martín/26, 61, 93, 152 bus. **Open** 10am-3pm Mon-Fri. **Map** p325 G12.

Western Union

Córdoba 975, entre Suipacha y Carlos Pellegrini, Microcentro (freephone 0800 800 3030/www. westernunion.com). Subte C, Lavalle/10, 59, 111 bus. **Open** 9am-8pm Mon-Fri. **Map** p325 G11.

Travellers' cheques & bureaux de change

Travellers' cheques are often refused by businesses and can be difficult and expensive to change in banks. There are various bureaux de change around the intersection of Sarmiento and Reconquista streets that will change them. Commission is usually around two per cent, with a minimum charge of US$5. Usual opening hours are 9am-6pm.

American Express

Arenales 707, y Maipú, Retiro (4310 3000). Subte C, San Martín/10, 17, 70, 152 bus. **Open** 10am-3pm Mon-Fri. **Map** p325 G11.
Will change AmEx travellers' cheques without charge.

Credit cards

Credit cards are accepted in most outlets; photo ID is usually required. Visa (V), MasterCard (MC) and American Express (AmEx) are the most accepted cards. Diners Club (DC) is also valid in a number of places, but check first.

Lost & stolen cards

American Express 0810 5552639.
Diners Club 0810 4442484.
MasterCard 4348 7070.
Visa 4379 3333.

Tax

Local sales tax is called IVA, aka *Impuestos a Valor Agregado*. It's a whopping 21 per cent, though as a rule it's always included on the bill or pricetag. The exception is hotel rates, which are generally listed without IVA in more expensive establishments. However, in our **Where to Stay** chapter (*see pp43-72*) we have quoted all prices with IVA included, so there's no nasty shock on the final bill. To find out how to claim back sales tax on your purchases *see p178*.

Natural hazards

Apart from a volatile economy and some vicious summer mosquitoes, Argentina is largely free of natural hazards. The only blip comes during June to October, when a strong wind from the south – La Sudestada – brings torrential rain and flash flooding to La Boca, Palermo and Belgrano.

Opening hours

Opening hours are extremely variable, but here are some general guidelines:

Banks

Generally open 10am-3pm weekdays, some an open hour earlier or close an hour later.

Bars

Most bars in Buenos Aires don't get busy until after midnight and many are open round the clock. Pubs, or evening bars, open around 6pm for happy hour (known here as 'after office'), or 8pm out of the centre, and most stay open till the crowds thin out.

Business hours

Ordinary office hours are 9am-6pm, with a lunchbreak from 1pm to 2pm.

Post offices

The Correo Central (Central Post Office; *see right*) is open 8am-8pm Mon-Fri and 8am-1pm Sat. Other branch post offices are open weekdays from 9am to 6pm.

Shops

Most malls open 10am-10pm, though there can be one hour's variation. The food court and cinemas stay open after the other shops. Shops on the street tend to open at 9am-10am and close at around 7pm.

Police

Public safety in the capital is the responsibility of the Policía Federal, divided into 53 *comisarías* (at least one per barrio), with a central police station. Tourists needing to report a crime should contact the **Comisaría del Turista**, where English speakers will be able to help. Alternatively you can head to the station in the barrio in which the incident occurred, however we strongly recommend the tourist police as the first port of call. *See p299* for emergency telephone numbers and details.

Comisaría del Turista

Avenida Corrientes 436, entre San Martín y Reconquista, Microcentro (0800 999 2838). Subte B, Florida/ 10, 93, 99 bus. **Open** 24 hrs daily. *Phone lines* 9am-8pm daily. **Map** p325 F11.
English-speaking staff are on hand to help tourists who've been robbed, ripped off or injured.

Departamento Central de Policía

Moreno 1550, entre Luis Sáenz Peña y Virrey Cevallos, Congreso (4370 5800 24hrs). Subte A, Sáenz Peña/39, 64, 86 bus. **Map** p325 F9. This is the central police station, but we still recommend you go to the Comisaría del Turista.

Comisaría 2ª (San Telmo)

Perú 1050, entre Carlos Calvo y Humberto 1°, San Telmo (4361 8054). Bus 24, 30, 126, 152. **Map** p324 D9.

Postal services

Numerous competitors offer postal, courier and express delivery services, but Correo Argentino is still the cheapest for domestic mail. A letter weighing up to 20 grams costs AR$1; from 20 to 150 grams costs AR$4. By airmail, an international letter of up to 20 grams costs AR$4, from 20 to 150 grams is AR$9.50. Expect it to take up to a fortnight to arrive. Registered post (essential for any document of value) costs AR$17 for up to 150 grams nationally, and from AR$19.75 to send a letter of the same weight internationally.

There are Correo Argentino branches throughout the city, *see left* for opening hours, and many larger *locutorios* (call centres) also offer some postal services.

If you want to receive post in Buenos Aires, get it sent directly to your hotel or to a private address if you have contacts here and then cross your fingers: packages and parcels of any value tend to go astray. For couriers and shippers *see p298*. There is a *poste restante* service at the Correo Central; it costs AR$5 to collect each piece of mail, which should be sent to:
Recipient's name,
Lista de Correos,
Correo Central,
Sarmiento 189,
(1003) Capital Federal,
Argentina.

Correo Central

Sarmiento 151, entre Leandro N Alem y Bouchard, Microcentro (4891 9191). Subte B, LN Alem/ 26, 93, 99, 152 bus. **Open** 8am-8pm Mon-Fri; 8am-1pm Sat. **Map** p325 F11.

Religion

Argentina is a secular country; the consitution insists on the separation of church and state and guarantees freedom of worship for citizens. Roman Catholicism is the official state religion, though only about 20 per cent of Argentinians attend church regularly. There are many synagogues in Once, and many other evangelical gatherings that occur in converted stores around BA. Here are a few addresses of places of worship around the city. For a more complete listing, check the local *Yellow Pages* (www.paginasamarillas. com.ar), look under 'Iglesias - Parroquias y Templos Religiosos'.

Anglican

Catedral Anglicana de San Juan Bautista *25 de Mayo 282, y Sarmiento, Microcentro (4342 4618). Bus 126, 130, 146, 152.* **Services** *English* 9.30am Sun. *Spanish* 11am Sun. **Map** p325 F11.

Buddhist

Templo Budista Honpa-Hongwanji *Sarandí 951, entre Carlos Calvo y Estados Unidos, San Cristobal (4941 0262). Subte E, Entre Ríos/12, 37, 126, 168 bus.* **Service** 5pm Sun. **Map** p325 F7.

Roman Catholic

Catedral Metropolitana *Avenida Rivadavia 412, y San Martín, Microcentro (4331 2845). Subte A, Plaza de Mayo or D, Catedral or E, Bolívar/24, 29, 64, 86 bus.* **Services** Spanish only 9am, 11am, 12.30pm, 6pm Mon-Fri; 11am, 6pm Sat; 11am, noon, 1pm, 6pm Sun. **Map** p325 F10.

Jewish

Gran Templo de la Asociación Comunidad Israelita Sefardí *Camargo 870, entre Gurruchaga y Serrano, Villa Crespo. Subte B, Malabia/15, 24, 57, 106, 110 bus.* **Services** 7.10am, 6.45pm Mon-Fri; 9am, 5.30pm Sat; 8am, 6.30pm Sun. **Map** p323 M3.

Muslim

Centro Islámico Ray Fahd
*Avenida Bullrich 55, y Libertador,
Palermo (4899 0201). Subte D,
Palermo/39, 60, 64, 130, 152
bus.* **Map** p327 N10.

Presbyterian

**Presbyterian Scottish Church of
Saint Andrew** *Avenida Belgrano
579, entre Bolívar y Perú, Monserrat
(4331 0308). Subte E, Piedras/24, 29,
86, 126 bus.* **Services** *English* 10am
Sun. *Spanish* 11.30am Sun.
Map p325 E10.

Safety

Continued economic hardship
in Buenos Aires has been
linked to a rise in street crime,
but with a little common sense
and a few basic precautions,
visitors should be able to avoid
any trouble. Avoid pulling out a
wallet stacked with bills, and
try not to flash expensive
jewellery and cameras too
obviously. Keep an eye on
belongings on public transport
and always use radio taxis.
Check your notes carefully, as
forgeries abound. One trick is
for taxi drivers to accept your
hundred peso bill, switch it
surreptitiously, and hand you
back a forged bill saying they
can't change your money.

Remember that while most
central areas are safe, more care
should be taken in the edgier
barrios of Constitución and La
Boca. Touristy San Telmo and
leafy Palermo can lull you into
a false sense of security, and
although violent crime is rare,
bag snatching, sadly, is not. If
you are actually threatened,
hand over your goods calmly:
BA has a gun problem. Football
games can also be dodgy.

Street aggression is most
commonly of the verbal kind,
especially for women. The best
response is to ignore someone –
if he's really annoying, walk
into a shop to lose him.

If you need to report a crime,
contact the **Comisaría del
Turista** (*see p303*) where
knowledgeable English-
speaking staff are on hand.

Smoking

Legislation in 2006 prohibited
smoking in all public
buildings, restaurants, bars,
shops and clubs, as well as on
public transport. Larger eating
and watering holes may have a
separate smokers' area, but in
general you'll have to head
outside for a fag, and in most
late-night bars and clubs the
ban is flagrantly ignored.
Despite an ambitious effort to
change public opinion, the
bottom line remains the same,
nicotine is in.

Study

Language classes

Every year new institutes
open, offering Spanish for
foreigners. There are huge
ranges in price and quality.

To organise an *intercambio*
or language exchange, check
noticeboards in universities.
There are usually lots of
willing partners. Institutes and
private teachers advertise in
the *Buenos Aires Herald*.

Ayres de Español

*Gurruchaga 1851, entre Costa Rica y
Nicaragua, Palermo Viejo (4834
6340/www.ayresdespanol.com.ar).
Subte D, Plaza Italia/36, 39, 55, 93,
160 bus.* **Open** 9am-6pm Mon-Fri.
Rates *Group classes* AR$40 per hr.
Private classes AR$60 per hr. **No
credit cards.** **Map** p323 M5.

Ibero

*Uruguay 150, entre Bartolomé Mitre
y J D Perón, Congreso (5218 0240/
www.iberospanish.com). Subte A,
Sáenz Pena/5, 7, 23, 26, 39, 102 bus.*
Open 9am-6pm Mon-Fri. **Rates**
Group classes US$120 20hrs per wk.
Private classes US$270 20 hrs per wk.
No credit cards. **Map** p325 G10.

UBA – Laboratorio de
Idiomas, Facultad de
Filosofía y Letras

*25 de Mayo 221, entre Perón y
Sarmiento, Centro (4343 5981/
1196/www.idiomas.filo.uba.ar). Bus
126, 130, 146, 152.* **Open** 9am-9pm
Mon-Fri. **Rates** *Group classes* from
AR$619 4hrs per wk for 17 wks or
8hrs per wk for 8 wks. **No credit
cards.** **Map** p325 F11.

Students' unions

FUBA (Federación
Universitaria de
Buenos Aires)

*3rd Floor, Azcuénaga 280, entre
Sarmiento y Perón, Once (4952
8080). Subte A, Alberti/24, 26, 101,
105 bus.* **Open** 9am-8pm Mon-Fri.
Map p326 I8.

Universities

There is both state-run and
private university education
available in Buenos Aires. The
**Universidad de Buenos
Aires** (UBA) is, in general, the
most academically respected.
Study at state-run UBA is free
but you will have to enrole,
usually during the summer
months. Visiting classes would
not be a problem although they
can get very cramped. Private
universities tend to have
greater numbers of classes
throughout the year, and better
facilities. Staff at Argentinian
universities are scandalously
underpaid; many are young
volunteers or assistants.

UBA (Departamento
de Títulos y Planes)

*Uriburu 950, entre Paraguay y
Marcelo T de Alvear, Barrio Norte
(4951 0634 ext 100 or 101). Subte
D, Facultad de Medicina/39, 60, 51,
132, 152, 194 bus.* **Open** noon-4pm
Mon, Thur. **Map** p326 I9.
If you want to study at UBA, contact
this department or go in person to
the Centro Cultural Ricardo Rojas
(*see p262*), which has general
information for the university.

Universidad Argentina
de la Empresa

*Lima 717, entre Independencia y
Chile, San Telmo (4372 5454/ www.
uade.edu.ar). Subte E, Independencia/
17, 59, 67, 105 bus.* **Open** 9am-8pm
Mon-Fri. **Map** p325 E9.
A business school with agreements
with universities in the US, Chile,
Brazil and Germany, among others.

Universidad
de Palermo

*Avenida Córdoba 3501, entre Mario
Bravo y Bulnes, Palermo (4964
4600/www.palermo.edu.ar). Bus 26,
36, 92, 128.* **Open** 9am-8pm Mon-
Fri. **Map** p326 K8.

Useful organisations

www.delestudiante. com
Listings of every university, degree and postgrad offered.

www.studyabroad.com
Information in English on studying around the world; includes Argentina.

Asatej
3rd Floor, Office 320, Florida 835, entre Córdoba y Paraguay, Microcentro (4511 8700/www. asatej.com). Subte B, Florida/10, 26, 93, 130, 152 bus. **Open** 9am-7pm Mon-Fri. **Map** p325 G11.
Student travel agency, with locations across town. ISIC cards issued here.

Telephones

Dialling & codes
All land-line numbers within Buenos Aires begin with either 4, 5 or 6 and consist of eight digits. To call a mobile phone, 15 must be added to the front of an eight-digit number. From overseas, dial your country's international dialling code followed by 54 11 and the eight-digit number. To call mobile phones from overseas, dial 54 9 11 and leave out the 15. To dial overseas from BA, dial 00 followed by the country code and number (Australia 61, Canada 1, Ireland 353, New Zealand 64, UK 44, USA 1).

Useful numbers:
Directory information 110
International operator 000
National operator 19
Repair service 114
Talking clock 113
Telecom/Telefónica commercial services 112
Telelectura 121. This is a free, 24hr service, which tells you the call charges within a billing period.

Call centres
BA is awash with *locutorios* (call centres), generally run by Telefónica or Telecom. Calls cost a few *centavos* more than from a public phone, but for a

seat, air-con and the guarantee that your last coin won't be gobbled, it's worth it. They offer fax services and often net access and post services.

Public phones are coin- or card-operated, sometimes both. Phonecards can be bought from kiosks.

Mobile phones
CDMA/TDMA is the predominant system, though it's cheaper to rent locally than bring your own phone. Most UK cellphones will not work.

Phonerental
San Martín 948, 3rd Floor, entre Paraguay y Marcelo T de Alvear, Retiro (24hr hotline 4311 2933/ www.phonerental.com.ar). Subte C, San Martín/10, 93, 30, 152 bus. **Open** 9am-6pm Mon-Fri. **Map** p325 G11.
Free phone rental, AR$1.25 per min air time charge, no minimum.

Time
The clocks have been known to go back and forward in a rather arbitrary manner, so the following time differences are not set in stone. Energy saving in 2008 means that the clocks in Argentina gain an hour in summer and lose one in winter. Thus, Argentina is three hours behind GMT during the southern hemisphere spring and autumn, two hours behind over the southern summer, and four hours behind GMT during the southern winter. But this may change again.

Tipping
Tips tend to be left in the same quantities as most developed countries. As a rule of thumb, leave 10 to 15 per cent in a bar, restaurant, or for any delivery service; in a cab, just round off the fare. In hotels, bellboys expect AR$1.50-$2 for helping with your bags. Ushers in cinemas expect the same. When checking out, it's normal to leave a small tip for the maids.

Toilets
You're probably more likely to be struck by lightning in BA than to find a clean and functioning public toilet. However, most bars and restaurants – albeit grudgingly – offer evacuatory relief to the public. All shopping centres have clean public toilets. And, of course, bathroom use is one of the few advantages conferred on the world by fast-food outlets.

Tourist information
The tourist board website is www.bue.gov.ar, and has an English version.

These are the official tourist information points:
Abasto de Buenos Aires *Avenida Corrientes y Agüero, Abasto (4959 3507). Subte B, Carlos Gardel/bus 24, 26, 124, 168.* **Open** 11am-9pm daily. **Map** p326 J8.
Florida *Avenida Roque Sáenz Peña y Florida, Microcentro (no phone). Subte D, Catedral/bus 24, 103, 130, 152.* **Open** 9am-6pm Mon-Fri; 10am-3pm Sat. **Map** p325 F10.
Recoleta *Avenida Quintana y Ortiz (no phone). Bus 17, 67, 124, 130.* **Open** 10am-8pm daily. **Map** p326 J11.
Retiro *Terminal de Ómnibus, Avenida Antártida Argentina y Calle 10 (4311 0528). Subte C, Retiro/Bus 92, 130, 152.* **Open** 7.30am-1pm Mon-Sat. **Map** p325 H12.
Puerto Madero *Dique 4, AM de Justo al 200 (4313 0187). Bus 4, 130, 152.* **Open** noon-6pm Mon-Fri; 10am-8pm Sat, Sun. **Map** p325 F12.
San Telmo *Defensa 1250, entre San Juan y Cochabamba (no phone). Bus 29, 64, 86, 130, 152.* **Open** noon-6pm Mon-Fri; 10am-7pm Sat, Sun. **Map** p324 D9.
San Isidro Turístico *Ituzaingó 608, y Libertador, San Isidro (4512 3209). Train Mitre or de la Costa to San Isidro/ 168, 660 bus.* **Open** 8.30-5pm Mon-Fri; 10am-5pm Sat, Sun.
For national tourist info, go to:
Secretaría de Turismo de la Nación *Avenida Santa Fe 883, entre Suipacha y Esmeralda, Retiro (4312 5611/15). Subte C, San Martín/ 59, 111, 132, 152 bus.* **Open** 9am-5pm Mon-Fri. **Map** p325 G11.
Freephone information line (8am-8pm Mon-Fri) 0800 999 2838.

Directory

Visas

Visas are not required by members of the European Community or citizens of the USA and Canada. Immigration grants you a 90-day visa on entry that can be extended by a quick exit out of the country – to Uruguay for example – or via the immigration service for AR$100. The fine for overstaying is AR$50; if you do overstay, arrive at the airport early so you can pay the fine.

More information about longer-stay visas for students or business travellers can be obtained from your nearest Argentinian Embassy.

Weights & measures

Argentina uses the metric system, though a few old measures still stand good in the countryside: horses are measured by *manos* (hands) and distances are sometimes measured by *leguas* (leagues).

When to go

Climate

Summer is December-March, and the winter season is July-October. The proximity to the River Plate and sea-level location make the city humid, so the summer heat and winter chill are felt more acutely.

You'll also hear plenty about a local obsession: *sensación térmica (see p38)*. This isn't the real temperature, but how hot it feels; so prepare yourself for a summer day and being told that it is 44°C (111°F)!

Spring and autumn are ideal times to visit – gorgeous weather and lots going on. At any time of year, be prepared for rain; heavy storms or a day or so of solid downpour are common. For meteorological information within BA, phone 4514 4253.

Public holidays

The following *feriados*, or public holidays, are fixed from year to year:
1 January (New Year's Day); **Jueves Santo** (Thursday before Easter); **Viernes Santo** (Good Friday); **1 May** (Labour Day); **25 May** (May Revolution Day); **9 July** (Independence Day); **8 December** (Day of the Immaculate Conception); **25 December** (Christmas).
For the following, the day of the holiday moves to the Monday before if it falls on a Tuesday or Wednesday, or to the Monday following if it falls Thursday to Sunday:
2 April (Falklands/Malvinas War Veterans Day); **20 June** (Flag Day); **17 August** (San Martin Memorial Day); **12 October** (Columbus Day).

Women

Argentinian men can be macho and flirtatious, but seldom behave agressively, making BA one of the safest cities for female travellers in Latin America.

A 24-hour hotline, 0800 666 8537, assists women in violent situations, with a network of organisations offering counselling and legal advice. The **Dirección General de la Mujer** (7th Floor, Carlos Pellegrini 211, Microcentro, 4393 6466) is a women's welfare commission.

Working in BA

Finding work as an English teacher is not difficult, but opportunities dry up from December to February when everyone goes on holiday. Pay averages AR$18-$30 an hour. It is best to contact an institute that either has public classes or offers lessons to companies in BA. Income can fluctuate due to class cancellations.

Apart from mixing cocktails or bussing tables, most other job opportunities are published in the *Buenos Aires Herald*.

Work permits

Most foreigners work on tourist visas, hopping to Uruguay and back every three months, though, strictly speaking, it's illegal.

To obtain a work permit, you need translated birth, police and medical certificates, sponsorship from an employer, bags of patience and at least AR$400. To facilitate the procedure, *escribanos* (notaries) will act on your behalf for a fee of AR$300-$500. Once your papers are in order, you have to exit the country in order to make the official application. Permits are valid for a year; renewal costs another AR$200.

Weather report

Month	Average high	Average low
January	30.4°C (87°F)	20.4°C (69°F)
February	28.7°C (84°F)	19.4°C (67°F)
March	26.4°C (80°F)	17°C (63°F)
April	22.7°C (73°F)	13.7°C (57°F)
May	19°C (66°F)	10.3°C (51°F)
June	15.6°C (60°F)	7.6°C (46°F)
July	14.9°C (59°F)	7.4°C (45°F)
August	17.3°C (63°F)	8.9°C (48°F)
September	18.9°C (66°F)	9.9°C (50°F)
October	22.5°C (73°F)	13°C (55°F)
November	25.3°C (78°F)	15.9°C (61°F)
December	28.1°C (83°F)	18.4°C (65°F)

Directory

Language & Vocabulary

Porteños living and working in tourist areas usually speak some English and generally welcome the opportunity to practise it with foreigners. However, a bit of Spanish goes a long way, and making the effort to use even a few phrases will be greatly appreciated and respected.

As in other Latin languages, there is more than one form of the second person (you) to be used according to the formality or informality of the situation. The most polite form is *usted*, and though it's not used among young people, it may be safer for a foreigner to err on the side of politeness. The local variant of the informal, the *voseo*, differs from the *tú* that you may know from European Spanish. Both forms are given here, *usted* first, then *vos*.

Pronunciation

Spanish is easier than some languages to get a basic grasp of, as pronunciation is largely phonetic. Look at the word and pronounce every letter, and the chances are you will be understood. As a rule, stress in a word falls on the penultimate syllable, otherwise an accent indicates stress. Accents are omitted on capital letters, though still pronounced. The key to learning Argentinian Spanish is to master the correct pronunciation of a few letters and vowels.

Vowels

Each vowel is pronounced separately and consistently, except in certain vowel combinations known as diphthongs, where they combine as a single syllable. There are strong vowels: a, e and o; and weak vowels: i and u. Two weak vowels, as in *ruido* (noise), or one strong and one weak, as in *piel* (skin), form a diphthong. Two strong vowels next to each other are pronounced as separate syllables (as in *poeta*, poet).

a is pronounced like the **a** in apple.
e is pronounced like the **a** in say.
i is pronounced like the **ee** in beet.
o is pronounced like the **o** in top.
u is pronounced like the **oo** in mood.
y is usually a consonant, except when it is alone or at the end of the word, in which case it is pronounced like the Spanish i.

Consonants

Pronunciation of the letters f, k, l, n, p, q, s and t is similar to English. y and ll are generally pronounced like the French *'je'*, in contrast to the European Spanish pronunciation. ch and ll have separate dictionary entries. ch is pronounced as in the English chair.
b is pronounced like its English equivalent, and is not distinguishable from the letter v. Both are referred to as **be** as in English bet. b is **long b** (called *b larga* in Spanish), v is known as **short b** (*b corta*).
c is pronounced like the **s** in sea when before **e** or **i** and like the English **k** in all others.
g is pronounced like a guttural English **h** like the **ch** in loch when before **e** and **i** and as a hard **g** like **g** in goat otherwise.
h at the beginning of a word is silent.
j is also pronounced like a guttural English **h** and the letter is referred to as **jota** as in English **h**otter.
ñ is the letter **n** with a tilde and is pronounced like **ni** in English onion.
r is pronounced like the English **r** but is rolled at the beginning of a word, and rr is pronounced like the English **r** but is strongly rolled.
x is pronounced like the **x** in taxi in most cases, although in some it sounds like the Spanish **j**, for instance in Xavier.

Basics

hello *hola*
good morning *buenos días*
good afternoon *buenas tardes*
good evening/night *buenas noches*
OK *está bien*
yes *sí*
no *no*
maybe *tal vez/quizá(s)*
how are you? *¿cómo le va?* or *¿cómo le va?*

how's it going? *¿cómo anda?* or *¿cómo andás?*
Sir/Mr *Señor*; **Madam/Mrs** *Señora*
please *por favor*
thanks *gracias*; **thank you very much** *muchas gracias*
you're welcome *de nada*
sorry *perdón*
excuse me *permiso*
do you speak English? *¿habla inglés?* or *¿hablás inglés?*
I don't speak Spanish *no hablo castellano*
I don't understand *no entiendo*
speak more slowly, please *hable más despacio, por favor* or *habla más despacio, por favor*
leave me alone (quite forceful) *¡déjeme!* or *¡déjame!*
have you got change? *¿tiene cambio?* or *¿tenés cambio?*
there is/there isn't *hay/no hay*
good/well *bien*
bad/badly *mal*
small *pequeño/chico*
big *grande*
beautiful *hermoso/lindo*
a bit *un poco*; **a lot/very** *mucho*
with *con*; **without** *sin*
also *también*
this *este*; **that** *ese*
and *y*; **or** *o*
because *porque*; **if** *si*
what? *¿qué?*; **who?** *¿quién?*; **when?** *¿cuándo?*; **which?** *¿cuál?*; **why?** *¿por qué?*; **how?** *¿cómo?*; **where?** *¿dónde?*;
where to? *¿hacia dónde?*
where from? *¿de dónde?*
where are you from? *¿de dónde es?* or *¿de dónde sos?*
I am English *soy inglés* (man) or *inglesa* (woman); **Irish** *irlandés*; **American** *americano/ norteamericano/estadounidense*; **Canadian** *canadiense*; **Australian** *australiano*; **a New Zealander** *neocelandés*
at what time/when? *¿a qué hora?/¿cuándo?*
forbidden *prohibido*
out of order *no funciona*
bank *banco*
post office *correo*
stamp *estampilla*

Emergencies

Help! *¡auxilio! ¡ayuda!*
I'm sick *estoy enfermo*
I need a doctor/policeman/ hospital *necesito un médico/un policía/un hospital*
there's a fire! *¡hay un incendio!*

On the phone

hello *hola*
who's calling? *¿quién habla?*
hold the line *espere en línea*

Getting around

airport *aeropuerto*
station *estación*
train *tren*
ticket *boleto*
single *ida*
return *ida y vuelta*
platform *plataforma/andén*
bus/coach station *terminal de colectivos/omnibús/micros*
entrance *entrada*
exit *salida*
left *izquierda*
right *derecha*
straight on *derecho*
street *calle*; avenue *avenida*;
motorway *autopista*
street map *mapa callejero*
road map *mapa carretero*
no parking *prohibido estacionar*
toll *peaje*
speed limit *límite de velocidad*
petrol *nafta*; unleaded *sin plomo*

Sightseeing

museum *museo*
church *iglesia*
exhibition *exhibición*
ticket *boleto*
open *abierto*
closed *cerrado*
free *gratis*
reduced *rebajado/con descuento*
except Sunday *excepto los domingos*

Accommodation

hotel *hotel*; bed & breakfast *pensión con desayuno*
do you have a room (for this evening/for two people)? *¿tiene una habitación (para esta noche/para dos personas)?*
no vacancy *completo/no hay habitación libre*; vacancy *desocupado/vacante*
room *habitación*
bed *cama*; double bed *cama matrimonial*
a room with twin beds *una habitación con dos camas*
a room with a bathroom/shower *una habitación con baño/ducha*
breakfast *desayuno*; included *incluido*
lift *ascensor*
air-conditioned *con aire acondicionado*

Shopping

I would like... *me gustaría...*
Is there a/are there any? *¿hay/habrá?*
how much? *¿cuánto?*
how many? *¿cuántos?*
expensive *caro*
cheap *barato*

with VAT *con IVA* (21 per cent valued added tax)
without VAT *sin IVA*
what size? *¿qué talle?*
can I try it on? *¿me lo puedo probar?*

Numbers

0 *cero*
1 *uno*
2 *dos*
3 *tres*
4 *cuatro*
5 *cinco*
6 *seis*
7 *siete*
8 *ocho*
9 *nueve*
10 *diez*
11 *once*; 12 *doce*; 13 *trece*; 14 *catorce*; 15 *quince*; 16 *dieciséis*; 17 *dieciete*; 18 *dieciocho*; 19 *diecinueve*; 20 *veinte*; 21 *veintiuno*; 22 *veintidós*
30 *treinta*
40 *cuarenta*
50 *cincuenta*
60 *sesenta*
70 *setenta*
80 *ochenta*
90 *noventa*
100 *cien*
1,000 *mil*
1,000,000 *un millón*

Days, months & seasons

morning *la mañana*
noon *mediodía*;
afternoon/evening *la tarde*
night *la noche*
Monday *lunes*
Tuesday *martes*
Wednesday *miércoles*
Thursday *jueves*
Friday *viernes*
Saturday *sábado*
Sunday *domingo*
January *enero*; February *febrero*; March *marzo*; April *abril*; May *mayo*; June *junio*; July *julio*; August *agosto*; September *septiembre*; October *octubre*; November *noviembre*; December *diciembre*
spring *primavera*
summer *verano*
autumn/fall *otoño*
winter *invierno*

Others

Argentina is Spanish-speaking. But as anyone arriving from Spain or Mexico can attest, the expressive, Italian-laced street slang of Buenos Aires known as *lunfardo*, can, at times, make communicating a confusing if not comical experience.

Talking among friends, *porteños* will start every few sentences with 'che' ('hey, you' or 'mate') in the monotonous way Southern California skateboarders say 'dude'. Of course, the most famous 'che', and everybody's buddy, was Ernesto 'Che' Guevara.

The real fun begins, though, when you start sifting through the more than 1,000 *lunfardo* words and expressions with which *porteños* liven up even the most mundane conversation. Many of them have their origins in the tango underworld at the beginning of the 20th century, but now are used even by presidents to get messages across in a typically straight-shooting manner.

A few choice words or expressions you might hear only in Argentina (and Uruguay) include: *laburo* (work), *piola* (cool), *cana* (police, jail), *chabón* (man, guy), *mina* (girl/chick), *faso* or *pucho* (cigarette), *chamuyar* (sweet talk, bullshit), *chapita* (crazy), *limado* (incapacitated by drugs), *birra* (beer), *bocha* (large quantity, as in money). Although many of the words have a macho connotation, as in *boludo* or *pelotudo* (big balls, used as an insult or to kid a friend), they also, illogically, can take a feminine form as in *boluda* or *pelotuda*.

Some local terms are so out of whack with traditional Spanish that using them incorrectly runs a risk of public ridicule. For example, in Mexico when you ask for a *paja*, you'd be given a straw, whereas to do the same in Argentina would be to confess you want a wank. Meanwhile, the Spanish verb *coger* (to take, or catch, as in a bus) means to fuck in Buenos Aires, inappropriate no matter what you think of public transport. Better to *tomar* a bus instead.

Further Reference

Books

Non-fiction

Jimmy Burns *The Land That Lost Its Heroes: Argentina, the Falklands, and Alfonsín* The essential analysis of *that* conflict.
S Collier, A Cooper, MS Azzi and **R Martin** *¡Tango!* Currently the definitive guide to tango in English, lavishly illustrated.
Ronald Dworkin (introduction) *Nunca Más: The Report of the Argentine National Commission on the Disappeared* Awful but necessary to read, the accounts of torture and murder perpetrated by the 1976-83 dictatorship.
Robert Farris Thompson *Tango: the Art History of Love* In this impassioned attempt to challenge the assumption that tango is a white European musical form, Thompson traces the aetiology of those twisting thighs back to sub-Saharan Africa.
Miranda France *Bad Times in Buenos Aires: A Writer's Adventures in Argentina* Insightful travelogue that has fun with the big Argentinian myths: shrinks, sex and machismo.
Uki Goñi *The Real Odessa* How Perón helped his Nazi mates find homes in Argentina after the war.
Diego Armando Maradona *El Diego* In Spanish – the best No.10, in his own inimitable words.
Gabriela Nouzeille and **Graciela Montaldo** (eds) *The Argentina Reader* Great collection of primary texts from 16th-century journals to sociological analyses of soccer.
VS Naipaul *The Return of Eva Perón* Old-style travel writing, full of sharp political observations on Argentina in the 1970s.
Richard W Slatta *Gauchos and the Vanishing Frontier* Puts the cowboys in their historical context.
Jason Wilson *Buenos Aires: A Cultural and Literary Companion* Open your eyes to the roots and remains of literary greats and their influence on the city.

Literature

Jorge Luis Borges *Selected Poems* Buenos Aires conjured up through the exquisitely crafted words of Argentina's literary hero.
Julio Cortázar *Hopscotch* The king of experiment's masterpiece jumps between BA and Paris.
Graham Greene *The Honorary Consul* Captures the conflicting currents of northern Argentinian society in the 1970s.

José Hernández *Martín Fierro* Epic 19th-century poem following the hoof prints of a persecuted gaucho.
Alejandro López *Die Lady Die* Camp, crossdressing and cumbia dominate this picaresque tale of a Ricky-Martin obssessed provincial girl let loose in big, bad BA.
Tomás Eloy Martínez *Santa Evita* A gripping tale of the afterlife of Eva Perón's corpse. Brilliantly revealing on the blurred boundaries between history and fiction in Argentina.
Manuel Vázquez Montalbán *The Buenos Aires Quintet* Detective Pepe Carvalho tries to find a relative in the city of the disappeared.
Ernesto Sábato *The Tunnel* The definitive existentialist portrait of Buenos Aires, with plenty of gloom and urban alienation.
Domingo Faustino Sarmiento *Facundo: Or, Civilization and Barbarism* A subjective assessment of the country during the era of Rosas and the provincial *caudillos*.

Film

Alejandro Agresti *Buenos Aires viceversa* Earthy but plot-driven Ken Loach-like work from one of the best young film directors around.
Tristán Bauer *Iluminados por el fuego* Award-winning drama about a Falklands War veteran who returns to the islands after one of his combat buddies commits suicide.
Fabián Belinsky *Nueve reinas* Two con-artists try to make a fast buck on the streets of Buenos Aires.
Daniel Burman *Derecho de familia* Comedy drama about a thirtysomething *porteño* coming to terms with the trials of fatherhood.
Adrián Caetano and **Bruno Stagnaro** *Pizza, birra, faso* Down and out in Buenos Aires with a gang of street urchins.
Juan Carlos Desanzo *Eva Perón* Esther Goris and Victor Laplace star in this local, no-frills biopic.
Lucrecia Martel *La niña santa* The story of the sexual awakening of a 16-year-old Catholic choir girl. *La Ciénaga* A disturbing domestic drama set in Salta province.
Alan Parker *Evita* Madonna, Antonio Banderas and Jimmy Nail… go on, you know you want to.
John Reinhardt *El día que me quieras* A 1935 black-and-white classic: Gardel goes to Hollywood.
Carlos Sorin *Bombón el perro* A warm, deadpan take on the everyday foibles of the human condition.
Damián Szifrón *Tiempo de valientes* A shrink turns unlikely hero in an amusing tale of police corruption.

Music

Bajofondo Tango Club This eponymous album brilliantly fuses electronic beats with tango classics.
Charly García *Piano Bar* A solo work, considered by many to be the *porteño* rock icon's best.
Carlos Gardel *20 Grandes Exitos* An absolute gem; the voice still comes through as the finest in tango and every track is a classic.
León Gieco *De Ushuaia a La Quiaca* A rocker's anthropological adventure in regional folk music.
Manal *Manal* The first, and perhaps, best blues disc in Spanish.
Daniel Melingo *Tangos Bajos* Tom Waits meets the tango traditions of Edmundo Rivero.
Miranda *Sin restricciones* The album that catapulted the masters of catchy pop into the big time in 2005.
Astor Piazzolla *Buenos Aires: Zero Hour* Late, subtle, stirring tango from the postmodern maestro.
Soda Stereo *Canción Animal* Finest hour from the stadium-filling trio who conquered Latin America.
Mercedes Sosa *Mujeres argentinas* The young voice of 'la Sosa'. Songs like 'Juana Azurduy' made history.
Sui Generis *Obras Cumbres* A double album of rock-folk tracks from the legendary teaming of Charly Garcia and Nito Mestre.
Carlos Libedinsky *Narcotango* Sexier than the Gotan Project, *tango electrónica* for dancers, dark bars and horizontal coupling too.
Yerba Brava *Corriendo la coneja* One of the best *cumbia villera* albums – rude, lewd, crude and shrewd.
Atahualpa Yupanqui *El payador perseguido* Master work from the folk poet and guitarist.

Websites

www.argentinesoccer.com Everything you need to know about the national obsession.
www.bue.gov.ar The official city government's site, includes details of cultural events.
www.whatsupbuenosaires.com Hip recommendations for eating, shopping, drinking and clubbing.
www.cinenacional.com Spanish-only Argentinian cinema site.
www.guiaoleo.com.ar Listings for almost every restaurant in town.
www.vinosdeargentina.com Official site for viticulture and the booming local wine scene.
http://argentina.indymedia.org/ Good for getting the lowdown on new politics and protest.

Index

Note: Page numbers in
bold indicate section(s)
giving key information
on a topic; *italics* indicate
photographs.

a

Abasto 115-116
   accommodation 69
   restaurants 159
Abasto shopping centre
   116, **178**, 215
Abierto Argentino
   de Polo 213
Abierto de Tenis de
   Buenos Aires 210
abortion 300
Academia Nacional del
   Tango 32, 33, 258
accessories shops 196-199
accident & emergency
   299-300
accommodation 44-72
   albergues transitorios
      40, 52
   best hotels 44
   by price
      budget 51, 53-55,
         59, 65-69, 72
      expensive 47-49, 55,
         57-59, 61-63, 69, 71
      luxury 47, 55, 57, 69
      moderate 49-51, 53,
         59, 65, 69
   high-end hotels 65
   *see also p315
      accommodation index*
Actors Studio, The 264
addresses 297
Aduana 96
Aeroparque Jorge
   Newbery 294
Aeropuerto Ministro
   Pistarini 294
age restrictions 297
AIDS & HIV 300
airports & airlines 294
albergues transitorios
   40, 52
Alfonsín, Raúl 17, 18
Almagro 117-118
   restaurants 159-161
Alvear Fashion
   & Arts 212
amusement parks 216
Aniversario
   de la Revolución
   de Mayo 211
antiques shops 205
aquariums *see* zoos
   & aquariums
archery 251
art *see* galleries; museums
ArteBA **211**, 227, *227*

Ashkenazi Templo
   de Paso 115
Astillero 257
Ateneo 109, 181
ATMs 302
Avenida Boedo 117
Avenida de Mayo
   83-84, *83*
Avenida Santa Fe 109

b

BA Today 23-27
bakeries 201
Ballet Argentino 264
Ballet del Mercosur 264
Banco de la Nación 81
banks 302
Bar Sur 259
barbers 203
Barra, La 289-291
Barracas 103, *103*
Basílica de Santo
   Domingo 95
Basílica del Espíritu
   Santo 114
Basílica del Santísimo
   Sacramento 91
Basílica Nuestra Señora
   de la Merced 87
Basílica Nuestra Señora
   del Pilar 105
Basílica Nuestra Señora
   del Rosario 95
basketball 248
Beach 282-284
beauty shops 203
beer *see* Quilmes
Belgrano 123-124
   accommodation 71
   cafés, bars & pubs 177
   restaurants 161-164
Bellsario Club
   de Cultura 261
Biblioteca Nacional
   106, 108
Biela, La 106
bike hire 77
boat trips & services
   272, 273, 295
Boca, La 101-103
Boca Juniors *see* football
Boca Tango 259
Bocca, Julio 264
bodegas 286-287
Boedo 117, *117*
Bombonera, La
   101-102, 248
books on Buenos
   Aires 309
bookshops 179-181
boxing 248
breakdown services 296
British Arts Centre
   (BAC) 92

Buenos Aires Design
   105, 205
Buenos Aires Rowing
   Club 269
Buenos Aires Tango
   Festival 28, **212**, 254
Buque Museo Fragata
   Presidente Sarmiento
   120, 121
bureaux de change 302
buses 294-295, 296
business 297-298

c

Caballito 117-118
   restaurants 159
Cabildo 81, 82
Cafés, Bars & Pubs
   165-177
   best bars 165
   cultural café crawl 175
   gay & lesbian 236-238
   *see also p315 cafés,
      bars & pubs index*
Calesita, La 255
Calle de los Titeres 216
Camarín de
   la Musas, El 264
Caminito 102, *102*
camping equipment 208
Cañitas, Las 114
   accommodation 69
   cafés, bars & pubs 177
   restaurants 156-159
Cañitas Creativa 114
Canto al Trabajo 96
car hire 296
Cariló 283
Carmelo 286-287
Carnaval 210, *211*
carnival 262-263, 264
Casa de la Cultura 83
Casa Foa 212
Casa Minima 96
Casa Rosada 81
Cataratas de
   Iguazú 274, *275*
Catedral de San
   Isidro 125, 240
Catedral Metropolitana 81
Catedral, La 256
CDs & records 207
cell phones 305
Cementerio de la Chacarita
   118, *118*
Cementerio de la Recoleta
   104, 106
Central Post Office 87
Centre, The 80-93
   accommodation 47-51
   cafés, bars & pubs
      167-169
   restaurants 129-133
Centro Cultural Borges 82,

87, **228**, *228*, **265**
Centro Cultural del Sur 82
Centro Cultural la
   Cooperación 82
Centro Cultural Recoleta
   82, **105**, **229**
Centro Cultural Ricardo
   Rojas 261, 265
Centro Cultural San
   Martín 82
Centro Cultural Torquato
   Tasso 241, 258
Centro Islámico Ray
   Fahd 114
Centro Metropolitano
   de Diseño 103
Centro Región Leonesa 256
Cervecería Munich 120
ceviche 157
Chacarita 118
Chachafaz, El 30
chemists 203, 300
Children 214-216
   indoors 215-216
   outdoors 214-215
   outside Buenos
      Aires 216
   shops 181-183
Chinatown 123
Chinese New Year 210
churches & cathedrals
   81, 95, 303-304
cinemas 225-226
circo criollo 265
Círculo Militar 91
circus performers 265
Ciudad Cultural Konex
   116, 264
classical music 239-240
climate 306
clothes shops 183-196
Club 69 *233*, 238
Club Atlético Fernández
   Fierro 258
Club de Amigos 251
Club Gricel 256
Clubs 217-222
   gay & lesbian 236-238
Código País 213
coffee 165
Colegiales restaurants
   161-164
Colonia del Sacramento
   285-286, *285*
Complejo Tango 259
conferences 297
Confitería Ideal 258
Congregación Sefardí 115
Congreso 84-85
Constitución 103, 295
   restaurants 133
consulates 299
consumer rights 298
contraception 300

Airline flights are one of the biggest producers of the global warming gas CO_2. But with **The CarbonNeutral Company** you can make your travel a little greener.

Go to **www.carbonneutral.com** to calculate your flight emissions then 'neutralise' them through international projects which save exactly the same amount of carbon dioxide.

Contact us at **shop@carbonneutral.com** or call into the office on **0870 199 99 88** for more details.

CarbonNeutral®flights

Advertisers' Index

Maps

Trips Out of Town

Embalse Salto Grande

Santana do Livramento

Rivera

Santa Fe

Paraná

Concordia

Salto

ENTRE RÍOS PROVINCE

Colón

Paysandú

URUGUAY

Rosario

Gualeguaychú

San Nicolás de los Arroyos

14

Fray Bentos

Mercedes

12

San Pedro

Río Paraná

Colón

Carmelo

San Antonio de Areco

Zárate

Campana (Arg.)

Carmen de Areco

9

Belén de Escobar

Capilla del Señor

Tigre

Colonia del Sacramento

San Andrés de Giles

Pilar

7

Junín

Mercedes

Luján

BUENOS AIRES CITY

See p320-1

1

Canelones

Minas

Rocha

La Paloma

Chivilcoy

LA PLATA

RÍO DE LA PLATA

Piriápolis

1

Maldonado

MONTEVIDEO

Punta del Es

Lobos

Límite del lecho y subsuelo

San Miguel del Monte

Saladillo

3

Chascomús

Límite exterior del Río de la Plata

Las Flores

11

Límite lateral marítimo argentino-uruguayo

BUENOS AIRES PROVINCE

San Clemente del Tuyú

Azul

11

Olavarría

Pinamar

A R G E N T I N A

Villa Gesell

Tandil

Mar de las Pampas

Laprida

2

Mar Azul

Tres Arroyos

Mar del Plata

3

11

Miramar

Necochea

ATLANTIC OCEAN

Monte Hermoso

| 0 | 100 miles |
| 0 | 200 km |

© Copyright Time Out Group 2008

VENEZUELA

COLOMBIA

GUYANA

SURINAM

GUAYANA FRANCESA

ECUADOR

PERU

BRAZIL

BOLIVIA

PARAGUAY

Puerto Iguazú

URUGUAY

Buenos Aires City

ARGENTINA

CHILE

| 0 | 1000 miles |
| 0 | 1000 km |

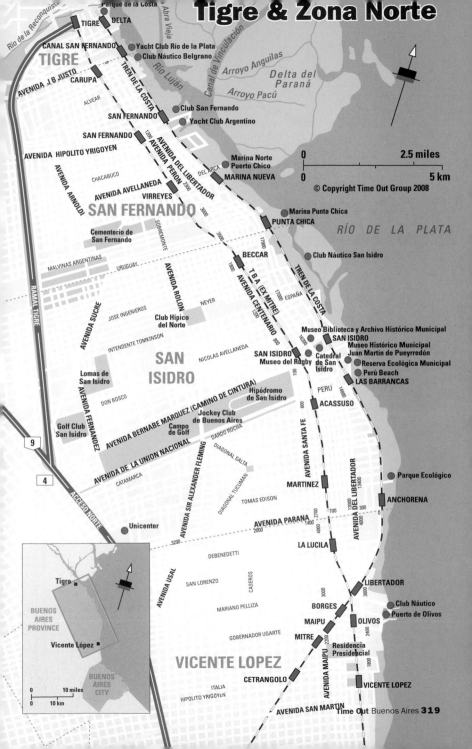

Tigre & Zona Norte

Parque de la Costa
TIGRE DELTA
CANAL SAN FERNANDO
TIGRE
Río de la Reconquista
Yacht Club Río de la Plata
Club Náutico Belgrano
AVENIDA J B JUSTO
CARUPA
Río Luján
Abra Vieja
Canal de Vinculación
Arroyo Anguilas
Delta del Paraná
Arroyo Pacú
ALVEAR
SAN FERNANDO
Club San Fernando
SAN FERNANDO
Yacht Club Argentino
AVENIDA HIPOLITO YRIGOYEN
1200
AVENIDA DEL LIBERTADOR
AVENIDA PERON
DEL ARCA
Marina Norte
Puerto Chico
MARINA NUEVA
CHACABUCO
2500
0   2.5 miles
0   5 km
© Copyright Time Out Group 2008
AVENIDA ARNOLDI
AVENIDA AVELLANEDA
VIRREYES
SAN FERNANDO
3000
Marina Punta Chica
PUNTA CHICA
RÍO DE LA PLATA
Cementerio de
San Fernando
SOBREMONTE
3500
17900
MALVINAS ARGENTINAS
URUGUAY
BECCAR
Club Náutico San Isidro
AVENIDA ROLON
AVENIDA SUCRE
JOSE INGENIEROS
NEYER
1800
AVENIDA CENTENARIO
T B A (EX MITRE)
1700
ESPAÑA
TREN DE LA COSTA
RAMAL TIGRE
INTENDENTE TOMKINSON
Club Hípico
del Norte
800
16200
Museo Biblioteca y Archivo Histórico Municipal
SAN ISIDRO
Museo Histórico Municipal
Juan Martin de Pueyrredón
Reserva Ecológica Municipal
Perú Beach
LAS BARRANCAS
SAN
ISIDRO
NICOLAS AVELLANEDA
SAN ISIDRO
Museo del Rugby
Catedral
de San
Isidro
100
Lomas de
San Isidro
DON BOSCO
Hipódromo
de San Isidro
PERU
AVENIDA FERNANDEZ
Golf Club
San Isidro
AVENIDA BERNABE MARQUEZ (CAMINO DE CINTURA)
Jockey Club
de Buenos Aires
Campo
de Golf
DARDO ROCHA
AVENIDA DE LA UNION NACIONAL
AVENIDA SIR ALEXANDER FLEMING
DIAGONAL SALTA
800
16900
ACASSUSO
9
CATAMARCA
DIAGONAL TUCUMAN
AVENIDA SANTA FE
4
ACCESO NORTE
TOMAS EDISON
MARTINEZ
AVENIDA DEL LIBERTADOR
13400
Parque Ecológico
ANCHORENA
700
13000
300
AVENIDA PARANA
2700
4000
0
Unicenter
1400
2000
LA LUCILA
3200
DEBENEDETTI
LIBERTADOR
3000
AVENIDA USAL
SAN LORENZO
CASEROS
3000
Club Náutico
Puerto de Olivos
Tigre
MARIANO PELLIZA
BORGES
OLIVOS
BUENOS
AIRES
PROVINCE
MAIPU
2400
GOBERNADOR UGARTE
MITRE
2200
Residencia
Presidencial
1800
Vicente López
AVENIDA MAIPU
VICENTE LOPEZ
10 miles
BUENOS
AIRES
CITY
CETRANGOLO
VICENTE LOPEZ
10 km
ITALIA
HIPOLITO YRIGOYEN
AVENIDA SAN MARTIN

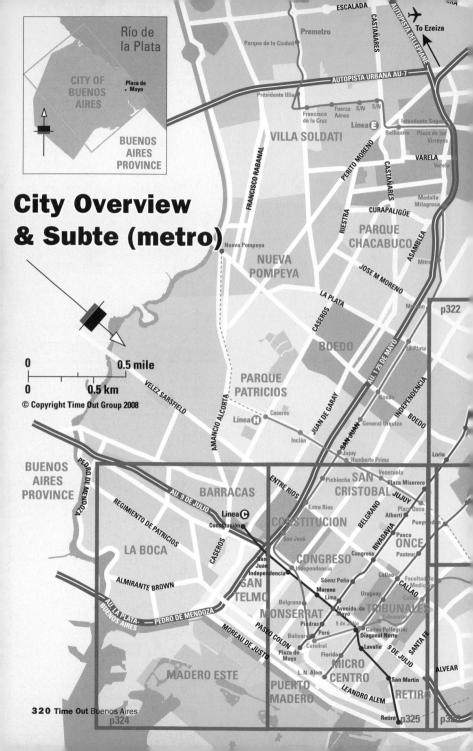

City Overview
& Subte (metro)

Río de
la Plata

CITY OF
BUENOS
AIRES

Plaza de
Mayo

BUENOS
AIRES
PROVINCE

0   0.5 mile
0   0.5 km
© Copyright Time Out Group 2008

ESCALADA
CASTAÑARES
To Ezeiza
AUTOPISTA DELLEPIANI
AUTOPISTA URBANA AU-7
Presidente Illia
Parque de la Ciudad
Premetro

Francisco
de la Cruz   Fuerza   S/N   S/N
                Aérea
                            Línea E   Intendente Saguier
VILLA SOLDATI   Balbastro   Plaza de los
                                         Virreyes
                                  VARELA
                             Varela
CASTAÑARES
PERITO MORENO
FRANCISCO RABANAL
RIESTRA   CURAPALIGÜE   Medalla
                                      Milagrosa
Nueva Pompeya   PARQUE
                 CHACABUCO   ASAMBLEA
NUEVA   Mitre
POMPEYA
                 JOSE M MORENO
            LA PLATA
CASEROS   Moreno
                         La Plata   p322
BOEDO
                         AU 1 25 DE MAYO
PARQUE   Caseros   INDEPENDENCIA
PATRICIOS   Boedo   BOEDO
AMANCIO ALCORTA   Línea H   Caseros
VELEZ SARSFIELD   JUAN DE GARAY
            Inclán   SAN JUAN General Urquiza
                      Jujuy
                      Humberto Primo   Loria
                  Pichincha Venezuela
                            Plaza Miserere
BUENOS   SAN   JUJUY
AIRES   ENTRE RIOS   CRISTOBAL
PROVINCE AU. 9 DE JULIO   Plaza Once
         BARRACAS   Entre Ríos Alberti Pueyrredón
PEDRO DE MENDOZA   BELGRANO ONCE
REGIMIENTO DE PATRICIOS   Línea C   RIVADAVIA   Pasco Pasteur
                 Constitución CONSTITUCION Congreso
LA BOCA   CASEROS   San José CONGRESO   Callao Facultad de
ALMIRANTE BROWN   Uruguay Medicina
         San   Sáenz Peña   CALLAO   Callao
         Juan Independencia Moreno
         Independencia   Lima   Avenida de TRIBUNALES
AU LA PLATA- SAN   Belgrano   Mayo Tribunales
BUENOS AIRES TELMO Perú 9 de Julio
PEDRO DE MENDOZA Piedras Carlos Pellegrini
         MONSERRAT Bolívar Diagonal Norte SANTA FE
MOREAU DE JUSTO PASEO COLON Catedral Lavalle 9 DE JULIO
                      Florida   ALVEAR
MADERO ESTE   BOLIVAR Plaza de MICRO
              Mayo   CENTRO
         PUERTO   L. N. Alem San Martín
         MADERO LEANDRO ALEM   RETIRO p325
320 Time Out Buenos Aires   Retiro p325
p324

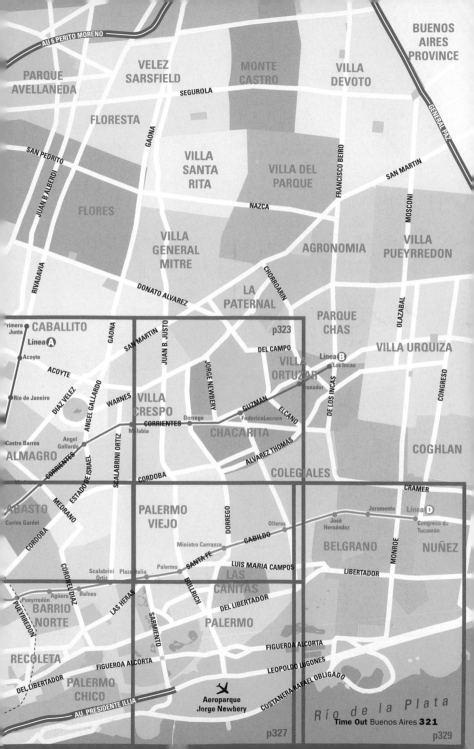

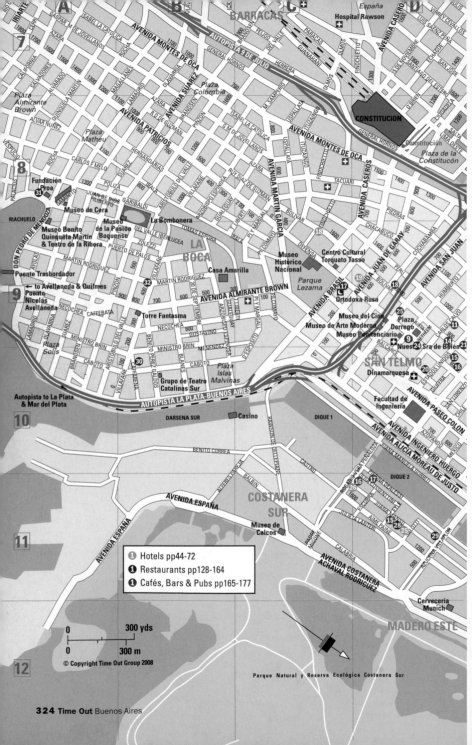

Hotels pp44-72
Restaurants pp128-164
Cafés, Bars & Pubs pp165-177

0 300 yds
0 300 m

© Copyright Time Out Group 2008

Parque Natural y Reserva Ecológica Costanera Sur

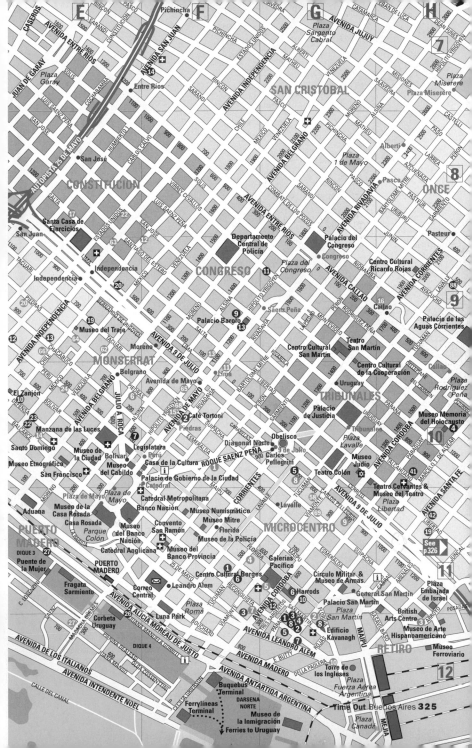

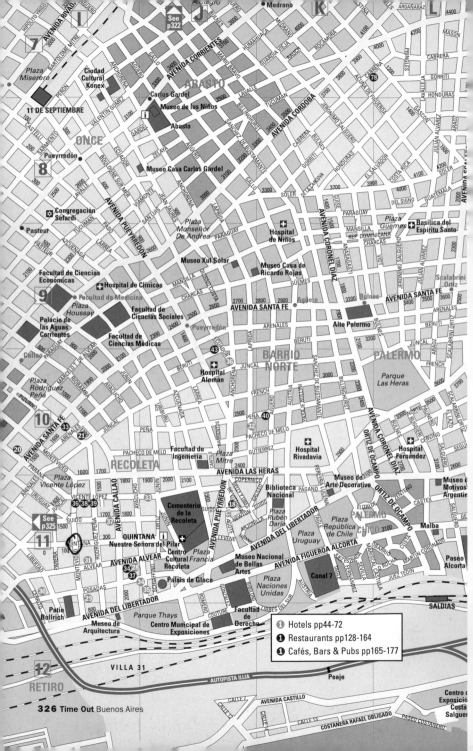

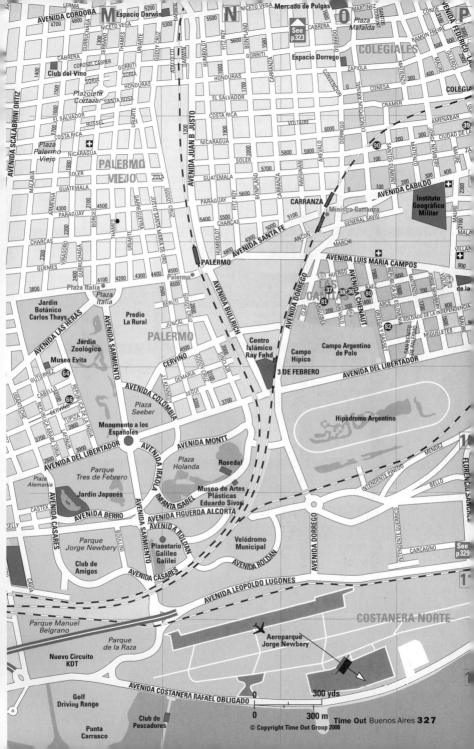

THE SHORTLIST

WHAT'S NEW | WHAT'S ON | WHAT'S BEST

- **POCKET–SIZE GUIDES**
- **WRITTEN BY LOCAL EXPERTS**
- **KEY VENUES PINPOINTED ON MAPS**

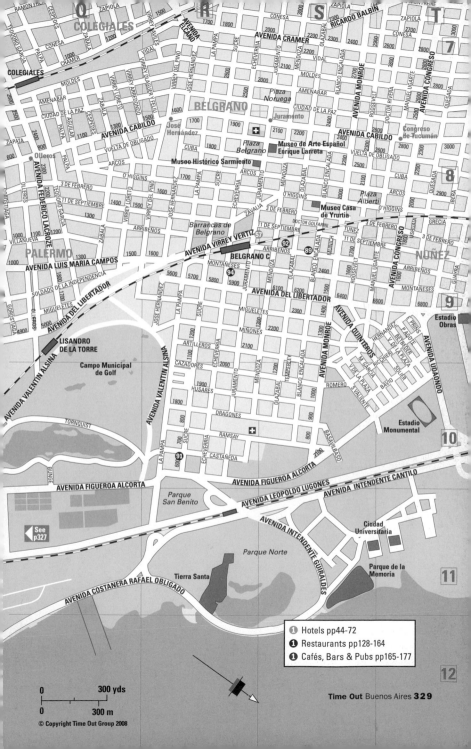

Q **R** **S** **T**

COLEGIALES

AVENIDA CRAMER

RICARDO BALBÍN

7

COLEGIALES

BELGRANO

Plaza
Noruega

AVENIDA CABILDO

Congreso
de Tucumán

José
Hernández

Plaza
Belgrano

Museo de Arte Español
Enrique Larreta

AVENIDA CABILDO

Museo Histórico Sarmiento

8

Museo Casa
de Yrurtia

Plaza
Alberti

PALERMO

Barrancas de
Belgrano

AVENIDA VIRREY VERTIZ

BELGRANO C

NÚÑEZ

LISANDRO
DE LA TORRE

AVENIDA LUIS MARÍA CAMPOS

AVENIDA DEL LIBERTADOR

9

Estadio
Obras

Campo Municipal
de Golf

AVENIDA VALENTÍN ALSINA

AVENIDA MONROE

AVENIDA QUINTEROS

AVENIDA UDAONDO

Estadio
Monumental

10

AVENIDA FIGUEROA ALCORTA

AVENIDA FIGUEROA ALCORTA

AVENIDA LEOPOLDO LUGONES

AVENIDA INTENDENTE CANTILO

See
p327

Parque
San Benito

Ciudad
Universitaria

Parque Norte

Tierra Santa

AVENIDA COSTANERA RAFAEL OBLIGADO

AVENIDA INTENDENTE GÜIRALDES

Parque de la
Memoria

11

12

❶	Hotels pp44-72
❶	Restaurants pp128-164
❶	Cafés, Bars & Pubs pp165-177

0   300 yds

0   300 m

© Copyright Time Out Group 2008

Time Out Travel Guides
Worldwide

All our guides are written by a team of **local experts** with a unique and stylish insider perspective. We offer essential tips, trusted advice and honest reviews for everything you need to know in the city.

Over 50 destinations available at all good bookshops and at timeout.com/shop

Time Out Guides

Street Index